ORAC

cle Press

Oracle Database 10*g* OCP Certification All-in-One

EXAM GUIDE

About the Authors

John Watson is an OCP DBA on 8.0, 8*i*, 9*i*, and 10*g* with the OCP special accreditation for Managing Oracle on Linux, and is a senior consultant with BPLC Management Consultants in South Africa. John worked for Oracle University in South Africa for four years (after doing time with Oracle Internal Support) where he taught the Database and Application Server curricula, and contributed towards developing course material and OCP questions.

Damir Bersinic, MCSE, MCDBA, MCT, CTT+, OCP DBA, regularly consults, teaches, and writes about topics related to Oracle, SQL Server, and general database technologies. He is the co-author of *Portable DBA: SQL Server, MCSA Windows Server 2003 Certification All-in-One Exam Guide,* and several other books on Oracle, SQL Server, Windows, and Active Directory. He lives and works in the Greater Toronto area in Canada. He can be reached by email at *dbersinic@hotmail.com.*

About the Contributor

Martin Bensch, MCSE and OCP DBA on 9*i* and 10*g*, is currently a senior lecturer and consultant at Global Bits THUTA, a certified Oracle Training Partner in South Africa. Previously Martin was a lecturer for Oracle University after serving three years as a senior technical consultant with Oracle's Global Education Services.

About the Technical Editor

Debra Wong, OCP DBA on 7.3, 8, 8*i*, 9*i*, and 10*g*, and an OCP certified Application Developer, is a technical lead for the Enterprise Database Architecture group at Marriott International. She has spent the majority of her career developing and maintaining host, PC-LAN, and Web-based database systems and is the author of *Oracle8 Backup and Recovery Exam Cram* and *Oracle8i Backup and Recovery Exam Cram.*

Oracle Press™

Oracle Database 10*g* OCP Certification All-in-One

EXAM GUIDE

John Watson, Damir Bersinic

McGraw-Hill/Osborne

New York • Chicago • San Francisco • Lisbon
London • Madrid • Mexico City • Milan • New Delhi
San Juan • Seoul • Singapore • Sydney • Toronto

The McGraw·Hill Companies

McGraw-Hill/Osborne
2100 Powell Street, 10th Floor
Emeryville, California 94608
U.S.A..

To arrange bulk purchase discounts for sales promotions, premiums, or fund-raisers, please contact **McGraw-Hill/Osborne** at the above address. For information on translations or book distributors outside the U.S.A., please see the International Contact Information page immediately following the index of this book.

Oracle Database 10g OCP Certification All-in-One Exam Guide

.34567890 CUS CUS 019876

Book p/n 0-07-225791-1 and CD p/n 0-07-225793-8
parts of
ISBN 0-07-007225790-3

Acquisitions Editor	**Proofreader**
Timothy Green	Stefany Otis
Project Editors	**Indexer**
Jody McKenzie, LeeAnn Pickrell	Valerie Perry
Acquisitions Coordinator	**Composition**
Jennifer Housh	Apollo Publishing Services
Technical Editor	**Cover Series Design**
Debra Wong	Damore Johann Design, Inc.
Copy Editor	**Series Design**
Robert Campbell	Peter F. Hancik, Lyssa Wald

This book was composed with Adobe® InDesign®.

I want to thank my reason for living, Silvia, for looking after me
(and our house, garden, cats, and dogs) for months
while I was working on this.

—John Watson

CONTENTS AT A GLANCE

CONTENTS

INTRODUCTION

There is an ever increasing demand for staff with IT industry certification. The benefits to employers are significant; employers can be certain that their staff has a certain level of competence. The benefits to the individuals, in terms of demand for their services, are equally great. Many employers are now requiring that technical staff have certifications, and many IT purchasers will not buy from firms that do not have certified staff. The Oracle certifications are among the most sought after. But apart from rewards in a business sense, knowing that you are among a relatively small pool of elite Oracle professionals and have proved your competence is a personal reward well worth attaining.

There are several Oracle certification "tracks." This book is concerned with the Oracle Database Administration certification track, specifically for release 10*g* of the database. There are three levels of DBA certification: Certified Associate (OCA), Certified Professional (OCP), and Certified Master (OCM). The OCA qualification is based on just one examination, and is covered in Part I of this book. OCP requires passing a second examination, based on content in Part II of this book. These examinations can be taken at any Prometric Testing Center, and consist of 60 or 70 questions to be completed in 90 minutes. OCM requires completing a further two-day evaluation at an Oracle testing center, involving simulations of complex environments and use of advanced techniques. This book will prepare you for passing the Oracle 10*g* Database Administrator Certified Associate (OCA) and Professional (OCP) examinations only.

To prepare for the OCA and OCP examinations, you can attend Oracle University instructor-led training courses, you can study Oracle University online learning material, or you can read this book. In all cases, you should also refer to the Oracle Documentation Library for detail of syntax. This book will be a valuable addition to other study methods, but it is sufficient by itself. It has been designed with the examination objectives in mind, although it does also include information that will be useful to you in the course of your work.

However, it is not enough to buy the book, place it under your pillow, and assume that knowledge will permeate into the brain by a process of osmosis: you must read it thoroughly, work through the exercises and sample questions, and experiment further with various commands. As you become more familiar with the Oracle environment, you will realize that there is one golden rule: When it doubt, try it out.

In a multitude of cases, you will find that a simple test that takes a couple of minutes can save hours of speculation and poring through manuals. If anything is ever unclear, construct an example and see what happens. This book was developed using Windows and Linux, but to carry out the exercises and your further investigations you can use any platform that is supported for Oracle.

Your initiation into the strange and magical world of Oracle Database Administration is about to begin—enjoy!

—*John Watson*

PART I

Oracle Database 10g Administrative I Exam

CHAPTER 1

Basic Oracle Concepts

In this chapter you will learn

- What a database is and what makes a database relational
- What SQL is
- Which database objects are supported in Oracle 10g
- What a database administrator does
- How the Oracle database fits into the Oracle product family

Someone once said that the best place to start is at the beginning. With Oracle, that means understanding where the idea of a relational database management system (RDBMS) came from and what a database is—in computer and everyday terms. Even though the material presented here may not be directly tested on the exam, this is assumed knowledge, however, so a quick read is probably a good idea.

Introduction to Databases and the Relational Model

In one form or another, databases have always been around, though their exact shape was not always easily recognizable. As long as some form of data had to be stored, there was always a method of storing it.

Databases, in their most simple form, are a mechanism for storing data. The data can be logical, like the values stored in a computer program, or may be physical, like a file or receipt. You probably have databases in existence all around you, but you may not see them as such. For example, the shoebox in which you've placed your tax receipts for the accountant is a database of your annual expenses. When you open a file cabinet and take out a folder, you are accessing a database. The content of the file folder is your data (e.g., your credit card statements, your bank statements, invoices, purchase orders, etc.). The file cabinet and drawers are your data storage mechanisms.

Before the advent of computers, all data was stored in some easily recognizable physical form. The introduction of computers simply changed the data from a physical form that you can touch and feel to a digital form that is represented by a series of 1's and 0's. Does the information that you display for an expense report on the computer screen differ greatly from the same information in the hard-copy version of the expense form? Perhaps the information is laid out differently than on the screen, but the key elements—who was paid, what amount, how much was the tax, what was the purpose of the expense, and so on—are all the same.

In looking at a database and its most basic set of characteristics, the following points hold true:

- A database stores data. The storage of data can take a physical form, such as a filing cabinet or a shoebox.

- Data is composed of logical units of information that have some form of connection to each other. For example, a genealogical database stores information on people as they are related to each other (parents, children, etc.).

- A database management system (DBMS) provides a method to easily retrieve, add, modify, or remove data. This can be a series of filing cabinets that are properly indexed, making it easy to find and change what you need, or a computer program that performs the same function.

When data began to move from a physical form to a logical form using computers, different theoretical versions of systems to manage data evolved. Some of the more common database management systems in use over the last 50 years include the *hierarchical, network,* and *relational.* Oracle is a relational database management system (RDBMS).

The Relational Model of Databases

The relational model for database management systems was proposed in the June 1970 issue of *Communications of the ACM*—the Association of Computing Machinery journal—by Dr. E.F. Codd, an IBM researcher, in a paper called "A Relational Model of Data for Large Shared Data Banks." For its time it was a radical departure from established principles because it stated that tables that have related data need not know where the related information is physically stored. Unlike previous database models, including the hierarchical and network models, which used the physical location of a record to relate information between two sets of data, the relational model stated that data in one table needed to know only the name of the other table and the value on which it is related. It was not necessary for data in one table to keep track of the physical storage location of the related information in another.

 NOTE The full text of Dr. E.F. Codd's paper "A Relational Model of Data for Large Shared Data Banks" can be found in the classics section of the ACM web site at www.acm.org/classics/nov95/toc.html.

The relational model broke all data down into collections of objects or relations that store the actual data (i.e., tables). It also introduced a set of operators to act on the related objects to produce other objects (i.e., join conditions to produce a new result set). Finally, the model proposed that a set of elements should exist to ensure data integrity so that the data would be consistent and accurate (i.e., constraints). Codd proposed a set of twelve rules that would allow designers to determine if the database management system satisfied the requirements of the relational model. Although no database today satisfies all twelve rules (because the database would run very slowly if it did, since theory is not always the same as practice), it is generally accepted that any RDBMS should comply with most of them.

The essence of the relational model is that data is made up of a set of relations. These relations are implemented as two-dimensional tables with rows and columns as shown in Figure 1-1. In this example, the Customers table stores information about clients we deal with—their customer ID, their company name, their address, and so on. The Orders table stores information about the client orders (but not the order line items—these are in another table), including the order data, the method of payment, the order date, and the ship date. The CustomerID column in both tables provides the relationship between the two tables and is the source of the relation. The tables themselves are stored in a database that resides on a computer. The physical locations of the tables need not be known—only their names.

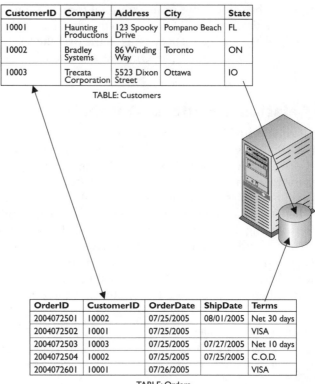

Figure 1-1

The Customers and Orders tables are related by CustomerID.

CustomerID	Company	Address	City	State
10001	Haunting Productions	123 Spooky Drive	Pompano Beach	FL
10002	Bradley Systems	86 Winding Way	Toronto	ON
10003	Trecata Corporation	5523 Dixon Street	Ottawa	IO

TABLE: Customers

OrderID	CustomerID	OrderDate	ShipDate	Terms
2004072501	10002	07/25/2005	08/01/2005	Net 30 days
2004072502	10001	07/25/2005		VISA
2004072503	10003	07/25/2005	07/27/2005	Net 10 days
2004072504	10002	07/25/2005	07/25/2005	C.O.D.
2004072601	10001	07/26/2005		VISA

TABLE: Orders

For a database to be considered relational, and because the physical location of rows is not something that a user querying data needs to know, the table must allow for each row to be uniquely identified. The column (or set of columns) that uniquely identifies a row is known as the *primary key*. Each table in a relational database (according to database theory) must have a primary key. In this way, you are certain that the specific value appears only once in the table. In Figure 1-1, the CustomerID column of the Customers table is a primary key, ensuring that each CustomerID appears only once in the table. For the Orders table, the OrderID is the primary key.

When relating tables together (the whole point of a relational database), the value of a primary key column in one table can be placed in a column in another table. The column in the second table holding the value is known as the *foreign key*. A foreign key states that the value in this column for a row exists in another table and must continue to exist, or else the relationship is broken. In Figure 1-1, the CustomerID column of the Orders table is a foreign key to the CustomerID column in the Customers table. In order for the relationship to be valid, any value placed in the CustomerID column of the Orders table must already exist in the CustomerID column of the Customers table. In other words, in order for a client to place an order, we need to know some basic information about them. If we don't have this information, the customer cannot place an order. Oracle enforces the primary key–foreign key relationship through the use of database constraints.

SQL: The Structured Query Language

All of the relations in a relational database are managed by a relational database management system. As indicated earlier, an RDBMS allows you to manipulate relational tables and their contents. It provides a language that allows you to create, modify, and remove objects in the database, as well as add, change, and delete data. The language that Oracle uses is the Structured Query Language, or SQL. SQL was originally developed by IBM, for whom E.F. Codd worked, and was first called Structured English Query Language (or SEQUEL, for short). The name has been shortened to Structured Query Language, or SQL, but it is still pronounced *sequel*.

SQL is actually a collection of several different "languages," each designed for a particular purpose. It is made up of the following:

- **Data definition language (DDL)**   DDL is used to create and modify database objects. DDL statements include CREATE, ALTER, DROP, RENAME, and TRUNCATE. If you need to add a new table to the database, you use the CREATE TABLE statement to perform this task. To remove an index, you use the DROP INDEX statement, and so on.

- **Data manipulation language (DML)**   DML is used to modify data in tables in the database. DML statements include INSERT, UPDATE, and DELETE, as well as extensions to control transactions in the database, including COMMIT, ROLLBACK, and SAVEPOINT. The SELECT statement used to query data in the database is not technically considered a DML command, although it is sometimes included with the definition of DML because it deals with the retrieval of data.

- **Data control language (DCL)**   DCL is used to configure security to perform database tasks and manipulate database objects. DCL statements include GRANT and REVOKE. Permissions can be granted to allow a user to perform a task such as creating a table, or to manipulate or query data, as by performing an insert into a table in the database.

Another characteristic of an RDBMS is that tables in a relational database do not have their relationship represented by data in one table storing the physical location of the data in a related table. As you can see in Figure 1-1, the Customers table and the Orders table are related by the data that exists in the CustomerID column of both tables. The physical location on disk of each table does not factor into the relationship between them. As long as a user querying the two tables knows the column that relates them, he/she is able to formulate a SQL statement that will extract the data satisfying the condition of that relationship (also known as the "join condition"). Should one of the tables be moved to a different hard disk used to store data in the database, the relationship will still hold true.

A third characteristic of an RDBMS is that the language used to manipulate the database has a rich and varied set of operators that can be used to manipulate the data and explore the relationships between the various tables. The SQL language allows you to determine, through the proper use of operators, data that is related between tables, data where the relationship does not hold true, and much more. The SQL language in its pure form does not, however, have any procedural elements of a programming language such as loops, conditional logic, and the use of variables. Oracle has extended SQL to include these elements through PL/SQL, a proprietary set of language elements that can be used to create stored procedures, triggers, and other subprograms.

RDBMSs have become popular in part for the preceding reasons. Nothing stays static for long in the database world. Oracle, the first commercially available relational database management system, has extended its database capabilities to support object features.

Object Relational Database Management System (ORDBMS)

Releases of Oracle prior to Oracle 8 were RDBMSs; that is, they followed the relational model and complied with its requirements, and often improved upon them. With the introduction of Oracle 8, Oracle was considered an object relational database management system—something that is even more true with Oracle 10g. An ORDBMS complies with the relational model but also extends it to support the newer object relational database model introduced in the 1980s.

An ORDBMS is characterized by a number of additional features, including these:

- **Support for user-defined datatypes**   This means that users can create their own datatypes based upon the standard Oracle datatypes or other user-defined datatypes. This feature allows for more accurate mapping of business objects to database features and can reduce the time it takes to maintain databases after they have been implemented.

- **Support for multimedia and other large objects**   Oracle 8 and subsequent releases up to 10g have full support for binary large objects, or BLOBs. This means that it is possible to store large amounts of information such as video clips, images, and large amounts of text in the column of a row. Even though earlier releases of Oracle had a similar feature, it lacked functionality and was not implemented in a way that conformed to object relational standards. The current implementation is much improved.

- **Full compatibility with relational database concepts**   Even though object extensions have been added to Oracle, in order for it to remain an ORDBMS, it needs to conform to the requirements of an RDBMS. Because of Oracle's strong legacy as an RDBMS, its object features can be leveraged along with the relational features to provide robust solutions.

The one thing that defines Oracle as an ORDBMS is its capability to allow you to create a user-defined datatype, which becomes an object in Oracle. For example, if you wanted to use a common definition for a telephone number in several tables (Customers, Suppliers, Employees, etc.) and wanted to be sure that any changes to its characteristics would be inherited by all tables using it, you could create a new datatype called "PhoneNumber" with the proper characteristics and then create the tables using the PhoneNumber datatype as one of the column definitions. If the rules for area codes, for example, changed, you could modify the attributes and methods of the PhoneNumber datatype and all tables would inherit the change.

Database Objects

Every RDBMS needs to support a minimum number of database objects in order to comply with the basic requirements for a relational database. Oracle supports these and many more. This chapter presents only a listing of those objects, while subsequent chapters will allow you to create and manipulate many of these objects.

Oracle's collection of database objects includes all of those that are needed for it to be called a relational database (tables, views, constraints, etc.) as well as others that go beyond what is required and are included because they provide additional functionality (packages, object types, synonyms, sequences, etc.). The full list of database objects that Oracle 10g supports appears in Table 1-1.

Object	Description
Table	A collection of columns and rows representing a single entity (e.g., customers, orders, employees, etc.).
Column	A single attribute of an entity stored in a table. A column has a name and a datatype. A table may have, and typically does have, more than one column as part of its definition.
Row	A single instance of an entity in a table, including all columns. For example, a student row will store all information about a single student, such as that student's ID, name, and address.
Cell	The term cell is used to refer to the intersection of a single column in a single row. For example, the CompanyName column for CustomerID 10002 in our example would be a cell holding that data—Bradley Systems.
Constraint	A database object that is used to enforce simple business rules and database integrity. Examples of constraints are PRIMARY KEY, FOREIGN KEY, NOT NULL, and CHECK.
View	A view is a logical projection of data from one or more tables as represented by a SQL statement stored in the database. Views are used to simplify complex and repetitive SQL statements by assigning those statements a name in the database.
Index	An index is a database object that helps speed up retrieval of data by storing logical pointers to specific key values. By scanning the index, which is organized in either ascending or descending order according to the key value, you are able to retrieve a row quicker than by scanning all rows in a table.

Table 1-1 Oracle 10g Database Objects

Object	Description
Index-organized table	A table whose physical storage is organized like an index. Unlike a regular table, where rows are inserted in no particular order and querying all rows will retrieve the data in random order, index-organized tables store data organized according to the primary key defined on the table. The difference between a table (referred to as storing data on a heap) and an index-organized table is like the difference between storing all of your receipts in a shoebox (i.e., in no specific order) and storing it chronologically according to the date the expense was incurred. Taking the receipts out of the shoebox will result in no specific logic in their retrieval, while doing the same when the receipts are organized chronologically will allow you to predict that the June 2 receipt will appear before the August 1 receipt.
Partition	Tables in Oracle 10g can be cut into pieces for more efficient physical storage. A partition (or subpartition) holds a subset of the table's data, typically on a separate physical disk, so that data retrieval is quicker either by allowing reads from more than one physical disk simultaneously (multipartition parallel reads) or by not reading a partition's data at all if it is not required to satisfy the query (partition elimination).
Cluster	A storage mechanism object that allows rows from more than one table to be physically stored together for quicker retrieval. For example, if you store the Order information (customer, payment info, delivery details, etc.) in one table and the line items (item, cost, sale price, quantity, etc.) in a different table, you will need to perform at least two reads to retrieve information about an order: one for the order info and the second for line item info. Creating both tables on the cluster organized by the order ID will allow Oracle to place the order and line item data for the same order ID on the same physical block, thereby reducing retrieval of that order's information to a single read. The downside of clusters is that they force you to preallocate a certain portion or all of the disk space they require when rows are added or the cluster is created.
Sequence	A sequence allows you to create and increment a counter that can be used to generate numerical values to be used as primary key values for a table.
Synonym	As in the English language, a synonym is another name for an existing object. Synonyms are used in Oracle as shorthand for objects with long names, or to make it easier to remember a specific object.
Stored procedure	A stored procedure is a collection of SQL and PL/SQL statements that perform a specific task, such as to insert a row into a table or to update data.
Trigger	A trigger is a special kind of stored procedure that cannot be invoked manually but rather is automatically invoked whenever an action is performed on a table. Triggers can be associated with a table and a corresponding action such as INSERT, UPDATE, or DELETE as well as system events such as user logon and logoff, or database STARTUP and SHUTDOWN.
Function	A function is a stored program that must return a value. Unlike stored procedures, which can have parameters passed to them and do not need to return any value as output, a function must return a value.

Table 1-1   Oracle 10g Database Objects *(continued)*

Object	Description
Package	A package is a collection of stored procedures and functions grouped under a common name. This allows you to logically group all program elements for a particular part of the database under a single name for maintenance and performance reasons.
User-defined datatype	A user-defined datatype is a database object that can be used in any table or another object definition. Using user-defined datatypes allows you to ensure consistency between tables and also lets you apply methods (i.e., actions that can be performed by the object) as part of the definition.
BLOB	A BLOB is a binary large object used to store video, images, and large amounts of text. BLOBs are defined as a column in a table and can be one of several datatypes: BLOB, CLOB, NCLOB, or BFILE.

Table 1-1   Oracle 10g Database Objects *(continued)*

Oracle also includes other objects that are beyond the scope of this book, including dimensions, directories, materialized views, and more. These objects are created for a specific purpose such as to facilitate data warehousing and their full coverage is beyond the scope of this book.

Each object in an Oracle database is owned by a user. A user defined in an Oracle database does not have to own any objects, but those that do are known as *schema users*. A *schema* is a collection of all objects owned by a particular user, including tables, indexes, views, and so on.

The Oracle Data Dictionary

As you may well imagine, a database may contain hundreds and even thousands of objects. Keeping track of all this information is the job of the Oracle data dictionary. A *data dictionary* in any database contains metadata information. Metadata is "data about data," or a set of tables and other database objects that store information about your own tables and database objects.

The data dictionary in Oracle is a set of tables, called base tables, which contain the most basic information about user-created database objects. These base tables are owned by an Oracle user called SYS, which is created when the database itself is created. The base tables are never accessed directly, as their names are cryptic by design to discourage users from querying and modifying them. To make it easier to access the data dictionary and get information on objects in the database, a series of views are created during the database creation process. These views are commonly referred to as data dictionary views.

Oracle has three sets of data dictionary views. They are as follows:

- **USER_ views**   These views allow users to get information on objects that are in their schema (i.e., objects that they have created and own).

- **ALL_ views** These views allow users to get information on objects that they own or that they have been given access to. The ALL_ views contain a subset of the information presented in the USER_ views for the same object and allow users to find out what other objects they are allowed to reference or manipulate in the database, in addition to the objects that they own.

- **DBA_ views** The DBA_ views, designed to be used by the database administrator (DBA) of the database, provide a full set of information for objects in the database, i.e., any object created by any user. Normal users do not have access to these views, as special privileges are needed to SELECT from them.

As you delve further in this book, you will be introduced to many DBA_ views to help you in your duties as a database administrator. But, what does a database administrator do in the Oracle world?

Responsibilities of a Database Administrator

One of my colleagues likes to comment that users of the databases for which he is responsible think they control the databases. The reality, as he quite correctly puts it (if in a control-freakish sort of way), is quite different. As a DBA, he can do whatever he wants in any database he is responsible for, so he's the one with control. Database administrators do have a great deal of power, but it is important to remember that with great power also comes great responsibility. Ultimately, the success and failure of a database to respond to user requirements and satisfy corporate objectives rests with the DBA. The DBA must take the blame and the praise for good or bad database management.

The kinds of tasks DBAs in the Oracle world are responsible for include the following:

- **Sizing and evaluating server hardware** As the individual responsible for the smooth operation of databases in your organization, you will be called upon to suggest the configuration of the server that will be used to run Oracle. Your experience will play a key role here in determining the amount of memory, hard disk, CPU, and other resources required to support the target database's operations. Understanding the architecture of Oracle and the data needs of the business and the application will help you perform this task.

- **Installing Oracle software and updates** After you buy the software, the first thing you need to do is bring it up. Installation of the Oracle software on the target platform is the job of the DBA. It usually involves more than putting in the CD and answering the prompts of the setup program because Oracle is a very powerful system comprising a complex piece of software that has many hooks and interactions with the operation system. Ensuring that the software is installed and working properly is a key to being a successful DBA.

- **Planning and designing the database structure** Once the software is installed, you need to make sure that the layout of the physical data structures and logical elements of Oracle is done in an optimal way. If this is not the case, performance will suffer and users will make their displeasure known. If you have properly sized the hardware, this should be an easy task, since you should have taken the database size and structure into account; if you inherited the environment, you may need to use your expertise to determine the optimal configuration.

- **Creating databases** As you will see in Chapter 3, this is a somewhat anticlimactic task. Creation of the database is the first step to administering it. Although relatively straightforward, the process can run into problems; with experience, however, you should grow well equipped to fix these problems.

- **Backing up databases and implementing other ways to safeguard the data** Once a database is in production and users are connecting to it, they may not take it well if the database becomes unavailable. Even worse, if data is lost it could mean lost productivity, sales, and customers. Ensuring that a database is always available to users, that data loss is minimized, and that recovery is quick and complete is perhaps one of the most important responsibilities of the DBA.

- **Creating and maintaining database users** Once a new user needs to gain access to the database or when the requirements and permissions of another user change, the DBA must be able to make the necessary security modifications to ensure appropriate access. In some cases, application developers may not make use of Oracle's built-in security fully, so being able to recognize these situations and take appropriate action is also necessary.

- **Implementing application and database designs** Organizations may purchase third-party software applications or hire database architects to design a database to suit a specific database requirement when in-house expertise is lacking. However, the actual implementation of these designs will be undertaken by the DBA, since the DBA will be responsible for ensuring that the database continues to work properly after the software vendor or database architect leaves.

- **Restoring and recovering databases** Sometimes things go wrong. Hardware fails, users improperly modify or delete data, or a natural disaster or some other calamity befalls the data center. Being able to recover from a variety of scenarios is critical. This is when the fault tolerance disaster recovery strategy is tested for real—but it should also be tested in mock scenarios to ensure it works. The DBA is the one that is answerable for their success or failure.

- **Monitoring and tuning database performance** In *Star Trek: The Next Generation* there is an episode where the Enterprise assists a stranded vessel. The vessel's occupants are somewhat lacking in both engineering and communication skills, but they do ask Captain Picard and Giordi to *make us go fast*. Your users will frequently comment that the database is not fast enough. Keeping those comments to a minimum and solving performance problems when (or before) they occur will reduce your stress level and increase job satisfaction.

As you can tell, the duties of a DBA are wide and varied. It is an exciting position whose goal can sometimes be summed up in one phrase: reduce the number of times the phone rings in a day. If you get a lot of phone calls from users or management, this is probably not a good sign and can make your day an unhappy one. Well-tuned databases on appropriate hardware with good disaster recovery and backup strategies will reduce your phone calls, make happy users, and increase your job satisfaction. Sounds simple, right?

The Oracle Product Family

As an Oracle database administrator, you may be responsible for a database that is actually part of another Oracle product or that complements or is relied upon by that other product. Oracle has long since become more than just a database company—though the Oracle database is at the heart of what Oracle Corporation does best. In addition to the database, Oracle Corporation also offers these products, among others:

- **Oracle E-Business Suite** Also referred to as Oracle Applications, the E-Business Suite is the premier enterprise resource planning (ERP) suite in the industry. Encompassing many modules, including financials, human resources, distribution, manufacturing, and many others, the E-Business Suite allows organizations to leverage Oracle technology to better run their businesses and increase profitability and customer satisfaction. Oracle E-Business Suite makes use of the Oracle database, Application Server, and Developer Suite to run and enhance the application.

- **Oracle Collaboration Suite** One of Oracle's newest products, Collaboration Suite encompasses e-mail, fax, calendaring, web conferencing, a files repository, voice mail, and other modules to provide a single integrated platform for an organization's collaboration and communication infrastructure. Like Oracle E-Business Suite, Collaboration Suite also incorporates the Oracle database and Application Server as its foundation.

- **Oracle Application Server** A Java 2 Enterprise Edition (J2EE)–certified server platform, Oracle Application Server integrates everything you need to deploy and develop web-based applications. Oracle Application Server includes a portal server and tools to develop portlets, Web Services capabilities, content management, support for forms-based applications using Oracle Forms, reporting using Oracle Reports, development using PL/SQL or Java, and many other features. It also includes the capability to configure and use a single sign-on server that interfaces with other third-party directory services such as Microsoft's Active Directory, Novell's NDS, and Sun's iPlanet.

- **Oracle Developer Suite**   If you need to develop applications for the Oracle database or Application Server, Oracle Developer Suite provides tools for the development of Java, PL/SQL, business intelligence, data warehousing, and other applications.

- **Oracle Consulting**   When you need assistance in your Oracle deployment, Oracle Consulting can provide the expertise and individuals to help your projects succeed.

- **Oracle University**   The training of customers and partners on Oracle products and technologies is the responsibility of Oracle University and its partners. Instructor-led and online courses are available.

More information on the products available from Oracle Corporation can be found on the Oracle web site at www.oracle.com.

Chapter Review

In this chapter you learned a bit about the history of the relational database management system (RDBMS) concept. You also learned that SQL is actually three languages: a data control language (DCL) for managing permissions on database objects, a data definition language (DDL) for creating and managing those objects, and a data manipulation language (DML) for adding, updating, or deleting data from the database, as well as controlling those transactions. You saw what objects may appear in an Oracle 10g database and read a brief description of each object, and you were briefed on your responsibilities as a database administrator. Finally, you learned that Oracle is not just a database company but one with a wealth and breadth of products and services. At this point, you're ready to start working with Oracle (after a few questions).

Questions

1. You need to recommend a platform for the deployment of your web-based application written in Java. You need to make the management of web page content easy as well as integrate security with your Active Directory infrastructure. Which Oracle product will satisfy your requirements? (Choose the best answer.)

   A. Oracle Database

   B. Oracle Application Server

   C. Oracle Collaboration Suite

   D. Oracle E-Business Suite

   E. Oracle Developer Suite

2. For which of the following types of information stored in a database would the use of a sequence be appropriate? (Choose two correct answers.)

     A. Invoice line item

     B. Invoice number

     C. Employee name

     D. Atomic element

     E. Customer identifier

3. What is a key benefit to making use of user-defined datatypes in Oracle? (Choose the best answer.)

     A. Ability to rename Oracle built-in datatypes

     B. Inheritance

     C. Polymorphism

     D. Consistency of similar data structures across multiple tables

     E. Easier maintenance of databases

4. Your organization has outgrown its hosted e-mail system. You also need to implement web conferencing. Development of an interface to your in-house telephone system will take place and needs to be integrated with a new voice mail platform. Your developers are versed in Java on a Linux platform. Which Oracle product provides the best fit for your organization's requirements? (Choose the best answer.)

     A. Oracle Database

     B. Oracle Application Server

     C. Oracle Collaboration Suite

     D. Oracle E-Business Suite

     E. Oracle Developer Suite

5. Which of the following is not typically a responsibility of an Oracle database administrator? (Choose the best answer.)

     A. Creating new users

     B. Creating database objects

     C. Installing Oracle software

     D. Application development to manipulate database data

     E. Backing up the database

Answers

1. **B.** Oracle Application Server provides a Java 2 Enterprise Edition (J2EE)–certified server for deploying your web-based application. It also includes a portal server for creating new content and a content management server for managing changes to content. Finally, the Oracle Internet Directory component allows for integration with third-party directory services to provide single sign-on functionality.

2. **B and E.** A sequence is an automatically generated chronological number, ideal for invoice numbers or unique identifiers for database data, such as a customer ID. Because a sequence is numeric in nature, it is not appropriate for text-based data such as an order line item, employee name, or atomic element.

3. **D.** Using a user-defined datatype, you can ensure that the same data is always stored the same way in all tables. In other words, a phone number will always have a consistent structure no matter what table it is in. It can make maintenance of the database easier as well, but this is a secondary benefit.

4. **C.** Oracle Collaboration Suite provides e-mail, fax, and voice mail functionality, as well as web conferencing, calendaring, and other features. Because it also includes Oracle Application Server, it is the perfect product for the development and deployment of a custom application to interface with the phone system.

5. **D.** The development of the application that will interface with the database and manipulate the data within it is not something that a DBA does. This task is performed by an application developer. The DBA is responsible for all other tasks listed in the question, including database security, software installation, backup and recovery, and the creation and management of database objects.

CHAPTER 2

Installing Oracle Database 10*g*

In this chapter you will learn how to
- Identify system requirements
- Use Optimal Flexible Architecture
- Install software with the Oracle Universal Installer
- Identify and configure commonly used environment variables

Understanding how a database works is a good starting point, but you actually need to get the software installed in order to see the real thing in action. Ironically, installing the software need not mean that you even create a database. Installing the Oracle 10g database software means that you now have the tools to create and manage databases at your disposal.

Oracle System Requirements

In order for Oracle 10g database software to be installed on a computer, you need to ensure that all the prerequisites are met. Oracle, because it runs on so many platforms, requires various forms of other software to be configured in order for it to work properly. This includes additional packages on Linux systems, specific services and software on Windows, kernel parameter sizing on Unix-based systems or any combination of these, as well as other, platform-specific environment settings and prerequisites.

Table 2-1 lists the minimum and recommended system requirements across most Oracle platforms. Notice that the CPU type and speed are not listed. This is because the operating system you are running will already determine which CPUs are supported. Oracle will work on the CPUs supported by the operating system you intend to run the software on. For a more specific list of system requirements, you should refer to the operating system–specific installation guide found on the installation CD or on the Oracle Technology Network (OTN) web site (www.oracle.com/technology/documentation/database10g.html).

As a general rule, the more RAM you have in the computer, the better it is for Oracle. RAM is the one resource that provides the best *bang for the buck* when it comes to performance of an Oracle database. If you plan on running many databases on the same server, increase the amount of RAM in the server to allow for smooth operation of all instances.

System Requirement	Minimum	Recommended
Random Access Memory (RAM)	512MB	1GB
Swap / Page File Space	1GB	Twice the size of RAM
Temp Space (/tmp or \TEMP)	400MB	1GB
Disk Space	1.5GB for Oracle software 1.5GB for starter database	1.5GB for Oracle software 1.5GB for starter database
Operating system and version	As specified in Oracle docs	As specified in Oracle docs

Table 2-1   Minimum and Recommended System Requirements for the Oracle 10g Database

EXAM TIP Oracle always recommends more RAM be available than specified in the system requirements. This avoids performance problems like paging and swapping due to lack of resources.

In terms of disk space, if you plan on having your databases grow, you should allocate additional disk space. The current thinking is *disk is cheap,* so add more space as needed to support the size of databases you plan on running. Adding more disk space can also allow you to more efficiently allocate that disk space for Oracle and take advantage of striping or other techniques to further improve performance.

Oracle 10g database is supported on many different operating systems and hardware platforms. While Linux and Windows may be the two most popular choices these days, Oracle is also available for Solaris, IBM AIX, HP-UX, HP (formerly Compaq) Tru64, and IBM z/OS (OS/390), as well as both 64-bit (AMD and Itanium) and 32-bit variants of Windows and Linux. When deciding on a specific version of an operating system, it is important to check Oracle's MetaLink support site (http://metalink.oracle.com) to ensure that your version of the operating system and platform is on the certified list. Oracle supports only certified versions of the operating system. For example, running Oracle on Red Hat's Fedora Project Linux is not officially supported, but Red Hat Linux Enterprise Edition AS and ES are supported. Always verify, either through the documentation or by checking on the Certify and Availability link on MetaLink, that you are installing Oracle on a supported platform.

 EXAM TIP The most up-to-date list of supported operating systems and versions can be found on Oracle's MetaLink support site.

Optimal Flexible Architecture

With the release of Oracle 8, Oracle introduced Optimal Flexible Architecture, or OFA. OFA is a method of naming mount points and directories and of organizing datafiles and database components to make it easy for a DBA to locate files and administer the database. The Oracle Universal Installer, when creating a starter database, will conform to OFA rules in the creation of that database. Furthermore, the Oracle Universal Installer will create a file and directory structure that will make compliance with OFA easy to achieve in the creation of additional databases using the Database Configuration Assistant.

The Optimal Flexible Architecture was developed by Oracle's consulting services to make the performance and monitoring of Oracle databases easier. OFA specifies that at least three sets of directories should be used to reduce contention and provide good performance. One set of directories will be used to store Oracle binary files such as the Oracle executables themselves, as well as associated support files that should normally not be changed. A second set of directories will be used to store controlfiles, redo log files, and other administrative files such as the parameter file for each database on the computer. Finally, a third set of directories will be used to store all the datafiles. Each set of directories should be on a separate physical hard disk, and further manual optimization may also be required to ensure good performance.

While OFA is not perfect, it does provide the basis for good performance and easier administration, including:

- A structured approach for locating the various files that are required and used by Oracle. This structured approach, when followed, will allow any DBA to easily become familiar with any database and server that they are asked to administer.

- Easier administration of databases while performing such tasks as backing up and restoring databases because of a familiar file and directory structure. If you need to create additional data files, you will also be able to figure out where to put the file by adhering to the OFA structure.

- Because the OFA configuration will make use of multiple physical disks on the computer, this will allow for improved performance of the databases that use it by reduced disk contention for datafiles, binary files, and redo log files. While simply adhering to OFA principles is not enough to guarantee optimal performance for your databases and server, it will provide a starting point for further performance monitoring and tuning.

- If you have multiple Oracle homes on the same computer or are running multiple versions of Oracle on the same computer, each version can adhere to OFA principles and thereby make it less likely that files required by one version of Oracle, or one Oracle package, will overwrite those of another version or package. OFA helps to separate potentially conflicting files, thereby making administration easier and contention less likely.

Directory and Mount Point Syntax

One of the things that makes OFA work well is a common naming scheme for mount points and directories (folders). Using a common naming methodology helps make it easier to organize and locate resources. The Oracle Database Configuration Assistant (DBCA) will create many of the OFA components when it is used to create a database in Oracle 10g. The Oracle Universal Installer used to install Oracle software will also create OFA-compliant structures within the mount points and directories you indicate as the base of the Oracle installation (ORACLE_BASE).

Recommendations for OFA-compliant naming scheme on a Linux/Unix platform include:

- Name all mount points using a combination of a common string constant and a variable value in the form /pm, where p is a string constant and m is a variable value. For example, /u01, /u02, /u03, etc., or /ora01, /ora02, /ora03 would be good choices. Using this convention makes it easy to add additional mount points that adhere to the naming convention.

- Within the mount points, name directories where Oracle software is installed in the form /pm/h/u/product/v, where /pm is the mount point as indicated in the preceding point, h is a standard directory name indicating a purpose such as app or db or home, u is the name of the owner of the directory (since multiple operating system users can install and own Oracle software), product is a literal, and v specifies the product version installed in the directory. For example, the location of the Oracle 10g database owned by an operating system user called "oracle" could be /u02/db/oracle/product/10.1.0. The location of an Oracle 10g Application Server installation could be /u01/app/oracle/product/9.0.4, or an Oracle 8i database could be /u01/db/oracle/product/8.1.7.

- Within the directory structure you would create an admin directory and additional subdirectories within the admin directory for storing specific file types used by Oracle. The full pathname would be /pm/h/admin/d/a, where admin is a literal, d is the SID (system identifier or name) of the database, and a is a subdirectory for a specific administrative file type. The common administration directories are shown in Table 2-2.

Subdirectory Name	Purpose	Example
adhoc	Ad hoc SQL and PL/SQL scripts for the database	/u02/db/admin/ocp10g/adhoc
arch	Location of archived redo log files	/u02/db/admin/ocp10g/arch
adump	Location of audit files—need to set AUDIT_FILE_DEST parameter first	/u02/db/admin/ocp10g/adump
bdump	Location of background process trace files and the alert log file. Set with the BACKGROUND_DUMP_DEST parameter	/u02/db/admin/ocp10g/bdump
cdump	Core dump file location. Set with the CORE_DUMP_DEST parameter	/u02/db/admin/ocp10g/cdump
create	Location of scripts used to create the database. DBCA places scripts in this location when you use it to create a new database	/u02/db/admin/ocp10g/create
exp	Recommended location of database export files created by the Export utility or Oracle Data Pump	/u02/db/admin/ocp10g/exp
logbook	Location of database history and status log files	/u02/db/admin/ocp10g/logbook
pfile	The parameter files used to start the database is placed here	/u02/db/admin/ocp10g/pfile
udump	User process trace files are located here. Set with the USER_DUMP_DEST parameter	/u02/db/admin/ocp10g/udump

Table 2-2 OFA-Compliant Administrative Directories and Their Contents

EXAM TIP The structure of the administrative directories of OFA is important for the effective administration of Oracle, and Oracle strongly recommends that it be used. DBAs are assumed to know the parameters to set in Oracle to ensure that the appropriate files are located in the OFA directory structure.

The naming of the mount points and directories is not enforced by Oracle. Rather, it is strongly recommended that you follow the recommendations to make it easier for you to identify what is installed on your computer's hard drive. In a Windows environment, the syntax is similar, though you could use drive letters for the mount points or mount the partition in an empty NTFS folder that serves as the base of your Oracle installation.

File-Naming Syntax

The final piece of a naming strategy needs to deal with the files located in the directories. For Oracle's datafiles, redo log files and controlfiles, the naming strategy starts with a directory naming component—the root of your database file structure (as opposed to the admin files outlined in the preceding section). The root of the datafile structure is a directory in the form /pm/q/d, where pm is the mount point, q is a literal indicating that the directory contains Oracle database data (e.g., "oradata" or "oracle"), and d is the name of the database sourced either from the DB_NAME parameter (recommended) or the ORACLE_SID environment variable. Examples include /u03/oradata/ocp10g and /u01/ORACLE/mydb.

It is possible, and quite common, to have data for a database on multiple mount points to spread the I/O workload across multiple physical disks and thereby provide better performance. For this reason, you will probably see the same directory name corresponding to a database on several mount points, such as /u02/oradata/ocp10g and /u03/oradata/ocp10g. This method can also be used to separate different Oracle database file types. These file types, and recommended naming convention are outlined in Table 2-3.

File Type	Purpose	Naming Convention
Controlfiles	Used to store information about the database, its files, and their status.	As control.ctl or control*nn*.ctl, where *nn* is a number (control01.ctl)
Redo log files	Store a record of changes to database data as they occur.	As redo*nn*.log, where *nn* is a number (redo01.log)
Datafiles	Store database data.	As *tablespacename*nn.dbf, where *tablespacename* is the name of the logical Oracle database storage structure and *nn* is a number ("system01.dbf" or "undo01.dbf")

Table 2-3 Recommended Naming Conventions for Oracle Database Files

An important point to remember is that only Oracle database files indicated in Table 2-3 should be stored in the OFA-compliant database file location. Storing other files makes it harder to keep track of which file is where. The administrative directory structure is used to store the other files used by an Oracle database and instance, whereas the database file location is used to store all files related to the Oracle database during normal operation—the control, redo log, and datafiles.

Installing Oracle Using the Oracle Universal Installer

Now that you are familiar with OFA and have decided upon the directory structure to be used for your Oracle installation, you can get the CDs out and are almost ready to install Oracle on your computer. Because Oracle is a complex piece of software running on many different operating systems, CPU architectures, and storage systems, additional requirements will need to be verified and tasks completed in order to ensure a successful installation.

Operating System Preparation

One of the first things you should do before installing the Oracle database software is to read the appropriate installation guide for your operating system and platform. These can be found on the Oracle Technology Network in the product documentation section for Oracle 10g database (www.oracle.com/technology/documentation/database10g.html). It is always a good idea to review the specific tasks that need to be performed on your environment because kernel parameters, other systems settings, and prerequisite software differ by platform. However, a couple of things are similar across all platforms.

 NOTE If you are installing Oracle on Linux, a special section of the OTN web site located at www.oracle.com/technology/tech/linux/install/index html deals with installing Oracle on Linux. Another good Linux resource is Werner Puschitz's Linux Page at www.puschitz.com (also linked from the OTN web site). Oracle-Base (www.oracle-base.com) is a good resource for Linux and other operating systems, as well as other Oracle product installation assistance.

Creating the User and Groups for Oracle

One of the first things you need to do before installing Oracle Database 10g is to create an operating system user and group that will own the Oracle software. The methods used depend on the operating system, but you should create at least one user (called **oracle** from here on in) and two groups, one to own the Oracle installation (**oinstall** will be used) and another to which users can be added for administering Oracle (**dba** is a commonly used group name).

For a Linux-based computer, you could issue the following commands while logged in as the **root** user to create the groups and users, as well as specifying the group ID and user ID values, the user's default home directory (-d /home/oracle) and the shell for the user (-s /bin/bash):

```
groupadd -g 500 oinstall
groupadd -g 501 dba
useradd -u 500 -g oinstall -G dba -d /home/oracle oracle -s /bin/bash
```

On Linux, in order to install Oracle you must log in as the **oracle** user. You will also need the **root** user to perform some configuration of the operating system, so make sure you know the **root** password or can have someone perform those tasks when needed. You cannot complete an install on Unix or Linux without performing the root-level operations.

NOTE If you will be installing Oracle on Linux and need some information on Linux commands, a couple of articles of value can be found at the Linux Technology Center on Oracle's web site: www.oracle.com/technology/tech/linux/index.html.

In Windows environments the DBA group needs to be a local group on the computer where Oracle is being installed and must be called **ORA_DBA**. It is important to note that you need not create this group before you install Oracle; it can be, and often is, created after Oracle is already installed. The only user requirement for installing Oracle on Windows is that the person installing the software must be logged in to the computer as a user that is a member of the local **Administrators** group.

Setting the Environment

In order for Oracle to operate properly after it is installed, a number of environment variables need to be configured for the **oracle** user. In Windows environments these requirements are automatically taken care of by Registry entries that Oracle creates when the software is installed, but in Unix and Linux these environment variables need to be configured manually. While no environment variables need to be configured when you are installing Oracle Database 10g and Oracle indicates that none should be set before starting the installation, setting them can ensure that Oracle performs properly during and after the install.

These are some variables that you may wish to set beforehand:

EXAM TIP You should be very familiar with these environment variables and their uses.

- **ORACLE_BASE** The root of an OFA-complaint Oracle directory structure for installation of all products on the computer. This environment variable specifies the directory where all Oracle products are installed on the computer, such as /opt/oracle.

- **ORACLE_HOME**   The home directory of the current Oracle installation. Typically specifies a directory under the path indicated by ORACLE_BASE such as $ORACLE_BASE/product/10.1.0 on a Linux or Unix system.

- **ORACLE_SID**   The identifier of the Oracle instance that you will connect to or create. In most environments it must be eight characters or less, beginning with a letter and containing letters and numbers. In Real Application Cluster environments it must be five characters or less. The default initial instance name is ORCL, though the ORACLE_SID must always be set to connect to an instance locally.

- **NLS_LANG**   Specifies the globalization settings for the Oracle installation in the form *language_territory.character_set*. The default value for NLS_LANG is "American_America.US7ASCII" in all environments except Windows, where this value is set to the regional settings specified for the operating system and keyboard setting.

NOTE If the keyboard setting in Windows is non-US English, then this will also cause Oracle to set the NLS_SORT value to be set to other than *binary*, thereby reducing optimizer effectiveness on character-based indexes. More information on how NLS_LANG and other NLS-related parameters work can be found in Chapter 21.

- **DISPLAY**   On Unix environments you need to indicate to the Oracle Universal Installer where to send graphical screen displays. The default behavior is to inherit the value of the DISPLAY environment variable from the operating system and send all output there. If you want to redirect the graphical display to an X Window terminal or some other location, you will need to set the DISPLAY environment variable in the form *hostname:display*, such as opus01.haunting.com:1.0. The user installing Oracle must have permissions to write to the display as well, which can be set using the `xhost` command in Unix-based environments.

NOTE To allow all users to write to a specific DISPLAY, the **root** user can issue the command `xhost +` to remove any security restrictions on that display. This is a security risk and should not be used as a permanent solution. Check the Linux/Unix documentation for more details on the proper usage of the `xhost` command.

EXAM TIP Understanding how to set the DISPLAY environment variable and use it during installation is worthwhile knowledge for the exam.

Before starting the installation of Oracle on Unix-based systems, it is a good idea to at least set the value of the ORACLE_HOME environment variable as the **oracle** user to tell Oracle where the software is to be installed and to create the directory path, as follows:

```
mkdir -p /opt/oracle/product/10.1.0
ORACLE_HOME=/opt/oracle/product/10.1.0 ; export ORACLE_HOME
```

Installing Oracle Software

Oracle is installed on all platforms by running the Oracle Universal Installer (OUI). This program is automatically invoked when you insert CD-ROM 1 of the installation media for Oracle Database 10g in the CD drive. You can also start it by issuing the `runInstaller` command from the CD-ROM on Unix-based systems or `setup.exe` from the root of the CD-ROM in Windows.

The Oracle Universal Installer

The Oracle Universal Installer is a Java-based application that looks and feels the same on all platforms. It includes a number of characteristics and features that facilitate a robust installation and configuration set:

- **Java-based design**   The Oracle Universal Installer is written in Java and looks and feels the same on any Oracle platform.

- **Dependency checking**   When you use OUI to install products on your computer, it will automatically check to see which other products might also need to be installed in order for your choice to function properly. The Universal Installer will then determine if the required components are already on the computer and select any it requires for installation.

- **Multiple Oracle home support**   OUI will keep track of all the Oracle home directories that exist on the target computer. Multiple Oracle homes are required if you want to install the Oracle database, Application Server, and other Oracle products and versions on the same computer. The Oracle Universal Installer will ensure that each product that requires a separate Oracle home will have it created and will keep track of which products and versions are installed where.

- **National language/globalization support**   When installing Oracle software, the Universal Installer will check to see what the computer's regional/ globalization settings are and configure itself to adhere to these settings. It will also do the same for the software that is being installed to ensure that the interactive experience that the user is expecting is delivered.

- **Web-based installation**   When you are prompted by the Oracle Universal Installer for the location of the software that you are installing, you can specify a physical or network disk location, or a URL where the files can be found. This allows you to create web pages that would be used to invoke the OUI and then point users to a server close to them that contains the package files for the application being installed. This can make large-scale deployments easier.

- **Unattended installation** The Oracle Universal Installer can be invoked from the command line and passed the name of a response file that has all the parameters required for the installation to proceed, as in this example:

```
runInstaller -responsefile respfile [-silent] [-nowelcome]
```

The `-nowelcome` command-line option tells the Oracle Universal Installer not to display the welcome screen when started. The default is to display the Oracle Universal Installer welcome screen. The `-silent` option tells the Oracle Universal Installer not to tell the user what is happening during the installation but to simply perform all of the tasks specified in the response file.

- **Intelligent uninstallation** Once you install the product using the Universal Installer, it keeps a record of the installation and allows you to uninstall a portion of the product or the product in its entirety. While performing an uninstall the Universal Installer will prompt you if you need to uninstall additional components, or if the uninstall will cause other products to fail, such that they must also be removed or the specific portion of the uninstall affecting them cancelled.

- **Support for user-defined packages** The Universal Installer allows you to add your own components to the list of packages to be installed when it is invoked. In this way you can install the Oracle server software and your own software at the same time. Furthermore, if specific utilities need to run during the installation process, the Universal Installer allows you to invoke them automatically from your installation script.

Installing Oracle Database 10g

The first thing that happens is that OUI performs a number of system checks to ensure that your computer is properly configured for Oracle and that you are logged in as a user with the appropriate privileges to perform the installation.

The tests that are to be performed are stored in a file called oraparam.ini located in the install directory of the first CD-ROM. It is possible to copy that file to another location and then make changes to the system prerequisite checks or other actions if you are familiar with editing its contents, though this is not recommended for users new to Oracle and OUI. You can then manually invoke the installer from the command line indicating which parameter file to use, as in the following example:

```
/mnt/cdrom/runInstaller -parameterFile /home/oracle/oraparam.ini
```

If you do not want the Oracle Universal Installer to perform any system checks, you can invoke it with the following command line:

```
/mnt/cdrom/runInstaller -ignoreSysPrereqs
```

In both of these examples /mnt/cdrom is the path to the CD-ROM root in a Red Hat Linux environment, and all commands and parameters are case sensitive.

EXAM TIP You should be familiar with at least the two `runInstaller` parameters indicated here and what they do.

After the system checks have been performed and passed (if things were not properly configured, OUI will raise an error and advise you of corrective action), the OUI welcome screen is displayed. Click Next to proceed.

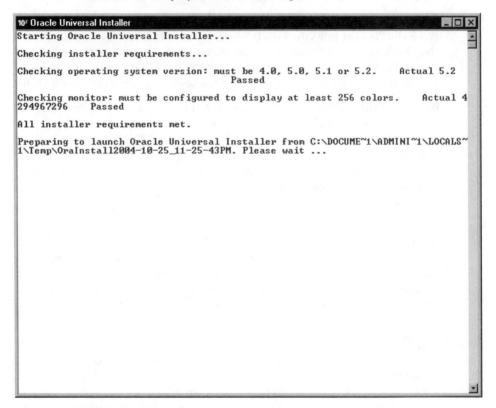

 NOTE The Oracle Installer on Windows has a Basic Installation option, in which it installs everything in a default location and optionally creates a starter database. If you choose this option, you will not be prompted for the other items discussed in the text that follows. Choosing the Advanced Installation option will prompt you for the items described herein.

If you are installing Oracle on a Unix-based system, you will next be asked to provide the location of the Oracle installation inventory used by the Oracle Universal Installer to keep track of the Oracle products installed on the computer, as well as the operating system group to be used to install Oracle products—the **oinstall** group referred to earlier. The default location for the inventory is $ORACLE_BASE/ oraInventory if the ORACLE_BASE environment variable is set; otherwise, another location will be indicated. Specify the inventory path and Oracle installation group and then click Next to continue.

 EXAM TIP You should be familiar with the workings of OUI on Unix-based platforms and the importance of the inventory location and files.

For Unix/Linux-based installations you will be prompted to run a script—orainstRoot.sh—as **root** from the Oracle inventory directory you specified earlier. This script needs to be run the first time any Oracle product is installed on a server. It will create the inventory points file called oraInst.loc, usually at the location specified by ORACLE_BASE—e.g., /opt/oracle/oraInst.loc—with a link to a file with the same name in the /etc directory on a Linux system. You will need to connect to your server as **root** (or open a terminal window in your X Window session and su to **root**) and run this script that creates additional directories and sets appropriate ownership and permissions on files. The contents of the script will be similar to this code listing:

```
#!/bin/sh
INVPTR=/etc/oraInst.loc
INVLOC=/opt/oracle/oraInst.loc
GRP=oinstall
PTRDIR="`dirname $INVPTR1";
#Create the software inventory location pointer file
if [ ! -d "$PTRDIR" ] ; then
  mkdir -p $PTRDIR
fi
echo "Creating the Oracle inventory pointer file ($INVPTR";
echo  inventory_loc=$INVLOC > $INVPTR
echo  inst_group=$GRP >\> $INVPTR
chmod 664 $INVPTR
# Create the Oracle inventory directory if it does not exist
if [ ! -d "$INVLOC" ] ; then
  echo "Creating the Oracle inventory directory ($INVLOC)";
  mkdir -p $INVLOC
  chmod 775 $INVLOC
fi
echo "Changing groupname of $INVLOC to oinstall.";
chgrp oinstall $INVLOC
if [ $? != 0 ] ; then
  echo "WARNING: chgrp of $INVLOC to oinstall failed!";
fi
```

After clicking OK to acknowledge that the script has been run successfully, you are then asked to confirm the source of the installation media and the destination Oracle home name and path. If you preset ORACLE_HOME, the destination path will be filled in and a suggested name for the Oracle home will be displayed. The Oracle home name and location will be placed by OUI into a file called /etc/oratab, which lists all the Oracle homes for all products installed by OUI as well as any manually added entries. This allows OUI to determine which products are found on the computer.

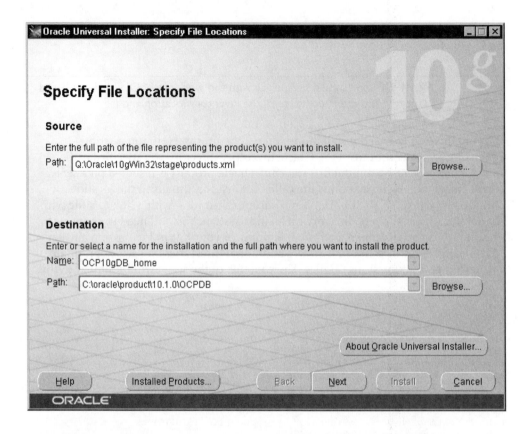

Clicking Next takes you to the product selection screen, allowing you to choose which edition of Oracle Database 10*g* to install on the computer. The default is Enterprise Edition, which includes such enterprise-level features as Oracle Data Guard (for the creation, management, and monitoring of standby databases for quick failover), several features that extend the security of Oracle databases (Oracle Advanced Security, Oracle Label Security, Enterprise User Security, Virtual Private Database, N-tier authentication, and Fine-Grained Auditing and Access Control), and some additional features to support enterprise data warehousing (Oracle Partitioning, Oracle OLAP, Transportable Tablespaces, and others). You can also select Custom, allowing you to choose components and features to install. You should always choose only the database edition you are licensed for and install only the features that your organization is licensed for. Make your choice and then click Next.

NOTE A Personal Edition of Oracle is also available. It includes all of the features of the Enterprise Edition and is designed for software development on a personal workstation.

 EXAM TIP A good understanding of the different editions of Oracle Database 10g is required for the exam.

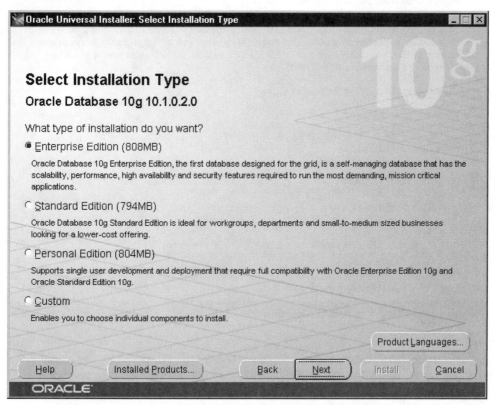

You will now have the option to create a starter database to use with Oracle or to bypass this option. You can always create a database later, but creating it during installation speeds up the process. Three preconfigured templates for a new database, which include database files, make the creation process quick, but you also have the option to create a custom database, which takes longer and will create the datafiles according to settings you specify. Make your selection and then click Next.

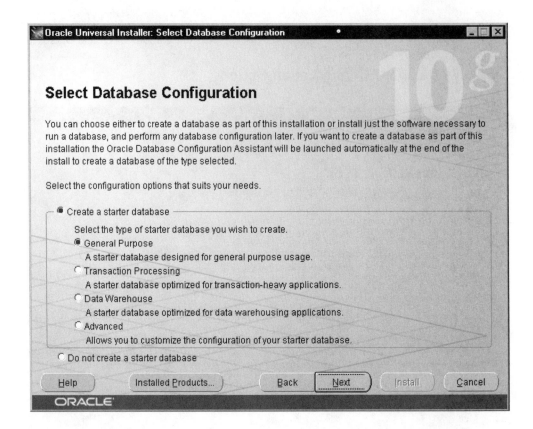

If you decided to create a starter database, you will be prompted for the global database name in the format *database.domain* and the database SID (or system identifier,) of one to eight characters starting with a letter. Defaults will be presented for these as well as for the character set to be used for the database (for which guidelines for making a good choice will be provided in Chapter 3). You will also be asked whether or not to include sample schemas in the database. Make your choices and then click Next.

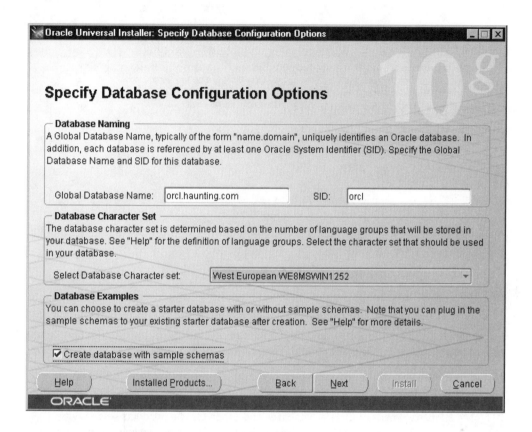

If you installed the agent for the Oracle Enterprise Manager Grid Control on the computer prior to installing Oracle Database 10g, you will have the option to use it for the management of this database; if not, you can select the Database Control to manage this database and instance. You also can specify an SMTP e-mail server and administrator e-mail address for notifications to be sent to. Click Next to continue.

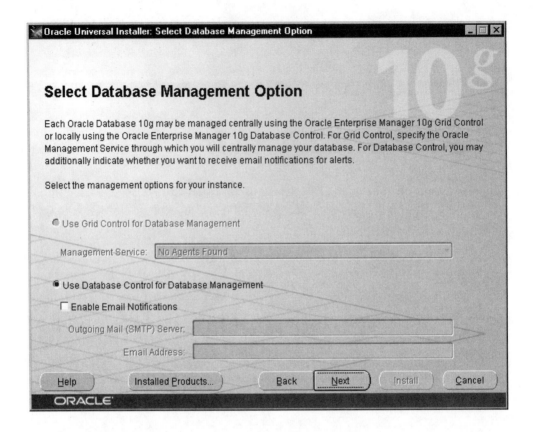

NOTE Enterprise Manager Grid Control provides enterprise-wide management of Oracle databases and other Oracle products—see www .oracle.com/enterprise_manager/index.html for more information. A thorough discussion is beyond the scope of the exam and the book.

The next screen will ask you how you want to store the database files: on the local file system using Automated Storage Management (ASM), whereby Oracle creates and manages the database files itself, providing striping and mirroring capabilities, or by using raw devices or partitions dedicated to Oracle—an advanced method. The easiest choice is always the local file system, though ASM has benefits worth considering, so a review of the *Oracle Database Administrators Guide* on setting up ASM may be worthwhile. You can find this manual on one of the CDs you were shipped or on OTN.

EXAM TIP Oracle datafiles can be stored using three methods: file system, ASM, and raw devices. The file system option also includes Oracle Cluster File System and third-party disk storage arrays.

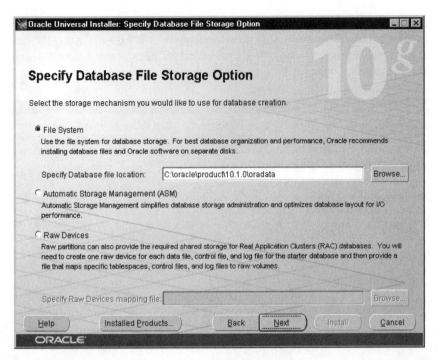

You next have the option to enable automatic backups. Typically it is a better idea to configure backups after you have properly added objects to your database and have it working as needed, so click Next on this screen to continue.

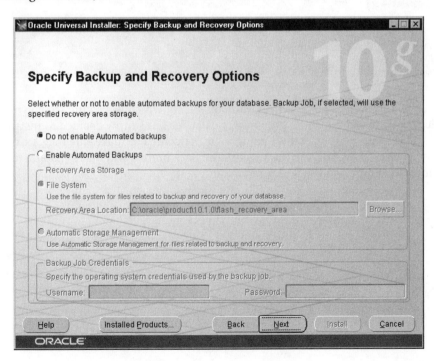

On the screen displayed you will need to specify the passwords for the Oracle users created initially. You can specify individual passwords for each user—the default and recommended method—or a single password for each of the accounts listed. Enter the appropriate passwords and confirm them and then click Next.

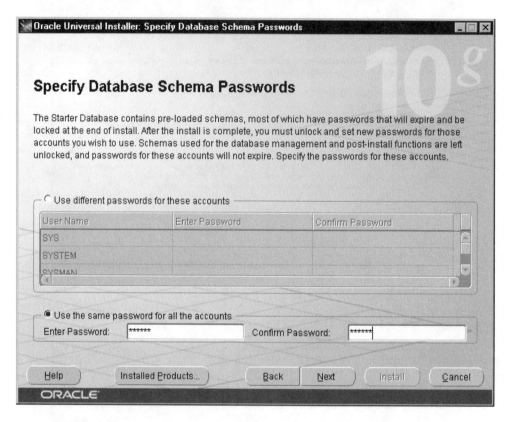

The next screen to appear is the Summary screen, which is also the screen you would see if you did not choose to create a database but simply decided to install Oracle. Review the actions that are going to be performed to make sure they are correct and then click Install. You can always click the Back button and make changes if you find incorrect entries on the Summary screen.

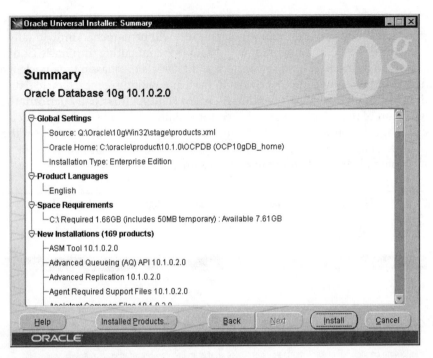

The Oracle Universal Installer starts the installation process and presents a status bar indicating how far along the installation is. You will also be presented with information on the location of the installation logfile at the bottom of the window so that you can check for any errors that may have occurred.

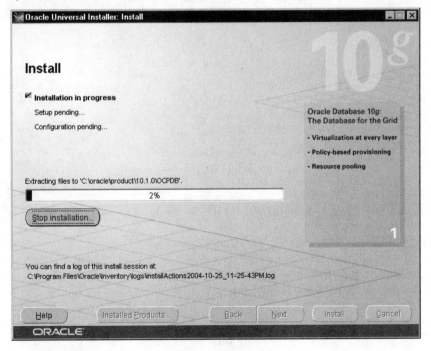

When the installation is ready to configure the database, and only if you selected a starter database, various configuration assistants will be launched individually including the *iSQL*Plus Configuration Assistant (for configuring the Oracle Containers for Java—OC4J—instance used to connect to the Oracle database), the Oracle Net Configuration Assistant (NETCA) to set up basic networking for the Oracle database, and the Oracle Database Configuration Assistant (DBCA) to actually perform the configuration of the database you selected for installation. You will be provided with a screen to notify you which assistants are being launched and their status. At their completion Oracle will specify if they succeeded or not, in which case you can retry the ones that failed, and then the install is complete.

 EXAM TIP Be familiar with what each configuration assistant does.

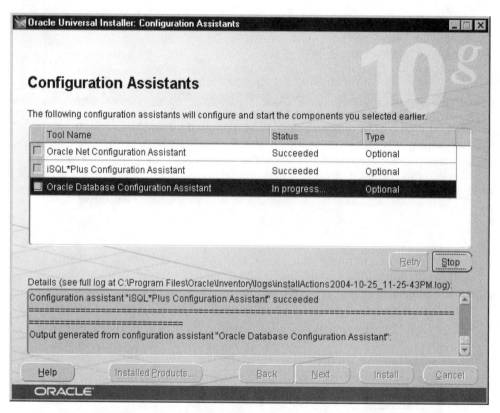

Once the Oracle Database Configuration Assistant has completed, you will be provided with information on the URL for the Oracle Enterprise Manager web site, as shown next, and have the option to unlock other user accounts in the database. Click OK to complete the database configuration.

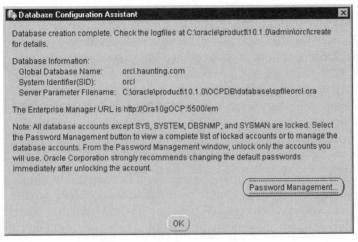

On Unix/Linux platforms you will also be asked to run a script called root.sh as the user **root**. This script is located in ORACLE_HOME directory and populates the /etc/oratab file with information on the Oracle homes and database instances on the computer. This information is used by Oracle Enterprise Manager and other administrative components to determine where databases are located, and whether or not they should be automatically started when the operating system starts. In Windows this information is located in the Registry, and no script needs to be run.

EXAM TIP Understand the importance, location, and contents of the oratab file.

The final screen will provide a summary of all URLs for the various products installed, including *i*SQL*Plus, Oracle Enterprise Manager, and Ultra Search. Make a note of these and then click Exit to complete the installation.

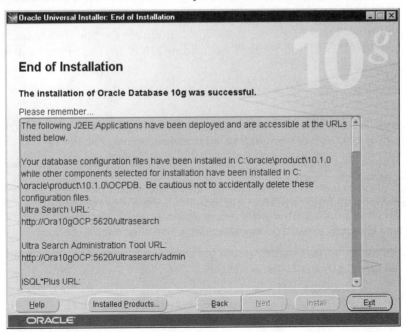

Exercise 2-1: Installing Oracle Database 10g

In this exercise you will install Oracle Database 10g on your computer and create the starter database. You can perform this task on either a Windows or Linux-based computer. Remember to create the user and group accounts and verify the system requirements prior to starting the installation. If you do not have the software, you can download Oracle Database 10g for your platform from the Oracle Technology Network (http://otn.oracle.com).

 NOTE Unix and Linux will be used interchangeably in this book. You should assume that when one is mentioned, both are included.

1. Log on to your computer as the **oracle** user (on Linux) or a user that is a member of the **Administrators** group on Windows.

2. Insert the Oracle Database 10g CD-ROM in the CD-ROM drive. The install program should start automatically. If not, execute `setup.exe` (Windows) or `runInstaller` from the root of the CD drive to invoke it.

3. If you are on Windows, choose the Advanced Installation option and click Next; for Linux click Next on the Welcome screen.

4. If you are installing on Linux, you will be asked to confirm the location of the inventory directory and the install group. Verify the information presented and click Next.

5. If you are installing on Linux and are asked to run a script as **root**, launch a new terminal window and run the script and then click Continue.

6. Verify the source and destination file locations in the Specify File Locations screen. Enter a name for the Oracle home (16 characters or less) and then click Next.

7. When prompted for the edition of Oracle to install, choose Enterprise Edition and then click Next.

8. The Oracle Universal Installer will perform prerequisite checks. If there are any errors, correct them and then click Next.

9. On the Select Database Configuration screen select a General Purpose starter database and then click Next.

10. Enter a database name and SID. Choose a database name in the format *database.domain* such as orcl.haunting.com and a SID name of ORCL. Leave the character set and other choices as is and click Next to continue.

11. When prompted whether to use the Database Control or Grid Control to manage the database, select Database Control and click Next.

12. On the File Storage Option screen, choose File System as the storage type and a path for the datafiles, or leave the default and click Next.

13. On the Backup and Recovery screen leave the default of no backups and click Next.

14. Select "Use the same password for all accounts" on the following screen and enter and confirm a password you will easily remember, such as "oracle." Then click Next.

15. Verify the installation parameters on the Summary screen and then click Install to begin the installation of Oracle Database 10g.

16. Monitor the installation on the following screen and then review activity as the configuration assistants are launched. This may take some time to complete. Acknowledge the completion of the Database Configuration Assistant by clicking OK on the dialog box presented and then review the information on ports configured. Click Exit to end the Oracle Universal Installer.

17. Start your web browser and navigate to http://localhost:5500/em to connect to the Enterprise Manager web site. Enter a username of SYSTEM with the password you specified in Step 14 and then click Login, acknowledge the licensing screen by clicking "I Agree" to display the EM web site for your database.

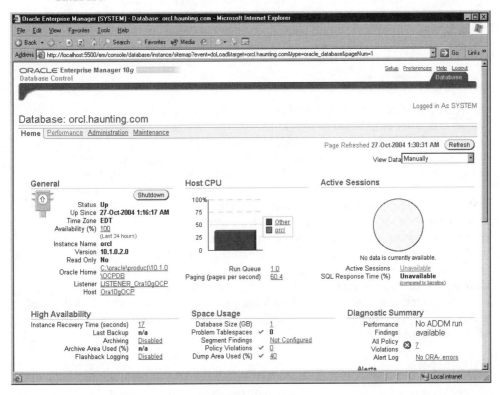

18. Close your browser. Congratulations—you have successfully installed Oracle Database 10g on your computer.

Post-Installation Tasks

If you installed Oracle on Windows, the Registry will have information on the path, environment variables, and other settings that need to be configured in order to run and manage the Oracle database on the computer. For Unix-based systems it is necessary to configure the **oracle** user's environment to administer and manage Oracle. One of the easiest ways to do this is to create a shell script or modify the user's login script with the appropriate settings.

The required settings include configuring ORACLE_HOME, ORACLE_BASE, ORACLE_SID, PATH, and other environment variables with the appropriate values. The following is a sample of a Linux .bash_profile login script used for the BASH shell with the appropriate settings to be used to manage the ORCL database created in the previous exercise. You can use it is as template to modify your own file.

```
# Oracle Settings
TMP=/tmp; export TMP
TMPDIR=$TMP; export TMPDIR
ORACLE_BASE=/opt/oracle; export ORACLE_BASE
ORACLE_HOME=$ORACLE_BASE/product/10.1.0/orcl; export ORACLE_HOME
ORACLE_SID=ORCL; export ORACLE_SID
PATH=$ORACLE_HOME/bin:/usr/sbin:$PATH; export PATH
LD_LIBRARY_PATH=$ORACLE_HOME/lib:/lib:/usr/lib; export LD_LIBRARY_PATH
CLASSPATH=$ORACLE_HOME/JRE:$ORACLE_HOME/jlib:$ORACLE_HOME/rdbms/jlib; export
CLASSPATH
LD_ASSUME_KERNEL=2.4.1; export LD_ASSUME_KERNEL
ulimit -u 16384 -n 65536
```

Chapter Review

Oracle Database 10g can be installed on many platforms, including Windows, Linux, and several varieties of Unix, as well as others. The Oracle Universal Installer is used to perform the installation and provides a similar interface on all Oracle platforms. Before installing Oracle, you will need to ensure your target computer and operating system satisfy the prerequisites, as well as perform some preconfiguration tasks.

Optimal Flexible Architecture is a set of standard directory and file naming conventions, as well as directory structures to make management of Oracle databases easier. Though using an OFA-compliant directory and file naming method is not enforced, it is strongly recommended to make your life easier.

Oracle Database 10g software is available in several editions, with Enterprise Edition providing all of the features and functions, while Standard Edition lacks some of the more advanced features such as Oracle OLAP and high-availability architecture.

Even though you have purchased the Enterprise Edition, you may not be licensed to use the additional-cost features, such as Oracle Advanced Security, Oracle Partitioning, or Oracle Data Mining.

Questions

1. You are asked to describe the benefits of the Oracle Universal Installer to your manager. Which of the following are key features of OUI? (Choose all correct answers.)

    A. OUI performs identically on all platforms on which Oracle runs.

    B. Web-based deployments can be performed using OUI.

    C. OUI is written using a .NET-based language ideal for Windows platforms.

    D. OUI is a text-based application not requiring a graphical display.

    E. Unattended installations can be performed using OUI.

2. The oratab file contains the following information. (Choose two correct answers.)

    A. A list of all Oracle products installed on the computer

    B. A list of all database instances and Oracle homes installed on the computer

    C. Version-specific information about each Oracle product and database on the computer

    D. Startup information for database instances on the computer

    E. Information to help Enterprise Manager manage Oracle databases on the computer

3. When installing Oracle on Unix-based systems, which of the following must you create before starting the installation? (Choose three correct answers.)

    A. The **root** user account

    B. The **oracle** user account

    C. The **oracle** group account

    D. The **oinstall** user account

    E. The **oinstall** group account

    F. The **dba** group account

4. Installing Oracle on a Windows computer requires that you be logged in as whom? (Choose the best answer.)

    A. The **oracle** user

    B. A user that is a member of the **Domain Admins** group

    C. A user that is a member of the **oinstall** group

    D. A user that is a member of the local **Administrators** group

    E. Any user with login privileges on the computer

5. Which of the following environment variables must be set on Unix-based computers before starting to install Oracle software? (Choose all correct answers.)

    A. ORACLE_HOME

    B. ORACLE_BASE

    C. ORACLE_SID

    D. LD_LIBRARY_PATH

    E. All of the above

    F. None of the above

6. When deciding between Enterprise Edition and Standard Edition of Oracle software, which of the following needed features would require that you purchase and install Enterprise Edition? (Choose two correct answers.)

    A. Real Application Clusters

    B. N-tier authentication

    C. Support of multiple CPUs on the server platform

    D. Oracle Enterprise Manager Database Control

    E. The ability to partition data in the database

7. Which of the following paths are consistent with Optimal Flexible Architecture? (Choose all correct answers.)

    A. /opt/oracle/ocsdb

    B. /opt/oracle/product/10.1.0/ocsdb

    C. /opt/oracle/admin/ocsdb/bdump

    D. /oracle/mydb

    E. /opt/oracle/admin/bdump

8. You are deciding on whether or not to implement Optimal Flexible Architecture for your Oracle installation. What are some of the considerations in favor of using OFA? (Choose all correct answers.)

    A. It provides a standardized directory structure, making files easier to find.

    B. It provides a standardized naming convention for Oracle executable files.

    C. It automatically spreads Oracle files across multiple disks when creating a new database using a standard directory structure.

    D. It makes all Oracle installations appear similar, reducing learning curves for database administration of many servers.

    E. It is required by Oracle.

9. You are installing Oracle Database 10g on a computer with the Red Hat Enterprise Linux ES 4 operating system. You are certain that the Oracle Universal Installer system check will fail on this operating system, but you want to install Oracle anyway. How would you invoke the OUI and force it not to perform system checks? (Choose the best answer.)

    A. `setup -ignorePreReqs`

    B. `setup -ignorePrereqs`

    C. `runInstaller -ignoreSysPrereqs`

    D. `runInstaller -ignoreSysprereqs`

    E. `runInstaller -bypassPrereqs`

    F. `setup -bypassPrereqs`

10. If you wanted to modify the file used by the Oracle Universal Installer with system prerequisite information, which file would you modify? (Choose the best answer.)

    A. oraparam.ini

    B. oraparam.ora

    C. oraparam.ins

    D. sysprereqs.ini

    E. sysprereqs.ora

    F. sysprereqs.ins

Answers

1. **A, B, and E.** Oracle Universal Installer is a graphical Java-based (not .NET-based) application that runs identically on all Oracle platforms. It allows the source location to be a URL, thereby allowing for web-based deployments, and it can be run unattended for silent installations.

2. **B and D.** The oratab file on a Unix-based system includes a list of database instances installed on the computer and an indicator whether or not the instance should be automatically started when the computer is booted. It does not contain a list of installed Oracle products (that's in the installer inventory location), any version-specific Oracle information, or Enterprise Manager configuration details.

3. **B, E, and F.** Installing Oracle on a Linux-based computer requires that you create the **oracle** user, and the **oinstall** (to own the Oracle installation information) and **dba** (for database administration) groups prior to starting the installation. The **root** user is created when you install the operating system, though that user is required to complete parts of the installation.

4. **D.** Installing Oracle on a Windows computer requires that you be logged in as a member of the local **Administrators** group. If you are logged in as a member of the **Domain Admins** group, you will also be able to install Oracle but will also have more privileges than needed, which may compromise security. The **oinstall** group and the **oracle** user are needed in Unix-based environments.

5. **F.** None of the environment variables must be set for Oracle to be installed on a Unix-based computer. However, in order to manage and administer the database, the ORACLE_HOME, ORACLE_SID and LD_LIBRARY_PATH variables may need to be set.

6. **B and E.** If you want to use N-tier authentication and partition table data in your database, you must install and purchase Enterprise Edition. All of the other features (RAC, multiple CPU support, and the Enterprise Manager Database Control) are available in Standard Edition.

7. **B and C.** While Oracle does not require you to use OFA, when you decide to use OFA the path and file naming conventions do set rules for usage. Only

"/opt/oracle/product/10.1.0/ocsdb" for an ORACLE_HOME path and "/opt/oracle/admin/ocsdb/bdump" for a background dump and log destination adhere to the naming conventions specified by OFA.

8. **A** and **D.** OFA is targeted at making administration of Oracle databases easier by making Oracle files easier to find on any platform and file system. In order to do this, it provides a standardized directory structure for Oracle installations that makes all Oracle installations similar, reducing learning curves for administrators. It is not required by Oracle, but highly recommended. OFA does not automatically spread files across multiple drives, nor does it provide a naming convention for Oracle executable files, but only Oracle data, redo, control, and other files attached to a database instance.

9. **C.** The `runInstaller -ignoreSysPrereqs` command will invoke OUI on a Linux computer, telling it not to check system prerequisites before performing the installation. OUI parameters are case-sensitive, making answer D incorrect, while "setup" is the command to invoke OUI on a Windows platform.

10. **A.** The oraparam.ini file contains the system prerequisite information used by OUI to verify the operating system and other requirements for installation.

CHAPTER 3

Creating an Oracle Database

In this chapter you will learn how to
- Create an Oracle database
- Explain the Oracle database architecture
- Explain the instance architecture
- Use the management framework
- Use DBCA to create a database
- Use DBCA to configure a database
- Use DBCA to drop a database
- Use DBCA to manage templates

This chapter goes through the theory and practice of creating a database: a review of the Oracle server architecture, followed by the mechanics of database creation with a look at the relevant tools, both GUI and command line, and the management options. But one immediate objective is to demystify the process. Creating a database is not a big deal. You can create twenty databases during a tea break (and you may well have to do this if you are, for example, supporting an IT teaching institution) once you understand what is required and have prepared appropriate scripts. Furthermore, do not worry about getting it right. Hardly anything is fixed at database creation time. It certainly makes sense to think about how your database will be structured, its purpose and environment, at creation time, but (with one exception) everything can be changed afterward. As a general rule, keep things as simple as possible at this stage. Get the thing created and working first, worry about configuring it for use later.

Architecture of the Oracle Server

An Oracle server consists of two entities: the instance and the database (as shown in Figure 3-1). They are separate, but connected. During the creation process, the instance is created first, and then the database. In a typical single instance environment the relationship of instance to database is one-to-one, a single instance connected to a single database, but always bear in mind that the relationship may be many-to-one: multiple instances on different computers opening a common database on a shared disk system. This is known as Real Application Clusters, or RAC. RAC gives amazing capabilities for performance, fault tolerance, and scalability (and possibly cost savings) and is integral to the Oracle's concept of the *grid*. With previous releases RAC (or its precursor, Oracle Parallel Server) was an expensive add-on, but with Database release 10g Standard Edition, RAC is bundled. This is an indication of how much Oracle Corporation

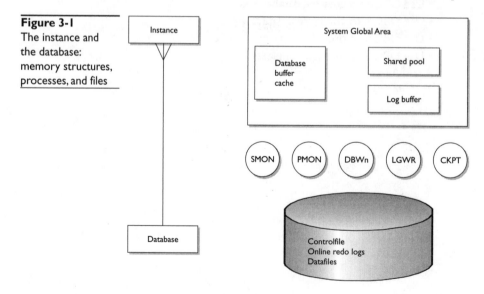

Figure 3-1
The instance and the database: memory structures, processes, and files

wants to push users toward the RAC environment. Standard Edition RAC is limited to computers with no more than two CPUs, and a maximum of four computers in the cluster, but even that gives access to a phenomenally powerful environment. RAC is an extra cost option for the Enterprise Edition, where the scalability becomes effectively limitless: bounded only by the capacities of the underlying operating system and hardware. It is also possible for one instance, through database links, to connect to multiple databases. For the most part, you will be dealing with the most common environment in this book: one instance on one computer, opening a database stored on local disks.

The *instance* consists of memory structures and processes. Its existence is transient, in your RAM and on your CPU(s). The *database* consists of physical files, on disk. Thus the lifetime of the instance is only as long as it exists in memory—it can be started and stopped. By contrast, the database, once created, persists indefinitely—until you deliberately delete the files that compose it. Within the physical structures of the database, which our system administrators see, are the logical structures that our end users (developers, business analysts, data warehouse architects, etc.) see. The Oracle architecture guarantees abstraction of the logical from the physical: there is no way that a programmer can determine where, physically, a bit of data is located. He/she addresses only logical structures, such as tables. Similarly, it is impossible for a system administrator to know what bits of data are in any physical structure: all he can see is the operating system files, not what is within them. Only you, the database administrator, is permitted (and required) to see both sides of the story. The data dictionary, which contains metadata describing the whole server, manages the relationship between physical and logical structures. Creating the data dictionary is an integral part of database creation. The final stages of the creation process make the newly created database usable, by generating various views and PL/SQL packages, and manageable, by generating the Enterprise Manager Database Control facility.

The Instance: Memory Structures and Processes

An Oracle instance consists of a block of shared memory known as the System Global Area, or SGA, and a number of processes. At a minimum, the SGA will contain three data structures: the shared pool, the database buffer cache, and the log buffer. It may, optionally, also contain a large pool, a Java pool, and a streams pool. Some of these SGA structures are fixed in size when you start the instance; others can be changed dynamically. But none are fixed at database creation time: you can stop the instance and restart it whenever you please, with a totally different memory configuration. You should remember, though, that if you are continually making memory configuration changes on a live system and those changes are of a type that requires the instance to be shut down, incurring downtime, your end users will not be happy with you.

 EXAM TIP Remember the three required elements of the SGA: the shared pool, the database buffer cache, and the log buffer.

The *shared pool* is further subdivided into a number of other structures. This book will only briefly mention two of the shared pool components: the library cache and the data dictionary cache. The *library cache* is a memory area for storing recently executed code, in its parsed form. Parsing is the conversion of code written by programmers into something executable, and it is a slow process that Oracle does on demand. By caching parsed code in the shared pool so that it can be reused without reparsing, performance can be greatly improved. The *data dictionary cache* stores recently used object definitions: descriptions of tables, indexes, users, and other metadata definitions. Keeping such definitions in memory, rather than having to read them repeatedly from the data dictionary on disk, enhances performance.

The *database buffer cache* is Oracle's work area for executing SQL. Users don't ever update data on disk. They copy data into the database buffer cache and update it there, in memory. Ideally, all the data that is frequently accessed will be in the database buffer cache, therefore minimizing the need for disk I/O.

The *log buffer* is a very small memory structure used as a short-term staging area for all changes that are applied to data in the database buffer cache. Chapter 9 will describe in detail how the log buffer and the database buffer cache are used when SQL statements retrieve and manipulate data.

The *large pool* is an optional area that, if created, will be used automatically by various processes that would otherwise take memory from the shared pool. You will be introduced to one of its main uses in Chapter 13 in the discussion on shared (or multithreaded) servers. The Recovery Manager, RMAN, covered in later chapters, will also use the large pool for its disk and tape I/O slave processes.

The *Java pool* is required only if your application is going to run Java stored procedures within the database: it is used for the heap space needed to instantiate the Java objects. However, a number of Oracle options are written in Java, so the Java pool is considered standard nowadays.

The *streams pool* is used by Oracle streams, an advanced tool that is beyond the scope of the exam or this book.

 TIP The sizing of SGA memory structures is critical for performance. In general, they should be large enough, but not too large. In addition to wasted memory, performance can degrade if too much memory is assigned to the SGA components.

Along with its SGA, the instance will also have, at a minimum, five processes: the system monitor, SMON; the process monitor, PMON; the database writer, DBWn (you may have up to ten of these); the log writer, LGWR; and the checkpoint process, CKPT. These are known as "background" processes, because they always exist while the instance is running, whether or not any sessions are actually logged onto the instance, or indeed even if a database has not yet been created or opened.

SMON's major function is opening the database: enabling the connection between the instance and a database. Chapter 5 will detail how it does this. During normal running, it carries out a number of monitoring and tidying-up operations.

PMON looks after user sessions, taking appropriate action if a session gets into trouble. For instance, if a user's PC reboots while the user is logged on to the database, PMON will detect this and tidy up whatever work the user had in progress.

The DBWn process or processes (by default, an instance will have one database writer per eight CPUs) is responsible for all writing to datafiles. Remember, no sessions ever update data on disk; they update only data in the database buffer cache: all updates are then funneled through the DBWn to disk. In general, DBWn writes as little and as rarely as possible. The assumption is that disk I/O is bad for performance, so Oracle keeps it to a minimum.

The LGWR propagates all changes applied to data in the database buffer cache to the online redo log files on disk. In contrast with DBWn, this disk write activity is done as near as possible in real time—and when you issue the COMMIT statement, it really is done in real time: it immediately flushes the changes from their small and temporary staging area, the log buffer in the SGA, to the online redo log files on disk. This is to ensure that all users' work is saved so that, in the event of damage to the database's datafiles, the changes can be applied to a restored backup. In this manner (as is covered in later chapters), Oracle can guarantee that data will never be lost.

The CKPT process is responsible for ensuring that, from time to time, the instance is synchronized with the database. In principle, the database is always out of date: there will be changes that have been applied in memory that have not yet been written to the datafiles by DBWn (though the changes themselves will have been streamed out to the online redo log files by LGWR as they happen). There are occasions when it is necessary to force a write of all changed data from the database buffer cache to the datafiles, to bring the database right up-to-date. The CKPT process controls the frequency of this.

 EXAM TIP Remember the five required background processes: system monitor, process monitor, database writer, log writer, and checkpoint process.

There are also a number of optional background processes (far more with 10*g* than with previous releases), some of which you will see in later chapters. Some of the background processes can be tuned. For example, you can decide how many database writer processes to launch, and you can (to a certain extent) control how frequently they will write changed data bocks from the database buffer cache to the datafiles. You do not need to consider this at database creation time: you can sort such things out later, always bearing in mind that some changes will require downtime.

The Database: Physical Structures

Three file types make up an Oracle database, along with a few others that exist externally to the database and, strictly speaking, are optional. The required files are the controlfiles, the online redo log files, and the datafiles. The external files are the initialization parameter file, the password file, and archived redo log files.

Every database has one *controlfile*, but a good DBA will always create multiple copies of the controlfile so that if one copy is damaged, the database itself will survive. If all copies of the controlfile are lost, it is possible (though perhaps awkward) to recover, but you should never find yourself in that situation. You don't have to worry about keeping multiplexed copies of the controlfile synchronized—Oracle will take care of that. The controlfile is small, but vital. It contains pointers to the rest of the database: the locations of the online redo log files and of the datafiles. It also stores information required to maintain database integrity: various critical sequence numbers and timestamps, for example. If you use the Recovery Manager, RMAN, then some backup information will also be stored in the controlfile. The controlfile will usually be no more than a few megabytes big, but you can't survive without it. Its maintenance is automatic; your only control is how many copies to have, and where to put them. If you get the number of copies, or their location, wrong at creation time, you can add or remove copies later, or move them around—but you should bear in mind that any such operations will require downtime.

Every database has at least two online *redo log files*, but as with the controlfile, a good DBA creates multiple copies of each online redo log file. The online redo logs store a continuous chain in chronological order of every change applied to the database. This will be the bare minimum of information required to reconstruct, or redo, changes. The redo log consists of groups of redo log files, each file being known as a *member*. Oracle requires at least two groups of at least one member each to function. You may create more than two groups for performance reasons, and more than one member per group for safety. The requirement for a minimum of two groups is in order that one group can accept the current changes while the other group is being backed up (or "archived," to use the correct term). One of the groups is the "current" group: changes are written to the current logfile group by LGWR. As user sessions update data in the database buffer cache, they also write out the minimal changes to the redo log buffer. LGWR continually flushes this buffer to the current online log group. Redo log files are fixed size; therefore, eventually the file members making up the current group will fill. LGWR will then perform what is called a *log switch*. It makes the second group current, and starts writing to that. If your database is configured appropriately, you will then archive (back up) the logfile members making up the first group. When the second group fills, LGWR will switch back to the first group, making it current, and overwriting it. Thus, the online redo log groups (and therefore the members making them up) are used in a circular fashion.

As with the controlfile, if you have multiple members per group (and you should!) you don't have to worry about keeping them synchronized. LGWR will ensure that it writes to all of them, in parallel, thus keeping them identical. If you lose one member of a group, as long as you have a surviving member, the database will continue to function.

The size and number of your online redo log file groups is a matter of tuning. In general, you will choose a size appropriate to the amount of activity you anticipate. A very busy database will require larger members than a largely static database. The number of members per group will depend on what level of fault tolerance is deemed appropriate. However, you don't have to worry about this at database creation time.

You can move your online redo log files around, add or drop them, and create ones of different sizes as you please at any time later on. Such operations are performed "online" and don't require downtime; therefore, they are transparent to the end users.

The third file type making up a database is the *datafile*. At a minimum, you must have two datafiles, to be created at database creation time. With previous releases of Oracle, you could create a database with only one datafile—10*g* requires two. You will, however, have many more than that when your database goes live, and you will usually create a few more to begin with.

Datafiles are the repository for data. Their sizes and number are effectively unlimited. A small database, of only a few gigabytes, might have just half a dozen datafiles of only a few hundred megabytes each. A larger database could have thousands of datafiles, whose size is limited only by the capabilities of the host operating system and hardware.

The datafiles are the physical structures visible to the system administrators. Logically, they are the repository for the segments containing user data that the programmers see, and also for the segments that make up the data dictionary. Datafiles can be renamed, resized, moved, added, or dropped at any time in the lifetime of the database, but remember that some operations on some datafiles may require downtime.

Logical Structures: Tablespaces and Segments

The physical structures that make up a database are visible as operating system files to your system administrators. Your users see logical structures such as tables. Oracle uses the term "segment" to describe any structure that contains data. Your typical segment is a table, containing rows of data, but there are more than a dozen possible segment types in an Oracle database. Of particular interest (for exam purposes) are table segments, index segments, and undo segments, all of which are investigated in detail in later chapters. For now, you don't need to know more than that tables contain rows of information; that indexes are a mechanism for giving fast access to any particular row; and that undo segments are data structures used for storing information that might be needed to reverse, or roll back, any transactions that you do not wish to make permanent.

System administrators see physical datafiles; programmers see logical segments. Oracle abstracts the logical storage from the physical storage by means of the tablespace. A *tablespace* is logically a collection of one or more segments, and physically a collection of one or more datafiles. Put in terms of relational analysis, there is a many-to-many relationship between segments and datafiles: one table may be cut across many datafiles; one datafile may contain bits of many tables. By inserting the tablespace entity between the segments and the files, Oracle resolves this many-to-many relationship.

A number of segments must be created at database creation time: these are the segments that make up the data dictionary. These segments are stored in two tablespaces, called SYSTEM and SYSAUX. The SYSAUX tablespace is new with 10*g*: in previous releases, the whole of the data dictionary went into SYSTEM. The database creation process must create at least these two tablespaces, with at least one datafile each, to store the data dictionary.

EXAM TIP The SYSAUX tablespace must be created at database creation time in Oracle 10g. If you do not specify it, one will be created by default.

The Data Dictionary

The data dictionary is metadata: data about data. It describes the database, both physically and logically, and its contents. User definitions, security information, integrity constraints, and (with release 10g) performance monitoring information are all part of the data dictionary. It is stored as a set of segments in the SYSTEM and SYSAUX tablespaces.

In many ways, the segments that make up the data dictionary are segments like any other: just tables and indexes. The critical difference is that the data dictionary tables are generated at database creation time, and you are not allowed to access them directly. There is nothing to stop an inquisitive DBA from investigating the data dictionary directly, but if you do any updates to it, you may cause irreparable damage to your database, and certainly Oracle Corporation will not support you. Creating a data dictionary is part of the database creation process. It is maintained subsequently by data definition language commands. When you issue the CREATE TABLE command, you are in fact inserting rows into data dictionary tables, as you are with commands such as CREATE USER or GRANT.

To query the dictionary, Oracle provides a set of views. The views come in three forms, prefixed DBA_, ALL_, or USER_. Most of the views come in all three forms. Any view prefixed USER_ will be populated with rows describing objects owned by the user querying the view, so no two people will see the same contents. If user SCOTT queries USER_TABLES, he will see information about his tables; if you query USER_TABLES, you will see information about your tables. Any view prefixed ALL_ will be populated with rows describing objects to which you have access. Thus ALL_TABLES will contain rows describing your own tables, plus rows describing tables belonging to anyone else that you have been given permission to see. Any view prefixed DBA_ will have rows for every object in the database, so DBA_TABLES will have one row for every table in the database, no matter who created it. These views are created as part of the database creation process, along with a large number of PL/SQL packages that are provided by Oracle to assist database administrators in managing the database and programmers in developing applications. PL/SQL code is also stored in the data dictionary.

 EXAM TIP Which view will show you *all* the tables in the database? Remember that the answer is DBA_TABLES, not ALL_TABLES.

Management Tools

Oracle database 10g provides two management environments: Enterprise Manager Database Control and Enterprise Manager Grid Control. Both are optional, but Oracle strongly advises you to use one or the other. Grid control is more complicated, and more capable. To use Grid Control, you must have already installed it somewhere on your network and installed the Grid Control Management agent on the computer where you are creating the database. You are going to create Database Control in this exercise, which is implemented as a set of tables and procedures within the database, generated at database creation time. Throughout this book, and for the purposes of the exam, Database Control is the tool to be used. Grid Control is undoubtedly more powerful, but it is not necessary in a straightforward environment; it also has licensing implications.

There are also numerous third-party products you can buy (and a few that you can download free of charge) to assist you in managing the Oracle environment. By all means investigate these, but Enterprise Manager in one of its two forms is Oracle's approved tool.

External Files

The remaining topic to cover before creating a database is the three file types that exist externally to the database: the parameter file, the password file, and the archive log files.

The parameter file defines the instance. You already know that an instance consists of memory structures and processes. The instance parameters specified in the parameter file control, among other things, how big the various memory structures should be, and how the background processes will behave. They also set certain limits, such as how many user sessions are permitted to log on to the instance concurrently. There are defaults for all parameters except one: DB_NAME, the name of the database to which the instance will connect. With this exception it is possible to start an instance relying totally on defaults, but such an instance will be useless for any practical purpose. Many parameters are dynamic, meaning that their values can be changed while the instance is running and the database is open, but some are fixed at instance startup. With one exception, all parameters can be changed subsequent to database creation by closing the database, shutting down the instance, editing the parameter file, and starting up again. The one exception is DB_BLOCK_SIZE, more on which later. You must create a parameter file and use it to build an instance in memory before creating a database.

TIP Parameters are divided into "basic" and "advanced." You will usually need to set the two dozen or so basic parameters, but the advanced ones (of which there are over two hundred) can often be left at default.

There are two types of parameter files: the old-fashioned static parameter file (usually called init<SID>.ora, where <SID> is the name of the instance) and the dynamic parameter file introduced with release 9*i* (called spfileSID.ora). A static parameter file is a simple text file that you create and edit with any ASCII editor you please, typically Notepad on Windows, or vi on Unix. It is read only once by the instance, at startup time. The dynamic parameter file is a binary file that is maintained and edited by Oracle itself, in response to commands you issue.

The password file causes much confusion in the Oracle world, particularly among computer auditors who do not understand its purpose. The problem it addresses is how to authenticate a user when the database is not open, or indeed before the database has even been created or an instance started. Users are nothing more than rows in a table in the data dictionary. You can see them and their encrypted passwords by querying the data dictionary view DBA_USERS. When you create a user, as you will in Chapter 7, you are simply inserting rows into the data dictionary. Now, it is a simple fact in the Oracle environment that if you have the privileges that let you start an instance and subsequently open or create a database, you can do absolutely anything within that database. It is therefore vitally important that Oracle should authenticate you, before letting you connect as such a user. But if the database is not already created and open, how can Oracle query the data dictionary to validate your username and password, and thus work out who you are and what you are allowed to do? To resolve this paradox, Oracle has provided two means of authentication that are not data dictionary based and therefore do not require the database to be open, or even to exist. These are operating system authentication and password file authentication.

For operating system authentication, Oracle delegates responsibility for identifying a user to the host operating system. At installation time (not database creation time!) you specified an operating system group name that would own the Oracle software, defaulting to dba on Unix, ORA_DBA on Windows. If you are logged on to the computer hosting the Oracle installation as a member of that group, then you will be allowed to connect (using appropriate syntax) to an instance, start it up, and open or create a database without any username/password prompt. Clearly, this relies totally on your operating system being secure, which it should be: that is out of Oracle's control and relies on decent system administration. But this mechanism can't work if you are connecting to the instance remotely, across a network: you will never actually log on to the operating system of the machine hosting the Oracle server, only to the machine where you are working. This is where the password file comes in: it is an operating system file, with usernames and passwords encrypted within it, that exists independently of the database. Using appropriate syntax, you can connect to an instance, respond to a prompt with a username/password combination that exists in the password file, start the instance, and open an existing database or create a new one. If you do not need to start the instance and open the database across a network but you can always log on to the computer hosting the Oracle installation, then a password file is not strictly necessary because you can use operating system authentication instead. However, for practical purposes, you will always have one.

Archive log files will be dealt with in detail in later chapters. They are copies of filled online redo log files: as the online logs are filled with changes, they should be copied to one or more destinations as archived logs, thus giving you a complete history of all changes applied to the database. While it is not an Oracle requirement to archive your online redo logs, in virtually all live installations it will certainly be a business requirement, as it is the archive logs that guarantee the impossibility of losing data.

Creating a Database

To create a database, there are a number of steps that must be followed in the correct order:

1. Create a parameter file and a password file.

2. Use the parameter file to build an instance in memory.

3. Issue the CREATE DATABASE command. This will generate, at a minimum, a controlfile; two online redo log files; two datafiles for the SYSTEM and SYSAUX tablespaces, and a data dictionary.

4. Run SQL scripts to generate the data dictionary views and the supplied PL/SQL packages.

5. Run SQL scripts to generate Enterprise Manager Database Control, along with any options (such as Java) that the database will require.

On Windows systems, there is an additional step because Oracle runs as a Windows service. Oracle provides a utility, ORADIM.EXE, to assist you in creating this service.

 EXAM TIP You can create a database with two words, CREATE DATABASE. There are defaults for everything.

These steps can be executed interactively from the SQL*Plus prompt or through a GUI tool, the Database Configuration Assistant (DBCA). Alternatively, you can automate the process by using scripts or a DBCA response file. Whatever platform you are running on, the easiest way to create a database is through the DBCA. You may well have run this as part of the installation. It will give you prompts that walk you through the whole process. It first creates a parameter file and a password file, and then it generates scripts that will start the instance, create the database, and generate the data dictionary, the data dictionary views, and Enterprise Manager Database Control. Alternatively, you can create the parameter file and the password file by hand and then do the rest from a SQL*Plus session. Many DBAs combine the two techniques: they use DBCA to generate the files and scripts and then look at them and perhaps edit them before running them from SQL*Plus.

DBCA is written in Java; it is therefore the same on all platforms. The only variation is that on Microsoft Windows you must be sitting in front of the machine where you are running it, because that is where the DBCA windows will open. On Unix, you run DBCA on the machine where you wish to create the database, but you can launch and control it from any machine that has an X server to display the DBCA windows. This is standard for the X Window System: you set an environment variable DISPLAY to tell the program where to send the windows it opens. For example,

```
export DISPLAY=10.10.10.65:0.0
```

will redirect all X windows to the machine identified by IP address 10.10.10.65, no matter which machine you are actually running DBCA on.

Exercise 3-1: Creating a Database with Database Configuration Assistant

In this exercise, you will first use DBCA to create a database and then inspect and interpret the scripts that it generates.

1. Log on to your computer as a member of the group that owns the Oracle software. By default, this will be the group dba on Unix, ORA_DBA on Windows.

2. Confirm that your ORACLE_HOME is set to point to the directory where your software is installed. On Unix, run

   ```
   echo $ORACLE_HOME
   ```

   On Windows, it will be the registry variable that was set at installation time.

3. Confirm that your search path includes the directory *bin* within your Oracle home. On Unix, display your search path with

   ```
   echo $PATH
   ```

   On Windows,

   ```
   echo %PATH%
   ```

   One additional required variable for Unix is DISPLAY. This must point to the terminal on which you are working. Show it with

   ```
   echo $DISPLAY.
   ```

   If you are working on the machine where you want to create the database, a suitable setting might be

   ```
   export DISPLAY=127.0.0.1:0.0
   ```

4. Launch DBCA. On Unix it is called dbca; on Windows it is dbca.bat. It is located in your ORACLE_HOME/bin directory, which must be in your search path.

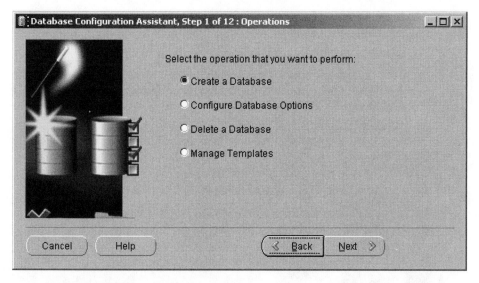

Database Configuration Assistant, Step 1 of 12 : Operations

Select the operation that you want to perform:

- Create a Database
- Configure Database Options
- Delete a Database
- Manage Templates

Cancel | Help | Back | Next

5. Respond to the prompts as follows:

   a. At the prompt "Select the operation you wish to perform," type **Create a database** and click Next.

   b. At the prompt "Select a template," type **Custom database** and click Next.

   c. Type **ocp10g** for both the Global database name and the SID, and then click Next.

   d. Select the checkboxes for "Configure the database with enterprise manager" and "Use database control for database management," but not the checkbox for "Use grid control for database management," and click Next.

   e. Do not select the checkboxes for "Enable email notification" or "Enable daily backup." Click Next.

   f. Select the checkbox for "Use the same password for all accounts" and enter the password as ORACLE. Enter it again to confirm, and click Next.

   g. Select "file system" as the storage mechanism, and click Next.

   h. Select "Use file locations from template" as the location for the database files, and click Next.

   i. Select the checkbox for "Specify flash recovery area" but not the checkbox for "Enable archiving," and click Next.

   j. De-select the checkboxes for "Oracle text," "Oracle OLAP," and "Oracle spatial." Select the check box for "Enterprise Manager Repository." In "Standard Database Components," de-select everything. Click Next.

k. Leave the Memory, Sizing, Character Sets, and Connection Mode on defaults, and click Next.

l. Leave the Database Storage on defaults, and click Next.

m. Select the check boxes for "Create database" and "Generate database creation scripts," de-select the checkbox for "Save as a database template." Click Next.

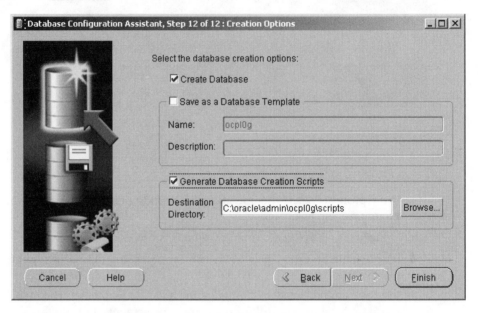

The final screen shows the details of the instance and the database that will be created. Depending on the speed of your computer, creation as suggested in this exercise (excluding all options) may take from fifteen to forty minutes.

The Database Creation Scripts

While the database is creating, take a look at database creation scripts that DBCA generated. DBCA will tell you where they are—typically, in the admin/<dbname>/ scripts directory (where <dbname> is the name of the database you are creating) beneath the directory where you installed Oracle. The init.ora file should look something like this:

```
##############################################################################
# Copyright (c) 1991, 2001, 2002 by Oracle Corporation
##############################################################################
###########################################
# Cache and I/O
###########################################
```

```
db_block_size=8192
db_cache_size=25165824
db_file_multiblock_read_count=16
##########################################
# Cursors and Library Cache
##########################################
open_cursors=300
##########################################
# Database Identification
##########################################
db_domain=""
db_name=ocp10g
##########################################
# Diagnostics and Statistics
##########################################
background_dump_dest=C:\oracle\admin\ocp10g\bdump
core_dump_dest=C:\oracle\admin\ocp10g\cdump
user_dump_dest=C:\oracle\admin\ocp10g\udump
##########################################
# File Configuration
##########################################
control_files=("C:\oracle\oradata\ocp10g\control01.ctl",
"C:\oracle\oradata\ocp10g\control02.ctl",
"C:\oracle\oradata\ocp10g\control03.ctl")
db_recovery_file_dest=C:\oracle\flash_recovery_area
db_recovery_file_dest_size=2147483648
##########################################
# Job Queues
##########################################
job_queue_processes=10
##########################################
# Miscellaneous
##########################################
compatible=10.1.0.2.0
##########################################
# Pools
##########################################
java_pool_size=0
large_pool_size=8388608
shared_pool_size=83886080
##########################################
# Processes and Sessions
##########################################
processes=150
##########################################
# Security and Auditing
##########################################
remote_login_passwordfile=EXCLUSIVE
##########################################
# Sort, Hash Joins, Bitmap Indexes
##########################################
pga_aggregate_target=25165824
sort_area_size=65536
##########################################
# System Managed Undo and Rollback Segments
##########################################
undo_management=AUTO
undo_tablespace=UNDOTBS1
```

Note that this is a static parameter file. Later in the process, it can be converted to a dynamic parameter file. These are the parameters that will be used to build the instance in memory. Two to emphasize at this point are DB_BLOCK_SIZE and CONTROL_FILES. DB_BLOCK_SIZE determines the size of the buffers in the database buffer cache. When the instance is instructed to create a database, this size will also be used to format the datafiles that make up the SYSTEM and SYSAUX tablespaces. It can never be changed after database creation. CONTROL_FILES is the pointer that allows the instance to find the database controlfile, including all the multiplexed copies. At this stage in our exercise, the controlfile does not exist: this parameter will tell the instance where to create it. Some of the other parameters are self-explanatory, but eventually you must refer to the Oracle Documentation Library (the volume you need is titled "Reference") and read up on all of them. All!

 EXAM TIP You can never change your database block size parameter after creation. All other parameters can be adjusted later.

The next file to inspect is ocp10g.bat (it will be a shell script on Unix):

```
mkdir C:\oracle\admin\ocp10g\bdump
mkdir C:\oracle\admin\ocp10g\cdump
mkdir C:\oracle\admin\ocp10g\create
mkdir C:\oracle\admin\ocp10g\pfile
mkdir C:\oracle\admin\ocp10g\udump
mkdir C:\oracle\flash_recovery_area
mkdir C:\oracle\oradata\ocp10g
mkdir C:\oracle\product\10.1.0\Db_1\database
set ORACLE_SID=ocp10g
C:\oracle\product\10.1.0\Db_1\bin\oradim.exe -new -sid OCP10G
-startmode manual -spfile
C:\oracle\product\10.1.0\Db_1\bin\oradim.exe -edit -sid OCP10G
-startmode auto -srvcstart system
C:\oracle\product\10.1.0\Db_1\bin\sqlplus /nolog
@C:\oracle\admin\ocp10g\scripts\ocp10g.sql
```

The script creates some directories, sets the ORACLE_SID environment variable, and then (because this example is Windows) uses the ORADIM.EXE utility to create the Windows service for the instance and put it on automatic start. Then it launches SQL*Plus and runs a SQL script called ocp10g.sql:

```
set verify off
PROMPT specify a password for sys as parameter 1;
DEFINE sysPassword = &1
PROMPT specify a password for system as parameter 2;
DEFINE systemPassword = &2
PROMPT specify a password for sysman as parameter 3;
DEFINE sysmanPassword = &3
PROMPT specify a password for dbsnmp as parameter 4;
DEFINE dbsnmpPassword = &4
host C:\oracle\product\10.1.0\Db_1\bin\orapwd.exe
file=C:\oracle\product\10.1.0\Db_1\database\PWDocp10g.ora
password=&&sysPassword force=y
```

```
@C:\oracle\admin\ocp10g\scripts\CreateDB.sql
@C:\oracle\admin\ocp10g\scripts\CreateDBFiles.sql
@C:\oracle\admin\ocp10g\scripts\CreateDBCatalog.sql
@C:\oracle\admin\ocp10g\scripts\emRepository.sql
@C:\oracle\admin\ocp10g\scripts\postDBCreation.sql
```

This script prompts for some passwords, already provided when you ran the DBCA. Then it calls the ORAPWD.EXE utility to create an external password file (the utility is orapwd on Unix). Then it calls another five SQL scripts. First, CreateDB.sql:

```
connect SYS/&&sysPassword as SYSDBA
set echo on
spool C:\oracle\product\10.1.0\Db_1\assistants\dbca\logs\CreateDB.log
startup nomount pfile="C:\oracle\admin\ocp10g\scripts\init.ora";
CREATE DATABASE "ocp10g"
MAXINSTANCES 8
MAXLOGHISTORY 1
MAXLOGFILES 16
MAXLOGMEMBERS 3
MAXDATAFILES 100
DATAFILE 'C:\oracle\oradata\ocp10g\system01.dbf' SIZE 300M
REUSE AUTOEXTEND ON NEXT  10240K MAXSIZE UNLIMITED
EXTENT MANAGEMENT LOCAL
SYSAUX DATAFILE 'C:\oracle\oradata\ocp10g\sysaux01.dbf' SIZE 120M REUSE
 AUTOEXTEND ON NEXT  10240K MAXSIZE UNLIMITED
DEFAULT TEMPORARY TABLESPACE TEMP TEMPFILE
 'C:\oracle\oradata\ocp10g\temp01.dbf' SIZE 20M REUSE AUTOEXTEND ON
NEXT  640K MAXSIZE UNLIMITED
UNDO TABLESPACE "UNDOTBS1" DATAFILE 'C:\oracle\oradata\ocp10g\undotbs01.dbf'
 SIZE 200M REUSE AUTOEXTEND ON NEXT  5120K MAXSIZE UNLIMITED
CHARACTER SET WE8MSWIN1252
NATIONAL CHARACTER SET AL16UTF16
LOGFILE GROUP 1 ('C:\oracle\oradata\ocp10g\redo01.log') SIZE 10240K,
GROUP 2 ('C:\oracle\oradata\ocp10g\redo02.log') SIZE 10240K,
GROUP 3 ('C:\oracle\oradata\ocp10g\redo03.log') SIZE 10240K
USER SYS IDENTIFIED BY "&&sysPassword" USER SYSTEM IDENTIFIED BY
 "&&systemPassword";
spool off
```

The script connects to the instance, using the syntax for password file authentication. Then the STARTUP NOMOUNT command builds the instance in memory, using the static parameter file you saw earlier. The significance of "NOMOUNT" will be dealt with in Chapter 5; for now, let it suffice that it is necessary, as there is no database to mount and open. And then at last we get the CREATE DATABASE command, which continues to the end of the file. The first section sets some overall limits for the database. They can all be changed subsequently, but if they are clearly inappropriate, it is a good idea to change them now, before creation. Two datafile specifications follow: these are the files that will be used for the SYSTEM and SYSAUX tablespaces. Next come specifications for a TEMPORARY tablespace and an UNDO tablespace (more on this in Chapter 16). Then a character set is specified. Until version 9*i* of the database, there was no method for changing the database character set after creation: it was therefore vital to get this right. With 9*i* and 10*g*, it is possible to change it later, but this is not an operation to embark on lightly—and in fact may not be feasible.

Get it right now! This area will be covered in detail in Chapter 21. Finally comes the specification for three online logfile groups, each consisting of one member, and the passwords for database users SYS and SYSTEM are initialized.

 TIP Be sure to change the passwords for all the standard users before the database goes live. You would be amazed at the number of live systems where this is not done.

This one file will create a database. After its successful execution, you will have an instance running in memory, and a database consisting of a controlfile and copies as specified by the CONTROL_FILES initialization parameter, and the datafiles and redo logs specified in the CREATE DATABASE command. A data dictionary will have been generated. But although the database has been created, it is unusable. The remaining scripts called by ocp10g.sql make the database usable:

- CreateDBfiles.sql creates another tablespace, to be used as a default storage location for user data.
- CreateDBcatalog.sql generates the data dictionary views and the PL/SQL supplied packages.
- emRepository.sql generates the Enterprise Manager Database Control tool.
- postDBcreation.sql tidies everything up.

And that's all there is to it: run DBCA, follow the prompts, and wait for it to finish. As a test, from an operating system prompt, set your ORACLE_SID environment variable and log on to your new database. For Windows,

```
C:\>
C:\>set ORACLE_SID=ocp10g
C:\>sqlplus sys/oracle as sysdba
SQL*Plus: Release 10.1.0.2.0 - Production on Sun Jul 25 12:34:14 2004
Copyright (c) 1982, 2004, Oracle.  All rights reserved.
Connected to:
Oracle Database 10g Enterprise Edition Release 10.1.0.2.0 - Production
With the Partitioning, OLAP and Data Mining options
SQL> select name,open_mode from v$database;
NAME       OPEN_MODE
---------  ----------
OCP10G      READ WRITE
SQL>
```

DBCA Additional Functions

The opening screen of DBCA gives you four options:

- Create A Database
- Configure Database Options

- Delete A Database

- Manage Templates

Configure Database Options helps you change the configuration of a database you have already created. In Exercise 3-1, you de-selected all the options; this was to make the creation as quick and simple as possible.

 TIP By de-selecting all the options, particularly those for "standard database components," creation time is reduced dramatically.

If you decide subsequently to install some optional features, such as Java or OLAP, running DBCA again is the simplest way to do it. An alternative method is to run the scripts to install the options by hand, but these are not always fully documented and it is possible to make mistakes; DBCA is better.

The Delete A Database radio button will prompt you for which database you wish to delete, and then give you one more chance to back out before it deletes all the files that make up the database and (for a Windows system) invokes ORADIM.EXE to delete the service as well.

Finally, you manage templates to store database definitions for use later. Remember that in the exercise, you chose to create a "custom" database. A custom database is not preconfigured; you chose it in order to see all the possibilities as you worked your way through DBCA. But apart from "custom," there were options for "data warehouse," "general purpose," and "transaction processing." If you take any of these, you'll be presented with an abbreviated version of the DBCA prompts that will create a database with different defaults, at least partly optimized for decision support systems (DSS, the data warehouse option), online transaction processing systems (OLTP, the transaction processing option), or mixed workload (the general purpose option). The final question when you created your database gave you the possibility of saving it as a template, that is, not to create it at all, but to save the definition for future use. DBCA will let you manage templates, either the presupplied ones or ones you create yourself, by copying, modifying, or deleting them. Templates can be extremely useful if you are in a position where you are frequently creating and re-creating databases that are very similar.

Chapter Review

This chapter began with a detailed description of the Oracle server architecture. A thorough understanding of this is essential for further progress. You must be familiar with the elements that make up an instance and a database: the memory structures, the processes, and the file types. Then there was a brief look at the purpose and contents of the data dictionary, and a brief discussion of the logical storage of segments within tablespaces. Finally you used the DBCA to create a database, and you walked through the various scripts and commands it generated for this purpose.

Questions

1. Which of the following memory structures are required, rather than optional, parts of the SGA? (Choose three answers.)

   A. Database buffer cache

   B. Java pool

   C. Large pool

   D. Redo log buffer

   E. Shared pool

   F. Streams pool

2. You are creating a database. Put these steps in the correct sequence:

   A. Build the data dictionary.

   B. Create a parameter file.

   C. Create the data dictionary views.

   D. Issue the CREATE DATABASE command.

   E. Issue the STARTUP NOMOUNT command.

3. If you do not specify a SYSAUX datafile on your CREATE DATABASE command, what will happen? (Choose the best answer.)

   A. The command will fail because SYSAUX is a required tablespace.

   B. The command will succeed, but you must add a SYSAUX tablespace after database creation.

   C. The command will succeed, and a default SYSAUX tablespace will be created for you.

   D. The command will succeed, but the whole data dictionary will be in the SYSTEM tablespace.

4. Which of the following can never be changed after database creation? (Choose the best answer.)

   A. Database block size

   B. Database character set

   C. Database name

   D. None of the above: nothing is fixed at database creation time

5. Which of the following is required to create a database? (Choose the best answer.)

   A. The operating system's root (for Unix/Linux) or Administrator (for Windows) password

   B. Execute permission on the DBCA

    C. At least as much RAM as the size of the SGA

    D. None of the above

6. On Unix/Linux, you launch the DBCA, and nothing happens. What could be the cause of this? (Choose the best answer.)

    A. You are not a member of the dba group.

    B. Your DISPLAY variable is not set to your terminal's address.

    C. You have not set your DISPLAY variable.

    D. You have not set your ORACLE_SID variable.

7. Which of the following files are optional? (Choose three answers.)

    A. Online redo log files

    B. Parameter file

    C. Password file

    D. SYSAUX tablespace datafile

    E. SYSTEM tablespace datafile

    F. UNDO tablespace datafile

8. If you do not specify an UNDO tablespace on your CREATE DATABASE command, what will happen? (Choose the best answer.)

    A. The command will fail because an UNDO tablespace is required.

    B. The command will succeed, and a default UNDO tablespace will be created for you.

    C. The command will succeed, but you must create an UNDO tablespace later.

    D. The command will succeed, and you may create an UNDO tablespace later.

9. You have created a database but cannot connect to it with Database Control. What could be the cause of this? (Choose the best answer.)

    A. You are not being authenticated by the operating system, or by password file authentication.

    B. You have not run the scripts to create Database Control.

    C. Grid control is a prerequisite for Database Control.

    D. You are not licensed to use Database Control.

10. When does the data dictionary get created? (Choose the best answer.)

    A. When you create a database

    B. When you run the post-creation scripts catalog.sql and catproc.sql, called by CreateDBcatalog.sql

    C. When the SYSTEM and SYSAUX tablespaces are created

    D. It does not need to be created; it is always available as part of the instance

11. Which of the following processes are optional? (Choose three answers.)

    A. Archive process

    B. Checkpoint process

    C. Database listener

    D. Grid Control Management Agent

    E. Log writer

    F. Process monitor

12. You created a database with two online redo log file groups, one member each. What must you do to provide fault tolerance? (Choose the best answer.)

    A. Add two more groups, to mirror the first two.

    B. Add one more member to each group.

    C. You can do nothing; these characteristics are fixed at creation time.

    D. You need do nothing; the second group already mirrors the first.

13. Which data dictionary view will show you all the tables in the database? (Choose the correct answer.)

    A. ALL_TABLES

    B. DBA_TABLES

    C. USER_TABLES

    D. None. To see all the tables, you must query the data dictionary directly.

14. Which of the following is not stored in the data dictionary? (Choose the best answer.)

    A. User definitions

    B. Supplied PL/SQL packages

    C. Data dictionary views

    D. None; they are all stored in the data dictionary

15. You de-selected the Oracle Java Virtual Machine when running DBCA, but you later wish to install it. What must you do? (Choose the best answer.)

    A. Create the Java pool in the database.

    B. Run scripts to create the JVM.

    C. Drop the database and re-create it with the JVM.

    D. Start the JVM background process.

Answers

1. **A, D, and E.** The remaining components are optional: a Java pool is required only if you are going to run Java; the large pool is a performance option; the streams pool is needed only if you using streams, an advanced option.

2. **B, E, D, A, and C.** You can't start up an instance until you have created a parameter file to define it. Then the CREATE DATABASE command will create your data dictionary. Only then can you run scripts to make the database usable.

3. **C.** The SYSAUX tablespace is needed at creation time; if you don't specify it, Oracle will create one for you.

4. **A.** This is the only setting that can never be changed without re-creation. Of course, there are plenty of other things that are very awkward to change.

5. **D.** The operating system root password may be required at installation time, but it isn't needed for creation. DBCA may be nice, but you don't have to use it. RAM is largely irrelevant; Oracle doesn't care if it is running in main memory or virtual memory.

6. **B.** With DISPLAY pointing to the wrong place, your X windows will appear there—where you can't see them. A and C will cause errors, and D is irrelevant; it gets set while running DBCA.

7. **B, C, and F.** You can add an UNDO tablespace later. The password file may be a practical necessity but is certainly not required. The parameter file is optional if you are using a static parameter file; you can delete it after starting the instance (though you wouldn't want to).

8. **D.** Unlike the SYSAUX tablespace, an UNDO tablespace really is optional, though as you'll see, it is a great performance and manageability feature.

9. **B.** The scripts to create the Enterprise Manager repository must be run before you can use Database Control.

10. **A.** Creation of a data dictionary is, more than anything else, what happens when you issue the CREATE DATABASE command.

11. **A, C, and D.** A listener may be needed for practical purposes (or users won't be able to connect), but it is optional. Archiving is also optional, though a very good idea. The Grid Control Agent is, of course, needed only if you want to use Grid Control.

12. **B.** Online redo log fault tolerance is provided by having multiple members per group.

13. **B.** This is a classic OCP trick question, pointing out that the names of the views are possibly ambiguous.

14. **D.** The catch here is that PL/SQL packages are stored in the data dictionary, even though they are owned by database users.

15. **B.** Though you could, of course, do it through DBCA—much simpler. A is the trick answer: you need a Java pool to run Java, not to create the JVM.

CHAPTER 4

Interfacing with the Oracle Database

In this chapter you will learn how to

- Use SQL*Plus and *i*SQL*Plus to access Oracle Database 10g
- Use SQL*Plus and *i*SQL*Plus to describe the logical structure of tables
- Use SQL to query, manipulate, and define data using SELECT, UPDATE/INSERT/ DELETE, and CREATE/ALTER/DROP
- Identify common database interfaces
- Describe a database transaction

After you have installed the Oracle Database 10g software and created a database, the next logical step is to be able to query the database for data. While querying the metadata (data about the data) in the database may seem a good starting point, the real value is in populating the database with data useful to your organization using data structures such as tables and views that logically make sense to your enterprise. The key language that you will use in doing all these tasks is SQL, the Structured Query Language. In order to interface with the database, you will make use of one or more Oracle tools built for that task: SQL*Plus, *i*SQL*Plus (a web-based version of SQL*Plus), or a third-party tool. This chapter will provide you with information on SQL as well as the tools to make effective use of it.

Using SQL

SQL was developed by IBM in the 1970s as a way to query relational data that can be used by individuals other than programmers. It was originally called Structured English Query Language (or SEQUEL for short), but eventually the English was dropped and we have SQL. SQL can be broken down into three basic sections or "languages": data definition language (DDL), data control language (DCL), and the data manipulation language (DML).

DDL statements do not deal with data directly; rather, they deal with the objects that hold and provide access to data. When you want to add, modify, or remove any object in the database (such as a table, a view, or an index), you must do so using a DDL statement. DDL includes all CREATE, ALTER, and DROP statements. Database creation begins with DDL statements; they build the entire framework of tables and constraints that will become the structure of the database. Before data can be added, you must have some place to add it to. Your users, normally, will not issue DDL statements, but you as a database administrator (DBA) and your database developers will perform them.

 EXAM TIP The three key DDL statements are CREATE, ALTER, and DROP. They are used to add, change, and remove objects from the database.

Database access is controlled by the data control language. Once an account is created for a user, that user can be given permission on the database using the GRANT statement or it can be taken away using the REVOKE statement. These two statements form the core of the DCL.

Two types of permissions can be granted and revoked: system and object permissions. System permissions enable a user to perform action on the database. Performing such activities as creating a table or index, or backing up the database, requires system permissions. Object permissions are applied to particular objects in the database, and these permissions may change depending on the type of object. For example, you could grant a particular user the permission to issue SELECT, INSERT, or UPDATE commands against a table, but an EXECUTE permission on a stored procedure. DCL statements are, for the most part, the job of the DBA. It is his or her job to create user accounts for every user and to assign those accounts the appropriate permissions.

EXAM TIP DCL statements are GRANT and REVOKE, which can be used to add or remove permissions for a user or role. System and object permissions are available. Object permissions can differ, depending on the type of object.

DML statements deal directly with data. Any manipulation or retrieval of data requires a DML statement. The key elements of the DML are SELECT, INSERT, UPDATE, and DELETE. These commands enable you to retrieve data from a table, add new data to a table, modify existing data, and delete rows from a table. DML also includes transactional control language elements consisting of COMMIT, ROLLBACK, and SAVEPOINT. These language elements help control the execution of DML statements by grouping them together into transactions. DML statements are the most common type of interaction with the database. It is the level of SQL that your users will be working in almost exclusively.

EXAM TIP This chapter will provide an overview of SQL and some of the key elements of the SQL language used by Oracle. The exam will test your ability to write correct SQL syntax, so you should review the Oracle Database 10g documentation for additional information on programming in SQL. SQL is a vast topic that cannot be adequately covered in a single chapter and has had thick books written about how to best make use of it.

The SELECT Statement

All SQL queries begin with the SELECT statement. This statement enables you to retrieve all data or only certain columns and rows in a table. It can also return data from more than one table. It enables you not only to retrieve data, but also to perform calculations on existing data and return the results of these calculations. The basic SELECT statement requires two elements: the select list and a FROM clause. This specifies what columns to retrieve and from where. Here is the basic format:

```
SELECT [DISTINCT] {* | column,[expression], . . . }
FROM table;
```

The select list can contain either the asterisk or a list of column names or expressions. The select list dictates *what* is returned by the query. The asterisk is simply shorthand, meaning all columns. For example, to retrieve information on all users in the database, you can issue the following SQL statement—the semicolon (;) is a line terminator:

```
SELECT * FROM DBA_USERS;
```

To list all users and their account lockout statuses, you can use an expression in the SELECT list and concatenate two columns in the table to provide the result, as well as alias the resulting column name, as in this example:

```
SELECT USERNAME || ' is ' || ACCOUNT_STATUS AS "User and Status" FROM DBA_USERS;
```

Limiting Rows Returned with the WHERE Clause

In all of the examples so far, the queries have limited which columns have been returned but have returned all rows in the table, but most of the time database queries return a specific set of data required by the user. For example, an order entry person taking an order on the phone will want to know the price of the specific product the customer is asking about instead of the price of all products. In SQL, you limit the number of rows returned with the use of a WHERE clause. In a SELECT statement, the WHERE clause is always placed after the FROM clause:

```
SELECT [DISTINCT] {* | column,[expression], . . . }
FROM table;
[WHERE condition1 [{AND | OR [NOT]} condition2 . . .] ]
```

The conditions of a WHERE clause consist of two expressions compared by an operator such as equal (=), not equal (<>), less than (<), or greater than (>), along with other operators such as BETWEEN, LIKE, and IN. When SQL processes the WHERE clause, it tests the value of each row in a column (or the result of each row in an expression) against a particular value. The query includes only rows that meet the condition in the result set. For example, to return the number of tables in the database owned by the user SYSMAN, a DBA could issue the following query:

```
SELECT COUNT(*) FROM DBA_TABLES WHERE OWNER = 'SYSMAN';
```

When you refer to character and date values in a WHERE clause, you must enclose them in single quotes. Numeric data does not require single quotes. If you omit the single quotes, Oracle attempts to interpret the value as a database object, and you will most likely receive an error. Furthermore, when using comparison operators with character data, you should always remember that Oracle is case-sensitive when performing character comparisons. These two queries will result in different sets of data returned—one with the rows and the other with no rows—just because of the difference in case for the value being retrieved:

```
SELECT COUNT(*) FROM DBA_OBJECTS WHERE OWNER='SYSMAN';
  COUNT(*)
----------
      1263
SELECT COUNT(*) FROM DBA_OBJECTS WHERE OWNER='sysman';
  COUNT(*)
----------
         0
```

An important point to remember is that Oracle is not case sensitive when it comes to the SQL syntax itself, just when comparing character values. Issuing the following commands will always result in the same data being retrieved:

```
SELECT COUNT(*) FROM DBA_OBJECTS WHERE OWNER='SYSMAN';
  COUNT(*)
----------
      1263

select count(*) from dba_objects where owner='SYSMAN';
  COUNT(*)
----------
      1263
```

Eliminating Duplicates in the Result Set

When you issue a SELECT statement, Oracle returns all rows that match the query. What if, however, you wanted a list only of all the users who own database objects? To create such a list, you have to use the DISTINCT keyword. When you include this keyword, Oracle sorts the result set and then returns only the first occurrence of each value returned by the query. To use the DISTINCT keyword, you place it in the SELECT list after the SELECT keyword. For example, to display the list of users who own objects in the database, you would issue the following command with the displayed result:

```
SQL> SELECT DISTINCT owner FROM DBA_OBJECTS;
OWNER
-----------------------------
DBSNMP
OUTLN
PUBLIC
SYS
SYSMAN
SYSTEM
WMSYS
7 rows selected.
```

If, on the other hand, you omitted the DISTINCT keyword, you would get a much larger number of rows (several thousand, in fact). It is important to remember that the DISTINCT keyword applies to the entire SELECT list. If you specify more than one column or expression in the SELECT list, the DISTINCT keyword will return the unique occurrences of the combination of all columns in the SELECT list. For example, issuing the following command will return the unique combination of owner and object_type from DBA_OBJECTS and return many more rows than the seven in the previous query:

```
SELECT DISTINCT owner, object_type FROM DBA_OBJECTS;
```

EXAM TIP DISTINCT will apply to the whole set of columns or expressions on the SELECT list.

Retrieving Data from More Than One Table

All SQL queries require two elements: a SELECT list specifying what to retrieve and a FROM clause specifying where to retrieve those items from. In all of the previous examples only one table is referenced in the FROM clause, but it is possible to include more than one table in the FROM clause of a query and then specify how the tables are related to form a join.

It is important to understand how to work with joins, not just because it is required for the exam, but because the majority of queries used in the real world will include joins. Even for DBAs it is necessary to write joins to extract data from Oracle's data dictionary. For example, if you wanted to retrieve a list of tablespaces and the names of their associated datafiles, you would need to write a query joining DBA_TABLESPACES and DBA_DATA_FILES.

Writing a join requires more than just a SELECT list and a FROM clause; it also requires a join condition. A join condition is a way to equate specific rows in one table with specific rows in another table. This condition is most often a primary key/ foreign key pair and is expressed in the WHERE clause (in all versions of Oracle) or in the ANSI JOIN syntax available in Oracle 9i and Oracle 10g. Therefore the join that would retrieve a list of tablespaces and their associated datafiles can be written two ways, as follows:

```
SELECT DBA_DATA_FILES.tablespace_name, file_name
FROM DBA_TABLESPACES, DBA_DATA_FILES
WHERE DBA_TABLESPACES.TABLESPACE_NAME=DBA_DATA_FILES.TABLESPACE_NAME;
```

```
SELECT DBA_TABLESPACES.tablespace_name, file_name
FROM DBA_TABLESPACES JOIN DBA_DATA_FILES
ON DBA_TABLESPACES.TABLESPACE_NAME = DBA_DATA_FILES.TABLESPACE_NAME;
```

The advantage of using the ANSI JOIN syntax is that it is easier to read and clearly specifies the join condition. You can also add a WHERE clause to further narrow down the query, while in the first syntax the WHERE clause and join condition are in the same place: the WHERE clause.

 EXAM TIP Oracle supports both the *classic* join syntax and the preferred ANSI join syntax.

Notice that the column `tablespace_name` in the SELECT list had to be qualified in both SQL statements, but the parent table could be either of the joined tables. This is because Oracle needs to be told which specific instance of the `tablespace_name` column you want to display because there are two, one in each table being joined. If you do not qualify the column name with the parent table name Oracle encounters an ambiguous reference and returns an error. However, if a column appears in only one table in the join, it does not need to be qualified, as is the case with the file_name column, since it exists only in the DBA_DATA_FILES table.

Another important thing to remember about joins is that the columns in the join condition do not need to be in the SELECT list; they can serve only to link the tables together. In fact, the join condition need not be specified at all, in which case you get what is known as a CROSS JOIN or Cartesian product where all rows in the first table are joined to all rows in the second table. While you may not think that this is useful, and in most cases it serves to simply cause excessive work for Oracle, cross-joins are very handy in data warehousing, where many tables are being related.

Not all joins are simple equijoins (joins whose join condition is based on the = operator) like the examples just shown. There are different join types that can return all matching data (inner joins, which can be equijoins or use other operators), more than the matching data (outer joins), and even data in two tables that is not related— i.e. the *unrelated* items—an extension of the outer join called the outer theta join. In the ANSI JOIN syntax you also have a NATURAL JOIN, which matches column names in the tables being related and then attempts to perform an equijoin based upon all matching column names in both tables. Finally, a SELECT statement can include more than one join so that it is possible to relate several tables in a single SQL statement.

 NOTE For more information on joins and join syntax, refer to the Oracle 10g *SQL Reference* documentation in the Oracle 10g documentation library that can be found at www.oracle.com/technology/documentation/database10g.html.

Sorting and Grouping Data

When you issue a SELECT statement in SQL, you receive a result set that contains all data in the table or tables that match the query. However, the order in which that data is returned is completely random. It is conceivably possible to issue the same query ten times and receive the same data back in ten different orders. When you want the data returned in a specific order, you must use the ORDER BY statement. With this statement, you specify the columns or expression that you want as the basis of your ordering. You can also specify whether you want the data sorted in ascending order (lowest to highest) or descending order (highest to lowest). You can order by a column of any datatype except for the large object datatypes (that is, CLOB, NCLOB, BLOB, BFILE, RAW, LONGRAW, and LONG). The default for character columns is to sort alphabetically in ascending order. To retrieve a list of tablespaces in alphabetical order and the associated datafiles, you can issue a query like this:

```
SELECT DBA_TABLESPACES.tablespace_name, file_name
FROM DBA_TABLESPACES JOIN DBA_DATA_FILES
ON DBA_TABLESPACES.TABLESPACE_NAME = DBA_DATA_FILES.TABLESPACE_NAME
ORDER BY DBA_TABLESPACES.TABLESPACE_NAME;
```

EXAM TIP The ORDER BY clause must always appear last in the SQL statement. You can order by any valid expression, such as a formula or calculation applied against the data.

To make things more interesting, the expression in the ORDER BY clause need not be in the SELECT list, JOIN condition, or WHERE clause. The data can be sorted using any valid expression and even columns not referenced in the query, such as this example, which sorts the output according to the size of the datafiles from largest to smallest:

```
SELECT DBA_TABLESPACES.tablespace_name, file_name
FROM DBA_TABLESPACES JOIN DBA_DATA_FILES
ON DBA_TABLESPACES.TABLESPACE_NAME = DBA_DATA_FILES.TABLESPACE_NAME
ORDER BY DBA_DATA_FILES.BYTES DESC;
```

Manipulating Data Using INSERT, UPDATE, and DELETE

The Oracle engine controls all access to the database and its data. This means that when you want to place or modify data in a table, you must instruct Oracle to make those changes for you. This is achieved through the INSERT, UPDATE, and DELETE statements. Because storing and manipulating data is the key function of an Oracle database, it is important to have a full understanding of how to issue these statements to work with and manage an Oracle database.

The INSERT Statement

In order to get data into tables, you must issue the correct DML statement. To add data to a table, you use the INSERT statement. The basic syntax for an INSERT statement is as follows:

```
INSERT INTO table [(column, [column . . . ])]
VALUES   (value [, value . . . ]);
```

You can insert data into only one table at a time using the INSERT statement. Thus, you can include only one table name in the INSERT statement. The VALUES keyword is followed by a list of values that are entered into the table in the same order as the columns for that table. When you are inserting character data or date data into a table, you must enclose this information in single quotes. Numeric data does not require single quotes. If you do not want to specify a value for a column in the table, you can assign it null by using the keyword NULL in place of data. NULL is the absence of a value and can be specified for any column that a NOT NULL constraint is not defined on.

NOTE NULL is a state of a column. A column can be NULL, in which case it does not have a value, or NOT NULL, if a value exists. When defining a table, it is possible to indicate whether a column must have a value or not by using the keywords NOT NULL or NULL, respectively, after the name and datatype of the column have been specified. Chapter 8 will provide more information on creating and managing tables.

PART I

If you plan to enter data into fewer columns than are defined for the table, you must include a column list after the table name. This list specifies the column or columns that you want to insert data into, and the order in which those columns appear in the VALUES list.

NOTE Oracle provides syntax allowing the insertion of data into more than one table using conditional logic. The INSERT ALL and INSERT FIRST statements can be used to add data to more than one table or the first table matching the criteria, something very useful in data warehousing environments where data loads are frequently performed.

The UPDATE Statement

In a transaction-oriented database such as an order entry system or an airline reservation system, data is constantly changing—shipping dates are added to orders, passengers change seat assignments, flights are rescheduled, and so on. To modify data after a row has been inserted into a table, you must use the UPDATE statement. The basic syntax for the UPDATE statement follows:

```
UPDATE table
SET column = value [, column = value, . . . ]
[WHERE condition];
```

It is possible to modify more than one column with a single UPDATE statement; however, you can update only one table at time. The WHERE condition in an UPDATE statement controls which rows are updated. An UPDATE statement updates all rows that match the WHERE condition. If the WHERE clause is omitted, all rows in the table are modified.

NOTE Oracle 10g also includes a MERGE INTO statement that allows you to update data in one table when matching data is found and INSERT data into another table when no match is found. This is also known as an UPSERT (UPDATE and INSERT). In fact, Oracle 10g enhanced the MERGE statement to allow conditional and optional extension clauses. The enhancements allow conditional updates and inserts and an optional delete clause when updating data (e.g., refresh existing row or delete obsolete row).

The DELETE Statement

Many databases will need to allow data to be removed as part of transactional processing, or to reduce the size of tables by taking data no longer needed out of the table. To remove a row from a table, you use the DELETE command. The basic syntax for the DELETE statement is as follows:

```
DELETE [FROM] table
[WHERE condition];
```

As with the UPDATE statement, the WHERE clause is used to control which rows are affected by the DELETE statement. If you omit the WHERE clause, the DELETE statement removes all rows from the table. If this is not your intention, you may remove data that others need and cause some work for yourself to recover the missing data. Luckily, there are commands in Oracle that determine whether or not to save your changes.

 EXAM TIP INSERT, UPDATE, and DELETE are always applied against data in one and only one table.

Transaction Control

Each DML statement in Oracle is a single operation that affects one or more rows. However, Oracle does not automatically save the changes you made, because it may be necessary for more than one INSERT, UPDATE, or DELETE statement to be executed for the data to be in a consistent and logical state. For example, consider the steps involved in a bank transfer, which requires that you reduce the balance of the source account and increase the balance of the target account in order for the transfer to be valid. If the statement reducing the balance of the source account succeeds and the second statement increasing the balance of the target account fails, there is a problem—someone is out some money. With a transaction, you can group these two operations into a single action. Transactions do more than just group statements together; they also ensure the logical consistency of the database and your data.

Transactional control in Oracle has been designed to meet the ACID test first suggested by Jim Gray and Andreas Reuter. ACID stands for "Atomicity," "Consistency," "Isolation," and "Durability," as defined here:

- **Atomicity**   The entire transaction must commit as a unit, or not at all.

- **Consistency**   The transaction must follow some logical rules. In the account transfer example, you are moving money from one location to another. Consistency, in this case, requires that money not be created or destroyed. It must be moved, and the amount credited must be the amount debited.

- **Isolation**   The process carrying out the transaction must have absolute control over all of the elements it is affecting. Oracle provides a concurrent environment through a locking mechanism. While a process has a row locked, it cannot be modified by another process. However, via the read consistency mechanism, other processes can see the data in the column before it was modified until the changes are committed to the database. This is achieved in Oracle through the use of the undo or rollback segment, which will be discussed in Chapter 16.

- **Durability**   Durability means that after a transaction completes (or *commits*), the data must remain that way and will be visible to all users. If changes need to be made, another transaction will need to be initiated.

Oracle does not commit a transaction and make changes permanent unless instructed to do so. For this reason, several commands exist to control transactions. A transaction implicitly starts when the DML statement is executed. It is not terminated until it is either committed or rolled back.

In Oracle SQL, you can explicitly control the end of a transaction using the COMMIT and ROLLBACK commands. When you issue a COMMIT statement, the changes made by the DML statement become permanent. When you issue a ROLLBACK, the changes are reversed. The advantage of this system is that it is possible to verify an operation before committing it. When you query the table that you have modified, Oracle displays the results of all DML statements within the transaction. These changes are not visible to other users until you either commit or roll back the transaction. This provides isolation. You can issue several DML statements, realize that you have made a mistake, and undo your actions without other users being aware of the change. To undo the changes, you simply issue a ROLLBACK statement.

 EXAM TIP The first DML statement issued starts a transaction. A transaction ends when a COMMIT or ROLLBACK is encountered, or an implicit COMMIT or ROLLBACK takes place. Implicit commits take place when the connection to the server is terminated normally, such as exiting a program. An implicit rollback takes place if the connection to the database is aborted for any reason.

At times, however, you may not want to roll back the entire transaction. For instance, you may want to verify each step of a multistep transaction and roll back individual steps. This level of transactional control can be achieved with the use of *savepoints*. Savepoints are named markers within the transaction that can be used as the target for a rollback. You set savepoints with the following syntax:

```
SAVEPOINT name;
```

After the savepoint is set, you can roll back to that point by including the TO operator and the name of the savepoint. After you issue a ROLLBACK TO statement, all DML statements before the savepoint are committed and all changes after the savepoint are rolled back. Also, all savepoints are erased and the current transaction is ended. If you want to make further changes, you must start a new transaction by issuing a DML statement.

Locking

Part of the ACID test was isolation, which implies that while a transaction is being processed, no other user can make changes to the data that is the subject of the transaction. Oracle controls this isolation with the use of locks. There are two types of locks in Oracle: shared locks and exclusive locks.

Shared locks are acquired when you issue a SELECT statement. Oracle locks the table to ensure that no one modifies its structure while you are using its data, but it does not place any locks on the rows being queried. Shared locks do not prevent other users from reading or modifying the data in the table, only from making changes to the table's structure using the ALTER TABLE command or from dropping the table using the DROP TABLE command. Multiple users can acquire share locks on the same data.

 EXAM TIP SELECT statements apply no locks to the rows being queried.

Exclusive locks are acquired when you issue a DML statement, and they are acquired for each row being modified. The exclusive lock prevents other users from acquiring exclusive locks on the data you are working with as part of your transaction until you issue a COMMIT or ROLLBACK statement. This prevents two users from attempting to update the same data at the same time. When a user attempts to update data that is locked by another user, the user must wait until the lock is removed.

 NOTE Oracle allows you to manually perform locking of a table using the LOCK TABLE command. As a general rule, applying your own manual locks is a bad idea because it will probably apply more locks on the data than Oracle would itself and therefore slow down processing. As a general rule, never apply locks manually.

Data Definition Language

Before you can add data to a table, you need to create the table in the database. Data definition language (DDL) commands are used to create, modify, and remove objects from a database. The three key DDL commands are:

- **CREATE** The CREATE statement adds a new object to the database. You use it to create new tables, views, stored procedures, and other objects. In order for the CREATE command to succeed, no other object with the same name can exist in the schema.

- **ALTER** The ALTER statement is used to change the characteristics of tables, indexes, and other objects in the database. The ALTER statement does not apply to all objects in the database.

- **DROP** The DROP statement is used to remove objects from the database. When used on tables, it also gets rid of any data that existed in the table. Once dropped, the referenced object is no longer available and any commands that attempt to make use of it will return an error.

 NOTE Creating, modifying, and dropping database objects will be covered in more detail in Chapter 8.

Names of objects in Oracle must follow certain rules; for instance, all object names must begin with a letter; may be from 1 to 30 characters in length; and may contain letters, numbers, the underscore character (_), the dollar sign symbol ($), or the pound sign symbol (#). Object names cannot be the same as any Oracle reserved word. Oracle reserved words include most commands (for example, SELECT, INSERT, DROP, GRANT), as well as the names of functions, and other language constructs. The complete list of Oracle reserved words can be found in the *SQL Reference Manual.* If you do not follow the rules and attempt to create an object, Oracle will generate an error.

An object name must not be the same as the name of another object owned by the same user. When you attempt to create an object with the same name as another in the same schema, Oracle generates an error. The names of objects in Oracle are case insensitive, so if you use uppercase only, lowercase only, or mixed case when you create an object, Oracle always returns the object name in uppercase.

Database, System, and Session Management Commands

Oracle also includes a number of special commands that are used to manage the instance, database, or user session. These include the ALTER DATABASE, ALTER SYSTEM, ALTER SESSION, and other commands.

The ALTER DATABASE command is used to make changes to the database as a whole or a part of it. For example, you can use the ALTER DATABASE command to indicate that one or more datafiles are the target of a backup, or to change the state of the database from one mode to another.

The ALTER SYSTEM command is used to change the state of the running instance. It can be used to change the values of Oracle initialization parameters either dynamically or in the SPFILE. The ALTER SYSTEM command can also be used to allow only database administrators to connect to the instance, as well as many other options.

The ALTER SESSION command allows a user to change the properties of his or her session. For example, provided the user has permissions to issue the command, it can be used to increase the amount of memory that is available for sorting or whether or not parallel executions can be used on queries, or how date and other data will be output.

Understanding PL/SQL

While SQL is a great language for retrieving data from a database and for adding, making changes to, or deleting the data, it does lack some important programming constructs. For example, SQL does not have any provisions to control execution flow or to store data in variables for later reuse or to perform specific actions if an error takes place. Oracle's solution to this problem was PL/SQL, which stands for Procedural Language Extensions to SQL.

Before the integration of the PL/SQL language in Oracle, applications were limited in how they could retrieve and manipulate database information. The two methods were to send a number of SQL statements to the server in a script file from an interactive tool like SQL*Plus or to embed those statements into a language precompiler called

Pro*C. The latter provided the desired processing power but was not trivial to implement. It took several lines of code to explain how to connect to the database, what statement to run, and how to use the results from that statement. There were also differences in the datatypes available in SQL and the precompiled language. PL/SQL addresses the limitations of both of these methods.

PL/SQL code must be written in specific pieces called *blocks*. Because PL/SQL is a compiled language, these blocks must be processed by a compiler before they can execute. Compilation is the process of checking to ensure that the objects referred to in the code exist and that the statements have a valid syntax. After this process is completed, the code can then run, but it must run within a PL/SQL engine. The PL/SQL engine is not a separate product from the Oracle server, but an integral part of the Oracle database that takes a PL/SQL block and executes it.

PL/SQL blocks come in two varieties: anonymous blocks and named blocks. *Anonymous* PL/SQL blocks are pieces of PL/SQL code that have no header with a name. As such, you send them to the PL/SQL engine through an interactive tool like SQL*Plus, and they run once. Remember that PL/SQL is a compiled language, so the block is compiled, is run, and then disappears. If you want to run it again, you have to send the entire block to the engine again, where it once again is compiled, is run, and then disappears. These anonymous blocks can be saved to script files in the operating system to make re-running them easier.

A *named* block can be "called" one or more times by its name. For this reason, the named blocks are often used to implement modularity within a program. The program can be broken down into several modules or subprograms, which can be called one or more times. There are four types of named subprograms in Oracle: procedures, functions, packages, and triggers. Procedures and functions are subprograms that can be created as objects in the database, in the schema of their owner. When this happens, they are called *stored subprograms*. The advantage of using stored subprograms is that they are compiled at creation time and then can be run many times without the processing overhead of recompiling. A package is a collection of procedures and functions and cannot be invoked by its name, but the individual subprograms within the package (the procedures or functions) can be called individually as long as they are preceded by the package name. Triggers are blocks of code that are automatically invoked when the triggering action takes place, such as inserting a row into a table or the user logging on to the database or a system error occurring.

All PL/SQL blocks have the same structure, including a declaration section for declaring variables and other identifiers (the DECLARE keyword starts this section), an executable section for the code to be run (BEGIN keyword), an exception section for trapping errors (EXCEPTION), and a block terminator indicated by the END keyword. Only the BEGIN and END (and the code between them) are required elements of an anonymous PL/SQL block.

 EXAM TIP A valid PL/SQL block requires only BEGIN and END statements and at least one line of valid code between them.

Each line of a PL/SQL block is terminated by a semicolon, and the entire block is treated by Oracle as a unit of execution, meaning it is run and completed and the results are then sent to the calling program or client tool. A sample of an anonymous PL/SQL block is as follows:

```
DECLARE
        Val1 NUMBER := 5;
        Val2 NUMBER := 2;
         TheAnswer NUMBER;
BEGIN
TheAnswer := Val1 + Val2;
DBMS_OUTPUT.PUT_LINE('The answer is ' || TheAnswer);
EXCEPTION
        WHEN ZERO_DIVIDE THEN
                DBMS_OUTPUT.PUT_LINE('Cannot divide by zero!');
END;
```

Named PL/SQL blocks have a similar structure but allow the passing of parameters into the block and, optionally, can return values back to the calling program. Functions must always return a value and specify a return type, whereas procedures and triggers do not need to. An example of the preceding anonymous PL/SQL block as a procedure is as shown next. Note that the DECLARE keyword is not required as the declaration section is assumed to follow the procedure name and parameter definition.

```
CREATE OR REPLACE PROCEDURE Add_Nums (Val1 IN NUMBER, Val2 IN NUMBER)
AS
        TheAnswer NUMBER;
BEGIN
TheAnswer := Val1 + Val2;
DBMS_OUTPUT.PUT_LINE('The answer is ' || TheAnswer);
EXCEPTION
        WHEN ZERO_DIVIDE THEN
                DBMS_OUTPUT.PUT_LINE('Cannot divide by zero!');
END;
```

To invoke the procedure and pass it the numbers to add, you would issue the following commands in SQL*Plus, iSQL*Plus, or another client query tool that supports Oracle:

```
execute Add_Nums(10,2);
```

Chapter 10 will provide greater insight into how to program PL/SQL to access and manipulate Oracle databases.

Query Tools in Oracle 10g

Oracle provides two key tools to send commands to the database to query its contents, create objects, administer the database and instance, and perform other manipulation: SQL*Plus and iSQL*Plus. SQL*Plus is a command-line tool executed on a client computer and is installed when the Oracle client software is installed; iSQL*Plus runs on the same computer as the database instance and is started as a service or background process on the host. Users access *i*SQL*Plus using Internet Explorer or any other supported web browser.

SQL*Plus

SQL*Plus is a tool with a number of features that can enhance development. The capability to save commands and use variables enables you to save and reuse common SQL statements. The capability to customize your environment and format your output enables you to write reports without purchasing a separate reporting tool. It is the main tool used to start up and shut down a database instance, and it includes a set of commands for managing the SQL*Plus environment as well as some useful shortcuts, such as the DESCRIBE SQL*Plus command to display the structure of a database object.

In SQL*Plus your last executable SQL statement or PL/SQL block is saved in a buffer that can be accessed and modified using the EDIT SQL*Plus command or other statements. You can use substitution variables in SQL statements and PL/SQL blocks to dynamically specify values for those variables when you execute the SQL statement. SQL*Plus also includes a set of commands that enables you to save commands to script files on disk, which can later be executed. You can also use the SPOOL SQL*Plus command to store the results of executions for logging or other purposes.

SQL*Plus includes a number of options for the SET command that allows you to configure your SQL*Plus environment so that it is best suited for you or affect how output is displayed. Those commands can be saved in a file called login.sql and will be executed whenever you start SQL*Plus to configure your SQL*Plus environment properly. The SHOW SQL*Plus command can be used to display the current settings. SQL*Plus also includes a set of commands that enable you to format your output and create formatted reports. Furthermore, the DBA can restrict the commands that users can execute in SQL*Plus by adding entries to the PRODUCT_USER_PROFILE table, which is owned by the SYSTEM schema.

In Windows environments there are two versions of SQL*Plus: the graphical one invoked from the Oracle program group when you install the Oracle software (called SQLPLUSW.EXE) and the command-line version also available on all Oracle platforms and invoked using the command `sqlplus`.

Exercise 4-1: Working with SQL*Plus

In this exercise you will invoke SQL*Plus from your Oracle host and execute and format a few queries.

1. Log on to your computer as the **oracle** user, i.e., the user who owns the Oracle software.

2. Invoke SQL*Plus from the command line by issuing the following command:

   ```
   $ sqlplus /nolog
   ```

3. Within SQL*Plus, connect to the default database instance as the user **system** with the appropriate password.

   ```
   SQL> connect system/oracle
   ```

4. Describe the structures of the DBA_TABLESPACES and DBA_DATA_FILES tables.

```
SQL> desc DBA_TABLESPACES;
SQL> desc dba_data_files;
```

5. Display the list of all tablespaces and their associated datafiles.

```
SQL> SELECT DBA_TABLESPACES.tablespace_name, file_name
  2  FROM DBA_TABLESPACES JOIN DBA_DATA_FILES
  3  ON DBA_TABLESPACES.TABLESPACE_NAME = DBA_DATA_FILES.TABLESPACE_NAME;
```

6. Format the output of the filename to be 55 characters wide and the tablespace name to be 20 characters long, and then reissue the query.

```
SQL> col file_name format a55
SQL> col tablespace_name format a20
SQL> SELECT DBA_TABLESPACES.tablespace_name, file_name
  2  FROM DBA_TABLESPACES JOIN DBA_DATA_FILES
  3  ON DBA_TABLESPACES.TABLESPACE_NAME = DBA_DATA_FILES.TABLESPACE_NAME
```

7. Return a list of all users who own objects in the database, with each user name appearing only once.

```
SQL> SELECT DISTINCT owner FROM DBA_OBJECTS;
```

8. Exit SQL*Plus.

```
SQL> exit;
```

*i*SQL*Plus

If you do not want to install the Oracle 10*g* client software on your computer (because it does take up a lot of disk space), there is a way to send queries to the database as well as execute scripts and do most things that you can do with SQL*Plus. This is by starting and using *i*SQL*Plus running on the Oracle server computer and then connecting to it using a web browser. Each installation of the Oracle 10*g* database will have *i*SQL*Plus available, though it needs to be started on the server first.

To start *i*SQL*Plus on a Linux system, log in to the computer where Oracle is installed as the **oracle** user, i.e., the owner of the Oracle installation, and while ensuring that the PATH includes $ORACLE_HOME/bin, issue the command

```
isqlplusctl start
```

If you want to stop *i*SQL*Plus on Linux, issue the command

```
isqlplusctl stop
```

On Windows systems *i*SQL*Plus runs as a service and can be started and stopped using the Services Microsoft Management Console (MMC) snap-in as shown in Figure 4-1. You can still use the `isqlplusctl` command to stop and start the service and check its status.

The best way to determine if *i*SQL*Plus is running, as well as to make use of it, is to connect to it using a web browser and then specify the URL in the form `http://<server>:<port>/isqlplus`, where `server` is the name or IP address of the computer on which Oracle is running and `port` is the TCP port number on which

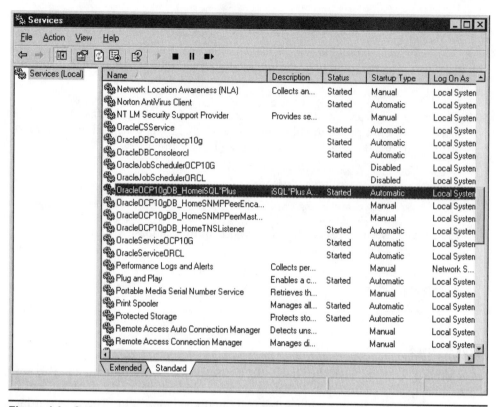

Figure 4-1 Startup and shutdown of *i*SQL*Plus is managed using the Services MMC snap-in in Windows.

*i*SQL*Plus is listening—usually 5560, as shown in Figure 4-2. If the Oracle Universal Installer detects that port 5560 is already in use, it will go to the next higher available port until it finds one that is free (5561, 5562, etc.). To determine what port is being used, you can always check the contents of the portlist.ini file in $ORACLE_HOME/install.

 EXAM TIP The default port number where *i*SQL*Plus is installed is 5560.

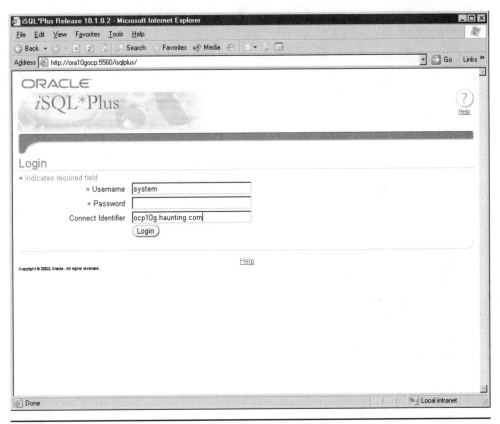

Figure 4-2 Use a web browser to connect to *i*SQL*Plus at the appropriate server port.

Once you have connected to *i*SQL*Plus, you need to specify an Oracle database username, password, and connect string. The connect string is the database you want to query and must be resolvable by the Oracle networking components of the computer where *i*SQL*Plus is running. If you leave the connect string blank, an attempt to connect to the default instance will be made, if one is defined. Once connected, you can issue and execute queries, load and run scripts, and save the commands to history for later recall or in a script from the main *i*SQL*Plus workspace shown in Figure 4-3.

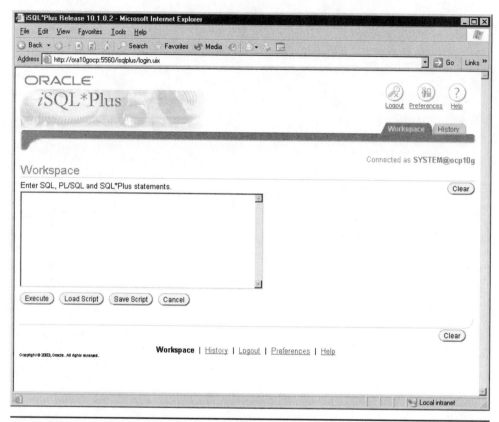

Figure 4-3   The *i*SQL*Plus main screen allows you to execute queries against the database.

Exercise 4-2: Working with *i*SQL*Plus

In this exercise you will connect to *i*SQL*Plus on your Oracle host using a browser and execute and format a few queries.

1. Start a web browser and connect to the *i*SQL*Plus URL on your Oracle database server, specifying the appropriate port number and machine name.

2. At the *i*SQL*Plus logon, enter **SYSTEM** as the username and the password you assigned as the password. Leave the Connect Identifier blank. Click the Login button to log on.

3. In *i*SQL*Plus, enter the command to describe the DBA_TABLESPACES table, and then click Execute. Do the same for the DBA_DATA_FILES table. (Hint: You can enter both commands and then click Execute to see both results at the same time.)

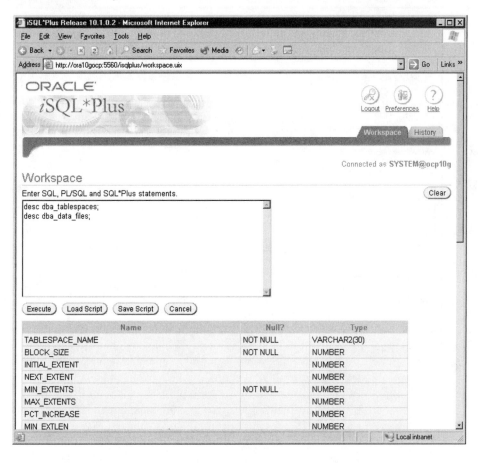

4. Click Clear to remove the previous commands and results, and then enter the SQL command to display a list of all tablespaces and their associated data files. Then click Execute.

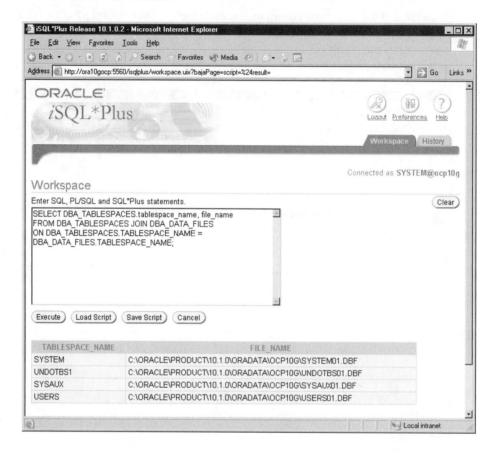

5. Modify the command to format the output of the filename to be 55 characters wide and the tablespace name to be 20 characters long. Then reissue the query.

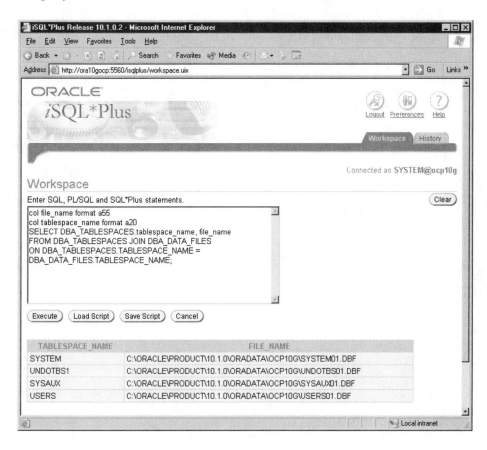

6. Clear out the previous results and then enter a command to return a list of all users who own objects in the database, with each username appearing only once.

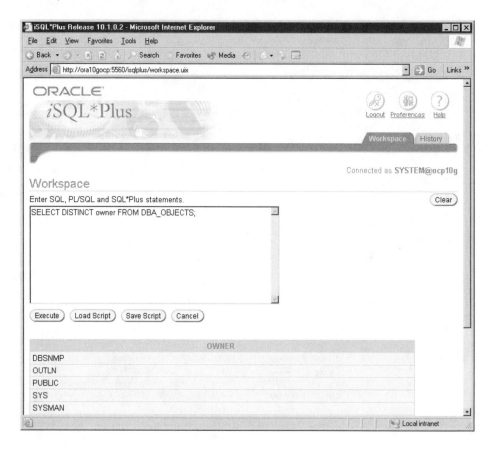

7. Click the History tab to view your session history.

8. Click Logout on the top right to end your *i*SQL*Plus session.

Other Methods to Interface with the Oracle Database

SQL*Plus and *i*SQL*Plus are not the only methods to interface with the Oracle database and manipulate the objects within it. Oracle databases can be accessed using Java and JDBC, programmatically using the Oracle Call Interface (OCI) application programming interface (API) and several other object interfaces and APIs, as well as by writing SQL statements in your 3GL code and then using precompilers like Pro*C++ to produce valid run-time calls.

Java in Oracle

Java is an industry-standard object-oriented programming language developed by Sun Microsystems. One of its major strengths is the ability to write programs on one supported Java platform, such as Windows, and have that code execute on other supported Java platforms. This is possible because Java includes a concept of a Java Virtual Machine, or JVM, which executes the code. The JVM runs on the target operating system but presents the same objects to the Java application, meaning that the programmer does not have to worry about programming for Windows or Unix— only about programming for the JVM.

Oracle has provided Java support since Oracle 8 and continues to enhance the Java capabilities of the database. Oracle 10g includes a JVM in the database (as did Oracle 8, 8i, and 9i) and allows you to program stored procedures and functions in Java that can be called from PL/SQL, and vice versa, by using Java Database Connectivity (JDBC). This provides the ability to make use of Java code and PL/SQL code interchangeably within the same database, and it is something that Oracle itself does. The JVM is installed and configured in the database when you create the database using the Database Configuration Assistant or run the appropriate scripts.

 EXAM TIP Oracle Database 10g includes a Java VM used to execute Java stored procedures and functions stored in the database. JDBC is used by the built-in JVM to manipulate database data.

Oracle Call Interface (OCI)

If you want to write C code in the same API that many of the Oracle tools and other programs are written in, you can make use of the Oracle Call Interface (OCI). OCI is a relatively low-level and complex API for advanced C and C++ programmers. Its main advantage is that it provides precise control over what is sent to Oracle and how the results are interpreted, and provides the best performance. In fact, all other Oracle APIs are built on top of OCI and make extensive use of it. Programming using OCI is the most efficient way to make use of third-generation languages (3GLs) like C and C++ for interfacing with Oracle.

EXAM TIP OCI is the fastest but the most difficult API to write Oracle applications in.

Other APIs

Oracle does not exist in a vacuum and needs to provide programmers with methods to interface with Oracle that make the most sense in their environments. For this reason, a number of other APIs are released and supported by Oracle, including these:

- **Java Database Connectivity (JDBC)** Oracle exposes the database for access by Java-based programs using JDBC. This means that developers can write programs in Java and query and manipulate Oracle databases by making a thin-client JDBC connection to Oracle. In fact, running Java stored procedures and functions in the Oracle JVM also makes use of JDBC to connect to the SQL engine within the Oracle database.

- **Pro*C/C++ and Pro*COBOL** Before the advent of PL/SQL and from the earliest days of the Oracle database, programmers had embedded SQL statements within their C or COBOL code and then run that code through a precompiler to produce code that would include run-time library calls for database access and compile properly with the C, C++, or COBOL compiler they were using. Pro*C/C++ and Pro*COBOL continue to be valid ways to embed SQL statements in 3GLs.

- **Oracle C++ Call Interface (OCCI)** C++ provides an object-oriented approach to programming, and OCCI provides object-oriented access to the Oracle database for C++ programmers. OCCI exposes many of the low-level functions of OCI while being easier for C++ programmers to work with than Pro*C++.

- **Open Database Connectivity (ODBC)** ODBC is a standard developed by Microsoft in the late 1980s to provide generic database access. It is still widely used by many programmers in Microsoft-centric organizations, though faster methods like .NET managed providers exist. In order to make use of ODBC to access an Oracle database, the Oracle 10*g* networking components must be installed on the computer running the ODBC-based application.

- **Oracle Data Provider for .NET (ODP.NET)** With the introduction of Visual Studio .NET, Microsoft also changed the way database access was handled in .NET-based applications. ODP.NET is a managed provider for Oracle database access that can be used in applications developed to the Microsoft .NET Framework.

- **Oracle Objects for OLE (OO4O)** Before .NET Microsoft Windows applications were written to take advantage of Object Linking and Embedding (OLE). OO4O allows for access to data stored in an Oracle database from pre-

.NET languages such as Visual Basic 6 or from any Microsoft-based scripting language such as Active Server Pages (ASP) or Visual Basic for Applications (VBA).

 EXAM TIP Developers using the Windows platform can program applications to access Oracle data using ODP.NET, OO4O, and ODBC, as well as any of the other APIs mentioned.

Oracle continues to enhance the methods that can be used to interface to the database and also has added support for access to Oracle data using FTP, HTTP, and Web Distributed Authoring and Versioning (WebDAV) when the XML DB feature of Oracle is installed and configured.

Chapter Review

Oracle provides a number of mechanisms to interact with the database and its data, including the SQL language, PL/SQL, Java, and other lower-level APIs such as OCI, OO4O, and ODP.NET, to name a few.

SQL is composed of three languages: DDL for creating and managing objects; DCL for granting and revoking permissions; and DML for adding, changing, and deleting data. Transaction control statements, including COMMIT and ROLLBACK, are used to control how data is saved to the database. SAVEPOINTs can be used to logically break a transaction into subparts that can be committed should later parts of the transaction fail.

PL/SQL contains language elements allowing a programmer to define variables and other identifiers, perform looping, conditionally execute statements according to the results of previous executions or the values of variables, and take advantage of other features familiar to programmers of any language. It is the foundation for programming powerful applications for Oracle. PL/SQL requires a PL/SQL engine for execution, which exists in the Oracle 10g database.

When executing queries against the database or PL/SQL blocks, you can make use of SQL*Plus on the client computer or iSQL*Plus using a web browser and connecting to the database server. Both provide similar functionality, but iSQL*Plus does not require that Oracle client software be installed on your computer.

Java can also be used to program database applications for Oracle. Oracle includes a Java Virtual Machine, allowing developers to create and execute Java procedures and functions in the database. JDBC is used to access and manipulate database data from Java.

Lower-level APIs can also be used to program applications that access an Oracle database. The Oracle Call Interface (OCI) is the fastest and most complicated of these; others include OO4O, ODP.NET, and ODBC, as well as precompilers such as Pro*C/C++ and Pro*COBOL.

Questions

1. You want to create an anonymous PL/SQL block to access data in your database based upon the value of a variable. In which section of the PL/SQL block would you need to define the variable? (Choose the best answer.)

   A. Declaration section

   B. Definition section

   C. Includable section

   D. Executable section

   E. Exception section

2. Which of the following APIs can you use to program an application on the Windows platform to access an Oracle database? (Choose all correct answers.)

   A. PL/SQL

   B. Oracle Objects for OLE

   C. Oracle Call Interface

   D. Java

   E. Oracle Data Provider for .NET

3. Given the following SQL statement, which line of code will cause the statement to fail? (Choose the best answer.)

   ```
   1    SELECT LastName, FirstName, Email
   2    FROM Customers, EmailUsers
   3    ON Customers.UserName = EmailUsers.UserName
   4    ORDER BY LastName ASC
   ```

   A. 1

   B. 2

   C. 3

   D. 4

   E. The statement will succeed

4. You need a mechanism to import data into Oracle from a legacy application and, using a value in one of the columns in the source data, add the row to one of several tables in your database. Which of the following can you use to satisfy your requirements? (Choose two correct answers.)

   A. PL/SQL

   B. MERGE INTO

   C. UPSERT

   D. INSERT

   E. INSERT ALL

   F. INSERT FIRST

5. Which of the following is not a valid SQL command? (Choose all correct answers.)

   A. SELECT

   B. COLUMN

   C. ROLLBACK

   D. DESCRIBE

   E. SAVEPOINT

6. Which of the following SQL statements will cause a transaction to be started? (Choose two correct answers.)

   A. INSERT

   B. SELECT

   C. COMMIT

   D. SAVEPOINT

   E. DELETE

   F. ROLLBACK

7. You issue the following SQL statement against your database to change the price of SKU 347711 from $90.75 to $99.75 without committing the change. At the same time another user queries the value of the same SKU. What will the result of that user's query be?

   ```
   UPDATE Products SET MSRP = 99.75 WHERE SKU=347711
   ```

   A. $90.75

   B. $99.75

   C. The user will wait until you commit your transaction before being displayed a value

   D. Oracle will return the error "ORA-20001: Current row locked by another process"

8. You attempt to connect to iSQL*Plus on your Oracle database server running on Linux and receive an error in your browser that the page cannot be opened. You suspect that iSQL*Plus is not started on the database server. Which of the following commands can you use to start the process? (Choose the best answer.)

   A. emctl start isqlplus

   B. emctl startup isqlplus

   C. isqlplusctl startup

   D. isqlplusctl start

   E. isqlplus start

9. Which of the following make it possible for Java procedures created and compiled in the Oracle 10*g* database to access data in the same database? (Choose the best answer.)

A. Java Virtual Machine

B. JDBC

C. PL/SQL engine

D. SQL engine

E. Java procedures cannot access database data in Oracle

10. On which line will the following PL/SQL block fail? (Choose the best answer.)

```
1    DECLARE
2      vNum NUMBER := 100;
3    BEGIN
4      vNum = vNum / 10;
5    END;
```

A. 1

B. 2

C. 3

D. 4

E. 5

F. The statement will succeed

Answers

1. **A.** You need to define all variables in your anonymous PL/SQL block following the DECLARE keyword in the declaration section of the PL/SQL block. The definition and includable sections do not exist. The executable section starts with the BEGIN keyword and includes the code being executed. The exception section is used to trap for expected errors in the code and starts with the EXCEPTION keyword.

2. **B, C, and E.** Any of the APIs available for Oracle can be used to program a Windows application to access Oracle data, including OO4O, OCI, ODP.NET, ODBC, and JDBC. You can also use precompilers to embed SQL code in your 3GL code. PL/SQL and Java are not APIs but programming languages and are therefore incorrect, since the question asked you to identify the APIs.

3. **C.** This SQL statement mixes *classic* join syntax with ANSI join syntax, making it invalid. The ON keyword can be used only in ANSI join syntax and must be preceded by the JOIN keyword between the table names. In *classic* join syntax the WHERE clause is used to specify the join condition and the ON keyword is invalid.

4. **A and F.** Because you need to add data to one of several tables, you need to perform conditional logic on each of the rows in the source table as they are read and then insert that row into the appropriate table. PL/SQL is a programming language with conditional logic capabilities and can be used to perform this task. You can also use the INSERT FIRST statement, which will add the data to the first table matching the conditions specified. INSERT ALL may insert data into more than one table, since all conditions are evaluated, whereas INSERT cannot perform any conditional logic. MERGE INTO performs an UPDATE and INSERT based upon data in an existing table, and there is no UPSERT statement in Oracle SQL.

5. **B and D.** COLUMN and DESCRIBE are not valid SQL statements but are valid SQL*Plus and iSQL*Plus commands to format the display of a column or provide information on the structure of a database object. SELECT, ROLLBACK, and SAVEPOINT are valid SQL commands in Oracle.

6. **A and E.** A transaction is started by any valid DML statement, including INSERT, UPDATE, and DELETE. A SELECT statement will execute a query against the database but not start a transaction. ROLLBACK and COMMIT will end a transaction but start another one. SAVEPOINT defines a named marker in your transaction that allows data before it to be committed and following it to be rolled back when the ROLLBACK TO *savepoint* statement is issued.

7. **A.** Oracle allows users to query the database even if changes to the data being queried are in process. The values returned will be those committed to the database at the time the query was issued, which in this case is $90.75, since the UPDATE was not yet committed.

8. **D.** The command to start iSQL*Plus on a Unix environment is `isqlplusctl start`. The `emctl` command is used to start Oracle Enterprise Manager and its controls and cannot be used to start iSQL*Plus. C and E are not correct syntax for starting iSQL*Plus.

9. **B.** Java Database Connectivity is used by Java procedures and functions created in the Oracle database to access the database data. The Java code will run in the JVM and then make JDBC calls for database data. The PL/SQL engine is not involved with Java in Oracle. The SQL engine is what JDBC uses to parse and execute the queries and send the results back to the Java code in the JVM.

10. **D.** The assignment operator in PL/SQL is `:=` and not just the equal sign. The equal sign (=) is a comparison operator. The rest of the PL/SQL block is valid.

CHAPTER 5

Managing Oracle Processes

In this chapter you will learn how to
- Control the database
- Start and stop *i*SQL*Plus
- Start and stop Enterprise Manager Database Control
- Start and stop the Oracle Listener
- Start up and shut down Oracle Database 10*g*
- Describe startup and shutdown options for the Oracle database
- Handle parameter files
- Locate and view the database alert log

A number of processes are required for an Oracle server to be working, and usable. To begin with, you need a user process. This is the process that the end user runs: in the last chapter, you saw SQL*Plus and *i*SQL*Plus, but of course for a production system with a full user interface, the user process will be much more complicated than either of those. Then there is the management process, in our case Database Control; the Database Listener, a process that responds to connection requests from remote user processes; and finally, the background processes that make up the instance itself. In this chapter, you will go through starting these processes and then look at how the database itself is opened for use.

Starting SQL*Plus

This couldn't be simpler. SQL*Plus is just an elementary process for issuing ad hoc SQL commands to a database. It is a client/server tool. On Windows systems, you have a choice between the character-based version, SQLPLUS.EXE, and the graphical version, SQLPLUSW.EXE. Both can be launched from a command prompt, or the standard installation of Oracle will have created a shortcut to SQLPLUSW.EXE in your Start menu. On Unix, there is just the one version, called sqlplus. On either operating system you will find the executable program in your ORACLE_HOME/bin directory.

A variation you need to be aware of is the NOLOG switch. By default, the SQL*Plus program immediately prompts you for an Oracle username, password, and database connect string. This is fine for regular end users, but it is useless for database administrators because it requires that the database be already open. To launch SQL*Plus without a login prompt, use the /NOLOG switch:

```
sqlplus /nolog
```

or for the Windows GUI version:

```
sqlplusw /nolog
```

This will give you a SQL prompt, from which you can connect with a variety of syntaxes, to be detailed in the sections that follow.

Starting *i*SQL*Plus

The *i*SQL*Plus program is a graphical version of SQL*Plus that runs as an Application Server service. End users connect to it from a browser, such as Internet Explorer. Conceptually, it is identical to SQL*Plus: it is a user process for issuing ad hoc SQL. The difference is that whereas the SQL*Plus user process is a single process on the client machine, *i*SQL*Plus divides the user process into two layers: a user interface layer running in the user's browser, which handles the bare bones of the graphical user interface (local window management, tracking mouse movements, keyboard control, and so on), and the application layer, which runs (typically) on a central server. It is this application layer product that we need to launch. Once running, it can be used by any browser anywhere. On Unix or Windows, launch the *i*SQL*Plus server with

```
isqlplusctl start
```

and stop it with

```
isqlplusctl stop
```

Alternatively, on Windows, you can start the *i*SQL*Plus server as a service, either through the Windows GUI or from the command line with `net start`.

To contact *i*SQL*Plus, issue the URL

```
http://<hostname.domain>:<port>/isqlplus
```

as shown in Figure 5-1, where <hostname.domain> is the address of the machine hosting your Oracle installation, and <port> is the IP port on which the *i*SQL*Plus server is listening. By default, this will be port 5560, but if your installation is nonstandard, it may be something different. Check the file portlist.ini in your ORACLE_HOME/install directory to see which port was

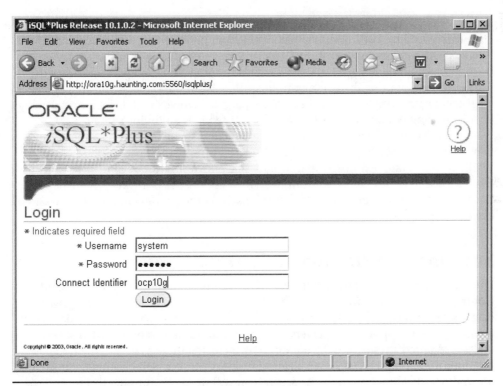

Figure 5-1   The *i*SQL*Plus logon screen—note the URL.

selected by the installer at install time. The *i*SQL*Plus tool is in fact implemented as a stand-alone OC4J application. (OC4J, Oracle Components for Java 2 Enterprise Edition, is Oracle's run-time environment for Java, normally shipped as part of the Application Server.)

 TIP Note that *i*SQL*Plus is a little more effort to start than SQL*Plus, but it can be vastly more convenient to use. For example, column formatting is much better. Furthermore, you do not need a single line of Oracle code installed on your client machine; all you need is a browser.

Starting the Database Listener

You will look at the Database Listener in much greater detail in Chapter 12, but for now, be content with just stopping and starting it, and checking its status. From the command line, use the Listener Control utility:

```
lsnrctl start <listener_name>
lsnrctl stop <listener_name>
lsnrctl status <listener_name>
```

The <listener_name> will default to LISTENER, and unless you have created additional listeners with different names, this will be fine, so you can leave it out.

Alternatively, if you have Database Control running, you can use it to control the listener instead of using the command-line utility. From the Database home page, click the listener name to go to the listener's home page and stop or start it from there. Finally, if you are using Windows, you can control the listener as a Windows service.

If your Database Listener is not running, no clients will be able to connect unless they are logged on to the server machine and are running their user process there, locally to the database. In particular, Database Control will not be able to connect to the database if the listener is not running. However, note that if you stop the listener, this will not affect already established sessions; it will mean only that no new sessions can be established.

Starting the Database Control Daemon

Enterprise Manager Database Control is an alternative to Enterprise Manager Grid Control. Unlike Grid Control, Database Control is limited to administering one database at a time, whereas Grid Control can be used to manage numerous databases at once, as well as application servers. Database Control is a web tool, consisting of tables and procedures within the database (you created these as part of the database creation process) and an OC4J application running on your database server. If there are multiple databases on the same server, you will need one running instance of the OC4J program for each one. You will contact them on a different port for each database. As with *i*SQL*Plus, your browser provides the user interface: the local window management and so on.

To start the Database Control process, whatever your platform, use the emctl utility:

```
emctl start dbconsole
```

and to stop the daemon or see if it is running,

```
emctl stop dbconsole
emctl status dbconsole
```

Alternatively, on Windows where emctl runs as a service, if you wish you can control it from the Services MMC snap-in, or the Computer Management MMC console. However, there are some possible complications, as shown in Figure 5-2.

First, if there are multiple databases on your server, you must set the ORACLE_ SID environment variable before starting Database Control. Second, Database Control does not like DHCP, or any other reason for changing the address of the server. Of course, this is not a problem for production systems, but it can be very annoying if you are using a laptop that is sometimes connected to a network and sometimes not. For this example in the figure, the database called ocp10g (there was already a database called orcl10g on the computer) was created while not attached to a network. Database Control therefore used a directory named after the localhost for its configuration data. Then the computer connected to a network, picked up a DHCP-issued address, and the user tried to start the dbconsole. As you can see, the first attempt to start dbconsole failed because the user had not set his ORACLE_SID environment variable. He fixed that and tried again; it then failed because Database Control next looked for its configuration information in a nonexistent directory whose name was derived from the newly acquired IP address. Then the user unplugged

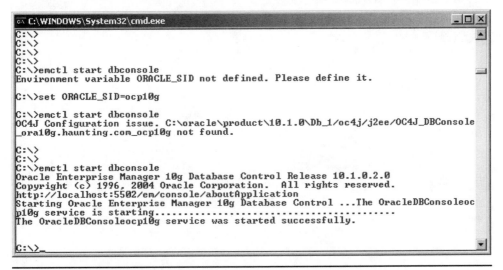

Figure 5-2 Some dbconsole startup problems

the network lead, and dbconsole started successfully. Your server should be configured with a static IP address to avoid this problem.

 TIP An undocumented environment variable, EMHOSTNAME, may help with changing an IP address. Set it to point to your local machine name before creating any databases, and then dbconsole should always look for that directory name for its config data.

Once the process is running, you contact it with the URL

```
http://<host.domain>:<port>/em
```

where <host.domain> is the address of your database server, as shown in Figure 5-3. The port will default to 5500 for your first database on the computer, 5501 for your second, and so on. If in any doubt, check the portlist.ini file as you did for *i*SQL*Plus.

 TIP There is a link in Database Control to navigate to *i*SQL*Plus.

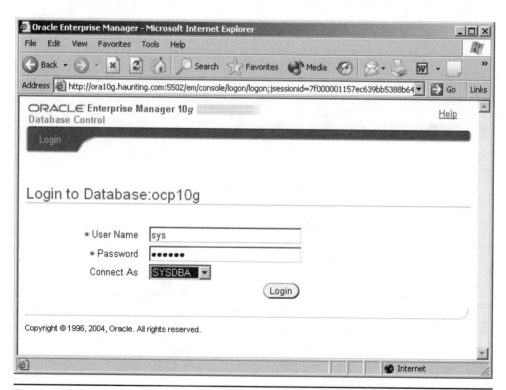

Figure 5-3 Database Control logon, showing the SYSDBA privilege selected. Note the URL.

Database Startup and Shutdown

To be precise, one does not start or stop a database: an instance may be started and stopped; a database is mounted and opened, and then dismounted and closed. This can be done from either SQL*Plus, using the STARTUP and SHUTDOWN commands, or through Database Control. The alert log will give details of all such operations.

Connecting with an Appropriate Privilege

Ordinary users cannot start up or shut down a database. This is because an ordinary user is authenticated against the data dictionary, and it is logically impossible for an ordinary user to start up (or create) a database, since the data dictionary cannot be read until the database is open. You must therefore connect with some form of external authentication, as discussed in Chapter 3: you must be authenticated either by the operating system, as being a member of the group that owns the Oracle software, or by giving a username/password combination that exists in the external password file. You tell Oracle that you wish to use external authentication by using appropriate syntax in the CONNECT command that you give in your user process. If you are using Database Control, it is easy: in the Connect As combo box you select either SYSOPER or SYSDBA (the difference will be defined shortly).

Database Control does not give you the option of using operating system authentication. This is because it always connects via a listener, as though it were a remote process. If your listener is not running or does not recognize the database you wish to connect to, you will not be able to use Database Control. If you are using SQL*Plus, the syntax of the CONNECT command tells Oracle what type of authentication you wish to use: the default of data dictionary authentication ("Normal" in Database Control parlance), password file, or operating system. These are the possibilities:

```
connect user/pass[@db]
connect user/pass[@db] as sysdba
connect user/pass[@db] as sysoper
connect / as sysdba
connect / as sysoper
```

The first example is normal, data dictionary, authentication. Oracle will validate the username/password combination against values stored in the data dictionary. The database must be open. Anyone connecting with this syntax cannot—no matter who he is—issue startup or shutdown commands. The second two examples instruct Oracle to go to the external password file to validate the username/password combination. The last two examples use operating system authentication: Oracle will go to the host operating system and check whether the operating system user running SQL*Plus is a member of the operating system group that owns the Oracle software, and if the user passes this test, he will be logged on as SYSDBA or SYSOPER without any need to give a username and password. A user connecting with any of the bottom four syntaxes will be able to issue startup and shutdown commands and will be able to connect no matter what state the database is in—it may not even have been created yet. Note that the first three examples can include a database connect string: this is necessary if the connection is to be made across a network. Naturally, this is not an option for operating system authentication, because operating system authentication relies on the user's being logged on to the machine hosting the Oracle server: he must either be working on it directly or have logged in to it with telnet or some similar utility.

SYSOPER and SYSDBA

These are special privileges with special capabilities. They can be enabled only when users are connecting with an external authentication method. SYSOPER has the ability to issue these commands:

```
STARTUP
SHUTDOWN
ALTER DATABASE [MOUNT | OPEN | CLOSE | DISMOUNT]
ALTER [DATABASE | TABLESPACE] [BEGIN | END] BACKUP
RECOVER
```

The SYSDBA privilege encompasses all of these commands but in addition has the ability to create a database, to do an incomplete recovery, and to create other SYSOPER and SYSDBA users.

 EXAM TIP SYSDBA and SYSOPER are not users; they are privileges that can be granted to users. By default, only user SYS has these privileges.

You may be wondering what Oracle user you are actually logging on as when you use operating system authentication. To find out, from a SQL*Plus prompt connect using the operating system authentication syntax just shown and then issue the show user command, as in Figure 5-4.

```
C:\WINDOWS\System32\cmd.exe - sqlplus /nolog                         _|□|×|
C:\>
C:\>
C:\>
C:\>
C:\>
C:\>sqlplus /nolog

SQL*Plus: Release 10.1.0.2.0 - Production on Sat Sep 11 12:55:40 2004

Copyright (c) 1982, 2004, Oracle.  All rights reserved.

SQL>
SQL> connect / as sysdba
Connected.
SQL>
SQL> show user
USER is "SYS"
SQL>
SQL> connect sys/oracle@ocp10g as sysoper
Connected.
SQL>
SQL> show user;
USER is "PUBLIC"
SQL>
SQL>
```

Figure 5-4 Use of external authentication

As you see, use of the SYSDBA privilege logs you on to the instance as user SYS, the most powerful user in the database and the owner of the data dictionary. Use of the SYSOPER privilege connects you as a user PUBLIC. PUBLIC is not a user in any normal sense but a notional user with administration privileges but (by default) no privileges that let him see or manipulate data. You should connect with either of these privileges only when you need to carry out procedures that no normal user can do.

Startup

Remember that the instance and the database are separate entities: they can exist independently of each other. The startup process is therefore staged: first you build the instance in memory, second you enable a connection to the database by mounting it, and third you open the database for use. At any moment, a database will be in one of four states:

- SHUTDOWN
- NOMOUNT
- MOUNT
- OPEN

When the database is in SHUTDOWN mode, all files are closed and the instance does not exist. In the NOMOUNT mode, the instance has been built in memory (the SGA has been created and the background processes started, according to whatever is specified in its parameter file) but no connection has been made to a database. It is indeed possible that the database does not yet exist. In MOUNT mode, the instance locates and reads the database control file. In OPEN mode, all database files are located and opened and the database is made available for use by end users. The startup process is staged: whenever you issue a startup command, it will go through these stages. It is possible to stop the startup part way. For example, if your control file is damaged, or a multiplexed copy is missing, you will not be able to mount the database, but by stopping in NOMOUNT mode, you may be able to repair the damage. Similarly, if there are problems with any datafiles or redo log files, you may be able to repair them in MOUNT mode before transitioning the database to OPEN mode.

At any stage, how does the instance find the files it needs, and exactly what happens? Start with NOMOUNT. When you issue a startup command, Oracle will attempt to locate a parameter file. There are three default filenames. On Unix they are

```
$ORACLE_HOME/dbs/spfile<SID>.ora
$ORACLE_HOME/dbs/spfile.ora
$ORACLE_HOME/dbs/init<SID>.ora
```

and on Windows,

```
%ORACLE_HOME%\database\SPFILE<SID>.ORA
%ORACLE_HOME%\database\SPFILE.ORA
%ORACLE_HOME%\database\INIT<SID>.ORA
```

TIP The spfile<SID>.ora file is undoubtedly the most convenient file to use as your parameter file. Normally, you will use spfile.ora only in a RAC environment, where one file may be used to start several instances. You will use an init<SID>.ora file only if for some reason you need to make manual edits: spfiles are binary files and cannot be edited by hand.

In all cases, <SID> refers to the name of the instance which the parameter file will start. This search order is important! Oracle will work its way down the list, using the first file it finds and ignoring the rest. If none of them exist, the instance will not start. The only files used in NOMOUNT mode are the parameter file and the alert log. The parameters in the parameter file are used to build the SGA in memory and to start the background processes. Entries will be written out to the alert log describing this process. Where is the alert log? In the location given by the BACKGROUND_DUMP_DEST parameter. If the log already exists, it will be appended to. Otherwise, it will be created. If any problems occur during this stage, trace files may also be generated in the same location.

 EXAM TIP An "init" file is known as a "static" parameter file, because it is read only once, at instance startup. An "spfile" is known as a "dynamic" parameter file, because Oracle continuously reads and updates it while the instance is running.

Once the instance is successfully started in NOMOUNT mode, it may be transitioned to MOUNT mode by reading the controlfile. It locates the controlfile by using the CONTROL_FILES parameter, which it knows from having read the parameter file used when starting in NOMOUNT mode. If the controlfile (or any multiplexed copy of it) is damaged or missing, the database will not mount and you will have to take appropriate action before proceeding further. All copies of the controlfile must be available and identical if the mount is to be successful.

As part of the mount, the names and locations of all the datafiles and online redo logs are read from the controlfile, but Oracle does not yet attempt to find them. This happens during the transition to OPEN mode. If any files are missing or damaged, the database will remain in MOUNT mode and cannot be opened until you take appropriate action. Furthermore, even if all the files are present, they must be synchronized before the database opens. If the last shutdown was orderly, with all database buffers in the database buffer cache being flushed to disk by DBWn, then everything will be synchronized: Oracle will know that all committed transactions are safely stored in the datafiles, and that no uncommitted transactions are hanging about waiting to be rolled back. However, if the last shutdown was disorderly (such as a power cut, or the server being rebooted), then Oracle must repair the damage. (You will go into the mechanism for this in Chapter 20.) The process that mounts and opens the database (and carries out repairs, if the previous shutdown was disorderly) is the SMON. Only after the database has been successfully opened will Oracle permit user sessions to be established.

Shutdown should be the reverse of startup. During an orderly shutdown, the database is first closed and then dismounted, and finally the instance is stopped. During the close phase, all sessions are terminated: active transactions are rolled back by PMON, completed transactions are flushed to disk by DBWn, and the datafiles and redo log files are closed. During the dismount, the controlfile is closed. Then the instance is stopped by deallocating the SGA and terminating the background processes. Now look at the syntax for startup and shutdown, beginning with how to connect.

Exercise 5-1: Starting Up and Shutting Down Your Database with SQL*Plus

Use SQL*Plus to start and stop the database. Alternatively, if your database is already running, stop it and then restart it with SQL*Plus. If you are working on Windows, make sure that the Windows service is running. It will be called

```
OracleServiceOCP10g
```

if your instance is called OCP10g. Start it through the Windows GUI, or from a command prompt with

```
net start OracleServiceOCP10g
```

The sequence of SQL*Plus commands is shown in Figure 5-5.

 TIP The Windows service may be configured to start the instance and open the database whenever you start the service. You can control this with the Registry variable ORA_OCP10G_AUTOSTART, setting it to TRUE or FALSE.

1. Launch SQL*Plus, using the /nolog switch.
   ```
   sqlplusw /nolog
   ```
2. Connect with operating system authentication.
   ```
   connect / as sysdba
   ```
3. Start the instance only.
   ```
   startup nomount;
   ```
4. Mount the database.
   ```
   alter database mount;
   ```
5. Open the database.
   ```
   alter database open;
   ```
6. Shut down, using the immediate option.
   ```
   shutdown immediate;
   ```
7. Connect with password file authentication.
   ```
   connect sys/oracle as sysdba;
   ```

8. Perform a complete startup, with one command.

```
startup;
```

9. Show the BACKGROUND_DUMP_DEST parameter.

```
show parameter background_dump_dest;
```

10. Navigate to the directory identified by the BACKGROUND_DUMP_DEST parameter. In it you will find your alert log, called alert_<SID>.log.

11. Open the alert log with any editor you wish and look at the last few dozen lines. You will see a history of the startup and shutdown commands, as well as information about the starting and stopping of the various background processes and a listing of the nondefault parameters read from the parameter file and used to build the instance in memory.

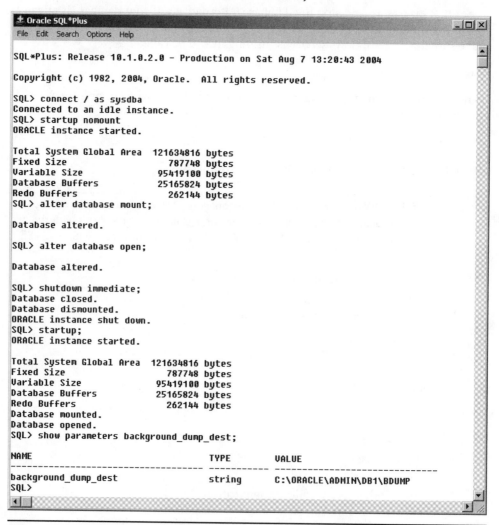

Figure 5-5 Startup/shutdown exercise

Shutdown

There are options that may be used on the shutdown command:

```
shutdown [normal | transactional | immediate | abort]
```

- **Normal** This is the default. No new user connections will be permitted, but all current connections are allowed to continue. Only once all users have (voluntarily!) logged off will the database actually shut down.

TIP Typically, a normal shutdown is useless: there is always someone logged on, even if it is only Database Control itself.

- **Transactional** No new user connections are permitted; existing sessions that are not in a transaction will be terminated; sessions currently in a transaction are allowed to complete the transaction and will then be terminated. Once all sessions are terminated, the database will shut down.
- **Immediate** No new sessions are permitted, and all currently connected sessions are terminated. Any active transactions are rolled back, and the database will then shut down.
- **Abort** As far as Oracle is concerned, this is the equivalent of a power cut. The instance terminates immediately. Nothing is written to disk; no file handles are closed; there is no attempt to terminate transactions that may be in progress in any orderly fashion.

TIP Using shutdown abort will not damage the database but will leave it in an inconsistent state; therefore, some operations (such as backups) are not advisable after an abort.

The "normal," "immediate," and "transactional" shutdown modes are usually referred to as "clean," "consistent," or "orderly" shutdowns. After all sessions are terminated, PMON will roll back any incomplete transactions. Then a checkpoint is issued (remember the CKPT process from Chapter 3?), forcing the DBWn process to write all updated data from the database buffer cache down to the datafiles. LGWR also flushes any change vectors still in memory to the logfiles. Then the file headers are updated, and the file handles closed. This means that the database is in a "consistent" state: all committed transactions are in the datafiles, there are no uncommitted transactions hanging about that need to be rolled back, and all datafiles and logfiles are synchronized.

The "abort" mode, often referred to as a "disorderly" shutdown, leaves the database in an "inconsistent" state: it is quite possible that committed transactions have been lost, because they existed only in memory and DBWn had not yet written them to the datafiles. Equally, there may be uncommitted transactions in the datafiles that have not yet been rolled back. This is the definition of a corrupted database: it may be missing committed transactions, or storing uncommitted transactions. These corruptions must be repaired by instance recovery. It is exactly as though the database server had been switched off, or perhaps rebooted, while the database was running.

Instance Recovery

You will find a full treatment of instance recovery in Chapter 20. For now, accept that the mechanisms of rollback and redo make it impossible to corrupt an Oracle database. DBAs do not say this just because they happen to work with Oracle; they say it because it is a fact. You can do horrible things to Oracle databases, but you will never manage to corrupt one. The mechanism of instance recovery absolutely guarantees that the database cannot be corrupted: committed transactions will always be reinstated; uncommitted transactions will always be backed out. If for some reason (always involving damage to disk files, which is out of Oracle's control) the instance recovery fails, then the database will not open until you have repaired the damaged files through the restore and recover routines that we deal with in later chapters. This impossibility of corruption is why people buy the Oracle database, and likewise why it isn't cheap.

 EXAM TIP If Oracle detects that instance recovery is necessary, it will happen automatically. There is no way to initiate it (or to cancel it) manually.

When an instance attempts to open a database, the SMON process checks the state of the datafiles and of the online redo log files. If the shutdown was disorderly, the fact will be immediately apparent at this time, and SMON will initiate the instance recovery process. Only once this has completed will the database open. Conversely, if the shutdown was orderly, SMON will detect this and open the database immediately. Thus you can always guarantee that an opened database has no corruptions, but the shutdown method chosen determines when corruptions are repaired.

With an orderly shutdown (normal, transactional, or immediate), any possible problems are fixed during the shutdown: incomplete transactions are rolled back, committed transactions are saved. The shutdown may take some considerable time as this is done, but the startup will be fast. With a disorderly shutdown (an abort, or perhaps a hardware failure or operating system crash) the shutdown is instantaneous, but the startup will be delayed while any problems are fixed by the instance recovery. It is possible to tune the speed of the shutdown/startup cycle, which will impact on the mean-time-to-recover, or MTTR, after a failure. The MTTR will often be specified in service level agreements.

Exercise 5-2: Starting Up and Shutting Down Your Database with Database Control

As in Exercise 5-1, become familiar with starting and stopping the instance and opening and closing the database.

1. Ensure that your Database Listener and Database Control processes are running, by entering

   ```
   lsnrctl status
   ```

   ```
   emctl status dbconsole
   ```

   from an operating system prompt.

2. Launch your browser, and contact Database Control with the appropriate URL, such as

   ```
   http://127.0.0.1:5501/em
   ```

3. Log on as in Figure 5-3. Click the SHUTDOWN button. Type in both operating system credentials and database credentials, as shown in Figure 5-6, and click OK.

TIP On Windows, the operating system account you use must have been granted the "Logon as a Batch Job" privilege. Note that by default, not even the Windows Administrator account has this privilege! Refer to your Windows documentation on how to grant this privilege; there are changes with different releases. On both Windows and Unix, the account should be a member of the group that owns the Oracle software.

4. Click Yes for an immediate shutdown. Note that the Advanced Options tab gives a choice of all four shutdown modes.

5. Refresh your browser (it may take a few moments) and you will see the screen shown in Figure 5-7.

6. Click Startup, and enter credentials as in Figure 5-6.

7. Click Yes to accept the default startup mode, which is "open."

TIP When you start and stop the database, Database Control does sometimes get confused about whether the database is actually up or down. This is perhaps hardly surprising, when you consider that a large part of Database Control actually resides within the database itself. If you realize (and it will be obvious) that this has happened, simply stop and start the dbconsole process with emctl, and reconnect with your browser.

8. When the database has opened, dbconsole will present you with a login screen. Log in as user SYSTEM.

9. From the database home page, take the Alert Log Content link in the Related Links section at the bottom of the page and examine the contents of the alert log.

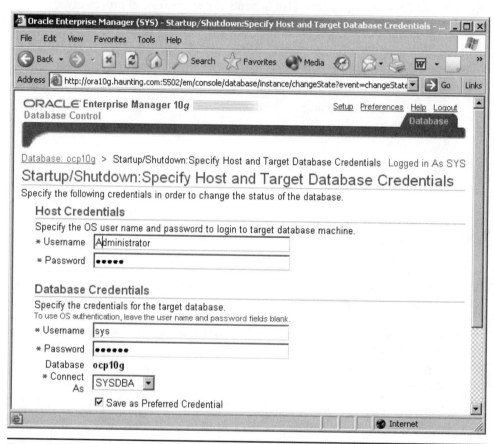

Figure 5-6   Oracle and OS credentials in dbconsole

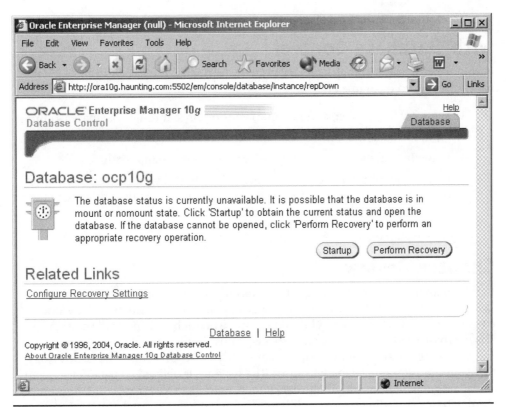

Figure 5-7 The dbconsole startup screen

The Initialization File

In Chapter 3, you saw a static initialization parameter file, init<SID>.ora. This was the only type of initialization file supported until release 9*i* of the Oracle database, but from 9*i* onward if you wish you can use a dynamic initialization file, spfile<SID>.ora. Most database administrators prefer to work with the dynamic file, and if you created your database with DBCA, your static file will have been converted to a dynamic file at the end of the creation process by the script postDBCreation.sql. If you examine this script, the conversion process is self-explanatory.

To view parameters, a static file can be inspected with any text editor you please, but a dynamic spfile can be inspected only from within the Oracle environment: it contains nonprintable characters and should never be edited by hand.

Exercise 5-3: Viewing Parameters with Database Control

In this exercise, you will look at your parameter settings and distinguish between the basic and advanced parameters.

1. Launch your browser, and log on to your instance through Database Control.
2. From the database home page, take the Administration tab.
3. In the Instance section, take the All Initialization Parameters link.
4. Inspect the values of the parameters used to control your instance. Note that of the more than two hundred and fifty parameters, less than thirty are classed as "basic."

Chapter Review

In this chapter you've gone through the details of launching the various processes involved in an Oracle database and its management. Remember that we have not covered the Grid Control—that is beyond the scope of this book, and of the examination. The database itself doesn't have any processes: it is simply a set of files. The processes are part of the instance, and you start them with a STARTUP command, issued from SQL*Plus, or through Database Control. The instance is defined by parameters in an initialization parameter file. The instance then attaches to a database: first it mounts the database, by reading the controlfile, and then it opens the database, by reading the datafiles and redo log files. In addition to starting the instance (and preferably before you start it), you must also start the Database Listener. Without a listener, you will not be able to connect with Database Control. The control processes are either Database Control, which requires you to start the OC4J engine within which it runs, or SQL*Plus, which runs as a self-contained program. An alternative to SQL*Plus is iSQL*Plus, an application server process that lets you connect to a database from a browser.

Questions

1. Which of the following commands will start the iSQL*Plus server process? (Choose the best answer.)
   A. `emctl start isqlplus`
   B. `isqlplusctl start`
   C. `isqlplus /nolog`
   D. `lsnrctl start isqlplus`

2. You issued the URL http://127.0.0.1:5500/em and received an error. What could be the problem? (Choose three answers.)
   A. You have not started the Database Listener.

B. You have not started the dbconsole.

C. The dbconsole is running on a different port.

D. You are not logged onto the database server node.

E. You have not started the Grid Control agent.

F. You have not started the database.

3. Which files must be synchronized for a database to open? (Choose the best answer.)

A. Datafiles, online redo log files, and the controlfile

B. The parameter file and the password file

C. All the multiplexed controlfile copies

D. None. SMON will synchronize all files by instance recovery after opening the database.

4. During the transition from NOMOUNT to MOUNT mode, which file or files are required? (Choose the best answer.)

A. Parameter file

B. Controlfiles

C. Online redo logs

D. Datafiles

E. All of the above

5. You shut down your instance with SHUTDOWN IMMEDIATE. What will happen on the next startup? (Choose the best answer.)

A. SMON will perform automatic instance recovery.

B. You must perform manual instance recovery.

C. PMON will roll back uncommitted transactions.

D. The database will open without recovery.

6. You have created two databases on your computer and want to use Database Control to manage them. Which of the following statements are correct? (Choose two answers.)

A. You cannot use Database Control, because it can manage only one database per computer.

B. You must use Grid Control, as you have multiple databases on the computer.

C. You must start one OC4J process and contact it on different ports for each database.

D. You must start one OC4J instance per database.

E. You must set the ORACLE_SID variable appropriately before starting an OC4J instance.

7. You issue the command SHUTDOWN, and it seems to hang. What could be the reason? (Choose the best answer.)

   A. You are not connected as SYSDBA or SYSOPER.

   B. There are other sessions logged on.

   C. You have not connected with operating system or password file authentication.

   D. There are active transactions in the database; when they complete, the SHUTDOWN will proceed.

8. What action should you take after terminating the instance with SHUTDOWN ABORT? (Choose the best answer.)

   A. Back up the database immediately.

   B. Open the database and perform database recovery.

   C. Open the database and perform instance recovery.

   D. None, but some transactions may be lost.

   E. None. Recovery will be automatic.

9. Using Database Control, you stop the Database Listener. Which of the following statements is true? (Choose the best answer.)

   A. Database Control will no longer be able to manage the database.

   B. Existing sessions will be terminated.

   C. No new sessions can be established.

   D. You must restart the listener with the lsnrctl utility.

10. Database Control is a multitier web application. Which tier is responsible for window management? (Choose the best answer.)

    A. The dbconsole middle tier

    B. The procedures within the database tier

    C. The client browser

    D. The OC4J application runtime environment

Answers

1. **B.** The emctl command is used to start the dbconsole, lsnrctl is used to start database listeners, and isqlplus from a command line won't do anything.

2. **B, C,** and **D.** Any of these could be a reason. A, E, and F are related to other processes.

3. **A.** These are the three file types that make up a database: datafiles, online redo log files, and the controlfile.

4. **B.** Remember which files are read at each stage: the parameter file at NOMOUNT, the online redo log files and the datafiles at OPEN.

5. **D.** This holds true because IMMEDIATE is a clean shutdown.

6. **D and E.** D is correct because one OC4J can only support one Database Control process to manage one database, and E is correct because without this the emctl utility will not know which OC4J to start.

7. **B.** This answer is correct because the default shutdown mode is NORMAL, which will wait for all sessions to log off.

8. **E.** It is vital to remember this! After a crash, or an abort, recovery is automatic and unstoppable. No data is ever lost, and you need take no action at all.

9. **C.** Without a listener there is no way to launch the server process needed for a session.

10. **C.** Your local window management is done by your local browser. The other answers refer to processes that reside on the application server tier (A and D), or within the database (B).

CHAPTER 6

Managing Oracle Storage Structures

In this chapter you will learn how to
- Define the purpose of tablespaces and datafiles
- Create tablespaces
- Manage tablespaces (alter, drop, generate DDL, take offline, put online, add datafiles, make read-only or read/write)
- Obtain tablespace information from Enterprise Manager and the data dictionary
- Drop tablespaces
- Describe the default tablespace

You have now created a database and know how to manage the instance to get access to the database data. The next logical step is to create storage structures in the database to hold your data and to ensure that those storage structures are managed efficiently. You don't want to overallocate disk space, and you don't want to underallocate. Furthermore, you want to ensure that the use of disk space is as efficient as possible for the type of database you will be managing and the disk resources available to you. Understanding how Oracle manages storage, both logically and physically, and understanding the different components involved in storing Oracle database data are some of the key concepts any DBA must master.

Oracle Storage Basics: Tablespaces and Datafiles

Storage in an Oracle database has two distinct "sides": physical and logical. *Physical* storage is how the storage components that make up an Oracle database at the operating system level are seen, normally, as a series of datafiles. *Logical* storage is how Oracle internally manages the objects that are stored in the database. The logical and physical storage structures in Oracle and their relationships can be expressed as a model shown in Figure 6-1.

Looking at the model of Oracle storage, a few key elements can be discerned, such as these:

- Every *database* must consist of one or more *tablespaces*. Every *tablespace* must belong to one and only one *database*.

- Every *tablespace* must consist of one or more *datafiles*. Each *datafile* must belong to one and only one *tablespace*.

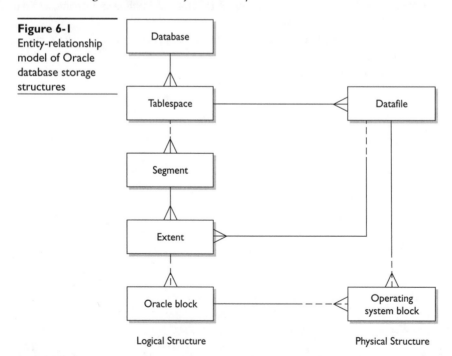

Figure 6-1
Entity-relationship model of Oracle database storage structures

- Every *datafile* must consist of one or more *operating system blocks*. Each *operating system block* may belong to one and only one *datafile*.

- Every *tablespace* may contain one or more *segments*. Every *segment* must exist in one and only one *tablespace*.

- Every *segment* must consist of one or more *extents*. Each *extent* must belong to one and only one *segment*.

- Every *extent* must consist of one or more *Oracle blocks*. Each *Oracle block* may belong to one and only one *extent*.

- Every *extent* must be located in one and only one *datafile*. The space in the *datafile* may be allocated as one or more *extents*.

- Every *Oracle block* must consist of one or more *operating system blocks*. Every *operating system block* may be part of one and only one *Oracle block*.

 EXAM TIP It is important to be clear on the physical and logical makeup of an Oracle database. Be familiar with the terms used in both.

Physical Storage Structures

The physical structure is what the operating system sees when "looking" at an Oracle database. Oracle physical storage is quite simple to understand and see: it is a collection of one or more datafiles. It is also possible for Oracle to make use of raw devices (partitions of a hard disk not managed by the operating system), but doing so introduces complexity when it comes to backup and recoverability. It is also possible for Oracle to manage physical storage itself through something called Automated Storage Management, or ASM, in which case the operating system is also not involved. However, by and large, most Oracle physical storage is made up of operating system datafiles.

Each datafile is composed of operating system blocks and is created on a disk partition or volume, all managed by the host operating system. This is the most common scenario and one that you will encounter most frequently.

Oracle Datafiles

Datafiles are operating system files that hold Oracle data. When you create a database, a number of datafiles are created to hold the data dictionary and the SYSAUX tablespace data, along with any other tablespaces you decided to create at that time. The datafiles consist of the header and the space that can be used to allocate extents to segments. In effect, most datafiles have three parts: the header, the extents (allocated space), and free (unallocated space).

The *header* of a datafile identifies it as part of a database and stores specifics of that datafile: which tablespace it belongs to and the last checkpoint performed. This way, Oracle can check that all files are synchronized when it starts up. If it detects that one of the files is older than the rest (or all files are older than the controlfile), it will assume that the file was restored from a backup and initiate recovery. The rest of the datafile consists of extents and free space, the management of which is performed by creating, dropping, and altering the logical storage components of Oracle: *segments.*

Each Oracle datafile belongs to one and only one tablespace and is made up of operating system blocks. As you will see later in this chapter, it is possible to specify growth characteristics for datafiles and resize them either manually or automatically. You can also take a datafile offline, making its contents unavailable, provided it does not belong to the SYSTEM tablespace.

Operating System Blocks

Operating system blocks are the minimum allocation unit for the file system. Each file system has its own minimum and default sizes, which often vary with the hard disk geometry and size, as well as the file system used to format the drive. Most systems will allow you to configure the block size when formatting the drive. It is a good idea to keep the operating system block size the same as the Oracle block size. So, if you are planning to add a drive in order to keep Oracle datafiles on it, and your database block size is 8KB, you may want to format the drive using 8KB blocks. However, because Oracle Database 10g allows you to create tablespaces with differing block sizes, you may want to ensure that the operating system block size is the same size as the largest database block. This way, for every Oracle I/O request the operating system needs to retrieve only one block.

Logical Storage Structures

As a DBA, you will be spending a great deal of your time looking at database storage from the logical point of view. You will be creating and managing tablespaces, segments, and extents and ensuring that the Oracle block size is efficiently configured for your database. The logical structure of the database is the left side of the model in Figure 6-1.

The *database* is the highest and final unit of organization for Oracle. It is self-contained and consists of at least three tablespaces (preferably more) in Oracle 10g (up from one in previous releases). In order to access database data, an instance must be started.

Tablespaces

Within a database the *tablespace* is the largest storage structure. A database in Oracle 10g must have at least three tablespaces: SYSTEM, SYSAUX, and one undo tablespace. These are created when you create the database; you create others for a specific purpose in order to manage your database objects and ensure the instance and database perform well. You should also create at least one additional tablespace for specific data: a temporary tablespace to hold temporary objects created when a sort takes place and cannot be completely performed in memory.

Tablespace Types   Tablespaces can be classified using many different criteria, the first of which is based upon the type of objects the tablespace stores: SYSTEM or non-SYSTEM. In Oracle 10g two tablespaces make up the SYSTEM type: SYSTEM and SYSAUX. All other tablespaces are classified as non-SYSTEM.

EXAM TIP Oracle Database 10g has two tablespaces that are considered part of the system: SYSTEM and SYSAUX. Previous releases of Oracle required only a SYSTEM tablespace.

The SYSTEM tablespace contains the data dictionary—internal tables that describe the structure of the database itself, all of the objects in it, users, roles, and privileges. When a user issues a query or a DML statement, the data dictionary is used in order to verify the user's permissions and find the data that belongs to the segment being queried or changed. When a DDL statement is processed, the internal tables are modified in order to reflect the change: CREATE, ALTER, or DROP. The SYSTEM tablespace also contains the SYSTEM undo or rollback segment (also called SYSTEM), which can be used only for operations on objects stored in the SYSTEM tablespace. User objects should be kept out of the SYSTEM tablespace in order to keep it operating efficiently.

EXAM TIP The SYSTEM tablespace is the location of the data dictionary in an Oracle database. The database cannot operate without a SYSTEM tablespace.

The SYSAUX tablespace is also considered a SYSTEM tablespace and is used to store statistical and other information that used to be kept in the SYSTEM tablespace in previous versions.

After you create the database, you will need to create additional tablespaces to store your data. The number of tablespaces you create and what is stored within them depend on what your database will be used for and the amount of data. Here are some of the guidelines to follow when creating additional tablespaces and to help with performance:

- **Separate data that will participate in resource contention** For example, a table and its indexes will normally be accessed simultaneously during inserts and updates, so to prevent a bottleneck, it is best to place them on different hard drives. One way to do this is to create different tablespaces—DATA and INDEX—to hold the data and then place each tablespace's datafiles on a different hard disk. This way, you can update both the table and its index simultaneously and not risk resource contention.

- **Separate objects that have different storage requirements** Keeping small tables and large tables on different tablespaces will provide better space management and performance. While extent management can be largely automated in Oracle 10g, there is no reason to make Oracle's job more difficult by placing dissimilar objects on the same tablespace.

- **Store different partitions in different tablespaces** One of the benefits of partitioning your data is to gain performance improvements for queries. Place each partition on a separate tablespace and, preferably, each tablespace's datafiles on a separate hard disk. In this way Oracle can read data from more than one hard disk at the same time when satisfying the query.

Tablespace Contents   A tablespace can store one of three types of segments: permanent, temporary, and undo. *Permanent* segments are what you expect to find in a database, such as a table or index. *Temporary* segments are those that exist for a short time and are then overwritten, such as a sort operation. *Undo* segments hold the before image of the data being modified so that other users can still have their queries answered even if the data is in the process of being changed.

 EXAM TIP Tablespaces can store one of three types of objects: permanent objects such as tables and indexes; temporary segments such as sort segments and temporary table data; and undo data used for transaction rollback or flashback queries.

When you create a user in Oracle, you specify the default tablespace that will be used to store extents for any segment the user creates, as well as a temporary tablespace to store temporary segments, although a global temporary tablespace defined for the database can be used as well.

All users share the undo tablespace, which is set by the DBA. To determine what the users' default and temporary tablespaces are, you can issue this query:

```
SQL> SELECT username, default_tablespace, temporary_tablespace
  2  FROM DBA_USERS;
USERNAME              DEFAULT_TABLESPACE        TEMPORARY_TABLESPACE
--------------------  ------------------------  ------------------------
SYS                   SYSTEM                    TEMP
SYSTEM                SYSTEM                    TEMP
OUTLN                 SYSTEM                    TEMP
DBSNMP                SYSAUX                    TEMP
SYSMAN                SYSAUX                    TEMP
MGMT_VIEW             SYSAUX                    TEMP
WK_TEST               SYSAUX                    TEMP
MDSYS                 SYSAUX                    TEMP
ORDSYS                SYSAUX                    TEMP
CTXSYS                SYSAUX                    TEMP
ANONYMOUS             SYSAUX                    TEMP
EXFSYS                SYSAUX                    TEMP
DMSYS                 SYSAUX                    TEMP
WMSYS                 SYSAUX                    TEMP
XDB                   SYSAUX                    TEMP
WKPROXY               SYSAUX                    TEMP
ORDPLUGINS            SYSAUX                    TEMP
SI_INFORMTN_SCHEMA    SYSAUX                    TEMP
OLAPSYS               SYSAUX                    TEMP
WKSYS                 SYSAUX                    TEMP
MDDATA                USERS                     TEMP
DIP                   USERS                     TEMP
SCOTT                 USERS                     TEMP
```

Tablespaces in Databases Created with the Database Configuration Assistant   A typical example of tablespaces that exist in most databases can be ascertained by looking at the tablespaces created when you use the Database Configuration Assistant. The DBCA will create a database with the following tablespaces, as shown in Figure 6-2.

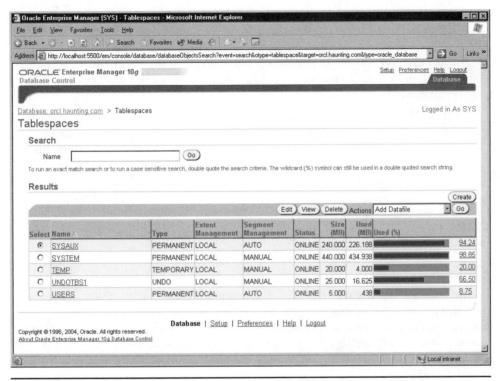

Figure 6-2 Tablespaces in a database created by the Database Configuration Assistant

- **SYSTEM**   Used to store the Oracle data dictionary and all objects in the SYS schema. Access to these objects is restricted to the user SYS and others that have been granted the DBA role, by default. Every database must have a SYSTEM tablespace.

- **SYSAUX**   The SYSAUX tablespace was introduced in Oracle Database 10*g* to store objects not owned by SYS but required in order for the database to function. In previous releases of Oracle these were stored in the SYSTEM tablespace; they include Oracle Enterprise Manager components, among others. Every Oracle 10*g* database must have a SYSAUX tablespace.

- **TEMP**   Used to store temporary objects and their data. Examples of these include the data portion of a global temporary table and sort segments created when a sort cannot be completely performed in memory. Every database should have a temporary tablespace, though it is not required, and one should be designated as the default temporary tablespace to be assigned to users if one is not specified when the user is created. Temporary tablespaces consist of tempfiles instead of datafiles. If no temporary tablespace is created, then temporary segments are created in the SYSTEM tablespace by default—a bad idea from a performance perspective.

- **UNDOTBS1** Used to store undo information for the database. Undo is data kept in the database to allow users to read rows that are in the process of being changed but whose transactions have not yet committed. This allows any user needing to get a read-consistent image of the data to avoid being held up by people changing the data. An undo tablespace is required in each database.

- **USERS** When a database user creates a segment, its data needs to be stored in a tablespace. The USERS tablespace serves this purpose. You can create additional tablespaces and allow users to store their segments in them, but one tablespace needs to be made the default users' tablespace, which the USERS tablespace is for nonsystem (i.e., not SYS or SYSTEM) users.

If you decided to load the example schemas when you created the database with DBCA, you will also have an EXAMPLE tablespace that stores those segments in the example schemas.

Segments

Within a tablespace, space is allocated to segments. A *segment* is an object in the database that requires storage, such as a table or an index. A *view,* on the other hand, is not a segment, since it does not store data; it is just a prewritten query that allows easy access to data stored in tables. Oracle allows you to create many different segment types. A query against the DBA_SEGMENTS view will display a list of segments created in the database, as follows:

```
SQL> SELECT DISTINCT segment_type FROM DBA_SEGMENTS;
SEGMENT_TYPE
------------------
CLUSTER
INDEX
INDEX PARTITION
LOB PARTITION
LOBINDEX
LOBSEGMENT
NESTED TABLE
ROLLBACK
TABLE
TABLE PARTITION
TYPE2 UNDO
```

This query shows only the segment types that exist in your database, not all possible types. How to manage many (but not all) of the segment types listed will be the discussion of several future chapters.

 EXAM TIP Any object requiring storage in a database is classified as a segment.

Extents

When space is allocated for segments in a tablespace, it is allocated an *extent* at a time. A segment consists of one or more extents, and when a segment (e.g., a table or an index) is created, at least one extent is allocated at creation time. Extents are made of contiguous data blocks and can be managed either manually by the DBA or automatically by Oracle, depending upon the conditions specified by the DBA, or Oracle defaults. Extents are created in the datafiles belonging to the tablespace on which the segment is defined. A segment can exist in only one tablespace, and an extent exists in a datafile belonging to the tablespace.

Extent Management in Tablespaces

When you create a tablespace, you can specify whether extents should be locally managed or dictionary-managed. *Locally managed* extents are more efficient and are recommended for all database data. In a tablespace where extents are locally managed, free extents are stored in a bitmap in the tablespace. Each bit in the bitmap represents a single database block or a multiple of database blocks if extent management has been configured to be of a uniform size or automatic. As an extent is allocated to a segment or freed up because a segment was dropped, truncated, or resized, the bitmap is updated to reflect the change.

 EXAM TIP Extents are a collection of contiguous blocks allocated to a segment. Extents can be managed locally in the tablespace (preferred) or in the dictionary (for backward compatibility).

Dictionary-managed tablespaces are the historical way of managing extents and require any allocation or deallocation of an extent to update a table in the data dictionary. This means that any time an extent is allocated to a table, the data dictionary must be touched to record the change. When a table is dropped or truncated, the data dictionary must be changed. Because of the amount of work required on the data dictionary when using dictionary-managed extents, they are no longer recommended and exist primarily for backward compatibility. All tablespaces should be created with local extent management.

 NOTE You can use Enterprise Manager or the DBMS_SPACE_ADMIN .TABLESPACE_MIGRATE_TO_LOCAL procedure to migrate a dictionary-managed tablespace to local extent management.

Database Blocks

A database *block* is the minimum unit of I/O in the database. When the database needs to read data, it cannot read just one row; it must read the entire block. The same happens with writing: even if only one row in a block is changed, the DBWn process has to write the entire block during the checkpoint. When a database is created, the default block size for tablespaces is specified. It is possible to have more than one block size specified for a database, but a tablespace and its datafiles will always only have one database block size. In other words, you specify the block size for the tablespace when you create it, or assume the database default. For a different tablespace you can specify a different block size. You cannot change the block size for a tablespace once it is created, except by dropping and re-creating it (and possibly losing all the tablespace contents).

Creating and Managing Tablespaces

There are two ways to create a tablespace in Oracle: using Oracle Enterprise Manager (OEM) or by issuing the CREATE TABLESPACE command in SQL*Plus or iSQL*Plus. The end result is the same, since OEM will send the appropriate command to the database to perform the operation.

The CREATE TABLESPACE Command

The CREATE TABLESPACE and CREATE TEMPORARY TABLESPACE commands allow you to create a tablespace using SQL*Plus or iSQL*Plus. Alternatively, you can create a tablespace from Enterprise Manager, which provides a nice point-and-click interface, and then optionally view the command sent to the Oracle server before it is executed.

The overall syntax of the command is somewhat complex because of the number of options available, but we will break it down into manageable chunks.

```
CREATE [BIGFILE | SMALLFILE] [TEMPORARY] TABLESPACE tablespace name
DATAFILE datafile spec | TEMPFILE tempfile spec
[MINIMUM EXTENT minimum extent size]
[BLOCKSIZE blocksize]
[[COMPRESS|NOCOMPRESS] DEFAULT STORAGE (default storage clause)]
[LOGGING|NOLOGGING]
[FORCE LOGGING]
[ONLINE|OFFLINE]
[EXTENT MANAGEMENT DICTIONARY |
    LOCAL [AUTOALLOCATE|UNIFORM SIZE size]]
[SEGMENT SPACE MANAGEMENT MANUAL|AUTO]
[FLASHBACK ON|OFF]
```

To create a tablespace, all you need is the name of the tablespace and the datafile specification; all other settings are left at Oracle defaults, as in this example:

```
CREATE TABLESPACE default_demo
DATAFILE '$ORACLE_BASE/oradata/default_demo01.dbf' SIZE 10M;
```

This one command did everything: physically created the datafile, created the tablespace, updated the controlfile and the data dictionary, and set all the defaults for the new tablespace.

 NOTE If the datafile already exists on disk, the creation of the tablespace will fail. You can specify the REUSE parameter to the datafile specification to instruct Oracle to overwrite any file with the same name as the datafile you want to create. This is useful when re-creating tablespaces that you dropped.

Perhaps the best way to create a tablespace in Oracle 10*g* is to use Enterprise Manager. With EM you can create a tablespace with an easy interface and also learn about the syntax to do so by displaying the SQL code to perform the action.

Exercise 6-1: Using Enterprise Manager to Create a Tablespace

In this exercise you will connect to Enterprise Manager and create a tablespace in your database.

1. Start a web browser and connect to the Enterprise Manager URL on your Oracle database server, specifying the appropriate port number and machine name.

2. Log in to your database as the user SYSTEM with the appropriate password. If you receive the licensing information page, click I Agree to continue.

3. On the Enterprise Manager main page, click the Administration hyperlink to display the Administration page.

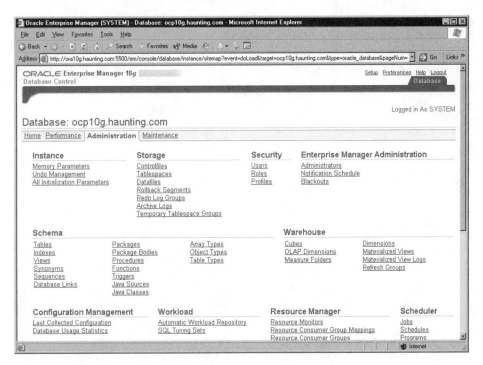

4. Click the Tablespaces hyperlink under Storage to display the current tablespaces in the database and their space utilization.

5. To create a new tablespace, click Create on the right side to bring up the Create Tablespace screen.

6. In the Name text box, enter the name of the tablespace you want to create, **OCP10gData**, for example. You will notice that you also have a number of selections to make regarding the tablespace characteristics, including extent management (local or dictionary), tablespace type (permanent, temporary, or undo), and status (read/write, read-only, or offline).

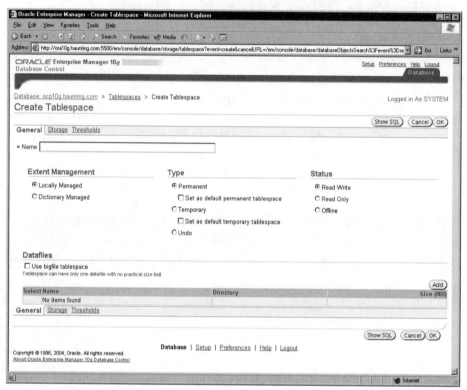

Permanent tablespaces are the default and can be used to hold segment data such as tables, indexes, and clusters. The majority of the tablespaces you create will be of the Permanent variety. If you select the Set As Default check box for the tablespace, any user created in the database that does not have a default tablespace specified at creation time will be assigned this tablespace as his default tablespace. Any segments the user creates will occupy space on this tablespace by default, unless a different tablespace is specified when the object is created.

Status determines the initial state of the tablespace after creation. Read/write means that objects can be created and otherwise modified on the tablespace and its contents can change. Read-only means that it cannot be written to, and offline means that the contents of the tablespace are not available. When creating a tablespace, it is best to choose Read Write; you can always change the status later.

Leave your tablespace at the default values of Locally Managed, Permanent, and Read Write.

7. Under the Datafiles heading you have the option to add one or more datafiles to the tablespace. If you select the Use Bigfile Tablespace check box, your tablespace can have only one datafile whose size limit is as large as the file system will allow. Bigfile tablespaces cannot be dictionary-managed.

   Leave the Use Bigfile Tablespace option unchecked and then click Add to bring up the Add Datafile page.

8. On the Add Datafile page, enter the name of the datafile for the tablespace and verify that the location provided is appropriate. Enterprise Manager will display the default location for datafiles according to OFA guidelines, typically the directory pointed to by the location $ORACLE_BASE/oradata/<db_name>. You also need to specify a file size or accept the default value. Under Storage you can specify whether or not to automatically grow the file (AUTOEXTEND) when it becomes full as well as how much to grow it by and whether or not to specify a maximum size the file can grow to. Autoextend allows you to automate file growth while at the same time optionally providing a limit on the growth so that a file does not occupy all available disk space.

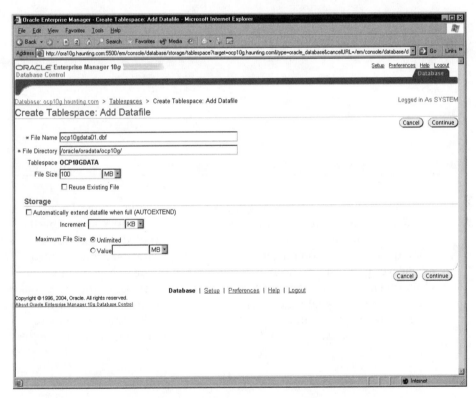

Leave the datafile size at the default of 100MB and specify autogrowth in increments of 50MB up to a maximum size of 500MB. Click Continue when done.

9. On the Create Tablespace page, click Show SQL to display the SQL commands that will be sent to the database to create the tablespace. Click Return when done reviewing the code.

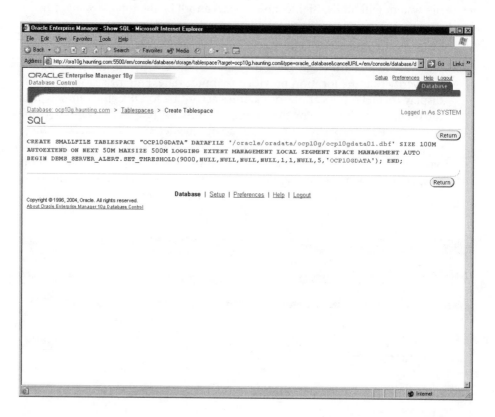

10. Click the Storage hyperlink to display the Storage Options page. Because you specified that the tablespace will be locally managed, here you can specify whether extent allocation will be automatically handled by Oracle based upon the data stored on the tablespace, in which case you cannot control extent sizing. If you want to make all extents the same size, you can specify Uniform sizing, which defaults to extent sizes of 1MB. Uniform sizing makes sense for temporary tablespaces and for those tablespaces where the data being stored is of the same row size (i.e., all large rows or all small rows, etc.). You cannot use automatic extent allocation for temporary tablespaces.

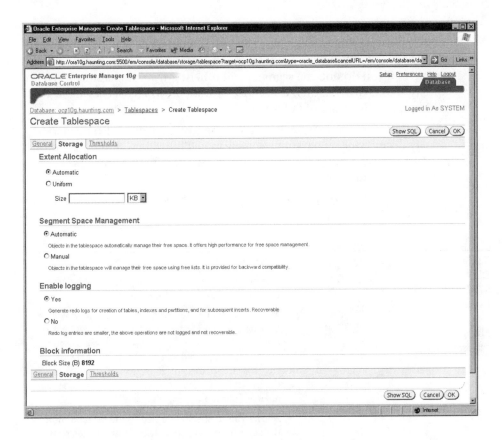

The second option on this screen deals with the way that space will be managed within the segment. With automatic segment space management Oracle will use bitmaps to determine which blocks are free and which contain large amounts of data. The amount of space that exists for inserting rows will be automatically tracked by the bitmap containing all blocks allocated to the segment. This is an efficient method that frees the DBA from setting segment space management parameters manually. Using manual space management requires the DBA or the creator of the segment to specify values for the PCTFREE, PCTUSED, FREELISTS, and FREELIST GROUPS parameters when creating the object and maintaining them as the volume of segment data increases.

EXAM TIP PCTFREE, PCTUSED, FREELISTS, and FREELIST GROUPS can be set only for dictionary-managed tablespaces.

The last section requires you to specify whether changes made to segments in the tablespace should be logged to the redo log files (LOGGING) or not (NOLOGGING). While you can specify this parameter when you create the segment, if you do not, the segment will inherit it from the tablespace. If you specify NOLOGGING, then it may not be possible to recover segments in the tablespace in the event of failure.

If you created a dictionary-managed tablespace, you would also need to specify default storage parameters using the DEFAULT STORAGE clause of the CREATE TABLESPACE command. Table 6-1 lists the parameters of the DEFAULT STORAGE clause and their values.

Specify automatic extent management, automatic segment management, and logging for the tablespace.

Table 6-1 DEFAULT STORAGE Parameters for Dictionary-Managed Tablespaces	Setting	Description
	MINEXTENTS	The number of extents each segment will be created with, which defaults to the minimum of 1.
	MAXEXTENTS	The maximum number of extents a segment will be allocated if necessary. The default value depends on the DB_BLOCK_SIZE setting, while the maximum is UNLIMITED. Avoid setting MAXEXTENTS to UNLIMITED, as this will allow a segment to take all the available space in the tablespace and can disrupt normal operation of the database.
	INITIAL	Allows you to specify the size of the first extent for the segment in bytes (use K or M as suffixes to the numeric value to specify KB or MB). The default is 5 database blocks, with a minimum of 2 database blocks.
	NEXT	Specifies the size of the second or subsequent extents in bytes, KB or MB.
	PCTINCREASE	Specifies how much bigger to make the third extent compared to the second extent, the fourth compared to the third, etc., as a percentage. For example, if PCTINCREASE is set to 20, the INITIAL and NEXT are set to 100K, the third extent will be 120K, the fourth, 144K, etc., rounded up to the next multiple of DB_BLOCK_SIZE. If PCTINCREASE is set to 0, SMON will not automatically coalesce the free space in the tablespace.

PART I

11. Click the Thresholds hyperlink to bring up the Thresholds page. Thresholds allow you to have Enterprise Manager warn you when space in the tablespace is getting used up. You can specify thresholds for the database, specify them for the individual tablespace, or disable them for the tablespace. Thresholds will be covered in more detail in Chapter 15. Leave the current settings at the default values and then click OK to create the tablespace.

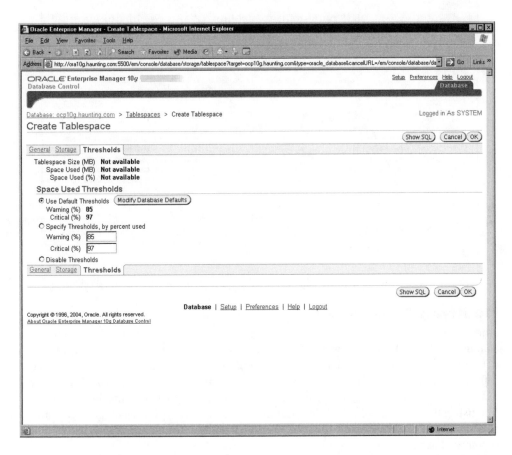

12. After a short delay, you will be presented with the Tablespaces page of Enterprise Manager, shown next, where the tablespace you just created is listed. You can also create more tablespaces or manage the ones that are there.

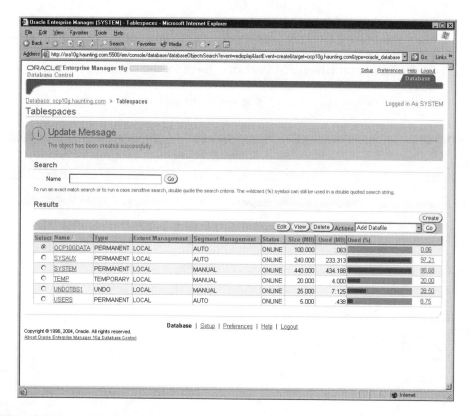

Modifying Tablespaces

Since databases generally are not static, you will from time to time need to make changes to the tablespaces you created. These can be common tasks such as adding datafiles to a tablespace or increasing the size of existing datafiles, taking a tablespace offline for maintenance or recovery purposes, or changing the mode from read/write to read-only or vice versa. All of these tasks can be accomplished from the command line using the ALTER TABLESPACE command or using Enterprise Manager. You can also rename a tablespace if needed, but this is generally not recommended after segments have been created on it.

Exercise 6-2: Using Enterprise Manager to Alter a Tablespace

In this exercise you will connect to Enterprise Manager and change the characteristics of the tablespace you created in the previous exercise.

1. Start a web browser and connect to the Enterprise Manager URL on your Oracle database server specifying the appropriate port number and machine name.

2. Log in to your database as the user SYSTEM with the appropriate password. If you receive the licensing information page, click I Agree to continue.

3. On the Enterprise Manager main page, click the Administration hyperlink to display the Administration page.

4. Click the Tablespaces hyperlink under Storage to display the current tablespaces in the database and their space utilization.

5. Select the tablespace created in the preceding exercise (OCP10GDATA, for example) and then click Edit to display the Edit Tablespace page. Note that the majority of options are grayed out except for the check box to make this the default tablespace for the database, and the various status options. This is because the extent management and type of tablespace cannot be modified after creation time; you must drop and then re-create the tablespace to change these.

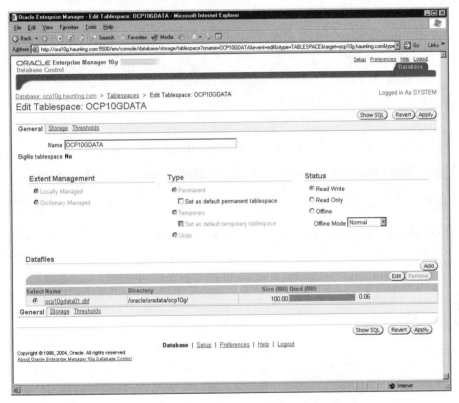

The normal mode of operation of a tablespace is read/write, meaning that objects can be created on the tablespace and their contents modified—data inserted, updated, or deleted. Making a tablespace read-only does not allow any changes to segment data on the tablespace but does allow SELECT statements to be executed against it. The read-only status of a tablespace does not prevent dropping objects created on the tablespace, since the object definition is not stored on the tablespace but rather in the data dictionary. Think of this as similar to the phone company changing your phone number—they have to come to the house to install the phones, but to change your phone number all they have to do is modify an entry at the central office to specify which number will cause your phone at home to ring.

6. Click the drop-down list box next to Offline Mode to display the four available modes. Taking a tablespace offline makes its contents unavailable until the tablespace is brought back online, but taking a tablespace offline should be done gracefully to prevent having to perform recovery when the tablespace is brought online. The NORMAL and IMMEDIATE options will issue a checkpoint before taking all datafiles belonging to the tablespace offline, although the IMMEDIATE option cannot be used if the database is in noarchivelog mode. Using the TEMPORARY option will gracefully take the datafiles offline and not require recovery unless one of the datafiles was already offline due to media failure, in which case recovery will be needed. FOR RECOVER is deprecated and should not be used; it is included for backward compatibility.

7. If you want to add a datafile to the tablespace, you can click Add. For now click Edit to display the Edit Datafile page. Notice that you can change the size of the datafile by entering a new value. You can specify a value smaller or larger than the existing file size, but no smaller than the amount of data physically in the file; otherwise, you receive the "ORA-03297: file contains used data beyond requested RESIZE value" error. You can also change autogrowth characteristics, rename the datafile, or change its location. Decrease the size of the datafile to 50MB and click Continue.

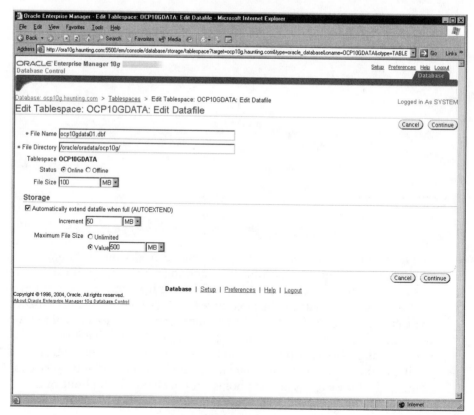

8. Click Show SQL to display the SQL code required to make your changes, as in this code listing example, and then click Return:

```
ALTER DATABASE DATAFILE '/oracle/oradata/ocp10g/ocp10gdata01.dbf' RESIZE 50M
```

9. Click Apply to save your changes.

10. Click the Tablespaces hyperlink at the top of the Enterprise Manager page to display the list of tablespaces in the database.

11. Click the drop-down list box next to Actions to display the list of available actions. Actions are activities that can be performed on the selected tablespace. They are described in more detail in Table 6-2.

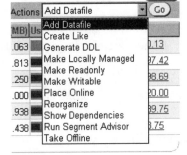

12. Close Enterprise Manager.

Table 6-2 Available Tablespace Actions	Action	Description
	Add Datafile	Allows you to add another datafile to the tablespace.
	Create Like	Uses the selected tablespace as a template for another tablespace. Characteristics such as extent and segment management, datafile location, and size are copied to the new tablespace.
	Generate DDL	Displays a page with the generated SQL statement used to re-create the tablespace.
	Make Locally Managed	Converts a dictionary-managed tablespace to a locally managed tablespace.
	Make Read Only	Makes a read/write tablespace read-only. Current transactions are allowed to complete, but no new transactions can be started on segment data in the tablespace. Also forces a checkpoint to update the controlfile and datafile headers. This action cannot be performed on UNDO, SYSTEM, and SYSAUX tablespaces.
	Make Writable	Allows writes on tablespace segment data.
	Place Online	Brings a currently offline tablespace online.
	Reorganize	Starts the Reorganization Wizard of Enterprise Manager to allow you to move objects around to make space utilization more efficient. This process can severely impact performance of tablespace data and should be performed during off-hours.
	Show Dependencies	Lists objects dependent on this tablespace (i.e., segments created on it) or objects the tablespace is dependent upon.
	Run Segment Advisor	Segment Advisor allows you to determine if segments on the tablespace have space available to be reclaimed for use by other objects.
	Take Offline	Takes a tablespace offline. Cannot be performed on the SYSTEM or SYSAUX tablespace.

Dropping Tablespaces

The DROP TABLESPACE command allows you to drop an existing tablespace in the database. To perform this action, you must have the DROP TABLESPACE system privilege. You can then issue the following command:

```
DROP TABLESPACE OCP10GDATA;
```

If there are objects in the tablespace, you will get the following error:

```
DROP TABLESPACE OCP10GDATA
*
ORA-01549: tablespace not empty, use INCLUDING CONTENTS option
```

If there are foreign key constraints that depend on tables on the tablespace, you can modify the syntax to drop those links too by using the following syntax:

```
DROP TABLESPACE OCP10GDATA INCLUDING CONTENTS CASCADE CONSTRAINTS;
```

EXAM TIP Tablespaces can be dropped only if they contain no permanent objects, unless the INCLUDING CONTENTS and CASCADE CONSTRAINTS parameters are specified.

The result of dropping a tablespace is that any reference to it is erased from the data dictionary and the controlfile of the database. The datafile is not actually deleted, so you will need to do that manually (though Enterprise Manager can be used to do that step as well).

EXAM TIP Dropping a tablespace from the command line does not remove the datafile from disk. Deleting a tablespace using Enterprise Manager provides the option to also delete the datafile.

Exercise 6-3: Using Enterprise Manager to Drop a Tablespace

In this exercise you will connect to Enterprise Manager and drop the tablespace you created earlier.

1. Start a web browser and connect to the Enterprise Manager URL on your Oracle database server, specifying the appropriate port number and machine name.

2. Log in to your database as the user SYSTEM with the appropriate password. If you receive the licensing information page, click I Agree to continue.

3. On the Enterprise Manager main page, click the Administration hyperlink to display the Administration page.

4. Click the Tablespaces hyperlink under Storage to display the current tablespaces in the database and their space utilization.

5. Select the tablespace created in Exercise 6-1 (OCP10GDATA, for example) and then click Delete to display the Delete Tablespace warning page. Read the warning and note that a backup should always be performed before deleting a tablespace in case you want to get the data back.

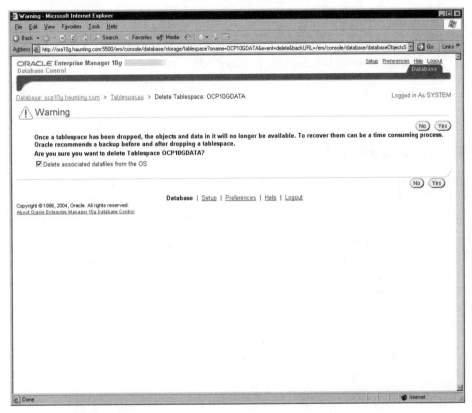

6. Ensure that the Delete Associated Datafiles From The OS check box is checked, and then click Yes to delete the tablespace.

7. Notice that the tablespace is no longer listed on the Tablespaces page. Verify at the operating system to ensure that the datafile is also removed.

8. Close Enterprise Manager.

Viewing Tablespace Information

The easiest way to view tablespace information is by using Enterprise Manager—selecting a tablespace and then clicking the View button is the best way to get full information on a tablespace. Oracle also includes a number of data dictionary and dynamic performance views that can be used to gather information on tablespaces.

To get a list of tablespaces in the database and their characteristics, you can use the DBA_TABLESPACES or V$TABLESPACE views. The DBA_TABLESPACES view provides information on tablespace storage characteristics not found in V$TABLESPACE.

For a list of datafiles, you can query the DBA_DATA_FILES view or the V$DATAFILE view. The DBA_DATA_FILES view will list the name of the tablespace to which the datafile belongs, whereas V$DATAFILE lists only the tablespace number, which must be joined to V$TABLESPACE to get the tablespace name, but V$DATAFILE provides more details on the file status.

 EXAM TIP The V$TABLESPACE, V$DATAFILE, and V$TEMPFILE views can be queried when the database is in a MOUNT state.

For temporary tablespaces, you can query the V$TEMPFILE and DBA_TEMP_FILES views to get a list of tempfiles and their storage characteristics.

Chapter Review

A database has a physical structure and a logical structure. From the physical point of view, the database consists of datafiles built out of operating system blocks. The logical representation of a database consists of tablespaces, which contain segments built out of extents. The smallest logical unit in the database is the database block.

A tablespace is the link between the physical and logical structures of a database. By using tablespaces, we can control the location of data and administer parts of the database separately.

A segment is an object that is allocated space in the datafiles. There are different types of segments: tables, indexes, rollback, temporary, and many others. A segment can be located in only one tablespace.

An extent is the unit of space allocation in a tablespace. An extent is a group of contiguous blocks and must exist in one datafile. Different extents belonging to the same segment can be located in different datafiles belonging to the same tablespace. Multiple segments cannot share an extent in Oracle.

A database block is the minimum unit of I/O within the database. The size of all blocks in the database is set at its creation and cannot be changed.

Tablespaces can be of different types: SYSTEM or non-SYSTEM, permanent or temporary, locally managed or dictionary-managed.

Tablespaces can contain permanent objects or temporary objects. Temporary objects are segments created for sort operations and temporary tables.

Tablespaces are created using the CREATE TABLESPACE command, either from the command line or using Enterprise Manager. When creating a tablespace, you need to specify the datafiles it will use, extent management characteristics, storage settings for the segments created in it, and whether it can be written to.

Datafiles can extend automatically if necessary by using the AUTOEXTEND clause in the datafile definition. When using AUTOEXTEND, make sure that you specify NEXT (how much the file will grow by) and MAXSIZE (the maximum size it will grow to) values so that a file does not occupy all available disk space.

You can increase the size of an existing tablespace by increasing the size of an existing datafile or adding new ones. You can make a tablespace unavailable by taking it offline using the ALTER TABLESPACE command. A tablespace that contains static or historical data should be made Read Only by using the ALTER TABLESPACE command. Read-only tablespaces do not need to be backed up regularly, and most changes to data are prevented. You can, however, drop an object located in a read-only tablespace.

If you no longer need a tablespace, it can be dropped. Dropping the tablespace does not delete the operating system files, but it does remove the tablespace from the controlfile and from the data dictionary. If the tablespace contains objects, you need to use the DROP TABLESPACE ... INCLUDING CONTENTS command.

In order to view information on your tablespaces and datafiles, you can use the DBA_TABLESPACES, DBA_DATA_FILES, and DBA_TEMP_FILES views. When the database is not open, you can query the V$TABLESPACE, V$DATAFILE and V$TEMPFILE views.

Questions

1. Which line of code will cause the following SQL statement to fail? (Choose the best answer.)

```
1      CREATE BIGFILE TABLESPACE OCP10gDATA
2      DATAFILE '/oracle/ocp10gdata/ocp10gdata02.dbf'
3      EXTENT MANAGEMENT LOCAL
4      FREELISTS 5
5      NOLOGGING;
```

   A. 1

   B. 2

   C. 3

   D. 4

   E. 5

   F. The statement will succeed

2. You have mounted the database but did not open it. Which views do you need to query if you need the locations of all datafiles and the names of the tablespaces they belong to? (Choose all correct answers.)

   A. V$DATAFILE

   B. DBA_DATA_FILES

   C. V$TABLESPACE

   D. DBA_TABLESPACES

   E. V$TEMPFILE

   F. DBA_TEMP_FILES

   G. V$UNDOFILE

3. You attempt to create a tablespace but receive an error that the datafile for the tablespace cannot be created. The size of the datafile you wanted to create is 3GB, and you specified the SMALLFILE option for the tablespace. You verify that the operating system directory where the file will reside is owned by the same user as Oracle and the user has full read/write permissions. You are logged

in to the database as the user SYSTEM, and there is plenty of disk space on the hard drive. What is the likely cause of the error? (Choose the best answer.)

A. You cannot create a file larger than 2GB in an Oracle database when specifying SMALLFILE.

B. The operating system cannot create a file larger than 2GB.

C. You must specify the WITH OVERWRITE option for the datafile specification.

D. You must specify the REUSE option for the datafile specification.

E. You must specify the AUTOEXEND option for the datafile specification.

4. You want to be able to re-create a tablespace quickly in case of failure but do not have the SQL code to perform the operation. What is the best way to determine which SQL statement will properly re-create the tablespace with all options correctly set? (Choose the best answer.)

A. Use the Generate DDL option of iSQL*Plus.

B. Use the Generate DDL option of Enterprise Manager.

C. Use the Create Like option of iSQL*Plus.

D. Use the Create Like option of Enterprise Manager.

E. Query the CODE column of the V$TABLESPACE view.

F. Query the TEXT column of the DBA_TABLESPACES view.

5. Which line of code will cause the following SQL statement to fail? (Choose the best answer.)

```
1    CREATE BIGFILE TABLESPACE OCP10gDATA
2    DATAFILE '/oracle/ocp10gdata/ocp10gdata02.dbf'
3    EXTENT MANAGEMENT DICTIONARY
4    FREELISTS 5
5    NOLOGGING;
```

A. 1

B. 2

C. 3

D. 4

E. 5

F. The statement will succeed

6. You determine that a datafile belonging to your ARCHIVE2002 tablespace is too large. You want to reduce the size of the datafile so that disk space is not wasted. This tablespace will not have any data added to it. When you use Enterprise Manager to reduce the size of the datafile belonging to the tablespace, you receive an error. What is the most likely cause? (Choose the best answer.)

A. You cannot reduce the size of datafiles in Oracle.

B. You cannot reduce the size of datafiles using Enterprise Manager.

   C. You do not have sufficient permissions to reduce the size of the file.

   D. The file does not exist.

   E. The file contains data beyond the size you want to reduce the file to.

7. You issue the following command to drop a tablespace and receive an error indicating that the tablespace cannot be dropped. What is the likely cause? (Choose the best answer.)

```
DROP TABLESPACE SYSAUX INCLUDING CONTENTS CASCADE CONSTRAINTS;
```

   A. System tablespaces cannot be dropped.

   B. You do not have permissions to drop the SYSAUX tablespace.

   C. Objects in other tablespaces depend on objects in the tablespace being dropped.

   D. You cannot drop objects in the tablespace that you did not create.

   E. The command should succeed.

8. You want to change extent management on your DATA09 tablespace from local to dictionary to match the other tablespaces in the DATA01–DATA08 range. Which method can be used to make this change? (Choose the best answer.)

   A. DBMS_SPACE_ADMIN.TABLESPACE_DICTIONARY_MANAGED

   B. DBMS_SPACE_ADMIN.TABLESPACE_MIGRATE_TO_DICITONARY

   C. Enterprise Manager

   D. ALTER TABLESPACE DATA09 EXTENT MANAGEMENT DICTIONARY

   E. You cannot convert a locally managed tablespace to dictionary management

9. What permissions are required to create a tablespace? (Choose all correct answers.)

   A. CREATE TABLESPACE

   B. MANAGE DATABASE

   C. DBA

   D. SYSDBA

   E. SYSOPER

10. What types of segments can tablespaces in Oracle Database 10g store? (Choose all correct answers.)

   A. Tables

   B. Sort segments

   C. Redo segments

   D. Undo segments

   E. DBA segments

   F. Clusters

Answers

1. **D.** When specifying local extent management in the creation of a tablespace, you cannot specify a dictionary-managed segment storage parameter as well. FREELISTS can be specified only when extent management is dictionary, so that part of the CREATE TABLESPACE statement would cause the entire statement to fail.

2. **A, C, and E.** Because the database is not yet in an OPEN state, any of the DBA_ data dictionary views are not yet accessible; they can be queries only when the database is in an open state. The V$TABLESPACE view will provide you a list of tablespaces. The V$DATAFILE and V$TEMPFILE views can be joined to the V$TABLESPACE view using the TS# column to retrieve a list of all tablespaces and their datafiles. There is no V$UNDOFILE view.

3. **D.** The most likely reason that you are receiving an error on the creation of the datafile for the tablespace is that a file with that name already exists. To correct this, you must specify the REUSE option on the datafile specification to have Oracle overwrite the existing file (or delete the file manually from the hard disk). Neither Oracle nor the operating system will prevent a file of 3GB being created for a SMALLFILE tablespace.

4. **B.** The Generate DDL option of Enterprise Manager will generate the SQL code to re-create the selected tablespace. You can then cut and paste this into a SQL script for later execution. There is no Generate or Create Like option in *i*SQL*Plus, and the Create Like option of Enterprise Manager will display a new page to enter the name of a tablespace with the same parameters as the one selected. There is no CODE column in the V$TABLESPACE or TEXT column in DBA_TABLESPACES.

5. **C.** In order to create a BIGFILE tablespace, you must specify local extent management and automatic segment space management. You cannot create a dictionary-managed BIGFILE tablespace.

6. **E.** Oracle allows you to reduce the size of datafiles, and this can be accomplished from the command line or using Enterprise Manager. If you are able to change the size of the file in Enterprise Manager, you have the necessary permissions to perform the action. The most likely reason you are unable to perform the action is that more data exists in the datafile than the size you want to reduce it to. Specify a larger value and try again.

7. **A.** SYSAUX is a system tablespace and cannot be dropped. The same holds true for the SYSTEM tablespace.

8. **E.** Once a tablespace is made locally managed, it is not possible to convert it to a dictionary-managed tablespace. There is no command or Enterprise Manager option to perform the change.

9. **A and C.** You must be granted either the CREATE TABLESPACE system permission or the DBA role to create a tablespace. There is no MANAGE DATABASE permission. The SYSOPER and SYSDBA roles provide permissions for managing the instance and database but do not specifically grant the holder the permission to create a tablespace.

10. **A, B, D,** and **F.** Tablespaces in Oracle can store tables, clusters (both are types of permanent segments, which also include indexes, partitions, and others), undo segments, and sort segments (a type of temporary segment). Redo segments and DBA segments do not exist. Redo is stored in the redo log files.

CHAPTER 7

Administering Database Users

In this chapter you will learn how to
- Create and manage database user accounts
- Create and manage roles
- Grant and revoke privileges
- Control resource usage by users

As a database administrator, you must ensure that individuals that need access to the database have the appropriate level of permission. This means creating users in the database to allow individuals to connect to the instance, as well as granting the appropriate system permissions to let users create and manage objects. Once a user creates an object, he can then grant others permissions to manipulate those objects; the DBA need not be involved in managing permissions to an individual user's objects. Finally, you want to ensure that no user can consume all database resources when issuing an errant SQL statement or by other means.

Creating and Managing Database Users

In order for anyone to be able to access the database, that person needs to be authenticated by Oracle as a valid database user. Applications can be configured to require each individual needing access to have a separate database account, or the application itself can connect to the database as a common user and handle application-level permissions internally. No matter which method is chosen, at least one database user will need to be created in the database to allow data manipulation.

Users and Schemas

When you create a database, depending on what options you have selected, a number of database users will be created but will be locked by default. Two database users are always created and are always unlocked: SYS and SYSTEM. The SYS user owns the data dictionary and all of its associated objects. The user SYSTEM has access to all objects in the database. The distinction between a user owning objects and a user only having access to objects that are owned by another user is an important one in Oracle.

Any user that has been given the permission to create objects and does so is said to own a schema. The *schema* is a collection of all objects that are owned by a user. The schema has the same name as the user. For example, if a database user called John created a table called Customers, John has now also created his schema and will be schema owner of the "John" schema. Anyone wanting to query the new table in John's schema can prefix the table name with the schema name and query the data as JOHN.CUSTOMERS (assuming John has granted them permissions to do so). If Damir wants to query the JOHN.CUSTOMERS table, he may do so if he has permissions. Damir does not have to be a schema owner like John, just a database user. In fact, the majority of users in a database are not schema owners (i.e., they do not own database objects) but are simply users accessing other schemas.

 EXAM TIP Any user that has created a database object (view, table, etc.) owns a schema and is considered a *schema user*.

To relate the concept of schema users and non-schema users to a real-world example, think of it as being similar to your still living with your parents. Your parents own the house that you live in, just as an Oracle user owns a schema. They allow you to live in the house (with or without cost), which makes you the non-schema user, since you do not own the house. In fact, they have given you permission to access objects in the house (your room, the bathroom, the kitchen, and—most important—the fridge), much as a schema owner grants privileges to other Oracle users to access a table or other object. The schema owner always has the option to revoke any privileges granted to objects in the database, just as a parent may have the option to kick you out of the house if you overstay your welcome.

Creating Users

Gaining access to an Oracle database requires that you have a user account in the database, which is created for you by the DBA. The DBA is an Oracle user who has been granted all permissions in the database because he owns the database. The user SYS in Oracle has that power and has also granted it to the SYSTEM user by granting SYSTEM the DBA role (roles will be explained in the next section of this chapter). SYS can also grant this authority to other Oracle users, so that not everyone needs to know the SYS or SYSTEM password. The password for the SYS user is always "change_on_install" by default, and for user SYSTEM, it is "manager" if you create the database from the command line using the CREATE DATABASE statement. If you use the Database Configuration Assistant to create a database, you will be prompted to specify passwords other than the default for these users. In any case, ensure that the default passwords are not the ones used for SYS or SYSTEM; otherwise, you are making a hacker's job rather easy.

 EXAM TIP Oracle Database 10g databases will typically have many more users besides SYS and SYSTEM defined when the database is created. The majority of these users will have their accounts locked and will need to be manually unlocked by the DBA or when running DBCA.

The command that creates a user in Oracle is the CREATE USER command. The syntax for this command is listed here, while Table 7-1 provides additional information on the various parameters for the CREATE USER command listed in the syntax.

```
CREATE USER username
IDENTIFIED [BY password | EXTERNALLY | GLOBALLY AS extname]
[DEFAULT TABLESPACE tablespacename]
[TEMPORARY TABLESPACE tablespacename]
[ACCOUNT LOCK | UNLOCK]
[PROFILE profilename | DEFAULT]
[PASSWORD EXPIRE]
[QUOTA num [K|M] | UNLIMITED ON tablespace
[QUOTA num [K|M] | UNLIMITED ON tablespace] ... ]
```

Parameter	Description
username	The name of the user to be created. The name must be specified and must be unique within the database. A username can be up to 30 characters long and must adhere to Oracle naming conventions (starts with a letter and may contain numbers; letters; or the symbols #, _, or $).
IDENTIFIED	Specifies how the user will have their authenticity validated. The three methods include: —**BY** *password*, where *password* represents a DBA-specified password of up to 30 characters. The database will check the credentials provided by the user against the username and passwords in the data dictionary and deny or grant access, depending upon whether or not a match is found. —**EXTERNALLY**, where the username will be authenticated by the operating system of the computer on which the database is running and Oracle will allow access if the operating system authenticates the user. In order to configure this type of authentication, some additional processes are involved. —**GLOBALLY AS** *extname*, where the username and password will be passed to the *extname* service for logon validation. This type of authentication requires external authentication mechanisms, such as a RADIUS server.
DEFAULT TABLESPACE	The name of a tablespace that will be used to store segments created by the user if no tablespace is specified at object creation time. If the DEFAULT TABLESPACE parameter is not specified at user creation time, the tablespace configured at the database level to be the database default tablespace will be used. If no database default tablespace is configured, this parameter defaults to SYSTEM. It is strongly recommended that you always specify a DEFAULT TABLESPACE for the user and assign the user a quota on this tablespace if you expect her to create segments.
TEMPORARY TABLESPACE	The name of a tablespace that will be used to store temporary segments, such as sort segments. If the TEMPORARY TABLESPACE parameter is not specified at user creation time, the tablespace configured at the database level to be the database temporary tablespace will be used. If no database temporary tablespace is configured, this parameter defaults to SYSTEM. It is strongly recommended that you specify a TEMPORARY TABLESPACE for the user.
ACCOUNT LOCK | UNLOCK	Allows you to explicitly lock or unlock a user account at creation time. The default for this parameter is UNLOCK, which means that a user can connect to the instance as soon as the account is created and the appropriate privileges granted.
PROFILE	Specifies the profile that will be assigned to the user. The profile will determine password management and, optionally, resource limits that will apply to the user. If this parameter is not specified, or if the keyword DEFAULT is used, the user will be assigned the DEFAULT profile.
PASSWORD EXPIRE	This parameter allows you to automatically expire the user's password at creation time, forcing them to change the password the first time a successful connection to the instance is established. The default behavior is not to expire the user's password, though use of this parameter is recommended.
QUOTA	Lets you configure a quota for the user on tablespaces in the database. The quota is specified in bytes, kilobytes (K), or megabytes (M). You should specify a quota on the user's DEFAULT TABLESPACE if you expect the user to create segments. You should not specify an UNLIMITED quota on a tablespace for a regular user.

Table 7-1   CREATE USER Command Parameters

You can also use Oracle Enterprise Manager to create a user, as well as see the syntax to perform the action. Enterprise Manager also allows the creation of users with similar settings as an already-existing database user.

Exercise 7-1: Using Enterprise Manager to Create a Database User

In this exercise you will connect to Enterprise Manager and create a database user.

1. Start a web browser and connect to the Enterprise Manager URL on your Oracle database server, specifying the appropriate port number and machine name.

2. Log in to your database as the user SYSTEM with the appropriate password. If you receive the licensing information page, click I Agree to continue.

3. On the Enterprise Manager main page, click the Administration hyperlink to display the Administration page.

4. Click the Users hyperlink under Security to display the users currently defined in the database and their statuses and parameters.

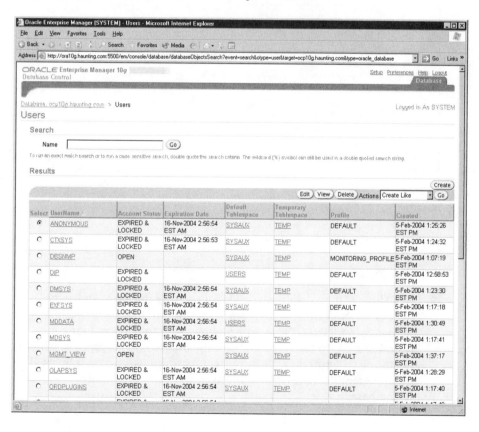

5. Click Create to display the Create User page.

6. Enter values for the parameters required, including a username and a password, confirming the password of your choice. Choose a default tablespace (use USERS if it exists; otherwise, use the flashlight to select a tablespace in the database) and a temporary tablespace (use TEMP if it exists), and ensure that the status is Unlocked and Expire Password Now is unchecked.

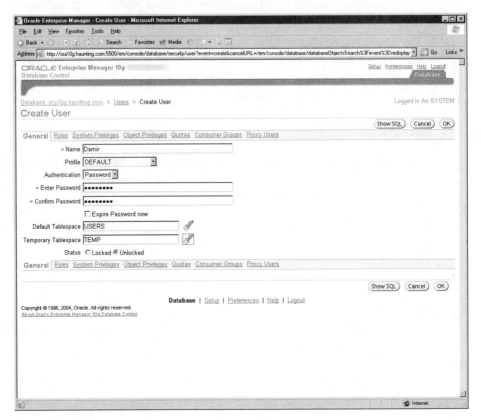

7. Click Show SQL to display the code for creating the user. Notice the "GRANT CONNECT TO <username>" portion of the code. This grants the user the CONNECT role, which allows him to connect to the instance. Without the CONNECT role granted, the user would get an error when attempting to connect to the instance. Creating a user account by itself does not grant the user permission to connect to the instance and access the database.

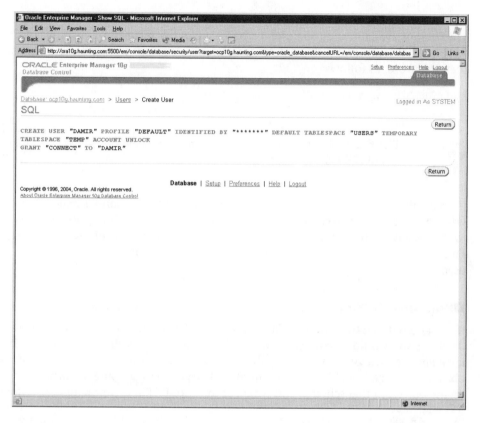

8. Click Return to return to the Create User page.

9. Click OK to create the User. You should be returned to the list of users with your user now visible in the list. Verify this and then close Enterprise Manager.

Modifying User Properties

While it is possible to have users never change anything for the duration of their existence in the database, this is probably not a good security practice, nor is it likely. Users may forget their password, or you may need to specify a different tablespace as the user's default tablespace, or grant new quotas or increased quotas for the user's objects, or lock out a user temporarily. The ALTER USER command can be used to accomplish these tasks. Its syntax is as follows:

```
ALTER USER username
IDENTIFIED [BY password | EXTERNALLY | GLOBALLY AS extname]
[DEFAULT TABLESPACE tablespacename]
[TEMPORARY TABLESPACE tablespacename]
[ACCOUNT LOCK | UNLOCK]
[PROFILE profilename]
[PASSWORD EXPIRE]
[QUOTA num [K|M] | UNLIMITED ON tablespace
[QUOTA num [K|M] | UNLIMITED ON tablespace] ... ]
```

As you can see, the syntax hardly varies from that of the CREATE USER command. The options available are the same. Perhaps one of the most useful features of the ALTER USER command is that a database user can also issue this command to change their password, as follows:

```
ALTER USER Damir IDENTIFIED BY newpassword;
```

EXAM TIP All user properties except the username can be modified using the ALTER USER command.

Note that the password itself is not masked when the command is issued. If you want the password masked, you can use the Edit User page in Enterprise Manager to change a user's password, though this is not a method the user himself could use. Enterprise Manager can also be used to perform any other action in modifying a user, such as assigning a quota.

Dropping Users

If you guessed that the DROP USER command is the one that removes a user from a database, you would be correct. However, the syntax is not as simple as "DROP USER *username*" because of the possibility that the user may have a schema. If a user owns objects in the database, his account cannot be dropped, because other users may depend on the objects in that schema. The syntax of the DROP USER command is as follows:

```
DROP USER username [CASCADE]
```

Oracle prevents you from dropping a user from a database whose schema contains objects. This is to ensure that objects created by one user and depended upon by another user's objects are not inadvertently removed from the database. Since the user and the schema are linked, dropping the user will also drop the schema. Oracle does not allow you to drop both the user and the schema, unless you specify the CASCADE option on the DROP USER command.

Using the CASCADE option will drop all objects, as well as any data contained in tables, that the user owns (i.e., that are in the user's schema). This can have drastic side effects in the database if not planned properly. It is always recommended that before dropping a user, you determine if the user owns any objects in the database, and if so, drop the objects after verifying that they are not depended upon by other users.

EXAM TIP To drop a schema user, you must specify the CASCADE option of the DROP USER command or, preferably, drop the user's objects first and then drop the user.

To find out which objects are owned by a user you wish to drop, you can query the DBA_OBJECTS view. If you get zero rows returned, as in the following example, you can safely drop the user:

```
SQL> SELECT OBJECT_NAME, OBJECT_TYPE FROM DBA_OBJECTS
  2  WHERE OWNER='DAMIR';

no rows selected
```

On the other hand, if you do get a list of objects back, you should also query the DBA_DEPENDENCIES view to determine which objects are dependent on those owned by the user you wish to drop.

Granting and Revoking Privileges

Once you have created user accounts in Oracle, you will need to allow those users to perform certain actions in the database or to access and manipulate objects in the database. This is accomplished through the granting and revoking of different privileges (or permissions). Oracle has two different types of privileges that can be granted: system privileges and object privileges. *System* privileges allow a user to perform certain database actions, such as create a table, or create an index, or even connect to the instance. *Object* privileges allow a user to manipulate objects, as by reading data through a view, executing a stored procedure, or changing data in a table. System privileges are granted to and revoked from users by the DBA, while object privileges are granted to and revoked from users by the owner of the object.

System Privileges

Oracle 10*g* has well over one hundred system privileges that can be granted to users, of which some of the most common are listed in Table 7-2. These privileges include the capability to create various database objects, modify the configuration of the database, and many more. The right to grant these privileges is restricted to the DBA by default, though these permissions can be granted to other users as well.

Granting System Privileges

You can grant system privileges either using the command line or through Oracle Enterprise Manager. The syntax for assigning system privileges is as follows:

```
GRANT privilege [, privilege, ...]
TO username [, username, ...]
[WITH ADMIN OPTION];
```

As you can see by this syntax, it is possible to grant multiple privileges to multiple users at the same time. The privileges granted to a user are immediately available to the user. This means that the user does not need to disconnect from the instance and log in again in order for the privilege change to take effect. Simply granting the privilege lets the user make use of it right away.

Privilege	Description
CREATE SESSION	Allows the grantee to connect to the database instance. After creating a new user, you need to grant the CREATE SESSION privilege; otherwise, the user will not be able to connect.
CREATE TABLE	Allows the grantee to create a table in her schema.
CREATE VIEW	Allows the grantee to create a view in her schema.
CREATE SYNONYM	Allows the grantee to create a private synonym in her schema.
CREATE PUBLIC SYNONYM	Allows the grantee to create a synonym in the SYS schema that can be used by any user in the database.
CREATE PROCEDURE	Allows the grantee to create a stored procedure or function in her schema.
CREATE SEQUENCE	Allows the grantee to create a sequence in her schema.
CREATE TRIGGER	Allows the grantee to create a trigger in her schema on a table in her schema.
CREATE USER	Allows the grantee to create another user in the database and specify the password and other settings at creation time.
ALTER USER	Allows the grantee who has been granted the privilege to modify the user information of another user in the database, including changing the user's password.
DROP ANY TABLE	Allows the grantee to drop any table in any schema in the database.
ALTER ANY TABLE	Allows the grantee to alter any table in any schema in the database.
BACKUP ANY TABLE	Allows the grantee to make a copy of any table in the database using the Export utility (exp).
SELECT ANY TABLE	Allows the grantee to issue a SELECT statement against any table in the database, whether or not permissions to the table have been explicitly granted to the grantee performing the action.
INSERT ANY TABLE	Allows the grantee to issue an INSERT statement against any table in the database, whether or not permissions to the table have been explicitly granted to the grantee performing the action.
UPDATE ANY TABLE	Allows the grantee to issue an UPDATE statement against any table in the database, whether or not permissions to the table have been explicitly granted to the grantee performing the action.
DELETE ANY TABLE	Allows the grantee to issue a DELETE statement against any table in the database, whether or not permissions to the table have been explicitly granted to the grantee performing the action.

Table 7-2 Commonly Granted System Privileges in Oracle 10g

For example, if you want to allow Damir to create tables, views, triggers, indexes, synonyms, and sequences in his schema, you can issue the following command:

```
GRANT CREATE TABLE, CREATE VIEW, CREATE SYNONYM,
CREATE SEQUENCE, CREATE TRIGGER, CREATE INDEX
TO Damir;
```

Just because a user has been granted a system privilege does not always mean that the user can exercise that privilege, as evident by this error indicating an insufficient quota for Damir on the USERS tablespace when Damir tries to connect to the instance and create a table:

```
SQL> connect Damir/newpass1@ocp10g.haunting.com
Connected.
SQL> CREATE TABLE DamirTable
  2    (DamirID number,
  3    Name varchar2(40));
CREATE TABLE DamirTable
*
ERROR at line 1:
ORA-01950: no privileges on tablespace 'USERS'
```

WITH ADMIN OPTION   When a user is granted a system privilege, the grantor (i.e., the person granting the privilege, typically the DBA) also has the option to allow the grantee (the person receiving the privilege, typically the user) to grant the same privilege to other users. If this is the result desired, the grantor can grant the privilege using the WITH ADMIN OPTION. When privileges are granted WITH ADMIN OPTION, this means that the grantor has decided that the grantee can be fully trusted by him as well as by the user that granted him the system privilege in the first place. In essence all users holding a system privilege WITH ADMIN OPTION are considered equal and can grant and revoke that privilege from anyone, including the person who granted it to them in the first place.

 EXAM TIP   The WITH ADMIN OPTION allows you to grant your grantee the ability to grant system privileges to other users.

Exercise 7-2: Using Enterprise Manager to Grant System Privileges

In this exercise you will connect to Enterprise Manager and create additional database users and grant them system privileges.

1. Start a web browser and connect to the Enterprise Manager URL on your Oracle database server, specifying the appropriate port number and machine name.

2. Log in to your database as the user SYSTEM with the appropriate password. If you receive the licensing information page, click I Agree to continue.

3. On the Enterprise Manager main page, click the Administration hyperlink to display the Administration page.

4. Click the Users hyperlink under Security to display the users currently defined in the database and their statuses and parameters.

5. Click Create to display the Create User page.

6. Fill in the values to create a new user called John with a password of "oracle," a default tablespace of USERS, and a temporary tablespace of TEMP. Ensure that the account is not locked and that the password is not set to expire; then click OK to create the user.

7. Create two additional users—Tim and Jessica—with the same settings as John.

8. Open another browser window and connect to *i*SQL*Plus for your database instance and log in as the user SYSTEM with the appropriate password.

9. Enter the following SQL statements in the Workspace window and then click Execute to run them:

```
GRANT CREATE TABLE TO JOHN WITH ADMIN OPTION
/
GRANT CREATE VIEW TO TIM
/
GRANT SELECT ANY TABLE TO JESSICA
/
```

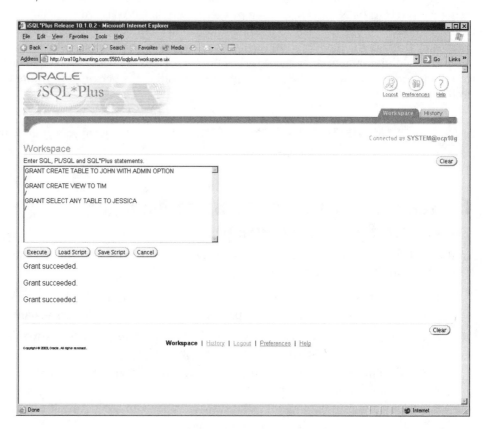

10. Log out from *i*SQL*Plus and then log in as John with the appropriate password.

11. Issue the following command to create a table and notice the error you receive due to an absence of quota on the tablespace:

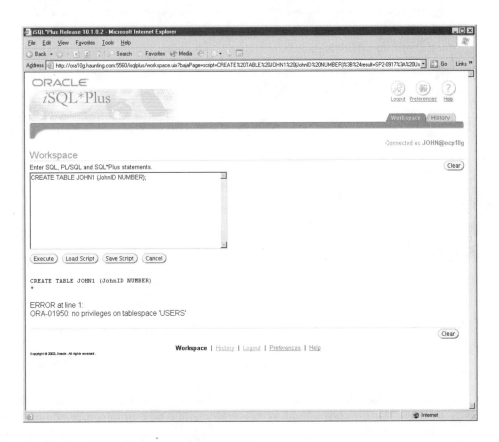

```
CREATE TABLE JOHN1 (JohnID NUMBER);
```

12. Go back to Enterprise Manager and select the user John in the user list; then click Edit.

13. Click the Quotas hyperlink for the user, and then for the Users tablespace select Value from the Quota drop-down. Enter **50** in the Value column to grant the user John a 50MB quota on the Users tablespace, as shown next, and then click Apply.

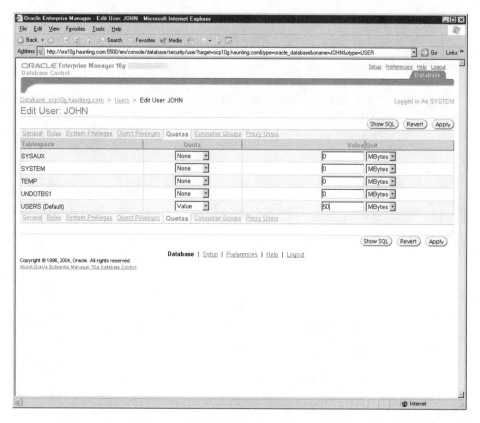

14. Modify the quota for the Users tablespace for users Tim and Jessica to also be 50MB.

15. In iSQL*Plus connected as John, attempt to re-create the John1 table again. Notice that the command succeeded, since John now has a quota on the Users tablespace.

16. Insert some data into the John1 table by issuing the following commands in iSQL*Plus and then clicking Execute:

```
INSERT INTO JOHN1 VALUES (100);
INSERT INTO JOHN1 VALUES (101);
INSERT INTO JOHN1 VALUES (102);
INSERT INTO JOHN1 VALUES (103);
INSERT INTO JOHN1 VALUES (104);
COMMIT;
```

17. Issue the command **GRANT CREATE TABLE TO TIM** to allow Tim to create tables, and then click Execute.

18. Log out from *i*SQL*Plus as John and log in as Tim.

19. Attempt to query data in the John1 table. Notice the error indicating that the object cannot be found, which really means you don't have permissions.

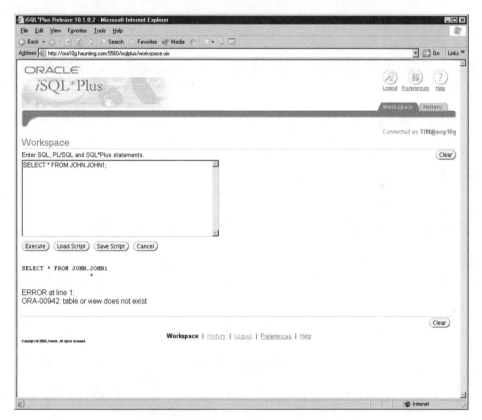

20. Issue the same CREATE TABLE JOHN1 command as previously while connected as Tim. Notice that it is possible to create two tables called John1 as long as they are in different schemas.

21. Log out of *i*SQL*Plus and log in again as Jessica.

22. Attempt to query the John1 tables in both the John and Tim schemas. Notice that you can perform these actions, since Jessica has been granted the SELECT ANY TABLE privilege.

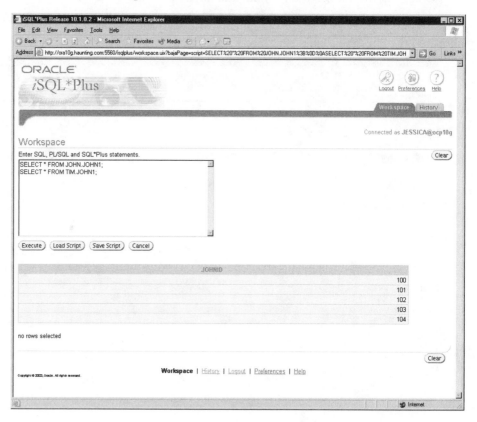

23. In Enterprise Manager, select Jessica and click View to display information on Jessica's user account and the privileges granted to her.

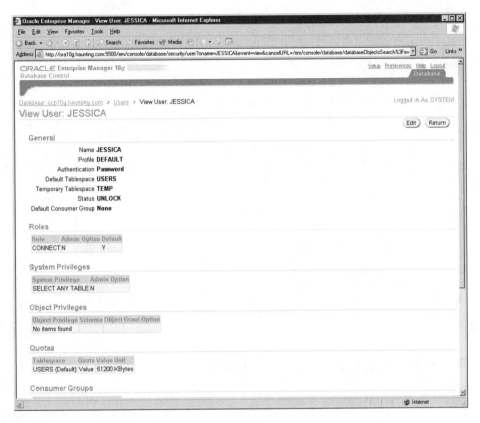

24. Log out of *i*SQL*Plus and Enterprise Manager.

Revoking System Privileges

If you do not want anyone to continue to have a system privilege granted to them, you can use the REVOKE command or Enterprise Manager to remove the privileges granted. The syntax of the REVOKE command to revoke system privileges is very similar to that of granting it and can be used to revoke one or more privileges from one or more users/grantees, as follows:

```
REVOKE privilege [, privilege, ...]
FROM username [, username, ...];
```

It is important to note one side effect when the WITH ADMIN OPTION is specified at the time a system privilege is granted. While the DBA may revoke the privilege granted to the user WITH ADMIN OPTION, if the user has granted that same privilege to others, it is not removed from those users that were granted the privilege. For example, if you give the key to your car to a friend and tell him that it is alright to make copies of the key, when you ask for the key back from your friend, you cannot, at the same time, get back all copies that were made by him and given to others. In order to get the other copies of the key back, you need to find out who has them. Similarly, in Oracle you need to query the data dictionary to determine which other users were granted the permission being revoked by the user from which it is being revoked.

 EXAM TIP Revoking system privileges from a user will not cascade to anyone the revokee granted the same system privilege if he had been granted the privilege WITH ADMIN OPTION.

Determining System Privileges Granted

If you want to find out which system privileges you have been granted, you can query the DBA_SYS_PRIVS (for all system privileges granted to all users) and USER_SYS_PRIVS (for system privileges granted to the currently logged-on user) data dictionary views. These views will let you see which privileges you have been granted and whether or not they have been granted WITH ADMIN OPTION. Only those system privileges that have been granted will appear on the list. Any privileges that have been revoked will not be listed, as Oracle does not keep track of permissions denied a user. The default for Oracle is to deny all actions except those explicitly granted; therefore, only those explicitly granted are listed.

To determine which privileges have been granted to individual users, you can use Enterprise Manager to display the user information, including privileges and quotas.

Object Privileges

Users in Oracle can also be granted object privileges. Object privileges allow a user to manipulate data in the database or perform an action on an object, such as executing a stored procedure. Unlike system privileges, which are granted by the DBA, object privileges need to be granted by the owner of the object.

Granting Object Privileges

The syntax to assign object privileges is as follows:

```
GRANT privilege [,privilege, ...] | ALL [(column[, column, ...])]
ON objectname
TO user | role | PUBLIC
[WITH GRANT OPTION];
```

The major difference in the syntax between system and object privileges is that the keyword ON needs to be specified to determine which object the privileges apply to. Furthermore, object privileges for views and tables can also specify which column of the view or table they should be applied to. The keyword ALL specifies that all privileges that apply to the object should be granted. The privilege can be granted to a user, a role (to be discussed later), or the keyword PUBLIC, which means all users in the database.

 EXAM TIP Object privileges are granted by the owner of the object.

The types of privileges that can be granted depend on the object that they are being granted on. For example, it makes no sense to grant the SELECT privilege to a stored procedure, while the SELECT privilege makes perfect sense on a table. The object privileges that can be granted and the object they can be granted to are outlined in Table 7-3. For example, you cannot issue an ALTER VIEW command, so therefore the ALTER privilege cannot apply to a view, and so on.

One privilege that requires a bit of an explanation is the REFERENCES privilege. The REFERENCES privilege is one that can be granted to a user to create a FOREIGN KEY on a column of a table. By granting the user the REFERENCES privilege, you do not need to allow the user to be able to see that data, as they would with the SELECT privilege, but are only allowing them to reference the data in the FOREIGN KEY. The SELECT permission alone is not sufficient to create a FOREIGN KEY or view that references a column in the table; the REFERENCES permission is also required. Even if the user has the SELECT permission on the table, the creation of a FOREIGN KEY or view will fail without the REFERENCES permission.

Table 7-3 Privileges and the Objects They Can Be Granted On	**Privilege**	**Granted On**
	SELECT	Table, view, sequence
	INSERT	Table, view
	UPDATE	Table, view
	DELETE	Table, view
	ALTER	Table, sequence
	INDEX	Table
	REFERENCES	Table
	EXECUTE	Procedure, function, package

NOTE It is generally not recommended, and often frowned upon, to grant object privileges at the column level. The management of many column-level privileges can become quite time consuming, as well as confusing. Generally, it is recommended that when you need to assign privileges to only certain columns of a table, you should create a view including only those columns and grant the appropriate permission on the view itself. This way, if you drop the view or remove permission from the view for a user, the management is easier and cleaner.

WITH GRANT OPTION   Similar to the WITH ADMIN OPTION of system privileges, the WITH GRANT OPTION on object privileges allows a user granted the privilege to grant it to someone else. The reason for doing this is to minimize the administrative burden of granting object privileges.

Revoking Object Privileges

Revoking object privileges has similar syntax to granting them, as follows:

```
REVOKE privilege [,privilege, ...] | ALL [(column[, column, ...])]
ON objectname
FROM user | role | PUBLIC
[CASCADE CONSTRAINTS];
```

Unlike the WITH ADMIN OPTION for system privileges, if an object privilege is revoked from a user to whom it was granted WITH GRANT OPTION, that privilege would also be removed from anyone that user granted the privilege to. For example, if Damir granted John the SELECT privilege on the DAMIR.JOHN1 table WITH GRANT OPTION, and John then granted the SELECT privilege to Tim, then if Damir issued the command REVOKE SELECT ON DAMIR.JOHN1 FROM JOHN, Tim would also no longer have the privilege. This is because when object privileges are revoked, the revoke also cascades to anyone that the privilege was granted to by the user from whom it is being revoked.

 EXAM TIP Object privileges revoked from a user to whom they were granted WITH GRANT OPTION will also be revoked from anyone the revokee granted them to; i.e., the revoke will cascade.

The CASCADE CONSTRAINTS option of the REVOKE command for object privileges is needed in those situations where a user has been granted REFERENCES permission on a table in your schema, and they have used this privilege to create a table with a FOREIGN KEY constraint depending upon the table you own. Attempting to revoke the REFERENCES privilege will generate an error:

```
ORA-01981: CASCADE CONSTRAINTS must be specified to perform this revoke
```

To correct the problem, simply reissue the command using the CASCADE CONSTRAINTS option. When using the CASCADE CONSTRAINTS option of the

REVOKE command for object privileges, verify that any FOREIGN KEY created in another schema referencing the table is no longer required. One of the things you do not want to do is break the database and invite inconsistent data by simply revoking an object privilege. If you do get the ORA-01981 error, query the data dictionary to determine which objects are referencing the table and notify those table's owners of your intentions prior to performing the action.

Determining the Object Privileges Granted

As for system privileges, Oracle also allows a user to determine which object privileges have been granted to him/her by querying the data dictionary, or by using Enterprise Manager. These are some of the data dictionary views that can be used to determine which privileges have been granted to a user or granted by the user:

- **USER_TAB_PRIVS_MADE**   Object privileges the user has granted to others on his schema objects

- **USER_TAB_PRIVS_RECD**   Privileges granted to the user to objects in other schemas

- **ALL_TAB_PRIVS_MADE**   Object privileges the user has granted to others on his and other schema objects

- **ALL_TAB_PRIVS_RECD**   Privileges granted to the user to objects in his and other schemas

- **USER_COL_PRIVS_MADE**   Column privileges granted by the user to tables in his schema

- **USER_COL_PRIVS_RECD**   Column privileges granted to the user to columns in tables in other schemas

- **ALL_COL_PRIVS_MADE**   Column privileges granted by the user to tables in his and other schemas

- **ALL_COL_PRIVS_RECD**   Column privileges granted to the user to columns in tables in his and other schemas

Exercise 7-3: Using Enterprise Manager to Grant Object Privileges

In this exercise you will connect to Enterprise Manager and grant and revoke privileges to users on schema objects and then test the results.

1. Start a web browser and connect to the Enterprise Manager URL on your Oracle database server, specifying the appropriate port number and machine name.

2. Log in to your database as the user SYSTEM with the appropriate password. If you receive the licensing information page, click I Agree to continue.

3. On the Enterprise Manager main page, click the Administration hyperlink to display the Administration page.

4. Click the Users hyperlink under Security to display the users currently defined in the database and their statuses and parameters.

5. Click the user Damir created in a pervious exercise to bring up the Edit User page.

6. Click the Object Privileges hyperlink to display the existing list of object privileges granted to the user. The list should be empty.

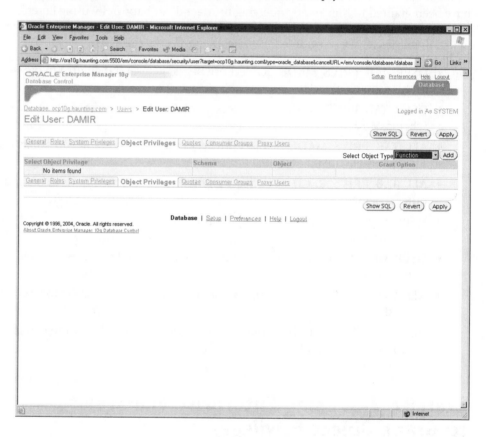

7. On the Select Object Type drop-down list box, select Table and then click Add to display the Add Table Object privilege page.

8. Enter **JOHN.JOHN1** as the table name (or use the flashlight to find the table in the data dictionary) and choose the SELECT, INSERT, UPDATE, and DELETE privileges from the list; then click Move.

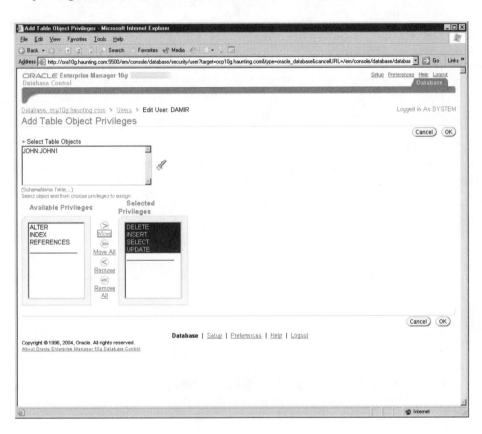

9. Click OK to save your changes and display the updated list of object privileges.

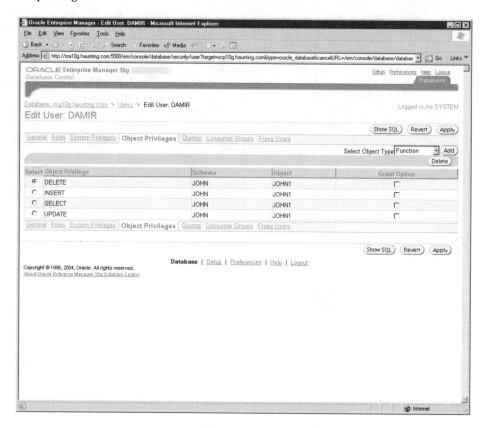

10. For the SELECT privilege check the check box under the Grant Option heading and then click Show SQL to display the SQL code to grant the privileges.

11. Click Return and then Apply to save your changes.

12. Invoke a browser and connect to *i*SQL*Plus and the database as DAMIR with the appropriate password.

13. Issue the command **SELECT * FROM JOHN.JOHN1** to make sure you can query the table you have just been granted privileges on. Also insert a row into the table, and delete and update a row to test all privileges.

14. Issue the command **GRANT SELECT ON JOHN.JOHN1 TO TIM** and verify that it succeeds.

15. Attempt to grant the INSERT privilege on the JOHN.JOHN1 table and review the error you receive.

16. From a different browser window and in another *i*SQL*Plus session, connect as Tim and attempt to query the JOHN.JOHN1 table.

17. As Tim, issue the command **CREATE VIEW JOHN1VIEW AS SELECT * FROM JOHN.JOHN1**. Remember that Tim has previously been granted the CREATE VIEW system privilege.

18. Issue the command **SELECT * FROM JOHN1VIEW** and see that all the data from the JOHN.JOHN1 table appears.

19. Attempt to insert a row in the JOHN.JOHN1 table. Notice the "ORA-01031: insufficient privilege" error message.

20. Log out of *i*SQL*Plus as Tim and log in as John with the appropriate password.

21. Issue the command **REVOKE ALL ON JOHN.JOHN1 FROM DAMIR**.

22. In the *i*SQL*Plus session where you are logged in as Damir, attempt to select from the JOHN.JOHN1 table. Notice the "ORA-00942: table or view does not exist" error.

23. Log out as Damir, log in to *i*SQL*Plus as Tim, and then attempt to query the JOHN1VIEW view. Notice the message indicating the view has an error. Attempt to SELECT from the JOHN.JOHN1 table and notice the error.

24. Issue the command **DROP VIEW JOHN1VIEW**.

25. Close all *i*SQL*Plus and Enterprise Manager sessions.

Creating and Managing Roles

Up to this point you have seen how to assign permissions to other users. In small environments assigning permissions directly to users may be sufficient, especially if new users need to be created in the database only occasionally. However, in more complex or larger environments, or those where users are added and deleted frequently, Oracle provides a mechanism to group permissions together and then assign the whole group of permissions to a user: the ROLE.

A role is a container that holds privileges. The main benefit of a role is that it simplifies the process of granting privileges to users. To make the process efficient, a DBA creates a role and then grants all of the privileges required by a user to perform a task to the role. If another user comes along that needs to perform the same task, instead of granting that user the permission explicitly, the DBA grants the user the role. Any privileges that have been granted to a role that has been granted to a user automatically apply to the user. Similarly, if you need to grant new privileges to users or revoke existing privileges from users, and if these were granted to a role rather than users, you need to grant or revoke the privileges only once—at the role level—instead

PART I

of numerous times. Furthermore, those privileges granted will be automatically active once the grant or revoke takes place. Changes to role privileges are dynamically modified for all users holding the role.

When you grant privileges to users, those privileges will be available no matter how the user accesses the database. This means that someone using a front-end client application that presents preconfigured forms may need the same level of privileges as someone connecting to the instance using *i*SQL*Plus and performing interactive queries. The problem with this is that a user of the front-end application could also connect to the instance and perform deletes, or other data manipulation, that may be more controlled through the front-end application. Roles, which can be selectively enabled and disabled, allow you to provide the user with additional privileges by enabling them when the user is using the front-end application, but not allow the user to have the same set of privileges if they connect to the instance using *i*SQL*Plus.

 EXAM TIP Roles are containers for privileges or other roles and can be authenticated externally.

Roles, in a similar fashion to database users, can be authenticated by the operating system instead of the Oracle server. Creating roles that are authenticated by the operating system allows you to create groups at the OS level and map their membership to roles in the database, and grant those individuals that are members of an OS group additional privileges. This can also allow you to have individuals who just joined your company, or have been moved into new positions within the organization, that have been granted certain group membership by the system administrator automatically inherit database privileges that can allow them to do their job (and you did not have to do anything). Of course, the other edge of this sword means that you, as a DBA, have now lost some control over who can perform certain actions in the database. In other words, having roles authenticated by the OS can be both good and bad, depending on how it is implemented.

When you revoke an object privilege from a user in Oracle, if that user was granted the privilege WITH GRANT OPTION, anyone that the user granted the privilege to will also have it revoked. With roles, there are no cascading revokes for object privileges granted to roles, because you cannot grant object privileges to a role WITH GRANT OPTION; the syntax is not allowed. However, you can grant a system privilege, or another role, to a role WITH ADMIN OPTION. Doing so allows anyone granted the role to grant those system privileges or roles to others.

Finally, the evaluation of roles by the database takes less work than evaluating privileges assigned to users directly. This means—in a nutshell—that roles provide better performance than granting privileges directly to users. This is because the privileges granted to a role can be cached in the data dictionary cache when they are first used and do not need to be reloaded, unless flushed out, the next time a user who has been assigned the role makes use of the privileges. Individual user privileges must be checked against the data dictionary each time a command is sent to the server, and will be cached only if they are frequently used.

Predefined Roles

Every Oracle 10g database, once created and once the CATPROC.SQL and CATALOG
.SQL scripts are run, will include a number of predefined roles. Some of these still exist
for backward compatibility with previous versions, whereas some are there to ease
administration and to provide the DBA with the necessary privileges to do his/her job.
In fact, the DBA gets all of the privileges required to manage the database through a
predefined role called, ironically enough, "DBA." Table 7-4 lists the predefined roles in
an Oracle 10g database. Other roles will be created as you install additional database
options or functionality.

In your database you may also find that other roles are created. They are most
likely there because you have enabled certain database functionality. For example, if
your database will host a Recovery Catalog to be used by Recovery Manager for storing
information about backup and restore operations, you may find that your database

Role	Privileges Granted
DBA	Almost all system privileges and some roles
SELECT_CATALOG_ROLE	Object privileges on the data dictionary. No system privileges
EXECUTE_CATALOG_ROLE	Object privileges on data dictionary packages, procedures and functions
DELETE_CATALOG_ROLE	DELETE ON SYS.AUD$ DELETE ON SYS.FGA_LOG$
EXP_FULL_DATABASE	Privileges to query any table or sequence, execute any procedure or type, and modify data dictionary objects when exporting data from the database
IMP_FULL_DATABASE	Privileges to create any object in any schema in the database, except the SYS schema when performing an import
CONNECT	ALTER SESSION CREATE CLUSTER CREATE DATABASE LINK CREATE SEQUENCE CREATE SESSION CREATE SYNONYM CREATE TABLE CREATE VIEW
RESOURCE	CREATE CLUSTER CREATE INDEXTYPE CREATE OPERATOR CREATE PROCEDURE CREATE SEQUENCE CREATE TABLE CREATE TRIGGER CREATE TYPE UNLIMITED TABLESPACE (when granted)

Table 7-4 Sample List of Predefined Roles in Oracle 10g and the Permissions Granted to Them

Role	Privileges Granted
AQ_ADMINISTRATOR_ROLE	Object privileges on Advanced Queuing objects CREATE EVALUATION CONTEXT CREATE RULE CREATE RULE SET DEQUEUE ANY QUEUE ENQUEUE ANY QUEUE MANAGE ANY QUEUE
AQ_USER_ROLE	EXECUTE ON SYS.DBMS_AQ EXECUTE ON SYS.DBMS_AQIN EXECUTE ON SYS.DBMS_AQJMS_INTERNAL EXECUTE ON SYS.DBMS_TRANSFORM
SCHEDULER_ADMIN	CREATE ANY JOB CREATE JOB EXECUTE ANY CLASS EXECUTE ANY PROGRAM MANAGE SCHEDULE (All are granted WITH ADMIN OPTION)
PUBLIC	No special permissions, but when permissions are granted to PUBLIC, all users inherit those permissions

Table 7-4 Sample List of Predefined Roles in Oracle 10g and the Permissions Granted to Them *(continued)*

includes the RECOVERY_CATALOG_OWNER role. If you use Oracle Enterprise Manager, you may also have an OEM_MONITOR role created, and so on. The number of predefined roles depends on the features selected and enabled.

If you find that these roles meet your needs, then you should make use of them. However, if you find that they do not provide all the functionality required, or they give away too many privileges, like CONNECT and RESOURCE, then do not use them but create your own roles and assign them the privileges you want users to have.

 EXAM TIP The CONNECT role is automatically granted to a user when the user is created with Enterprise Manager. Be aware of the privileges this provides the user.

Creating Roles

Like most other security-related items in Oracle, you can create roles from the command line using *i*SQL*Plus or with Enterprise Manager. In order to create a role, you must have been assigned the CREATE ROLE system privilege, or the DBA role. The syntax for the CREATE ROLE command is

```
CREATE ROLE rolename
[NOT IDENTIFIED | IDENTIFIED
BY password | EXTERNALLY | GLOBALLY];
```

The name of each role must be unique in the database and cannot be the same as that of an existing user, since users and roles are both stored in the same place in the data dictionary. When you issue the CREATE ROLE command, the default is to create a role with the name specified and not require any authentication to have the role enabled for the user. However, if you want to enable the role through an application, you can specify a password for the role by using the IDENTIFIED BY clause followed by the password.

You can also have the role IDENTIFIED EXTERNALLY, which means that the user must be a member of an operating system group with a name that corresponds to the role in order for it to be enabled. In order for roles to be authenticated by the operating system, you need to set the Oracle initialization parameter OS_ROLES to TRUE (the default is FALSE). Once you have decided that you want to support roles that are IDENTIFIED EXTERNALLY, you will need to create groups on the server where the database resides with a naming convention as follows:

```
ora_<SID>_<ROLE>[_[d][a]]
```

The naming convention is used to ensure that the proper group membership can be assigned at the OS level to users that need the roles. The parts that make up the group name have these meanings:

- **<SID>** The value of the ORACLE_SID parameter for the instance to which the user will be connecting. It should ideally be the same as the name of the database. On Windows this value is not case sensitive; it is case sensitive on most other platforms.

- **<ROLE>** The name of the role you created in the database to be IDENTIFIED EXTERNALLY. In order for operating system authentication to work, the role must still be created in the database, as well as the group being created at the operating system.

- **d** Indicates that the role specified by the <ROLE> portion will be a default role for the user. If either **a** or **d**, or both, are specified, they must be preceded by an underscore.

- **a** Indicates that the role specified by the <ROLE> portion will be granted to the user WITH ADMIN OPTION. If either **a** or **d**, or both, are specified, they must be preceded by an underscore.

For example, if you create a role in the OCP10G database called JuniorAdmin that will be identified externally, and if you want that role to be the default role for some users and the default role but granted WITH ADMIN OPTION to others, you would create two groups at the OS level called "ora_OCP10G_JuniorAdmin_d" and "ora_OCP10G_JuniorAdmin_da."

Modifying Roles

Once a role is created, its authentication method can be changed after the fact using Enterprise Manager or by issuing the ALTER ROLE command:

```
ALTER ROLE rolename
[NOT IDENTIFIED | IDENTIFIED
BY password | EXTERNALLY | GLOBALLY];
```

Changes to role permissions or who it is granted to are done using the standard GRANT and REVOKE commands.

Granting and Revoking Permissions for Roles

You grant permissions to roles just as you grant them to users: using Enterprise Manager or the GRANT command. Permissions are revoked the same way as well: using the REVOKE command. The syntax for granting system permissions to roles is as follows:

```
GRANT system_priv [, system_priv, ...]
      TO role | PUBLIC [, role | PUBLIC, ...]
       [WITH ADMIN OPTION];
```

For granting object privileges to roles the syntax is as follows:

```
GRANT ALL [PRIVILEGES] | object_priv [(column, column, ...)]
      [, object_priv [(column, column, ...(] , ...]
ON [schema_name.]object_name
TO role | PUBLIC [, role | PUBLIC, ...];
```

Notice that you cannot grant object privileges WITH GRANT OPTION to roles, but you can grant system privileges WITH ADMIN OPTION.

To revoke system and object privileges from roles, the syntax is similar to revoking those same privileges from a user. For system privileges:

```
REVOKE system_priv | role_name [, system_priv | role_name, ...]
      FROM role | PUBLIC [,role | PUBLIC, ...];
```

And for object privileges:

```
REVOKE ALL [PRIVILEGES] | object_priv [, object_priv, ...]
ON [schema_name.]object_name
FROM role | PUBLIC [,role | PUBLIC, ...]
[CASCADE CONSTRAINTS]
```

Granting and Revoking Roles for Users

Once you have created a role and granted the role its further roles, along with the object and system privileges desired, you next need to assign the role to users that you want to inherit all the privileges that the role has. To do so, you use the GRANT command or Oracle Enterprise Manager. The syntax of the GRANT command to grant roles to users (as well as other roles) is

```
GRANT role_name [, role_name, ...]
      TO user_name | role | PUBLIC [, user_name | role | PUBLIC, ...]
      [WITH ADMIN OPTION];
```

If you grant a role WITH ADMIN OPTION, you are allowing the user to whom you are granting the role to also grant the role (and all its associated privileges) to others. In order to grant a role to a user or another role, you need to be the owner of the role (i.e., you are the user that issued the CREATE ROLE command) or have been granted the GRANT ANY ROLE privilege by the DBA.

Just as you can grant a role to a user, you can also revoke the role to remove all of the role's privileges from the user using the REVOKE command or Oracle Enterprise Manager. The syntax of the REVOKE command is again similar to what you have seen previously, as follows:

```
REVOKE role_name [, role_name, ...]
     FROM user_name | role | PUBLIC [, user_name | role | PUBLIC, ...];
```

If you revoke the role from a user, the role's permissions will not be immediately taken away from the user, unless the user disconnects from the instance or disables the role. However, the user will not be able to reenable the role on the next connection attempt or by using the SET ROLE command once it has been revoked.

Setting a User's Default Roles

Once you grant a role to a user, it is automatically configured to be a default role. This means that when the user connects to the instance, the role will automatically be enabled for the user and any privileges that the role has been granted will be available to the user. However, if you want some of the roles granted to the user to be active only when the user connects to the instance, you need to modify the set of default roles that are automatically enabled.

 EXAM TIP All roles granted to a user are considered the user's default roles unless otherwise specified by the ALTER USER command or Enterprise Manager.

The ALTER USER command, or Oracle Enterprise Manager, can be used to manage a user's default roles. The syntax of the ALTER USER command to manage a user's default role list is as follows:

```
ALTER USER username DEFAULT ROLE
     role [, role, ...] | ALL [EXCEPT role [, role, ...]] | NONE;
```

If you do not want Oracle to enable all roles that a user has been granted, you must use the ALTER USER command to disable any roles that you do not want the user to have when they connect to the instance. You can then programmatically enable the roles or have the user issue the SET ROLE command to enable those roles that you disabled by default.

If you grant the user a role that requires a password, and if you make that role a default role, the user will not be required to enter a password in order to make use of the privileges granted to the role. In essence, making a role that has a password a default role for the user bypasses the password requirement. In this way some users may have the role and its privileges when they connect, by default, while other users will be required to enable the role manually and specify a password in order to access the privileges granted the role.

You can also disable all roles that have been assigned to the user by using the NONE option when specifying which roles are default roles. After doing so, all roles granted to the user will be disabled and will need to be enabled using the SET ROLE command. The user will have only the capability to perform actions according to those system and object privileges that have been assigned directly to him/her, or to PUBLIC.

Enabling and Disabling Roles

One of the major benefits of roles is the ability to selectively grant and revoke a set of privileges by enabling and disabling roles that contain them. While a user is connected to the instance, your application (typically) can issue the SET ROLE command, or execute the DBMS_SESSION.SET_ROLE package procedure, to enable or disable roles dynamically. A role that was created with a password will need to have the password specified when it is enabled. This allows you to further control the enabling of roles by users by ensuring that roles are enabled only while a particular application is being used to connect to the database. The syntax for the SET ROLE command is as follows:

```
SET ROLE ALL [EXCEPT role_name [,role_name]] | NONE |
role_name [IDENTIFIED BY password] [, role_name [IDENTIFIED BY password, ...];
```

If you want to disable a role for a user, you need to issue the SET ROLE command, or execute the DBMS_SESSION.SET_ROLE procedure a second time, omitting the role that you do not want the user to have enabled. In other words, there is no "UNSET ROLE" command or its equivalent.

Dropping Roles

If you no longer need a role that you have been using, you can drop it from the database by issuing the DROP ROLE command, or by using Oracle Enterprise Manager. In order to drop a role, you must be the user who created the role, have been granted the DROP ANY ROLE system privilege, or have been granted the role WITH ADMIN OPTION. If any of these is not true, the command will fail and the role will not be dropped. The syntax of the DROP ROLE command is as follows:

```
DROP ROLE role_name;
```

When you drop a role, any user or role to which the role being dropped has been granted will have it revoked at the time the role is dropped. Any privileges that the role granted its holders will also be revoked at the time the role is dropped.

Exercise 7-4: Using Enterprise Manager to Create and Manage Roles

In this exercise you will connect to Enterprise Manager and create a role, assign it permissions, grant the role to a user, and then test the results.

1. Start a web browser and connect to the Enterprise Manager URL on your Oracle database server, specifying the appropriate port number and machine name.

2. Log in to your database as the user SYSTEM with the appropriate password. If you receive the licensing information page, click I Agree to continue.

3. On the Enterprise Manager main page, click the Administration hyperlink to display the Administration page.

4. Click the Roles hyperlink under Security to display the roles currently defined in the database and their statuses and parameters.

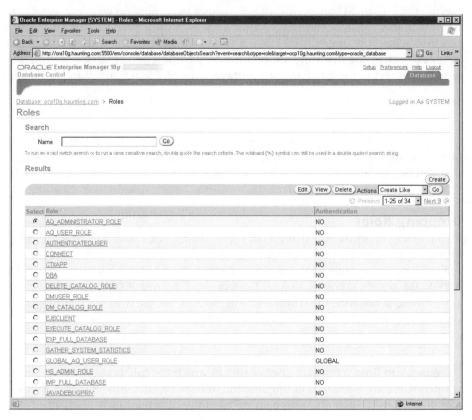

5. Click Create to display the Create Role page.

6. Enter **OCP10GROLE** as the role name and then expand the Authentication drop-down list box and select None.

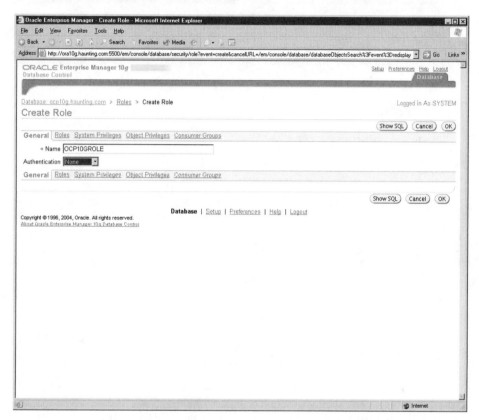

7. Click the Object Privileges hyperlink and grant the role OCP10GROLE all permissions on the JOHN.JOHN1 table.

8. Click System Privileges and grant the role OCP10GROLE the CREATE VIEW privilege.

9. Click Show SQL to display the SQL code to create the role and grant it privileges.

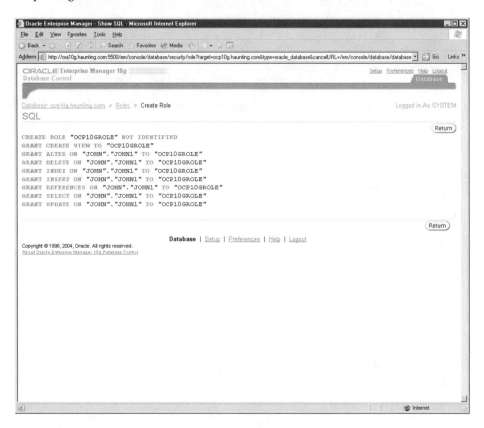

10. Click Return and then OK to create the role OCP10GROLE.

11. Click the database hyperlink at the top left of the page, then Administration, then Users, and then the user Tim.

12. Verify that Tim does not have permissions on the JOHN.JOHN1 table by invoking *i*SQL*Plus in another browser session and issue a SELECT statement to query the table.

13. In Enterprise Manager, grant Tim the role OCP10GROLE.

14. In *i*SQL*Plus, log out and then log in as Tim and verify that you can SELECT from the JOHN.JOHN1 table.

15. Exit Enterprise Manager and *i*SQL*Plus.

Using Profiles to Control Resource Usage

One aspect of the Oracle security domain deals with ensuring that password management and account lockout policies for the database are adhered to. These may be set at the enterprise level and need to be enforced at the database level. Furthermore, as a DBA, you may need to ensure that a database is available to all users and that no one user is able to invoke a SELECT statement that performs a large query and consumes all system resources, as an example. The creation and management of account lockout and password policies, as well as limiting resource usage for a user's session or an individual SQL statement, is handled in Oracle by the use of profiles.

A *profile* is an Oracle object that allows you to set both password management and resource limits. In every Oracle database a single profile is created when you create the database. This profile, called DEFAULT, places no limits on password and account lockout, or on resource utilization. You can change the settings of the DEFAULT profile to conform to your requirements, and they will then be applied to all users in the database assigned the DEFAULT profile.

A database administrator may create additional profiles dealing with password or account lockout issues, resource management settings, or both. Once created, a profile can be assigned to a user account as it is created, or it can be assigned to the user with the ALTER USER command. Any settings in the profile will then apply to the user the next time he/she connects to the database. A user may have only one profile active at one time, so you need to ensure that the settings within the profile match the requirements of each user.

When deciding to make use of profiles, it is important to understand what settings are always applied and which require that you change your database and instance configuration. Because of the very nature of security requirements, Oracle ensures that password management and account lockout settings in profiles are always enforced. Any settings dealing with security policy are considered important enough that simply configuring them enables them. The utilization of system resources, such as CPU and disk I/O, is not automatically enforced by Oracle. In order to have these aspects of a profile limit a user's actions, you need to enable them by setting them in the parameter file (SPFILE or INIT.ORA file) or by changing the value of the RESOURCE_LIMIT initialization parameter to TRUE with the ALTER SYSTEM command.

 EXAM TIP Resource limits are enforced only when the RESOURCE_LIMIT system initialization parameter is set to TRUE. It is FALSE by default.

Resource Limits Enforceable Using Profiles

Oracle profiles also allow you to limit the use of system resources by a user. The limit can be specified for the session (known as a *per session* limit) or for a single SQL statement (known as a *per call* limit). Table 7-5 lists the resource limits that can be enforced in Oracle 10g.

Setting	Description
CPU_PER_SESSION	The total CPU time, measured in hundredths of a second, that a user is allowed to consume during a session. Once the limit is reached, the user's session is terminated with an Oracle server error message. To reset this limit, the user needs to disconnect from the instance and connect again.
CPU_PER_CALL	The total CPU time, measured in hundredths of a second, that a user is allowed to consume for a single SQL statement. Once the limit is reached, the SQL statement is aborted and the transaction it is a part of is rolled back. The user's session remains connected. The limit is reset on every call to the database.
SESSIONS_PER_USER	The maximum number of concurrent sessions that a user may have at one time.
CONNECT_TIME	The maximum amount of time, specified in minutes, that a user may remain connected to the instance.
IDLE_TIME	The maximum amount of time, specified in minutes, that a user's session may remain connected to the instance while not performing any database activity.
LOGICAL_READS_PER_SESSION	The number of blocks (both physical—from disk—and logical—from the database buffer cache) that the user is allowed to read during their session. Once the number of blocks specified by this parameter are read, the user will need to start another session in order to access data in the database.
LOGICAL_READS_PER_CALL	The number of blocks (both physical—from disk—and logical—from the database buffer cache) that the user is allowed to read when executing a SQL statement. Once the number of blocks specified by this parameter are read, the SQL statement will be terminated and any transaction that it is a part of will be rolled back.
PRIVATE_SGA	In a Multi-Threaded Server (MTS) environment, this parameter specifies the maximum number of bytes that a user's session can occupy in the SGA. If you are not connected to the database instance with an MTS connection, this parameter is ignored.
COMPOSITE_LIMIT	Specifies a numerical value that is the weighed average of four resource limits: CPU_PER_SESSION CONNECT_TIME LOGICAL_READS_PER_SESSION PRIVATE_SGA Setting COMPOSITE_LIMIT will allow Oracle to monitor all four of these parameter values; when the combination of all exceeds the value specified by COMPOSITE_LIMIT, the user's session will be terminated.

Table 7-5 Profile Resource Limits

Creating, Altering, and Dropping Profiles

You can create, alter, and drop profiles using the CREATE PROFILE, ALTER PROFILE, and DROP PROFILE commands or by using Oracle Enterprise Manager. Profiles, once created, are not used until they are assigned to users. Once a profile is created, its limits can be modified and then those changes will apply to all users assigned the profile the next time the users connect to the server (i.e., the changes are not applied to any logged-on users). Dropping a profile requires that no users be assigned the profile, unless the CASCADE option is specified. If you use the CASCADE option of the DROP PROFILE command, users to whom the profile was assigned will automatically have the default profile assigned.

To create a profile, issue the CREATE PROFILE command, whose syntax is as follows when dealing with resource limits. Password limits will be discussed in Chapter 11 and are not shown here.

```
CREATE PROFILE profile_name LIMIT
      [SESSIONS_PER_USER            value]
      [CPU_PER_SESSION              value]
      [CPU_PER_CALL                 value]
      [CONNECT_TIME                 value]
      [IDLE_TIME                    value]
      [LOGICAL_READS_PER_SESSION    value]
      [LOGICAL_READS_PER_CALL       value]
      [COMPOSITE_LIMIT              value]
[PRIVATE_SGA                  bytes [K|M]]
```

You can specify the keyword UNLIMITED for any profile limit to not have any limitation imposed for that resource. Specifying the keyword DEFAULT for any limit when creating or altering a profile will assign the value of the DEFAULT profile for the resources. This way, you can have some limits specific to a profile and others at the same value for all users. If the DEFAULT profile imposes a limit, specifying DEFAULT for the profile you are creating will impose the same limit.

To modify a profile, you issue the ALTER PROFILE command, whose options are the same as the CREATE PROFILE command. As indicated earlier, any changes to the profile limits do not take effect until the next time the user to whom the profile applies logs on. Any existing user session will not be affected by the profile change.

The DROP PROFILE command deletes a profile and optionally, if the CASCADE option is specified, assigns the DEFAULT profile to any users for whom the profile was active when it was dropped. The syntax of the DROP PROFILE command is

```
DROP PROFILE profile_name [CASCADE]
```

You cannot drop the DEFAULT profile, since it must exist in the database. You also should not drop the MONITORING_PROFILE, because it is needed by Oracle to perform system monitoring functions in the database.

If you want to determine the currently configured profile values, you can query the DBA_PROFILES data dictionary view or use Enterprise Manager to display the information.

Assigning Profiles to Users

Users are assigned profiles when they are either created or altered via the command interface or Enterprise Manager. You can use the ALTER USER command at any time to assign a profile to an existing user. Only one profile is active for a user at any time, so it is not possible for a user to be assigned more than one profile. The profile limits apply each time the user connects to the instance and creates a session, and they are enforced for the duration of the session.

 EXAM TIP A user has only one profile active at any time.

To assign a profile called DBA_PROFILE to the user John, who already exists in the database, you can issue the following command:

```
ALTER USER JOHN PROFILE DBA_PROFILE
```

If you create a new user called Stephen and want to assign him the DBA_PROFILE, you can issue the following command:

```
CREATE USER STEPHEN IDENTIFIED BY ORACLE PROFILE DBA_PROFILE
```

Exercise 7-5: Using Enterprise Manager to Create and Manage Profiles

In this exercise you will connect to Enterprise Manager and create a profile, assign resource limits to it, assign the profile to a user, view profile information, and test the results.

1. Start a web browser and connect to the Enterprise Manager URL on your Oracle database server, specifying the appropriate port number and machine name.

2. Log in to your database as the user SYSTEM with the appropriate password. If you receive the licensing information page, click I Agree to continue.

3. On the Enterprise Manager main page, click the Administration hyperlink to display the Administration page.

4. Click the Profiles hyperlink under Security to display the profiles currently defined in the database. There should be two: DEFAULT and MONITORING_ PROFILE.

5. Click Create to create a new profile called DBA_PROFILE and assign it a connect time value of UNLIMITED, an idle time of 15 minutes, and a concurrent sessions value of UNLIMITED. Leave all other settings at the value of DEFAULT.

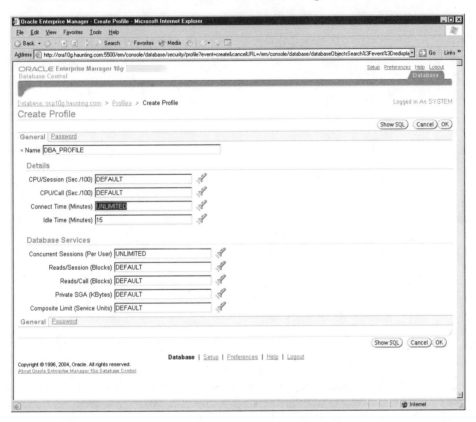

6. Click Show SQL to view the SQL code to perform the action and then click Return and then OK to create the profile.

7. On the profile list page, select DEFAULT and then click Edit. Modify the value of the default profile to specify a connect time of 600 minutes, an idle time of 30 minutes, and a concurrent sessions value of 1. Then click Apply to save your changes. Click the Profiles hyperlink to return to the list of profiles.

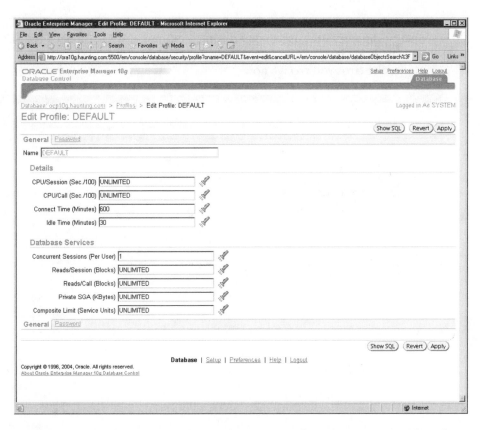

8. Open another browser window and connect to the instance using *i*SQL*Plus as the user John with the appropriate password.

9. Open another browser window and once again attempt to connect to the instance using *i*SQL*Plus as John. Notice that you do not receive an error message and John is able to connect. That is because resource limits have not been configured to be enforced on this instance. Log out of *i*SQL*Plus as John but keep the browser window open.

10. In another browser window, connect to the instance using *i*SQL*Plus as SYSTEM with the appropriate password and issue the command **ALTER SYSTEM SET RESOURCE_LIMIT=TRUE**. Attempt to log in as John for the second time. Notice the error you receive now.

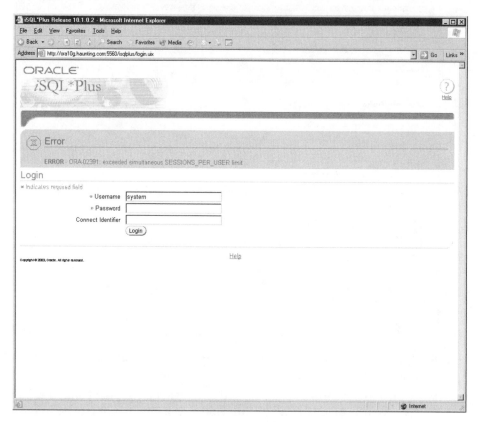

11. As user SYSTEM turn off resource limits by issuing the command **ALTER SYSTEM SET RESOURCE_LIMIT=FALSE** and close that *i*SQL*Plus session. Also log out of all other *i*SQL*Plus sessions and return to the Enterprise Manager console.

12. Navigate to the Administration page in Enterprise Manager and click Users under Security.

13. Click the user Damir and on the Edit User page select the drop-down list box next to Profile and assign Damir the DBA_PROFILE. Then click Apply. Return to the Users page and edit the user John, assigning him the DBA_PROFILE.

14. Return to the Administration page and then select Profiles under Security. Select the DBA_PROFILE and in the Actions drop-down list box select Show Dependencies. Then click Go.

15. On the Show Dependents page, click the Dependents hyperlink to see which users have been assigned the DBA_PROFILE (the objects that these users own will also be displayed as part of the dependency tree). Click OK to return to the Profiles page.

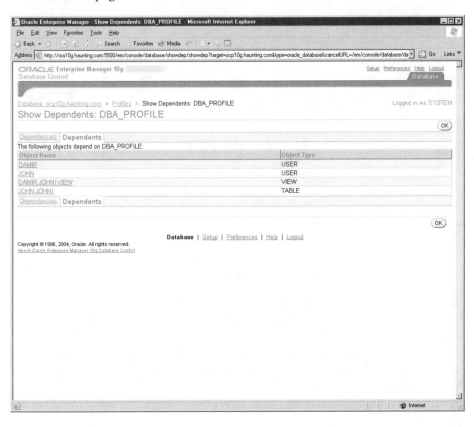

16. Select DBA_PROFILE and then click Delete. Notice the error you receive, indicating that the profile cannot be dropped, since it is assigned to users.

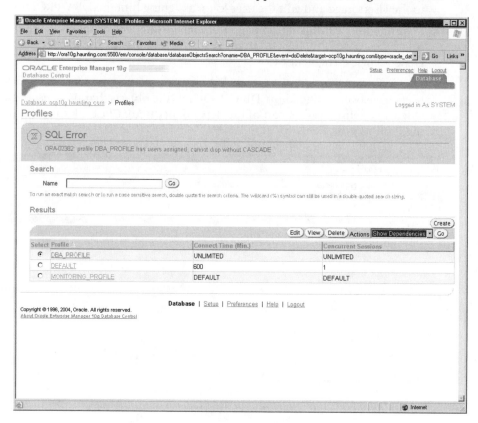

17. In another browser window, invoke *i*SQL*Plus, connect to the instance as SYSTEM, and issue the command **DROP PROFILE DBA_PROFILE CASCADE**. Then exit *i*SQL*Plus.

18. In Enterprise Manager, navigate to the Users page for Damir and John and notice that the DEFAULT profile is now assigned to the users. Exit Enterprise Manager when done.

Chapter Review

In order for an individual to access database data a user account must be created for him and appropriate privileges assigned. Database administrators can use the CREATE USER command or Enterprise Manager to create and manage user accounts and assign them privileges, a default tablespace, a temporary tablespace, quotas, and profiles. Users who have been granted permission to create objects are called "schema users," since the collection of objects they create is considered their "schema."

Two kinds of privileges exist in Oracle: system privileges, which allow you to perform an action such as create a table or drop an index, and object privileges, which allow you to manipulate objects, for instance, to SELECT from a table or EXECUTE a procedure. System privileges are granted by the DBA role and anyone who has had them granted WITH ADMIN OPTION. Object privileges are granted by the owner of the object and anyone granted those permissions WITH GRANT OPTION. Privileges can be revoked using the REVOKE command and, for object privileges only, will also be revoked from anyone the revokee granted them to.

In many environments it is preferable to create roles to hold both system and object privileges that need to be assigned to users. Permission assignment is simplified because only the role needs to be granted to a user. Any permission changes on the role automatically are changed for all users holding the role. A user may have several roles active at one time and may have other roles made active during a session using the SET ROLE command or the DBMS_SESSION.SET_ROLE package procedure.

Profiles allow a DBA to control resource usage by users when activated with the RESOURCE_LIMIT initialization parameter. A user may have only one profile active at a time, and any profile changes do not take effect until a user assigned the profile creates a new session on the instance. If a profile is dropped using the CASCADE option, the DEFAULT profile, which must exist, is assigned to all users.

Questions

1. You have created a new user called George. You have assigned George the RESTRICTED_ACCESS user profile. The profile settings have all limits configured as DEFAULT except for a concurrent sessions limit whose value is set to 1. George asks you to help with a problem, and when you arrive at his desk, you notice that he has several SQL*Plus sessions open, all of which are connected to the instance with his user account. You suspect that your profile limits are not being enforced. Which of the following should you investigate to determine the cause of the problem? (Choose two correct answers.)

   A. DBA_USER_LIMITS table

   B. RESOURCE_LIMIT initialization parameter

   C. DBA_PROFILE_LIMITS data dictionary view

   D. DBA_PROFILES data dictionary view

   E. V$LIMITS dynamic performance view

2. Which line of code will cause the following SQL statement to fail? (Choose the best answer.)

```
1       CREATE USER Sam
2       IDENTIFIED EXTERNALLY BY $amP@ssw0rd
3       DEFAULT TABLESPACE Users
4       TEMPORARY TABLESPACE User_Temp
5       QUOTA 2048MB ON APPS_DATA
```

A. 1

B. 2

C. 3

D. 4

E. 5

F. The statement will succeed

3. You have been asked to provide additional information to your manager on how system privileges can be assigned and behave. Which of the following statements about system privileges are true? (Choose all correct answers.)

A. System privileges can be granted to others if you use the WITH ADMIN OPTION.

B. System privileges can be granted to others if you use the WITH GRANT OPTION.

C. Only the DBA can grant system privileges, since the DBA owns the database.

D. System privileges can be granted only by the owner of the database.

E. When revoked for a user, system privileges will also be revoked for any user to whom that revokee granted them.

F. When revoked for a user, system privileges will not be revoked for any user to whom that revokee granted them.

4. How would a user change his active profile? (Choose the best answer.)

A. `ALTER USER SET PROFILE=NewProfile`

B. `ALTER SYSTEM SET PROFILE=NewProfile`

C. `ALTER SESSION SET PROFILE=NewProfile`

D. `ALTER DATABASE SET PROFILE=NewProfile`

E. A user cannot change his active profile

5. If you create a profile and specify limits for only some of the profile settings, what value will be automatically assigned to any resource limit you do not include in your CREATE PROFILE statement? (Choose the best answer.)

A. DEFAULT

B. 0

C. UNLIMITED

    D. UNKNOWN

    E. You must specify a value for all profile limits

6. If you do not specify a TEMPORARY TABLESPACE when creating a new user account, what will be the value of this parameter when the user is created? (Choose the best answer.)

    A. SYSTEM

    B. TEMP

    C. NULL

    D. Database default temporary tablespace

    E. You must specify a value for TEMPORARY TABLESPACE

7. Which of the following commands can a new user called Anthony issue after successfully connecting to the instance and establishing a user session? (Choose all correct answers.)

    A. `ALTER USER Anthony PASSWORD EXPIRE;`

    B. `ALTER USER Anthony QUOTA 2M ON SYSTEM;`

    C. `ALTER USER Anthony ACCOUNT LOCK;`

    D. `ALTER USER Anthony TEMPORARY TABLESPACE TEMP;`

    E. `ALTER USER Anthony IDENTIFIED BY NEWPASS;`

8. While passing by Benjamin's desk, you notice that he is using SQL*Plus to query data in your TempOrders table. You did not grant Benjamin privileges to issue SELECT statements against your TempOrders table. Why is Benjamin able to query your table? (Choose all correct answers.)

    A. A user to whom you granted the SELECT privilege on the table also granted it to Benjamin.

    B. Benjamin is a DBA and can query any table in the database.

    C. You granted Benjamin the UPDATE privilege on the TempOrders table, which automatically grants the SELECT privilege.

    D. Benjamin has been granted the SELECT ANY TABLE privilege by the DBA.

    E. Benjamin has been granted the SELECT privilege on your TempOrders table by a user to whom you granted the SELECT privilege WITH ADMIN OPTION.

9. Which of the following statements will fail when granting privileges to the role QueryRole? (Choose the best answer.)

    A. `GRANT CONNECT TO QueryRole;`

    B. `GRANT CONNECT TO QueryRole WITH ADMIN OPTION;`

    C. `GRANT SELECT ON Orders TO QueryRole;`

    D. `GRANT SELECT ON Orders TO QueryRole WITH GRANT OPTION;`

    E. `GRANT DBA TO QueryRole WITH ADMIN OPTION;`

10. When creating a user using Enterprise Manager instead of the CREATE USER statement, which additional privileges are granted to the user? (Choose the best answer.)

    A. SELECT_CATALOG_ROLE

    B. SYSDBA

    C. CONNECT

    D. RESOURCE

    E. DBA

Answers

1. **B and D.** You can query the DBA_PROFILES data dictionary view to determine the settings of all profiles in the database, including the one George is supposed to have assigned to him. The RESOURCE_LIMIT initialization parameter must be set to TRUE for the concurrent sessions limit to be enforced, so you need to verify this setting in the running instance and in the SPFILE. DBA_USER_LIMITS, DBA_PROFILE_LIMITS, and V$LIMITS views do not exist.

2. **B.** When you create a user, you can specify at most one authentication method. This SQL statement specified both EXTERNALLY and password (BY $amP@ssw0rd) authentication at the same time, which would generate an error when the command was executed.

3. **A and F.** If you have been granted a system privilege WITH ADMIN OPTION, you can also grant the same privilege to others and specify the WITH ADMIN OPTION. The WITH GRANT OPTION applies to object privileges and not system privileges. If system privileges are revoked for a user to whom they were granted WITH ADMIN OPTION, they will not be revoked for other users to whom the revoke granted them; there are no cascading revokes for system privileges. The DBA is a role and is not the only one that can grant system privileges, and neither is the user SYS (the database owner), in that anyone holding the DBA role can grant them, since the DBA role has system privileges granted to it WITH ADMIN OPTION.

4. **E.** A user cannot himself change his active profile. Only the DBA can modify a user's profile or the profile limits.

5. **A.** If you do not specify a value for a limit in your profile, it will automatically be assigned the value of DEFAULT. This means that Oracle will enforce whatever value exists for the limit in the DEFAULT profile.

6. **D.** The currently defined database default temporary tablespace will be assigned to the user if you do not specify a TEMPORARY TABLESPACE for the user. If no database default temporary tablespace is defined, the user will be assigned SYSTEM as the temporary tablespace.

7. **E.** Anthony, like any new user who has been configured with password authentication, has the ability to change his password at any time. No other changes to the user account are allowed to be performed by the user himself.

8. **B and D.** Benjamin can query your TempOrders table only if he is a DBA, who automatically has the SELECT ANY TABLE privilege, or if Benjamin has been granted the SELECT ANY TABLE privilege by the DBA. Another user to whom you only granted the SELECT privilege could not grant it to Benjamin unless you specified the WITH GRANT OPTION. Granting the UPDATE privilege on the table does not automatically grant the SELECT privilege.

9. **D.** It is not possible to grant object privileges to roles WITH GRANT OPTION, so this statement will fail. All other statements will succeed, assuming you have the privileges required to perform the operation.

10. **C.** Using Enterprise Manager to create a user will automatically grant the user the CONNECT role, which includes the CREATE SESSION privilege, so the user is able to connect to the instance right away. This role also includes the privileges to create tables, views, synonyms, sequences, and other database objects, which may or may not be desired for all users.

CHAPTER 8

Managing Database Objects

In this chapter you will learn how to
- Create and modify tables
- Define constraints
- View the attributes of a table
- View the contents of a table
- Create indexes and views
- Name database objects
- Select appropriate datatypes
- Create and use sequences

In a typical database, the greater part of the data is stored in tables. This chapter covers the syntax for creating tables with columns of various datatypes, and also creating some associated objects: the constraints that guarantee that the rows inserted into tables conform to certain business rules; the indexes that enhance the performance of retrieving rows from tables; and the views that can conceal the underlying table structures from end users. Finally, you will see how to create sequences: data structures that can deliver numbers that are guaranteed to be unique.

All these objects are stored in schemas: a schema is associated with a user—create a user, and a schema is automatically created.

Bear in mind that the topics covered in this chapter are very large, and that this is only a superficial introduction.

Users, Schemas, and Schema Objects

A user is a person, uniquely identified by username, who exists within the database. Chapter 7 covered the techniques for creating users and giving them the privileges that allow them to connect to the database, and then create and use objects. When a user is created, a schema is created too. A schema consists of the objects owned by a user; initially, it will be empty. As far as SQL is concerned, a schema is nothing more than a container for tables, views, code, and other database elements.

Users and Schemas

Some schemas will always be empty: the user will never create any objects, because he does not need to and (if he is set up correctly) will not have the necessary privileges anyway. Users such as this will have been granted permissions, either through direct privileges or through roles, to use code and access data in other schemas, owned by other users. Other users may be the reverse of this: they will own many objects but will never actually log on to the database. They need not even have been granted the CREATE SESSION privilege, so the account is effectively disabled (or indeed it can be locked); these schemas are used as repositories for code and data, accessed by others.

Schema objects are objects with an owner. The unique identifier for an object of a particular type is not its name; it is its name, prefixed with the name of the schema to which it belongs. Thus the table HR.REGIONS is a table called REGIONS that is owned by user HR. There could be another table SYSTEM.REGIONS that would be a completely different table (perhaps different in both structure and contents) owned by user SYSTEM and residing in his schema.

A number of users (and their associated schemas) are created automatically at database creation time. Principal among these are SYS and SYSTEM. User SYS owns the data dictionary: a set of tables (in the SYS schema) that define the database and its contents. SYS also owns several hundred PL/SQL packages: code that is provided for the use of the Oracle kernel, database administrators, and developers. Objects in the SYS schema should never be modified with DML commands. If you were to execute DML against the data dictionary tables, you would run the risk of corrupting the data dictionary, with disastrous results. You update the data dictionary by running DDL commands (such as CREATE TABLE), which provide a layer of abstraction between you and the data dictionary itself. The SYSTEM schema stores various additional objects used for administration and monitoring.

Depending on the options selected during database creation, there may be more users created, perhaps up to thirty in total. These users are used for storing the code and data required by various options. For example, the user MDSYS stores the objects used by Oracle Spatial, an option that extends the capabilities of the Oracle database to manage geographical information.

Naming Schema Objects

A *schema* object is an object that is owned by a user. The database will also contain non-schema objects: these may be objects that have nothing to do with users, such as tablespaces, or in some cases they are objects owned by SYS and directly accessible by all users; examples of the latter include public synonyms and public database links that can be used by all users regardless of privileges.

To view schema objects through database control, take the appropriate link for the type of object of interest from the Schema section in the Administration window, as in Figure 8-1, and you will be prompted for various search criteria.

All schema object names must conform to certain rules:

- The name may be from one to thirty characters long, with the exception of database link names, which may be up to 128 characters long.

- Reserved words (such as SELECT) cannot be used as object names.

- All names must begin with a letter from A through Z.

- Names can only use letters, numbers, the underscore (_), the dollar sign ($), or the hash symbol (#).

- Lowercase letters will be converted to uppercase.

By enclosing the name within double quotes, all these rules (with the exception of the length) can be broken, but to get to the object subsequently, it must always be specified with double quotes, as in the examples in Figure 8-2. Note that the same restrictions apply to column names.

Although tools such as SQL*Plus will automatically convert lowercase letters to uppercase, unless the name is enclosed within double quotes, remember that object names are always case sensitive. In this example, the two tables are completely different:

```
ocp10g> create table lower(c1 date);
Table created.
ocp10g> create table "lower"(col1 varchar(2));
Table created.
ocp10g> select table_name from dba_tables where
  2  lower(table_name) = 'lower';
TABLE_NAME
------------------------------
lower
LOWER
```

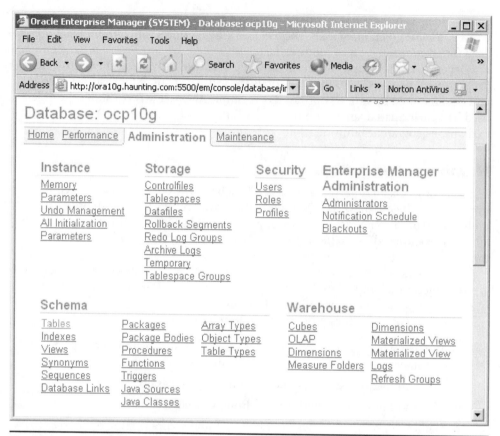

Figure 8-1 Schema objects manageable with Database Control

 TIP While it is possible to use lowercase names and nonstandard characters (even spaces), it is considered bad practice, because of the confusion it can cause.

Object Namespaces

It is often said that the unique identifier for an object is the object name, prefixed with the schema name. While this is generally true, for a full understanding of naming it is necessary to introduce the concept of a namespace. A *namespace* defines a group of object types, within which all names must be uniquely identified—by schema and name. Objects in different namespaces can share the same name.

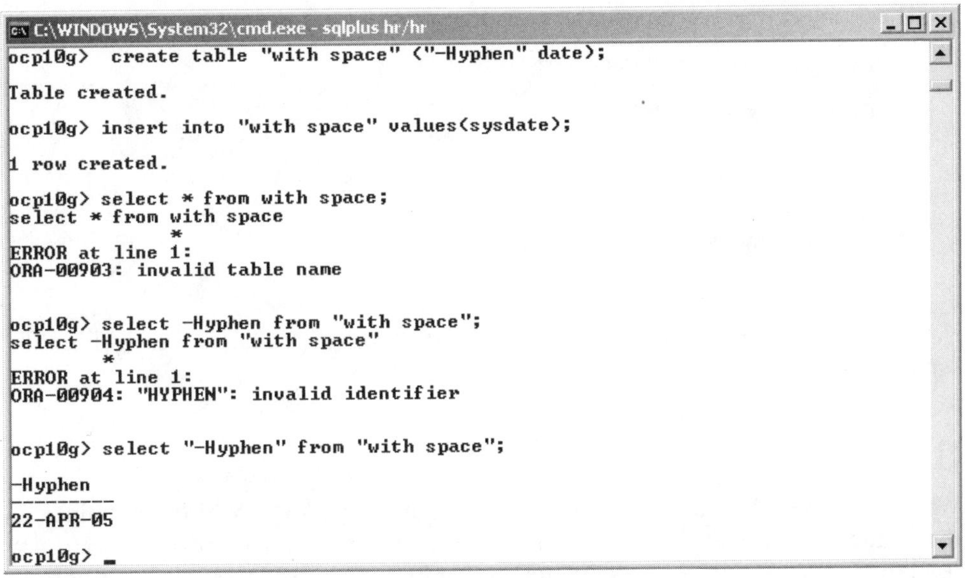

```
C:\WINDOWS\System32\cmd.exe - sqlplus hr/hr                         _ □ ×
ocp10g>  create table "with space" ("-Hyphen" date);

Table created.

ocp10g> insert into "with space" values(sysdate);

1 row created.

ocp10g> select * from with space;
select * from with space
             *
ERROR at line 1:
ORA-00903: invalid table name


ocp10g> select -Hyphen from "with space";
select -Hyphen from "with space"
       *
ERROR at line 1:
ORA-00904: "HYPHEN": invalid identifier


ocp10g> select "-Hyphen" from "with space";

-Hyphen
---------
22-APR-05

ocp10g> _
```

Figure 8-2   Using double quotes to use nonstandard names

These object types all share the same namespace:

- Tables
- Views
- Sequences
- Private synonyms
- Stand-alone procedures
- Stand-alone stored functions
- Packages
- Materialized views
- User-defined types

Thus it is impossible to create a view with the same name as a table; at least, it is impossible if they are in the same schema. And once created, SQL statements can address a view as though it were a table. The fact that tables, views, and private synonyms share the same namespace means that you can set up several layers of abstraction between what the users see and the actual tables, which can be invaluable for both security and for simplifying application development.

These object types each have their own namespace:

- Indexes
- Constraints
- Clusters
- Database triggers
- Private database links
- Dimensions

Thus it is possible for an index to have the same name as a table, even within the same schema.

Datatypes

When creating tables, each column must be assigned a datatype, which determines the nature of the values that can be inserted into the column. These datatypes are also used to specify the nature of the arguments for PL/SQL procedures and functions. When selecting a datatype, you must consider the data that you need to store and the operations you will want to perform upon it. It may be possible to change a column to a different datatype after creation, but this is not always easy. Space is also a consideration: some datatypes are fixed length, taking up the same number of bytes no matter what data is actually in them; others are variable. If a column is not populated, then Oracle will not give it any space at all; if you later update the row to populate the column, then the row will get bigger, no matter whether the datatype is fixed length or variable. Tables 8-1 through 8-4 describe the various internal datatypes, grouped by character data, numeric data, date-time data, and large objects.

Datatype	Description
VARCHAR2	Variable-length character data from 1 byte to 4KB. The data is stored in the database character set.
NVARCHAR2	As VARCHAR2, but the data is stored in the alternative national language character set: one of the permitted Unicode character sets.
CHAR	Fixed-length data in the database character set. If the data is not the length of the column, then it will be padded with spaces.
RAW	Variable-length binary data from 1 byte to 2KB. Unlike the CHAR and VARCHAR datatypes, RAW data is not converted by Oracle Net from the database's character set to the user process's character set on select or the other way on insert.

Table 8-1   Datatypes for Alphanumeric Data

Datatype	Description
NUMBER	Numeric data for which you can specify precision and scale. The precision can range from 1 to 38, and the scale can range from –84 to 127.
FLOAT	This is an ANSI datatype, for floating-point numbers with precision of 126 binary (or 38 decimal). Oracle also provides BINARY_FLOAT and BINARY_DOUBLE as alternatives.
INTEGER	Equivalent to NUMBER, with scale zero.

Table 8-2   Datatypes for Numeric Data, All Variable Length

TIP   For ISO/ANSI compliance, you can specify a VARCHAR datatype, but any columns of this type will be automatically converted to VARCHAR2.

Oracle provides a range of type-casting functions for converting between datatypes, and in some circumstances it will do automatic type casting. Figure 8-3 illustrates both techniques.

Datatype	Description
DATE	This is either length zero, if the column is empty, or 7 bytes. All DATE data includes century, year, month, day, hour, minute, and second. The valid range is from January 1, 4712 B.C. to December 31, 9999 A.D.
TIMESTAMP	This is length zero if the column is empty, or up to 11 bytes depending on the precision specified. Similar to DATE, but with precision of up to nine decimal places for the seconds, six places by default.
TIMESTAMP WITH TIMEZONE	As TIMESTAMP, but the data is stored with a record kept of the time zone to which it refers. The length may be up to 13 bytes depending on precision. This datatype lets Oracle determine the difference between two times by normalizing them to UTC, even if the times are for different time zones.
TIMESTAMP WITH LOCAL TIMEZONE	As TIMESTAMP, but the data is normalized to the database time zone on saving. When retrieved, it is normalized to the time zone of the user process selecting it.
INTERVAL YEAR TO MONTH	Used for recording a period in years and months between two DATEs or TIMESTAMPs.
INTERVAL DAY TO SECOND	Used for recording a period in days and seconds between two DATEs or TIMESTAMPs.

Table 8-3   Datatypes for Date and Time Data, All Fixed Length

Datatype	Description
CLOB	Character data stored in the database character set, size effectively unlimited: 4GB multiplied by the database block size.
NCLOB	As CLOB, but the data is stored in the alternative national language character set: one of the permitted Unicode character sets.
BLOB	As CLOB, but binary data that will not undergo character set conversion by Oracle Net.
BFILE	A locator pointing to a file stored on the operating system of the database server. The size of the files is limited to 4GB.
LONG	Character data in the database character set, up to 2GB. All the functionality of LONG (and more) is provided by CLOB; LONGs should not be used in a modern database, and if your database has any columns of this type, they should be converted to CLOB.
LONG RAW	As LONG, but binary data that will not be converted by Oracle Net. Any LONG RAW columns should be converted to BLOBs.

Table 8-4 Large Object Datatypes

In the example shown in the figure, the first insert uses type-casting functions to convert the character data entered to the datatypes specified for the table columns. The second insert attempts to insert character strings into all three columns, but the

```
Oracle SQL*Plus                                                         _ □ ×
File  Edit  Search  Options  Help
ocp10g> create table typecast(datecol date,numcol number,vcharcol varchar2(20));

Table created.

ocp10g> alter session set nls_date_format='dd-mm-yy';

Session altered.

ocp10g> insert into typecast values
  2  (to_date('23-04-05'),to_number('1000'),'done correctly');

1 row created.

ocp10g> insert into typecast values('24-04-05','1000','automatic casting');

1 row created.

ocp10g> select * from typecast;

DATECOL       NUMCOL UCHARCOL
--------   ---------- --------------------
23-04-05         1000 done correctly
24-04-05         1000 automatic casting

ocp10g> |
```

Figure 8-3 Use of type-casting functions and automatic type casting

insert still succeeds because Oracle can convert datatypes automatically if necessary, and if the format of the data is suitable.

 TIP Do not rely on automatic type casting. It can impact on performance and may not always work. The Oracle environment is strongly typed, and your programmers should respect this.

Creating Tables

The syntax for creating a table requires giving the table a name (which must be unique within the schema to which the table belongs) and specifying one or more columns, each with a datatype. It is also possible to specify constraints when creating a table; alternatively, constraints can be added later. There are many examples in this book of creating tables from the SQL*Plus command line (there have already been two examples in this chapter!) but it can also be done through Database Control. Database Control provides a fully functional menu-driven interface for creating and editing table structures, and also for managing the constraints, indexes, and views that will be based on the tables.

The CREATE TABLE command can be quite complex (when you look it up in the "SQL Reference" volume of the Documentation Library, you will see that it takes up 72 pages) and includes a vast range of options for specifying physical and logical attributes. Most of the examples given in this book are very simple; this is a little more complicated:

```
ocp10g> create table emp
   2   (empno number(6)
   3   constraint emp_empno_pk primary key
   4   using index
   5   create index emp_empno_pk on emp(empno) tablespace idx_ts),
   6   firstname varchar2(20),
   7   lastname varchar2(25)
   8   constraint emp_last_name_nn not null,
   9   hire_date date default sysdate,
  10   salary number(8,2),
  11   managerid number(6)
  12   constraint emp_managerid_fk references emp(empno),
  13   deptno number(4)
  14   constraint emp_deptno_fk references dept(deptno),
  15   photo blob,
  16   resume clob,
  17   email varchar2(25),
  18   constraint emp_salary_min check (salary >= 0),
  19   constraint emp_email_uk unique (email))
  20   lob (photo, resume) store as
  21   (tablespace example chunk 4096);
Table created.
```

Lines 2, 3, 4, and 5 define a numeric column EMPNO, which is to be used as a primary key. Rather than letting Oracle create the primary key index using its defaults, the USING INDEX clause can specify a full index creation command.

Lines 7 and 8 demonstrate creating a NOT NULL constraint.

Line 9 creates a column with a default value to be applied at insert time, if the column is not populated by the INSERT statement.

Line 10 creates a numeric column with a precision of two decimal places.

Lines 11 and 12 create a column with a self-referencing foreign key constraint: each employee must have a valid manager, who is also an employee. Constraints of this nature can impact on the order in which rows can be inserted. Lines 13 and 14 create a foreign key constraint to a different table.

Lines 15 and 16 create two large object columns.

Lines 18 and 19 demonstrate creating constraints on columns defined earlier. The UNIQUE constraint will force the creation of an index, using defaults.

Finally, lines 20 and 21 specify some storage options for the large objects.

To reach the table management window of Database Control, from the database home page take the Administration tab, then the Tables link in the Schema section. Enter whatever search criteria are needed to locate the table of interest, and then open the Actions drop-down box to see what possibilities are available, as in Figure 8-4.

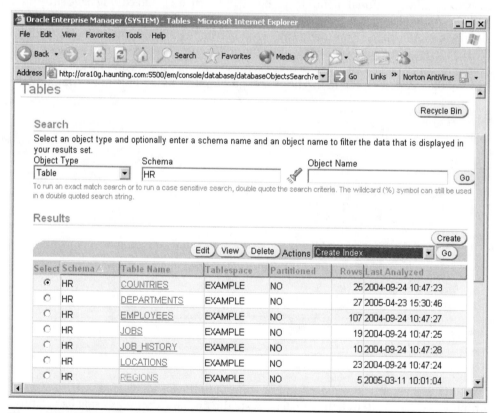

Figure 8-4   The Database Control Tables window

These are the actions:

- **CREATE LIKE**   Create a new table based on the same structure as the selected table.
- **CREATE INDEX**   Define and generate an index on the table.
- **CREATE SYNONYM**   Create a logical name, or alias, that can be used as a pseudonym for the table.
- **CREATE TRIGGER**   Create a block of PL/SQL code that will run automatically whenever DML is executed against the table.
- **GATHER STATISTICS**   Analyze the contents of the table, to gather statistics to be used by the optimizer to work out how best to access the table.
- **GENERATE DDL**   Reverse-engineer the table's structure, to generate a CREATE TABLE statement that could be used to re-create the table.
- **GRANT PRIVILEGES**   Give users permission to read or alter the data in the table.
- **REORGANIZE**   Run a wizard to go through the process of reorganizing the data in a table to move the table, or to change its structure.
- **RUN SEGMENT ADVISOR**   Use the advisor to generate a recommendation for whether the table should be shrunk.
- **SHRINK SEGMENT**   Use the online reorganization tool to reclaim wasted space from a segment.
- **SHOW DEPENDENCIES**   Display all the objects that are in some way related to the table and could therefore be affected by any action on the table.
- **VIEW DATA**   Run a wizard to assist with querying and displaying the contents of the table.
- **FLASHBACK TABLE**   Reverse all DML operations against the table, in reverse chronological order, to take the table back to a previous state.
- **FLASHBACK BY ROW VERSIONS**   Query historical data, to display previous versions of rows.

Creating Constraints

Table constraints are a means by which the database can enforce business rules and guarantee that the data conforms to the entity-relationship model determined by the system's analysis that defines the application data structures. For example, the business analysts of your organization may have decided that every customer and every invoice must be uniquely identifiable by number; that no invoices can be issued to a customer before he has been inserted; and that every invoice must have a valid date and a value greater than zero. These would be implemented by creating primary key constraints on the CUSTOMER_NUMBER column of the CUSTOMERS table and the INVOICE_NUMBER column of the INVOICES table, a foreign key constraint on the INVOICES table referencing the CUSTOMERS table, a not-null constraint on the INVOICE_DATE column of the INVOICES table (the DATE datatype will itself ensure that any dates are valid automatically—it will not accept invalid dates), and a check constraint on the AMOUNT column on the INVOICES table.

If any DML is executed against a table with constraints defined, if the DML violates a constraint then the whole statement will be rolled back automatically. If the statement is part of a multistatement transaction, then the statements that have already succeeded will remain intact, but uncommitted.

These constraints are supported by Oracle:

- **UNIQUE**   No two rows can have the same value for a UNIQUE column. However, NULL values are permitted; indeed, multiple rows can have NULL values.

- **NOT NULL**   The column must have a value.

- **PRIMARY KEY**   The primary key is the means of locating a row: the value must be both UNIQUE and NOT NULL.

- **CHECK**   A CHECK constraint can be used to enforce simple rules, such as ranges of values. The internal implementation of NOT NULL is in fact a preconfigured CHECK constraint.

Exercise 8-1: Creating Tables and Constraints

Use Database Control to create two tables with constraints, and validate the structures with SQL*Plus.

1. Connect to your database as user SYSTEM using Database Control.

2. From the database home page, take the Administration tab, and then the Tables link in the Schema section. Click Create.

3. On the Create Table: Table Organization window, select the Standard, Heap Organized radio button, and click Continue.

4. On the Create Table window, enter the name **CUSTOMERS**, and define two columns, as in Figure 8-5.

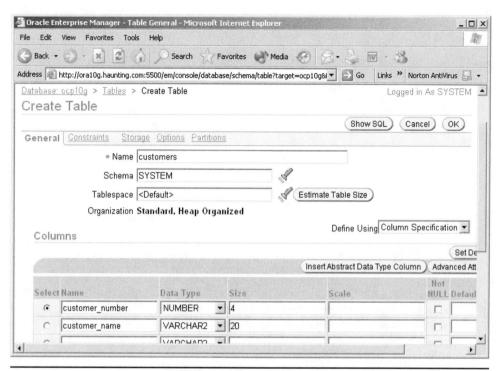

Figure 8-5 Creating the CUSTOMERS table

5. Create a second table, INVOICES, as in Figure 8-6. Note that the Not Null check box has been selected for the INVOICE_DATE column.

6. To add a primary key constraint to the CUSTOMERS table, navigate to the Tables window as in Step 2, and search for the table called CUSTOMERS. Select it, and click Edit. Select the Constraints tab.

7. Select PRIMARY from the drop-down box, and click Add.

8. Choose CUSTOMER_NUMBER as the column on which to base the constraint, leave all other options on default, and click OK, as in Figure 8-7. Click Apply to create the constraint.

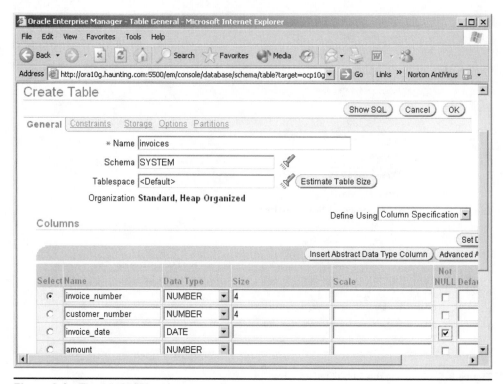

Figure 8-6 The INVOICES table

9. Repeat the process to add a primary key constraint to the INVOICES table, using the INVOICE_NUMBER column.

10. To add the foreign key constraint connecting INVOICES to CUSTOMERS, fill in the Add FOREIGN Constraint window as in Figure 8-8. Click Apply to create the constraint.

11. To add the check constraint ensuring that the AMOUNT is greater than zero, fill in the Add CHECK Constraint window as in Figure 8-9. Click OK and Apply.

12. Connect to your database as user SYSTEM with SQL*Plus.

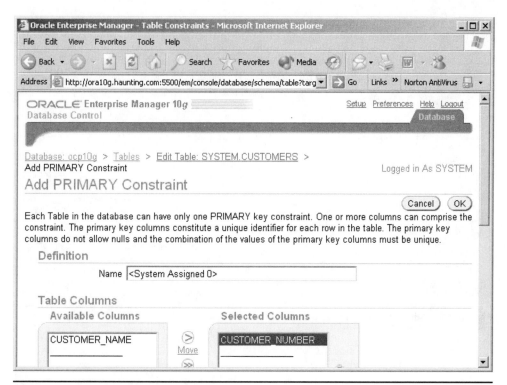

Figure 8-7 Adding a primary key constraint

13. Insert some valid data as follows:

```
insert into customers values(1,'John');
insert into customers values(2,'Damir');
insert into invoices values(10,1,sysdate,100);
insert into invoices values(11,2,sysdate,200);
commit;
```

14. Demonstrate the effectiveness of the constraints by attempting to insert some data that violates them, such as

```
ocp10g> insert into customers values(1,'McGraw');
ocp10g> insert into invoices values (30,3,sysdate,50);
ocp10g> insert into invoices values(10,1,sysdate,0);
```

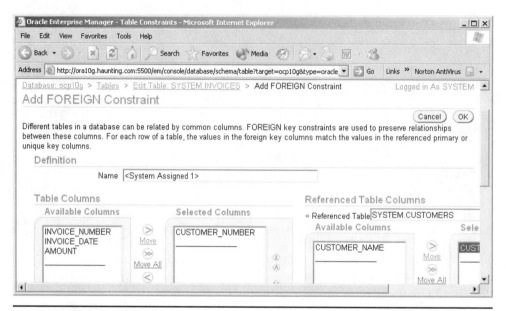

Figure 8-8   Adding a foreign key constraint

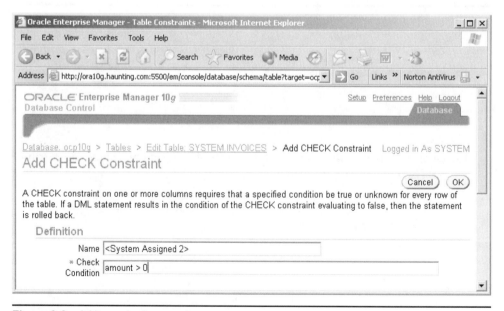

Figure 8-9   Adding a check constraint

Creating Indexes

Indexes have a dual purpose: to enhance the performance of retrieving rows, and to enforce constraints. When you define a unique or primary key constraint on a column (or on a number of columns), Oracle will check whether an index already exists on the column(s), and if it does not, an index will be created for you.

Indexes can be based on one column, on several columns, or on functions applied to columns: there are no restrictions regarding datatype or column order. A table can have any number of indexes, and they are maintained automatically to keep them synchronized with the table.

When deciding on your indexing strategy, you must consider the nature of access to the data. As a general rule, indexes will improve performance of retrieving individual rows but will tend to reduce the performance of executing DML against them. So indexes will help SELECT statements but hinder INSERT statements. They will assist with finding rows to be updated or deleted but will work against the efficiency of actually doing the UPDATE or DELETE. It is not necessary for programmers to know the name of an index, or even that it exists. For all retrieval operations, the Oracle optimizer will make an intelligent decision about whether or not to use any available indexes, but for DML it has no choice: indexes must always be maintained.

To create an index from the command line, use the CREATE INDEX command.

For example, to index the CUSTOMER_NAME column of the CUSTOMERS table used in the previous exercise, you could use this command:

```
ocp10g> create index name_idx on customers(customer_name);
```

Alternatively, it can be done through Database Control as in Figure 8-10.

To see what indexes exist on a table, query the DBA_INDEXES data dictionary view:

```
ocp10g> select index_name from dba_indexes where owner='SYSTEM'
  2  and table_name='CUSTOMERS';
INDEX_NAME
------------------------------
NAME_IDX
SYS_C0010004
```

The first index listed is that created on the CUSTOMER_NAME column. The second, SYS_C0010004, is the index created automatically by Oracle when the primary key constraint on the CUSTOMER_NUMBER column was defined. Primary key constraints require an index, and if one does not exist, one is created for you, with a system-generated name.

TIP System-generated names are cryptic; therefore, DBAs typically provide descriptive names, which help during the investigation of constraint violations and other error conditions.

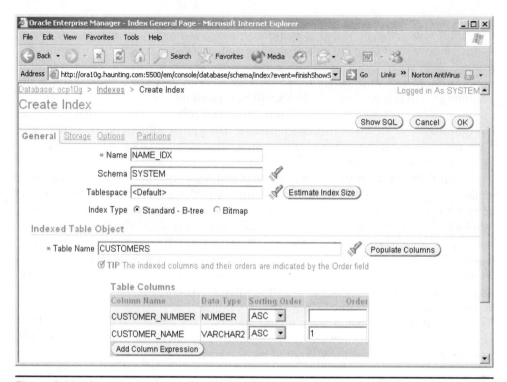

Figure 8-10   Creating an index on the CUSTOMER_NAME column

Creating Views

A *view* is a means of presenting data to your users. Rather than having your programmers address actual tables, they can address views instead. This can shield them from the complexities of the underlying data structures and can also be used for security: the views can conceal certain rows or columns. The tables on which a view is based are referred to as either the "detail" tables or the "base" tables.

A view is in fact a query—a SELECT statement stored within the data dictionary. Whenever a user addresses a view, using the same syntax as to address a table, the query runs to generate a result set, and the user's statement executes against this set. Note that there are no performance benefits. In order to simplify data access, a view might join many tables and perform aggregations or sorts to produce a simple result set; this will take some time, and it must be done every time the view is queried.

Whether or not DML statements can be executed against a view depends on how complicated is the query on which the view is based.

For example, a simple view defined by a query against just one detail table can be used for DML:

```
ocp10g> create view emp_30 as
  2  select * from employees where department_id=30;
View created.
ocp10g> select first_name,last_name from emp_30;
FIRST_NAME           LAST_NAME
-------------------- -------------------------
Den                  Raphaely
Alexander            Khoo
Shelli               Baida
3 rows selected.
ocp10g> delete from emp_30 where last_name='Raphaely';
1 row deleted.
```

A more complex view cannot support DML, as is the case with this example, which joins two tables and performs an aggregation:

```
ocp10g> create view dept_sal as
  2  select department_name,sum(salary) tot_sal from departments
  3  join employees using(department_id) group by department_name;
View created.
ocp10g> select * from dept_sal;
DEPARTMENT_NAME                  TOT_SAL
------------------------------ ----------
Accounting                        20300
Administration                     4400
Purchasing                        13900
Sales                            304500
Shipping                         156400
5 rows selected.
ocp10g> update dept_sal set tot_sal=tot_sal*1.1;
update dept_sal set tot_sal=tot_sal*1.1
      *
ERROR at line 1:
ORA-01732: data manipulation operation not legal on this view
```

 TIP By creating INSTEAD OF triggers on views, your programmers can convert unexecutable DML commands against complex views into executable DML against the detail tables.

Views can also be created and edited through Database Control, as in Figure 8-11.

Views can be created from detail tables in any schemas, providing that the owner of the view has been granted privileges to see the tables. Then the owner of the view can grant other users permission to see the view. This establishes a layer of abstraction between users and the tables that is useful for security: users can only ever get to data through views, and need not be given permissions against the tables themselves.

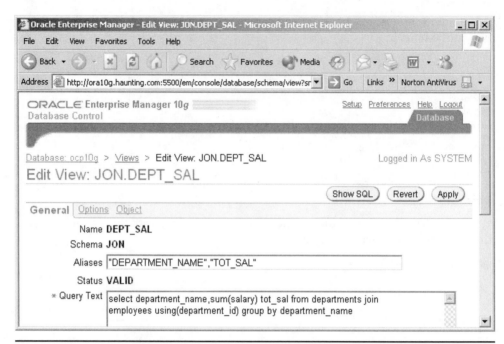

Figure 8-11　Editing the DEPT_SAL view with Database Control

Creating and Using Sequences

There are many cases in a typical database system where unique numbers are required. Typically, this is for primary key values. For instance, the business analysts of a sales organization may have decided that every invoice issued must have a unique invoice number. Relying on the data entry staff to supply unique numbers is impractical, so the database must generate them instead. A sequence is defined with a starting point and an increment, both defaulting to one.

To read a value from the sequence (which will cause it to increment, ready for the next usage—either by the same session or any other session), use the NEXTVAL pseudo-column:

```
ocp10g> create sequence inv_nos start with 1 increment by 1;
Sequence created.
ocp10g> select inv_nos.nextval from dual;
   NEXTVAL
----------
         1
ocp10g> select inv_nos.nextval from dual;
   NEXTVAL
----------
         2
```

Selecting the NEXTVAL from a sequence will increment it automatically; there is no way to roll back this increment, and it is immediately visible to all other sessions that may be selecting from the same sequence. This means that there will be gaps in the sequence of numbers used.

TIP You can increase the performance of sequences by using the CACHE clause when you create them, but this can result in more gaps. This is of no significance to the database, but some auditors get upset about gaps in sequences.

Exercise 8-2: Using Constraints, Views, and Sequences

Create a sequence to generate unique invoice numbers, and create a view to join your INVOICES and CUSTOMERS tables.

1. Connect to your database as user SYSTEM using SQL*Plus.

2. Create a sequence. Since the previous exercise issued invoice numbers 10 and 11, start the sequence at 12.

```
ocp10g> create sequence inv_nos start with 12;
```

3. Use the sequence to enter new invoices, with unique numbers.

```
ocp10g> insert into invoices values (inv_nos.nextval,1,sysdate,150);
ocp10g> insert into invoices values (inv_nos.nextval,2,sysdate,250);
```

4. Create a view to display invoices with the customers' names, and select from it.

```
ocp10g> create view cust_inv as
  2  select invoice_number,customer_name,amount from
  3  invoices join customers using (customer_number);
View created.
ocp10g> select * from cust_inv;
INVOICE_NUMBER CUSTOMER_NAME               AMOUNT
-------------- -------------------- ----------
            10 John                        100
            11 Damir                       200
            12 John                        150
            13 Damir                       250
```

5. Tidy up.

```
ocp10g> drop table invoices;
ocp10g> drop table customers;
ocp10g> drop view cust_inv;
ocp10g> drop sequence inv_nos;
```

Note that there is no need to drop any constraints or indexes: they are dropped automatically along with the tables.

Chapter Review

This chapter has introduced tables, along with the commonly used associated objects: constraints, indexes, and views. Also shown were sequences, typically used for generating unique values for inserts into primary key–constrained columns. All these objects are "schema" objects, meaning that they must belong to a user; they cannot exist independently. A schema object must have a unique name within its namespace and schema; some objects, such as indexes, have their own namespace; others, such as tables and views, share a namespace.

Tables are defined with one or more columns, which can be any of Oracle's supported internal datatypes. Oracle is a strongly typed environment, and datatypes must match; however, in some circumstances Oracle can do automatic type casting to avoid errors when users attempt, for example, to insert a numeric value into a character column.

Constraints are defined on tables to enforce business rules. Unique and primary key constraints are enforced through the use of indexes: if an index does not exist on the constrained column(s), one will be created for you. You can also create additional indexes to enhance performance.

In many cases, the table structure within a database may be overly complex. Views can conceal these complexities by presenting the data in a simplified form. Some views can be treated exactly as though they were tables; others can only be selected from, DML being impossible. Views are also invaluable for security: users can be granted permissions against views, without being granted permissions against their detail (or "base") tables.

Questions

1. Which of these statements will fail because the table name is not legal? (Choose two answers.)

    A. `create table "SELECT" (col1 date);`

    B. `create table "lower case" (col1 date);`

    C. `create table number1 (col1 date);`

    D. `create table 1number(col1 date);`

    E. `create table update(col1 date);`

2. Several object types share the same namespace and therefore cannot have the same name in the same schema. Which of the following object types is not in the same namespace as the others? (Choose the best answer.)

    A. Index

    B. PL/SQL stored procedure

    C. Synonym

    D. Table

    E. View

3. Which of the following is not supported by Oracle as an internal datatype? (Choose the best answer.)

    A. CHAR

    B. FLOAT

    C. INTEGER

    D. STRING

4. You need to record date/time values, with a precision of one second. What would be a suitable datatype for a single column to store this information?

    A. DATE

    B. TIMESTAMP

    C. Either DATE or TIMESTAMP

    D. You must develop your own user defined datatype, because the internal types store either the date or the time.

5. Which types of constraint require an index? (Choose all that apply.)

    A. CHECK

    B. NOT NULL

    C. PRIMARY KEY

    D. UNIQUE

6. A transaction consists of two statements. The first succeeds, but the second (which updates several rows) fails part way through because of a constraint violation. What will happen? (Choose the best answer.)

    A. The whole transaction will be rolled back.

    B. The second statement will be rolled back completely, and the first will be committed.

    C. The second statement will be rolled back completely, and the first will remain uncommitted.

    D. Only the one update that caused the violation will be rolled back; everything else will be committed.

    E. Only the one update that caused the violation will be rolled back; everything else will remain uncommitted.

7. Which of the following statements is correct about indexes? (Choose the best answer.)

    A. An index can be based on multiple columns of a table, but the columns must be of the same datatype.

    B. An index can be based on multiple columns of a table, but the columns must be adjacent and specified in the order that they are defined in the table.

    C. An index cannot have the same name as a table, unless the index and the table are in separate schemas.

    D. None of the above statements is correct.

8. For what purposes might you choose to create views? (Choose two answers.)

   A. To enhance security

   B. To present data in a simple form

   C. To improve performance

   D. To save result sets of commonly executed queries

9. You insert a row using a sequence INV_NOS and then roll back the insert, as follows:

```
ocp10g> insert into invoices values (inv_nos.nextval,1,sysdate,150);
1 row created.
ocp10g> rollback;
Rollback complete.
```

Before this transaction, the sequence was at value 10. What will be the next value it will issue? (Choose the best answer.)

   A. 10

   B. 11

   C. 12

   D. It depends on how the sequence was created

Answers

1. **D and E.** D violates the rule that a table name must begin with a letter, and E violates the rule that a table name cannot be a reserved word. Both rules can be bypassed by using double quotes.

2. **A.** Indexes have their own namespace.

3. **D.** There is no STRING datatype.

4. **C.** Both DATE and TIMESTAMP columns always record the date and the time to a precision of at least one second.

5. **C and D.** These are enforced with indexes, which will be created automatically if they do not exist.

6. **C.** SQL is a set-oriented language: it is impossible for a statement to be partially completed. Transactions can be incomplete, but COMMIT is all or nothing.

7. **D.** None of these are restrictions on index creation.

8. **A and B.** Views are about usability, not performance. D applies to materialized views, not to views per se.

9. **D.** The sequence will have been incremented, and the increment does not get rolled back, but you do not know what the next value will be, unless you know what STEP was defined when the sequence was created.

CHAPTER 9

Manipulating Database Data

In this chapter you will learn how to
- Manipulate data through SQL using INSERT, UPDATE, and DELETE
- Use Data Pump to export data
- Use Data Pump to import data
- Load data with SQL Loader
- Create directory objects

Chapter 4 offers a brief look at the SQL syntax for the SELECT, INSERT, UPDATE, and DELETE commands but doesn't go into what actually happens in memory and on disk when these commands are executed. Similarly, Chapter 8 shows the syntax for creating tables but doesn't look at how data is actually entered into and retrieved from them. This chapter will make good these gaps by walking through the whole process, including the generation of undo (which enables the rollback command) and of redo (which enables commit and recovery operations). As a precursor for this, you will review some of the principles of a relational database to which all databases (not just Oracle's) must conform. Then the chapter finishes with a look at the tools provided by Oracle for bulk data loading and unloading operations: Data Pump and SQL*Loader.

Database Transactions

This is not the place to go into detail on the relational database transactional paradigm—there are any number of academic texts on this, and there is not enough space to cover this topic in a practical guide—but a quick review of transaction theory is necessary before looking at how Oracle has implemented transaction management and the data manipulation language (DML). Oracle's mechanism for transactional integrity combines undo segments and redo log files: this mechanism is undoubtedly the best of any database yet developed, and it conforms perfectly to the international standards for data processing. Other database vendors comply with the same standards with their own mechanisms, but with varying levels of effectiveness. In brief, any relational database must be able to pass the *ACID test*.

A Is for Atomicity

The principle of *atomicity* states that all parts of a transaction must complete, or none of them. For example, if your business analysts have said that every time you change an employee's salary you must also change his grade, then the "atomic" transaction will consist of two updates. The database must guarantee that both go through, or neither. If only one of the updates were to succeed, you would have an employee on a salary that was incompatible with his grade: a data corruption, in business terms. If anything (anything at all!) goes wrong before the transaction is complete, the database itself must guarantee that any parts that did go through are reversed: this must happen automatically.

But although an atomic transaction sounds small (like an atom), it could be enormous. To take another example, it is logically impossible for the nominal ledger of an accounting package to be half in August and half in September: the end-of-month rollover is therefore (in business terms) one atomic transaction, which may affect millions of rows in thousands of tables and take hours to complete (or to roll back, if anything goes wrong).

The rollback of an incomplete transaction may be manual (as when you issue the ROLLBACK command), but it must be automatic and unstoppable in the case of an error. Oracle guarantees atomicity absolutely through the use of undo segments, dealt with in detail in Chapter 16.

C Is for Consistency

The principle of *consistency* states that the results of a query must be consistent with the state of the database at the time the query started. Imagine a simple query that averages the value of a column of a table. If the table is large, it will take many minutes to pass through the table. If other users are updating the column while the query is in progress, should the query include the new or the old values? Should it include rows that were inserted or deleted after the query started? The principle of consistency requires that the database ensure that changed values are not seen by the query: it will give you an average of the column as it was when the query started, no matter how long the query takes or what other activity is occurring on the tables concerned.

Through the use of undo segments Oracle guarantees that if a query succeeds, the result will be consistent. However, if your undo segments are incorrectly configured, the query may not succeed: a famous Oracle error, "ORA-1555 snapshot too old," is raised. This used to be an extremely difficult problem to fix with earlier releases of the database, but from release 9*i* onward you should always be able to avoid it.

I Is for Isolation

The principle of *isolation* states that an incomplete (that is, uncommitted) transaction must be invisible to the rest of the world. While the transaction is in progress, only the one session that is executing the transaction is allowed to see the changes: all other sessions must see the unchanged data, not the new values. The logic behind this is, first, that the full transaction might not go through (remember the principle of atomicity?) and that therefore no other users should be allowed to see changes that might be reversed. And second, during the progress of a transaction the data is (in business terms) incoherent: there is a short time when the employee has had his salary changed, but not his grade. Transaction isolation requires that the database must conceal transactions in progress from other users: they will see the preupdate version of the data until the transaction completes, when they will see all the changes as a consistent set. Again, Oracle guarantees transaction isolation through use of undo segments.

D Is for Durability

The principle of *durability* states that once a transaction completes with a COMMIT, it must be impossible for the database to lose it. During the time that the transaction is in progress, the principle of isolation requires that no one (other than the session concerned) can see the changes it has made so far. But the instant the transaction completes, it must be broadcast to the world, and the database must guarantee that the change is never lost: a relational database is not allowed to lose data. Oracle fulfils this requirement through the use of logfiles. Logfiles come in two forms: online redo log files, and archive redo log files. These are dealt with in detail in Chapter 18. For now, remember that it is impossible for a properly configured Oracle database to lose data. Of course, data can be lost through user error: inappropriate DML, or dropping objects. But as far as Oracle and the DBA are concerned, such events are transactions like any other: according to the principle of durability, they are absolutely nonreversible.

TIP If a database ever loses data, Management's first, and fully justified, reaction is to fire the DBA. Everyone knows that a properly configured Oracle database won't lose data; therefore, it must be the administrator's fault. Careers have been broken for this reason.

Executing SQL statements

The whole of the SQL language is only a dozen or so commands. The ones we are concerned with here are

- SELECT
- INSERT
- UPDATE
- DELETE
- COMMIT
- ROLLBACK

Remember that from release 9*i* Oracle has included a very efficient and powerful MERGE command, but since the end result of a merge is identical to a combination of INSERT, UPDATE, and DELETE, there is no need to discuss it here.

Executing a SELECT Statement

The SELECT command retrieves data. A SELECT statement is executed in stages: the server process executing the statement will first check whether the blocks containing the data required are already in memory, in the database buffer cache. If they are, then execution can proceed immediately. If they are not, the server must locate them on disk and copy them into the database buffer cache.

 EXAM TIP Always remember that server processes read blocks from datafiles into the database buffer cache, but DBWn writes blocks from the database buffer cache to the datafiles.

Once the data blocks required for the query are in the database buffer cache, any further processing (such as sorting or aggregation) is carried out in the PGA of the session. When the execution is complete, the result set is returned to the user process.

How does this relate to the ACID test? For read consistency, if the query encounters a block that has been changed since the time at which the query started, the server process will go to the undo segment that protected the change, locate the old version of the data, and (for the purposes of the current query only) roll back the change. Thus any changes initiated after the query commenced will not be seen. Clearly, if the data needed to do this rollback is no longer in the undo segments, this mechanism will not work. That is when you get "ORA-1555: snapshot too old."

Executing an Update Statement

For any DML operation, it is necessary to work on both data blocks and undo blocks, and also to generate redo: the A, C, and I of the ACID test require generation of undo; the D requires generation of redo.

 EXAM TIP Remember, "undo" is not the opposite of "redo"! Redo protects *all* block changes, no matter whether it is a change to a block of a table segment, an index segment, or an undo segment. As far as redo is concerned, an undo segment is just another segment, and any changes to it must be made durable.

The first step in executing DML is the same as executing SELECT: the required blocks must be found in memory or copied into memory from disk. The only change is that an empty (or expired—more of that in Chapter 16) block of an undo segment is needed too. From then on, things are a bit more complicated.

First, locks must be placed on any rows and associated index keys that will be affected by the operation. This process is covered in Chapter 17.

Then the redo is generated: the server process writes to the log buffer the changes that are going to be applied to the data blocks. This generation of redo is applied to both table block changes and undo block changes: if a column is to be updated, then the new value of the column is written to the log buffer (which is the change that will be applied to the table block), and also the old value (which is the change that will be applied to the undo block). If the column is part of an index key, then the changes to be applied to the index are also written to the log buffer, together with an undo block change to protect the index changes.

Having generated the redo, the update is carried out in the database buffer cache: the block of table data is updated with the new version of the changed column, and the old version of the changed column is written to the block of an undo segment. From this point until the update is committed, all queries from other sessions addressing the changed row will be redirected to the undo data. Only the session that is doing the update will see the actual current version of the row in the table block. The same principle applies to any associated index changes.

As a simple example, consider this statement:

```
update emp set sal=sal*1.1 where empno=7934;
```

To execute this statement, the block of table data containing the row for employee number 7934 (and possibly several other rows too, if the rows are smaller than the block) is copied into the database cache and a block of an undo segment is copied into the cache. Then your server process writes to the log buffer the old version of the sal column (which is the change to be applied to the block of undo) and the new version of the sal column (which is the change to be applied to the block of table data). Finally, the blocks themselves are updated. And remember that because SQL is a set-oriented language, if there were many rows in the emp table with the same empno, they would all be updated by the one statement. But because empno will be a primary key, that can't happen.

Executing Insert and Delete Statements

Conceptually, INSERT and DELETE are managed in the same fashion as an UPDATE. Redo generation is exactly the same: all changes to be made to data and undo blocks are first written out to the log buffer. The difference is in the amount of undo generated. When a row is inserted, the only undo generated consists of writing out the new rowid to the undo block. This is because to roll back an INSERT, the only information Oracle requires is the rowid, so that a

```
delete from <table> where rowid=<rowid of the new row>
```

statement can be executed. For a DELETE, the whole row is written to the undo block, so that the deletion can be rolled back if need be by inserting the complete row back into the table.

A more normal DELETE statement might be

```
delete from emp where empno=7934;
```

which will delete the one row (if 7934 really is unique) from the table, writing it out to the undo block as it does it.

TIP Always include a WHERE clause in any UPDATE (or DELETE) statement; otherwise, you will UPDATE (or DELETE) every row in the table.

Executing a Rollback

Remember that if anything goes wrong, rollback of transactions in progress is completely automatic, carried out by background processes. For example, if the session that initiated the transaction fails (perhaps the PC running the user process reboots, or the network link goes down), then the PMON will detect that there is a problem, and roll back the transaction. If the server reboots, then on startup SMON will detect the problem and initiate a rollback. A manual rollback requires the user to issue the ROLLBACK command. But however the rollback is initiated, the mechanism is identical: in the case of an UPDATE, the pre-update versions of the columns are copied from the undo block back to the table blocks. To roll back an INSERT, Oracle retrieves the rowid of the inserted row from the undo block and uses it as the key for a delete on the table. To roll back a DELETE, Oracle constructs a complete insert statement from the data in the undo block. Thus, Oracle's implementation of the ROLLBACK command is to use undo data to construct and execute another statement that will reverse the effect of the first statement.

TIP A rollback will itself generate more redo as it executes, perhaps rather more than the original statement.

If you do omit a WHERE clause—as by saying `delete from emp;`—and so delete all of the several million rows in the table, you can roll back the changes. During the deletion, your server process will have copied the rows to an undo segment as it deleted them from the table: ROLLBACK will insert them back into the table, and no one will ever know you made the mistake. Unless, of course, you typed COMMIT....

Executing a Commit

Commit processing is where many people (and even some experienced DBAs) show an incomplete, or indeed completely inaccurate, understanding of the Oracle architecture. When you say COMMIT, all that happens physically is that LGWR flushes the log buffer to disk. DBWn does absolutely nothing. This is one of the most important performance features of the Oracle database.

To make a transaction durable, all that is necessary is that the changes that make up the transaction be on disk: there is no need whatsoever for the actual data to be on disk. If the changes are on disk, in the form of multiplexed redo log files, then in the event of damage to the database the transaction can be reinstantiated by restoring the datafiles from a backup taken before the damage occurred and applying the changes from the redo log. This process is covered in detail in later chapters; for now, just hang on to the fact that a COMMIT involves nothing more than flushing the log buffer to disk, and flagging the transaction as complete.

This is why a transaction involving millions of updates in thousands of tables over many minutes or hours can be committed in a fraction of a second. Because LGWR writes in very nearly real time, virtually all the transaction's changes are on disk already. When you say COMMIT, LGWR actually does write in real time: your session will hang until the write is complete. This delay will be the length of time it takes to flush the last bit of redo from the log buffer to disk, which will take only milliseconds. Your session is then free to continue, and from then on all other sessions will no longer be redirected to the undo blocks when they address the changed table, unless the principle of consistency requires it.

 EXAM TIP What does DBWn do when you say commit? Absolutely nothing.

Having said that DBWn has nothing to do with commit processing, it does of course write changed, or "dirty," blocks to disk—eventually. The algorithm used is intended to ensure that while changed blocks do get to disk, they will not be written so quickly as to impact on normal working. If DBWn never wrote blocks to disk, there would be a huge amount of work for it to do when a checkpoint was finally needed. The exception is when a checkpoint is issued: these are the rare occasions (typically, only during an orderly shutdown of the database and instance) when CKPT instructs DBWn to write all dirty blocks to the datafiles.

EXAM TIP In normal running, DBWn writes only a few dirty buffers to disk; when a checkpoint is signaled, it writes all dirty buffers to disk.

Where there is often confusion is that the stream of redo written out to the redo log files by LGWR will contain changes for both committed and uncommitted transactions. Furthermore, at any given moment DBWn may or may not have written out changed blocks of data segments or undo segments to the datafiles for both committed and uncommitted transactions. So in principle, your database on disk is corrupted: the datafiles may well be storing uncommitted work and be missing committed changes. But in the event of a crash, the stream of redo on disk always has enough information to reinstantiate any committed transactions that are not in the datafiles (by use of the changes applied to data blocks), and to reinstantiate the undo segments (by use of the changes applied to undo blocks) needed to roll back any uncommitted transactions that are in the datafiles.

DDL and Transaction Control

The COMMIT and ROLLBACK statements apply only to DML. You cannot roll back a DDL statement: once executed, it is immediately durable. If it were possible to see the source code for (for example) the CREATE TABLE command, it would be obvious why. When you create a table, you are in fact doing a transaction against some data dictionary tables: at the very least, you are inserting a row into SYS.TAB$, a data dictionary table with one row to define every table in the database, and one or more rows into SYS.COL$, a data dictionary table with one row for the definition of every column of every table in the database. Then the command concludes with a COMMIT. This is to protect the data dictionary: if the COMMIT were not built into the CREATE TABLE command, the possibility of an incomplete transaction would arise, and an incomplete transaction in the data dictionary could have appalling side effects.

The So-Called "Auto-Commit"

To conclude this discussion of commit processing, it is necessary to remove any confusion about what is often called "auto-commit," or sometimes "implicit commit." You will often hear it said that in some situations Oracle will "auto-commit." One of these situations is when doing DDL, as just described; another is when you exit from a user process such as SQL*Plus.

Quite simply, there is no such thing as an automatic commit. When you execute a DDL statement, a perfectly normal COMMIT is included in the source code that implements the DDL command. But what about when you exit from your user process? If you are using SQL*Plus on a Windows terminal (never mind what operating system the database server is running) and you issue a DML statement followed by an "exit," your transaction will be committed. This is because a COMMIT statement is built into the SQL*Plus "exit" command: if we could see the source code, it would be obvious. But what if you click in the top-right corner of the SQL*Plus window? The window will close, and if you log in again, you will see that the transaction has been rolled back. This is because the programmers who wrote SQL*Plus for Microsoft Windows included a ROLLBACK statement in the code that is executed when you close the window. By contrast, if you are using the X Window version of SQL*Plus, you will find that closing the window commits the transaction. So whether you get an "auto-commit" when you exit from a program in various ways is entirely dependent on how your programmers wrote the exit code. The Oracle server will simply do what it is told to do.

Of course, a disorderly exit from the user process, such as killing it with an operating system utility, will be detected by PMON, and an active transaction will always be rolled back.

Exercise 9-1: Transaction Isolation, Read Consistency, and COMMIT

It is time to experiment with some SQL commands, and particularly to illustrate some aspects of transaction control. For this exercise, open two SQL*Plus sessions (or iSQL*Plus if you prefer), log on as the same user in both sessions, and run the commands that follow in the two sessions.

In Your First Session	In Your Second Session
`create table t1 as select * from all_users;`	
`select count(*) from t1;`	`select count(*) from t1;`
Results are the same in both sessions.	
`delete from t1;`	
`select count(*) from t1;`	`select count(*) from t1;`
Results differ because of the principle of isolation.	
`rollback;`	
`select count(*) from t1;`	`select count(*) from t1;`
Results are the same in both sessions.	
`delete from t1;`	
`select count(*) from t1;`	`select count(*) from t1;`
`create view v1 as select * from t1;`	
`select count(*) from t1;`	`select count(*) from t1;`
`rollback;`	
`select count(*) from t1;`	`select count(*) from t1;`
Oh dear! The DDL statement committed the transaction, so it can't be rolled back.	
`drop view v1;`	
`drop table t1;`	

DML and Integrity Constraints

By default, integrity constraints are always enforced during DML, at statement execution time. When an integrity constraint is violated by a statement, the whole statement is rolled back. For example, a statement that attempts to update many rows might successfully update a number of rows but then hit a problem: execution will cease, and the successful updates already carried out by the statement will be reversed. It makes no difference what the problem is. For instance, it could be an integrity constraint or perhaps a space problem.

 EXAM TIP If one statement in a multistatement transaction violates a constraint, only that one statement is rolled back; the rest of the transaction remains intact and uncommitted.

The various constraint errors that can be raised by the various DML statements are summarized next, with examples of the messages.

Constraint	Possible Errors
Foreign key	INSERT and UPDATE on the child table: the value must exist in the parent table. *Error:* ORA-02291: integrity constraint (SCOTT.FK_DEPTNO) violated - parent key not found UPDATE and DELETE on the parent table: there must be no dependent rows in the child table. *Error:* ORA-02292: integrity constraint (SCOTT.FK_DEPTNO) violated - child record found
Not null	INSERT and UPDATE: cannot insert without a value, or modify the value to null. *Error:* ORA-01400: cannot insert NULL into ("SCOTT"."EMP"."EMPNO")
Unique	INSERT and UPDATE: cannot have any value that already exists in the table. Multiple nulls are permitted. *Error:* ORA-00001: unique constraint (SCOTT.PK_DEPT) violated
Primary key	Equivalent to a unique constraint modified with a not-null constraint: both sets of rules apply. *Error:* Same as for unique

 TIP Programmers should trap these errors in their exceptions clauses and take appropriate action to deal with the problem.

Data Pump

In the normal course of events, ordinary SELECT and DML commands are used to extract data from the database and to insert data into it, but there are occasions when you will need a much faster method for bulk operations. There are many reasons why it may be desirable to extract large amounts of data and the associated object definitions from a database in a form that will allow them to be easily loaded into another. One obvious purpose is backup, but there are others, such as archiving of historical data before deleting it from the live system, or to transfer data between production and test environments, or between an online system and a data warehouse.

Historically, Oracle provided the Export and Import utilities. These were effective (and they are still available with release 10*g*), but they suffer from the limitation of being client/server tools: they are just user processes, like any other. The Export utility connects to the database via a server process and issues SELECT statements: the data retrieved by the server process is passed back to the Export user process, where it is formatted and written out to a disk file. Similarly, the Import utility user process logs onto the instance via a server process and then reads the disk file produced by Export and constructs DDL and insert statements to create tables and other objects and load the data into them. Release 10*g* introduces the Data Pump facility. Functionally, the results are the same as the old Export/Import utilities: large amounts of data can be extracted from one database and transferred into another. But the implementation is totally different, and far superior. Note also that the Data Pump and Export/Import dump file formats are completely different. Data Pump export command-line options are shown in Figure 9-1.

Data Pump Architecture

Data Pump is a server-side utility. You initiate Data Pump jobs from a user process, either SQL*Plus or through Enterprise Manager, but all the work is done by server processes. This improves performance dramatically over the old Export/Import utilities, because the Data Pump processes running on the server have direct access to the datafiles and the SGA; they do not have to go via a session. Also, it is possible to launch a Data Pump job and then detach from it, leaving it running in the background. You can reconnect to the job to monitor its progress at any time.

There are a number of processes involved in a Data Pump job, two queues, a number of files, and one table. First, the processes.

The user processes are expdp and impdp (for Unix) or expdp.exe and impdp.exe (Windows). These are used to launch, control, and monitor Data Pump jobs. Alternatively, there is an Enterprise Manager interface, which will be described later. The expdp or impdp user process establishes a session against the database through

Figure 9-1 Data Pump export command-line options

a normal server process. This session then issues commands to control and monitor Data Pump jobs. When a Data Pump job is launched, at least two processes are started: a Data Pump Master process (the DM*nn*) and one or more worker processes (named DW*nn*). If multiple Data Pump jobs are running concurrently, each will have its own DM*nn* process and its own DW*nn* processes. As the name implies, the master process controls the workers. If you have enabled parallelism, then each DW*nn* may make use of two or more parallel execution servers (named P*nnn*.)

Two queues are created for each Data Pump job: a control queue and a status queue. The DM*nn* divides up the work to be done and places individual tasks that make up the job on the control queue. The worker processes pick up these tasks and execute them, perhaps making use of parallel execution servers. This queue operates on a deliver-exactly-once model: messages are enqueued by the DM*nn* and dequeued by the worker that picks them up. The status queue is for monitoring purposes: the DM*nn* places messages on it describing the state of the job. This queue operates on a publish-and-subscribe model: any session (with appropriate privileges) can query the queue to monitor the job's progress.

The files generated by Data Pump come in three forms: SQL files, dump files, and log files. SQL files are DDL statements describing the objects included in the job. You can choose to generate them (without any data) as an easy way of getting this information out of the database, perhaps for documentation purposes or as a set of scripts to re-create the database. Dump files contain the exported data. This is formatted with XML tags. The use of XML means that there is a considerable overhead in dump files for describing the data. A small table like the REGIONS table in the HR sample schema will generate a 94KB dump file, but while this overhead may seem disproportionately large for a tiny table like that, it becomes trivial for larger tables. The log files describe the history of the job run.

EXAM TIP Remember the three Data Pump file types: SQL files, log files, and dump files.

Finally, there is the control table. Created for you by the DM*nn* when you launch a job, it is used both to record the job's progress and to describe it. It is included in the dump file as the final item of the job.

Directories

Data Pump reads and writes files in an Oracle directory. An Oracle directory gives a layer of abstraction between the user and the operating system: you as DBA create a directory within the database, which points to a physical path within the operating system file system. Directories can be created either from a SQL*Plus prompt as shown in Figure 9-2 or from within Database Control. To see information about directories, query the view DBA_DIRECTORIES. Each directory has a name, an owner, and the physical path to which it refers. Note that Oracle does not verify whether the path exists when you create the directory—if it does not, or if the operating system user who owns the Oracle software does not have permission to read and write to it, you will only get an error when you actually use Data Pump. Having created a directory, you must give the Oracle user who will be running Data Pump permission to read and write to it, just as your system administrators must give the operating system user permission to read and write to the physical path.

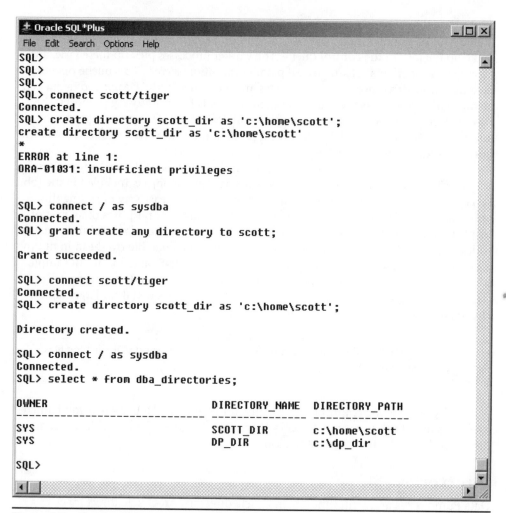

Figure 9-2 Creating directories from the command line

 EXAM TIP Oracle directories are always owned by user SYS, but to create them, you must have been granted the appropriate privilege, CREATE DIRECTORY.

Directories can be contrasted with the initialization parameter UTL_FILE_DIR. This is a parameter that allows Oracle, through PL/SQL procedures, to write to the file system of the database server machine, but it is a far cruder method: it is not possible to grant permissions within Oracle on UTL_FILE_DIR directories. Thus, if the parameter is set to

```
UTL_FILE_DIR=/tmp
```

then any Oracle user can completely fill your /tmp directory. Furthermore, if it is set to

```
UTL_FILE_DIR=*
```

then anyone can write to any directory that the Oracle owner has permission on, which is a shocking security risk.

 TIP Writing to the UTL_FILE_DIR is usually done with the PL/SQL package UTL_FILE. Make sure that execute permissions on this package are strictly limited.

Direct Path or External Table Path?

Data Pump has two methods for loading and unloading data: the direct path, and the external table path. The direct path bypasses the database buffer cache. For an export, Data Pump reads the datafiles directly from disk, extracts and formats the content, and writes it out as a dump file. For an import, Data Pump reads the dump file, uses its content to assemble blocks of table data, and writes them directly to the datafiles. The write is above the "high-water mark" of the table. The high-water mark is a marker in the table above which no data has ever been written. Once the load is complete, Data Pump shifts the high-water mark up to include the newly written blocks, and the rows within them are then visible to other users. This is the equivalent of a COMMIT. No undo is generated, and if you wish, you can switch off the generation of redo as well. Direct path is therefore extremely fast, and furthermore, it should have no impact on your end users because interaction with the SGA is kept to a minimum.

The external table path uses the database buffer cache. Even though Data Pump is manipulating files that are external to the database, it uses the database buffer cache as though it were reading and writing an internal table. For an export, Data Pump reads blocks from the datafiles into the cache through a normal SELECT process. From there, it formats the data for output to a dump file. During an import, Data Pump constructs standard insert statements from the content of the dump file and executes them by reading blocks from the datafiles into the cache, where the insert is carried out in the normal fashion. As far as the database is concerned, external table Data Pump jobs look like absolutely ordinary (though perhaps rather large) SELECT or INSERT operations. Both undo and redo are generated, as they would be for any normal DML statement. Your end users may well complain while these jobs are in progress! Commit processing is absolutely normal.

So what determines whether Data Pump uses the direct path or the external table path? You as DBA have no control: Data Pump itself makes the decision according to the complexity of the objects. Only simple structures, such as heap tables without active triggers, can be processed through the direct path; more complex objects such as clustered tables force Data Pump to use the external table path because it requires interaction with the SGA in order to resolve the complexities. In either case, the dump file generated is identical.

EXAM TIP The external table path insert uses a regular commit, like any other DML statement. A direct path insert does not use a commit: it simply shifts the high-water mark of the table to include the newly written blocks.

Using Data Pump in Network Mode

It is possible to use Data Pump to transfer data from one database to another, without staging the data on disk at all. Consider this example of launching Data Pump from the command-line utility impdp:

```
impdp userid=scott/tiger tables=dept,emp network_link=L1 directory=dp_dir
```

This command will launch a Data Pump export against the local database, logging on as user SCOTT with password TIGER. The Data Pump job will then read two tables, DEPT and EMP, in SCOTT's schema and transfer them across the network to the database identified by the database link L1, where a Data Pump import job will insert the data. The export and the import processes will run concurrently, the one feeding the other. Note that even though the data is never written out as an operating system file, it is still necessary to specify a directory, in order that Data Pump can write out logging information.

 TIP A database link defines a path to a remote database.

Exercise 9-2: Using Data Pump Export Through Enterprise Manager Database Control

This exercise will create a table and export it using the Database Control interface to Data Pump.

1. Create a directory to be used by Data Pump. For example, from a command prompt,

   ```
   md c:\dp_dir
   ```

2. Using SQL*Plus, log on to your instance as user SYSTEM and create a table to be used for testing Data Pump.

   ```
   create table dp_test as select * from all_users;
   select count * from dp_test;
   ```

3. Still within SQL*Plus, create the Oracle directory to be used by Data Pump and grant all users permission to read and write to the directory.

```
create directory dp_dir as 'c:\dp_dir';
grant all on directory dp_dir to public;
exit;
```

4. Log on to Database Control as user SYSTEM.

5. From the database home page, click the Maintenance tab.

6. In the Utilities section, click the Export To Files link.

7. On the Export: Export Type window shown here, select Tables and enter an operating system username and password with read/write permissions on the directory specified in Step 3.

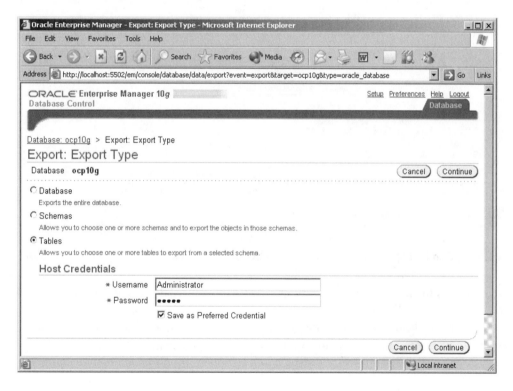

8. On the Export: Add Tables window shown here, click Add, and specify SYSTEM as the schema and "DP_TEST" as the table. Click Select and Next.

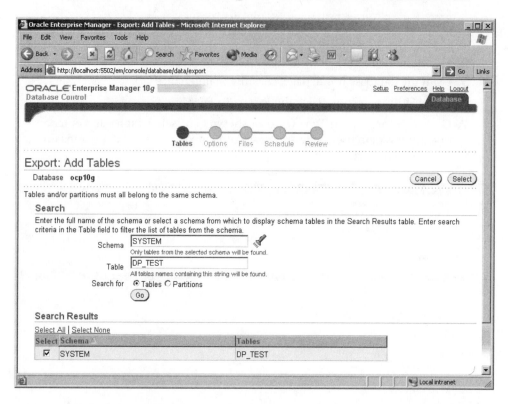

9. On the Export: Options window, choose the directory DP_DIR as the location for the logfile, and click Next.

10. On the Export: Files window, choose the directory DP_DIR as the location and click Finish.

11. In the Export: Review window shown next, take a look at the script that has been generated to see how you would run the job using the Data Pump API, and click Submit Job.

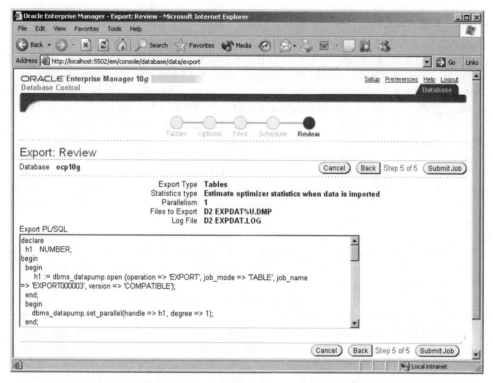

12. On the Status window, click OK.

13. From an operating system prompt, navigate to the directory specified in Step 3. There will be a file EXPDAT01.DMP, which is the export dump file, and a logfile, EXPDAT.LOG. Examine the logfile to check that the job did complete successfully.

Exercise 9-3: Using Data Pump Import Through impdp

This exercise will use the command-line utility impdp to bring the exported table back into the database with Data Pump.

1. Log in to the instance as user SYSTEM through SQL*Plus, and drop the table created in Exercise 9-2:

```
drop table dp_test;
exit;
```

2. From an operating system prompt, issue this command:

```
impdp userid=system/oracle dumpfile=expdat01.dmp directory=dp_dir
```

3. When the import has completed, connect to the instance with SQL*Plus as SYSTEM and confirm that the table has been imported successfully.

```
select count(*) from dp_test;
```

SQL*Loader

Data Pump reads and writes files in an Oracle proprietary format: it is used to transfer data into and out of, or between, Oracle databases. But in many cases you will be faced with a need to do a bulk upload of datasets generated from some third-party system. This is where SQL*Loader comes in. The input files may be generated by anything, but so long as the layout conforms to something that SQL*Loader can understand, it will upload the data successfully. Your task as DBA is to configure a SQL*Loader controlfile that can interpret the contents of the input datafiles; SQL*Loader will then insert the data, either using direct path or via the database buffer cache, in a similar fashion to Data Pump. The crucial differences are, first, that SQL*Loader can read any file no matter what its source, and second, that it is a user process like any other; unlike Data Pump, it is not a server-side utility. It establishes a session against the instance and the database via a server process.

SQL*Loader uses a number of files. The *input datafiles* are the source data that it will upload into the database. These must conform to an agreed format. The *controlfile* is a text file written by the DBA with directives telling SQL*Loader how to interpret the contents of the input files, and what to do with the rows it extracts from them. *Logfiles* summarize the success (or otherwise) of the job, while detailing any errors. Rows extracted from the input files may be rejected by SQL*Loader (perhaps because they do not conform to the format expected by the controlfile) or by the database (for instance, insertion might violate an integrity constraint); in either case, they are written out to a *bad file*. If rows are successfully extracted from the input but rejected because they did not match some record selection criterion, they are written out to a *reject file*. SQL*Loader command-line options are shown in Figure 9-3.

The SQL*Loader Controlfile

The controlfile is a text file instructing SQL*Loader on how to process the input datafiles. It is possible to include the actual data to be loaded on the controlfile, but you would not normally do this; usually, you will create one controlfile and reuse it, on a regular basis, with different input datafiles. The formats that SQL*Loader can understand are fixed record format, variable record format, and stream record format. Remember that the examples following are very simple: the variety of input formats that SQL*Loader can understand is limited only by your ingenuity in constructing a controlfile.

The fixed record format is the most straightforward, as well as the fastest to process. Each row of data is a fixed length, terminated with a carriage return character. Within the rows, you use some character as a field delimiter. A fixed record controlfile such as this,

```
load data
infile 'fixed.dat' "fix 15"
into table names
fields terminated by ','
(first,last)
```

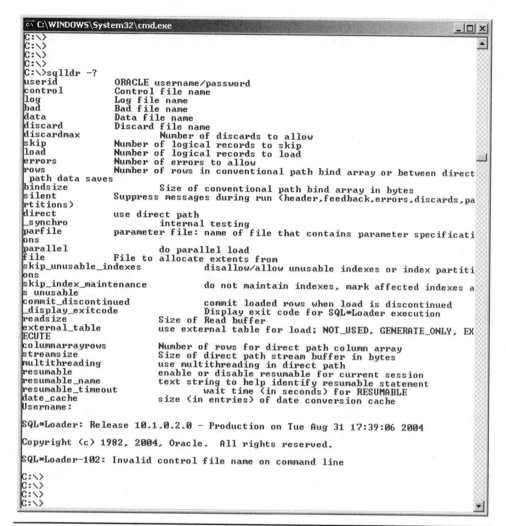

Figure 9-3 The SQL*Loader command-line options

will read the file fixed.dat, parse it into rows 15 bytes long (note that the 15 bytes must include one for the carriage return row terminator), divide the rows into two fields, and insert them into the columns "first" and "last" of the table "names." A matching input datafile, called test.dat, could be

```
John,Watsonaaa
Damir,Bersinic
McGraw,Hillaaa
```

Variable records include an entry at the head of each row to state how long the row is. The length of this entry is included in the controlfile. The controlfile might be

```
load data
infile 'names.dat' "var 3"
into table names
fields terminated by ','
(first,last)
```

and a matching datafile would be

```
012John,Watson
015Damir,Bersinic
012McGraw,Hill
```

Note that the length of each row is a three-digit number, as specified in the controlfile, and must include a character for the carriage return. Variable record format is not as fast as fixed format but is faster than stream format.

Stream format requires SQL*Loader to do the most work. Rather than being given any information about the length of the rows, SQL*Loader must scan each row for the record terminator. This is the most flexible format but also the slowest to process. The controlfile might be

```
load data
infile 'names.dat' "str '\n'"
into table names
fields terminated by ','
(first,last)
```

Note the use of the newline character, specified as "\n". If you are familiar with the C programming language, that will not be new. If not, note that a number of nonprintable characters, such as the newline character, can be specified in this way: a leading backslash, then a letter used to indicate the nonprintable character. The combination "\n" is the most commonly used row delimiter (it indicates a line break), but tabs or form feed characters can be used as well. A matching datafile for the preceding controlfile might take the form

```
John,Watson
Damir,Bersinic
McGraw,Hill
```

As you can see, this format of input datafile is the easiest to generate. But it is also the slowest to process.

TIP It may be very difficult to get a controlfile right, but once you have it, you can use it repeatedly, with different input datafiles for each run. It is then the responsibility of the feeder system to produce input datafiles that match your controlfile, rather than the other way around.

It is necessary to study the Utilities Manual for a full description of all the formatting capabilities of SQL*Loader, but in general you can assume that it is possible to construct a controlfile that will understand just about any input datafile. However, do not think that it is always easy.

Loading Methods

As with Data Pump, it is possible to use either a direct path or a conventional path for loading data into database tables. But also as with Data Pump, there are restrictions. Unlike when using Data Pump, you must tell SQL*Loader to use the direct path: add the keyword DIRECT to the controlfile or optionally specify DIRECT=Y on the SQL*Loader command line. Remember that a conventional load is a straightforward insert, whereas for a direct load, the server process supporting the SQL*Loader session assembles blocks in memory and writes them directly to the datafiles, bypassing the database buffer cache. Here is a comparison of direct and conventional loads:

Conventional Path Load	Direct Path Load
Uses COMMIT to make the insert permanent	Uses a "data save" to include the new blocks in the table
Generates undo and redo	Does not generate undo, and redo generation is optional
All constraints enforced	Only primary key, unique, and not-null constraints enforced
Insert triggers fire	Insert triggers do not fire
Works for all tables	Can be used only for heap tables
No table locks	Table is locked for DML during the duration of the load

TIP Direct Path loading is fast, but it has limitations!

Exercise 9-4: Using SQL*Loader

This exercise will insert some more rows into the table created in Exercise 9-2.

1. Using a text editor (such as Windows Notepad), create a SQL*Loader controlfile, called STREAMIN.CTL, as follows:

```
load data
infile 'STREAMIN.DAT' "str \n"
append
into table dp_test
fields terminated by ','
(username,user_id)
```

Note that the "append" keyword allows SQL*Loader to insert into a table that already contains rows.

2. Using a text editor as before, create the input datafile, to be called STREAMIN .DAT, as follows:

```
John,100
Damir,200
McGraw,9999
```

3. From an operating system prompt, issue this command:

```
sqlldr userid=system/oracle control=STREAMIN.CTL
```

4. Log in to your instance with SQL*Plus, and confirm that the three new rows have been inserted into the table:

```
select * from dp_test
```

Chapter Review

In this chapter you learned the internal mechanisms that Oracle uses to ensure transactional consistency, according to the requirements of the relational database model, and looked at what actually happens, in memory and on disk, when SQL statements are executed. Following this investigation on executing individual DML statements, you saw how the Data Pump and SQL*Loader utilities can be used for bulk operations.

Questions

1. You issue a COMMIT command. Which of the following statements is correct? (Choose two correct answers.)

   A. DBWn writes the changed blocks to the datafiles.

   B. LGWR writes the changes to the logfiles.

   C. CKPT synchronizes the database buffer cache with the datafiles.

   D. The transaction is made durable.

   E. The transaction can be rolled back.

2. You issue an UPDATE command, and then a COMMIT. Put the following actions in the correct order:

   A. Data blocks are copied from the datafiles into the database buffer cache.

   B. Data blocks in the cache are updated.

   C. The log buffer is updated.

   D. The changed blocks are flushed to disk.

   E. The log buffer is flushed to disk.

3. User JOHN updates some rows and asks user DAMIR to log in and check the changes before he commits them. Which of the following statements is true? (Choose the best answer.)

   A. DAMIR can see the changes but cannot alter them because JOHN will have locked the rows.

   B. DAMIR will not be able to see the changes.

   C. JOHN must commit the changes, so that DAMIR can see them and if necessary roll them back.

   D. JOHN must commit the changes so that DAMIR can see them, but only JOHN can roll them back.

4. User JOHN updates some rows but does not commit the changes. User DAMIR queries the rows that JOHN updated. Which of the following statements is true? (Choose three correct answers.)

   A. DAMIR's query will be redirected to the redo logs to show the original version of the rows.

   B. DAMIR's session will roll back JOHN's changes to show the original version of the rows.

   C. JOHN must commit the changes before DAMIR can see them.

   D. DAMIR cannot see the rows that were updated, because they will be locked.

   E. If DAMIR's query started after JOHN's update, the principle of read consistency means that he cannot see JOHN's changes.

   F. If DAMIR's query started after JOHN's update, the principle of isolation means that he cannot see JOHN's changes.

5. You are using Data Pump to upload rows into a table, and you wish to use the direct path. Which of the following statements is correct? (Choose three answers.)

   A. You must include the "DIRECT" keyword in the Data Pump controlfile.

   B. This is not possible if the table is in a cluster.

   C. You must disable insert triggers on the table first.

   D. You must enable insert triggers on the table first.

   E. You have no control over this; Data Pump will use the direct path automatically if it can.

   F. Direct path is slower than the external table path because it doesn't cache data in memory.

6. You issue an INSERT command and then attempt to SELECT the rows you inserted before committing them. Which of the following is true? (Choose the best answer.)

   A. You must commit the insert before you can see the rows.

   B. You will see the new rows, even though they are uncommitted.

    C. You must terminate the transaction with a COMMIT or ROLLBACK before you can issue a SELECT statement.

    D. You will see the new rows because your session will read them from an undo segment.

7. You issue an INSERT statement, and it fails with the message "ORA-02291: integrity constraint (HR.EMP_DEPT_FK) violated - parent key not found." Which of the following statements is true? (Choose the best answer.)

    A. The transaction will have been rolled back.

    B. The statement will have been rolled back.

    C. You must create an index on the parent table before you can find parent keys.

    D. All of the above are correct.

8. Which of the following is not a Data Pump file type? (Choose the best answer.)

    A. Dump file

    B. Logfile

    C. Controlfile

    D. SQL file

9. You launch a Data Pump export job to export a number of tables, which runs for several hours. Which of the following is true? (Choose the best answer.)

    A. The tables being exported will be locked throughout the run.

    B. Transactions against the tables committed during the run will be included in the export.

    C. Transactions against the tables (committed or not) during the run will not be included in the export.

    D. SQL executed against the tables during the run will be written out to a SQL file.

    E. The DDL describing the tables will be written out to a SQL file.

10. Using SQL*Loader, place these file formats in order of speed to process, from slowest to fastest:

    A. Fixed record format

    B. Stream record format

    C. Variable record format

11. You want to transfer a large amount of data from one database to another: both databases are on the same machine. What should be the quickest method? (Choose the best answer.)

    A. Use the Export/Import utilities.

    B. Use Data Pump to write out the data, and a SQL*Loader direct load to bring it in.

    C. Use Data Pump in network mode.

    D. Use Data Pump export to write out the data and then Data Pump import to read it in.

12. Which of the following is not a SQL*Loader file? (Choose one answer.)

    A. Bad file

    B. Controlfile

    C. Discard file

    D. Good file

    E. Logfile

13. You create a directory with the statement

```
create directory dp_dir as 'c:\tmp';
```

but when you try to use it with Data Pump, there is an error. Which of the following could be true? (Choose three answers.)

    A. The Oracle software owner has no permissions on c:\tmp.

    B. The Oracle database user has no permissions on dp_dir.

    C. The path c:\tmp does not exist.

    D. The path c:\tmp must exist, or the "create directory" statement would have failed.

    E. If you use Data Pump in network mode, then there will be no need for a directory.

    F. Issuing the command `grant all on 'c:\tmp' to public;` may solve some permission problems.

14. You launch a Data Pump job with expdp and then exit from the session. Which of the following is true? (Choose two answers.)

    A. The job will terminate.

    B. The job will continue running in the background.

    C. You cannot monitor the job once you have exited.

    D. You can reattach to the job to monitor it.

    E. The job will pause but can be restarted.

15. You run SQL*Loader on your PC, to insert data into a remote database. Which of the following is true? (Choose the best answer.)

    A. The input datafiles must be on your PC.

    B. The input datafiles must be on the server.

    C. Direct load is possible only if the input datafiles are on the server.

    D. Direct load is only possible if you run SQL*Loader on the server, not on the PC.

Answers

1. **B and D.** When you say commit, LGWR flushes the log buffer to disk, and the transaction is made durable.

2. **A, C, B, E, and D.** Remember that everything happens in memory first, and that your server process writes to the log buffer before writing the database buffer cache. Then on commit, the log buffer is flushed to disk. The data blocks may not be written for some time.

3. **B.** The principle of isolation means that only JOHN can see his uncommitted transaction; DAMIR will not be able to see the changes.

4. **B, C, and F.** B is correct because that is how Oracle provides transaction isolation. C is correct, again, because of isolation being maintained until commit. F is correct because the principle of isolation, not read consistency, means that DAMIR cannot see JOHN's changes.

5. **B, C, and E.** B and C are correct because these are two of the limitations. E is correct because this is a feature of Data Pump.

6. **B.** A session can always see its own transactions, committed or not.

7. **B.** The statement that throws an error is rolled back automatically; the rest of the transaction remains intact and uncommitted.

8. **C.** The controlfile is wrong: it is used for SQL*Loader, not Data Pump. The other three file types are those that Data Pump can generate.

9. **C.** Transactions against the affected tables during a long-running Data Pump export job will not be included in the export file: the job is protected from any changes.

10. **A, C, and B.** This is the correct order because SQL*Loader will process fixed-length record format faster than variable-length record format or stream record format.

11. **C.** Using Data Pump in network mode avoids the need to stage data on disk: there is no reason not to use it when the databases are on the same machine.

12. **D.** The "good file" is not a SQL*Loader file. SQL*Loader does not produce a file like this—only the other four.

13. **A, B, and C.** A and B could be reasons: remember to distinguish between the operating system user who owns the software, and the Oracle user who only exists within the database. C could also be a reason: at directory creation time, Oracle does not check that the physical path is valid.

14. **B and D.** Data Pump jobs run independently of the session that launched them, making it possible to disconnect from the job and then to reconnect for monitoring purposes.

15. **A.** The input datafiles must be on your PC, because it is the SQL*Loader user process that reads the input datafiles.

CHAPTER 10

Programming Oracle with PL/SQL

In this chapter you will learn how to
- Identify PL/SQL objects
- Describe triggers and triggering events
- Identify configuration options that affect PL/SQL performance

PL/SQL is a programming language developed specifically for the Oracle database. It extends the SQL language by providing procedural structures, and facilities for generating user interface code. Theoretically, a database administrator may not need to be an expert in PL/SQL; programming work should be done by the development staff. But in practice, the more PL/SQL a DBA knows, the better. At the very least, you will need to be able to identify PL/SQL objects that have problems (as is detailed in Chapter 14). Furthermore, at most Oracle installations, the DBA will be expected to assist programmers with writing code and when necessary to create PL/SQL objects as well.

Programming Languages and the Oracle Database

The Oracle database, like all ISO-compliant relational databases, supports the use of Structured Query Language, or SQL. SQL is a set-oriented language designed for retrieving and manipulating data in a client/server environment. It is very efficient at this, but there are many occasions when your programmers will want to manipulate rows one at a time, rather than in groups. Also, SQL does not have any facilities for designing user interfaces. By contrast, procedural languages can manipulate individual rows. They have commands that will allow navigation from one row to another, and can include flow control structures.

SQL and Procedural Languages

To combine the advantages of SQL's set-oriented structures with the control facilities of a procedural language, your programmers need to use a language with elements of both. The universally accepted approach is to embed SQL commands in procedural code. There are two approaches to this. The pure client/server approach is to run the procedural code on a client machine (either a user's terminal or an application server) and send the SQL commands it generates to the database server for execution. An alternative is to run the procedural code, as well as the SQL, within the database. In some ways, the second approach is more efficient: there is no network overhead, and all the code is centrally stored and managed. But it means that the language is proprietary: it will run within the database that is designed to run it, and nowhere else. A second possible problem is that all the processing workload is concentrated within the database.

PL/SQL is Oracle's proprietary third-generation language, which runs within the database. You can use it to retrieve and manipulate data with SQL, while using procedural constructs such as IF...THEN...ELSE or FOR or WHILE. The PL/SQL code can be stored on a client machine and sent to the server for execution (this is known as "anonymous" PL/SQL), or it can be stored within the database as a named block of code.

From release 8i of the Oracle database, it is also possible to use Java within the database. Like PL/SQL, Java can be used to provide a blend of procedural code with SQL statements. Since Java can run either on a client machine (typically, an application server) or within the database, it gives you the option of distributing the processing workload—at the cost of increased network traffic. And unlike PL/SQL, it is a nonproprietary industry standard: if your application is written in Java, it should be portable to any Java-compliant database. But Java is a much lower-level language and will often have a longer development cycle.

The choice of language is dependent on many factors, but PL/SQL should always be considered in the Oracle environment. It is a very quick and easy language to work with, and all DBAs should be familiar with it—if only to assist programmers.

Stored and Anonymous PL/SQL

PL/SQL runs within the database, but it can be stored on either the client or the server. PL/SQL code can also be entered interactively from a SQL*Plus prompt. Stored PL/SQL is loaded into the database and stored within the data dictionary as a named PL/SQL object. When it is saved to the database, it is compiled: the compilation process checks for syntactical errors and also picks up errors relating to the data objects the code addresses. This saves time when the code is actually run and means that programmers should pick up errors at compilation time, before users hit them. Code stored remotely, or ad hoc code issued at the SQL*Plus prompt, is compiled dynamically: this impacts on performance and also raises the possibility that unexpected errors might occur.

Figure 10-1 shows an example of running an anonymous PL/SQL block and of creating and running a stored procedure. The anonymous block in the figure creates a variable called INCREASE with the DECLARE statement and sets it to 10. Then the

```
Oracle SQL*Plus                                          _ □ x
File  Edit  Search  Options  Help
ocp10g> declare increase number := 10;
  2   begin
  3   update emp set sal=sal*(100+increase)/100;
  4   commit;
  5   end;
  6   /

PL/SQL procedure successfully completed.

ocp10g> create procedure inc_sal(increase number) as
  2   begin
  3   update emp set sal=sal*(100+increase)/100;
  4   commit;
  5   end;
  6   /

Procedure created.

ocp10g> execute inc_sal(10);

PL/SQL procedure successfully completed.

ocp10g> |
```

Figure 10-1   Anonymous and stored PL/SQL

procedural code (within the BEGIN...END statements) uses the variable within a SQL statement that updates the sal column of the emp table.

The second example in the figure creates a procedure called INC_SAL, stored within the data dictionary. It takes a numeric argument called INCREASE and uses this in a SQL UPDATE statement. Then the procedure is invoked with the EXECUTE command, passing in a value for the argument.

These examples are very simple, but they should illustrate how anonymous PL/SQL runs just once and therefore must be compiled at execution time, whereas stored PL/SQL can be compiled in advance and then executed many times.

 TIP Anonymous PL/SQL is less efficient than stored PL/SQL and also causes problems with source code management, as the code may be distributed across many machines.

PL/SQL Objects

There are five types of PL/SQL object:

- Procedure
- Function
- Package
- Package body
- Trigger

All of these are schema objects stored within the data dictionary. PL/SQL can also be used to create object types and the methods to manipulate them, but this is beyond the scope of the OCP examination.

Procedures, Functions, and Packages

Procedures and functions carry out user-defined actions. Packages are collections of procedures and functions, grouped together for manageability. To create these PL/SQL objects, you can use Enterprise Manager Database Control, SQL*Plus, or a tool specifically designed for generating PL/SQL code, such as Oracle's Procedure Builder or various third-party products.

 TIP SQL*Plus and Database Control are only suitable for small-scale PL/SQL development. For real work, your programmers will need a proper IDE (interactive development environment) tool that will assist with syntax checking, debugging, and source code management.

Procedures and Functions

A *procedure* is a block of code that carries out some action. It can, optionally, be defined with a number of *arguments*. These arguments are replaced with the actual parameters given when the procedure is invoked. The arguments can be IN arguments, meaning that they are used to pass data into the procedure, or OUT arguments, meaning that they are modified by the procedure and after execution the new values are passed out of the procedure. Arguments can also be IN-OUT, where the one variable serves both purposes. Within a procedure, you can define any number of variables that, unlike the arguments, are private to the procedure. To run a procedure, either call it from within a PL/SQL block or use the interactive EXECUTE command.

A *function* is similar in concept to a procedure, but it does not have OUT arguments and cannot be invoked with the EXECUTE command. It returns a single value, with the RETURN statement.

Anything that a function can do, a procedure could also do. Functions are generally used to support specific operations: small code blocks, that will be used many times. Procedures are more commonly used to divide code into modules, and may contain long and complex processes.

Figure 10-2 shows an example of creating and invoking a function. The first line is an instruction to create the function, or if it already exists, to overwrite it. The function takes one numeric argument and will return a varchar2 value. Within the BEGIN...END is the procedural code, which includes the flow control construct IF...THEN...ELSE... END IF.

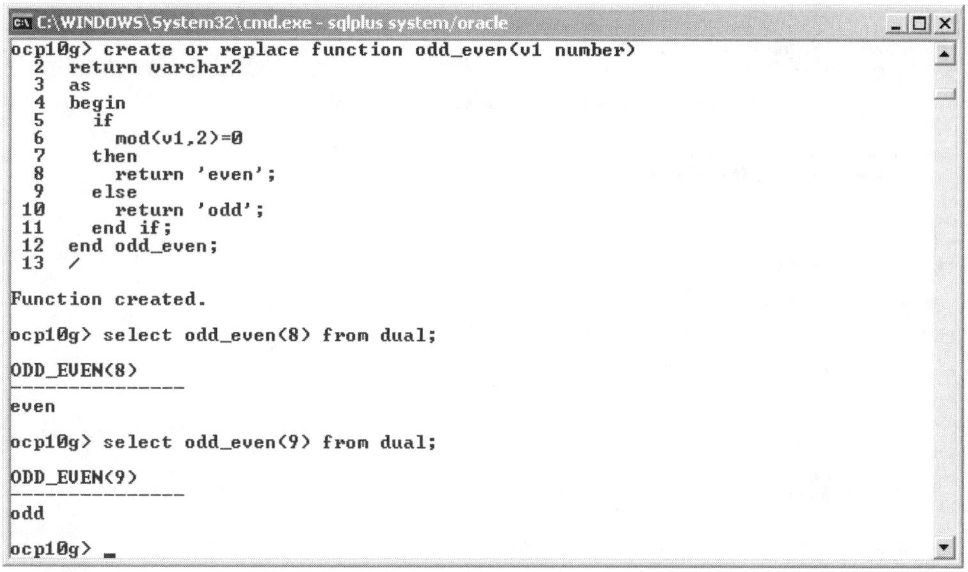

```
C:\WINDOWS\System32\cmd.exe - sqlplus system/oracle
ocp10g> create or replace function odd_even(v1 number)
  2    return varchar2
  3    as
  4    begin
  5      if
  6        mod(v1,2)=0
  7      then
  8        return 'even';
  9      else
 10        return 'odd';
 11      end if;
 12    end odd_even;
 13    /

Function created.

ocp10g> select odd_even(8) from dual;

ODD_EVEN(8)
---------------
even

ocp10g> select odd_even(9) from dual;

ODD_EVEN(9)
---------------
odd

ocp10g>
```

Figure 10-2   Creating and using a function with SQL*Plus

TIP If you use CREATE, rather than CREATE OR REPLACE, you will have to drop the object first if it already exists.

Figure 10-3 shows an example of creating and invoking a procedure. The procedure uses a looping construct to call a statement a variable number of times, dependent on the value of the parameter passed to the IN argument.

 TIP Some people get very upset about terminology. To summarize, an "argument" is the variable defined when you create a function or procedure; a "parameter" is the value passed to the argument when you run the function or procedure.

Packages

To group related procedures and functions together, your programmers create packages. A *package* consists of two objects: a specification and a body. A package specification lists the functions and procedures in the package, with their call specifications: the arguments and their datatypes. It can also define variables and constants accessible to all the procedures and functions in the package. The package body contains the PL/SQL code that implements the package: the code that creates the procedures and functions.

```
C:\WINDOWS\System32\cmd.exe - sqlplus system/oracle                    _ □ ×

ocp10g> create or replace procedure ins_ints(v1 in number)
  2   as
  3   begin
  4   for i in 1..v1 loop
  5   insert into integers values(i,odd_even(i));
  6   end loop;
  7   end ins_ints;
  8   /

Procedure created.

ocp10g> execute ins_ints(5);

PL/SQL procedure successfully completed.

ocp10g> select * from integers;

        C1 C2
---------- -----
         1 odd
         2 even
         3 odd
         4 even
         5 odd

ocp10g>
```

Figure 10-3 Creating and executing a procedure with SQL*Plus

To create a package specification, use the CREATE PACKAGE command. For example,

```
ocp10g> create or replace package numbers
  2  as
  3  function odd_even(v1 number) return varchar2;
  4  procedure ins_ints(v1 in number);
  5  end numbers;
  6  /
Package created.
```

Then to create the package body, use the CREATE OR REPLACE PACKAGE BODY statement to create the individual functions and procedures.

Several hundred PL/SQL packages are provided as standard with the Oracle database. Many are documented in the "PL/SQL Packages and Types Reference" manual. These supplied packages are, for the most part, created when you create a database. Some of them are for the use of the database administrator (such as the DBMS_WORKLOAD_REPOSITORY package, which lets you manage the Automatic Workload Repository); others are for your developers (such as the DBMS_OUTPUT package, that lets them write to a session's user process).

To invoke a packaged procedure, you must prefix the procedure name with the package name. For example,

```
ocp10g> exec dbms_output.put_line('message to the user');
```

will run the PUT_LINE procedure in the DBMS_OUTPUT package.

Exercise 10-1: Creating and Using Functions, Procedures, and Packages

Use Database Control to create PL/SQL objects and execute them from SQL*Plus.

1. Connect to your database as user SYSTEM using SQL*Plus.

2. Create a table to be used for this exercise.

   ```
   ocp10g> create table integers (c1 number,c2 varchar2(5));
   ```

3. Connect to your database as user SYSTEM using Database Control.

4. From the database home page, take the Administration tab and then the Packages link in the Schema section. Click Create.

5. In the Create Package window, enter **NUMBERS** as the package name, and the source code for the package as in Figure 10-4. Click OK to create the package.

6. From the database home page, take the Administration tab and then the Package bodies link in the Schema section. Click Create.

7. In the Create Package Body window, enter **NUMBERS** as the package name, and the source code for the package body as in Figure 10-5. Click OK to create the package body.

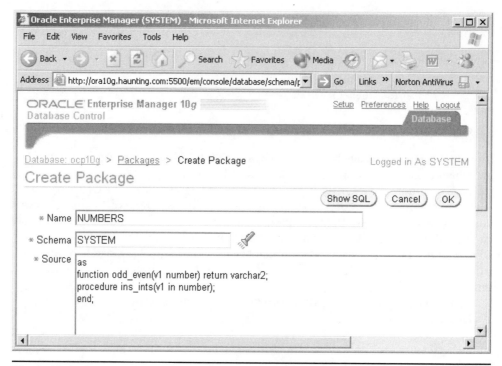

Figure 10-4 Creating a package specification with Database Control

8. In your SQL*Plus session, describe the package, execute the procedure, and check the results.

```
ocp10g> desc numbers;
PROCEDURE INS_INTS
 Argument Name                 Type                In/Out Default?
 ------------------------       -------------------  ------ --------
 V1                            NUMBER               IN
FUNCTION ODD_EVEN RETURNS VARCHAR2
 Argument Name                 Type                In/Out Default?
 ------------------------       -------------------  ------ --------
 V1                            NUMBER               IN
ocp10g> execute numbers.ins_ints(5);
PL/SQL procedure successfully completed.
ocp10g> select * from integers;
        C1 C2
---------- -----
         1 odd
         2 even
         3 odd
         4 even
         5 odd
5 rows selected.
```

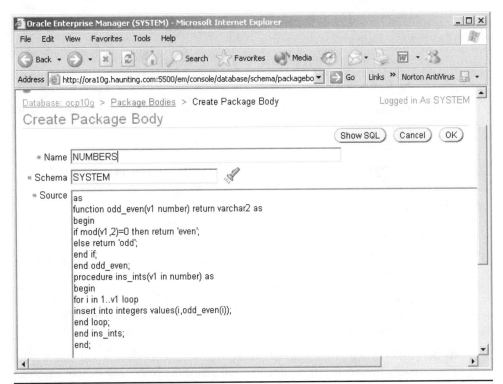

Figure 10-5   Creating a package body with Database Control

Database Triggers

Database triggers are a special category of PL/SQL object, in that they cannot be invoked
manually. A trigger runs (or "fires") automatically when a particular action is carried out
or a certain situation arises; this is the triggering event. There are a number of possible
triggering events. For many of them, the trigger can be configured to fire either before
or after the event. It is also possible to have both before and after triggers defined for
the same event. The DML triggers, which fire when rows are inserted, updated, or
deleted, can be configured to fire once for each affected row, or once per statement
execution.

All triggers have one factor in common: their execution is completely beyond the
control of the user who caused the triggering event. He may not even know that the
trigger fired. This makes triggers admirably suited to auditing user actions, as will be
described in Chapter 11. These are the more commonly used triggering events:

- Execution of INSERT, UPDATE, and DELETE DML commands
- Execution of CREATE, DROP, ALTER, and TRUNCATE DDL commands

- Session logon and logoff
- Database startup and shutdown
- Suspension of a statement because of a space problem
- Detection of a server error

Note that there is no such thing as a trigger on SELECT, though in Chapter 11 you will see how fine-grained auditing (FGA) can be used to produce a similar effect.

There are numerous uses for triggers. Here are some examples:

- **Auditing users' actions**   A trigger can capture full details of what was done and who did it, and write them out to an audit table.

- **Executing complex edits**   An action on one row may, in business terms, require a number of associated actions on other tables. The trigger can perform these automatically.

- **Security**   A trigger can check the time, the user's IP address, the program he is running, and any other factors that should limit what s/he can do.

- **Enforcing complex constraints**   An action may be fine in terms of the constraints on one table, but may need to be validated against the contents of several other tables.

Consider an HR system. Before an employee is deleted from the current employees' table, it is necessary to transfer all his details from a number of tables to archive tables. This could be enforced by creating a trigger as follows:

```
create or replace trigger archive_emp
before delete on current_emps
for each row
begin
archive_emp(:old.employee_id);
end;
```

Whenever any session deletes rows from the CURRENT_EMPS table, before each row is actually deleted the procedure ARCHIVE_EMP will execute, taking the EMPLOYEE_ID of the row being deleted as its parameter. This procedure will do whatever is necessary to archive an employee's data. This illustrates an important point: it is generally considered good practice to keep triggers small, and to do the bulk of the work with a stored procedure.

 EXAM TIP It is impossible to run a trigger by any means other than its triggering event.

Exercise 10-2: Using DML Triggers

Create a trigger to validate data, before committing it.

1. Connect to your database as user SYSTEM using SQL*Plus.

2. Create a trigger on the INTEGERS table as follows:

```
ocp10g> create or replace trigger oe_check
  2   after insert or update on integers
  3   for each row
  4   begin
  5   if mod(:new.c1,2)=0 then
  6   dbms_output.put_line(:new.c1||' is even');
  7   else
  8   dbms_output.put_line(:new.c1||' is odd');
  9   end if;
 10   end;
 11   /
Trigger created.
```

3. Enable printing to the screen for your SQL*Plus session.

```
ocp10g> set serveroutput on;
```

4. Test the effect of the trigger as follows:

```
ocp10g> insert into integers values(2,'odd');
2 is even
1 row created.
ocp10g> rollback;
Rollback complete.
ocp10g> insert into integers values(3,'odd');
3 is odd
1 row created.
ocp10g> commit;
Commit complete.
```

Note that because triggers fire as part of the transaction, it is possible to roll back the incorrect insertion.

5. Connect to your database as user SYSTEM using Database Control.

6. From the database home page, take the Administration tab and then the Triggers link in the Schema section.

7. In the Search window, select Object Type as Trigger, Schema as SYSTEM, and Object Name as OE_CHECK. Then click Go.

8. Click View to see the source code of the trigger, as in Figure 10-6. Note that it is "Valid," meaning that it has compiled correctly, and "Enabled," meaning that it will fire.

9. Tidy up.

```
ocp10g> drop trigger oe_check;
ocp10g> drop table integers;
ocp10g> drop package numbers;
```

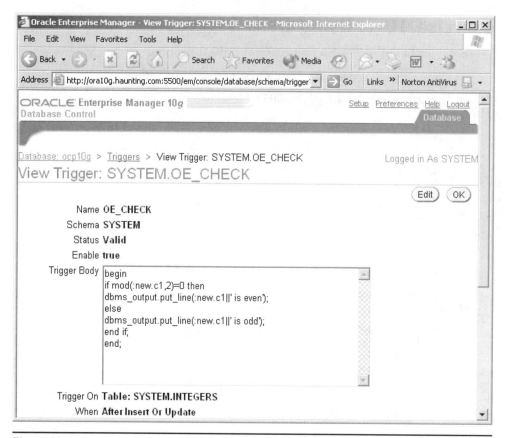

Figure 10-6 Displaying a trigger with Database Control

Instance Parameters for PL/SQL

The performance of PL/SQL code can be influenced by some instance parameters:

- **PLSQL_V2_COMPATIBILITY, default FALSE** Setting this to TRUE forces Oracle to allow some abnormal behavior that was legal in earlier releases. Use this only if it is necessary for backward compatibility.

- **PLSQL_DEBUG, default FALSE** Setting this to true forces Oracle to compile PL/SQL in a manner that will store additional information that may assist with debugging. This would not normally be set on a production system.

- **PLSQL_OPTIMIZE_LEVEL, default 2** Level 2, the highest, enables the use of all the compiler's optimization features; this gives the best run-time performance but perhaps increases compilation time. Lower settings (0 or 1) will result in quicker compilation but possibly slightly degraded execution. If the production system is doing a large amount of compilation (anonymous PL/SQL, for example), then it might be necessary to change this.

- **PLSQL_WARNINGS, default DISABLE:ALL**   This controls which messages should be displayed by the PL/SQL compiler. Other settings will cause the compiler to generate messages that may be of value when debugging code. This would not normally be set on a production system.

- **PLSQL_CODE_TYPE, default INTERPRETED**   The default setting means that PL/SQL code is compiled only down to byte code. Then when invoked, this is interpreted. Setting this to NATIVE, in conjunction with the parameter that follows, instructs Oracle to precompile the PL/SQL code to C code, and then to compile and link this with the C compiler and linker provided by your server's operating system. This may improve performance.

- **PLSQL_NATIVE_LIBRARY_DIR, default NULL**   Specifies the operating system path to store the dynamic link libraries that are generated by native PL/SQL compilation.

In most cases, the default settings for all these instance parameters will be suitable. On a production system, you may wish to consider setting the PLSQL_CODE_TYPE to NATIVE; this is in fact recommended for Oracle E-Business Suite running in a 10*g* database. Details of how to do this are given in the *PL/SQL Users Guide and Reference* manual.

Chapter Review

PL/SQL is a proprietary language for use with an Oracle database. It provides procedural constructs that can be used in conjunction with SQL statements. PL/SQL is usually used to write stored procedures and functions: these are compiled and stored within the data dictionary of the database and for ease of management can be grouped into packages. A package consists of a package specification, which publishes the call specifications of the procedures and functions, and a package body, which implements them.

A special type of PL/SQL object is the trigger. Triggers are PL/SQL code blocks that cannot be invoked on demand: they run automatically when their triggering event occurs.

The default mode for running PL/SQL is through an interpreter. It is compiled down to byte code, but no further. If you wish, and if you have a C compiler and a linker available, you can convert your PL/SQL code to C code, compile and link it, and save it as a dynamically linkable shared object library.

Questions

1. Which of the following, if any, can be PL/SQL objects? (Choose all that apply.)

   A. Constraints

   B. Functions

   C. Package bodies

   D. Package specifications

   E. Procedures

   F. Sequences

   G. Triggers

   H. Views

2. Which of the following PL/SQL objects can be invoked with the EXECUTE command? (Choose the best answer.)

   A. Functions

   B. Packages

   C. Procedures

   D. Triggers

   E. All of the above

3. Where does PL/SQL code run? (Choose the best answer.)

   A. Within the session's user process

   B. Within the data dictionary

   C. Within the instance

   D. It depends on whether the PL/SQL is anonymous or stored

4. Which PL/SQL object types can be packaged? (Choose all that apply.)

   A. Anonymous PL/SQL blocks

   B. Functions

   C. Procedures

   D. Triggers

5. When PL/SQL is compiled, where is the resulting code stored? (Choose the best answer.)

   A. In the data dictionary

   B. As an operating system file

   C. In the default tablespace of the user who owns the code

   D. It depends on the PLSQL_CODE_TYPE parameter

Answers

1. **B, C, D, E,** and **G.** All these are created with PL/SQL; the others, with SQL.

2. **C.** Only procedures can be invoked with the EXECUTE command. Functions are called by other statements, and triggers fire automatically. Packages can't be executed at all, unlike the procedures and functions they contain.

3. **C.** PL/SQL runs within the instance. It may be invoked by a user process, and it is stored in the data dictionary. Whether the code is anonymous or stored, it still runs in the instance.

4. **B** and **C.** Packages consist of one or more procedures and functions. Anonymous blocks must be converted to procedures before they can be packaged, and while triggers can call packaged code, they cannot themselves be included within a package.

5. **D.** It depends on the PLSQL_CODE_TYPE setting. Native compiled code is stored in an operating system file, while interpreted code is stored in the data dictionary.

CHAPTER 11

Securing the Oracle Database

In this chapter you will learn how to
- Apply the principal of least privilege
- Manage default user accounts
- Implement standard password security features
- Audit database activity
- Register for security updates

The safest principle to follow when determining access to computer systems is that of "least privilege": no one should have access to anything beyond the absolute minimum needed to perform their work, and anything not specifically allowed is forbidden. The Oracle database conforms to this, in that by default no one can do anything at all with the exception of the two users SYS and SYSTEM. No other users can even connect, not even those created by the standard database creation routines.

Once users are given permission to connect and to see and manipulate data, the database provides facilities for controlling passwords and for tracking what people are doing. But before going into that, there are certain "best practices" that should be applied to tighten up the default security levels.

Adjusting Default Security Settings

A database created with the Database Configuration Assistant, DBCA, will, depending on the options selected, have more than a dozen user accounts. Access to these accounts must be controlled—by default, there is no access to most of them. The user accounts you create subsequent to database creation should have their privileges restricted: by default, they may have capabilities that you are not expecting. It is vital to control these if there is any possibility of users connecting with tools (such as SQL*Plus) that let them issue ad hoc SQL and PL/SQL commands.

Default Users

To see the users in your database and the status of the accounts, query the DBA_USERS view:

```
ocp10g> select username,account_status from dba_users;
USERNAME              ACCOUNT_STATUS
-------------------   --------------------------------
SYS                   OPEN
SYSTEM                OPEN
OUTLN                 EXPIRED & LOCKED
DIP                   EXPIRED & LOCKED
DBSNMP                OPEN
WMSYS                 EXPIRED & LOCKED
EXFSYS                EXPIRED & LOCKED
SI_INFORMTN_SCHEMA    EXPIRED & LOCKED
ORDPLUGINS            EXPIRED & LOCKED
ORDSYS                EXPIRED & LOCKED
MDSYS                 EXPIRED & LOCKED
DMSYS                 EXPIRED & LOCKED
CTXSYS                EXPIRED & LOCKED
XDB                   EXPIRED & LOCKED
ANONYMOUS             EXPIRED & LOCKED
OLAPSYS               EXPIRED & LOCKED
MDDATA                EXPIRED & LOCKED
WKPROXY               EXPIRED & LOCKED
WKSYS                 EXPIRED & LOCKED
WK_TEST               EXPIRED & LOCKED
SYSMAN                OPEN
<output truncated...>
```

With the exception of four users, all the users created by DBCA have their accounts marked as EXPIRED & LOCKED. "Expired" refers to the password: the first time a user logs on to the database with that username, he will be prompted to change the password. "Locked" means that it is impossible to connect with that account anyway; it must be unlocked before it can be used.

The passwords for the usable default accounts (SYS, SYSTEM, DBSNMP, and SYSMAN) are set at database creation time. This was covered in Chapter 3. The other accounts have well-known passwords: they are the same as the username. If you decide to unlock the accounts, you will be forced to change the password immediately, as in Figure 11-1.

TIP The DBSNMP and SYSMAN accounts are for the use of Enterprise Manager, either Grid Control or Database Control. To change their passwords, you must use the `emctl` utility.

It should only be necessary to unlock a default account in exceptional circumstances. These accounts are used to store data and code required by certain options within the database, not for users to connect to. For example, the MDSYS schema stores the objects required by the Oracle Spatial option, which extends the capabilities of the database to manage geographical information. Users can make use of the spatial option without needing to connect to the schema.

TIP Even the demonstration schemas (HR, OE, and so on) are locked after you create them.

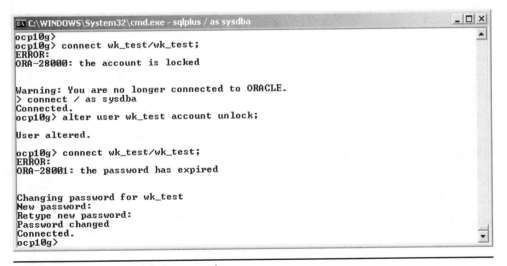

Figure 11-1 Opening a default account for use

When you create accounts for your users, always check whether they are actually needed for connections, or whether they are only to be used for storing data. In many systems, there will be hardly any accounts that must be opened for logon. For example, in an Oracle 11i E-Business Suite database, it may be that only two accounts (APPS and APPLSYSPUB) are actually used for connections. The numerous other accounts (GL, AR, AP, and dozens more) may be used only for storing application data. In this type of application environment, you delegate responsibility for security to the application.

If your database was created from the SQL*Plus command line, security may be much weaker than using DBCA. For example, the SYS and SYSTEM passwords may be on the very well-known defaults of CHANGE_ON_INSTALL and MANAGER respectively. On a frightening number of production systems, these defaults are never changed.

Public Privileges

There is a pseudo-user called PUBLIC. Any privileges granted to PUBLIC have, in effect, been granted to every user; every account you create will have access to these privileges. By default, the public user has a large number of privileges. In particular, he has execute permission on a number of PL/SQL utility packages, as shown in Figure 11-2.

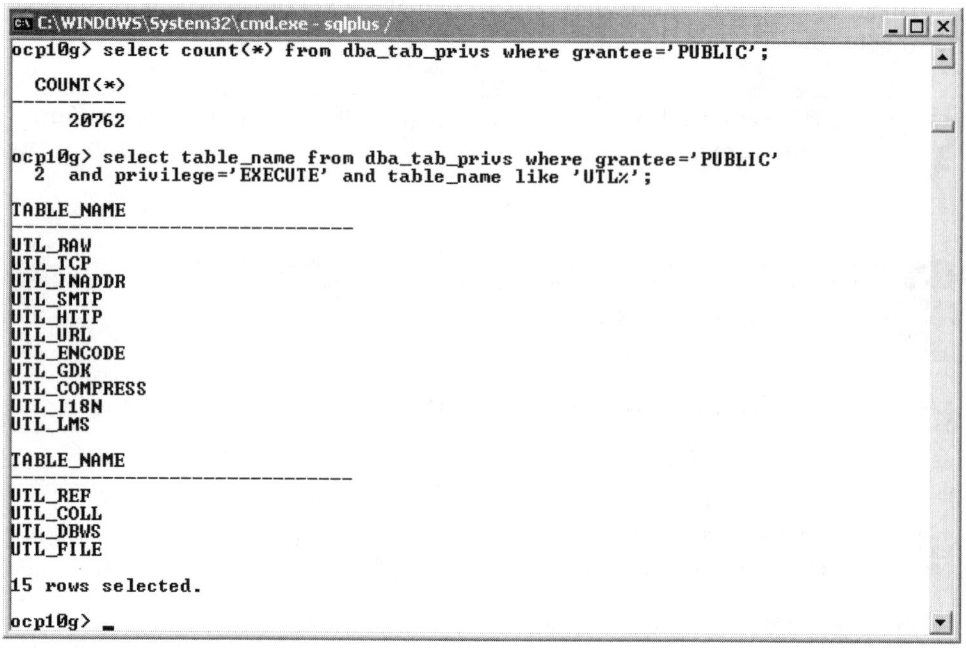

```
C:\WINDOWS\System32\cmd.exe - sqlplus /                                  _ □ ×
ocp10g> select count(*) from dba_tab_privs where grantee='PUBLIC';

  COUNT(*)
----------
     20762

ocp10g> select table_name from dba_tab_privs where grantee='PUBLIC'
  2  and privilege='EXECUTE' and table_name like 'UTL%';

TABLE_NAME
------------------------------
UTL_RAW
UTL_TCP
UTL_INADDR
UTL_SMTP
UTL_HTTP
UTL_URL
UTL_ENCODE
UTL_GDK
UTL_COMPRESS
UTL_I18N
UTL_LMS

TABLE_NAME
------------------------------
UTL_REF
UTL_COLL
UTL_DBWS
UTL_FILE

15 rows selected.

ocp10g> _
```

Figure 11-2 Privileges granted to PUBLIC

You should always consider revoking the execution privileges on the UTL packages, though remember that application software may assume that the privilege is there. Revoke the privilege as follows:

```
SQL> revoke execute on utl_file from public;
```

These are some of the more dangerous packages listed in Figure 11-2:

- **UTL_FILE** This allows users to read and write any file and directory that is accessible to the operating system user under whose identity the Oracle processes are running. This includes all the database files and the ORACLE_ HOME directory. On Windows systems, this is particularly dangerous, as many Windows databases run with Administrator privileges. The package is to a certain extent controlled by the UTL_FILE_DIR instance parameter, discussed in a following section.

- **UTL_TCP** This allows users to open TCP ports on the server machine for connections to any accessible address on the network. The interface provided in the package only allows connections to be initiated by the PL/SQL program; it does not allow the PL/SQL program to accept connections initiated outside the program. Nonetheless, it does allow malicious users to use your database as the starting point for launching attacks on other systems, or for transmitting data to unauthorized recipients.

- **UTL_SMTP** Written using UTL_TCP calls, this package lets users send mail messages. It is restricted by the UTL_SMTP_SERVER instance parameter, which gives the address of the outgoing mail server, but even so, you probably do not want your database to be used for exchange of mail messages without your knowledge.

- **UTL_HTTP** This too is written with UTL_TCP calls. It allows users to send HTTP messages and receive responses, in effect, converting your database into a web browser.

Always remember that, by default, these packages are available to absolutely anyone who has a logon to your database, and furthermore that your database may have a number of well-known accounts with well-known passwords.

Security Critical Instance Parameters

Some parameters are vital to consider for securing the database. The defaults are usually fine, but in some circumstances (for which there should always be a good business case), you may need to change them. All of the parameters described here are static: you must restart the instance for a change to take effect. This is intended to give extra security, as it reduces the likelihood that they can be changed temporarily to an inappropriate setting without the DBA being aware of it.

UTL_FILE_DIR

The UTL_FILE_DIR instance parameter defaults to NULL and is therefore not a security problem. But if you need to set it, take care. This parameter gives PL/SQL access to the file system of the server machine, through the UTL_FILE supplied package. The package has procedures to open a file (either a new file or an existing one) and read from and write to it. The only limitation is that the directories listed must be accessible to the Oracle owner.

The difficulty with this parameter is that, being set at the instance level, it offers no way to allow some users access to some directories and other users access to other directories. All users with execute permission on the UTL_FILE package have access to all the directories listed in the UTL_FILE_DIR parameter.

The parameter takes a comma-separated list of directories and is static. To set it, follow the syntax in this example, which gives access to two directories, and restart the instance:

```
SQL> alter system set utl_file_dir='/oracle/tmp','/oracle/interface' scope=spfile;
```

 TIP The UTL_FILE_DIR parameter can include wildcards. Never set it to '*', because that will allow all users access to everything that the database owner can see, including the ORACLE_HOME and all the database files.

REMOTE_OS_AUTHENT and OS_AUTHENT_PREFIX

The REMOTE_OS_AUTHENT instance parameter defaults to FALSE. This controls whether a user can connect to the database from a remote computer without the need to give a password. The reasons for wanting to do this have largely disappeared with modern computer systems, but the capability is still there.

In the days before all users had intelligent terminals, such as PCs, it was customary for users to log on directly to the database server machine, and therefore to be authenticated by the server's operating system. They would then launch their user process on the server machine and connect to the database. In order to avoid the necessity for users to provide usernames and passwords twice (once for the operating system logon, and again for the database logon), it was common to create the Oracle users with this syntax:

```
SQL> create user jon identified externally;
```

This delegates responsibility for authentication to the server's operating system. Any person logged on to the server machine as operating system user "jon" will be able to connect to the database without the need for any further authentication:

```
$ sqlplus /
Connected to:
Oracle Database 10g Enterprise Edition Release 10.1.0.2.0 - Production
With the Partitioning, OLAP and Data Mining options
```

```
SQL> show user;
USER is "JON"
SQL>
```

This is secure, as long as your server's operating system is secure. As networking became more widespread, it became common to separate the user process workload from the server process workload by having users log on to a different machine dedicated to running user processes, which would connect to the server over Oracle Net (or SQL*Net, as it was then known). Since the user no longer logs on to the server's operating system, external authentication can't be used—unless you use the REMOTE_OS_AUTHENT parameter. Setting this to TRUE means that user JON can connect without a password from any machine where he is logged on as operating system user "jon." This is only secure as long as no one has access to the network from a machine with an insecure operating system (such as a PC).

 TIP It is generally considered to be bad practice to enable remote operating system authentication.

The OS_AUTHENT_PREFIX instance parameter is related to external authentication, either local or remote. It specifies a prefix that must be applied to the operating system username before it can be mapped onto an Oracle username. The default is "OPS$". In the preceding example, it is assumed that this parameter has been cleared, with

```
SQL> alter system set os_authent_prefix='' scope=spfile;
```

Otherwise, the Oracle username would have had to be OPS$JON.

O7_DICTIONARY_ACCESSIBILITY

The O7_DICTIONARY_ACCESSIBILITY instance parameter controls the effect of granting object privileges with the ANY keyword. It defaults to FALSE. You can give user JON permission to see any table in the database with

```
SQL> grant select any table to jon;
```

but do you want him to be able to see the data dictionary tables as well as the user tables? Probably not; some of them contain sensitive data, such as unencrypted passwords or source code that should be protected.

O7_DICTIONARY_ACCESSIBILITY defaults to false, meaning that the ANY privileges exclude objects owned by SYS, thus protecting the data dictionary; JON can see all the user data, but not objects owned by SYS. If you change the parameter to TRUE, then ANY really does mean ANY, and JON will be able to see the data dictionary as well as all user data.

It is possible that some older application software may assume that the ANY privileges include the data dictionary, as was always the case with release 7 of the

Oracle database (hence the name of the parameter). If so, you have no choice but to change the parameter to TRUE until the software is patched up to current standards.

 TIP Data dictionary accessibility is sometimes a problem for application installation routines. You may have to set O7_DICTIONARY_ACCESSIBILITY to true while installing a product, and then be able to put it back on default when the installation is finished.

If you have users who really do need access to the data dictionary, rather than setting O7_DICTIONARY_ACCESSIBILITY to true, consider granting them the SELECT ANY DICTIONARY privilege. This will let them see the data dictionary and dynamic performance views, but they will not be able to see any user data—unless you have specifically granted them permission to do so. This might apply, for example, to the staff of an external company you use for database administration support: they need access to all the data dictionary information, but they have no need to view your application data.

REMOTE_LOGIN_PASSWORDFILE

The remote REMOTE_LOGIN_PASSWORDFILE instance parameter controls whether it is possible to connect to the instance as a user with the SYSDBA privilege over the network. With this parameter on its default of NONE, the only way to get a SYSDBA connection is to log on to the operating system of the server machine as a member of the operating system group that owns the Oracle software. This is absolutely secure—as long as your server operating system is secure, which it should be.

Setting this parameter to either EXCLUSIVE or SHARED gives users another way in: even if they are not logged on to the server as a member of the Oracle software owning group, or even if they are coming in across the network, they can still connect as SYSDBA if they know the appropriate password. The passwords are embedded, in encrypted form, in an operating system file in the Oracle home directory: $ORACLE_HOME/dbs on Unix, or %ORACLE_HOME%\database on Windows. A setting of SHARED means that all instances running of the same Oracle home directory will share a common password file. This will have just one password within it for the SYS user that is common to all the instances. EXCLUSIVE means that the instance will look for a file whose name includes the instance name: PWD<SID>.ora on Windows, orapw<SID> on Unix, where <SID> is the instance name. This file will have instance-specific passwords.

The password file is initially created by running the orapwd utility from an operating system prompt. This will create the file and embed within it a password for the SYS user. Subsequently, you can add other users' passwords to the file, thus allowing them to connect as SYSDBA or SYSOPER as well. Review the scripts in Chapter 3 for an example of the syntax for creating a password file. To add another user to the file, grant him either the SYSDBA or SYSOPER privilege, as in Figure 11-3. The V$PWFILE_USERS view shows you which users have their passwords entered in the password file, and whether they have the SYSOPER privilege, the SYSDBA privilege, or both.

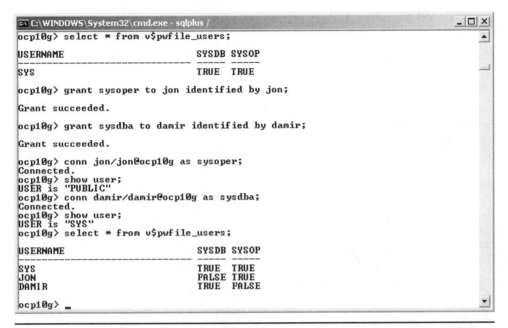

Figure 11-3   Managing the password file with SQL*Plus

Note that when connecting as SYSDBA, even though you use a username and password, you end up connected as user SYS; when connecting as SYSOPER, you are in fact connected as the PUBLIC user.

Password Profiles

Most organizations will have a security policy that has rules for, among other things, password and account management. If your organization does not have such a policy, someone should be writing one—perhaps it should be you. The security policy will be driven by business requirements, but also by legal necessities that will vary from one country to another and according to the business environment.

In many cases the security of an application will be controlled by the application itself, in which case the DBA will have little control of it: the principle of least privilege should be applied by the application designers. But it is always necessary to control what users can do if they can connect directly with their own schema usernames with user processes (such as SQL*Plus) that allow them freedom to issue ad hoc SQL and PL/SQL calls. To assist with managing database username security, a standard feature of the Oracle database is user profiles.

Profiles can also be used to limit resource usage, shown as the kernel limits in the next section. To enable resource profiles, the instance parameter RESOURCE_LIMIT must be set to TRUE. Password profiles are always enabled, irrespective of this parameter.

Password Profile Limits

The password profile facility is being used in all databases whether you know it or not.
Every user (even SYS) is assigned to a profile: by default, to the profile called DEFAULT.
To confirm this, issue this query:

```
SQL> select username,profile from dba_users;
```

You will see that all users are assigned to a profile called DEFAULT. The DEFAULT
profile has, by default, no limits, as is shown by this query against the DBA_PROFILES
view:

```
ocp10g> select * from dba_profiles where profile ='DEFAULT';
PROFILE      RESOURCE_NAME              RESOURCE LIMIT
----------   ------------------------   -------- ----------
DEFAULT      COMPOSITE_LIMIT            KERNEL   UNLIMITED
DEFAULT      SESSIONS_PER_USER          KERNEL   UNLIMITED
DEFAULT      CPU_PER_SESSION            KERNEL   UNLIMITED
DEFAULT      CPU_PER_CALL               KERNEL   UNLIMITED
DEFAULT      LOGICAL_READS_PER_SESSION  KERNEL   UNLIMITED
DEFAULT      LOGICAL_READS_PER_CALL     KERNEL   UNLIMITED
DEFAULT      IDLE_TIME                  KERNEL   UNLIMITED
DEFAULT      CONNECT_TIME               KERNEL   UNLIMITED
DEFAULT      PRIVATE_SGA                KERNEL   UNLIMITED
DEFAULT      FAILED_LOGIN_ATTEMPTS      PASSWORD UNLIMITED
DEFAULT      PASSWORD_LIFE_TIME         PASSWORD UNLIMITED
DEFAULT      PASSWORD_REUSE_TIME        PASSWORD UNLIMITED
DEFAULT      PASSWORD_REUSE_MAX         PASSWORD UNLIMITED
DEFAULT      PASSWORD_VERIFY_FUNCTION   PASSWORD NULL
DEFAULT      PASSWORD_LOCK_TIME         PASSWORD UNLIMITED
DEFAULT      PASSWORD_GRACE_TIME        PASSWORD UNLIMITED
16 rows selected.
```

The kernel limitations are to do with how much processing capacity a session is
allowed to consume, and are of no concern here. It is the password limits that are
relevant to security:

- **FAILED_LOGIN_ATTEMPTS**   After this number of consecutive connect
  requests with an incorrect password, the account will be locked. This will
  prevent hackers from trying numerous common passwords in an attempt
  to guess the correct one. The counter is reset after a successful connection.

- **PASSWORD_LOCK_TIME**   The number of days for which the account will be
  locked if the FAILED_LOGIN_ATTEMPTS limit is reached. If days are unsuitable
  as units, use appropriate arithmetic. For instance, one day has one thousand
  four hundred and forty minutes, so setting the PASSWORD_LOCK_TIME
  to (30/1440) is equivalent to thirty minutes; enough to foil a hacker who is
  throwing a dictionary at your database, without inconveniencing forgetful
  users too much.

- **PASSWORD_LIFE_TIME**   The number of days that will pass before the user
  is prompted to change his password.

- **PASSWORD_GRACE_TIME**   The number of days following a successful login after the expiration of PASSWORD_LIFE_TIME. The grace time starts after the login, even if the password has already expired.

- **PASSWORD_REUSE_TIME**   The time in days that must elapse before a password can be reused. This prevents users from bypassing the PASSWORD_ LIFE_TIME limit setting by "changing" their password to what it was in the first place.

- **PASSWORD_REUSE_MAX**   The number of times that a password can be reused, irrespective of the PASSWORD_REUSE_TIME setting.

- **PASSWORD_VERIFY_FUNCTION**   As detailed in the next section, this is a PL/SQL function that will perform complexity checks (or any other checks that may be needed) whenever a password is changed.

When setting these limits, you must consider them together: there is little point in setting a PASSWORD_LOCK_TIME unless you also set FAILED_LOGIN_ATTEMPTS. In addition to using profiles to expire passwords and lock accounts automatically, you can also do it manually:

```
SQL> alter user jon password expire;
```

will generate a prompt to change password the next time user JON logs in, and

```
SQL> alter user jon account lock;
```

will lock JON's account immediately. Neither command will affect JON's session(s) if he is currently connected.

The Password Verify Function

Any user can change his password at any time—or an administrator can change it for him. A password profile can include a reference to a PL/SQL function, known as the password verify function. This is a function that will execute whenever a user with that profile changes his password or has it changed by an administrator. The function must reside in the SYS schema and accept three arguments: the username, the new password, and the old password. It must return TRUE or FALSE; if it returns FALSE, the password change is rejected.

A demonstration function is provided as part of the standard Oracle installation. To create it, connect as SYS and run a script. On Unix,

```
SQL> @?/rdbms/admin/utlpwdmg.sql
```

or on Windows,

```
SQL> @?\rdbms\admin\utlpwdmg.sql
```

The script is well documented; before running it, you should study it to check whether it really does meet your requirements. If not, create your own script to fit your needs. The function it creates performs these checks on the new password and will reject the change if it fails any of them:

- The password may not be the same as the username. The check is not case sensitive; the username and password are converted to lowercase before the comparison.

- The password must be at least four characters long.

- The password, again converted to lowercase, is checked against a hard-coded list of half a dozen commonly used passwords. This list is certainly inadequate for production systems. If you have rules regarding common passwords, you may have to adjust the code to point to an appropriately populated table.

- The password is checked to ensure that it contains at least one digit, one upper- or lowercase letter, and one punctuation mark. The punctuation marks are a hard-coded list.

- The password must contain at least three characters that are different from the old password, or be at least three characters longer. The check is based on the position of the characters in the string.

The script will also adjust the default profile to enable use of the verify function that it creates, and set some password limits. Again, you must check the script before running it to ensure that it really does meet your requirements.

Creating, Assigning, and Modifying Password Profiles

Determining the password policy for your organization is not part of the DBA's role. The requirements will be dependent on the business and legal needs and may well be detailed by your computer auditors, or a security group. In many cases, the security policy will be enforced at the application level, but in an environment where it is possible for users to connect to the database using Oracle usernames, password profiles are the tool to implement the policy.

Since all users are automatically assigned to the profile called DEFAULT, the quickest way to implement a security policy is to alter the DEFAULT profile. Then all users will pick up the changes at their next login. This is what the UTLPWDMG.SQL script described previously does. The final command in the script is

```
ALTER PROFILE DEFAULT LIMIT
PASSWORD_LIFE_TIME 60
PASSWORD_GRACE_TIME 10
PASSWORD_REUSE_TIME 1800
PASSWORD_REUSE_MAX UNLIMITED
FAILED_LOGIN_ATTEMPTS 3
PASSWORD_LOCK_TIME 1/1440
PASSWORD_VERIFY_FUNCTION verify_function;
```

Running this command will generate a "change password" prompt for all users after sixty days, with an additional ten days to make the change before the account is locked. Passwords cannot be reused for another eighteen hundred days. After three consecutive incorrect passwords, the account will be locked for one minute. Any password change will be checked by a function called SYS.VERIFY_FUNCTION.

Applying one profile to all users may not be a suitable solution. For example, it is not uncommon to have a public account on a database with a well-known password with very restricted privileges: perhaps it can search a catalog of products, or a telephone directory, but do nothing more. This account would need a profile with no limits. Other users with higher levels of access might require tighter controls. In such an environment, you must create multiple profiles and assign different users to them. The different profiles can even have different verify functions.

Profiles can be created, modified, assigned to users, and dropped using SQL*Plus commands or with Database Control. From SQL*Plus, use the commands

```
CREATE PROFILE...;
ALTER PROFILE...;
DROP PROFILE...;
```

to manage profiles, and

```
ALTER USER <username> PROFILE <profilename>;
```

to assign a profile to a user.

Exercise 11-1: Creating and Using Password Profiles

Create a profile with strict limits, and assign a user to it. Demonstrate the effect.

1. Connect to your database as user SYSTEM with Database Control.

2. From the database home page, take the Administration tab and then the Profiles link in the Security section.

3. Click Create to reach the Create Profile window, and enter **STRICT** as the profile name. Take the Password link to reach the password controls window.

4. Set limits for your STRICT profile as in Figure 11-4. Users assigned to this profile will have to change their passwords after two weeks, and they will have three days to do so. A password can only ever be used once, and after two failed login attempts the account will be locked—but only for one minute.

5. Click Show SQL, examine the CREATE PROFILE command being generated, and click Return.

6. Click OK to create the profile.

7. Return to the Administration page of Database Control, and take the Users link in the Security section.

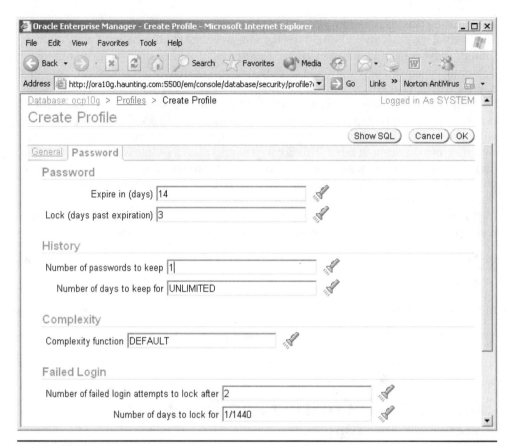

Figure 11-4   Setting password limits with Database Control

8. On the Users window, find the SYSTEM user, select his radio button, and click Edit.

9. In the Edit User: SYSTEM window, select the STRICT profile and expire the password, as in Figure 11-5.

10. Click Show SQL, examine the ALTER USER command being generated, and click Return.

11. Click Apply to make the change.

12. Connect to your database as user SYSTEM using SQL*Plus. Note that you immediately receive a warning that the password has expired, and that you are already in the "grace" period of three days.

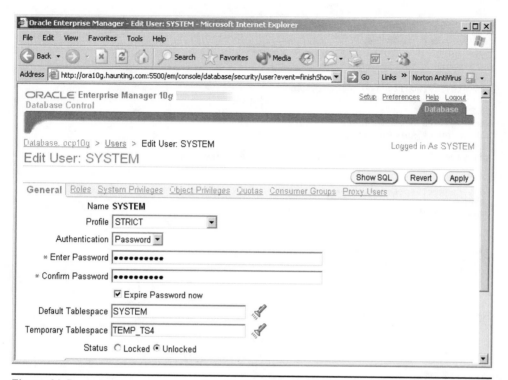

Figure 11-5 Assigning a user to a profile with Database Control

13. Attempt to change the password to the value it is already (in the example here, it is ORACLE) with

```
SQL> alter user system identified by oracle;
```

You will receive an error,

```
ORA-28007: the password cannot be reused
```

14. Enter a different password. (Remember it!) For the following examples, it was set to MANAGER.

15. Attempt to connect three times with the wrong password. At the third attempt, you will be told that the account is locked, as in Figure 11-6. Wait at least one minute, and then connect with the correct password.

16. Tidy up by assigning SYSTEM back to the default profile and dropping the STRICT profile.

```
SQL> alter user system profile default;
SQL> drop profile strict;
```

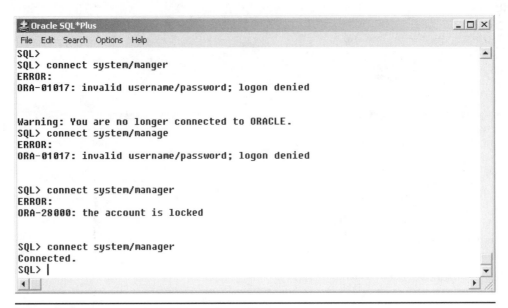

Figure 11-6   An account locked by use of a profile

Auditing

No matter how good your security policies are, there will be occasions when a policy is not enough. You will have to accept that users have privileges that could be dangerous. All you can do is monitor their use of those privileges and track what they are actually doing with them. The most extreme example of this is you, the database administrator. Anyone with the SYSDBA privilege can do anything within the database. For your employers to have confidence that you are not abusing this power (which cannot be revoked, or you couldn't do your job), it is necessary to audit all SYSDBA activity. For normal users, you may also wish to track what they are doing. You may not be able to prevent them from breaking company rules on access to data, but you can track the fact that they did it.

Apart from SYSDBA auditing, Oracle provides three auditing techniques:

- Database auditing can track the use of certain privileges, the execution of certain commands, access to certain tables, or logon attempts.

- Value-based auditing uses database triggers. Whenever a row is inserted, updated, or deleted, a block of PL/SQL code will run that can (among other things) record complete details of the event.

- Fine-grained auditing allows tracking access to tables according to which rows (or which columns of the rows) were accessed. It is much more precise than either database auditing or value-based auditing, and it can limit the number of audit records generated to only those of interest.

TIP Auditing of any type increases the amount of work that the database must do. In order to limit this workload, you should focus your auditing closely and not track events of minimal significance.

Auditing SYSDBA Activity

There is an instance parameter AUDIT_SYS_OPERATIONS. If it is set to TRUE (the default is FALSE), then every statement issued by a user connected AS SYSDBA or AS SYSOPER is written out to the operating system's audit trail. This gives a complete record of all work done by the DBA. Clearly, the audit trail must be protected: if it were possible for the DBA to delete the audit records, there would be no point in creating them.

This brings up the question of "separation of duties." Your system needs to be configured in such a way that the DBA has no access to the audit records that track his activity: they should be accessible only to the computer's system administrator. If the DBA were also the system administrator, then the auditing would be useless. For this reason, a decent computer auditor will always state that the DBA must not have the Unix "root" password (or the Windows "Administrator" password), and the system administrator must not have the Oracle SYSDBA password.

The destination of the SYS audit records is platform specific. On Windows, it is the Windows Application Log; on Unix it is controlled by the AUDIT_FILE_DEST parameter. This parameter should point to a directory on which the Oracle owner has write permission (so that the audit records can be written by the instance) but the Unix ID used by the DBA does not, so that he cannot adjust the audit records by hand.

Database Auditing

Before setting up database auditing, an instance parameter must be set: AUDIT_TRAIL. This has four possible values:

- **NONE (or FALSE)** Database auditing is disabled, no matter what auditing you attempt to configure.

- **OS** Audit records will be written to the operating system's audit trail: the Application Log on Windows, or the AUDIT_FILE_DEST directory on Unix.

- **DB (or TRUE)** The audit records are written to a data dictionary table, SYS.AUD$. There are views that let you see the contents of this table.

- **DB_EXTENDED** As DB, but including information on the SQL statements with bind variables that generated the audit records.

Having set the AUDIT_TRAIL parameter, you can use database auditing to capture login attempts, use of system and object privileges, and execution of SQL commands. Furthermore, you can specify whether to audit these events when they succeeded, when they failed because of permissions, or both. Auditing commands that did not succeed can be particularly valuable: any records produced will tell you that users are attempting to break their access rights.

Database auditing is configured using the AUDIT command.
Use of privileges can be audited with, for example,

```
ocp10g> audit create any trigger;
ocp10g> audit select any table by session;
```

Your programmers may have been granted the CREATE ANY TRIGGER privilege because they will be creating triggers on other schemas' tables as part of their work, but it is a dangerous privilege that could be used maliciously. So you certainly need to know when they use it. Similarly, some staff will need the SELECT ANY TABLE and UPDATE ANY TABLE privileges in order to sort out problems with transactions that have gone wrong, but whenever they use these privileges, a record must be kept so that they will be deterred from accessing data unless they have a legitimate reason. In general, the ANY privileges should be restricted and granted only under exceptional circumstances.

By default, auditing will generate an audit record for every occurrence of the event. This is equivalent to appending BY ACCESS to the AUDIT command. Appending the keywords BY SESSION to the AUDIT command will restrict the audit output to only one record per logon, no matter how often the audit condition is met.

Auditing can also be object-oriented:

```
ocp10g> audit insert on ar.hz_parties whenever successful;
ocp10g> audit all on ar.ra_interface_lines_all;
```

The first of these examples will generate audit records whenever a row is inserted in the named table. The WHENEVER SUCCESSFUL keywords restrict audit records to those where the operation succeeded; the alternative syntax is WHENEVER NOT SUCCESSFUL. By default, all operations (successful or not) are audited. The second example will audit all DDL statements executed against the named table.

Logons are audited with AUDIT SESSION. For example,

```
ocpt10g> audit session whenever not successful;
```

Session auditing records each connection to the database. The NOT SUCCESSFUL keywords restrict the output to only failed attempts. This can be particularly useful: recording failures will indicate if attempts are being made to break into the database.

If auditing is to the operating system (because the AUDIT_TRAIL parameter is set to OS), then view the files created in the operating system audit trail to see the results of the audits. If it is to the data dictionary (AUDIT_TRAIL=DB), then you can see the entries through data dictionary views. The critical view is the DBA_AUDIT_TRAIL view. This will show all audit trail entries, no matter what type of audit it was; of necessity, the view is very generic, and not all columns will be populated for each audit trail entry. Table 11-1 is an extract from the *Oracle Database 10g Reference*, describing the view.

The other audit views (DBA_AUDIT_OBJECT, DBA_AUDIT_STATEMENT, and DBA_AUDIT_SESSION) each show a subset of the DBA_AUDIT_TRAIL view, only displaying certain audit records and the columns relevant to them.

Column	Description
OS_USERNAME	Operating system login username of the user whose actions were audited
USERNAME	Name (not ID number) of the user whose actions were audited
USERHOST	Client host machine name
TERMINAL	Identifier of the user's terminal
TIMESTAMP	Date and time of the creation of the audit trail entry (date and time of user login for entries created by AUDIT SESSION) in the local database session time zone
OWNER	Creator of the object affected by the action
OBJ_NAME	Name of the object affected by the action
ACTION	Numeric action type code. The corresponding name of the action type is in the ACTION_NAME column
ACTION_NAME	Name of the action type corresponding to the numeric code in the ACTION column
NEW_OWNER	Owner of the object named in the NEW_NAME column
NEW_NAME	New name of the object after a RENAME or the name of the underlying object
OBJ_PRIVILEGE	Object privileges granted or revoked by a GRANT or REVOKE statement
SYS_PRIVILEGE	System privileges granted or revoked by a GRANT or REVOKE statement
ADMIN_OPTION	Indicates whether the role or system privilege was granted with the ADMIN option
GRANTEE	Name of the grantee specified in a GRANT or REVOKE statement
AUDIT_OPTION	Auditing option set with the AUDIT statement
SES_ACTIONS	Session summary (a string of 16 characters, one for each action type in the order ALTER, AUDIT, COMMENT, DELETE, GRANT, INDEX, INSERT, LOCK, RENAME, SELECT, UPDATE, REFERENCES, and EXECUTE. Positions 14, 15, and 16 are reserved for future use. The characters are: – (None) S (Success) F (Failure) B (Both)
LOGOFF_TIME	Date and time of user logoff
LOGOFF_LREAD	Logical reads for the session
LOGOFF_PREAD	Physical reads for the session
LOGOFF_LWRITE	Logical writes for the session
LOGOFF_DLOCK	Deadlocks detected during the session

Table 11-1 The Columns of the DBA_AUDIT_TRAIL View from the *Oracle Database 10g Reference Manual*

Column	Description
COMMENT_TEXT	Text comment on the audit trail entry, providing more information about the statement audited Also indicates how the user was authenticated. The method can be one of the following: DATABASE—Authentication was done by password NETWORK—Authentication was done by Oracle Net Services or the Advanced Security option PROXY—Client was authenticated by another user; the name of the proxy user follows the method type
SESSIONID	Numeric ID for each Oracle session
ENTRYID	Numeric ID for each audit trail entry in the session
STATEMENTID	Numeric ID for each statement run
RETURNCODE	Oracle error code generated by the action. Some useful values: 0—Action succeeded 2004—Security violation
PRIV_USED	System privilege used to execute the action
CLIENT_ID	Client identifier in each Oracle session
SESSION_CPU	Amount of CPU time used by each Oracle session
EXTENDED_TIMESTAMP	Timestamp of the creation of the audit trail entry (timestamp of user login for entries created by AUDIT SESSION) in UTC (Coordinated Universal Time) time zone
PROXY_SESSIONID	Proxy session serial number, if an enterprise user has logged in through the proxy mechanism
GLOBAL_UID	Global user identifier for the user, if the user has logged in as an enterprise user
INSTANCE_NUMBER	Instance number as specified by the INSTANCE_NUMBER initialization parameter
OS_PROCESS	Operating system process identifier of the Oracle process
TRANSACTIONID	Transaction identifier of the transaction in which the object is accessed or modified
SCN	System change number (SCN) of the query
SQL_BIND	Bind variable data of the query
SQL_TEXT	SQL text of the query

Table 11-1 The Columns of the DBA_AUDIT_TRAIL View from the *Oracle Database 10g Reference Manual (continued)*

Value-Based Auditing

The database auditing described previously can catch the fact that a command was executed against a table, but not necessarily the rows that were affected. For example, issuing AUDIT INSERT ON HR.EMPLOYEES will cause an audit record to be generated whenever a row is inserted into the named table, but the record will not include the actual values of the row that was inserted. On occasion, you may want to capture these. This can be done by using database triggers.

A database trigger is a block of PL/SQL code that will run automatically whenever an insert, update, or delete is executed against a table. This trigger can do almost anything; in particular, it can write out rows to other tables. These rows will be part of the transaction that caused the trigger to execute, and will be committed when the rest of the transaction is committed. There is no way that a user can prevent the trigger from firing: if you update a table with an update trigger defined, that trigger will execute.

Consider this trigger creation statement:

```
ocp10g> CREATE OR REPLACE TRIGGER system.creditrating_audit
  2   AFTER UPDATE OF creditrating
  3   ON oe.customers
  4   REFERENCING NEW AS NEW OLD AS OLD
  5   FOR EACH ROW
  6   BEGIN
  7   IF :old.creditrating != :new.creditrating THEN
  8   INSERT INTO system.creditrating_audit
  9   VALUES (sys_context('userenv','os_user'), sysdate,
 10   sys_context('userenv','ip_address'),
 11   :new.cust_id ||' credit rating changed from
 12   '||:old.creditrating||
 13   ' to '||:new.creditrating);
 14   END IF;
 15   END;
 16   /
```

The first line names the trigger, which is in the SYSTEM schema. Lines 2 and 3 give the rule that determines when the trigger will execute: every time the CREDITRATING column of a row in OE's CUSTOMERS table is updated. There could be separate row-level triggers defined to manage inserts and deletes, or actions on other columns. Line 7 supplies a condition: if the CREDITRATING column were not actually changed, then the trigger will exit without doing anything. But if the CREDITRATING column were updated, then a row is inserted into another table designed for trapping audit events. Lines 9 and 10 use the SYS_CONTEXT function to record the user's operating system username and the IP address of the terminal he was using when he executed the update. Lines 11, 12, and 13 record the employee number of the row updated, and the old and new values of the CREDITRATING column. Database auditing as described previously could have captured all this information, except for the actual values: which employee was updated, and what the change actually was.

TIP Auditing through triggers is a much slower process than database auditing, but it does give you more information.

Fine-Grained Auditing (FGA)

Database auditing can capture all accesses to a table, whether SELECT or DML operations. But it cannot distinguish between rows, even though it might well be that only some rows contain sensitive information. Using database auditing, you may have to sift through a vast number of audit records to find the few that have significance. Fine-grained auditing, or FGA, can be configured to generate audit records only when certain rows are accessed, or when certain columns of certain rows are accessed. It can also run a block of PL/SQL code when the audit condition is breached.

FGA is configured with the package DBMS_FGA. To create an FGA audit policy, use the ADD_POLICY procedure, which takes these arguments:

Argument	Description
OBJECT_SCHEMA	The name of the user who owns the object to be audited. This defaults to the user who is creating the policy.
OBJECT_NAME	The name of the table to be audited.
POLICY_NAME	Every FGA policy created must be given a unique name.
AUDIT_CONDITION	An expression to determine which rows will generate an audit record. If left NULL, access to any row is audited.
AUDIT_COLUMN	A list of columns to be audited. If left NULL, then access to any column is audited.
HANDLER_SCHEMA	The username that owns the procedure to run when the audit condition is met. Default is the user who is creating the policy.
HANDLER_MODULE	A PL/SQL procedure to execute when the audit condition is met.
ENABLE	By default, this is TRUE: the policy will be active and can be disabled with the DISABLE_POLICY procedure. If FALSE, then the ENABLE_POLICY procedure must be used to activate the policy.
STATEMENT_TYPES	One or more of SELECT, INSERT, UPDATE, or DELETE to define which statement types should be audited. Default is SELECT only.
AUDIT_TRAIL	Controls whether to write out the actual SQL statement and its bind variables to the FGA audit trail. The default is to do so.
AUDIT_COLUMN_OPTS	Determines whether to audit if a statement addresses any or all of the columns listed in the AUDIT_COLUMNS argument. Options are DBMS_FGA.ANY_COLUMNS, the default, or DBMS_FGA_ALL_COLUMNS.

The other DBMS_FGA procedures are to enable, disable, or drop FGA policies. To see the results of fine-grained auditing, query the DBA_FGA_AUDIT_TRAIL view:

```
ocp10g> desc dba_fga_audit_trail;
Name                           Null?    Type
------------------------------ -------- -------------------------
SESSION_ID                     NOT NULL NUMBER
TIMESTAMP                               DATE
DB_USER                                 VARCHAR2(30)
OS_USER                                 VARCHAR2(255)
USERHOST                                VARCHAR2(128)
CLIENT_ID                               VARCHAR2(64)
EXT_NAME                                VARCHAR2(4000)
OBJECT_SCHEMA                           VARCHAR2(30)
OBJECT_NAME                             VARCHAR2(128)
POLICY_NAME                             VARCHAR2(30)
SCN                                     NUMBER
SQL_TEXT                                NVARCHAR2(2000)
SQL_BIND                                NVARCHAR2(2000)
COMMENT$TEXT                            VARCHAR2(4000)
STATEMENT_TYPE                          VARCHAR2(7)
EXTENDED_TIMESTAMP                      TIMESTAMP(6) WITH TIME ZONE
PROXY_SESSIONID                         NUMBER
GLOBAL_UID                              VARCHAR2(32)
INSTANCE_NUMBER                         NUMBER
OS_PROCESS                              VARCHAR2(16)
TRANSACTIONID                           RAW(8)
STATEMENTID                             NUMBER
ENTRYID                                 NUMBER
```

Exercise 11-2: Enabling Auditing

Enable both database auditing and fine-grained auditing, and use data dictionary views to see the results.

1. Connect to your database as SYSDBA using SQL*Plus.

2. Set the AUDIT_TRAIL instance parameter to enable auditing to the data dictionary. As this is a static parameter, you must use the SCOPE clause and restart the instance.

    ```
    ocp10g> conn / as sysdba
    Connected.
    ocp10g> alter system set audit_trail=db scope=spfile;
    System altered.
    ocp10g> startup force;
    ```

3. Connect to your database as user SYSTEM using SQL*Plus.

4. Create a table and insert some rows as follows:

    ```
    ocp10g>  create table audit_test(name varchar2(10),salary number);
    ocp10g> insert into audit_test values('McGraw',100);
    ocp10g> insert into audit_test values('Hill',200);
    ```

5. Enable database auditing of access to the table.

    ```
    ocp10g> audit select, update on system.audit_test;
    ```

6. Execute some statements against the table.

```
ocp10g> select * from audit_test;
ocp10g> update audit_test set salary=50 where name='McGraw';
```

7. Query the DBA_AUDIT_TRAIL view to see the results of the auditing.

```
ocp10g> select username, userhost, os_username,
ses_actions, obj_name from dba_audit_trail;
USERNAME USERHOST         OS_USERNAME SES_ACTIONS       OBJ_NAME
-------- ------------     ----------- ----------------- ----------
SYSTEM   WORKGROUP\PC1 PC1\Guest      ---------SS-----  AUDIT_TEST
```

This shows that the Oracle user SYSTEM, while logged onto a machine called PC1 in the Windows workgroup called WORKGROUP as the local Windows user Guest, executed one or more SELECT and UPDATE statements successfully against the table called AUDIT_TEST. To decode the SES_ACTIONS column, refer to the documentation extract in the preceding section that describes the view.

8. Create an FGA policy to capture all SELECTs against the AUDIT_TEST table that read the SALARY column, if the salary retrieved is greater than 100, with this procedure call:

```
ocp10g> exec dbms_fga.add_policy(-
> object_schema=>'system',-
> object_name=>'audit_test',-
> policy_name=>'high_sal',-
> audit_condition=>'salary > 100',-
> audit_column=>'salary',-
> statement_types=>'select');
```

9. Run some queries against the table.

```
ocp10g> select * from audit_test;
ocp10g> select salary from audit_test where name='Hill';
ocp10g> select salary from audit_test where name='McGraw';
ocp10g> select name from audit_test;
```

10. Query the fine-grained audit trail.

```
ocp10g> select os_user,db_user,sql_text from dba_fga_audit_trail;
OS_USER        DB_USER SQL_TEXT
------------   ------- ----------------------------------------
ORA10G\Guest SYSTEM   select * from audit_test
ORA10G\Guest SYSTEM   select salary from audit_test where
                      name='Hill'
```

Note that only the first and second queries from Step 9 generated audit records, and that the actual statement used can be retrieved.

11. Tidy up by canceling the database auditing, dropping the FGA policy, and dropping the table.

```
ocp10g> noaudit select,update on system.audit_test;
ocp10g> exec dbms_fga.drop_policy(object_name=>'audit_test',-
> policy_name=>'high_sal');
ocp10g> drop table audit_test;
```

Security Updates

Oracle Corporation issues regular security updates. These are usually in the form of patches that you must apply to your Oracle software. Wherever possible, patches should be installed as patch sets. A patch set is a collection of patches that you install with the Oracle Universal Installer; it will have been through thorough integration testing, and the installation will update the version numbers of the components being patched. In exceptional cases when you cannot wait for a patch set to be issued, you may need to install an interim patch; this is installed with the OPatch utility. Generally speaking, it should not be necessary to install interim patches.

To assist with identifying and downloading patches, you can use Database Control. The Enterprise Manager repository stores critical patch advisory information, which can be automatically refreshed so that you will be informed whenever a new security patch is released.

From the database home page, take the Oracle Metalink Credentials link in the Critical Patch Advisories section. This will take you to the Patching Setup window, where you can enter your Metalink credentials. Once you have done this, the Enterprise Manager job Refresh From Metalink will run automatically, by default once a day. This job is configured by the Scheduler, to be described in Chapter 36.

Chapter Review

Security for all computer systems should be managed by the principle of "least privilege": give users the bare minimum of permissions they need to do their jobs. A first step for this in the Oracle environment is limiting the CONNECT capability, and the privileges granted to the PUBLIC user.

Having determined which users must connect, force them to change passwords in accordance with whatever policy is in place in your organization. If users can only connect through an application, the application should take care of this, but if it is possible for users to connect directly, then the password profile facility will help enforce such policies within the database.

In many cases, limiting access rights is not enough: you will have to accept that users do have permissions that could be abused. This is where auditing comes in: you accept the fact that users must be able to see and manipulate data as part of their work, but through auditing you track the work they are doing. This means that if a user does go beyond the limits of what he is meant to do, you can identify that this is happening and take appropriate action.

The database provides three forms of auditing. Database auditing can track access to objects, use of privileges, and logins; but it does not capture the actual statements issued. Database triggers execute whenever a DML operation is executed against a table: they can capture full details of the DML operation. But they cannot track SELECT statements. Fine-grained auditing has elements of both database auditing and auditing with triggers: it can capture actual statements, and it works for SELECT as well as for DML.

Questions

1. A user complains that he cannot connect, though he is certain he is using the correct password. You query the DBA_USERS views, and see that his account has a STATUS of EXPIRED & LOCKED. What does this mean? (Choose the best answer.)

   A. The account is locked because the password has expired.

   B. You can reset the password to unlock the account.

   C. If you unlock the account, the user will be able to log in if the password grace period has not expired.

   D. The account has expired and must be unlocked to reactivate it.

2. Under what circumstances could you set the REMOTE_LOGIN_PASSWORDFILE instance parameter to EXCLUSIVE? (Choose two correct answers.)

   A. You will need a SYSDBA connection when you are logged on to a machine other than the server.

   B. You want to disable operating system authentication.

   C. You want to add users to the password file.

   D. You want to prevent other users from being added to the password file.

3. Password profiles can enforce policies on password management. Which of the following statements, if any, are correct? (Choose all that apply.)

   A. Profiles can prevent a user from changing his password.

   B. A profile can be used to configure an account that you can connect to without a password.

   C. Profiles can be used to track password changes.

   D. Profiles can control how long an account is locked for following repeated failed logins.

   E. The FAILED_LOGIN_ATTEMPTS profile limit will lock an account only if the failed login attempts are consecutive.

   F. The PASSWORD_GRACE_TIME profile limit controls the number of days before password expiration during which you will be prompted to change your password.

4. If you want a block of PL/SQL code to run whenever certain data is accessed with SELECT, what auditing technique could you use? (Choose the best answer.)

   A. Database auditing

   B. Fine-grained auditing

   C. Database triggers

   D. You cannot do this

5. What is necessary to audit actions done by a user connected with the SYSDBA privilege? (Choose the best answer.)

   A. Set the AUDIT_SYS_OPERATIONS instance parameter to TRUE.

   B. Use database auditing to audit use of the SYSDBA privilege.

   C. Set the REMOTE_LOGIN_PASSWORDFILE instance parameter to NONE, so that SYSDBA connections can only be made with operating system authentication. Then set the AUDIT_TRAIL parameter to OS, and make sure that the DBA does not have access to it.

   D. This is not possible: any user with SYSDBA privilege can always bypass the auditing mechanisms.

Answers

1. **C.** "Expired" refers to the password; "Locked" refers to the account. These are managed independently, so if you unlock the account the password will still be expired—but if the password's grace period is still in effect, which starts after the first successful login after the password expires, the user will be able to connect.

2. **A and C.** Enabling a password file (with EXCLUSIVE or SHARED) means that you can administer the database remotely, and (unlike SHARED) an EXCLUSIVE file can have names other than SYS added to it.

3. **D and E.** The profile directive PASSWORD_LOCK_TIME controls how long an account is locked following repeated failed logins, but they must be consecutive failed logins to cause the account to lock.

4. **B.** Fine-grained auditing can be used to give an effect similar to a trigger on SELECT statements.

5. **A.** This is all that is necessary: all statements issued as SYSDBA will then go to the operating system audit trail.

CHAPTER 12

Configuring Oracle Networking

In this chapter you will learn how to
- Use Database Control to create additional listeners
- Use Database Control to create Oracle Net service aliases
- Use Database Control to configure connect-time failover
- Use Listener features
- Use the Oracle Net Manager to configure client and middle-tier connections
- Use tnsping to test Oracle Net connectivity
- Describe Oracle Net services
- Describe Oracle Net names resolution methods

Networking is an integral part of the client/server database architecture that is fundamental to all modern relational databases. The Oracle database had the potential for client/server computing from the beginning (the first release, in 1978, made a separation between the Oracle code and the user code), but it was only with version 4 in 1984 that Oracle introduced interoperability between PC and server. True client/ server support came with version 5, in 1986. This chapter introduces the Oracle Net services. Oracle Net was previously known as Sqlnet, and you will still hear many DBAs refer to it as such. But before going into the detail of Oracle Net, this chapter has a review of how Oracle implements the client/server paradigm: a full understanding of this is essential if one is to appreciate what Oracle Net is doing for you.

Oracle's Implementation of the Client/Server Paradigm

There are many layers between the user and the database. In the Oracle environment, no user ever has direct access to the database—nor does the process that he is running. Client/server architecture guarantees that all access to data is controlled by the server.

A user interacts with a user process: this is the software that he runs on his local terminal. For example, it could be Microsoft Access plus an ODBC driver on a Windows PC; it could be something written in C and linked with the Oracle Call Interface (or OCI) libraries; it could even be our old friend SQL*Plus. Whatever it is, the purpose of the user process is to prompt the user to enter information that the process can use to generate SQL statements. In the case of SQL*Plus, the process merely waits for you to enter a SQL statement or SQL*Plus command; a more sophisticated user process will paint a proper data entry screen, validate your input, and then, when you click the Submit button, construct the statement and send it off to the server process.

The server process is a process running on the database server machine that executes the SQL it receives from the user process. This is your basic client/server split: a user process generating SQL, a server process executing it. The execution of a SQL statement goes through four stages: parse, bind, execute, and fetch.

In the parse phase your server process works out what the statement actually means, and how best to execute it. Parsing involves interaction with the shared pool of the instance: shared pool memory structures are used to convert the SQL into something that is actually executable.

In the bind phase, any variables are expanded to literal values. Then the execute phase will require more use of the instance's SGA, and possibly of the database.

During the execution of a statement, data in the database buffer cache will be read or updated and changes written to the redo log buffer, but if the relevant blocks are not in the database buffer cache, your server process will read them from the datafiles. This is the first point in the execution of a statement where the database itself is involved;

PART I

all the work so far has occurred in the instance. Chapter 9 covered in full detail how the instance interacts with the database via its background processes, the LGWR and the DBWn, to write information from the instance memory to the database. And finally, the fetch phase of the execution cycle is where the server process sends the result set generated by the statement's execution back to the user process, which should then format it for display.

Oracle Net provides the mechanism for launching a server process to execute code on behalf of a user process. This is establishing a session. Then Oracle Net is responsible for maintaining the session: transmitting SQL from user process to server process, and fetching results from the server process back to the user process through the sequence shown in Figure 12-1.

So to summarize, a user interacts with a user process; a user process interacts with a server process, via Oracle Net; a server process interacts with the instance; and the instance, via its background processes, interacts with the database. Your client/server split is between the user process generating SQL and the server process executing it. This split will usually be physical as well as logical: there will be a local area network between the machines hosting the user processes and the machine hosting the server side. But it is quite possible for this link to be wide area, or conversely to run the user processes on the server machine. Oracle Net is responsible for establishing a session, and then for the ongoing communication between the user process and the server process.

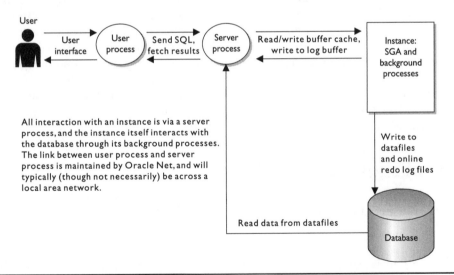

Figure 12-1   The database is protected from users by several layers of segregation.

A Word on Oracle Net and Communication Protocols

Oracle Net is a layered protocol: it runs on top of whatever communications protocol is supported by your operating system. Historically, Sqlnet could work with all the popular protocols (with the exception of NETBIOS/NETBEUI, which has too limited functionality to be used for large database systems), but in release 10g Oracle's network support is limited to TCP, Named Pipes (or NMP), and the new Sockets Direct Protocol (or SDP) over InfiniBand high-speed networks. The secure sockets variants of these protocols can also be used. All operating systems also have an Inter-Process Communication (or IPC) protocol proprietary to the operating system—this is also available to Oracle Net for local connections where the user process is on the same machine as the server.

This layering of Oracle Net on top of whatever is provided by your operating system gives Oracle platform independence. You as DBA do not need to know anything about the underlying network: you configure Oracle Net to use whatever protocol has been configured by your network administrators, and you need not concern yourself with what is happening beneath. TCP is, for better or worse, undoubtedly the most popular protocol worldwide, so that is the one used in the examples that follow.

With regard to conformance with the Open Systems Interconnection (or OSI) seven-layer model to which all IT vendors are supposed to comply, Oracle Net maps onto layers five, six, and seven: the session, presentation, and application layers. The protocol adapters installed with the standard Oracle installation provide the crossover to layer four, the transport layer, provided by your operating system. Thus Oracle Net is responsible for establishing sessions between end systems once TCP (or whatever else you are using) has established a layer four connection. The presentation layer functions are handled by the Oracle Net Two-Task Common (or TTC) layer. TTC is responsible for any conversions necessary when data is transferred between the user process and the server process, such as character set changes. Then the application layer functions are the user and server processes themselves.

Establishing a Session

When a user, through his user process, wishes to establish a session against an instance, he will issue a command something like

```
SQL> CONNECT SCOTT/TIGER@OCP10G
```

Of course, if he is using a properly written user interface, he won't type in those words—he will be prompted to enter the details into a logon screen—but one way or another that is the command the user process will generate. It is now time to go into what actually happens when that command is processed. First, break down the command into its components. There is a database username ("SCOTT"), followed by a database password ("TIGER"), and the two are separated by a "/" as a delimiter. Then there is an "@" symbol, followed by a connect string, "OCP10G". The "@" symbol is an indication to the user process that a network connection is required. If the "@" and the connect string are omitted, then the user process will assume that the instance you wish to connect to is running on the local machine, and that the always-available IPC protocol can be used. If the "@" and a connect string are included, then the user process will assume that you are requesting a network connection to an instance on a remote machine—though in fact, you could be bouncing off the network card and back to the machine you are logged on to.

Connecting to a Local Instance

Even when you connect to an instance running on your local machine, you still use Oracle Net. All Oracle sessions use a network protocol, but for a local connection the protocol is IPC: this is the protocol provided by your operating system that will allow processes to communicate within the host machine. This is the only type of connection that does not require a listener; indeed, local connections do not require any configuration at all. The only information needed is to tell your user process which instance you want to connect to. Remember that there could be several instances running on your local computer. You give the process this information through an environment variable. Figure 12-2 shows examples of this in Linux; Figure 12-3 is the same thing on Windows.

Name Resolution

When connecting using Oracle Net, the first stage is to work out exactly what you want to connect to. This is the process of name resolution. If your connect statement includes the connect string "@OCP10g", Oracle Net has to work out what is meant by "OCP10g". This means that the string has to be resolved into four pieces of information: the protocol you want to use (in modern times, one can usually assume that this is TCP), the IP address on which the database listener is running, the port that the listener is monitoring for incoming connection requests, and the name of the instance (which need not be the same as the connect string) to which you wish to connect. There are variations: rather than an IP address, the connect string can include a hostname, which then gets further resolved to an IP address by a DNS server. Rather than specifying an instance by name, the connect string can include the name of a "service," which (in a RAC environment) could be made up of a number of instances. You can configure a number of ways of resolving connect strings to address and instance names, but one way or another the name resolution process gives your user process enough information to go across the network to a database listener, and request a connection to a particular instance.

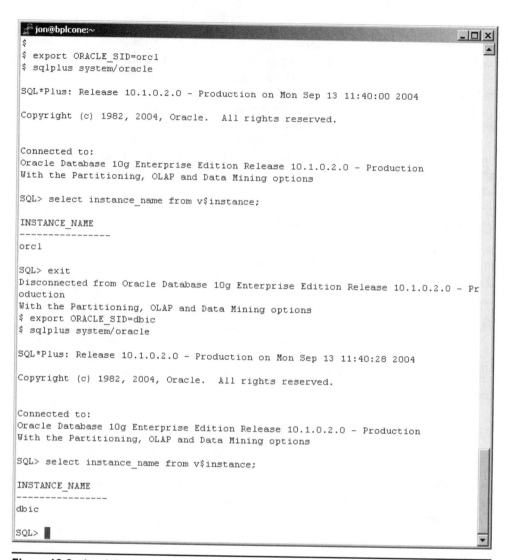

Figure 12-2   Local database connections—Linux

Launching a Server Process

The database listener, running on the server machine, uses one or more protocols to monitor one or more ports on one or more network interface cards for incoming connection requests. You can further complicate matters by running multiple listeners on one machine, and any one listener can accept connection requests for a number of instances. When it receives a connect request, the listener must first validate whether the instance requested is actually available. Assuming that it is, the listener will launch

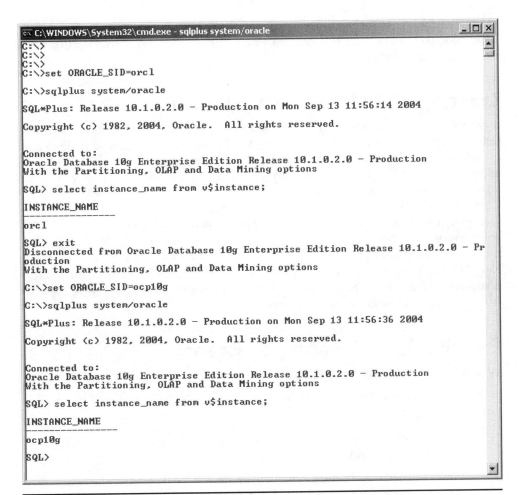

Figure 12-3 Local database connections—Windows

a new server process to service the user process. Thus if you have a thousand users logging on concurrently to your instance, you will be launching a thousand server processes. This is known as the "dedicated server" architecture, where each user process is given a server process, dedicated to its session (in the next chapter you'll see the "shared server" alternative).

In the TCP environment, each dedicated server process launched by a listener will acquire a unique TCP port number. This will be assigned at process startup time by your operating system's port mapping algorithm. The port number gets passed back to the user process by the listener (or on some operating systems the socket already opened to the listener is transferred to the new port number), and the user process can then communicate directly with its server process. The listener has now completed its work and waits for the next connect request. If the listener is not running, no new server processes can be launched, but this will not affect any existing sessions that have already been established.

Creating and Managing a Listener

A listener is defined in a file: the listener.ora file whose default location is in the ORACLE_HOME/network/admin directory. As a minimum, the listener.ora file must include a section for one listener that states its name and the protocol and listening address it will use. You can configure several listeners in the one file, but they must all have different names and addresses.

As with other files used to configure Oracle Net, this file can be very fussy about seemingly trivial points of syntax, such as case sensitivity, white spaces, and abbreviations. For this reason, many DBAs do not like to edit it by hand (though there is no reason not to). Oracle provides three graphical tools to manage Oracle Net: Database Control, the Net Manager, and the Net Configuration Assistant. There is considerable overlap between the functionality of these tools, though there are a few things that can be done only in one or the other.

Exercise 12-1: Creating a Listener with Database Control

In this exercise, you will create a new listener using Database Control, and inspect the listener.ora file.

1. In your browser, connect to Database Control and log in to your instance as user SYSTEM with the SYSDBA privilege.

2. From the database home page, in the General section select the link LISTENER_<hostname>, where <hostname> is the name of your computer.

3. Select the Net Services Administration link in the Related Links section.

4. Choose Listeners from the Administer drop-down box and click Go.

5. Click Create.

6. Enter an operating system username and password.

7. Enter **LIST2** as the listener name.

8. Add a listening address:

    Protocol: TCP
    Port: 1522 (or any other available port)
    Host: Your computer name

9. Click OK to save the new listener definition.

10. To start the new listener, select Start/Stop from the Actions drop-down list and click Go.

11. From an operating system prompt, navigate to your ORACLE_HOME/network/ admin directory. This will be something like

```
c:\oracle\product\10.1.0\db_1\NETWORK\ADMIN
```

on Windows, or

```
/oracle/product/10.1.0/db_1/network/admin
```

on Unix. There, inspect the file listener.ora. The contents will resemble

```
# listener.ora Network Configuration File:
C:\oracle\product\10.1.0\Db_1\NETWORK\ADMIN\listener.ora
# Generated by Oracle configuration tools.
LISTENER =
  (DESCRIPTION =
    (ADDRESS = (PROTOCOL = TCP)(HOST = ora10g)(PORT = 1521))
  )
LIST2 =
  (DESCRIPTION =
    (ADDRESS = (PROTOCOL = TCP)(HOST = ora10g)(PORT = 1522))
  )
```

12. To confirm that your new listener is running, from an operating system prompt run the lsnrctl utility, as in Figure 12-4.

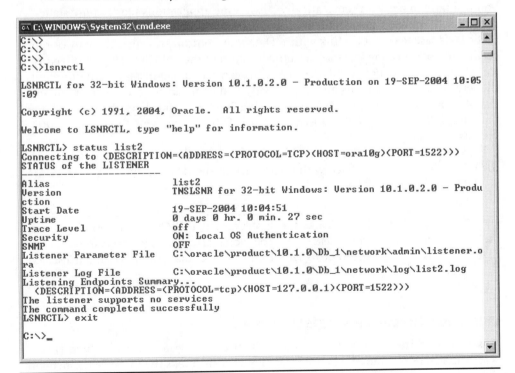

Figure 12-4 Use of the lsnrctl utility

Database Registration

A listener is necessary to spawn server processes against an instance. In order to do this, it needs to know what instances are available on the computer on which it is running. A listener finds out about instances by the process of "registration."

 EXAM TIP The listener and the instance must be running on the same computer, unless you are using RAC. In a RAC environment, any listener on any computer in the cluster can connect you to any instance on any computer.

There are two methods for registering an instance with a database: static and dynamic registration. For *static* registration, you hard-code a list of instances in the listener.ora file. *Dynamic* registration means that the instance itself, at startup time, locates a listener and registers with it.

Static Registration

As a general rule, dynamic registration is a better option, but there are circumstances when you will resort to static registration. Dynamic registration was introduced with release 8*i*, but if you have older databases that your listener must connect users to, you will have to register them statically. Also, some applications may require static registration: typically, management tools. To register an instance statically, take the Static Database Registration link within Database Control, and enter the name of the service, the name of the instance, and the location of the ORACLE_HOME directory for that instance, as shown in Figure 12-5. In a simple, single-instance, environment the service name and the instance name will often be the same, but if you are in any doubt about this, log in to your instance using SQL*Plus and check the values of the parameters INSTANCE_NAME and SERVICE_NAMES by querying the V$PARAMETER view as shown in Figure 12-6.

If SERVICE_NAMES was not set in your parameter file, it will have defaulted to the INSTANCE_NAME suffixed with the DB_DOMAIN. The default for DB_DOMAIN is NULL.

 TIP In previous releases, the default for DB_DOMAIN was ".world". This is not a very helpful default. It is common practice either to set it to null (which is the 10g default) or to set it to the name of the host on which the instance is running.

Dynamic Instance Registration

This is the preferred method by which an instance will register with a listener. There is an initialization parameter LOCAL_LISTENER, which tells the instance the network

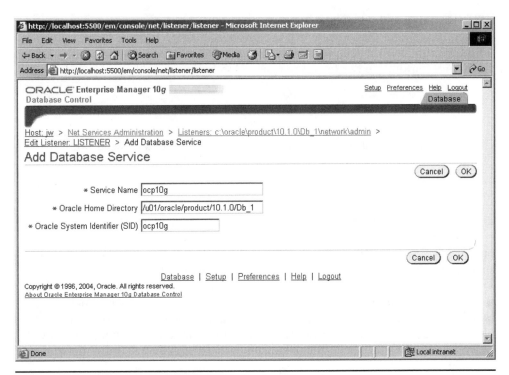

Figure 12-5 Static instance registration with Database Control

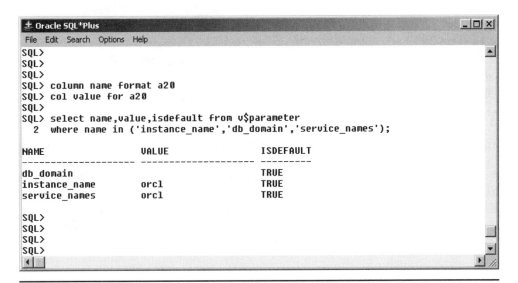

Figure 12-6 Confirming your instance and service names

address that it should contact to find a listener with which to register. At instance startup time, the PMON process will use this parameter to locate a listener and inform it of the INSTANCE_NAME and SERVICE_NAMES. At any time subsequent to instance startup, you can force a re-registration by executing the command

```
SQL> alter system register;
```

 TIP You will need to re-register your instance with the listener with "alter system" if you have restarted the listener, or if you started the database instance before starting the listener.

Dynamic registration is a better option than static registration because it ensures that only running instances are registered with the listener, and also that there are no errors in the instance and service names. It is all too easy to make mistakes here, particularly if you are editing the listener.ora file by hand. Also, when the instance shuts down, it will de-register from the listener automatically.

From release 9i onward, dynamic registration requires no configuration at all if your listener is running on the default port, 1521. All instances will automatically look for a listener on the localhost on that port and register themselves if they find one. However, if your listener is not running on the default port, you must specify where the listener is by setting the parameter local_listener and re-registering, for example,

```
SQL> alter system set local_listener=list2;
SQL> alter system register;
```

In this example, the local_listener has been specified by name. This name needs to be resolved into an address in order for the instance to find the listener and register itself; you'll see how to do this soon, but first take a more detailed look at the listener control utility, lsnrctl.

The Listener Control Utility

You can start and stop listeners through Database Control, but there is also a command-line utility, lsnrctl (lsnrctl.exe on Windows). You can run lsnrctl commands directly from an operating system prompt as in Figure 12-7, or through a simple user interface as in Figure 12-8. For all the commands, you must specify the name of the listener, if it is not the default name of LISTENER. The following figures show how to check the status of a listener and to stop and start it, issuing the commands either from the operating system prompt or from within the user interface.

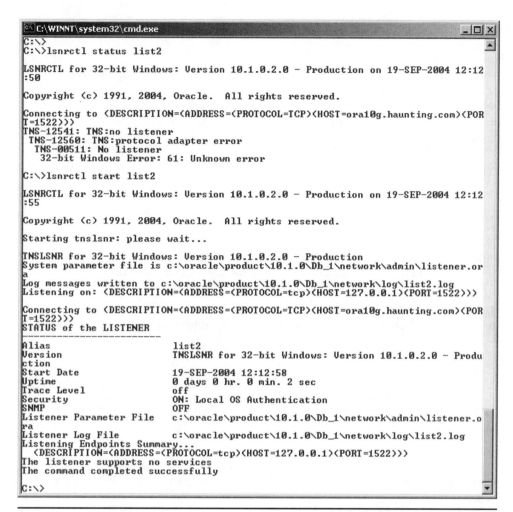

```
C:\WINNT\system32\cmd.exe                                              _ □ x

C:\>
C:\>lsnrctl status list2

LSNRCTL for 32-bit Windows: Version 10.1.0.2.0 - Production on 19-SEP-2004 12:12
:50

Copyright (c) 1991, 2004, Oracle.  All rights reserved.

Connecting to (DESCRIPTION=(ADDRESS=(PROTOCOL=TCP)(HOST=ora10g.haunting.com)(POR
T=1522)))
TNS-12541: TNS:no listener
 TNS-12560: TNS:protocol adapter error
  TNS-00511: No listener
   32-bit Windows Error: 61: Unknown error

C:\>lsnrctl start list2

LSNRCTL for 32-bit Windows: Version 10.1.0.2.0 - Production on 19-SEP-2004 12:12
:55

Copyright (c) 1991, 2004, Oracle.  All rights reserved.

Starting tnslsnr: please wait...

TNSLSNR for 32-bit Windows: Version 10.1.0.2.0 - Production
System parameter file is c:\oracle\product\10.1.0\Db_1\network\admin\listener.or
a
Log messages written to c:\oracle\product\10.1.0\Db_1\network\log\list2.log
Listening on: (DESCRIPTION=(ADDRESS=(PROTOCOL=tcp)(HOST=127.0.0.1)(PORT=1522)))

Connecting to (DESCRIPTION=(ADDRESS=(PROTOCOL=TCP)(HOST=ora10g.haunting.com)(POR
T=1522)))
STATUS of the LISTENER
------------------------
Alias                     list2
Version                   TNSLSNR for 32-bit Windows: Version 10.1.0.2.0 - Produ
ction
Start Date                19-SEP-2004 12:12:58
Uptime                    0 days 0 hr. 0 min. 2 sec
Trace Level               off
Security                  ON: Local OS Authentication
SNMP                      OFF
Listener Parameter File   c:\oracle\product\10.1.0\Db_1\network\admin\listener.o
ra
Listener Log File         c:\oracle\product\10.1.0\Db_1\network\log\list2.log
Listening Endpoints Summary...
  (DESCRIPTION=(ADDRESS=(PROTOCOL=tcp)(HOST=127.0.0.1)(PORT=1522)))
The listener supports no services
The command completed successfully

C:\>
```

Figure 12-7   Using lsnrctl commands from the operating system prompt to check the status and then starting the listener LIST2

Note that the status command always tells you the address on which the listener is accepting connection requests, the name and location of the listener.ora file that defines the listener, and the name and location of the logfile for the listener. Also, in the examples in the figures, the listener LIST2 "supports no services." This is because there are no services statically registered in the listener.ora file for that listener, and

```
C:\WINNT\system32\cmd.exe                                           _|□|x|
C:\>
C:\>
C:\>lsnrctl

LSNRCTL for 32-bit Windows: Version 10.1.0.2.0 - Production on 19-SEP-2004 12:14
:36

Copyright (c) 1991, 2004, Oracle.  All rights reserved.

Welcome to LSNRCTL, type "help" for information.

LSNRCTL> status list2
Connecting to (DESCRIPTION=(ADDRESS=(PROTOCOL=TCP)(HOST=ora10g.haunting.com)(POR
T=1522)))
STATUS of the LISTENER
------------------------
Alias                     list2
Version                   TNSLSNR for 32-bit Windows: Version 10.1.0.2.0 - Produ
ction
Start Date                19-SEP-2004 12:12:58
Uptime                    0 days 0 hr. 1 min. 44 sec
Trace Level               off
Security                  ON: Local OS Authentication
SNMP                      OFF
Listener Parameter File   c:\oracle\product\10.1.0\Db_1\network\admin\listener.o
ra
Listener Log File         c:\oracle\product\10.1.0\Db_1\network\log\list2.log
Listening Endpoints Summary...
  (DESCRIPTION=(ADDRESS=(PROTOCOL=tcp)(HOST=127.0.0.1)(PORT=1522)))
The listener supports no services
The command completed successfully
LSNRCTL> stop list2
Connecting to (DESCRIPTION=(ADDRESS=(PROTOCOL=TCP)(HOST=ora10g.haunting.com)(POR
T=1522)))
The command completed successfully
LSNRCTL> exit

C:\>
C:\>_
```

Figure 12-8   Using the lsnrctl user interface to check the status and then stopping the listener LIST2

no instances have dynamically registered either. Figure 12-9 uses both the status and services commands to show the state of the listener after an instance has registered dynamically.

In Figure 12-9, the output of the status command tells you that the listener supports two services: orcl and orclXDB. The orcl service is the regular database service: this listener is prepared to launch server processes for sessions against the orcl service. But what does the orcl service actually consist of? That is shown by the output of the services command, which shows you that the orcl service consists of one instance, also called orcl. In a RAC environment, it would be possible for one service to consist of multiple instances.

The second service shown, orclXDB, is the XML database service—an advanced feature provided as standard with a 10g database.

```
C:\WINNT\system32\cmd.exe - lsnrctl                              _ |□| x|
LSNRCTL>                                                                ▲
LSNRCTL> status list2
Connecting to <DESCRIPTION=<ADDRESS=<PROTOCOL=TCP><HOST=ora10g.haunting.com><POR
T=1522>>>
STATUS of the LISTENER
-------------------------
Alias                     list2
Version                   TNSLSNR for 32-bit Windows: Version 10.1.0.2.0 - Produ
ction
Start Date                19-SEP-2004 12:22:24
Uptime                    0 days 0 hr. 3 min. 3 sec
Trace Level               off
Security                  ON: Local OS Authentication
SNMP                      OFF
Listener Parameter File   c:\oracle\product\10.1.0\Db_1\network\admin\listener.o
ra
Listener Log File         c:\oracle\product\10.1.0\Db_1\network\log\list2.log
Listening Endpoints Summary...
  <DESCRIPTION=<ADDRESS=<PROTOCOL=tcp><HOST=127.0.0.1><PORT=1522>>>
Services Summary...
Service "orcl" has 1 instance(s).
  Instance "orcl", status READY, has 1 handler(s) for this service...
Service "orclXDB" has 1 instance(s).
  Instance "orcl", status READY, has 1 handler(s) for this service...
The command completed successfully
LSNRCTL>
LSNRCTL> services list2
Connecting to <DESCRIPTION=<ADDRESS=<PROTOCOL=TCP><HOST=ora10g.haunting.com><POR
T=1522>>>
Services Summary...
Service "orcl" has 1 instance(s).
  Instance "orcl", status READY, has 1 handler(s) for this service...
    Handler(s):
      "DEDICATED" established:0 refused:0 state:ready
          LOCAL SERVER
Service "orclXDB" has 1 instance(s).
  Instance "orcl", status READY, has 1 handler(s) for this service...
    Handler(s):
      "D000" established:0 refused:0 current:0 max:1002 state:ready
          DISPATCHER <machine: JW, pid: 940>
          <ADDRESS=<PROTOCOL=tcp><HOST=jw><PORT=1831>>
The command completed successfully
LSNRCTL>                                                                ▼
```

Figure 12-9 The services command gives fuller information than the status command.

Techniques for Name Resolution

At the beginning of this chapter you saw that to establish a session against an instance, your user process must issue a connect string. That string resolves to the address of a listener and the name of an instance or service. In the discussion of dynamic instance registration, you saw again the use of a logical name for a listener, which needs to be resolved into a network address in order for an instance to find a listener with which to register. Oracle provides four methods of name resolution: Easy Connect, local naming, directory naming, and external naming. It is probably true to say that the majority of Oracle sites use local naming, but there is no question that directory naming is the best method for a large and complex installation.

Easy Connect

The Easy Connect name resolution method is new with release 10g. It is very easy to use; it requires no configuration at all. But it is limited to one protocol: TCP. The other name resolution methods can use any of the other supported protocols, such as TCP with secure sockets, or Named Pipes. Another limitation is that Easy Connect cannot be used with any of Oracle Net's more advanced capabilities, such as load balancing or connect-time failover across different network routes. It is fair to say that Easy Connect is a method you as DBA will find very handy to use, but that it is not a method of much use to your end users. Easy Connect is enabled by default. You invoke it with a syntax such as this as your connect string:

```
SQL> connect scott/tiger@ora10g.haunting.com:1522/ocp10g
```

In this example, SQL*Plus will use TCP to go to port 1522 on the IP address ora10g .haunting.com. Then if there is a listener running on that port and address, it will ask the listener to spawn a server process against an instance that is part of the service ocp10g. Easy Connect can be made even easier:

```
SQL> connect scott/tiger@ora10g.haunting.com
```

will also work, but only if the listener is using port 1521, and the service name registered with the listener is ora10g.haunting.com: the same as the computer name.

Local Naming

With local naming the user supplies an alias, known as an Oracle Net service alias, for the connect string, and the alias is resolved by a local file into the full network address (protocol, address, port, and service or instance name.) This local file is the infamous tnsnames.ora file that has caused DBAs much grief over the years. Consider this example of a tnsnames.ora file:

```
ocp10g =
  (DESCRIPTION =
    (ADDRESS_LIST =
      (ADDRESS = (PROTOCOL = TCP)(HOST = ora10g.haunting.com)(PORT = 1521))
    )
    (CONNECT_DATA =
      (service_name = ocp10g)
    )
  )
test =
  (DESCRIPTION =
    (ADDRESS_LIST =
      (ADDRESS = (PROTOCOL = TCP)(HOST = serv2.haunting.com)(PORT = 1521))
    )
    (CONNECT_DATA =
      (sid = testdb)
    )
  )
```

This tnsnames.ora file has two Oracle Net service aliases defined within it: ocp10g and test. These aliases are what your users will provide in their connect statements. The first entry, ocp10g, simply says that when the connect string "@ocp10g" is issued, your user process should use the TCP protocol to go to the machine ora10g.haunting .com, contact it on port 1521, and ask the listener monitoring that port to establish a session against the instance with the service name ocp10g. The second entry, test, directs users to a listener on a different machine and asks for a session against the instance called testdb.

 TIP There need be no relationship between the alias, the service name, and the instance name, but for the sake of your sanity you will usually keep them the same.

Local naming supports all protocols and all the advanced features of Oracle Net, but maintaining tnsnames.ora files on all your client machines can be an extremely time-consuming task. The tnsnames.ora file is also notoriously sensitive to apparently trivial variations in layout. Using the GUI configuration tools will help avoid such problems.

Directory Naming

Directory naming points the user toward an LDAP directory server to resolve aliases. LDAP (the Lightweight Directory Protocol) is a widely used standard that Oracle (and other mainstream software vendors) is encouraging organizations to adopt. To use directory naming, you must first install and configure a directory server somewhere on your network. Oracle provides an LDAP server (the Oracle Internet Directory) as part of the Oracle Application Server, but you do not have to use that; if you already have a copy of Microsoft Active Directory, that will be perfectly adequate. IBM and Novell also sell directory servers conforming to the LDAP standard.

Like local naming, directory naming supports all Oracle Net features, but unlike local naming, it offers a central repository, the directory server, for all your name resolution details. This is much easier to maintain than many tnsnames.ora files distributed across your whole user community.

External Naming

External naming is conceptually similar to directory naming, but it uses third-party naming services such as Sun's Network Information Services (NIS+) or the Cell Directory Services (CDS) that are part of the Distributed Computing Environment (DCE).

Configuring Service Aliases

Having decided what name resolution method to use, your next task is to configure the clients to use it. You can do this through Database Control, but since Database Control is a server-side process, you can only use it to configure clients running on the database server. An alternative is to use the Net Manager, a stand-alone Java utility shipped with all the Oracle client-side products.

To launch the Net Manager, run `netmgr` from a Unix prompt, or on Windows you will find it on the Start menu.

The Net Manager menu tree has three branches. The Profile branch is used to set options that may apply to both the client and the server sides of Oracle Net and can be used to influence the behavior of all Oracle Net connections. This is where, for example, you can configure detailed tracing of Oracle Net sessions. The Service Naming branch is used to configure client-side name resolution, and the Listeners branch is used to configure database listeners.

When you take the Profile branch as shown in Figure 12-10, you are in fact configuring a file called sqlnet.ora. This file exists in your ORACLE_HOME/network/admin directory. It is optional—there are defaults for every sqlnet.ora directive—but you will usually configure it, if only to select the name resolution method.

In the Profile branch, you will see all the available naming methods, with two (TNSNAMES and EZCONNECT) selected by default: these are Local Naming and Easy

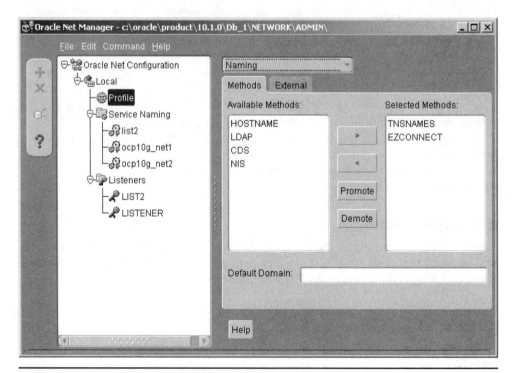

Figure 12-10   Net Manager's Profile editor

Connect. The external methods are NIS and CDS. LDAP is Directory Naming, and HOSTNAME is a previous version of Easy Connect that is retained for backward compatibility.

Then you need to configure the individual Oracle Net service aliases. This is done in the Service Naming branch, which in fact creates or edits the Local Naming tnsnames.ora file that resides in your ORACLE_HOME/network/admin directory. If you are fortunate enough to be using Directory Naming, you do not need to do this: choosing LDAP in the Profile as your naming method is enough.

Exercise 12-2: Creating an Oracle Net Service Alias

Use the Net Manager to create and test an Oracle Net service alias. This alias will connect you to your database through the listener LIST2 that you configured in Exercise 12-1.

1. Launch the Net Manager. On Unix, run netmgr from an operating system prompt. On Windows, it will be on the Start menu, in Oracle's Configuration and Migration Tools submenu.

2. Highlight the Service Branch, and click the "+" symbol on the left of the window to add a new alias.

3. Enter **ocp10g_1522** as the Net Service Name, and click Next.

4. Select TCP/IP as the protocol, and click Next.

5. Enter the name of your server machine as the Host Name and **1522** as the Port Number, and click Next.

6. Enter **ocp10g** as the Service Name, and click Next.

7. Click the Test button. This will attempt to connect using the alias you have created. The test should fail, because even though the newly created alias does resolve to the address of the listener LIST2, the listener does not have your instance registered.

8. Close the Test window, and from the File menu select Save Network Configuration. Note the directory path at the top of Net Manager's window: this is where the Oracle Net files will be saved.

Exercise 12-3: Configuring Dynamic Service Registration

In this exercise you will set the local_listener parameter for your instance so that it will register with your nondefault listener LIST2. Then check that the registration has occurred and test the connection you created in Exercise 12-2. Finally, put everything back to normal.

1. Using SQL*Plus, connect to your instance as user SYSTEM, and issue the commands

```
SQL> alter system set local_listener='ocp10g_1522';
SQL> alter system register;
```

2. From an operating system prompt, use lsnrctl to check that your instance has registered dynamically with your list2 listener.

```
C:\> lsnrctl services list2
```

3. Test the alias by connecting using SQL*Plus.

```
SQL> connect system/oracle@ocp10g_1522;
```

4. Reset your instance to use the default listener by putting the local_listener parameter back to default, and re-register it.

```
SQL> alter system set local_listener='';
SQL> alter system register;
```

Advanced Connection Options

Network connectivity is critical for making your database available to your users, and your network administrators may well have configured redundancy in the network; if so, Oracle Net can take advantage of this. Consider an environment where your database server is dual homed: it has two network interface cards, on two different subnets. This means that there are two routes by which user processes can connect to the instance. You should then configure Oracle Net such that all incoming connection requests will be load-balanced across the two routes. Furthermore, if one route is unavailable (perhaps there is a routing problem, or the network interface card is down), you need to ensure that all connection requests are sent through the surviving route.

First, you will need to configure the listeners to monitor both network cards. You may do this either by configuring one listener with two listening addresses, or by creating a second listener to monitor the second address. Then connect-time fault tolerance and load balancing are configured on the client side, by setting up the service alias appropriately. Consider this example of a tnsnames.ora file:

```
ocp10g_net1 =
  (DESCRIPTION =
    (ADDRESS_LIST =
      (ADDRESS = (PROTOCOL = TCP)(HOST = ora10g_net1.haunting.com)(PORT = 1521))
    )
    (CONNECT_DATA =
      (service_name = ocp10g)
    )
  )
ocp10g_net2 =
  (DESCRIPTION =
    (ADDRESS_LIST =
      (ADDRESS = (PROTOCOL = TCP)(HOST = ora10g_net2.haunting.com)(PORT = 1521))
    )
    (CONNECT_DATA =
      (service_name = ocp10g)
```

```
    )
  )
ocp10g_either =
  (DESCRIPTION =
    (ADDRESS_LIST =
      (load_balance=on)
      (failover=on)
      (ADDRESS = (PROTOCOL = TCP)(HOST = ora10g_net1.haunting.com)(PORT = 1521))
      (ADDRESS = (PROTOCOL = TCP)(HOST = ora10g_net2.haunting.com)(PORT = 1521))
    )
    (CONNECT_DATA =
      (service_name = ocp10g)
    )
  )
```

The service alias ocp10g_net1 requests a connection to the service ocp10g via the IP address for ora10g_net1.haunting.com. Alias ocp10g_net2 requests the same service, but via a different IP address. But the service alias ocp10g_either includes both addresses in its address_list. Note the directives load_balance=on and fail_over=on. The first of these instructs the user process to select one address randomly. This will result in half your users hitting the database server through one address, and half through the other: the network load will be evenly balanced across your database server's two network cards. The second directive instructs the user process to try the other address if the first one it randomly selected fails, thus giving you fault tolerance as well as load balancing. You can configure aliases such as this manually, or through the Database Control or Net Manager tools, as shown in Figure 12-11.

Another common network problem is security and firewalls. Oracle provides a utility, the Connection Manager, that can act as a proxy server. It is a specialized listener that will (typically) run on a firewall bastion host. It will accept Oracle Net connection requests from the external network and forward them to a database server on the internal network. All traffic for connections established in this manner is subsequently routed through the Connection Manager. To configure use of such a system, create a service alias such as this:

```
ocp10g_from_outside =
  (DESCRIPTION =
    (ADDRESS_LIST =
      (source_route=on)
      (ADDRESS = (PROTOCOL = TCP)(HOST = firewall.haunting.com)(PORT = 1521))
      (ADDRESS = (PROTOCOL = TCP)(HOST = ora10g.haunting.com)(PORT = 1521))
    )
    (CONNECT_DATA =
      (service_name = ocp10g)
    )
  )
```

This example shows an alias ocp10g_from_outside that is intended to be used by users coming into your systems from the Internet. It includes the directive source_route=on. This instructs the user process to go to the first address in the list, which is the address of a Connection Manager running on your firewall. The Connection Manager will then forward the connection to the listener identified by the second

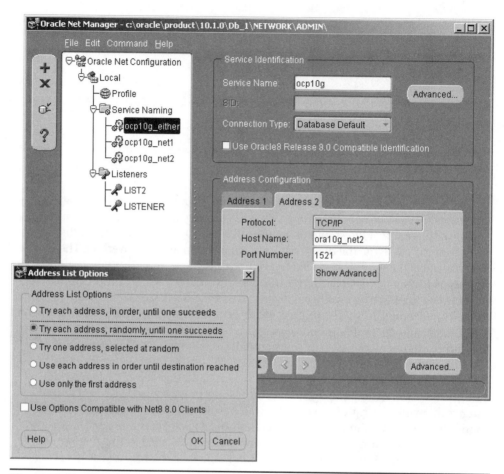

Figure 12-11   Using Net Manager to configure connect time fault tolerance and load balancing

address, which is your database server on your intranet. Then the Connection Manager will proxy all traffic to and fro.

As with load balancing and fault tolerance, you can create an alias like this by editing the tnsnames.ora file by hand, or through the GUI tools. In Figure 12-11, you would select "Use each address in order until destination reached" to achieve this result.

Testing Your Oracle Net Connections

Of course, you can test your connections by using SQL*Plus and attempting to log on through an alias. But Oracle provides two utilities specifically for testing. You have already seen one: the Test command within the Net Manager. You are prompted to use this whenever you create a service alias, or you can invoke it by highlighting an alias and selecting Test Service from the Command drop-down menu. The Net Manager test does an end-to-end check: from the client machine where you are running Net Manager it will attempt to log on to the instance, thus confirming that the alias is syntactically correct; that the alias does resolve to the address of a listener; that the listener is running and does know about the service requested; that the instance making up that service is running; that the database the service connects to is open. When attempting a logon, the Net Manager test will use the username/password SCOTT/TIGER, the old demonstration database user. If SCOTT does not exist in your database, the test will fail with an error to that effect—do not worry about this; the fact that the database could respond with an error is proof enough that you can connect to it.

The second test is the command-line utility tnsping (it is tnsping.exe on Windows). Unlike the Net Manager test, tnsping only tests connectivity as far as the listener.

The first test in Figure 12-12 failed because the alias used could not be resolved: it does not exist in the tnsnames.ora file. The second test corrects the alias, but fails because the listener is not running. Then after starting the listener, the third test succeeds.

```
C:\WINNT\system32\cmd.exe                                                    _|□|×|
C:\>
C:\>
C:\>tnsping ocp10

TNS Ping Utility for 32-bit Windows: Version 10.1.0.2.0 - Production on 19-SEP-2
004 17:23:38

Copyright (c) 1997, 2003, Oracle.  All rights reserved.

Used parameter files:
c:\oracle\product\10.1.0\Db_1\network\admin\sqlnet.ora

TNS-03505: Failed to resolve name

C:\>tnsping ocp10g

TNS Ping Utility for 32-bit Windows: Version 10.1.0.2.0 - Production on 19-SEP-2
004 17:23:44

Copyright (c) 1997, 2003, Oracle.  All rights reserved.

Used parameter files:
c:\oracle\product\10.1.0\Db_1\network\admin\sqlnet.ora


Used TNSNAMES adapter to resolve the alias
Attempting to contact (DESCRIPTION = (ADDRESS_LIST = (ADDRESS = (PROTOCOL = TCP)
(HOST = 127.0.0.1)(PORT = 1521))) (CONNECT_DATA = (SERVICE_NAME = ocp10g)))
TNS-12541: TNS:no listener

C:\>tnsping ocp10g

TNS Ping Utility for 32-bit Windows: Version 10.1.0.2.0 - Production on 19-SEP-2
004 17:23:59

Copyright (c) 1997, 2003, Oracle.  All rights reserved.

Used parameter files:
c:\oracle\product\10.1.0\Db_1\network\admin\sqlnet.ora


Used TNSNAMES adapter to resolve the alias
Attempting to contact (DESCRIPTION = (ADDRESS_LIST = (ADDRESS = (PROTOCOL = TCP)
(HOST = 127.0.0.1)(PORT = 1521))) (CONNECT_DATA = (SERVICE_NAME = ocp10g)))
OK (40 msec)

C:\>
```

Figure 12-12   Test results for tnsping

EXAM TIP The tnsping utility does a handshake with the listener but does not test whether the instance is running and the database is open. Only the Net Manager test does that.

Chapter Review

This chapter has covered the theory behind Oracle Net and how to configure client/server connections. You have seen how Oracle Net is controlled by a set of files: the server-side listener.ora file, which defines listeners, and the client-side tnsnames.ora file, which provides a name resolution capability for the most commonly used name resolution method: local naming. There is also the sqlnet.ora file, an optional file for either the client or server side. There are graphical configuration tools for managing Oracle Net, which you are strongly advised to use in order to avoid problems with connectivity that can be very difficult to resolve. Finally, you saw some of the more advanced capabilities of Oracle Net, and the testing tools to test Oracle Net connections.

Questions

1. Which protocols can Oracle Net 10g use? (Choose four answers.)
   A. TCP
   B. UDP
   C. SPX/IPX
   D. SDP
   E. TCP with secure sockets
   F. Named Pipes
   G. LU6.2
   H. NetBIOS/NetBEUI

2. Where is the division between the client and the server in the Oracle environment? (Choose the best answer.)
   A. Between the instance and the database
   B. Between the user and the user process
   C. Between the server process and the instance
   D. Between the user process and the server process
   E. The client/server split varies depending on the stage of the execution cycle

3. Which of the following statements about listeners is correct? (Choose the best answer.)
   A. A listener can connect you to one instance only.
   B. A listener can connect you to one service only.

    C. Multiple listeners can share one network interface card.

    D. An instance will accept connections only from the listener specified on the LOCAL_LISTENER parameter.

4. You have decided to use local naming. Which files must you create on the client machine? (Choose the best answer.)

    A. tnsnames.ora and sqlnet.ora

    B. listener.ora only

    C. tnsnames.ora only

    D. listener.ora and sqlnet.ora

    E. None. You can rely on defaults if you are using TCP and your listener is running on port 1521.

5. If you stop your listener, what will happen to sessions that connected through it? (Choose the best answer.)

    A. They will continue if you have configured failover.

    B. They will not be affected in any way.

    C. They will hang until you restart the listener.

    D. You cannot stop a listener if it is in use.

    E. The sessions will error out.

6. If you stop a Connection Manager, what will happen to sessions that connected through it? (Choose the best answer.)

    A. They will continue if you have configured failover.

    B. They will not be affected in any way.

    C. You cannot stop a Connection Manager if it is in use.

    D. The sessions will error out.

7. If you are running your user process on the same machine as the instance you wish to connect to, which of the following is correct? (Choose two answers.)

    A. You do not need to go via a listener.

    B. You can only use the IPC protocol.

    C. You cannot use the IPC protocol.

    D. You do not need to use Oracle Net at all.

    E. You do not need to configure Oracle Net at all.

8. Your organization has many databases on many servers, and a large number of users. The network environment is always changing. What would be the best naming method to use? (Choose the best answer.)

    A. Easy Connect, because it means that you don't have to maintain tnsnames .ora files.

    B. Directory naming, because it centralizes the naming information.

    C. Local naming, because each user can maintain his own configuration files locally.

    D. External naming, because you can rely on a third-party product to maintain the configuration information.

9. Your server is using a European character set, and your client is using an American character set. How will Oracle Net handle this? (Choose the best answer.)

    A. It cannot; you must change the character set of the database or of the client.

    B. The underlying network protocol will handle the conversion.

    C. Oracle Net will handle the conversion.

    D. The application software must do any necessary conversion.

10. Why might you set up multiple listeners for one instance? (Choose the best answer.)

    A. You can't; there can be only one local listener.

    B. To provide fault tolerance and load balancing.

    C. If the listeners are on separate computers, you will get better performance.

    D. To spread the workload of maintaining sessions across several processes.

11. The tnsping utility reports that an alias is fine, but you can't connect with SQL*Plus. What might be the reason? (Choose two answers.)

    A. You are using a bad username/password combination, but tnsping tested with a correct one.

    B. The listener is running, but the instance isn't.

    C. The database is in mount mode.

    D. SQL*Plus is using one name resolution method; tnsping is using another.

12. Which configuration tools can be used to start a listener? (Choose two answers.)

    A. Database Control

    B. The Net Manager

    C. The lsnrctl utility

    D. SQL*Plus

13. Consider this tnsnames.ora file:

```
test =
 (description =
   (address_list =
     (address = (protocol = tcp)(host = serv2)(port = 1521))
   )
   (connect_data =
     (service_name = prod)
   )
 )
prod =
 (description =
```

```
      (address_list =
        (address = (protocol = tcp)(host = serv1)(port = 1521))
      )
      (connect_data =
        (service_name = prod)
      )
   )
 dev =
  (description =
     (address_list =
        (address = (protocol = tcp)(host = serv3)(port = 1521))
     )
     (connect_data =
        (service_name = prod)
     )
  )
```

Which of the following statements is correct? (Choose the best answer.)

A. All the aliases will connect to the same service.

B. The aliases will all go to different services.

C. The first and third aliases will fail, because the alias name doesn't match the service name.

D. There will be a port conflict, because all aliases use the same port.

E. None of the above.

14. Consider this line from a listener.ora file:

```
l1=(description=(address=(protocol=tcp)(host=serv1)(port=1521)))
```

What will happen if you issue this connect string:

```
connect scott/tiger@l1
```

A. You will be connected to the instance l1.

B. You will be connected to an instance only if dynamic instance registration is working.

C. You can't tell; it depends on how the client side is configured.

D. If you are logged on to the server machine, IPC will connect you to the local instance.

E. The connection will fail if the listener is not started.

15. Consider these four initialization parameters:

```
instance_name=PRD
db_name=PROD
db_domain=WORLD
local_listener=''
service_names=production
```

What service name will be registered with a listener on port 1521? (Choose the best answer.)

A. PRD.WORLD

B. PROD.WORLD

C. production

D. None, because the local_listener parameter has been disabled.

Answers

1. **A, D, E, and F.** The four protocols supported by Oracle Net 10g are TCP, SDP, TCP with secure sockets, and Named Pipes. Previous releases supported other protocols.

2. **D.** The client/server split is between user process and server process.

3. **C.** One network interface card can support many listeners, provided they use different ports.

4. **C.** The only required file is tnsnames.ora.

5. **B.** A listener establishes connections; it does not maintain them. Therefore B is correct, and the others are wrong.

6. **D.** A Connection Manager is responsible for maintaining connections: all traffic goes through it. So D is correct because the sessions will fail.

7. **A and E.** All connections use Oracle Net, but they need not use a network and for local connections you need do no configuration.

8. **B.** Directory naming is intended for exactly the environment described and is the best answer.

9. **C.** Character set conversion is done by the Two-Task Common layer of Oracle Net.

10. **B.** Multiple listeners can provide connect-time fault tolerance and load balancing.

11. **B and C.** The tnsping utility tests only the handshake between user process and listener, not the onward connection to the instance, so B and C are both possibilities.

12. **A and C.** Listeners can be started with Database Control or the lsnrctl utility.

13. **B.** Each alias specifies a different host.

14. **C.** You have no idea what will happen, without knowing how the client is configured.

15. **C.** The SERVICE_NAMES parameter is used to register the instance.

CHAPTER 13

Managing Shared Servers

In this chapter you will learn how to
- Configure Oracle shared servers
- Identify when to use Oracle shared servers
- Monitor shared servers
- Describe the shared server architecture

Chapter 12 went through the dedicated server architecture, which is the default Oracle configuration: for each session against an instance, the listener will spawn a server process. The alternative is the shared server architecture: rather than spawning server processes on demand for each session, you prespawn a small number of server processes, to be shared by all your database sessions. This chapter will explain the shared server architecture, teach you how to configure and monitor it, and give some guidelines on when to use it. Always remember that shared server is an option that you only use if you have to—there are many installations where it is not applicable, but it is a feature that all DBAs should be aware of and is considered important for examination purposes.

The Limitations of the Dedicated Server Architecture

The standard dedicated server architecture requires that the database listener should spawn a dedicated server process for each concurrent connection to the instance. These server processes will persist until the session is terminated. You can see the processes being launched and terminated at the operating system level. On Unix, use the ps command to display them, as in Figure 13-1.

```
 ora10g.haunting.com                                                    _ □ ×
$
$
$ ps -ef|grep ocp10g
ora10g     6248     1   0 14:58 ?        00:00:00 ora_pmon_ocp10g
ora10g     6250     1   0 14:58 ?        00:00:00 ora_mman_ocp10g
ora10g     6252     1   0 14:58 ?        00:00:00 ora_dbw0_ocp10g
ora10g     6254     1   0 14:58 ?        00:00:00 ora_lgwr_ocp10g
ora10g     6256     1   0 14:58 ?        00:00:00 ora_ckpt_ocp10g
ora10g     6258     1   0 14:58 ?        00:00:00 ora_smon_ocp10g
ora10g     6260     1   0 14:58 ?        00:00:00 ora_reco_ocp10g
ora10g     6262     1   0 14:58 ?        00:00:00 ora_cjq0_ocp10g
ora10g     6276     1   0 14:58 ?        00:00:01 oracleocp10g (DESCRIPTION=(LOCAL
=YES)(ADDRESS=(PROTOCOL=beq)))
ora10g     6294     1   0 14:58 ?        00:00:00 ora_qmnc_ocp10g
ora10g     6298     1   0 14:58 ?        00:00:00 ora_mmon_ocp10g
ora10g     6300     1   0 14:58 ?        00:00:00 ora_mmnl_ocp10g
ora10g     6320     1   0 14:58 ?        00:00:00 ora_q000_ocp10g
ora10g     6332     1   0 14:59 ?        00:00:00 ora_q001_ocp10g
ora10g     6345     1   0 14:59 ?        00:00:01 ora_j000_ocp10g
ora10g     6981     1   0 15:04 ?        00:00:00 oracleocp10g (LOCAL=NO)
ora10g     7003     1   0 15:04 ?        00:00:00 oracleocp10g (LOCAL=NO)
ora10g     7023  3751   0 15:04 pts/4    00:00:00 grep ocp10g
$
$ ▉
```

Figure 13-1 Using ps and grep to display all the processes that are part of the instance called ocp10g

Each oracleocp10g process is an Oracle dedicated server; the other processes are the background processes that make up the instance. Two of the server processes, with process ID numbers 6981 and 7003, include "(LOCAL=NO)," which is an indication that the server process is servicing a remote user process. The other server process, number 6276, says "(DESCRIPTION=(LOCAL=YES) (ADDRESS=(PROTOCOL=beq)))," which is an indication that the user process is running on the same machine as the server and did not come in through a listener. If you launch some more SQL*Plus sessions, locally or remote, you will see more server processes appearing on the ps listing.

On Windows, the server processes are not actual operating system processes; they are threads within the single oracle.exe process, but the principle is exactly the same. Within your Windows Task Manager, if you choose to display the thread count (on the Processes tab, click View | Select Columns | Thread Count), you will see that the number of threads increases by one for each concurrent logon. If you have the Windows Resource Kit, or some similar tool, you can look inside the oracle.exe file for more detailed information on the names of the threads being launched, similar to that displayed by the Unix ps command.

 TIP Some DBAs refer to server processes as "shadow" processes.

As more users log on to your instance, more server processes get launched. This is not a problem as far as Oracle is concerned. The database listener can launch as many processes as required, though there may be limits on the speed with which it can launch them. If you have a large number of concurrent connection requests, your listener will have to queue them up. You can avoid this by running multiple listeners on different ports and load-balancing between them. Then once the sessions are established, there is no limit to the number that PMON can manage. But your operating system may well have limits on the number of processes that it can support, limits to do with context switches and with memory.

A computer can only do one thing at a time, unless it is an SMP machine, in which case each CPU can only do one thing at a time. The operating system simulates concurrent processing by using an algorithm to share CPU cycles across all the currently executing processes. This algorithm, often referred to as a time-slicing or time-sharing algorithm, takes care of allocating a few CPU cycles to each process in turn. Switching one process off CPU in order to put another process on CPU is called a *context switch*. Context switches are very expensive: the operating system has to do a lot of work to restore the state of each process as it is brought onto CPU and then save its state when it is switched off the CPU. As more users connect to the instance, the operating system has to context-switch between more and more server processes. Depending on your operating system, this can cause a severe degradation in performance. A decent mainframe operating system can context-switch between tens of thousands of processes without problems, but newer (and simpler) operating systems such as Unix and

Windows may not be good at running thousands, or even just hundreds, of concurrent processes. This is very much platform specific, but performance may degrade dramatically because a large proportion of the computer's processing capacity is taken up with managing the context switches, leaving a relatively small amount of processing capacity available for actually doing work.

There may also be memory problems as more sessions are established. The actual server processes themselves are not an issue, because all modern operating systems use shared memory when the same process is loaded more than once. So launching a thousand server processes should take no more memory than launching one. The problem comes with the Program Global Area, or PGA. The PGA is a block of memory associated with each server process, to maintain the state of the session and as a work area for operations such as sorting rows. Clearly, the PGAs cannot be in shared memory: they contain data unique to each session. This is why your system may begin to swap as more users log on: each session will require its own PGA.

So in the dedicated server environment, performance may degrade if your operating system has problems managing a large number of concurrent processes, and the problem will be exacerbated if your server machine has insufficient memory. Note that it doesn't really matter whether the sessions are actually doing anything or not. Even if the sessions are idle, the operating system must still bring them on and off CPU and possibly page the appropriate PGA into main memory from swap files, according to its time-slicing algorithm. There comes a point when, no matter what you do in the way of hardware upgrades, performance begins to degrade because of operating system inefficiencies in managing context switches and paging. These are not Oracle's problems, but to overcome them Oracle offers the option of the shared server architecture. This allows a large number of user processes to be serviced by a relatively small number of shared server processes, thus reducing dramatically the number of processes that the server's operating system has to manage. As a fringe benefit, memory usage may also reduce.

The Shared Server Architecture

One point to emphasize immediately is that shared server (known as the multithreaded server, or MTS, in earlier releases) is implemented purely on the server side. The user process and the application software have no way of telling that anything has changed. The user process issues a connect string that must resolve to the address of a listener and the name of a service (or of an instance). In return, it will receive the address of a server-side process that it will think is a dedicated server. It will then proceed to send SQL statements and receive back result sets: as far as the user process is concerned, absolutely nothing has changed. But the server side is very different.

Shared server is implemented by additional processes that are a part of the instance. They are background processes, launched at instance startup time. There are two new process types, dispatchers and shared servers. There are also some extra queue memory structures within the SGA, and the database listener modifies its behavior for shared server. When an instance that is configured for shared server starts up, in addition to the usual background processes, one or more dispatcher processes also start. The dispatchers, like any other TCP process, run on a unique TCP port allocated by your operating system's port mapper: they contact the listener and register with it, using the LOCAL_LISTENER parameter (remember that from Chapter 12?) to locate the listener. One or more shared server processes also start. These are conceptually similar to a normal dedicated server process, but they are not tied to one session. They will receive SQL statements, parse and execute them, and generate a result set—but they will not receive the SQL statements directly from a user process; they will read them from a queue that will be populated with statements from any number of user processes. Similarly, the shared servers don't fetch result sets back to a user process directly; instead, they put the result sets onto a response queue.

The next question is, how do the user-generated statements get onto the queue that is read by the server processes, and how do results get fetched to the users? This is where the dispatchers come in. When a user process contacts a listener, rather than launching a server process and connecting it to the user process, the listener passes back the address of a dispatcher. If there is only one dispatcher, the listener will connect it to all the user processes. If there are multiple dispatchers, the listener will load-balance incoming connection requests across them, but the end result is that many user processes will be connected to each dispatcher. Each user process will be under the impression that it is talking to a dedicated server process, but it isn't; it is sharing a dispatcher with many other user processes. At the network level, many user processes will have connections mutexed through the one port used by the dispatcher.

 EXAM TIP A session's connection to a dispatcher persists for the duration of the session, unlike the connection to the listener, which is transient.

When a user process issues a SQL statement, it is sent to the dispatcher. The dispatcher puts all the statements it receives onto a queue. This queue is called the "common" queue, because all dispatchers share it. No matter which dispatcher a user process is connected to, all statements end up on the common queue.

All the shared server processes monitor the common queue. When a statement arrives on the common queue, the first available shared server picks it up. From that point on execution proceeds through the usual parse-bind-execute cycle, but when it comes to the fetch phase, it is impossible for the shared server to fetch the result set back to the user process because there is no connection between the user process and the shared server. So instead, the shared server puts the result set onto a response queue that is specific to the dispatcher that received the job in the first place. Each dispatcher monitors its own response queue, and whenever any results are put on it, the dispatcher will pick them up and present them back to the user process that originally issued the statement.

 EXAM TIP There is a common input queue shared by all dispatchers, but each dispatcher has its own response queue.

A result of the mechanism of dispatchers and queues is that any statement from any user process could be executed by any available shared server. This raises the question of how the state of the session can be maintained. It would be quite possible for a user process to issue, for example, a SELECT FOR UPDATE, a DELETE, and a COMMIT. In a normal dedicated server connection, this isn't a problem, because the PGA (which is tied to the one server process that is managing the session) stores information about what the session was doing, and therefore the dedicated server will know what to COMMIT and what locks to release. The PGA for a dedicated server session will store the session's session data, its cursor state, its sort space, and its stack space. But in the shared server environment, each statement might be picked off the common queue by a different shared server process, which will have no idea what the state of the transaction is. To get around this problem, a shared server session stores most of the session data in the shared pool, rather than in the PGA. Then whenever a shared server picks a job off the common queue, it will go to the SGA and connect to the appropriate block of memory to find out the state of the session. The memory used in the SGA for each shared server session, known as the User Global Area (UGA), includes all of what would have been in a PGA with the exception of the session's stack space. This is where the memory saving will come from. Oracle can manage memory in the shared pool much more effectively than it can in many separate PGAs.

 EXAM TIP In shared server, what PGA memory structure does not go into the SGA? The stack space.

Configuring Shared Server

Being a server-side capability, shared server entails no client configuration at all beyond perfectly normal client-side Oracle Net, as detailed in Chapter 12. On the server side, shared server has nothing to do with the database—only the instance. The listener will be automatically configured for shared server through dynamic instance registration. It follows that shared server is configured through instance initialization parameters. Only one is required, though there are a few optional ones as well. The shared server parameters are shown in Table 13-1.

 TIP Advanced or not, you should always set SHARED_SERVERS, DISPATCHERS, and LARGE_POOL_SIZE if you are using shared server. And you should always set PROCESSES and SESSIONS in any case. You must also set LOCAL_LISTENER if your listener is not using port 1521.

The first parameter to consider is SHARED_SERVERS. This controls the number of shared servers that will be launched at instance startup time. Shared server uses a queuing mechanism, but the ideal is that there should be no queuing: there should always be a server process ready and waiting for every job that is put on the common queue by the dispatchers. Therefore, SHARED_SERVERS should be set to the maximum

Parameter	Required for Shared Server?	Basic or Advanced?
SHARED_SERVERS	No	Basic
DISPATCHERS	Yes	Advanced
MAX_SHARED_SERVERS	No	Advanced
MAX_DISPATCHERS	No	Advanced
LOCAL_LISTENER	No	Advanced
LARGE_POOL_SIZE	No	Advanced
CIRCUITS	No	Advanced
SHARED_SERVER_SESSIONS	No	Advanced
PROCESSES	No	Basic
SESSIONS	No	Basic

Table 13-1   Instance Parameters for Shared Server

number of concurrent requests that you expect. But if there is a sudden burst of activity, you don't have to worry too much, because Oracle will launch additional shared servers, up to the value specified for MAX_SHARED_SERVERS. By default, SHARED_SERVERS is 1 if DISPATCHERS is set. MAX_SHARED_SERVERS defaults to one-eighth of the PROCESSES parameter.

The DISPATCHERS parameter controls how many dispatcher processes to launch at instance startup time, and how they will behave. This is the only required parameter. There are many options for this parameter, but usually two will suffice: how many to start, and what protocol they should listen on. Among the more advanced options are ones that allow you to control the port and network card on which the dispatcher will listen, and the address of the listener(s) with which it will register, but usually you can let your operating system's port mapper assign a port, and use the LOCAL_LISTENER parameter to control which listener the dispatcher(s) will register with. MAX_DISPATCHERS sets an upper limit to the number of dispatchers you can start, but unlike shared servers, Oracle will not start extra dispatchers on demand. You can, however, launch additional dispatchers at any time up to this limit.

LOCAL_LISTENER is a parameter you saw with regard to dynamic instance registration. It tells the instance the address of a listener that it should register with. In the shared server environment, the dispatchers will also use this parameter to register themselves; otherwise, the listener would not know where the dispatchers were. During the lifetime of the instance, the dispatchers continually update the local listener with data on how many sessions they are servicing, so that the listener can always direct a new incoming connection request to the least busy dispatcher.

The LARGE_POOL_SIZE parameter is not required, but you should always set it. A large part of a session's PGA, known as the UGA, is stored in the SGA if the session is coming in through the shared server mechanism. By default, the UGAs for all your sessions go into the shared pool. If you have many shared server sessions, this will put a lot of strain on the shared pool, both in terms of memory demand and management as memory is being allocated and deallocated on demand. But if you specify the LARGE_POOL_SIZE parameter, you create a separate area of memory in the SGA that will be used for the UGAs instead of the shared pool. This will take a lot of strain off the shared pool.

The CIRCUITS and SHARED_SERVER_SESSIONS parameters limit how many users are allowed to connect through the shared servers. A circuit is one connection to a dispatcher and will usually map onto one session, but if your programmers are writing code using appropriate OCI calls, they can channel several logical sessions through one physical circuit. By default, there are no limits on the number of circuits or shared server sessions.

Finally, two more basic parameters: The SESSIONS and PROCESSES parameters are not necessarily related to shared server, but this is an appropriate time to discuss them. The PROCESSES parameter sets a limit on the number of operating system processes (or threads on Windows) that can connect to the SGA. This total must be large enough to allow for the background processes and all dedicated server processes. Shared servers and dispatchers also count against the total. So in a dedicated server environment, this is one way of limiting the number of concurrent connections. SESSIONS is applied at the Oracle level rather than the operating system level; it limits the number of concurrent logons to the instance, irrespective of whether each logon is through a dedicated server or through a shared server.

 TIP The defaults for SESSIONS and PROCESSES are not suitable for most modern databases. You should always consider how many concurrent users you expect, and set them appropriately.

Exercise 13-1: Configuring and Verifying Shared Server

In this exercise, you will convert your instance to use shared server, and demonstrate that it is working.

1. Log on to your instance with SQL*Plus, and issue the following commands to set parameters to enable the shared server:

```
alter system set dispatchers='(protocol=tcp)(dispatchers=2)' scope=spfile;
alter system set shared_servers=3 scope=spfile;
startup force;
```

2. Issue this query to confirm that the dispatchers and shared servers have started:

```
select program from v$process;
```

Note that there are two processes, d000 and d001, that are the two dispatchers, and three shared server processes, s000, s001, and s002.

3. Use lsnrctl to confirm that the dispatchers have registered with your listener: from an operating system prompt, enter

```
lsnrctl services
```

The output will resemble that in Figure 13-2.

Note that the two dispatchers have registered themselves but have not yet established any sessions.

4. Launch a new SQL*Plus session, and log on to your instance through the listener.

```
sqlplus system/oracle@ocp10g
```

5. Query V$CIRCUIT to confirm that your connection has been established as a circuit: a connection through a shared server.

```
select dispatcher,saddr,circuit from v$circuit;
```

One row will be returned, showing which dispatcher your new session has come through and the session address.

6. Repeat Steps 4 and 5 several times until you have a number of concurrent sessions, and observe how the new connections are balanced across the two dispatchers.

```
C:\WINDOWS\System32\cmd.exe                                         _ □ X

C:\>
C:\>lsnrctl services

LSNRCTL for 32-bit Windows: Version 10.1.0.2.0 - Production on 25-SEP-2004 15:28
:16

Copyright (c) 1991, 2004, Oracle.  All rights reserved.

Connecting to (DESCRIPTION=(ADDRESS=(PROTOCOL=IPC)(KEY=EXTPROC)))
Services Summary...
Service "PLSExtProc" has 1 instance(s).
  Instance "PLSExtProc", status UNKNOWN, has 1 handler(s) for this service...
    Handler(s):
      "DEDICATED" established:0 refused:0
        LOCAL SERVER
Service "ocp10g" has 1 instance(s).
  Instance "ocp10g", status READY, has 3 handler(s) for this service...
    Handler(s):
      "DEDICATED" established:0 refused:0 state:ready
        LOCAL SERVER
      "D000" established:0 refused:0 current:0 max:1002 state:ready
        DISPATCHER <machine: ORA10G, pid: 3784>
        (ADDRESS=(PROTOCOL=tcp)(HOST=ora10g)(PORT=1040))
      "D001" established:0 refused:0 current:0 max:1002 state:ready
        DISPATCHER <machine: ORA10G, pid: 3080>
        (ADDRESS=(PROTOCOL=tcp)(HOST=ora10g)(PORT=1070))
Service "ocp10gXDB" has 1 instance(s).
  Instance "ocp10g", status READY, has 0 handler(s) for this service...
The command completed successfully

C:\>_
```

Figure 13-2 Dispatchers registered with a database listener

Monitoring the Shared Server

There are a number of views that will inform you of the state of your shared server environment.

V$CIRCUIT will have one row for each current connection through the shared server. The column CIRCUIT is the unique identifier, and there are join columns to V$SESSION (column SADDR) and V$DISPATCHER (column DISPATCHER) that will let you map sessions to dispatchers.

V$SHARED_SERVER will tell you the status of each shared server process. Perhaps the most useful columns are IDLE and BUSY, which show how much time each process has spent actually servicing requests rather than waiting for jobs to arrive on the common queue.

V$DISPATCHER has one row per dispatcher. Again, the key columns are IDLE and BUSY.

V$SHARED_SERVER_MONITOR has just one row, showing the maximum number of connections and sessions (usually these figures will be the same) that have ever come through the shared server. Also, there are figures for how many shared server processes have been launched dynamically. If this figure is greater than zero, clearly you did not start enough in the first place.

The final view is V$QUEUE. This will have one row for the common queue, and one row for each dispatcher's response queue. The critical column is QUEUED, which shows the number of items on the queues right now. Remember that the ideal is no queuing. If there are items on the common queue, that indicates that you do not have enough shared servers to clear it, and if there are items on the response queues, that indicates that your dispatchers are overloaded.

TIP There is a view V$MTS, provided for backward compatibility, which is identical to V$SHARED_SERVER_MONITOR and a lot shorter to type.

When to Use the Shared Server

You will not find a great deal of hard advice in the Oracle documentation on when to use shared server, or how many dispatchers and shared servers you'll need. The main point to hang on to is that shared server is a facility you use because there is a need for it. It increases scalability when there are hundreds or thousands of concurrent users, at the cost of increasing the number of CPU cycles needed for any one statement execution, because it has to go via queues. But overall, the scalability of your system will increase dramatically because the efficiency of the operating system will be greatly improved. You will be able to put many more requests per second through the instance, because the operating system will not have to spend such a large proportion of CPU time on context switches.

 TIP It is often said that you should think about using shared server when your number of concurrent connections is in the low hundreds. If you have less than one hundred concurrent connections, you almost certainly don't need it. But if you have more than a thousand, you probably do. The critical factor is whether your operating system performance is beginning to degrade because of excessive context switches.

What Applications Are Suitable for Shared Server?

Consider an OLTP environment, such as hundreds of telephone operators in a call center. Each operator may spend one or two minutes per call, collecting the caller details and entering them into the user process. Then when s/he clicks the Submit button, the user process constructs an insert statement and sends it off to the server process. The server process might go through the whole parse/bind/execute/fetch cycle for the statement in just a few hundredths of a second. Clearly, no matter how fast the clerks work, their server processes are idle 99.9 percent of the time. But the operating system still has to switch all those processes on and off CPU, according to its time-sharing algorithm. By contrast, consider a data warehouse environment. Here, users submit queries that may run for a long time. The batch uploads of data will be equally long running. Whenever one of these large jobs is submitted, the server process for that session could be working flat out for hours on just one statement.

It should be apparent that shared server is ideal for managing many sessions doing short transactions, where the bulk of the work is on the client side of the client/server divide. In these circumstances, one shared server will be able to service dozens of sessions. But for batch processing work, dedicated servers are much better. If you submit a large batch job through a shared server session, it will work, but it will tie up one of the processes from your small pool of shared server processes for the duration of the job, leaving all your other users to compete for the remaining shared servers. The amount of network traffic involved in batch uploads from a user process and in fetching large result sets back to a user process will also cause contention for dispatchers.

A second class of operations that are better done through a dedicated server is database administration work. Index creation, table maintenance operations, and backup and recovery work through the Recovery Manager (covered in later chapters) will perform much better through a dedicated server. And it is logically impossible to issue startup or shutdown commands through a shared server: the shared servers are part of the instance and thus not available at the time you issue a startup command. So the administrator should always have a dedicated server connection.

How to Control Use of Shared Servers

If you are running your user process locally on the server machine, you can bypass the shared server simply by using a direct connection. From a SQL*Plus prompt, issue the command

```
SQL> connect sys/oracle as sysdba
```

and you will get a dedicated server, because you have not specified a network alias that would go via a listener. All local connections, not just yours as sysdba, will do this. But most of your users will be coming in across a network through a listener.

An application has no way of controlling whether it is using a shared server or a dedicated server, but as DBA you can control this through Oracle Net. If dispatchers and shared servers are available, by default every connection through the listener will use them. This default can be overridden by the connection details you specify in the client side tnsnames.ora file, configured either by hand or through the Net Manager as in Figure 13-3.

Note that choosing a connection type is an example of something that can be done if you are using local or directory naming, but not with Easy Connect. Easy Connect will always use shared server if it is available.

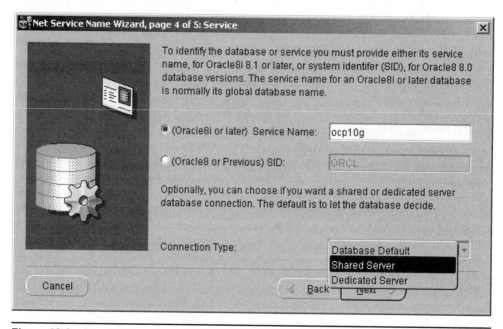

Figure 13-3   Selecting the connection type in the Net Manager

Exercise 13-2: Configuring a Client to Choose the Connection Type

In this exercise, create two new service aliases, one specifying dedicated server, the other specifying shared server. Test the effect, and then put your instance back to dedicated server only.

1. Using whatever text editor you wish, open your tnsnames.ora file in your ORACLE_HOME/network/admin directory.

2. Substituting your server's hostname for the HOST, add these two entries to your tnsnames.ora file:

```
ocp10g_ded =
  (DESCRIPTION =
    (ADDRESS_LIST =
      (ADDRESS = (PROTOCOL = TCP)(HOST = ora10g.haunting.com)(PORT = 1521))
    )
    (CONNECT_DATA =
      (SERVER = DEDICATED)
      (SERVICE_NAME = ocp10g)
    )
  )
ocp10g_mts =
  (DESCRIPTION =
    (ADDRESS_LIST =
      (ADDRESS = (PROTOCOL = TCP)(HOST = ora10g.haunting.com)(PORT = 1521))
    )
    (CONNECT_DATA =
      (SERVER = SHARED)
      (SERVICE_NAME = ocp10g)
    )
  )
```

Note that both aliases request the same service, ocp10g, but that the connect_data sections demand either a dedicated server (alias ocp10g_ded) or a connection through a shared server (alias ocp10g_mts).

3. At the operating system level, note how many processes there are in your instance. On Unix, use ps as in previous Figure 13-1. On Windows, use the Task Manager to display the number of threads in the oracle.exe process.

4. Launch a SQL*Plus session through a dedicated server.

```
SQL> connect system/oracle@ocp10g_ded
```

5. Repeat Step 3, and note that an extra server process (or thread) has been started.

6. Launch a SQL*Plus session through a shared server.

```
SQL> connect system/oracle@ocp_10g_mts
```

7. Repeat Step 3, and note that the process (or thread) count has not changed.

8. Return your instance to dedicated server only, and restart it.

```
connect / as sysdba;
alter system set dispatchers='' scope=spfile;
alter system set shared_servers=0 scope=spfile;
startup force;
```

Chapter Review

The shared server is an advanced option that many databases will never need to use, but if you do need it, the benefits can be immense. By use of initialization parameters, you instruct the instance to launch one or more dispatchers and shared server processes. The dispatchers register with a listener, and the listener will then concurrently connect many user processes to each dispatcher. The user processes submit statements to the dispatchers, which put them on a common queue that is serviced by a pool of shared servers. After executing the statements, the shared servers put the result set on a response queue, which the dispatcher then fetches back to the user process.

Questions

1. Which of these memory structures is not stored in the SGA for a shared server session? (Choose the best answer.)

   A. Cursor state

   B. Sort space

   C. Stack space

   D. Session data

2. Match the object to the function:

Object	Function
A. Common queue	a. Connects users to dispatchers
B. Dispatcher	b. Stores jobs waiting for execution
C. Large pool	c. Executes SQL statements
D. Listener	d. Stores results waiting to be fetched
E. Response queue	e. Receives statements from user processes
F. Shared server	f. Stores UGAs accessed by all servers

3. Which of the following is incorrect about memory usage? (Choose the best answer.)

   A. For dedicated server sessions, the server processes will not use shared memory.

   B. PGA memory is always outside the system global area.

    C. Shared server queues are created in the large pool, if a large pool has been defined. Otherwise, they are in the shared pool.

    D. For shared server sessions, UGAs are always stored in the SGA.

4. Which of the following statements are true about dispatchers? (Choose two answers.)

    A. Dispatchers don't handle the work of users' requests; they only interface between user processes and queues.

    B. Dispatchers share a common response queue.

    C. Dispatchers load-balance connections between themselves.

    D. Listeners load-balance connections across dispatchers.

    E. You can terminate a dispatcher, and established sessions will continue.

5. Which of the following statements about shared servers are true? (Choose the best answer.)

    A. All statements in a multistatement transaction will be executed by the same server.

    B. If one statement updates multiple rows, the work may be shared across several servers.

    C. The number of shared servers is fixed by the SHARED_SERVERS parameter.

    D. Oracle will spawn additional shared servers on demand.

6. You can monitor the shared server environment through a number of views. Which of the following statements is correct? (Choose two correct answers.)

    A. You can monitor how busy your shared servers are by querying V$SHARED_SERVER_MONITOR.

    B. V$PROCESS will have a row for each shared server.

    C. V$PROCESS will have a row for each dispatcher.

    D. V$CIRCUIT will show you how busy each shared server session is.

7. You query V$QUEUE and see that that the common queue has no messages waiting, but the response queues do. What action should you take? (Choose the best answer.)

    A. You need do nothing; queuing is a normal part of shared server operation.

    B. You should consider adding more shared servers.

    C. You should consider adding more dispatchers.

    D. You should create a large pool, to relieve the strain on the shared pool.

8. After configuring shared server, you find that there are still dedicated servers being spawned. What might be the reason for this? (Choose the best answer.)

    A. Your users are making local connections.

    B. The application is demanding dedicated servers.

    C. Large batch jobs are being run.

    D. Oracle has spawned dedicated servers, because you set the SHARED_
       SERVER parameter too low.

9. If you have multiple listeners, what will your dispatchers do? (Choose two
   answers.)

    A. All dispatchers will dynamically register with all listeners, automatically,
       if they are running on port 1521.

    B. Dispatchers can register with only one listener; otherwise, load balancing
       would not be possible.

    C. The dispatchers will load-balance themselves across the listeners.

    D. The dispatchers will register with whatever listener is nominated in the
       LOCAL_LISTENER parameter.

    E. You can control which listener each dispatcher will register with.

10. Your database is used for a mixture of OLTP, DSS, and batch processing.
   Would you advise use of shared server? (Choose the best answer.)

    A. Yes, but only for the OLTP work.

    B. Yes, if the batch and DSS users come though a different dispatcher from
       the OLTP users.

    C. No, because the mixed workload will cause problems.

    D. No, unless the work can be partitioned such that the OLTP work is in the
       day and the batch and DSS work at night to avoid contention.

11. There is one required parameter for shared server. Which is it?

    A. DISPATCHERS

    B. LARGE_POOL_SIZE

    C. PROCESSES

    D. SESSIONS

    E. SHARED_SERVERS

12. Which of the following operations cannot be done through a shared server
   connection? (Choose the best answer.)

    A. Backup and restore

    B. Shutdown and startup

    C. Physical operations, such as creating data files

    D. Large batch jobs

    E. Index creation

13. Which of the following is correct regarding memory usage? (Choose the best answer.)

    A. Overall memory demand should decrease because the number of server processes will be reduced when using the shared server option.

    B. Overall memory demand should decrease if you change to shared server, because you can reduce the size of the SGA.

    C. You should increase the size of the SGA if you convert to shared server.

    D. Implementing shared server will reduce the size of sessions' UGAs.

14. You have many sessions connected to one dispatcher. What is happening at the network level?

    A. Each session connects to the dispatcher on a unique TCP port.

    B. All the sessions connect to the dispatcher on one TCP port.

    C. The initial connection is always to one port; then the established connection is on a unique port.

    D. The connections are made and broken on demand, through a queuing mechanism.

15. You want to ensure that you have a dedicated server connection. Which of the following connection methods will give you this? (Choose two answers.)

    A. Using Easy Connect, because it can't use advanced features such as shared server

    B. Making a local connection that bypasses the listener

    C. Embedding the SERVER=DEDICATED directive in the service alias you use

    D. Connecting AS SYSDBA, which will always give a dedicated connection so that you can issue startup and shutdown commands

Answers

1. C. The stack space is not stored in the SGA.

2. A-b. The common queue is shared for all statements.
   B-e. The dispatchers receive statements from user processes.
   C-f. If created, the large pool is where the UGAs are stored.
   D-a. The listener establishes sessions by connecting users to dispatchers.
   E-d. Each dispatcher has its own response queue for result sets.
   F-c. Shared servers execute statements as normal.

3. C. This the correct answer, because it confuses memory used for queues with memory used for UGAs.

4. **A and D.** Dispatchers are the intermediaries between user processes and queues, and listeners will load-balance incoming connection requests across dispatchers.

5. **D.** This statement is the correct answer, though ideally you will have set SHARED_SERVERS high enough to satisfy the demand.

6. **B and C.** V$PROCESS does have an entry for every process, though you would normally use V$DISPATCHER and V$SHARED_SERVER if those were the processes you were interested in.

7. **C.** If responses are backing up, this implies that the dispatchers are too busy to clear their queues promptly.

8. **A.** This is the only possible reason, unless you, the DBA, have configured client-side Oracle Net to request dedicated sessions.

9. **D and E.** The dispatchers will by default register with the listener specified by the LOCAL_LISTENER parameter, but you can override this when you set the DISPATCHERS parameter.

10. **A.** Shared server is generally not recommended for work that may entail long running statements, but is excellent for the short queries and transactions typical of OLTP sessions.

11. **A.** This is the correct answer, but you should always configure the other parameters as well.

12. **B.** This is the only correct answer because shutdown and startup cannot be executed via the shared server.

13. **C.** You will need to increase the SGA, to provide space for the session UGAs— stored in the shared pool, or (preferably) in the large pool.

14. **B.** All sessions are mutexed through one port.

15. **B and C.** Bypassing the listener will always result in a dedicated server process being launched, or you can demand this in your TNS connection details.

CHAPTER 14

Managing Database Performance

In this chapter you will learn how to
- Troubleshoot invalid and unusable objects
- Gather optimizer statistics
- View performance metrics
- React to performance issues

Performance monitoring can take two general forms: reactive or proactive. The "reactive" approach means taking some action when or after a problem manifests itself; "proactive" means to identify pending issues before they become problems. Clearly, proactive monitoring is the ideal technique to minimize the impact of problems on end users, but reactive monitoring is also necessary in many cases. Chapter 15 goes through the use of the server alert system and the Automatic Database Diagnostic Monitor to assist with proactive monitoring, while this chapter concentrates on identifying problems after they have occurred.

Two types of problems are addressed: objects that have become useless, and drops in performance. Procedural objects, views, materialized views, and indexes can be invalidated if the objects to which they refer are changed in certain ways; when this happens, this should be detected and fixed. Performance of SQL statements is critically dependent on statistics that the optimizer uses to design efficient execution plans. Collection of statistics can be manual or automatic.

If, after gathering statistics, performance is still an issue, then various metrics can be used to drill down to the cause of the problem.

Invalid Objects

Stored PL/SQL is code stored and compiled within the data dictionary, as PL/SQL objects. This code can take these forms:

- Procedures
- Functions
- Triggers
- Packages
- Object types

Most, if not all, of these procedural objects will refer to data objects, such as tables. When a procedural object is compiled, the compiler checks the data objects to which it refers in order to confirm that their definition is correct for the code and whether the privileges are appropriate.

For example, if the code refers to a column, the column must exist or the code will not compile. If any of the data objects to which a procedural object refers change after the procedural object has been compiled, then the procedure will be marked INVALID. Procedural objects may also be invalid for more mundane reasons: perhaps the programmer made a simple syntactical mistake. In that case, the object will be created INVALID and will be useless.

The same situation can occur with views. When created they may be fine, but they will be invalidated if the tables on which they are based have their definitions changed.

 EXAM TIP Oracle will always attempt to recompile invalid PL/SQL objects and views automatically, but this may not succeed. You do not have to do it manually—though it may be advisable to do so.

Identifying Invalid Objects

Objects can be created invalid because of programmer error, or they can become invalid some time after creation. The view DBA_OBJECTS (and the derived views ALL_OBJECTS and USER_OBJECTS) has a column, STATUS, which should ideally always be VALID. To identify all invalid objects in the database, as user SYSTEM or another privileged user run the query

```
SQL> select owner,object_name,object_type from dba_objects where
status='INVALID';
```

If any objects are listed by this query, the first question to ask is whether the object was ever valid. It may never have worked and not be needed, in which case the best thing to do may be to drop it. But if, as is likely, you do not know if the object was ever valid, then a sensible first step is to attempt to compile it. The first time an invalid object is accessed, Oracle will attempt to compile it automatically, but if the compilation fails, the user will receive an error. Clearly, it is better for the DBA to compile it first; then, if there is an error, he can try to fix it before a user notices. Even if the object does compile when it is accessed, there may be a delay while the compilation takes place; it is better for perceived performance if this delay is taken by the DBA in advance.

Invalid objects can also be displayed through Database Control. From the database home page, take the Administration tab, and then select whatever object type you are interested in from the Schema section. All the objects of that type will be displayed, as in Figure 14-1, with the status.

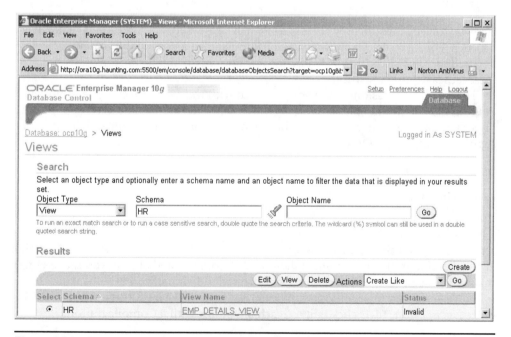

Figure 14-1 The status of a view, displayed by Database Control

Repairing Invalid Objects

To compile procedural objects, use the ALTER...COMPILE; command. For example,

```
SQL> alter procedure hr.add_reg compile;
```

will attempt to compile the procedure ADD_REG in the HR schema, and

```
SQL> alter view rname compile;
```

will compile the view RNAME. If the compilation succeeds, you have no further problems. If it fails, then you need to work out why. If a procedure does not compile, use the SQL*Plus command SHOW ERRORS to see why not. (Unfortunately, SHOW ERRORS is not supported for views.)

Often a useful starting point in identifying the cause of compilation errors is to use the DBA_DEPENDENCIES view, described here:

```
ocp10g> desc dba_dependencies;
 Name                               Null?     Type
 ---------------------------------- --------  -------------
 OWNER                              NOT NULL  VARCHAR2(30)
 NAME                               NOT NULL  VARCHAR2(30)
 TYPE                                         VARCHAR2(17)
 REFERENCED_OWNER                             VARCHAR2(30)
 REFERENCED_NAME                              VARCHAR2(64)
 REFERENCED_TYPE                              VARCHAR2(17)
 REFERENCED_LINK_NAME                         VARCHAR2(128)
 DEPENDENCY_TYPE                              VARCHAR2(4)
```

For every object, identified by NAME, there will be rows for each object on which it depends. For example, if a view retrieves columns from a dozen tables, they will each be listed as a REFERENCED_NAME. If a view does not compile, then investigating these tables would be sensible.

There will be occasions when you are faced with the need to recompile hundreds or thousands of invalid objects. Typically, this occurs after an upgrade to an application, or perhaps after applying patches. Rather than recompiling them individually, use the supplied utility script. On Unix,

```
SQL> @?/rdbms/admin/utlrp
```

or on Windows,

```
SQL> @?\rdbms\admin\utlrp
```

This script, which should be run when connected AS SYSDBA, will attempt to compile all invalid objects. If after running it there are still some invalid objects, you can assume that they have problems that should be addressed individually.

You can also recompile objects with Database Control. Having identified an INVALID object, as in Figure 14-1, click Edit to reach a window with a Compile button.

Exercise 14-1: Repairing Invalid Objects

Create some objects, force them to go invalid, and fix the problem.

1. Using SQL*Plus, connect to your database as user SYSTEM.

2. Create a user to be used for this exercise; grant him the DBA privilege.

```
SQL> grant dba to testuser identified by testuser;
```

3. Connect as TESTUSER, and create some objects.

```
SQL> conn testuser/testuser
Connected.
ocp10g> create table testtab(n1 number,d1 date);
Table created.
ocp10g> insert into testtab values(1,sysdate);
1 row created
ocp10g> create or replace view v1 as select d1 from testtab;
View created.
ocp10g> create or replace procedure p1 as
  2  cnt number;
  3  begin
  4  select count(*) into cnt from testtab;
  5  end;
  6  /
Procedure created.
```

4. Confirm the status of the objects.

```
SQL> select object_name,object_type,status from user_objects;
```

They will all have the STATUS of VALID.

5. Perform a DDL command on the table.

```
SQL> alter table testtab drop column d1;
```

6. Re-run the query from Step 4. Note that both the procedure and the view are now INVALID.

7. Re-compile the procedure:

```
SQL> alter procedure p1 compile;
Procedure altered.
```

This succeeds, because dropping a column does not mean that the procedure (which does not actually reference any columns by name) cannot run.

8. Re-compile the view.

```
ocp10g> alter view v1 compile;
Warning: View altered with compilation errors.
```

This fails, because a column on which the view is based no longer exists.

9. To diagnose the problem, query the DBA_DEPENDENCIES view.

```
ocp10g> select referenced_name,referenced_owner,referenced_type
  from user_dependencies where name='V1';
```

REFERENCED_NAME	REFERENCED_OWNER	REFERENCED_TYPE
TESTTAB	TESTUSER	TABLE
D1	TESTUSER	NON-EXISTENT

This shows that the view refers to a table, TESTTAB, and a nonexistent object called D1.

10. To pinpoint the exact problem, retrieve the code on which the view is based.

```
ocp10g>  select text from user_views where view_name='V1';
TEXT
----------------------------------------
select d1 from testtab
```

The problem is now apparent: the view references a valid table, but the column it needs no longer exists.

11. To fix the problem, add the column back to the table and recompile.

```
ocp10g> alter table testtab add (d1 date);
Table altered.
ocp10g> alter view v1 compile;
View altered.
```

12. Confirm that all the objects are now valid by re-running the query from Step 4.

13. Tidy up by dropping view and procedure (the table will be used in the next exercise).

```
SQL> drop view v1;
SQL> drop procedure p1;
```

Unusable Indexes

If a procedural object, such as a stored PL/SQL function or a view, becomes invalid, the DBA does not necessarily have to do anything: the first time it is accessed, Oracle will attempt to recompile it, and this may well succeed. But if an index becomes unusable for any reason, it must always be repaired explicitly before it can be used.

An index consists of the index key values, sorted into order, each with the relevant rowid. The rowid is the physical pointer to the location of the row to which the index key refers. If the rowids of the table are changed, then the index will be marked as unusable. This could occur for a number of reasons. Perhaps the most common is that the table has been moved, with the ALTER TABLE...MOVE command. This will change the physical placement of all the rows, and therefore the index entries will be pointing to the wrong place. Oracle will be aware of this and will therefore not permit use of the index.

Identifying Unusable Indexes

In earlier releases of the Oracle database, it was more than likely that users would detect unusable indexes because their sessions would return errors. When executing SQL statements, if the session attempted to use an unusable index it would immediately return an error, and the statement would fail. Release 10g of the database changes this behavior. If a statement attempts to use an unusable index, the statement will revert to an execution plan that does not require the index. Thus, statements will always succeed—but perhaps at the cost of greatly reduced performance. This behavior is controlled by the instance parameter SKIP_UNUSABLE_INDEXES, which defaults to TRUE. The exception to this is if the index is necessary to enforce a constraint: if the index on a primary key column becomes unusable, the table will be locked for DML.

 TIP If you wish your database to react as earlier releases, where unusable indexes would cause errors, issue the command ALTER SYSTEM SET SKIP_UNUSABLE_INDEXES=FALSE;

To detect indexes which have become unusable, query the DBA_INDEXES view:

```
SQL> select owner, index_name from dba_indexes where status='UNUSABLE';
```

The status of indexes is also displayed by Database Control, as in Figure 14-2.

Repairing Unusable Indexes

Indexes are marked unusable if the rowid pointers are no longer correct. To repair the index, it must be re-created with the ALTER INDEX...REBUILD command. This will make a pass through the table, generating a new index with correct rowid pointers for each index key. When the new index is completed, the original unusable index is dropped.

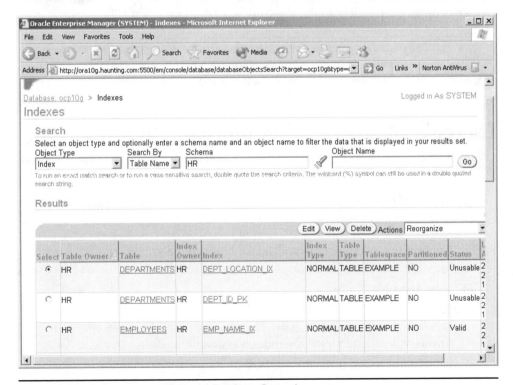

Figure 14-2 Index status as shown by Database Control

TIP While an index rebuild is in progress, additional storage space is required.

The syntax of the REBUILD command has several options. The more important ones are TABLESPACE, ONLINE, and NOLOGGING. By default, the index will be rebuilt within its current tablespace, but by specifying a table space with the TABLESPACE keyword, it can be moved to a different one. Also by default, during the course of the rebuild the table will be locked for DML. This can be avoided by using the ONLINE keyword. The NOLOGGING keyword instructs Oracle not to generate redo for the index rebuild operation. This will make the rebuild proceed much faster, but it does mean that the tablespace containing the index should be backed up immediately. Until the tablespace is backed up, the index will not survive media damage requiring use of restore and recovery.

EXAM TIP Enabling NOLOGGING disables redo generation only for the index rebuild. All subsequent DML against the index will generate redo as normal.

As an alternative to rebuilding unusable indexes with SQL*Plus, you can use Database Control. In the Indexes window, select Reorganize in the Actions drop-down box, as shown in Figure 14-2. Then in the Reorganize Objects: Options window you can select options equivalent to the keywords available at the SQL*Plus prompt.

TIP Rebuilding indexes may also be necessary as part of normal database maintenance. Indexes become inefficient with time, particularly if there are many deletions, or updates that affect the key values of rows.

Exercise 14-2: Repairing Unusable Indexes

Create indexes, force them to become unusable, and repair them using SQL*Plus and Database Control.

1. In your SQL*Plus session, connect as TESTUSER and create two indexes.

```
SQL> create index d1_idx on testtab(d1);
SQL> create index n1_idx on testtab(n1);
```

2. Confirm the index creation and status. Both will be VALID.

```
SQL> select index_name,status from user_indexes;
```

3. Move the table.

```
SQL> alter table testtab move;
```

4. Run the query from Step 2 again. The move of the table, which changed any rowids, will have rendered the indexes unusable, as shown in Figure 14-3.

5. Rebuild one index, using the NOLOGGING and ONLINE options.

```
SQL> alter index n1_idx rebuild online nologging;
```

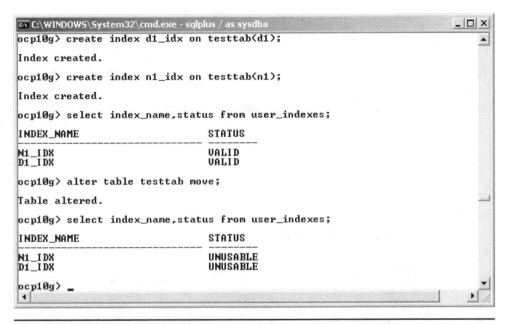

```
C:\WINDOWS\System32\cmd.exe - sqlplus / as sysdba                    _ □ X

ocp10g> create index d1_idx on testtab(d1);

Index created.

ocp10g> create index n1_idx on testtab(n1);

Index created.

ocp10g> select index_name,status from user_indexes;

INDEX_NAME                      STATUS
------------------------------  -------
N1_IDX                          VALID
D1_IDX                          VALID

ocp10g> alter table testtab move;

Table altered.

ocp10g> select index_name,status from user_indexes;

INDEX_NAME                      STATUS
------------------------------  -------
N1_IDX                          UNUSABLE
D1_IDX                          UNUSABLE

ocp10g> _
```

Figure 14-3   Indexes becoming unusable

6. Connect to your database as user SYSTEM using Database Control.

7. From the database home page, take the Administration tab and then the
   Indexes link in the Schema section.

8. In the Search section of the Indexes window, enter **TESTUSER** as the Schema,
   and click Go. This will show the two indexes on the TESTTAB table, one of
   which, D1_IDX, is still unusable.

9. Select the radio button for the unusable index, select Reorganize in the
   Actions drop-down box, and click Go to launch the Reorganize Objects
   Wizard.

10. Click Next, leave all the options on default, and click Next again to generate
    the reorganization script and reach the Impact Report window, shown in
    Figure 14-4. This should confirm that there is sufficient free space for the
    operation to proceed. Click Next to proceed.

11. On the Reorganize Objects: Schedule window, leave everything on default to
    run the job immediately, and click Next to reach the Review window.

12. In the Review window, click Submit Job to rebuild the index.

13. In your SQL*Plus session, confirm that the index is now valid by running the
    query from Step 2.

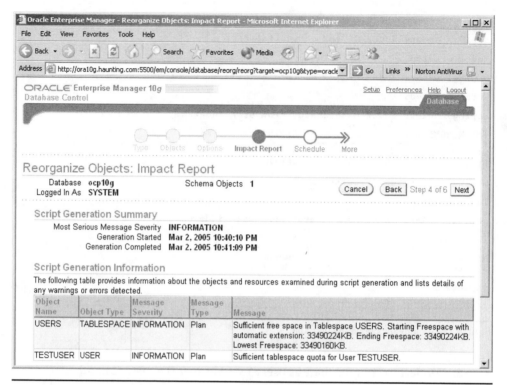

Figure 14-4 The impact analysis of an index rebuild operation

Optimizer Statistics

Any one SQL statement may be executable in a number of different ways. For example, it may be possible to join tables in different orders; there may be a choice of whether to use indexes or table scans; or some execution methods may be more intensive in their use of disk I/O as against CPU resources.

The choice of execution plan is critical for performance. In an Oracle database, the standard behavior is for execution plans to be developed dynamically by the optimizer.

The optimizer relies heavily on statistics to evaluate the effectiveness of many possible execution plans and to choose which plan to use. For good performance, it is vital that these statistics be accurate. There are many types of statistics, but chief among these are the object statistics that give details of the tables that the SQL statements address.

 TIP Statistics are not relevant to PL/SQL, only to SQL, so analysis will not improve PL/SQL performance. But most PL/SQL will include calls to SQL statements: statistics are as important for these statements as for any others.

Object Statistics

Analyzing a table gathers statistics on the table that will be of use to the optimizer. The statistics, visible in the DBA_TABLES view, include

- The number of rows in the table
- The number of blocks (used and never used) allocated to the table
- The amount of free space in the blocks that are being used
- The average length of each row
- The number of "chained" rows—rows cut across two or more blocks, either because they are very long or because of poor storage settings

Apart from statistics regarding the table as a whole, each column of the table is also analyzed. Column statistics are visible in the DBA_TAB_COLUMNS view and include

- The number of distinct values
- The highest and lowest values
- The number of nulls
- The average column length

When a table is analyzed, its indexes are also examined. The statistics on indexes are shown on the DBA_INDEXES view and include

- The depth of the index tree
- The number of distinct key values
- The clustering factor—how closely the natural order of the rows follows the order of the index keys

These statistics, which are stored within the data dictionary, give the optimizer the information it needs to make vital decisions about how best to execute SQL statements. If statistics are missing or incorrect, performance may degrade dramatically.

It is also possible to gather statistics on indexes. These are displayed in the INDEX_STATS view; they include

- The number of index entries referring to extant rows
- The number of index entries referring to deleted rows

This information is of value because of the manner in which indexes are maintained: when rows are deleted, the index keys remain; after a prolonged period, indexes can become inefficient due to the amount of space occupied by these references to deleted rows.

EXAM TIP In addition to the table statistics shown in DBA_TABLES, the index and column statistics in DBA_INDEXES and DBA_TAB_COLUMNS are also gathered whenever you analyze a table.

Gathering Statistics

Object statistics are not real-time: they are static, which means that they become out of date as DML operations are applied to the tables. It is therefore necessary to gather statistics regularly, to ensure that the optimizer always has access to statistics that reflect reasonably accurately the current state of the database. Statistics can be gathered manually, or the process can be automated. Manual statistics gathering can be done either with the ANALYZE command or by executing procedures in the DBMS_STATS package, as in Figure 14-5, or else through Database Control.

In Figure 14-5, first the table REGIONS is analyzed, using the ANALYZE command. The keywords COMPUTE STATISTICS instruct Oracle to analyze the whole table, not just a proportion of it. The following query shows that there are four rows in the table. Then there is a row inserted, but the statistics haven't been updated in real time: the number of rows is incorrect, until the table is analyzed again, this time with the DBMS_STATS.GATHER_TABLE_STATS procedure. There are numerous arguments that can be supplied to the GATHER_TABLE_STATS procedure to control what it does; this is the simplest form of its use.

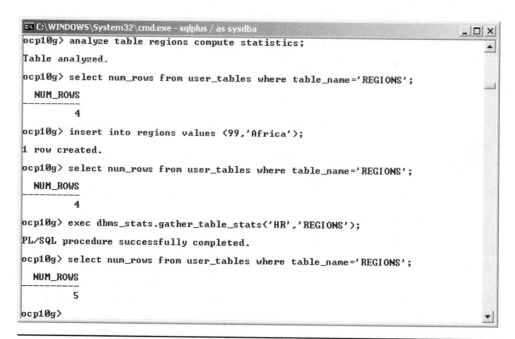

Figure 14-5   Gathering statistics from the SQL*Plus prompt

Gathering statistics will improve performance, but the actual gathering may impose a strain on the database that will have a noticeable effect on performance while the analysis is in progress. This paradoxical situation raises two questions. First, how frequently should statistics be gathered? The more frequently this is done, the better performance may be—but if it is done more frequently than necessary, performance will suffer needlessly. Second, what proportion of an object needs to be analyzed to gain an accurate picture of it? Analyzing a huge table may be a long and resource-intensive process; it may well be that analyzing a representative sample of the object would be enough for the optimizer and would not impose such a strain on the database.

 TIP The DBMS_STATS procedures can take many arguments to influence the depth of the analysis, far more than the older ANALYZE command.

You can also manually gather statistics through Database Control. To analyze a table, select Tables from the Schema section in the Administration window, choose the table, and take the Gather Statistics option in the Actions drop-down box. You will receive a warning stating that "Oracle recommends you to use automated tasks to generate statistics regularly within maintenance windows." This is a strong hint that Oracle Corporation believes you should automate the gathering of statistics, rather than gathering them on an ad hoc basis. If the database was created with the Database Configuration Assistant, or DBCA, automatic statistics gathering will have been configured, as a job managed by the Scheduler. The Scheduler will be described in detail in Chapter 36.

Alternatively, you can launch the Gather Statistics Wizard by taking the Maintenance tab from the database home page, and the Gather Statistics link in the Utilities section. You will, however, receive the same warning. The wizard prompts you through the process of setting the various options for what and how to analyze, and when to run the task. It finally shows you the procedure call that will be used.

The example in Figure 14-6 shows the use of the GATHER_SCHEMA_STATS procedure, which will analyze all the objects belonging to one user. Taking the arguments in turn,

- OWNNAME specifies the schema to be analyzed.
- ESTIMATE_PERCENT controls how much of the tables to analyze. The setting given instructs Oracle to make an intelligent guess at the amount needed for a meaningful sample.
- GRANULARITY refers to how best to analyze objects consisting of a number of subobjects, such as a table that is divided into partitions. The setting given lets Oracle decide.
- BLOCK_SAMPLE determines whether the table should be sampled by row or by block. The default, by row, is more accurate but possibly more time consuming.

- CASCADE controls whether to analyze any dependent objects, such as the indexes of tables.

- DEGREE controls the number of parallel execution servers to use for the task. The setting given lets the optimizer decide on the best number.

- METHOD_OPT controls for which columns to build up histograms, and how many buckets they should have. The setting given lets Oracle decide.

- OPTIONS determines which objects to analyze. The setting given instructs Oracle to analyze all objects that have no statistics, and also all objects where Oracle considers the statistics to be out-of-date.

This example illustrates that you can delegate all decisions on what needs to be analyzed, in what way, and to what depth to Oracle itself. If a command such as the one just described is run sufficiently frequently, it should ensure that the optimizer always has the statistics it needs, without overburdening the database by gathering statistics unnecessarily.

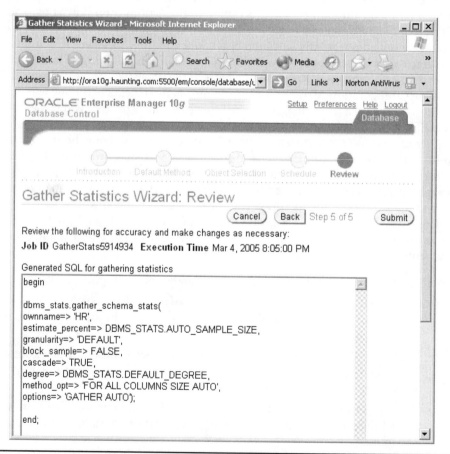

Figure 14-6   A DBMS_STATS procedure call generated by the Gather Statistics Wizard

The remaining point to consider is how frequently to run the command. The automatic statistics gathering configured by the DBCA will do this every weekday night, and again at the weekend. To see the job details, you must connect to Database Control as user SYS as SYSDBA. From the database home page, take the Administration tab, and then the Jobs link in the Scheduler section to see the page shown in Figure 14-7.

The GATHER_STATS_JOB shown in the figure will run the procedure DBMS_STATS.GATHER_STATS_JOB_PROC. This is a procedure specially designed for running automatically through the Scheduler. It will analyze the whole database, using automation options similar to those described for earlier Figure 14-6, and in addition it will analyze the objects that Oracle considers to be most in need of analysis first. The schedule it will run on, the MAINTENANCE_WINDOW_GROUP, instructs the Scheduler to run the job every night and weekend, during the preconfigured WEEKEND_WINDOW and WEEKNIGHT_WINDOW windows. The job will run with a priority, controlling its use of system resources, determined by the AUTO_TASKS_JOB_CLASS, which should ensure that it does not impact adversely on other users. Full details of how the Scheduler can be configured (including the use of Windows and Job Classes) will be given in Chapter 36.

 EXAM TIP Object statistics are not real-time: they are static until refreshed by a new analysis. If this is not done with sufficient frequency, they will grow seriously out-of-date and the optimizer may consequently develop inappropriate execution plans.

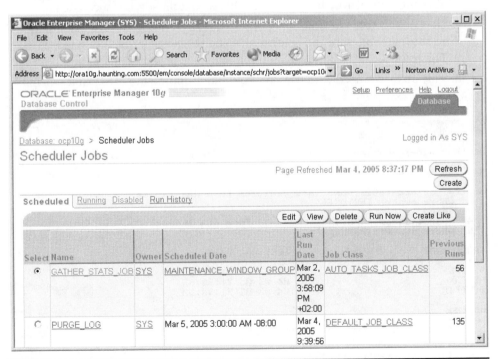

Figure 14-7 The jobs configured to run by SYS

Exercise 14-3: Automating Statistics Collection

Create a scheduled job to gather statistics on the TESTTAB table. The job will carry out a complete analysis of the table and its indexes, and also develop histograms on the columns used as index keys.

1. Connect to your database as user TESTUSER using Database Control.

2. Take the Administration tab, then the Jobs link in the Scheduler section to reach the Scheduler Jobs window.

3. Click Create to reach the Create Job window. In the General section, enter the Name as **Analyze testtab**, and leave everything else on default.

4. In the Command section, replace the sample code with this:
   ```
   begin
   dbms_stats.gather_table_stats(
   ownname=>'TESTUSER',
   tabname=>'TESTTAB',
   estimate_percent=>100,
   cascade=>true,
   method_opt=>'for all indexed columns size auto');
   end;
   ```

5. Take the Schedule link to reach the Schedule window. Leave everything on default, to run the job once only right away, and return to the Scheduler Jobs window.

6. Take the Run History link, and you will see that the job has succeeded.

7. In your SQL*Plus session, set your NLS_DATE_FORMAT session parameter to show the full time and confirm that statistics were indeed collected, as in Figure 14-8.

8. Tidy up by connecting as user SYSTEM and dropping the TESTUSER schema.
   ```
   SQL> drop user 'TESTUSER' cascade;
   ```

```
ocp10g>
ocp10g> alter session set nls_date_format='dd-mm-yy hh24:mi:ss';

Session altered.

ocp10g> select table_name,last_analyzed from dba_tables
  2  where owner='TESTUSER'
  3  union
  4  select index_name,last_analyzed from dba_indexes
  5  where owner='TESTUSER';

TABLE_NAME                        LAST_ANALYZED
--------------------------------  --------------------
D1_IDX                            04-03-05 21:38:53
N1_IDX                            04-03-05 21:38:53
TESTTAB                           04-03-05 21:38:52

ocp10g> _
```

Figure 14-8   Verifying statistics collection

Performance Metrics

Oracle collects hundreds of performance metrics. These are accumulated as statistics in memory and periodically flushed to the data dictionary, from which they can be analyzed by various Advisors. The mechanism for this and a description of the capabilities of the advisors appear in Chapter 15. But it is also possible to view the performance metrics interactively: querying various dynamic performance views will show you the real-time values of statistics, and by using Database Control, you can see them converted into more meaningful graphics.

Remember that in the Oracle environment a distinction is made between "statistics" and "metrics." A statistic is a raw figure, which may be useless in itself. A metric is a statistic converted into something meaningful. For example, the number of disk reads carried out by the instance is a statistic that does not convey any performance monitoring information, but the number of disk reads per transaction or per second is a useful metric.

Viewing Statistics with the Dynamic Performance Views

There are more than three hundred dynamic performance views. You will often hear them referred to as the "Vee dollar" views, because their names are prefixed with "V$". In fact, the "Vee dollar" views are not views at all; they are synonyms for views that are prefixed with "V_$", as shown in Figure 14-9.

The dynamic performance views give access to a phenomenal amount of information about the instance, and (to a certain extent) about the database. The majority of the views are populated with information from the instance, the remainder are populated from the controlfile. All of them give real-time information. Dynamic performance views that are populated from the instance, such as V$INSTANCE or V$SYSSTAT, are

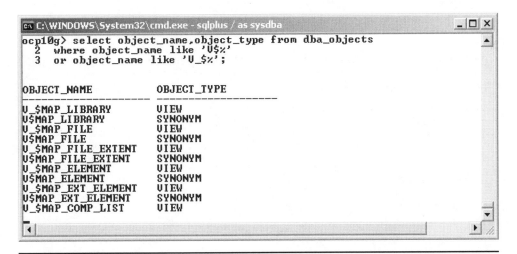

Figure 14-9 The V$ views

available at all times, even when the instance is in NOMOUNT mode. Dynamic performance views that are populated from the controlfile, such as V$DATABASE or V$DATAFILE, cannot be queried unless the database has been mounted, which is when the controlfile is read. By contrast, the data dictionary views (prefixed DBA, ALL, or USER) can only be queried after the database—including the data dictionary—has been opened.

 EXAM TIP Dynamic performance views are populated from the instance or the controlfile; DBA_, ALL_, and USER_ views are populated from the data dictionary.

The dynamic performance views are created at startup, updated during the lifetime of the instance, and dropped at shutdown. This means that they will contain values that have been accumulated since startup time: if your database has been open for six months nonstop, they will have data built up over that period. After a shutdown/startup, they will start from the beginning again. While the totals may be interesting, they will not tell you anything about what happened during certain defined periods, when there may have been performance issues. For this reason, it is generally true that the dynamic performance views give you statistics, not metrics. The conversion of these statistics into metrics is a skilled and sometimes time-consuming task, made much easier by the self-tuning and monitoring capabilities of release 10g of the database.

As an example of a dynamic performance view, you cannot do better than V$SYSSTAT, described here:

```
ocp10g> desc v$sysstat;
 Name                                      Null?    Type
 ----------------------------------------- -------- -------------
 STATISTIC#                                         NUMBER
 NAME                                               VARCHAR2(64)
 CLASS                                              NUMBER
 VALUE                                              NUMBER
 STAT_ID                                            NUMBER
```

This shows over three hundred statistics that are fundamental to monitoring activity:

```
ocp10g> select name, value from v$sysstat;
NAME                                VALUE
----------------------------------- ----------
logons cumulative                         356
logons current                             34
opened cursors cumulative              154035
opened cursors current                   5490
user commits                             2502
user rollbacks                            205
user calls                              37574
recursive calls                       6446648
recursive cpu usage                     39263
session logical reads                 4613746
session stored procedure space              0
<output truncated...>
```

Another critical view is V$SYSTEM_WAIT_CLASS, which summarizes the various categories of problems that can cause sessions, or the whole database, to run slowly:

```
ocp10g> select wait_class,time_waited from v$system_wait_class
  2  order by time_waited;
WAIT_CLASS           TIME_WAITED
-------------------- -----------
Network                       32
Application                   44
Configuration               1545
Concurrency                 4825
Commit                      5212
Other                      10483
System I/O                 41787
User I/O                  102743
Idle                    13087012
```

This query shows that the worst problems since the instance started have been "Idle" events. These are not problems: they are events such as server processes waiting to receive SQL statements from user processes. The worst real problem is disk I/O caused by user sessions, followed by disk I/O by the instance itself.

Viewing Metrics with Database Control

The Database Control interface converts statistics to metrics. To reach the metrics display, take the All Metrics link in the Related Links section of the database home page. From there, take the link for the area of interest and drill down to the individual metric. For example, in the preceding query you can see that there have been 2502 commits by user sessions. But this figure is since the instance was started; it says nothing about the rate of activity. Figure 14-10 shows the metric, User Commits (per second): this gives more useful information, in this case, that activity has fallen off dramatically in the last ten minutes.

Reacting to Performance Issues

In an ideal world, you would not react to performance issues; you would have anticipated them before they occurred. In practice, though, all database administrators rely to a certain extent on real-time figures to identify problem areas. Database Control provides an extremely simple interface to diagnose causes of performance problems. From the database home page, take the Performance tab, as in Figure 14-11. This will show a set of five graphs, correlating activity against time:

- The run queue length, which indicates whether the server machine's CPU resources are being strained
- The paging rate, which will increase if the server is short of memory
- The count of database sessions waiting, and why

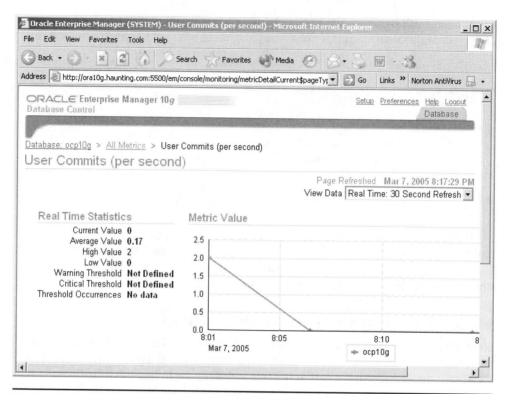

Figure 14-10   A real-time metric, viewed with Database Control

- The number of logins and transactions per second
- The number of physical reads and amount redo generated by second

Of these, the first and last pairs are informative, but it is the middle graph, of sessions waiting, that is diagnostic. The waiting sessions are grouped into color-coded classes showing why the sessions are waiting. In the figure, the worst problems can immediately be seen as user I/O and system I/O. Taking the link for any one class will generate a graph breaking down the figure into individual wait events. For instance, the user I/O wait class is divided into I/O related to table scans and I/O related to index lookups.

Having identified the problem areas, the next step is to resolve them. For this, the advisors described in the next chapter will be of great assistance.

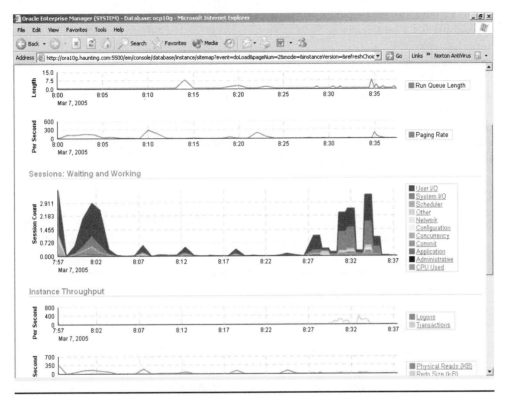

Figure 14-11 Performance metrics displayed graphically

Chapter Review

Objects can become not valid. PL/SQL procedural objects will become INVALID if the objects on which they depend are changed. Indexes will become UNUSABLE if the tables they are based on undergo certain operations. In either case, you can ignore the problem and the application may continue to function. But it may run with reduced performance as objects are compiled dynamically, and as the optimizer resorts to full table scans rather than index lookups. It is also possible that the application will fail if the procedural objects do not recompile successfully, or if the indexes are needed to enforce constraints. These damaged objects should be identified and fixed before their state impacts on end users.

When the optimizer develops execution plans, it relies heavily on statistics. Object statistics give the optimizer the information it needs to determine the most efficient way to execute a statement. You should gather statistics regularly, either by invoking the commands interactively or by using a scheduled job. Failure to do this will result in performance degradation, as the optimizer develops execution plans that are not appropriate to the current state of the data.

Oracle gathers hundreds of statistics. Interpreting these requires converting them into metrics. A metric is a meaningful figure that relates statistics to each other, or to time; metrics are what you need for tuning. The hundreds of dynamic performance views accumulate statistics from the time the instance starts; they are cleared on shutdown. Database Control can show these statistics converted into metrics, which are the starting point for problem resolution and tuning.

Questions

1. If you create a table and a procedure that refers to it, and then change the definition of the table, what will happen when you try to run the procedure? (Choose the best answer.)

    A. The procedure will recompile automatically and run successfully.

    B. The procedure will fail until you recompile it.

    C. The procedure will run with reduced performance until you analyze the table.

    D. The procedure may or may not compile, depending on the nature of the change.

2. If a SELECT statement attempts to use an UNUSABLE index, what will happen? (Choose the best answer.)

    A. The statement will fail.

    B. The statement will succeed, but at reduced performance.

    C. The index will be rebuilt automatically if possible.

    D. It depends on the SKIP_UNUSABLE_INDEXES parameter.

3. You determine that an index is unusable, and decide to rebuild it. Which of the following statements, if any, are correct? (Choose all that apply.)

    A. The NOLOGGING and ONLINE keywords cannot be used together when rebuilding the index.

    B. A rebuild may require double the disk space while it is in progress.

    C. If you do not use the ONLINE keyword during a rebuild, the table will be unavailable for SELECT and DML statements.

    D. The NOLOGGING keyword applied to a rebuild means that DML against the index will not generate redo.

4. You can analyze an index with the ANALYZE INDEX command, or with the DBMS_STATS.GATHER_INDEX_STATS procedure. Which view will be populated after this? (Choose the best answer.)

   A. INDEX_STATS

   B. DBA_INDEXES

   C. DBA_IND_COLUMNS

   D. DBA_INDEX_STATS

5. Object statistics are gathered and become out of date. What will cause them to be gathered again? (Choose two correct answers.)

   A. The optimizer can be configured to gather statistics automatically when it considers them out of date.

   B. You can configure a Scheduler job to gather statistics automatically.

   C. You can always force the gathering of statistics by using the ANALYZE command.

   D. Applying the GATHER AUTO option to the DBMS_STATS.GATHER_DATABASE_STATS procedure will force collection of statistics for all objects.

6. From where are dynamic performance views populated? (Choose all correct answers.)

   A. The instance

   B. The controlfile

   C. The data dictionary

   D. The Automatic Workload Repository

7. When you shut down an instance, what happens to the information in the dynamic performance views? (Choose the best answer.)

   A. It is lost.

   B. It is saved to the Automatic Workload Repository by the MMON process.

   C. It is saved to the controlfile.

   D. It depends on the method of shutdown: a crash or SHUTDOWN ABORT will lose it; otherwise, it will be saved.

8. If a primary key index becomes unusable, what will the effect be upon an application that uses it? (Choose the best answer.)

   A. SELECT will succeed, but perhaps at reduced performance.

   B. DML commands will succeed, but perhaps at reduced performance.

   C. The primary key constraint can no longer be enforced.

   D. All of the above.

Answers

1. **D.** Oracle will attempt to recompile automatically, but this may or may not succeed.

2. **D.** The instance parameter SKIP_UNUSABLE_INDEXES controls this behavior. Depending on this, the statements will either fail or run by resorting to full table scans.

3. **B.** A rebuild needs space for both the old and the new index while it is in progress.

4. **B.** This view could also have been populated by analyzing the table on which the index is based.

5. **B and C.** The Scheduler can be configured to run a statistics gathering job automatically, or the statistics can be gathered interactively at any time.

6. **A and B.** Dynamic performance views are populated from either the instance or the controlfile.

7. **A.** Information in the dynamic performance views exists only for the lifetime of the instance: it is lost on shutdown, no matter how it occurs.

8. **A.** If the SKIP_UNUSABLE_INDEXES instance parameter is on default, then SELECT statements will still succeed, by resorting to full table scans. Most DML statements will fail in this situation. The only exception is UPDATE statements that do not affect the key columns.

CHAPTER 15

Monitoring Oracle

In this chapter you will learn how to

- Set warning and critical alert thresholds
- Collect and use baseline metrics
- Use tuning and diagnostic advisors
- Use the Automatic Database Diagnostic Monitor (ADDM)
- Manage the Automatic Workload Repository
- Describe server-generated alerts

The manageability infrastructure provided with Oracle Database 10g can be used to automate a significant amount of the database administrator's day-to-day work. With earlier releases, monitoring the database in order to pick up developing problems before they become critical took much time. Identifying and diagnosing performance issues was not only time-consuming but also required much skill. Use of the alert system and the diagnostic advisors, installed as standard in every 10g database, frees the DBA from the necessity of devoting a large mount of effort to this work.

Throughout all the discussions of tuning, remember that tuning relies on the use of metrics. A metric is a statistic converted into something meaningful. An example of a statistic is the number of disk reads. This by itself is useless; what you need to know is the number of disk reads per second, or perhaps per statement. In earlier releases of the database, it was the DBA who has to convert statistics into metrics; now much of this work is done for you, by the advisors.

The graphical interface to the advisors, accessed through Database Control, is covered in this chapter. There are also APIs and views that an experienced DBA may wish to use instead; these are described in later chapters. At the heart of all the tools, both graphical and otherwise, is the Automatic Workload Repository, or AWR.

The Automatic Workload Repository

Oracle collects a vast amount of statistical information regarding performance and activity. This information is accumulated in memory and periodically written to disk: to the tables that make up the AWR. Eventually, it is aged out and overwritten.

Gathering Statistics

The level of statistics gathered is controlled by the instance parameter STATISTICS_ LEVEL. This can be set to BASIC, or to TYPICAL (which is the default), or to ALL. The TYPICAL level will force the collection of all the statistics that are needed for normal tuning, without collecting any whose collection would impact adversely on performance. The BASIC level will disable virtually all statistics, with no appreciable performance benefit. The ALL level will collect extremely detailed statistics on SQL statement execution: these may occasionally be necessary if you are doing advanced SQL statement tuning, but they may cause a slight performance drop while being collected.

 TIP During normal running, leave the STATISTICS_LEVEL on TYPICAL, the default.

Statistics are accumulated in memory, in data structures within the SGA. There is no performance impact to this, because the statistics merely reflect what the instance is doing anyway. Periodically (by default, once an hour) they are flushed to disk, to the AWR. This is known as a "snapshot." The flushing to disk is done by a background process: the manageability monitor, or MMON. This use of a background process is the key to the efficiency of the statistics collection process. In earlier releases of the database, accessing performance tuning statistics was only possible by running queries against various views—the V$ views. Populating these views was an expensive process. The DBA had to launch a session against the database and then issue a query. The query forced Oracle to extract data from the SGA and present it to the session in a view. This approach is still possible—all the old views, and many more, are still available—but the AWR approach is far more efficient.

The MMON has direct access to the memory structures that make up the SGA, and therefore the statistics within them. It can extract data from the SGA without the need to go via a session. The only overhead is the actual writing of the data to the AWR. By default this occurs only once an hour and should not therefore have a noticeable effect on run-time performance.

EXAM TIP Statistics are saved as a snapshot to the AWR by the MMON process, by default every sixty minutes.

The Size and Location of the AWR

The AWR is a set of tables located in the SYSAUX tablespace; these tables cannot be relocated. They exist in the SYSMAN schema. You can log on to the database as user SYSMAN, but this should never be necessary because Oracle Corporation does not support access to the AWR tables with SQL*Plus, or indeed with any tools other than the various APIs provided in the form of DBMS packages or through various views. The most straightforward way to access AWR information is through Database Control.

Snapshots are kept in the AWR, by default, for seven days. This period is configurable. As a rough guide for sizing, if the snapshot collection is left on every hour and the retention time is left on seven days, then the AWR may well require between 200MB and 300MB of space in the SYSAUX tablespace. But this figure is highly variable and will to a large extent depend on the number of sessions.

To administer the AWR with Database Control, take the Administration tab from the database home page, and then the Automatic Workload Repository link in the Workload section. The Automatic Workload Repository window, as in Figure 15-1, shows the current settings and lets you adjust them.

Adjusting the AWR settings to save snapshots more frequently will make problem diagnosis more precise. If the snapshots are several hours apart, you may miss peaks of activity (and consequent dips in performance). But gathering snapshots too frequently will increase the size of the AWR and could possibly impact on performance due to the increased workload of collecting and saving the information.

EXAM TIP The AWR is located in the SYSAUX tablespace and cannot be relocated to anywhere else.

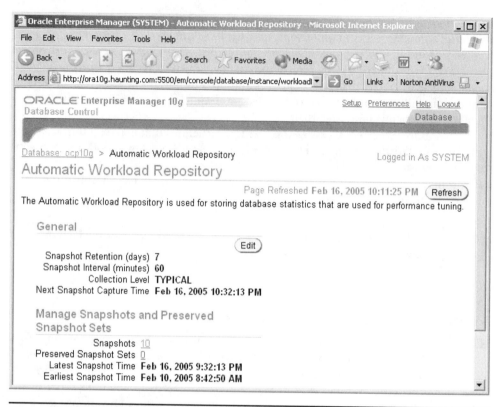

Figure 15-1 The AWR administration window

Preserving Snapshots

Snapshots are purged after a certain period, by default, after seven days. For long-term tuning, it is necessary to keep snapshots over a longer period. You may, for example, want to keep the snapshots collected during each month-end processing run, so that you can compare the performance of the month-end batch jobs over a year. To do this, take the link next to "Preserved snapshot sets" in Figure 15-1. You will be presented with a list of all the snapshots currently in the AWR; choose the ones you wish to keep indefinitely.

Creating preserved snapshots means that you can always compare current performance with performance at a point in the past. This is vital for proper trend analysis. The reports themselves are kept by default for thirty days, but if you preserve the snapshots, you can always regenerate the reports.

 EXAM TIP By default, AWR snapshots are kept for a week and ADDM reports for thirty days.

The Diagnostic and Tuning Advisors

The database comes preconfigured with a set of advisors. First among these is the Automatic Database Diagnostic Monitor, or ADDM. Studying ADDM reports, which are generated automatically whenever an AWR snapshot is taken, will usually be a regular part of the DBA's routine. The ADDM reports are of great value in themselves and will highlight problems within the database and suggest solutions, but in many cases, its recommendations will include suggesting that you run one or more other advisors. These advisors must be invoked manually, but they can give much more precise diagnostic information and advice than the ADDM.

To use the advisors, in Database Control take the Advisor Central link in the Related Links section. The Advisor Central window gives you the options of viewing the results of previous advisor tasks, or of using any of the seven advisors:

- The Automatic Database Diagnostic Monitor (the ADDM)
- The SQL Tuning Advisor
- The SQL Access Advisor
- The Memory Advisor
- The Mean Time to Recover (MTTR) Advisor
- The Segment Advisor
- The Undo Advisor

At this stage, it is only necessary to study the ADDM. The other advisors will be dealt with in detail in later chapters.

The Automatic Database Diagnostic Monitor

The ADDM is run automatically by the MMON whenever a snapshot is taken. As with all the advisors, it takes statistics and other information from the AWR. The automatically generated ADDM reports always cover the period between the current snapshot and the previous one, so by default, you will have access to reports covering every hour. You can invoke the ADDM manually to generate a report covering the period between any two snapshots, if you want to span a greater period. The ADDM is triggered by automatic snapshots and also if you gather a snapshot manually. The reports are purged by default after thirty days.

 EXAM TIP The ADDM is launched by MMON whenever a snapshot is gathered.

To view the ADDM reports, take the Advisor Central link from the database home page. The Advisor Central window will show you the most recent runs of each advisor, as in Figure 15-2.

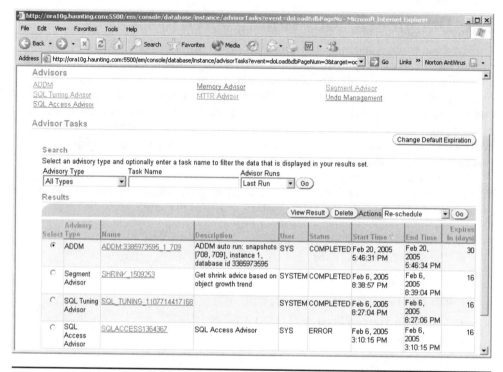

Figure 15-2 The Advisor Central

Select the report's radio button and click View Report to see the summary report, as in Figure 15-3. Drill down to the individual recommendations for precise advice.

The ADDM will often recommend running another advisor. In the preceding example, selecting the fourth recommendation, for segment tuning, gives the result shown in Figure 15-4.

The SQL Tuning and Access Advisors

A basic principle of performance tuning is to start at the beginning. This means that performance should be considered from the very beginning of the system development cycle, with the business analysis that determines the business processes to be automated. Performance also needs to be considered subsequently, during both the systems analysis that generates an ideal model and the system design that represents a compromise, adapting the ideal model to circumstances. Then the program designers should keep performance in mind when writing in code. In a perfect world, the DBA would be involved in all these stages, but frequently you will be asked to manage a system that is already completed. It will therefore be too late to influence the analysis and design stages, but you can still detect problems and possibly fix them by identifying high-

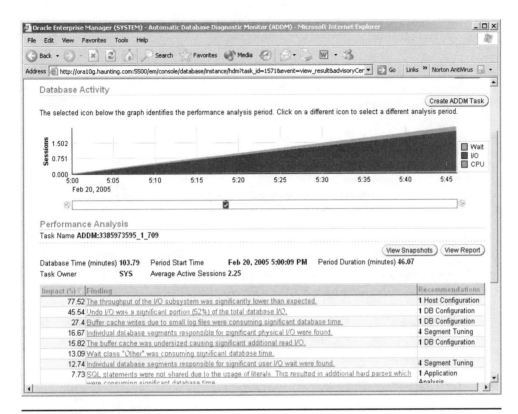

Figure 15-3 The ADDM report summary

load SQL and suggesting improvements. The SQL Tuning Advisor is your tool for
doing this.

The SQL Tuning Advisor takes as its input a set of one or more SQL statements
and investigates their structure and manner of execution. Known as a SQL Tuning Set,
this can be created from the SQL recently executed, SQL stored in the AWR snapshots,
or a hypothetical workload. The advice may include

- Gathering optimizer statistics on the objects addressed
- Generating SQL profiles, with statistics on statement execution
- Changing the code to use more efficient SQL constructs
- Rewriting the code to remove possible design errors

The SQL Access Advisor also takes SQL Tuning Sets as its input. It investigates
whether the SQL execution performance could be improved by adding indexes or
materialized views, and also whether some indexes and materialized views are in fact
a hindrance and should be dropped. In general, indexes and materialized views will
improve the performance of SELECT statements, but it is possible that maintaining

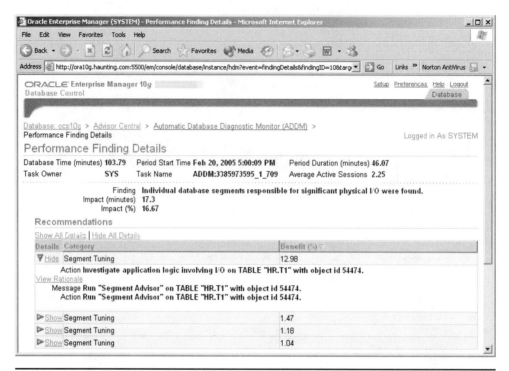

Figure 15-4 A recommendation to invoke another advisor

them will be detrimental for DML commands. Indexes enhance performance by giving faster access to individual rows, obviating the need for full table scans. Materialized views enhance performance by, in effect, pre-running all or part of a query. When working out how best to execute a statement, the optimizer will look at the structure of the objects and their statistics and make an intelligent decision about whether to use any available indexes and materialized views. The SQL Access Advisor goes further than this: it estimates whether performance could be improved by creating additional indexes and materialized views, and it also can recommend dropping ones that exist but are not being used.

The Memory Advisors

There are graphical advisors that will predict the effect of varying the amount of memory allocated to the database buffer cache and the shared pool, and also the total amount of memory available for the PGAs of all the database sessions. The buffer cache advisor, which graphs expected disk reads against the size of the cache, is shown in Figure 15-5.

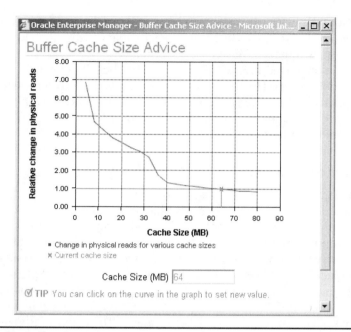

Figure 15-5   The buffer cache advisor

In this example, the buffer cache is currently 64MB. The curve shows that increasing it would produce only a marginal reduction in disk reads. It could even be reduced by a few megabytes without disk reads increasing too much, but to reduce it below 40MB would be disastrous.

A result like this is typical for the memory advisors: as more memory is allocated to an SGA structure or to the PGA, performance will improve, but with diminishing returns. If it is necessary to reduce memory usage, perhaps because the system is swapping, then memory can be saved—but if you go too far, performance will degrade.

The Mean Time to Recover Advisor

After an instance crash, such as a power cut or the server being rebooted without shutting down the database, the instance must be recovered. This recovery process, detailed in Chapter 18, is completely automatic. For now, let it suffice that the recovery process ensures that no matter what is happening in the database, it is impossible to corrupt it by crashing the instance. You can switch off the server while hundreds of users are logged on and executing statements, and the database will not be affected: the instance recovery process will repair any damage. But while the instance will always be recovered, it may take a considerable time. This is the Mean Time to Recover (MTTR).

The MTTR will often be built into service level agreements. It can be controlled by the instance parameter FAST_START_RECOVERY_TARGET, set in seconds. In general, the shorter the time this parameter is set to, the quicker it will be to open the database after a crash, but the worse online performance will be. The problem is that in order to minimize recovery time, Oracle must write more data to disk than it would do otherwise: this may impact adversely on performance.

The decision on the required MTTR is not one for the DBA to make; it is determined by business requirements. However, it is possible for the DBA to show what the effect will be of a particular MTTR target in terms of additional disk I/O. The MTTR Advisor graphs the expected change in disk I/O against various settings for the FAST_START_RECOVERY_TARGET instance parameter.

The Segment Advisor

Segments grow automatically. As rows are inserted into table segments and index keys inserted into index segments, the segments fill, and then Oracle will allocate more extents as necessary. Segments do not shrink automatically.

DML operations on the rows in table segments, such as DELETE and possibly UPDATE, cause blocks within the segment to empty, as rows are removed or reduced in size. This space that is freed up will be reused by subsequent INSERT commands, but it is still possible for a table to end up occupying far more space than is needed for its current contents. DML on rows will also affect the associated index segments, and the effects may be worse than on table segments. The algorithms that Oracle applies to reuse space in index segments can result in large amounts of wasted space that cannot be reused.

The Segment Advisor will inspect segments and determine whether the amount of space allocated to the segment that is not being used is sufficiently great that the SHRINK SPACE operation could be usefully applied to it. The algorithms used do not rely purely on the amount of "wasted" space: they also take account of the pattern of activity on the segment. If, for example, history shows that a table frequently has a large number of rows inserted and then deleted, the Advisor may not necessarily recommend that it should be shrunk: just because there is unused space in the segment now, the Advisor knows that it could be needed again. This is possible because the Advisor has access to the AWR, which will have such historical information.

The Undo Advisor

Undo data is generated by all DML commands. The length of time that the undo data is retained for is, at a minimum, the length of the transaction. It will, however, frequently be necessary to store undo data for some considerable time after the transaction has finished. This is to satisfy the need for consistent reads: the C of the ACID test. This requirement is determined by the length of the longest-running queries executed against the database. In order to prevent the "ORA-1555: snapshot too old" error, the undo tablespace must be large enough to retain enough undo data to prevent this. If you intend to make use of the Flashback Query capability of the database (which will be detailed in Chapter 29), it may be necessary to retain undo data for considerably longer.

PART I

The algorithm to size the undo tablespace is based on the rate of undo generation per second and the number of seconds of data it is necessary to store to meet the requirements of long-running queries, and possibly the use of Flashback Query. The Undo Advisor shows a graph of the necessary size of the undo tablespace for various undo retention times.

Exercise 15-1: Generating an ADDM Report

Gather an AWR snapshot, simulate a workload, gather another snapshot, and view the ADDM report.

1. Connect to your database as user SYSTEM with SQL*Plus.

2. Force the creation of an AWR snapshot.

```
SQL> exec dbms_workload_repository.create_snapshot;
```

3. Simulate a workload by creating a table and running this anonymous PL/SQL block to generate some activity:

```
SQL>  create table tmptab as select * from all_objects;
SQL> begin
  2  for i in 1..10 loop
  3 insert into tmptab select * from all_objects;
  4 delete from tmptab;
  5 end loop;
  6 commit;
  7 /
```

4. Repeat the command from Step 2 to generate another snapshot.

5. Connect to your database as user SYSTEM using Database Control.

6. Take the Advisor Central link in the Related Links section on the database home page. The first report listed will be the ADDM report generated as a result of the snapshot, as in Figure 15-6.

7. Select the radio button for the latest ADDM report, and click View Result. The report should resemble Figure 15-7.

8. Study the report. In the example, the worst problem (as shown in the graph) is disk I/O; the findings at the bottom of the screen show the causes of this I/O problem. Double-click the findings links for further details.

NOTE Your results may differ from those in the example, depending on your database configuration; if the report shows no problems, edit the code in Step 3 to force more activity, and repeat the exercise.

9. Tidy up by dropping the TMPTAB table.

```
SQL> drop table tmptab;
```

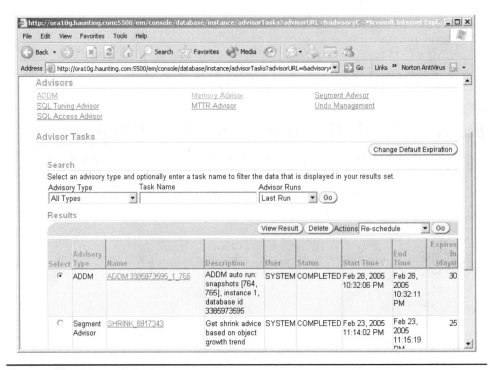

Figure 15-6 Advisor Central

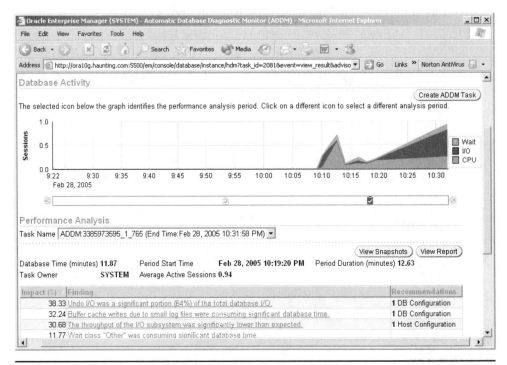

Figure 15-7 An ADDM report

Server-Generated Alerts

A large amount of a DBA's work has always involved monitoring the database to pick up potential problems before they become serious. This proactive monitoring is far better for your user community than reactive monitoring, where you wait for a problem to arise before addressing it. Previous releases of the database did provide tools to assist with monitoring, but they were client/server tools: they connected to the database through a server process, as does any other session. Release 10g comes with a server-based alert system designed to assist you with proactive monitoring by taking over the task of monitoring and informing you of problems. It is installed and enabled automatically; all you have to do is configure it.

The Alert System Architecture

A 10g database monitors itself. The manageability monitor, the MMON background process, observes the instance and the database. If certain metrics deviate excessively from expected levels, the MMON will raise an alert. The alerts raised by the MMON are placed on a queue, the ALERT_QUE in the SYS schema.

Queues are implemented by the Advanced Queueing option. Queues are a mechanism for sessions or processes to communicate with each other. One process can enqueue a message (write it to the queue), and another process can de-queue the message (read it from the queue). Depending on options used, the de-queueing can either remove the message from the queue or leave it there for another process to read as well.

To see alert messages, you must subscribe to the alert queue. You can use the advanced queueing API (the DBMS_AQ package) to write your own routines for viewing alerts, but the easiest way to view alerts is through Database Control, which subscribes to the queue automatically.

Alerts are of two forms: threshold, or stateful, and non-threshold, or stateless. Threshold alerts must be configured by setting values for some metric to be monitored, such as the percentage of space used in a tablespace. When this threshold is crossed, the alert will be raised and will persist until some action is taken (such as adding space to the tablespace) to cause the metric to drop below the triggering value. The non-threshold alerts are triggered by an event that happens but does not persist, such as an "ORA-1555: snapshot too old" error.

 EXAM TIP Alerts are sent by the MMON background process and displayed by Database Control.

Setting Thresholds

To configure the settings for the threshold alerts, navigate to the Manage Metrics window in Database Control, as in Figure 15-8.

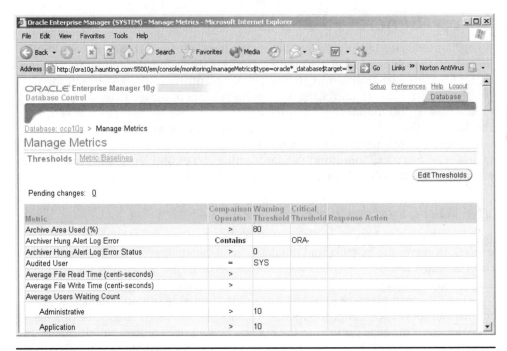

Figure 15-8 The alert thresholds

Some alerts are preconfigured with thresholds; others must be set before they will be enabled. For example, the "Tablespace percent full" alert is by default set to send a warning alert when a tablespace reaches 85 percent full and a critical alert when it reaches 97 percent full, but the "Average File Read Time" alert is not configured by default; as shown in Figure 15-8, it is null unless you set it. To change a threshold, click Edit Thresholds, and set whatever values are appropriate for a warning and a critical alert to be raised.

Using Baselines

Rather than comparing metrics to values you have chosen by hand, you can allow Oracle to raise alerts based on deviations from a time when performance was known to be acceptable. This saves the necessity of working out what the thresholds should be. To do this, create a "baseline." To use baselines,

1. From the database home page, take the Manage Metrics link in the Related Links section and then the Metric Baselines link. Click Create.

2. Specify a date and hour when performance and workload were normal, as shown in Figure 15-9, provide warning and critical percentage deviations from this norm, and click Go to display all the metrics that can be used for comparisons. Deselect the ones you are not concerned with.

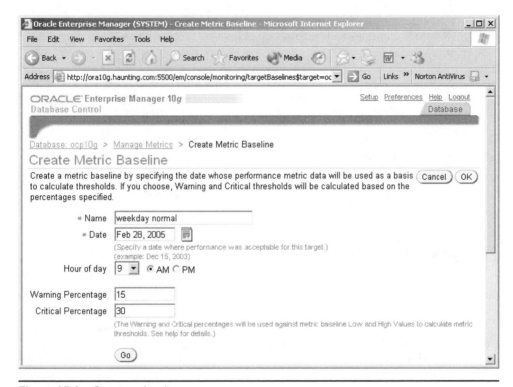

Figure 15-9   Creating a baseline

3. Click OK to save the baseline.

4. To copy the thresholds from the baseline to the Edit Thresholds window, select the baseline and click Copy Thresholds From Metric Baseline.

Exercise 15-2: Configuring Alerts

Configure the "User Commits (per second)" alert, and monitor it being raised.

1. Connect to your database with Database Control as user SYSTEM.

2. From the database home page, take the Manage Metrics link in the Related Links section.

3. Click Edit Thresholds to reach the Edit Thresholds window.

4. Scroll down to the "User Commits (per second)" alert, and set the warning and critical values to 1 and 4. These are artificially low thresholds that it will be simple to cross. Click OK to save this change.

5. Connect to your database as user SYSTEM with SQL*Plus, and issue the COMMIT command a few times quickly.

```
SQL> commit;
Commit complete.
SQL> /
Commit complete.
SQL> /
Commit complete.
SQL> /
Commit complete.
```

6. In your Database Control session, within a few seconds you will see that the alert has been raised.

7. Tidy up by returning to the Edit Thresholds window and clearing the threshold values.

Chapter Review

This chapter has introduced some of the self-management capabilities of the database: the Automatic Database Diagnostic Monitor (ADDM), the various advisors, and the server alert system. All of these will be revisited in later chapters.

Central to the self-management capability is the Automatic Workload Repository (AWR). This is a store of statistical information regarding performance and activity. It is populated automatically by "snapshots" of information, gathered from the instance at regular intervals by the MMON process. Whenever a snapshot is taken, MMON also runs the ADDM to generate a report.

The server alert system is also implemented by MMON: it will monitor the instance and the database and if certain metrics cross certain thresholds, it will raise an alert message via a queueing system. These alerts can be seen through Database Control.

Questions

1. Classify the following measures as being statistics or metrics. There are three of each.

A. Tablespace used, megabytes

B. Tablespace space used, percentage

C. Disk reads since instance startup

D. User rollbacks per second

E. Maximum concurrent sessions

F. Redo generated per transaction

2. Where is the Automatic Workload Repository stored? (Choose the best answer.)

A. In the SYSAUX tablespace

B. In the SYSTEM tablespace

C. In the System Global Area

D. You can choose the location at database creation time and relocate it subsequently.

3. When are AWR snapshots taken? (Choose the best answer.)

A. Every hour

B. Every ten minutes

C. On demand

D. By a regular schedule, and on demand

4. Which process generates ADDM reports? (Choose the best answer.)

A. Database Control

B. MMON, the manageability monitor

C. SMON, the system monitor

D. RMAN, the Recovery Manager

5. For how long are AWR snapshots and ADDM reports retained? (Choose the best answer.)

A. By default, both snapshots and reports are kept for thirty days, unless purged earlier or flagged for retention.

B. Snapshots are kept until purged, reports are not stored; they are generated on demand.

C. By default, snapshots are kept for seven days, and reports for 30 days.

D. Snapshots are stored in the SGA and are dropped on shutdown. Reports are stored until purged in the AWR.

6. Which process raises alerts? (Choose the best answer.)

A. MMON, the manageability monitor

B. Database Control

C. The server process that detects the problem

D. SMON, the system monitor

7. Database release 10g ships with a number of advisors. Match the advisors, a to d, listed below with a function, A to D.

Advisor	Function
a. Memory Advisor	A. Recommendations on creating segments
b. Segment Advisor	B. Advice on shrinking objects that are wasting space
c. SQL Access Advisor	C. Predictions of the space needed to retain expired undo data for a period of time
d. Undo Advisor	D. Advice on how best to size certain SGA components

8. What are the default warning and critical alert levels for the "Tablespace percent full" alert? (Choose the best answer.)

A. This alert is disabled until you set the thresholds

B. 85% and 97%

C. 85% and 100%

D. 97% and 10%

9. Some alerts are stateful, meaning they persist until cleared; others are cleared immediately. Which of the following, if any, are stateless? (Choose all that apply.)

A. Snapshot too old

B. Tablespace full

C. Database down

D. User commits per second

10. With regard to the collection of monitoring information, put these steps in the correct order:

A. Data accumulates in the SGA.

B. MMON generates an ADDM report.

C. MMON writes data to the AWR.

D. Reports are purged.

E. Snapshots are purged.

Answers

1. A statistic is a raw figure; a metric is a statistic related to another statistic. So the statistics are **A**, **C**, and **E**, none of which have significance by themselves. The metrics are **B**, which compare space used to total space; **D**, which relates the number of rollbacks to time; and **F**, which correlates the number of redo writes with the number of transactions.

2. **A.** The AWR is in the SYSAUX tablespace, not the SYSTEM tablespace. The SGA is only a temporary store of statistics that will be transferred to the AWR, and it cannot be relocated.

3. **D.** The default schedule for AWR snapshots is every hour, but this can be changed. You can also request a snapshot at any time.

4. **B.** ADDM reports are generated by MMON whenever a snapshot is taken. Database Control is used for viewing the reports. SMON does monitor the instance but it does not report on it. RMAN, the Recovery Manager, has nothing to do with ADDM.

5. **C.** AWR snapshots are retained for seven days, ADDM reports for 30 days. These defaults can be changed.

6. **A.** MMON raises alerts. Database Control and your server process report alerts; they don't raise them. And in spite of its name, SMON has nothing to do with the alert system.

7. **a-D.** The Memory Advisor predicts the effect of changing the instance parameters that control the size of SGA components.

   b-B. The Segment Advisor inspects segments and reports on whether they have a significant amount of wasted space.

   c-A. The Access Advisor can recommend creating (or dropping) indexes and materialized views.

   d-C. The Undo Advisor calculates the undo space needed to meet various undo retention targets.

8. **B.** 85% and 97% are the database defaults for warning and critical alerts on tablespace usage.

9. **A.** The only correct answer is snapshot too old. This occurs, and is gone.

10. **A, C, B, E, D.**

CHAPTER 16

Managing Undo

In this chapter you will learn how to
- Monitor and administer undo
- Configure undo retention
- Guarantee undo retention
- Use the Undo Advisor
- Describe the relationship between undo and transactions
- Size the undo tablespace

Chapter 9 describes what happens in memory and on disk when you execute INSERT, UPDATE, or DELETE statements: the manner in which changed data is written to blocks of table and index segments and the old version of the data is written out to blocks of an undo segment. It also covered the theory behind this, summarized as the ACID test that every relational database must pass. In this chapter you will see the practicalities of how undo data is managed. But first, a review of the purpose of undo.

Undo Data: Why and What Is It?

Undo data is the information needed to reverse the effects of DML statements. It is often referred to as "rollback data," but try to avoid that term. In earlier releases of Oracle, the terms "rollback data" and "undo data" were used interchangeably, but from 9i onward they are different. Whenever a transaction changes data, the pre-update version of the data is written out to a rollback segment or to an undo segment. The difference is crucial. Rollback segments can still exist, but with release 9i of the database Oracle introduced the undo segment as an alternative. Oracle strongly advises that all databases should use undo segments—rollback segments are retained for backward compatibility, but they are not referenced in the OCP exam and are therefore not covered in this book. But even though "rollback" as a noun should no longer be used in the Oracle environment, "roll back" as a verb is as relevant as ever.

To roll back a transaction means to use data from the undo segments to construct an image of the data as it was before the transaction occurred. This is usually done automatically to satisfy the requirements of the ACID test, but the flashback capability (introduced with 9i and greatly enhanced with 10g) leverages the power of the undo mechanism by giving you the option of querying the database as it was at some time in the past. (Flashback through use of undo segments is detailed in Chapter 29.) And of course, any user can use the ROLLBACK command interactively to back out any DML statements that s/he has issued and not committed.

The ACID test requires, first, that Oracle keep pre-update versions of data in order that incomplete transactions can be reversed, either automatically in the case of an error or on demand through the use of the ROLLBACK command. This type of rollback is permanent and published to all users. Second, for read consistency, the database must be able to present a query with a version of the database as it was at the time the query started. The server process running the query will go to the undo segments and construct what is called a "read consistent" image of the blocks being queried, if they were changed after the query started. This type of rollback is temporary and visible only to the session running the query. Third, undo segments are also used for transaction isolation. This is perhaps the most complex use of undo data. The principle of isolation requires that no transaction can be in any way dependent upon another, incomplete, transaction. In effect, even though a multiuser database will have many transactions in progress at once, the end result must be as though the transactions were executing one after another. The use of undo data combined with row and table locks (you will see how locking is implemented in Chapter 17) guarantees transaction isolation: the impossibility of incompatible transactions. Even though several transactions may be running concurrently, isolation requires that the end result must be as if the transactions were serialized.

From 9*i* onward, undo data can also be used for flashback queries. This is a completely optional but very powerful tool that allows users to query a past image of the database. You will see some uses of this in Chapter 29. For flashback queries, undo data is used to construct a version of one or more tables as they were at some previous time by applying undo data. As with rollback for the purposes of consistency, rollback for flashback purposes is only temporary, and visible only to the session concerned.

As a final word on "rollback" as opposed to "undo," observe the results of a query against DBA_SEGMENTS as shown in Figure 16-1. This shows that within the database there are one or more segments of type ROLLBACK, and one or more of type TYPE2 UNDO. So rollback segments do still exist in a 10*g* database, but for only one purpose. Undo segments can exist only in an undo tablespace; this is one of their features. But at database creation time, there may not be an undo tablespace. Therefore, at creation time, Oracle creates a single old-fashioned rollback segment in the SYSTEM tablespace, along with the data dictionary. This is used during database creation, but never in normal running. All user transactions will use undo segments, listed in DBA_SEGMENTS as segment_type TYPE2 UNDO.

 TIP If you ask Oracle Product Development "What is a TYPE1 UNDO segment?" the reply will be, "That's a ROLLBACK segment."

If your database has been converted to use undo segments and automatic undo management, any existing rollback segments will be in offline mode and cannot be set online, so you might as well get rid of them. Use of undo segments is incompatible

```
C:\WINDOWS\System32\cmd.exe - sqlplus / as sysdba

SQL>
SQL>
SQL>
SQL> select distinct segment_type from dba_segments;

SEGMENT_TYPE
------------------
CLUSTER
INDEX
INDEX PARTITION
LOB PARTITION
LOBINDEX
LOBSEGMENT
NESTED TABLE
ROLLBACK
TABLE
TABLE PARTITION
TYPE2 UNDO

11 rows selected.

SQL>
SQL>
SQL>
SQL>
```

Figure 16-1 Segment types within a 10*g* database

with use of rollback segments: it is one or the other, depending on the setting of the UNDO_MANAGEMENT parameter.

Undo Tablespaces

Starting with the Oracle9i release, the management of undo data, by means of the new segment type "undo," can be completely automatic. The only control you as DBA have is whether to use undo segments rather than rollback segments, and if so which tablespace to keep them in, and how big this tablespace should be. The size of the tablespace will determine how much undo data is actually kept—a topic discussed later in this chapter.

One feature of undo segments is that they can exist only in a tablespace created specially for that purpose, whereas rollback segments could be created in any tablespace. You will always create an undo tablespace, possibly at database creation time. You may well create more than one, but if you do, only one of them will be used at any given moment. The only exception to this rule is a RAC database, where each instance opening the clustered database will use its own undo tablespace. You can create an undo tablespace from the SQL*Plus command line, through Database Control.

 EXAM TIP There may be multiple undo tablespaces in a database, but only one is active at a given point in time.

An undo tablespace is in many ways a tablespace like any other, but there are some limitations. It must be created as permanent, locally managed, with automatic extent allocation (remember these attributes from Chapter 6?). After creation, management commands are generally limited to physical operations. You can add, move, or resize datafiles in an undo tablespace, but you cannot, for example, make an undo tablespace read-only. If it is the active undo tablespace, you cannot take it offline or drop it.

Exercise 16-1: Creating an Undo Tablespace with Database Control

Use Database Control to create an undo tablespace, and verify the configuration from SQL*Plus.

1. Connect to your instance as user SYSTEM with Database Control.

2. From the Maintenance tab in the Storage section, take the Tablespaces link.

3. Click Create.

4. Enter **UNDO2** as the tablespace name, and set the radio buttons to Extent Management "Locally Managed," Type "Undo," and Status "Read Write."

5. At the bottom of the screen, click Add to specify a datafile.

6. Enter **UNDO2-01.DBF** as the File Name, leave everything else on default, and click Continue.

7. On the Create Tablespace screen, click Show SQL, and study the statement used to create your undo tablespace. Click Return to return to the Create Tablespace screen, and click OK to create the tablespace.

8. Connect to your instance as user SYSTEM through SQL*Plus.

9. Run this query, which will return one row for each tablespace in your database:

```
select tablespace_name,contents,retention from dba_tablespaces;
```

and note that your new tablespace has contents UNDO, meaning that it can only be used for undo segments, and that retention is NOGUARANTEE, a topic covered shortly.

10. Run this query, which will return one row for each rollback or undo segment in your database:

```
select tablespace_name, segment_name, status from dba_rollback_segs;
```

and note that a number of undo segments have been created automatically in your new undo tablespace, but that they are all offline. Also note that the names of the automatic undo segments are in the form of "_SYSSMUn\$,$" where n is the undo segment number (usn).

Transactions and Undo Segments

When a transaction starts, Oracle will assign it to one (and only one) undo segment. Any one transaction can be protected by only one undo segment; it is not possible for the undo data generated by one transaction to cut across multiple undo segments. This is not a problem, because undo segments are not fixed in size. So if a transaction does manage to fill its undo segment, Oracle will automatically add another extent to the segment so that the transaction can continue. It is possible for multiple transactions to share one undo segment, but in normal running this should not occur. A tuning problem common with rollback segments was estimating how many rollback segments would be needed to avoid excessive interleaving of transactions within rollback segments without creating so many as to waste space. One feature of undo management is that Oracle will automatically generate new undo segments on demand, in an attempt to ensure that it is never necessary for transactions to share undo segments. If Oracle has found it necessary to extend its undo segments or to generate additional segments, when the workload drops Oracle will shrink and drop the segments, again automatically.

 EXAM TIP No transaction can ever cut across multiple undo segments.

As a transaction updates table or index data blocks, the information needed to roll back the changes is written out to blocks of the assigned undo segment. Oracle guarantees absolutely the A, for atomicity, of the ACID test, meaning that all the undo data must be retained until a transaction commits. By default, Oracle does not however guarantee the C, for consistency, of the ACID test. Oracle guarantees consistency to the extent that if a query succeeds, the results will be consistent with the state of the database at the time the query started—but it does not guarantee that the query will actually succeed. This means that undo data can be divided into two parts. "Active" undo is undo data that might be needed to roll back transactions in progress. This data can never be overwritten, until the transaction completes. "Expired" undo is undo data from committed transactions that Oracle is no longer obliged to store—though it might be needed for consistent reads, if there are any long-running queries in progress. This data can be overwritten if Oracle needs the space for another active transaction.

The fact that undo information expires on commit means that undo segments can be used in a circular fashion. Eventually, the whole of the undo tablespace will be filled with undo data, so when a new transaction starts, or a running transaction generates some more undo, the undo segment will "wrap" around, and the oldest undo data within it will be overwritten—always assuming that this oldest data is not part of a long-running uncommitted transaction, in which case it would be necessary to extend the undo segment instead.

With the old, manually managed rollback segments, a critical part of tuning was to control which transactions were protected by which rollback segments. A rollback segment might even be created and brought online specifically for one transaction. Automatically managed undo segments make all of that unnecessary, because you as DBA have no control over which undo segment will protect any one transaction. Don't worry about this; Oracle does a better job than you ever could. But if you wish, you can still find out which segment has been assigned to each transaction by querying the view V$TRANSACTION, which has join columns to V$SESSION and DBA_ROLLBACK_SEGS as shown in Figure 16-2, thus letting you build up a complete picture of transaction activity in your database: how many transactions there are currently running, who is running them, which undo segments are protecting those transactions, when the transactions started, and how many blocks of undo each transaction has generated.

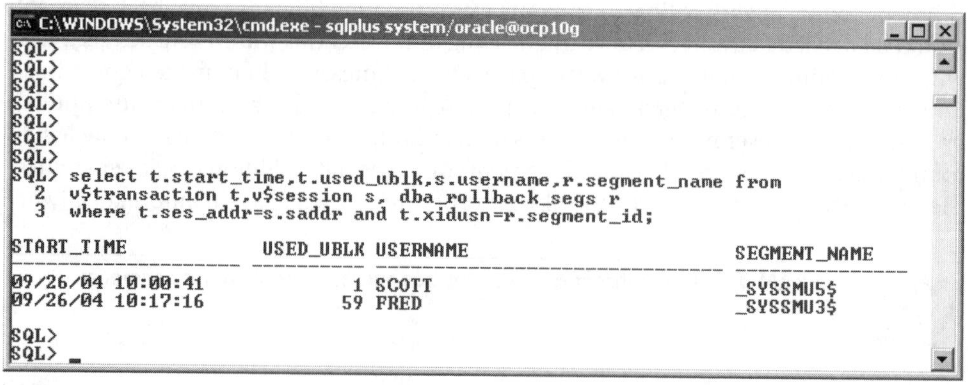

Figure 16-2   Query showing details of transactions in progress

Managing Undo

A major feature of undo segments is that they are managed automatically, but you must set the limits within which Oracle will do its management. After considering the nature and volume of activity in your database, you set certain instance parameters and adjust the size of your undo tablespace in order to achieve your objectives.

Error Conditions Related to Undo

The principles are simple: first, there should always be sufficient undo space to allow all transactions to continue, and second, there should always be sufficient undo data for all queries to succeed. The first principle requires that your undo tablespace be large enough to accommodate the worst case for undo demand. It should have enough space allocated for the worst case—the peak usage of active, or unexpired, undo data generated by your transaction workload. Note that this might not be during the peak number of concurrent transactions; it could be that during normal running you have many small transactions, but the total undo they generate might be less than that generated by a single end-of-month batch job. The second principle requires that there be additional space in the undo tablespace to store expired undo data that might be needed for read consistency, so that long-running queries will not fail with a famous Oracle error ORA-1555, snapshot too old.

   If a transaction runs out of undo space, it will fail with the error ORA-30036, unable to extend segment in undo tablespace. The statement that hit the problem is rolled back, but the rest of the transaction remains intact and uncommitted. The algorithm that assigns space within the undo tablespace to undo segments means that this error condition will arise only if the undo tablespace is absolutely full of unexpired undo data. If a query fails on consistent read with "snapshot too old," it means that the query hit a block that had been changed since the query started, but when it went to the undo segment to find the pre-update version of the data, that bit of undo data had been overwritten.

Parameters for Undo Management and Retention Guarantee

There are three initialization parameters controlling undo: UNDO_MANAGEMENT, UNDO_TABLESPACE, and UNDO_RETENTION.

   UNDO_MANAGEMENT defaults to "manual," meaning that Oracle will not use undo segments at all. This is for backward compatibility, and if you use this, you will have to do a vast amount of work creating and tuning rollback segments. Don't do it. Oracle strongly advises setting this parameter to "auto" to enable automatic undo management through the use of undo segments. In this case, DBAs relinquish undo segment management to Oracle. This parameter is static, meaning that if it is changed, the change will not come into effect until the instance is restarted. The other parameters are dynamic—they can be changed while the instance is running.

If you are using UNDO_MANAGEMENT=AUTO, you must also specify UNDO_TABLESPACE. This parameter nominates a tablespace, which must have been created as an undo tablespace, as the active undo tablespace. All the undo segments within it will be brought online (that is, made available for use) automatically.

 TIP Having several undo tablespaces available enables you to switch and use a different tablespace with a different sizing configuration for OLTP or batch purposes.

Finally, UNDO_RETENTION, set in seconds, is usually optional. It specifies a target for keeping expired undo data. If, for example, your longest running query is thirty minutes, you would set this parameter to 1800. Oracle will then attempt to keep all undo data for at least 1800 seconds, and your query should therefore never fail with ORA-1555. If, however, you do not set this parameter, or if you set it to zero, Oracle will still keep data for as long as it can anyway. The algorithm controlling which expired undo data is overwritten first will always choose to overwrite the oldest bit of data; therefore, UNDO_RETENTION is always at the maximum allowed by the size of the tablespace.

 TIP Some queries can be very long-running indeed. Queries lasting several hours to days are not unheard of. You will need an undo tablespace the size of Jupiter if you are going to run such queries successfully during normal transaction processing. You may want to consider limiting the DML workload during long reporting runs.

Where the UNDO_RETENTION parameter is not optional is if you have configured guaranteed undo retention. The default mode of operation for undo is that Oracle will favor transactions over queries. If the sizing of the undo tablespace is such that a choice has to be made between the possibility of a query failing with ORA-1555 and the certainty of a transaction failing with ORA-30036, Oracle will choose to let the transaction continue by overwriting committed undo data that a query might need. In other words, the UNDO_RETENTION is only a target that Oracle will try to achieve. But there may be circumstances when successful queries are considered more important than successful transactions. An example might be the end-of-month billing run for a utilities company, when it might be acceptable for transactions to be blocked for a few hours while the reports are generating. Another case is if you are making use of flashback queries, which rely on undo data. This is covered in Chapter 29.

With the 10g release, there is an option to guarantee undo retention. This means that undo data will never be overwritten until the time specified by the UNDO_RETENTION parameters has passed. Retention guarantee is enabled at the tablespace level via the Retention Guarantee clause. This attribute can be specified at undo tablespace creation time, or an undo tablespace can be altered later to enable it. Once you activate an undo tablespace for which a retention guarantee has been specified, all queries will complete successfully, provided they finish within the undo retention time; you will never have "snapshot too old" errors again. The downside is that transactions may fail for lack of undo space because Oracle cannot overwrite committed undo data until the retention time has passed.

EXAM TIP You can alter a tablespace to guarantee undo retention from SQL*Plus, but not through Database Control.

A database might have one tablespace used in normal operations where undo retention is not guaranteed, and another to be used during month-end reporting where retention is guaranteed. Such a system could be set up as shown in Figure 16-3.

Sizing and Monitoring the Undo Tablespace

The undo tablespace should be large enough to store the worst case of all the undo generated by concurrent transactions, which will be active undo, plus enough expired undo to satisfy the longest-running query. In an advanced environment, you may also have to add space to allow for flashback queries as well. The algorithm is simple: calculate the rate at which undo is being generated at your peak workload, and multiply by the length of your longest query.

There is a view, V$UNDOSTAT, that will tell you all you need to know. There is also an advisor within Database Control that will present the information in an immediately comprehensible way.

Figure 16-4 shows the undo management screen of Database Control. To reach this, take the Administration tab from the database home page, and then the Undo Management link in the Instance section. The configuration section of the screen shows that the undo tablespace currently in use is called UNDOTBS1, and it is 25MB big.

```
C:\WINDOWS\System32\cmd.exe - sqlplus / as sysdba
SQL>
SQL>
SQL> --create the tablespaces
SQL> create undo tablespace undo_noguarantee datafile 'undo_ng01.dbf' size 10m;

Tablespace created.

SQL> create undo tablespace undo_guarantee datafile 'undo_g01.dbf' size 10m;

Tablespace created.

SQL> alter tablespace undo_guarantee retention guarantee;

Tablespace altered.

SQL> --then for normal running.
SQL> alter system set undo_tablespace=undo_noguarantee;

System altered.

SQL> --and for end-of-month reporting.
SQL> alter system set undo_tablespace=undo_guarantee;

System altered.

SQL>
SQL>
```

Figure 16-3 Undo management from the command line

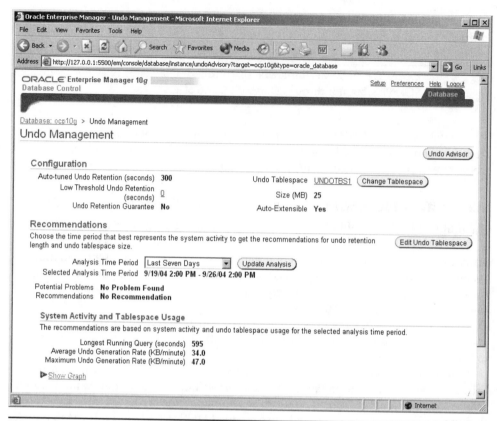

Figure 16-4 Undo management through Database Control

Undo guarantee has not been set, but the datafile(s) for the tablespace is auto-extensible. Making your undo datafiles auto-extensible will ensure that transactions will never run out of space, but Oracle will not extend them merely to meet the undo retention target. However, you should not rely on the auto-extend capability: your tablespace should be the correct size to begin with. The Change Tablespace button will issue an ALTER SYSTEM command to activate an alternative undo tablespace.

The System Activity and Tablespace Usage section of the screen tells you that the peak rate for undo generation was only 47KB per minute, and the longest running query was 595 seconds. It follows that the minimum size of the undo tablespace to prevent errors would be, in bytes,

47000 / 60 * 595 = 466083

or less than half a megabyte. If the current size were less than that, this would be pointed out in the Recommendations section.

To view the undo advisor, click Advisor.

The graph in Figure 16-5 projects the length of time for which undo could be stored against the size of the undo tablespace, given the (extremely low) rate of undo generation seen on the previous screen. For example, the graph shows that if you were to increase the size of the undo tablespace to 20GB, it could store undo data going back 542,091 minutes (about a year, which should be enough for anyone).

To obtain comparable information through SQL*Plus, query the V$UNDOSTAT view.

Dropping and Shrinking Undo Segments

When an undo tablespace is created, Oracle will create a pool of undo segments within it. If the number of concurrent transactions exceeds the number of segments in this pool, Oracle will create more. Also, if a transaction's undo data exceeds the size of its undo segment, the segment will be extended. In normal running, if the undo tablespace is under space pressure, Oracle will automatically transfer extents of expired undo data from one undo segment to another if necessary, to ensure that undo segments do have

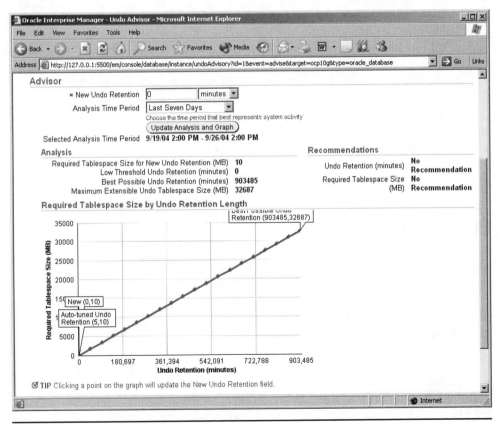

Figure 16-5 Database Control's undo advisor

enough space for the active undo being generated by currently running transactions. An additional mechanism for resizing, and indeed dropping, undo segments is driven by the system monitor process, SMON. Once every twenty-four hours, SMON will inspect the undo tablespaces and drop segments that were created to satisfy a peak demand but are no longer needed. At the same time, any excessively large segments will be shrunk.

Exercise 16-2: Monitoring Undo with SQL*Plus

Use SQL*Plus to monitor undo generation, long queries, and undo errors.

1. Connect to your instance with SQL*Plus as user SYSTEM.

2. Set up your session for displaying dates conveniently.

   ```
   SQL> alter session set nls_date_format='dd-mm-yy:hh24:mi:ss';
   ```

3. Query V$UNDOSTAT as follows:

   ```
   SQL> select begin_time, end_time, undoblks, maxquerylen, ssolderrcnt,
   nospaceerrcnt from v$undostat;
   ```

4. Interpret the results of the query. Note that the view has one row per ten-minute interval, showing you how much undo was generated, in blocks; how long the longest query was, in seconds; and whether there were any "snapshot too old" errors, or errors from transactions running out of undo space.

5. Calculate the minimum necessary size in bytes for your undo tablespace that will prevent errors, given your current activity data, with this query:

   ```
   select
   (select max(undoblks)/600 * max(maxquerylen) from v$undostat)
   *
   (select value from v$parameter where name='db_block_size')
   from dual;
   ```

Chapter Review

Undo management was, with releases prior to 9i, one of the most taxing problems facing database administrators. From 9i onward, you have the option of using automatic undo management. This is an option Oracle strongly recommends. Undo management is implemented by setting initialization parameters: UNDO_MANAGEMENT=AUTO will enable automatic management of undo segments, which are created and managed automatically in an undo tablespace nominated by the parameter UNDO_TABLESPACE.

The problems to be addressed are transactions running out of space for their undo data, and queries failing because expired undo data has been overwritten. Both of these problems should be mitigated by sizing the undo tablespace appropriately in conjunction with proper initialization parameter configuration. The information you need to calculate the necessary size of your undo tablespace is available in views, or through Database Control.

Questions

1. If an undo segment fills up, what will happen? (Choose the best answer.)

   A. Another undo segment will be created automatically.

   B. The undo segment will increase in size.

   C. The undo tablespace will extend, if its datafiles are set to auto-extend.

   D. Transactions will continue in a different undo segment.

2. When a DML statement executes, what happens? (Choose the best answer.)

   A. Both the data and the undo blocks on disk are updated, and the changes are written out to the redo stream.

   B. The old version of the data is written to an undo segment, and the new version is written to the data segments and the redo log buffer.

   C. Both data and undo blocks are updated, and the updates also go to the log buffer.

   D. The redo log buffer is updated with information needed to redo the transaction, and the undo blocks are updated with information needed to reverse the transaction.

3. You have decided to implement automatic undo management. Which of these steps is optional? (Choose two answers.)

   A. Set the parameter UNDO_MANAGEMENT.

   B. Create an undo tablespace.

   C. Restart the instance.

   D. Set the parameter UNDO_RETENTION.

   E. Take any rollback segments offline.

4. Which of the following statements are correct about undo? (Choose three answers.)

   A. One undo segment can protect many transactions.

   B. One transaction can use many undo segments.

   C. One database can have many undo tablespaces.

   D. One instance can have many undo tablespaces.

   E. One undo segment can be cut across many datafiles.

   F. Undo segments and rollback segments cannot coexist.

5. Even though you are using automatic undo segments, users are still getting "snapshot too old" errors. What could you do? (Choose three answers.)

   A. Increase the UNDO_RETENTION parameter.

   B. Set the RENTENTION_GUARANTEE parameter.

    C. Tune the queries to make them run faster.

    D. Increase the size of the undo tablespace.

    E. Use Database Control to enable retention guarantee.

    F. Use SQL*Plus to enable retention guarantee.

    G. Increase the size of your undo segments.

6. Your undo tablespace has ten undo segments, but during a sudden burst of activity you have twenty concurrent transactions. What will happen? (Choose the best answer.)

    A. Oracle will create another ten undo segments.

    B. The transactions will be automatically balanced across the ten undo segments.

    C. Ten transactions will be blocked until the first ten commit.

    D. What happens will depend on your UNDO_RETENTION setting.

7. Which view will help you decide how much undo space is needed to protect your transaction workload? (Choose the best answer.)

    A. V$TRANSACTION

    B. V$UNDOSTAT

    C. V$UNDO_ADVICE

    D. V$UNDO_ADVISOR

    E. DBA_ROLLBACK_SEGS

8. Which view will tell you about your undo segments? (Choose the best answer.)

    A. V$UNDOSTAT

    B. DBA_ROLLBACK_SEGS

    C. DBA_UNDO_SEGS

    D. V$UNDO_TABLESPACE

9. Your users are reporting "ORA-1555: Snapshot too old" errors. What might be the cause of this? (Choose the best answer.)

    A. You are not generating snapshots frequently enough.

    B. The undo data is too old.

    C. Relevant undo data is not available for user transactions.

    D. Your undo tablespace is retaining data for too long.

10. You want to ensure that both long-running queries and large transactions will always succeed. How should you set up undo? (Choose the best answer.)

    A. Assign transactions to one undo tablespace, and queries to another.

    B. Enable the retention guarantee setting for your undo tablespace.

    C. Enable auto-extend on the undo tablespace datafiles.

    D. This situation may be impossible to resolve.

11. First, user JOHN initiates a query. Second, user DAMIR updates a row that will be included in the query. Third, JOHN's query completes. Fourth, DAMIR commits his change. Fifth, JOHN runs his query again. Which of the following statements are correct? (Choose three answers.)

    A. The principle of consistency means that both of JOHN's queries will return the same result set.

    B. When DAMIR commits, the undo data is flushed to disk.

    C. When DAMIR commits, the undo becomes inactive.

    D. JOHN's first query will use undo data.

    E. JOHN's second query will use undo data.

    F. The results of the two queries will be different.

12. Your undo tablespace consists of one datafile on one disk, and transactions are failing for lack of undo space. The disk is full. You have enabled retention guarantee. Any of the following options could solve the problem, but which would cause downtime for your users? (Choose the best answer.)

    A. Create another, larger, undo tablespace and use `alter system set undo_tablespace=...` to switch to it.

    B. Move the datafile to a disk with more space, and use `alter database resize datafile...` to make it bigger.

    C. Reduce the undo_retention setting with `alter system set undo_retention=....`

    D. Disable retention guarantee with `alter tablespace...retention guarantee`.

13. Your undo tablespace has ten undo segments. What will happen if more than ten users start transactions concurrently? (Choose the best answer.)

    A. Automatic undo management will manage the interleaving of the transactions' undo data in the ten segments.

    B. Additional undo segments will be created, automatically.

    C. All the transactions will run, unless you have set retention guarantee.

    D. Only ten transactions will run; the others will be queued.

    E. Only ten transactions will run; the others will fail for lack of undo space.

14. Examine this query and result set:

```
SQL> select BEGIN_TIME,END_TIME,UNDOBLKS,MAXQUERYLEN from V$UNDOSTAT;
BEGIN_TIME         END_TIME             UNDOBLKS MAXQUERYLEN
------------------ ------------------ ---------- -----------
02-10-04:11:35:55 02-10-04:11:41:33      14435          29
02-10-04:11:25:55 02-10-04:11:35:55     120248         296
02-10-04:11:15:55 02-10-04:11:25:55     137497          37
02-10-04:11:05:55 02-10-04:11:15:55     102760        1534
02-10-04:10:55:55 02-10-04:11:05:55     237014         540
02-10-04:10:45:55 02-10-04:10:55:55     156223        1740
02-10-04:10:35:55 02-10-04:10:45:55     145275         420
02-10-04:10:25:55 02-10-04:10:35:55      99074         120
```

The block size of the undo tablespace is 4KB. Which of the following would be the optimal size for the undo tablespace? (Choose the best answer.)

A. 1GB

B. 2GB

C. 3GB

D. 4GB

15. Which of the following could be a contributing factor to "snapshot too old" errors? (Choose the best answer.)

A. Long-running transactions

B. Too low a setting for UNDO_RETENTION

C. Use of "set transaction read only"

D. All of the above

Answers

1. **B.** Undo segments increase in size on demand, according to the volume of undo data being generated by the transaction.

2. **C.** Both data and undo blocks are updated, and the updates also go to the log buffer. As far as the mechanism of redo is concerned, an undo segment is just another segment, and changes to it must be protected in the same way that changes to data segments are protected.

3. **D and E.** The parameter UNDO_RETENTION is not required, nor is it necessary to take any rollback segments offline—they will be off-lined automatically. In fact, you would usually drop any rollback segments completely.

4. **A, C, and E.** It is possible for one undo segment to protect many transactions, though Oracle will try to prevent it. It is also true that one database can have many undo tablespaces, though only one tablespace will be made active at any moment by the instance. And like any other segment, an undo segment may have extents in any of the datafiles that make up its tablespace.

5. **C, D, and F.** It may be helpful to do any of these things, though tuning the queries is probably the best first step. If that cannot be done, then make the undo tablespace larger. If there are still problems, consider using retention guarantee—though that may impact DML work.

6. **A.** Oracle will create as many undo segments as needed for concurrent transactions.

7. **B.** It is V$UNDOSTAT that shows the amount of undo being generated per second and the length of your queries.

8. **B.** DBA_ROLLBACK_SEGS is the view that tells you about your undo segments: both the online segments in the active undo tablespace, and the offline segments in any inactive undo tablespace. It will also have details of any rollback segments that may exist in the database.

9. **C.** If a session requires undo data for read consistency, and that data is no longer available in the undo tablespace because it has been overwritten, then the session will receive an ORA-1555 error and the statement will fail.

10. **D.** Unfortunately, these two needs may be impossible to reconcile. The only solution may be to address the business processes that cause this situation to arise.

11. **C, D, and F.** Undo becomes inactive once the transaction completes, though it may be needed for read consistency (C). Also, JOHN's first query must not see DAMIR's changes (D). And by default, Oracle does not provide read consistency across a series of SELECT statements—so the two queries will give different results (F).

12. **B.** This is the only option that would cause downtime, because you can't move a datafile without taking it offline. All the other operations can be done during normal running.

13. **B.** Oracle will create undo segments as needed for concurrent transactions in an attempt to ensure that it is never necessary for transactions to share an undo segment.

14. **C.** To calculate, take the largest figure for UNDOBLKS, divide by 600 to get the rate of undo generation in blocks per second, multiply by the block size, and multiply by the largest figure for MAXQUERYLEN.

15. **C.** "Set transaction read only" for a series of statements will require extensive use of undo data.

CHAPTER 17

Dealing with Locking

In this chapter you will learn how to
- Detect and resolve lock conflicts
- Manage deadlocks
- Describe the relationship between transactions and locks
- Explain lock modes within the Oracle Database 10g

In any multiuser database application it is inevitable that, eventually, two users will wish to work on the same row at the same time. This is a logical impossibility, and the database must ensure that it is a physical impossibility. The principle of transaction isolation—the *I* of the ACID test—requires that the database guarantee that one session cannot see or be affected by another session's transaction until the transaction has completed. To accomplish this, the database must serialize concurrent access to data; it must ensure that even though multiple sessions have requested access to the same rows, they actually queue up and take turns.

Serialization of concurrent access is accomplished by record and table locking mechanisms. Locking in an Oracle database is completely automatic. Generally speaking, problems only arise if software tries to interfere with the automatic locking mechanism, or if programmers write poor code.

Shared and Exclusive Locks

The standard level of locking in an Oracle database guarantees the highest possible level of concurrency. This means that if a session is updating one row, the one row is locked, and nothing else. Furthermore, the row is locked only to prevent other sessions from updating it; other sessions can read it at any time. The lock is held until the transaction completes, either with a COMMIT or a ROLLBACK. This is an "exclusive" lock: the first session to request the lock on the row gets it, and any other sessions requesting write access must wait. Read access is permitted, though if the row has been updated by the locking session, as will usually be the case, then any reads will involve the use of undo data to make sure that reading sessions do not see any uncommitted changes.

Only one session can take an exclusive lock on a row, or a whole table, at a time, but "shared" locks can be taken on the same object by many sessions. It would not make any sense to take a shared lock on one row, because the only purpose of a row lock is to gain the exclusive access needed to modify the row. Shared locks are taken on whole tables, and many sessions can have a shared lock on the same table. The purpose of taking a shared lock on a table is to prevent another session from acquiring an exclusive lock on the table: you cannot get an exclusive lock if anyone else already has a shared lock. Exclusive locks on tables are required to execute DDL statements. You cannot issue a statement that will modify an object (for instance, dropping a column of a table) if any other session already has a shared lock on the table.

To execute DML on rows, a session must acquire exclusive locks on the rows to be changed, and shared locks on the tables containing the rows. If another session already has exclusive locks on the rows, the session will hang until the locks are released by a COMMIT or a ROLLBACK. If another session already has a shared lock on the table and exclusive locks on other rows, that is not a problem. An exclusive lock on the table would be, but the default locking mechanism does not lock whole tables unless this is necessary for DDL statements.

TIP It is possible to demand an exclusive lock on a whole table, but this has to be specifically requested, and programmers should have a good reason for doing it.

DML and DDL Locks

All DML statements require at least two locks: an exclusive lock on each row affected, and a shared lock on the table containing the row. The exclusive lock prevents another session from interfering with the row, and the shared lock prevents another session from changing the table definition with a DDL statement. These locks are requested automatically. If a DML statement cannot acquire the exclusive row locks it needs, then it will hang until it gets them.

To execute DDL commands requires an exclusive lock on the object concerned. This cannot be obtained until all DML transactions against the table have finished, thereby releasing both their exclusive row locks and their shared table locks. The exclusive lock required by any DDL statement is requested automatically, but if it cannot be obtained—typically, because another session already has the shared lock granted for DML—then the statement will terminate with an error immediately.

Exercise 17-1: Automatic and Manual Locking

Demonstrate the effect of automatic shared and exclusive locks, using DML and DDL commands.

1. Connect to your database with SQL*Plus as user SYSTEM.

2. Create a table, and insert a row into it.

   ```
   ocp10g> create table t1(c1 number);
   Table created.
   ocp10g> insert into t1 values(1);
   1 row created.
   ocp10g> commit;
   Commit complete.
   ```

3. Open a second session, again connecting with SQL*Plus as user SYSTEM.

4. In session 1, issue a DML command that will take an exclusive lock on the row and a shared lock on the table.

   ```
   ocp10g> update t1 set c1=2 where c1=1;
   1 row updated.
   ```

5. In session 2, issue a DDL statement against the table.

   ```
   ocp10g> alter table t1 add (c2 date);
   alter table t1 add (c2 date)
   *
   ERROR at line 1:
   ORA-00054: resource busy and acquire with NOWAIT specified
   ```

   The attempt to add a column to the table fails, because the exclusive table lock necessary for a DDL statement conflicts with the shared lock already granted for a DML statement. Note that whereas a DML statement will wait and continually retry until it gets its lock (in other words, it hangs), DDL statements terminate immediately with an error.

6. In session 1, commit the transaction.

```
ocp10g> commit;
Commit complete.
```

7. In session 2, repeat Step 5. This time it will succeed because there are no shared DML locks blocking the exclusive DDL lock.

8. In session 1, lock the whole table.

```
ocp10g> lock table t1 in exclusive mode;
Table(s) Locked.
```

9. In session 2, insert a row. The session will hang.

```
ocp10g> insert into t1 values (1,sysdate);
```

10. In session 1, release the table lock by issuing a COMMIT. Note that a ROLLBACK would do just as well.

```
ocp10g> commit;
Commit complete.
```

11. Session 2 will now be released, and the insert will complete; issue a COMMIT to terminate the transaction and release the row exclusive lock.

12. Leave both sessions open; they will be used in later exercises.

The Enqueue Mechanism

Requests for locks are queued. If a session requests a lock and cannot get it because another session already has the row or object locked, the session will wait. It may be that several sessions are waiting for access to the same row or object; in that case, Oracle will keep track of the order in which the sessions requested the lock. When the session with the lock releases it, the next session will be granted it, and so on. This is known as the "enqueue" mechanism.

If you do not want a session to queue up if it cannot get a lock, the only way to avoid this is to use the WAIT or NOWAIT clause of the SELECT...FOR UPDATE command. A normal SELECT will always succeed, because SELECT does not require any locks, but a DML statement will hang. The SELECT...FOR UPDATE command will select rows and lock them in exclusive mode. If any of the rows are locked already, the SELECT...FOR UPDATE statement will be queued and the session will hang until the locks are released, just as a DML statement would. To avoid sessions hanging, use either SELECT...FOR UPDATE NOWAIT or SELECT...FOR UPDATE WAIT <n>, where <n> is a number of seconds. Having obtained the locks with either of the SELECT... FOR UPDATE options, you can then issue the DML commands with no possibility of the session hanging.

Exercise 17-2: The SELECT...FOR UPDATE Command

Use the SELECT...FOR UPDATE command to control enqueue waits.

1. In your first SQL*Plus session, select and lock both the rows in the T1 table.

```
ocp10g> select * from t1 for update;
        C1 C2
---------- ---------
         2
         1 09-FEB-05
```

2. In your second session, attempt to lock the rows, but use the NOWAIT keyword to terminate the statement immediately if the locks cannot be obtained.

```
ocp10g> select * from t1 for update nowait;
select * from t1 for update nowait
              *
ERROR at line 1:
ORA-00054: resource busy and acquire with NOWAIT specified
```

The statement fails immediately, and the session can continue.

3. In your second session, try to lock the rows again but specify a time-out of ten seconds.

```
ocp10g> select * from t1 for update wait 10;
select * from t1 for update wait 10
              *
ERROR at line 1:
ORA-30006: resource busy; acquire with WAIT timeout expired
```

The session hangs for ten seconds before the statement fails and the session is freed.

4. Repeat Step 3, but before the ten seconds expire issue a COMMIT in your first session. Session 2 will then continue.

```
ocp10g> select * from t1 for update wait 10;
        C1 C2
---------- ---------
         2
         1 09-FEB-05
```

5. Release the locks obtained by session 2 by issuing a COMMIT.

Lock Contention

When a session requests a lock on a row or object and cannot get it because another session has an exclusive lock on the row or object, it will hang. This is lock contention, and it can cause the database performance to deteriorate appallingly as all the sessions queue up waiting for locks. Some lock contention may be inevitable, as a result of normal activity: the nature of the application may be such that different users will require access to the same data. But in many cases, lock contention is caused by program and system design.

The Oracle database provides utilities for detecting lock contention, and it is also possible to solve the problem in an emergency. A special case of lock contention is the "deadlock," which is always resolved automatically by the database itself.

 TIP Lock contention is a common reason for an application that performs well under testing to grind to a halt when it goes into production and the number of concurrent users increases.

The Causes of Lock Contention

It may be that the nature of the business is such that users do require write access to the same rows at the same time. If this is a limiting factor in performance of the system, the only solution is business process re-engineering, to develop a more efficient business model. But although some locking is a necessary part of business data processing, there are some faults in application design that can exacerbate the problem.

Long-running transactions will cause problems. An obvious case is where a user updates a row and then does not commit the change. Perhaps s/he even goes off to lunch, leaving the transaction unfinished. You cannot stop this from happening if users have access to the database with tools such as SQL*Plus, but it should never occur with well-written software. The application should take care that a lock is only imposed just before an update occurs, and released (with a COMMIT or ROLLBACK) immediately afterward.

Poorly written batch processes can also cause problems, if they are coded as long transactions. Consider the case of an accounting suite nominal ledger: it is a logical impossibility in accountancy terms for the ledger to be partly in one period and partly in another, so the end-of-month rollover to the next period is one business transaction. This transaction may involve updating millions of rows in thousands of tables and take hours to complete. If the rollover routine is coded as one transaction with a COMMIT at the end, millions of rows will be locked for hours, but in accountancy terms, this is what should happen. Good program design would avoid the problem by updating the rows in groups, with regular commits, but the programmers will also have to take care of simulating read consistency across transactions and handling the situation where the process fails part way through. If it were one transaction, this wouldn't be a problem: the database would roll it back. If it is many small transactions, they will have to manage a ledger that is half in one period and half in another. These considerations should not be a problem: your programmers should bear in mind that long transactions impact on the usability of the system, and design their systems accordingly.

Third-party user process products may impose excessively high locking levels. For example, some application development tools always do a SELECT...FOR UPDATE to avoid the necessity of re-querying the data and checking for changes. Some other products cannot do row-level locking: if a user wants to update one row, the tool locks a group of rows—perhaps dozens or even hundreds. If your application software is written with tools such as these, the Oracle database will simply do what it is told to do: it will impose numerous locks that are unnecessary in business terms. If you suspect that the software is applying more locks than necessary, investigate whether it has configuration options to change this behavior.

Finally, make sure your programmers are aware of the capabilities of the database. A common problem is repeatable reads. Consider this example:

```
ocp10g> select * from regions;
 REGION_ID REGION_NAME
---------- ------------------------
         1 Europe
         2 Americas
         3 Asia
         4 Middle East and Africa
ocp10g> select count(*) from regions;
  COUNT(*)
----------
         5
```

How can this be possible? The first query (the detail report) shows four rows, and then the second query (the summary report) shows five. The problem is that during the course of the first query, another session inserted and committed the fifth row. One way out of this would be to lock the tables while running the reports, thus causing other sessions to hang. A more sophisticated way would be to use the SET TRANSACTION READ ONLY statement. This will guarantee (without imposing any locks) that the session does not see any DML on any tables, committed or not, until it terminates the read-only transaction with a COMMIT or ROLLBACK. The mechanism is based on use of undo segments and is the same as that used for Flashback Query, detailed in Chapter 29.

Detecting Lock Contention

To reach the Database Control lock manager, take the Performance tab from the database home page, and then the Database Locks link in the Additional Monitoring Links section. Figure 17-1 shows the Database Locks window, with Blocking Locks selected. There may be any number of locks within the database, but it is usually only the locks that are causing sessions to hang that are of interest. These are known as *blocking* locks.

In the figure, there is one problem. Session number 138, logged on as user HR, is holding an exclusive lock on one or more rows of the table HR.REGIONS. This session is not hanging; it is operating normally. But session number 162, logged on as user SYSTEM, is blocked; it is waiting for an exclusive lock on one or more of the rows locked by session 138. Session 162 is hanging at this moment, and it will continue to hang until session 138 releases its locks by terminating its transaction with a COMMIT or a ROLLBACK.

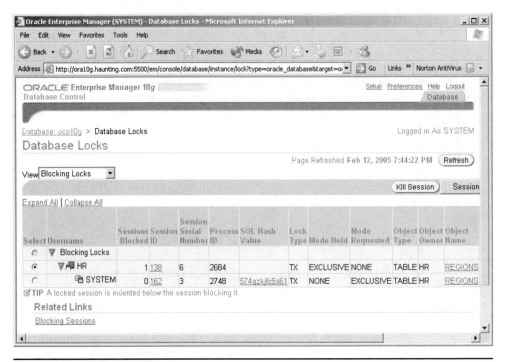

Figure 17-1 Showing locks with Database Control

Resolving Lock Contention

Lock contention is a natural consequence of many users accessing the same data concurrently. The problem can be exacerbated by badly designed software, but in principle lock contention is part of normal database activity. It is therefore not possible for the DBA to resolve it completely; s/he can only identify that it is a problem, and suggest to system and application designers that they bear in mind the impact of lock contention when designing data structures and programs.

In an emergency, however, it is possible for the DBA to solve the problem by terminating the session, or sessions, that are holding too many locks for too long. When a session is terminated forcibly, any locks it holds will be released as its active transaction is rolled back. The blocked sessions will then become free and can continue.

To terminate a session, use either Database Control or the ALTER SYSTEM KILL SESSION command. In the preceding example, if you decided that the HR session is holding its lock for an absurd period of time, you would select the radio button for the session and click the KILL SESSION button. HR's transaction will be rolled back, and SYSTEM's session will then be able to take the lock(s) it requires and continue working.

Exercise 17-3: Detecting and Resolving Lock Contention

Use Database Control to detect a locking problem, and resolve it with SQL*Plus.

1. Using your first session, lock all the rows in the T1 table.

```
ocp10g> select * from t1 for update;
        C1 C2
---------- ---------
         2
         1 09-FEB-05
```

2. In your second session, attempt to update a row.

```
ocp10g> update t1 set c2=sysdate where c1=2;
```

The session will hang.

3. Connect to your database as user SYSTEM with Database Control.

4. Navigate to the Database Locks window by taking the Performance tab from the database home page and then the Database Locks link in the Additional Monitoring Links section.

5. Observe that the second session is shown as waiting for an EXCLUSIVE lock. This will be the hanging session. The first session is the one holding the lock that is causing the problem.

6. Note the Session ID and Session Serial Number of the blocking session—138 and 6 in the example in Figure 17-1.

7. Launch a third SQL*Plus session and connect as user SYSTEM.

8. In your third session, issue this command, substituting your blocking session's session and serial number:

```
ocp10g> alter system kill session '138,6';
System altered.
```

9. Note that in your second session, the update has now succeeded.

10. In your first session, issue any statement you please; you will get the message "ORA-00028: your session has been killed," indicating that you have been forcibly disconnected.

Deadlocks

It is possible to construct a scenario where two sessions block each other in such a fashion that both will hang, each waiting for the other to release its lock. This is known as a *deadlock*. Deadlocks are not the DBA's problem; they are caused by bad program design and are resolved automatically by the database itself. Information regarding deadlocks is written out to the alert log, with full details in a trace file; as part of your daily monitoring, you will pick up the occurrence of deadlocks and inform your developers that they are happening.

If a deadlock occurs, both sessions will hang, but only for a brief moment. One of the sessions will detect the deadlock within seconds, and it will roll back the statement that caused the problem. This will free up the other session, returning the message "ORA-00060: Deadlock detected." This message must be trapped by your programmers in their exceptions clauses, which should take appropriate action.

 EXAM TIP You can do nothing about deadlocks other than report them; they are resolved automatically by the database.

It must be emphasized that deadlocks are a program design fault. They occur because the code attempts to do something that is logically impossible. Well-written code will always request locks in a sequence that cannot cause deadlocks to occur, or will test whether incompatible locks already exist before requesting them.

Exercise 17-4: Automatic Deadlock Resolution

Using the first and second sessions you have open from previous exercises, force a deadlock, and observe the reporting through trace files.

1. In your first session, lock a row with an update statement.

```
ocp10g> update t1 set c2=sysdate where c1=1;
1 row updated.
```

2. In your second session, lock the other row.

```
ocp10g> update t1 set c2=sysdate where c1=2;
1 row updated.
```

3. In your first session, request a lock on the row already locked by the second session, by issuing the statement in Step 2. The session will hang.

4. In your second session, issue the statement in Step 1, to complete the construction of the deadlock by requesting a lock on the row already locked by your first session.

5. Within a second or two, your first session will come free with an ORA-00060 message.

```
ocp10g> update t1 set c2=sysdate where c1=2;
update t1 set c2=sysdate where c1=2
         *
ERROR at line 1:
ORA-00060: deadlock detected while waiting for resource
```

Note that the other session is still hanging.

6. Open your alert log with any editor you please (remember, it is located in the directory specified by the BACKGROUND_DUMP_DEST instance parameter, and named alert_<instance name>.log) The final entry will resemble this:

```
Mon Feb 14 09:27:03 2005
ORA-00060: Deadlock detected. More info in file
/oracle/product/10.1.0/admin/ocp10g/udump/ocp10g_ora_420.trc.
```

7. Open the trace file listed. Note that it is in the directory specified by the USER_DUMP_DEST instance parameter. It will include information such as

```
*** 2005-02-14 09:27:03.242
*** ACTION NAME:() 2005-02-14 09:27:03.212
*** MODULE NAME:(SQL*Plus) 2005-02-14 09:27:03.212
*** SERVICE NAME:(SYS$USERS) 2005-02-14 09:27:03.212
*** SESSION ID:(133.26) 2005-02-14 09:27:03.212
DEADLOCK DETECTED
Current SQL statement for this session:
update t1 set c2=sysdate where c1=2
The following deadlock is not an ORACLE error. It is a
deadlock due to user error in the design of an application
or from issuing incorrect ad-hoc SQL. The following
information may aid in determining the deadlock:
```

8. Interpret the deadlock information: it gives the statement that caused the problem, as well as information on which program module caused the problem. In particular, note the phrase "The following deadlock is not an ORACLE error. It is a deadlock due to user error in the design of an application or from issuing incorrect ad-hoc SQL." This places the responsibility squarely on the programmers, which is where it belongs.

9. Tidy up: issue a commit in all sessions, and drop the table.

Chapter Review

Locking is implemented by the enqueue mechanism, which tracks what locks have been requested, and the order in which they were requested. Sessions will hang while waiting for an enqueue.

Row and table locking can be completely automatic in the Oracle environment. The default level of locking delivers the highest possible level of concurrency: individual rows are locked exclusively, which is necessary for transaction integrity, and tables are only ever locked in shared mode, in order to protect the structure of the objects being manipulated. Programmers can impose higher levels of locking if they wish; whole tables can be locked indefinitely.

Locks are a part of normal DML activity and should not be a problem, but if a lock persists for an undue period, the contention may cause problems. To resolve lock contention, you can kill the session holding the locks. A special case of lock contention is the deadlock. This should never occur: it is caused by poor programming that sets up a logically impossible situation. Oracle itself will resolve deadlocks by rolling back one of the statements that caused it.

Questions

1. Which of the following commands will impose one (or more) exclusive row lock(s)? (Choose all that apply.)

   A. ALTER TABLE EMP ADD COLUMN DOB(DATE);

   B. UPDATE EMP SET SAL=SAL*1.1;

    C. UPDATE EMP SET SAL=SAL*1.1 WHERE EMPNO=7839;

    D. SELECT * FROM EMP WHERE EMPNO=7839 FOR UPDATE;

    E. DROP TABLE EMP;

    F. CREATE INDEX ENAME_IDX ON EMP(ENAME);

2. Study the following sequence:

```
ocp10g> select * from emp where empno=7839 for update nowait;
select * from emp where empno=7839 for update nowait
              *
ERROR at line 1:
ORA-00054: resource busy and acquire with NOWAIT specified
```

    What best describes the situation? (Choose the best answer.)

    A. The row for employee number 7839 is already locked exclusively, and your session will hang until the lock is released.

    B. The NOWAIT keyword cannot be combined with an UPDATE.

    C. Another session has an exclusive lock either on the row for employee 7839 or on the whole EMP table.

    D. There is already a shared lock on the row for employee 7839, which is incompatible with the share mode lock required by SELECT...FOR UPDATE.

3. If several sessions request an exclusive lock on the same row, what will happen? (Choose the best answer.)

    A. The first session to request the lock will get an exclusive lock; the others will be granted shared locks.

    B. The first session will get an exclusive lock. When it releases the lock, an exclusive lock will be granted randomly to one of the other sessions.

    C. Oracle will keep track of the order in which each session requested the exclusive lock, and pass it on as sessions release the lock.

    D. A session cannot request an exclusive lock on a row if another session already has an exclusive lock on it.

4. Which of the following statements is correct regarding deadlocks? (Choose the best answer.)

    A. Deadlocks cannot happen in an Oracle database; they are prevented automatically.

    B. Deadlocks can happen in an Oracle database, but they are resolved automatically.

    C. If a deadlock occurs, it is the programmer's responsibility to resolve it, not the DBA's.

    D. A deadlock can be resolved by killing the sessions that locked each other.

5. If a session issues a single-row UPDATE command and hangs because the row concerned is locked by another session, for how long will it hang? (Choose the best answer.)

   A. It will not hang at all if the NOWAIT keyword was specified.

   B. It will hang until the locking session terminates its transaction, unless WAIT <n> was specified, where <n> is a number of seconds.

   C. It will hang until the locking session releases its lock by issuing another DML statement.

   D. It will not hang; it will take a shared lock and continue to work by using undo data.

   E. None of the above is correct.

Answers

1. **B, C,** and **D.** All DML commands require exclusive row locks, and all DDL commands require exclusive table locks.

2. **C.** SELECT...FOR UPDATE requests an exclusive row lock, which will fail if another session already has an exclusive row lock on the row, or if the whole table is locked. The first choice is wrong because it describes the behavior if the NOWAIT option were not used; the second is wrong because SELECT... FOR UPDATE is actually the only case where NOWAIT can be used. Finally, SELECT...FOR UPDATE requires an exclusive lock, not a shared lock.

3. **C.** The enqueue mechanism tracks the order in which locks were requested.

4. **B.** Deadlocks are resolved by the database automatically. The third choice is correct insofar as deadlocks are usually a programming fault, but wrong because no one needs to resolve them. Finally, no session need be killed; it is only necessary to roll back a statement.

5. **E.** None of the answers is correct. Both A and B are wrong because WAIT and NOWAIT can only be applied to SELECT statements. C is wrong because another DML statement will not release a lock; only COMMIT or ROLLBACK will do that. D is wrong because DML cannot use undo data; the answer would be correct if it were a SELECT statement.

CHAPTER 18

Configuring the Database for Backup and Recovery

In this chapter you will learn how to

- Describe the basics of database backup, restore, and recovery
- Identify the types of failure that may occur in an Oracle database
- Describe ways to tune instance recovery
- Identify the importance of checkpoints, redo log files, and archived log files
- Configure archivelog mode
- Configure a database for recoverability

Perhaps the most important aspect of a database administrator's job is to ensure that the database does not lose data. The mechanisms of redo and undo ensure that it is absolutely impossible to corrupt the database no matter what the DBA does, or does not do. After working through the section of this chapter headed "Instance Recovery" you will be able to prove this. However, it is possible for an Oracle database to lose data if the DBA does not take appropriate precautions. From release 9i onward, an Oracle database can be configured so that no matter what happens the database will never lose a single row of committed data. It is also possible to configure an environment for 100 percent availability. This chapter will go through the concepts behind Oracle's backup and recovery mechanisms: the enabling structure within which you will configure whatever level of data security and availability is demanded by your organization. But first, a summary of what you are trying to achieve with your backup and recovery strategy.

Backup and Recovery Issues

This is an area where the DBA cannot work in isolation. The amount of downtime and data loss that an organization can stand is a matter for the business analysts, not the DBA. The business analysts in conjunction with the end users will determine the requirement, and the DBA will then configure the database appropriately. To do this, s/he will require the cooperation of the system administrators and other support staff. Sometimes there will be budget constraints to consider: a zero data loss and hundred percent uptime environment will be far more expensive to configure than an environment that does not have such guarantees. Performance may also tend to degrade as the uptime and data loss requirements become more demanding.

The end result of considering the business requirements, performance, and financial considerations is often a compromise. It is vitally important that this be documented, usually in the form of a service level agreement that details exactly what is being done, and what the effects will be of various types of failure. For the DBA, there is no such thing as "good" or "bad" database administration in this environment; there is only whether the procedures he or she is following confirm to the service level agreement, or not. This protects the DBA from criticism (you can't be fired for doing what it has been agreed that you will do) and guarantees the end users the level of service that they have agreed they require. The three areas of a service level agreement relevant to backup and recovery are the mean time between failures (the MTBF), the mean time to recover (the MTTR), and loss of data. Your objective as DBA is to increase the MTBF while reducing the MTTR and data loss.

MTBF refers to how frequently the database becomes unavailable. For some organizations, the database must be available all the time. Real-time systems, such as satellite flight control or process control in an oil refinery, must run all the time; even a few minutes failure can be catastrophic. Oracle provides two advanced options that can contribute to 100 percent availability: RAC and Streams. A *RAC*, or clustered, database consists of one physical database opened by multiple instances on multiple computers. If any one computer or instance fails, the database remains open for use through a surviving instance. RAC protects against hardware, operating system, and software failure. The Streams environment consists of two or more databases on separate computers, which may be geographically widely separated. The Streams mechanism takes care of keeping the two databases synchronized, in real time if necessary. Users can connect to either, and changes made on each database are published to the other database. If one database becomes unavailable for any reason, work can continue on the other. Streams goes further than RAC for fault tolerance, because it protects against disk and network failure as well as hardware, operating system, and software failure.

MTTR refers to the length of downtime following a failure. For many organizations, this is actually more significant than losing data. For example, every minute that the billing system for a telco is unavailable could mean subscribers are getting free cell phone calls, and extended downtime could cost a lot more money than losing a few minutes of data. Clearly the ideal is to have the system available all the time, but when it does fail, it is your duty to bring it back up with minimal delay. A critical part of reducing MTTR is practice. When a database crashes, you will be under enormous pressure to open it as soon as possible. It is vital to be prepared. You do not want to be looking up things in manuals before taking appropriate action. Practice, practice, practice—if you can't test recovery on a live system, test on a backup system. Run simulations of all possible types of failure, and prepare for all eventualities.

The third objective is to minimize data loss. Some organizations cannot stand any data loss whatsoever. For example, a stock trading system must not lose a trade. It might be preferable to have no trades taking place—temporarily close the exchange—than to take the risk of losing a transaction. In other environments it may be acceptable to lose a few hours of data, but make sure that this is documented. From release 9i onward, an Oracle database can be configured for zero data loss, under any circumstances whatsoever. This is done through Data Guard. In a Data Guard system the live database, known as the primary, is protected by one or more standby databases. The standby is continually updated with all the changes applied to the primary. These changes can be propagated in real time if necessary.

These three advanced options—RAC, Streams, and Data Guard—all have performance implications (which may be for better or for worse, depending on how things are set up and what the objective is) and should not be embarked upon lightly. They are beyond the scope of the OCP examination, but knowledge of them is required for Oracle University's more advanced qualifications.

Any fault-tolerant environment will rely heavily on hardware redundancy. This is where you cannot work independently of the system administrators. If a datafile becomes unavailable because of a disk failure, your database will also (at least partially) become unavailable. Your objective of increasing the MTBF must be aligned with your system administrators' targets for disk redundancy and replacement. Similarly, you are totally dependent on the network. If your users cannot connect, they will not care whether the reason is that a router has failed. Your targets for the database must be set with the whole IT environment in mind, and the service level agreements must make this clear. Your role as DBA is to ensure that you can meet the agreed standards for uptime and data loss, no matter what the nature of the failure.

TIP You will find that the DBA is expected to know about everything. Not just the database, but also the hardware, the network, the operating system, the programming language, and the application. Sometimes only the DBA can see the totality of the environment, but no one can know it all; so work with the appropriate specialists, and build up a good relationship with them.

Categories of Failures

Failures can be divided into a few broad categories. For each type of failure, there will be an appropriate course of action to resolve it. Each type of failure may well be documented in a service level agreement; certainly the steps to be followed should be documented in a procedures manual.

Statement Failure

An individual SQL statement can fail for a number of reasons, not all of which are within the DBA's domain—but even so, s/he must be prepared to fix them. The first level of repair will be automatic. Whenever a statement fails, the server process executing the statement will detect the problem and roll back the statement. Remember that a statement might attempt to update many rows and fail part way through execution; all the rows that were updated before the failure will have their changes reversed through use of undo. This will happen automatically. If the statement is part of a multistatement transaction, all the statements that have already succeeded will remain intact, but uncommitted. Ideally, the programmers will have included exception clauses in their code that will identify and manage any problems, but there will always be some errors that get through the error handling routines. As shown in Figure 18-1, there are four common causes of statement failure: invalid data, insufficient privileges, space allocation problems, and logic errors. You will read about each of them next.

A common cause of statement failure is *invalid data*, usually a format or integrity constraint violation. A well-written user process will avoid format problems, such as attempting to insert character data into a numeric field, but they can often occur when doing batch jobs with data coming from a third-party system. Oracle itself will try to solve formatting problems by doing automatic type casting to convert data types on the fly, but this is not very efficient and shouldn't be relied upon. Constraint violations will be detected, but Oracle can do nothing to solve them. Clearly, problems caused by invalid data are not the DBA's fault, but you must be prepared to deal with them by working with the users to validate and correct the data, and with the programmers to try to automate these processes.

A second class of non–DBA related statement failures consists of *logic errors* in the application. Programmers may well develop code that in some circumstances is impossible for the database to execute. A perfect example is the deadlock that you saw in the last chapter. A deadlock is not a database error; it is an error caused by programmers writing code that permits an impossible situation to arise. Another example would be if the application attempts to insert a child row before the parent row.

```
C:\WINDOWS\System32\cmd.exe - sqlplus / as sysdba                    _ □ X
SQL>
SQL> --invalid data: there is already a department 10
SQL> insert into dept values (10,'Sales','UK');
insert into dept values (10,'Sales','UK')
*
ERROR at line 1:
ORA-00001: unique constraint (SCOTT.PK_DEPT) violated


SQL> --insufficient privileges: not allowed to insert into hr.regions
SQL> insert into hr.regions values (99,'Southern Africa');
insert into hr.regions values (99,'Southern Africa')
           *
ERROR at line 1:
ORA-01031: insufficient privileges


SQL> --space problem: the tablespace is full
SQL> create table too_big (c1 varchar2(1)) storage (initial 1000m);
create table too_big (c1 varchar2(1)) storage (initial 1000m)
*
ERROR at line 1:
ORA-01659: unable to allocate MINEXTENTS beyond 12 in tablespace USERS


SQL> --logic problem: the code can't handle two Smiths
SQL> declare v_sal number;
  2   begin
  3    select salary into v_sal from hr.employees where last_name='Smith';
  4   end;
  5   /
declare v_sal number;
*
ERROR at line 1:
ORA-01422: exact fetch returns more than requested number of rows
ORA-06512: at line 3


SQL> _
```

Figure 18-1   Examples of statement failures

Space management problems are frequent, but they should never occur. A good DBA will monitor space usage proactively and take action before problems arise. Space-related causes of statement failure include inability to extend a segment because the tablespace is full; running out of undo space; insufficient temporary space when running queries that use disk sorts; a user hitting his quota limit; or an object hitting its maximum extents limit. Database Control includes the undo advisor, the segment advisor, the Automatic Database Diagnostic Monitor, and the alert mechanism, all described in previous chapters, which will help to pick up space-related problems before they happen. The effect of space problems that slip through can perhaps be alleviated by setting datafiles to auto-extend, or by enabling resumable space allocation (as detailed in Chapter 32), but ideally, space problems should never arise in the first place.

TIP Issue the command `alter session enable resumable`, and from then on the session will not signal errors on space problems but instead hang until the problem is fixed. You can enable resumable for the whole instance with the RESUMABLE_TIMEOUT parameter.

Statements may fail because of *insufficient privileges*. Remember from Chapter 7 how privileges let a user do certain things, such as select from a table or execute a piece of code. When a statement is parsed, the server process checks whether the user executing the statement has the necessary permissions. This type of error indicates that the security structures in place are inappropriate, and the DBA (in conjunction with the organization's security manager) should grant appropriate system and object privileges.

 EXAM TIP Remember that there are four common causes of statement failure: invalid data, insufficient privileges, space allocation problems, and logic errors.

User Process Failure

A user process may fail for any number of reasons, including the user exiting abnormally instead of logging out, the terminal rebooting, or the program causing an address violation. Whatever the cause of the problem, the outcome is the same. The PMON background process periodically polls all the server processes to ascertain the state of the session. If a server process reports that it has lost contact with its user process, PMON will tidy up. If the session was in the middle of a transaction, PMON will roll back the transaction and release any locks. Then it will terminate the server process and release the PGA back to the operating system.

This type of problem is beyond the DBA's control, but s/he should watch for any trends that might indicate a lack of user training, poorly written software, or perhaps network or hardware problems.

Network Failure

In conjunction with the network administrators, it should be possible to configure Oracle Net such that there is no single point of failure. The three points to consider are listeners, network interface cards, and routes.

A database listener is unlikely to crash, but there are limits to the amount of work that one listener can do. A listener can service only one connect request at once, and it does take an appreciable amount of time to launch a server process and connect it to a user process. If your database experiences high volumes of concurrent connection requests, users may receive errors when they try to connect. You can avoid this by configuring multiple listeners (each on a different address/port combination) and using connect-time load balancing, as discussed in Chapter 12, to spread the workload across them all.

At the operating system and hardware levels, network interfaces can fail. Ideally, your server machine will have at least two network interface cards, for redundancy as well as performance. Create at least one listener for each card.

Routing problems or localized network failures can mean that even though the database is running perfectly, no one can connect to it. If your server has two or more network interface cards, they should ideally be connected to physically separate subnets. Then on the client side configure connect-time fault tolerance as well as load balancing, as described in Chapter 12. This step not only balances the network traffic across all available routes and devices but also permits the user processes to try a series of routes until they find one that is working.

 TIP The network fault tolerance for a single-instance database is only at connect time; a failure later on will disrupt currently connected sessions, and they will have to reconnect. In a RAC environment, it is possible for a session to fail over to a different instance, and the user may not even notice.

User Errors

Historically, user errors were undoubtedly the worst errors to manage. Release 10g of the database improves the situation dramatically. The problem is that user errors are not errors as far as the database is concerned. Imagine a conversation on these lines:

> User: "I forgot to put a WHERE clause on my UPDATE statement, so I've just updated a million rows instead of one."
>
> DBA: "Did you say COMMIT?"
>
> User: "Oh, yes."
>
> DBA: "Um...."

As far as Oracle is concerned, this is a transaction like any other. The "D" for "Durable" of the ACID test states that once a transaction is committed, it must be immediately broadcast to all other users and be absolutely nonreversible. But at least with DML errors such as the one dramatized here, the user does get the chance to roll back his statement if he realizes that it was wrong before committing. But DDL statements don't give you that option. For example, if a programmer drops a table when he thinks he is logged onto the test database but is actually logged onto the production database, there is a COMMIT built into the DROP TABLE command. That table is gone; you can't roll back DDL.

The ideal solution to user errors is to prevent them from occurring in the first place. This is partly a matter of user training, but more especially of software design: no user process should ever let a user issue an UPDATE statement without a WHERE clause. But even the best-designed software cannot prevent users from issuing SQL that is inappropriate to the business. Everyone makes mistakes. Oracle provides a number of ways whereby you as DBA may be able to correct user errors, but this is often extremely difficult—particularly if the error isn't reported for some time. The possible techniques, dealt with in detail in later chapters, are flashback query (see Chapter 29), flashback drop (also Chapter 29), the Log Miner, incomplete recovery (as in Chapter 27), and the Flashback Database (Chapter 28).

Flashback query is running a query against a version of the database as it existed at some time in the past. The read-consistent version of the database is constructed, for your session only, through the use of undo data. Figure 18-2 shows one of many uses of flashback query. The user has "accidentally" deleted every row in the EMP table and committed the delete. Then s/he retrieves the rows by querying a version of the table as it was five minutes previously.

Flashback drop reverses the effect of a DROP TABLE command, as shown in Figure 18-3. In previous releases of the database, a DROP command did what it says: it dropped all references to the table from the data dictionary. There was no way to reverse this. Even flashback query would fail, because the flashback query mechanism does need the data dictionary object definition. But in release 10g the implementation of the DROP command has changed: it no longer drops anything; it just renames the object so that you will never see it again, unless you specifically ask to.

The Log Miner is an advanced tool that extracts information from the online and archived redo logs. Redo includes all changes made to data blocks. By extracting the changes made to blocks of table data, it is possible to reconstruct the changes that were made—thus, redo can be used to bring a restored backup forward in time. But the redo stream also has all the changes made to undo blocks, and it is therefore possible to construct the changes that would be needed to reverse transactions, even though they have been committed. Conceptually, the Log Miner is similar to flashback query: the information to reverse a change is constructed from undo data, but whereas flashback query uses undo data that is currently in the undo segments, Log Miner extracts the undo data from the redo logs. This means that Log Miner can go back in time indefinitely, if you have copies of the relevant logs. By contrast, flashback query can go back only as far as your undo tablespace will allow.

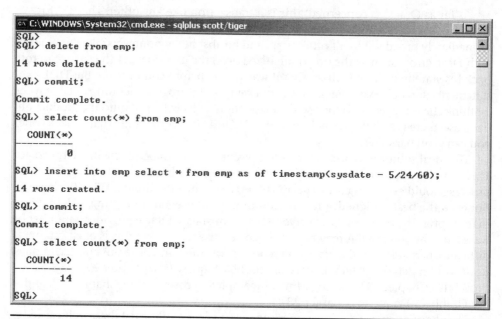

```
C:\WINDOWS\System32\cmd.exe - sqlplus scott/tiger
SQL>
SQL> delete from emp;

14 rows deleted.

SQL> commit;

Commit complete.

SQL> select count(*) from emp;

  COUNT(*)
----------
         0

SQL> insert into emp select * from emp as of timestamp(sysdate - 5/24/60);

14 rows created.

SQL> commit;

Commit complete.

SQL> select count(*) from emp;

  COUNT(*)
----------
        14

SQL>
```

Figure 18-2   Correcting user error with flashback query

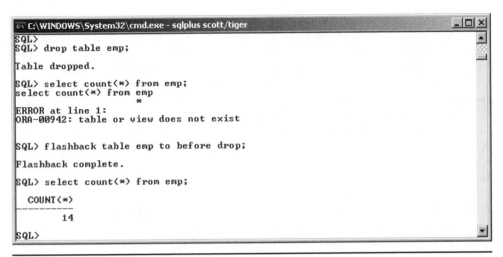

Figure 18-3 Correcting user error with flashback drop

Incomplete recovery and flashback database are much more drastic techniques for reversing user errors. With either approach, the whole database is taken back in time to before the error occurred. The other techniques just described let you reverse one bad transaction, while everything else remains intact. But if you ever do an incomplete recovery or a flashback of the whole database, you will lose all the work done from time you go back to—not just the bad transaction.

Media Failure

Media failure means damage to disks, and therefore the files stored on them. This is not your problem—but you must be prepared to deal with it. The point to hang on to is that damage to any number of any files is no reason to lose data. With release 9*i* and later, you can survive the loss of any and all of the files that make up a database without losing any committed data—if you have configured the database appropriately. Prior to 9*i*, complete loss of the machine hosting the database could result in loss of data; the Data Guard facility, not covered in the OCP curriculum, can even protect against that.

Included in the category of "media failure" is a particular type of user error: system or database administrators accidentally deleting files. This is not as uncommon as one might think (or hope).

TIP On Unix, the rm command has been responsible for any number of appalling mistakes. You might want to consider, for example, aliasing the rm command to rm −i to gain a little peace of mind.

When a disk is damaged, one or more of the files on it will be damaged, unless the disk subsystem itself has protection through RAID. Remember that a database consists of three file types: the controlfile, the online redo logs, and the datafiles. The controlfile and the online logs should always be protected through multiplexing. If you have multiple copies of the controlfile on different disks, then if any one of them is damaged you will have a surviving copy. Similarly, multiple copies of each online redo log mean that you can survive the loss of any one. Datafiles can't be multiplexed (other than through RAID, at the hardware level); therefore, if one is lost, the only option is to restore it from a backup. This introduces the concept of "recovery." The restored backup will be out-of-date; "recovery" means applying changes extracted from the redo logs (both online and archived) to bring it forward to the state it was in at the time the damage occurred.

Recovery requires the use of archived redo logs. These are the copies of online redo logs, made after each log switch. After restoring a datafile from backup, the changes to be applied to it to bring it up-to-date are extracted, in chronological order, from the archive logs generated since the backup was taken. Clearly, you must look after your archive logs because if any are lost, the recovery process will fail. Archive logs are initially created on disk, and because of the risks of losing disk storage, they, just like the controlfile and the online logfiles, should be multiplexed: two or more copies on different devices.

So to protect against media failure, you must have multiplexed copies of the controlfile, the online redo log files, and the archive redo log files. You will also take backups of the controlfile, the datafiles, and the archive log files. You do not back up the redo logs; they are, in effect, backed up when they are copied to the archive logs. Datafiles cannot be protected by multiplexing; they need to be protected by hardware redundancy: either conventional RAID systems or Oracle's own Automatic Storage Management (ASM) detailed in Chapter 33.

Instance Failure

An *instance failure* is a disorderly shutdown of the instance, popularly referred to as a crash. This could be caused by a power cut, by switching off or rebooting the server machine, or by any number of critical hardware problems. In some circumstances one of the Oracle background processes may fail; this will also trigger an immediate instance failure. Functionally, the effect of an instance failure, for whatever reason, is the same as issuing the SHUTDOWN ABORT command. You may hear people talking about "crashing the database" when they mean issuing a SHUTDOWN ABORT command.

After an instance failure, the database may well be missing committed transactions and storing uncommitted transactions. This is the definition of a corrupted database. This situation arises because the server processes work in memory: they update blocks of data and undo segments in the database buffer cache, not on disk. DBWn then, eventually, writes the changed blocks down to the datafiles. The algorithm that DBWn uses to select which dirty buffers to write is oriented toward performance, and it results in the blocks that are least active getting written first; after all, there would be little point in writing a block that is getting changed every second. But this means that at any given moment there may well be committed transactions that are not yet in the datafiles and uncommitted transactions that have been written: there is no correlation between a COMMIT and a write to the datafiles. But of course, all the changes that have been applied to both data and undo blocks are already in the redo logs.

Remember the description of commit processing detailed in Chapter 9: when you say COMMIT, all that happens is that LGWR flushes the log buffer to the current online redo log files. DBWn does absolutely nothing on COMMIT. So for performance reasons, DBWn writes as little as possible as rarely as possible; this means that the database is always out-of-date. But LGWR writes with a very aggressive algorithm indeed. It writes as nearly as possible in real time, and when you (or anyone else) say COMMIT, it really does write in real time. This is the key to instance recovery. Oracle accepts the fact that the database will be corrupted after an instance failure, but there will always be enough information in the redo log stream on disk to correct the damage.

Instance Recovery

The rules to which a relational database must conform, as formalized in the ACID test, require that it may never lose a committed transaction, and never show an uncommitted transaction. Oracle conforms to the rules perfectly. If the database is corrupted, Oracle will detect the fact and perform instance recovery to remove the corruptions. It will reconstitute any committed transactions that had not been saved to the datafiles at the time of the crash, and it will roll back any uncommitted transactions that had been written to the datafiles. This instance recovery is completely automatic; you can't stop it, even if you want to. If the instance recovery fails, which will only happen if there is media failure as well as an instance failure, you cannot open the database until you have used media recovery techniques to restore and recover the damaged files. The final step of media recovery is automatic instance recovery.

The Mechanics of Instance Recovery

Because instance recovery is completely automatic, it can be dealt with fairly quickly, unlike media recovery, which will take several chapters. In principle, instance recovery is nothing more than using the contents of the online logfiles to rebuild the database buffer cache to the state it was in before the crash. This will replay all changes extracted from the redo logs that refer to blocks that had not been written to disk at the time of the crash. Once this has been done, the database can be opened. At that point, the database is still corrupted, but there is no reason not to allow users to connect, because the instance (which is what users see) has been repaired. This phase of recovery, known as the roll forward, reinstates all changes: changes to data blocks and changes to undo blocks, for both committed and uncommitted transactions. Each redo record has the bare minimum of information needed to reconstruct a change: the block address, and the new values. During roll forward, each redo record is read, the appropriate block is loaded from the datafiles into the database buffer cache, and the change is applied. Then the block is written back to disk.

Once the roll forward is complete, it is as though the crash had never occurred. But at that point, there will be uncommitted transactions in the database—these must be rolled back, and Oracle will do that automatically in the rollback phase of instance recovery. However, that happens after the database has been opened for use. If a user connects and hits some data that needs to be rolled back but hasn't yet been, this is not a problem; the roll forward phase will have populated the undo segment that was protecting the uncommitted transaction, so the server can roll back the change in the normal manner for read consistency.

Instance recovery is automatic, and unavoidable, so how do you invoke it? By issuing a STARTUP command. Remember from Chapter 5, on starting an instance, the description of how SMON opens a database. First, it reads the controlfile when the database transitions to mount mode. Then in the transition to open mode, SMON checks the file headers of all the datafiles and online redo log files. At this point, if there had been an instance failure, it is apparent because the file headers are all out of sync. So SMON goes into the instance recovery routine, and the database is only actually opened after the roll forward phase has completed.

 TIP You never have anything to lose by issuing a STARTUP command. After any sort of crash, try a STARTUP and see how far it gets. It might get all the way.

The Impossibility of Database Corruption

It should now be apparent that there is always enough information in the redo log stream to reconstruct all work done up to the point at which the crash occurred, and furthermore that this includes reconstructing the undo information needed to roll back transactions that were in progress at the time of the crash. But for the final proof, consider this scenario.

User JOHN has started a transaction. He has updated one row of a table with some new values, and his server process has copied the old values to an undo segment. But before these updates were done, his server process wrote out the changes to the log buffer. User DAMIR has also started a transaction. Neither has committed; nothing has been written to disk. If the instance crashed now, there would be no record whatsoever of either transaction, not even in the redo logs. So neither transaction would be recovered, but that is not a problem. Neither was committed, so they should not be recovered: uncommitted work must never be saved.

Then user JOHN commits his transaction. This triggers LGWR to flush the log buffer to the online redo log files, which means that the changes to both the table and the undo segments for both JOHN's transaction and DAMIR's transaction are now in the redo log files, together with a commit record for JOHN's transaction. Only when the write has completed is the "commit complete" message returned to JOHN's user process. But there is still nothing in the datafiles. If the instance fails at this point, the roll forward phase will reconstruct both the transactions, but when all the redo has been processed, there will be no commit record for DAMIR's update; that signals SMON to roll back DAMIR's change, but leave JOHN's in place.

But what if DBWR has written some blocks to disk before the crash? It might be that JOHN (or another user) was continually requerying his data, but that DAMIR had made his uncommitted change and not looked at the data again. DBWn will therefore decide to write DAMIR's changes to disk in preference to JOHN's; DBWn will always tend to write inactive blocks rather than active blocks. So now, the datafiles are storing DAMIR's uncommitted transaction but missing JOHN's committed transaction. This is as bad a corruption as you can have. But think it through. If the instance crashes now— a power cut, perhaps, or a shutdown abort—the roll forward will still be able to sort out the mess. There will always be enough information in the redo stream to reconstruct committed changes; that is obvious, because a commit isn't completed until the write is done. But because LGWR flushes *all* changes to *all* blocks to the logfiles, there will also be enough information to reconstruct the undo segment needed to roll back DAMIR's uncommitted transaction.

So to summarize, because LGWR always writes ahead of DBWn, and because it writes in real time on commit, there will always be enough information in the redo stream to reconstruct any committed changes that had not been written to the datafiles, and to roll back any uncommitted changes that had been written to the datafiles. This instance recovery mechanism of redo and rollback makes it absolutely impossible to corrupt an Oracle database.

 EXAM TIP Can a SHUTDOWN ABORT corrupt the database? Absolutely not! It is impossible to corrupt the database. Nonetheless, it is not good practice.

Tuning Instance Recovery

A critical part of many service level agreements is the MTTR, the mean time to recover after various events. Instance recovery guarantees no corruption, but it may take a considerable time to do its roll forward before the database can be opened. This time is dependent on two factors: how much redo has to be read, and how many read/write operations will be needed on the datafiles as the redo is applied. Both these factors can be controlled by checkpoints.

A *checkpoint* guarantees that as of a particular time, all data changes made up to a particular SCN, or System Change Number, have been written to the datafiles by DBWn. In the event of an instance crash, it is only necessary for SMON to replay the redo generated from the last checkpoint position. All changes, committed or not, made before that position are already in the datafiles; so clearly, there is no need to use redo to reconstruct the transactions committed prior to that. Also, all changes made by uncommitted transactions prior to that point are also in the datafiles, so there is no need to reconstruct undo data prior to the checkpoint position either; it is already available in the undo segment on disk for the necessary rollback.

The more up-to-date the checkpoint position is, the faster the instance recovery. If the checkpoint position is fully up-to-date, no roll forward will be needed at all; the instance can open immediately and go straight into the rollback phase. But there is a heavy price to pay for this. To advance the checkpoint position, DBWn must write changed blocks to disk. Excessive disk I/O will cripple performance. But on the other hand, if you let DBWn get too far behind, so that after a crash SMON has to process hundreds of megabytes of redo and do millions of read/write operations on the datafiles, the MTTR following an instance failure can stretch into hours.

Tuning instance recovery time used to be largely a matter of experiment and guesswork. It has always been easy to tell how long the recovery actually took: just look at your alert log, and you will see the time when the STARTUP command was issued and the time that the startup completed, with information about how many blocks of redo were processed, but until release 9*i* of the database it was almost impossible to calculate in advance. Version 9*i* introduced a new parameter, FAST_START_MTTR_TARGET, that makes controlling instance recovery time a trivial exercise. You specify it in seconds, and Oracle will then ensure that DBWn writes out blocks at a rate sufficiently fast that if the instance crashes, the recovery will take no longer than that number of seconds. So the smaller the setting, the harder DBWn will work in an attempt to minimize the gap between the checkpoint position and real time. But note that it is only a target—you can set it to an unrealistically low value, which, no matter what DBWn does, is impossible to achieve. Database Control also provides an MTTR advisor, which will give you an idea of how long recovery would take if the instance failed. More detailed information can be obtained from the view V$INSTANCE_RECOVERY.

Exercise 18-1: Instance Recovery and the MTTR

This exercise demonstrates the effect of checkpointing on the MTTR following an instance failure.

1. Using SQL*Plus, connect as user SYSTEM.

2. Disable checkpoint tuning by setting the FAST_START_MTTR_TARGET parameter to zero.

   ```
   SQL> alter system set fast_start_mttr_target=0;
   ```

3. Simulate a workload by creating a table and starting a transaction.

   ```
   SQL> create table t1 as select * from all_objects where 1=2;
   SQL> insert into t1 select * from all_objects;
   ```

4. Run a query to see how much work would be required to recover the instance if it crashed right now.

   ```
   SQL> select RECOVERY_ESTIMATED_IOS, ACTUAL_REDO_BLKS, ESTIMATED_MTTR
        from v$instance_recovery;
   ```

   The query shows how many read/write operations would be required on the datafiles and how many blocks on redo would have to be processed during an instance recovery. The ESTIMATED_MTTR column shows, in seconds, how long the recovery would take.

5. Commit the transaction, and re-run the query from Step 2. Note that nothing much has changed: COMMIT has no effect on DBWn and will not advance the checkpoint position.

6. Issue a manual checkpoint.

```
SQL> alter system checkpoint;
```

This may take a few seconds to complete, as DBWn flushes all changed blocks to disk.

7. Re-run the query from Step 2. Note that the RECOVERY_ESTIMATED_IOS and ACTUAL_REDO_BLKS columns have dropped substantially, perhaps to zero. The ESTIMATED_MTTR column may not have reduced, because this column is not updated in real time.

8. Tidy up by dropping the table.

```
SQL> drop table t1;
```

The MTTR Advisor

Database Control has an interface to the FAST_START_MTTR_TARGET parameter, and to the V$INSTANCE_RECOVERY view. From the database home page, take the Advisor Central link and then the MTTR advisor to get a window that displays the current estimated recovery time and gives the option of resetting the parameter (see Figure 18-4).

Configuring a Database for Recoverability

To guarantee maximum recoverability for a database, the controlfiles must be multiplexed; the online redo logs must be multiplexed; the database must be running in archivelog mode, with the archive log files also multiplexed; and finally there must be regular backups, which are the subject of Chapter 19, with more detail in Chapter 24.

Protecting the Controlfile

The controlfile is small, but vital. It is used to mount the database, and while the database is open, the controlfile is continually being read and written. If the controlfile is lost, it is possible to recover; but this is not always easy, and you should never be in that situation, because there should always be at least two copies of the controlfile, on different physical devices.

 EXAM TIP You can have up to eight multiplexed copies of the controlfile.

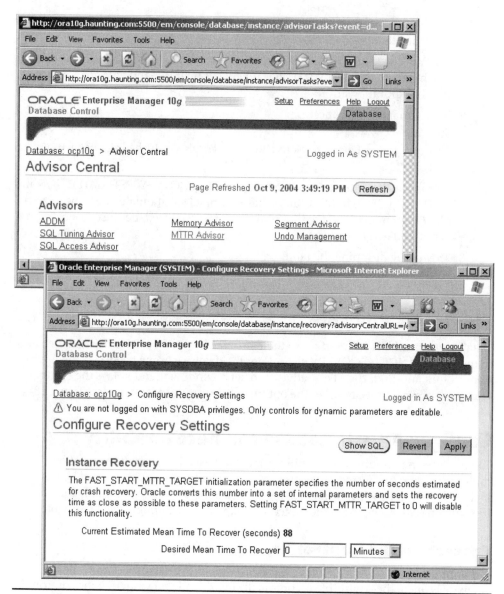

Figure 18-4 The MTTR advisor

In an ideal world, not only will each copy of the controlfile be on a different disk, but each of the disks will be on a different channel and controller if your hardware permits this. However, even if your database is running on a computer with just one disk (on a small PC, for instance) you should still multiplex the controlfile to different directories. There is no general rule saying that two copies is too few, or eight copies is too many, but there will be rules set according to the business requirements for fault tolerance.

TIP Your organization will have standards, such as "every production database will have three controlfiles on three different disks." If your organization does not have such standards, someone should agree and write them. If necessary, you should.

Provided that the controlfile is multiplexed, recovering from media damage that results in the loss of a controlfile is a trivial matter. Oracle ensures that all copies of the controlfile are identical, so just copy a surviving controlfile over the damaged or missing one. But damage to a controlfile does result in downtime. The moment that Oracle detects that a controlfile is damaged or missing, the instance will terminate immediately with an instance failure.

If you create a database with the DBCA, by default you will have three controlfiles, which is probably fine; but they will all be in the same directory, which is not so good. To move or add a controlfile, first shut down the database. No controlfile operations can be done while the database is open. Second, use an operating system command to move or copy the controlfile. Third, edit the CONTROL_FILES parameter to point to the new locations. If you are using a static initSID.ora parameter file, just edit it with any text editor. If you are using a dynamic spfileSID.ora parameter file, start up the database in NOMOUNT mode, and issue an `alter system set control_files=...` command as shown in Figure 18-5. Fourth, open the database as normal.

TIP There are no restrictions on naming for controlfile copies other than whatever is a legal name for your operating system, but you should adhere to some standard. Your organization may well have a standard for this already.

Protecting the Online Redo Log Files

Remember that an Oracle database requires at least two online redo log file groups to function, so that it can switch between them. You may need to add more groups for performance reasons, but two are required. Each group consists of one or more members, which are the physical files. Only one member per group is required for Oracle to function, but at least two members per group are required for safety.

TIP Always have at least two members in each logfile group, for security. This is not just data security; it is job security, too.

The one thing that a DBA is not allowed to do is to lose all copies of the current online logfile group. If that happens, you will lose data. The only way to protect against data loss when you lose all members of the current group is to configure a

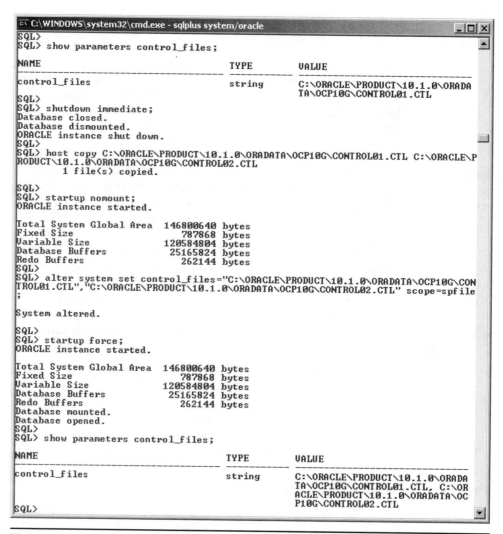

```
C:\WINDOWS\system32\cmd.exe - sqlplus system/oracle                          _ □ ×

SQL>
SQL> show parameters control_files;

NAME                                       TYPE        VALUE
------------------------------------------ ----------- ------------------------------
control_files                              string      C:\ORACLE\PRODUCT\10.1.0\ORADA
                                                       TA\OCP10G\CONTROL01.CTL
SQL>
SQL> shutdown immediate;
Database closed.
Database dismounted.
ORACLE instance shut down.
SQL>
SQL> host copy C:\ORACLE\PRODUCT\10.1.0\ORADATA\OCP10G\CONTROL01.CTL C:\ORACLE\P
RODUCT\10.1.0\ORADATA\OCP10G\CONTROL02.CTL
        1 file(s) copied.

SQL>
SQL> startup nomount;
ORACLE instance started.

Total System Global Area  146800640 bytes
Fixed Size                   787868 bytes
Variable Size             120584804 bytes
Database Buffers           25165824 bytes
Redo Buffers                 262144 bytes
SQL>
SQL> alter system set control_files="C:\ORACLE\PRODUCT\10.1.0\ORADATA\OCP10G\CON
TROL01.CTL","C:\ORACLE\PRODUCT\10.1.0\ORADATA\OCP10G\CONTROL02.CTL" scope=spfile
;

System altered.

SQL>
SQL> startup force;
ORACLE instance started.

Total System Global Area  146800640 bytes
Fixed Size                   787868 bytes
Variable Size             120584804 bytes
Database Buffers           25165824 bytes
Redo Buffers                 262144 bytes
Database mounted.
Database opened.
SQL>
SQL> show parameters control_files;

NAME                                       TYPE        VALUE
------------------------------------------ ----------- ------------------------------
control_files                              string      C:\ORACLE\PRODUCT\10.1.0\ORADA
                                                       TA\OCP10G\CONTROL01.CTL, C:\OR
                                                       ACLE\PRODUCT\10.1.0\ORADATA\OC
                                                       P10G\CONTROL02.CTL
SQL>
```

Figure 18-5   Multiplexing the controlfile

Data Guard environment for zero data loss, which is not a trivial exercise. Why is it so critical that you do not lose all members of the current group? Think about instance recovery. After a crash, SMON will use the contents of the current online logfile group for roll forward recovery, to repair any corruptions in the database. If the current online logfile group is not available, perhaps because it was not multiplexed and media damage has destroyed the one member, then SMON cannot do this. And if SMON cannot correct corruptions with roll forward, you cannot open the database.

Just as with multiplexed copies of the controlfile, the multiple members of a logfile group should ideally be on separate disks, on separate controllers. But when considering disk strategy, think about performance as well as fault tolerance. In the discussion of commit processing in Chapter 9, it was made clear that when a COMMIT is issued, the session will hang until LGWR has flushed the log buffer to disk. Only then is "commit complete" returned to the user process, and the session allowed to continue. This means that writing to the online redo log files is one of the ultimate bottlenecks in the Oracle environment: you cannot do DML faster than LGWR can flush changes to disk. So on a high-throughput system, make sure that your redo log files are on your fastest disks served by your fastest controllers. Related to this, try not to put any datafiles on the same devices; if the one LGWR process has to compete for disk I/O resources with DBWn and many server processes, performance may degrade.

If a member of a redo log file group is damaged or missing, the database will remain open if there is a surviving member. This contrasts with the controlfile, where damage to any copy will crash the database immediately. Similarly, groups can be added or removed and members of groups can be added or moved while the database is open, as long as there are always at least two groups, and each group has at least one valid member.

If you create a database with DBCA, by default you will have three groups, but they will have only one member each. You can add more members (or indeed whole groups) either through Database Control or from the SQL*Plus command line. There are two views that will tell you the state of your redo logs. V$LOG will have one row per group, and V$LOGFILE will have one row per logfile member. Examine Figure 18-6.

Figure 18-6 Online redo log configuration

The first query shows that this database has three logfile groups. The current group—the one LGWR is writing to at the moment—is group 3; the other groups are inactive, meaning first that the LGWR is not writing to them and second that in the event of an instance failure, SMON would not require them for instance recovery. In other words, the checkpoint position has advanced into group 3. The SEQUENCE# column tells us that there have been 94 log switches since the database was created. This number is incremented with each log switch. The MEMBERS column shows that each group consists of only one member—seriously bad news, which should be corrected as soon as possible.

The second query shows the individual online redo log files. Each file is part of one group, identified by GROUP#, and has a unique name. The STATUS column should always be null, as shown. If the member has not yet been used, typically because the database has only just been opened and no log switches have occurred, the status will be STALE; this will be there only until the first log switch. If the status is INVALID, either the member has just been created (in which case it will clear after a log switch into it) or you have a problem.

TIP As with the controlfile, Oracle does not enforce any naming convention for logfiles, but most organizations will have standards for this.

Then there is an

```
alter system switch logfile;
```

command to force a log switch, which would happen automatically eventually if there were any DML in progress once the current group was full. The log switch, either automatic or manual, causes the LGWR to start writing out redo data to the next online logfile group.

The last query shows that after the log switch, group 1 is now the current group that LGWR is writing to at log switch sequence number 95. The previously current group, group 3, has status ACTIVE. This means that it would still be needed by SMON for instance recovery if the instance failed now. In a short time, as the checkpoint position advances, it will become INACTIVE. Issuing an

```
alter system checkpoint;
```

command would force the checkpoint position to come up-to-date, and group 3 would then be inactive immediately.

The number of members per group is restricted by settings in the controlfile, determined at database creation time. Turn back to Chapter 3 and the CREATE DATABASE command called by the CreateDB.sql script; the MAXLOGFILES directive limits the number of groups that this database can have, and the MAXLOGMEMBERS directive limits the maximum number of members of each group. The DBCA defaults for these (16 and 3 respectively) may well be suitable for most databases, but if they prove to be inappropriate, it is possible to re-create the controlfile with different values. However, as with all controlfile operations, this will require downtime.

Exercise 18-2: Multiplexing the Redo Log

This exercise will add a member to each online redo log group through Database Control and then confirm the addition from SQL*Plus. The assumption is that there is currently only one member per group, and that you have three groups; if your groups are configured differently, adjust the instructions accordingly.

1. Using Database Control, log on as user SYSTEM.

2. From the database home page, take the Administration tab, and then the Redo Log Groups link in the Storage section.

3. Select the first group, and click Edit.

4. In the Redo Log Members section, click Add. The Add Redo Log Member page appears.

5. Enter a filename **REDO01b.LOG** for the new member for group 1.

6. Click Continue.

7. Click Show SQL and study the command that will be executed, and then click Return.

8. Click Apply to execute the command—or Revert if you would rather return to Step 4.

9. Take the Redo Log Groups link at the top of the screen to the Redo Log Groups window, and repeat Steps 3–8 for the other groups.

10. Using SQL*Plus, connect as user SYSTEM and issue these queries to confirm the creation of the new members:

    ```
    SQL> select group#,sequence#,members,status from v$log;
    SQL> select group#,status,member from v$logfile;
    ```

    The result will show the new members with status INVALID. This is not a problem; it happens merely because they have never been used.

11. Issue the following command three times, to cycle through all your logfile groups:

    ```
    SQL> alter system switch logfile;
    ```

12. Reissue the second query in Step 10 to confirm that the status of all your logfile group members is now null.

Archivelog Mode and the Archiver Process

Oracle guarantees that your database is never corrupted, through the use of the online redo log files to repair any corruptions caused by an instance failure. This is automatic, and unavoidable. But to guarantee no loss of data following a media failure, it is necessary to have a record of all changes applied to the database since the last backup of the database; this is not enabled by default. The online redo log files are overwritten as log switches occur; the transition to archivelog mode ensures that no online redo log file is overwritten unless it has been copied as an archive log first. Thus there will be a series of archive log files that represent a complete history of all changes ever applied to the database. If a datafile is damaged at any time, it will then be possible to restore a backup of the datafile and apply the changes from the archive log redo stream to bring it up-to-date. By default, a database is created in noarchivelog mode; this means that online redo log files are overwritten by log switches with no copy being made first. It is still impossible to corrupt the database, but data could be lost if the datafiles are damaged by media failure. Once the database is transitioned to archivelog mode, it is impossible to lose data as well—provided that all the archive log files generated since the last backup are available.

Once a database is converted to archivelog mode, a new background process will start, automatically. This is the archiver process, ARCn. By default Oracle will start two of these processes, but you can have up to ten. In earlier releases of the database it was necessary to start this process either with a SQL*Plus command or by setting the initialization parameter LOG_ARCHIVE_START, but a 10g instance will automatically start the archiver if the database is in archivelog mode.

TIP In archivelog mode, recovery is possible with no loss of data up to and including the last commit. Most production databases are run in archivelog mode.

The archiver will copy the online redo log files to an archive log file after each log switch, thus generating a continuous chain of logfiles that can be used for recovering a backup. The name and location of these archive log files is controlled by initialization parameters. For safety the archive logfiles can be multiplexed, just as the online logfiles can be multiplexed, but eventually, they should be migrated to offline storage, such as a tape library. The Oracle instance takes care of creating the archive logs with the ARCn process, but the migration to tape must be controlled by the DBA, either through operating system commands or by using the Recovery Manager utility RMAN (described in later chapters) or another third-party backup software package.

The transition to archivelog mode can be done only while the database is in mount mode after a clean shutdown, and it must be done by a user with a SYSDBA connection. It is also necessary to set the initialization parameters that control the names and locations of the archive logs generated. Clearly, these names must be unique, or archive logs could be overwritten by other archive logs. To ensure unique filenames, it is possible to embed variables such as the log switch sequence number in the archive log file names (see Table 18-1).

The minimum archiving necessary to ensure that recovery from a restored backup will be possible is to set one archive destination. But for safety, it will usually be a

Variable	Description
%d	A unique database identifier, necessary if multiple databases are being archived to the same directories.
%t	The thread number, visible as the THREAD# column in V$INSTANCE. This is not significant, except in a RAC database.
%r	The incarnation number. This is important if an incomplete recovery has been done, as described in Chapter 27.
%s	The log switch sequence number. This will guarantee that the archives from any one database do not overwrite each other.

Table 18-1 Variables That May Be Used to Embed Unique Values in Archive Log File Names

requirement to multiplex the archive log files by specifying two or more destinations, ideally on different disks served by different controllers. From 9*i* onward, it is possible to specify up to ten archive destinations, giving you ten copies of each filled online redo log file. This is perhaps excessive for safety. One archive destination? Good idea. Two destinations? Sure, why not. But *ten*? This is to do with Data Guard. For the purposes of this book and the OCP exam, an archive log destination will always be a directory on the machine hosting the database, and two destinations on local disks will usually be sufficient. But the destination can be an Oracle Net alias, specifying the address of a listener on a remote computer. This is the key to zero data loss: the redo stream can be shipped across the network to a remote database, where it can be applied to give a real-time backup. Furthermore, the remote database can (if desired) be configured and opened as a data warehouse, meaning that all the query processing can be offloaded from the primary database to a secondary database optimized for such work.

Exercise 18-3: Transition the Database to Archivelog Mode

Convert your database to archivelog mode, and set parameters to enable archiving to two destinations. The instructions for setting parameters in Step 3 assume that you are using a dynamic spfile; if your instance is using a static pfile, make the edits manually instead.

1. Create two directories with appropriate operating system commands. For example, on Windows,

```
c:\> md c:\oracle\archive1
c:\> md c:\oracle\archive2
```

or on Unix,

```
$ mkdir /oracle/archive1
$ mkdir /oracle/archive2
```

2. Connect with SQL*Plus as user SYS with the SYSDBA privilege.

```
SQL> connect / as sysdba
```

3. Set the parameters to nominate two destination directories created in Step 1 and to control the archive log file names. Note that it is necessary to include a trailing slash character on the directory names (a backslash on Windows).

```
SQL> alter system set log_archive_dest_1='location=/oracle/archive1/' scope=spfile;
SQL> alter system set log_archive_dest_2='location=/oracle/archive2/' scope=spfile;
SQL> alter system set log_archive_format='arch_%d_%t_%r_%s.log' scope=spfile;
```

4. Shut down the database cleanly.

```
SQL> shutdown immediate;
```

5. Start up in mount mode.

```
SQL> startup mount;
```

6. Convert the database to archivelog mode.

```
SQL> alter database archivelog;
```

7. Open the database.

```
SQL> alter database open;
```

8. Confirm that the database is in archivelog mode and that the archiver is running with these two queries.

```
SQL> select log_mode from v$database;
SQL> select archiver from v$instance;
```

9. Force a log switch.

```
SQL> alter system switch logfile;
```

10. The log switch will have forced an archive to both the destinations. Confirm this from within the Oracle environment with this query:

```
SQL> select name from v$archived_log;
```

and then from an operating system prompt confirm that the files listed by this query were in fact created.

Chapter Review

This chapter covered the concepts and architecture that underpin Oracle's recovery capabilities. A thorough understanding of this is essential before proceeding to the details of backup and recovery techniques. You have seen the various types of failure that can occur, and how the database and the DBA manage them. In particular, the instance recovery mechanism makes it absolutely impossible to corrupt an Oracle database. Then the mechanism of archiving makes it impossible to lose data, provided that you do not lose your current, unarchived, online redo log file group, and that you have adequate backups. To protect the online redo logs, you should multiplex them onto different disks. It is also good practice to multiplex the controlfile and the archive log files.

Questions

1. Which of the following files should be multiplexed, for safety? (Choose two answers).

    A. Archive log files

    B. Controlfile

    C. Initialization file

    D. System tablespace datafiles

2. You want to add a controlfile copy. Which of these sequences is correct and sufficient? (Choose the best answer.)

    A. Copy the controlfile, and issue an `alter system...` command to change the CONTROL_FILES parameter.

    B. Mount the database to read the controlfile, and issue an `alter database...` command to add a new copy.

    C. Copy the controlfile, shut down the database, start up in nomount mode, issue an `alter system...` command to change the CONTROL_FILES parameter, and open the database.

    D. Start up in nomount mode, copy the controlfile, issue an `alter system...` command to change the CONTROL_FILES parameter, and open the database.

    E. Issue an `alter system...` command to change the CONTROL_FILES parameter, shut down the database, copy the controlfile, and start up the database.

3. You want to multiplex a redo log group. Will this involve downtime? (Choose the best answer.)

    A. Yes, because logfiles can't be manipulated while the database is open.

    B. No, you can always reconfigure logfiles online.

    C. No, if your database is in archivelog mode.

    D. Yes, because database logging is controlled by static parameters.

4. If an online logfile gets damaged, what might happen next? (Choose the best answer.)

    A. The instance will terminate as soon as the corruption is detected.

    B. The instance will continue to run, if the group is multiplexed.

    C. If you have more than two surviving logfile groups, the instance will continue to run.

    D. The instance will terminate, unless you are in archivelog mode.

5. If your database is in archivelog mode, how can you force an archive?

   A. Issue an alter database switch `logfile` command.

   B. Issue an alter system switch `logfile` command.

   C. Issue an alter system `log_archive_start` command.

   D. There is no command to force an archive; they happen automatically.

6. You are concerned that performance is poor. What might you do to address this? (Choose two answers.)

   A. Increase the FAST_START_MTTR_TARGET setting.

   B. Reduce the FAST_START_MTTR_TARGET setting.

   C. Carry out manual checkpoints, to advance the checkpoint position.

   D. Give each logfile group its own disk, to avoid contention between groups.

   E. Ensure that members of the same redo group are on separate disks.

   F. Take the database out of archivelog mode.

7. After a crash, you issue a STARTUP command. Put the events that follow in the correct order:

   A. Normal users can connect.

   B. SMON carries out roll forward.

   C. SMON performs rollback.

   D. The instance starts in nomount mode.

   E. The database is mounted.

   F. The database is opened.

8. Which of the following circumstances could result in a corrupted database? (Choose the best answer.)

   A. Loss of all copies of the current logfile group

   B. Loss of all copies of the controlfile

   C. A crash during an instance recovery

   D. Loss of the system tablespace and the undo tablespace

   E. None. It is impossible to corrupt an Oracle database.

9. Neither your controlfile, nor your online logs, nor your archive logs are multiplexed. To multiplex them, which will require downtime? (Choose the best answer.)

   A. Archive logs

   B. Controlfile

   C. Redo logs

   D. None. All these operations can be done online.

10. You are using SQL*Plus from a PC, and the PC reboots while you are in the middle of a transaction. What will happen at the server side? (Choose the best answer.)

    A. Your server process will detect the problem and roll back the transaction.

    B. SMON will detect the problem and roll back the transaction.

    C. PMON will detect the problem and roll back the transaction.

    D. The SQL*Plus auto-commit will commit your transaction.

    E. The statement you were executing will be rolled back, but the rest of the transaction will remain intact.

11. On querying V$LOG, you see that you have one logfile group whose status is "ACTIVE." Which of the following statements are true? (Choose two answers.)

    A. This is the group to which LGWR is writing redo.

    B. In the event of a crash, SMON would use this group for recovery.

    C. The group has not yet been archived.

    D. Completing a checkpoint would change the status to null.

    E. This group was in use before the last log switch.

12. While executing a multirow update statement, you hit a constraint violation. What will happen next?

    A. The update that hit the problem will be rolled back, but the rest of the statement will remain intact.

    B. The whole statement will be rolled back.

    C. The whole transaction will be rolled back.

    D. It depends on whether you have issued the `alter session enable resumable` command.

13. From the following table, match the appropriate solution to each possible problem.

Problem	Solution
A. Accidentally dropping a table	a. Mirroring with RAID
B. Committing a bad transaction	b. Enable resumable
C. Datafiles filling up	c. Flashback drop
D. Deleting a datafile	d. Flashback query
E. Losing a disk	e. Restore and recover
F. Omitting a "where" clause on a delete	f. Rollback

14. A multiplexed copy of the controlfile gets damaged while the instance is shut down. Which of the following statements is true? (Choose the best answer.)

   A. The database can be opened immediately if there is a surviving copy of the controlfile.

   B. In mount mode, you can change the CONTROL_FILES parameter to remove the reference to the damaged copy of the controlfile, and then open the database.

   C. You can replace the damaged file with a surviving copy of the controlfile and then open the database.

   D. After restoring the controlfile, SMON will recover it as part of the instance recovery process.

15. The MTTR advisor will tell you.... (Choose two answers.)

   A. The estimated MTTR

   B. The value of the FAST_START_MTTR_TARGET parameter

   C. What the FAST_START_MTTR_TARGET should be set to

   D. How the MTTR will change, depending on the rate of redo generation

   E. How many I/Os on datafiles and how much redo would be processed in the event of an instance failure

Answers

1. **A, B.** You can, and should, also multiplex your online redo log files. You can't multiplex the initialization file or any datafiles, except through hardware mirroring techniques.

2. **E.** Physical operations on the controlfile may be carried out only while the database is closed, and note that because the CONTROL_FILES parameter is static, the "`alter system...`" command must specify "`... scope=spfile`".

3. **B.** The online redo log can always be managed while the database is open (unlike the controlfile).

4. **B.** As long as there is at least one surviving member of each online redo log file group, the database can remain open. It will terminate only if every member of a group is damaged—or if the only member of a non-multiplexed group is damaged.

5. **B.** A log switch will force an archive, and you effect a log switch with `alter system...`, not `alter database....`

6. **A and E.** You must ensure that members of the same redo group are on separate disks to avoid the contention that arises between members of the same group.

Increasing the FAST_START_MTTR_TARGET setting may also help, by reducing the pressure on DBWn, though instance recovery times may suffer.

7. **D, E, B, F, A, C.** The roll forward is done in mount mode, then the rollback is done after the database is opened for use.

8. **E.** It is impossible to corrupt an Oracle database: the mechanism of undo and redo guarantees that incomplete transactions will always be rolled back and that committed transactions will always survive.

9. **B.** It is only the controlfile that cannot be manipulated while the database is open.

10. **C.** A part of PMON's role is to detect this exact type of problem and to tidy up after a session fails because of problems with the user process.

11. **B and E.** The checkpoint position has not yet advanced through the ACTIVE group and on to the CURRENT group; therefore both groups would be needed in the event of a recovery being necessary. Generally, the only ACTIVE group will be that in use just prior to the last switch.

12. **B.** The whole statement will be rolled back, but any earlier statements in the transaction remain intact and uncommitted.

13. **A-c; B-d; C-b; D-e; E-a; F-f**

14. **C.** All copies of the controlfile are identical, so you can replace the damaged file with a surviving copy of the controlfile and then open the database.

15. **A and B.** The mean-time-to-recover advisor tells you how long it would take to open the database if it were to crash right now, and the current setting of the FAST_START_MTTR_TARGET instance parameter. Ideally, the former will always be less than the latter.

CHAPTER 19

Backing Up an Oracle Database

In this chapter you will learn how to
- Create consistent database backups
- Back up your database without shutting it down
- Create incremental backups
- Automate database backups
- Monitor the flash recovery area
- Describe the difference between image copies and backup sets
- Describe the different types of database backups
- Back up a controlfile to trace
- Manage backups

The second part of the OCP curriculum goes into great detail on backup and recovery options and techniques. For the first exam, it is only necessary to be familiar with some theory and with basic use of Database Control to carry out a backup, as described in this chapter, and simple restore and recovery, as described in Chapter 20. But as you study this material, remember that there is much more information to come.

Backup Tools

Backups can be made using straightforward operating system utilities, such as copy or WinZip on Windows, or cp, tar, or cpio on Unix. However, Oracle strongly recommends the use of the Recovery Manager, RMAN. RMAN is now in its fourth generation. Originally introduced with release 8.0—and perfectly functional then—it has been substantially enhanced through releases 8i, 9i, and now 10g. A persistent problem with RMAN was the user interface, but it is fair to say that all UI problems have been fixed in 10g. In later chapters you will see some advanced features that are better accessed from the RMAN command line, but basic backup and recovery can now be done through the Database Control RMAN interface.

One particular feature of RMAN is its integration with third-party tape libraries. Large computer installations will have one or more tape robots. These are very expensive pieces of equipment that may be fitted with many tape drives and storage for thousands of tape cartridges. The tape robot will be controlled by software capable of automatically locating and loading tapes as needed for any backup and restore operation. The ideal situation is that the physical realities of device drivers, tape cartridge locations, filenames, and so on be completely invisible to anyone making use of the tape library; RMAN can provide this abstraction, provided that your system administrators installed the appropriate drivers, which will be supplied by the manufacturer of the tape library. Thus RMAN can be integrated with all the popular tape library control systems, such as those sold by Compaq, IBM, or Veritas, to give the DBA complete control of the tape library, without him needing to know anything about it.

RMAN can back up datafiles, the controlfile, archive logs, and the server parameter file (the spfile). The backups can go to disk or tape. There is a fully functional and platform-independent scripting language, as well as a published API.

To conclude this discussion, Oracle provides backup and recovery capabilities using standard operating system commands, or using RMAN—but RMAN is the recommended tool and the one this book and the OCP exam focus on. RMAN can be used as a transparent interface to a third-party tape library control system, allowing you to automate completely the backup and recovery process. There are both command-line and graphical interfaces to RMAN; at this point, you will study the graphical interface provided by Database Control. The command-line interface will come later.

Concepts and Terminology

There are many options for your backup and recovery strategy, some of which are available only through RMAN backups, while others are available when using operating commands as well. Furthermore, some options are available only if your database is running in archivelog mode. But first, a summary of the various concepts and terms used in the Oracle environment to describe different types of backups.

Whole or Partial Backups

The first choice to be made is whether a backup should be of the entire database, or just a part of it. A *whole* backup is a backup of all the datafiles, the controlfile, and (if you are using it) the spfile. Remember that as all multiplexed copies of the controlfile are identical, it is necessary to back up only one of them. You do not back up the online redo logs! Online redo log files are protected by multiplexing, and optionally, by archiving. Also, note that only datafiles for permanent tablespaces can be backed up. The tempfiles used for your temporary tablespaces cannot be backed up by RMAN, nor can they be put into backup mode for an operating system backup.

A *partial* backup will include one or more datafiles and/or the controlfile. A partial backup will, inevitably, not be synchronized with the rest of the database. It is a copy of just a part of the database, at a particular moment in time. If it is ever necessary to restore a file from a partial backup, it will have to be synchronized with the rest of the database before it can be used. This means applying changes from the archived and online redo log files to bring it up to date.

 EXAM TIP Partial backups are valid only if your database is in archivelog mode.

Whole or partial backups can be made with RMAN or with operating system commands, while the database is open or closed. But if a partial backup is to be valid—whichever tool you use—the database must be running in archivelog mode. Partial backups of a database in noarchivelog mode are useless, except for very specific purposes such as transporting datafiles to a different database. As a general rule, if your database is not running in archivelog mode, you must always do whole backups.

Full or Incremental Backups

A *full* backup, which may be whole or partial, is a complete copy of one or more datafiles. Every block of the datafile is backed up. An *incremental* backup is a backup of just some of the blocks of a datafile: only the blocks that have been changed or added since the last full backup will be included. This is an example of where RMAN is superior to operating system utilities. RMAN is an Oracle product and is therefore capable of identifying changes within datafiles. Whenever a block is updated, the SCN of the change is embedded in the block header; this means that RMAN can determine which blocks have changed since the last full backup was done. So far as the operating system is concerned, if there has been any change to the file—perhaps just one block out of millions—then the file has been updated, and the whole thing must be backed up.

 EXAM TIP Incremental backups can be done only with RMAN, not with operating system commands.

Incremental backups will generally be much smaller than full backups, and they may be significantly faster. Either way, the strain on your tape I/O systems will be much reduced. Many system administrators try to avoid incremental backups because in the event of a restore operation they have to ensure that the correct full backup is located, and then the appropriate incremental backups applied. The bookkeeping necessary to keep track of a system of full and incremental backups can be awkward to maintain. RMAN makes this process completely automatic. There is no need to track which tapes contain which full or incremental backup—RMAN knows, and if it is linked to a tape library, it will load the appropriate tapes and extract and apply the appropriate backups without any user intervention at all.

Incremental backups can be done whether the database is open or closed, and whether it is in archivelog or noarchivelog mode. But they can be done only by RMAN.

 TIP A number of third-party products claim to be able to back up Oracle databases. In most cases, they make use of RMAN.

Offline or Online Backups

An *offline* backup is a backup taken while the database is closed. You may hear offline backups referred to as "closed," "cold," or "consistent" backups. The term "closed" is self-explanatory, and "cold" is just slang, but "consistent" requires an understanding of the Oracle architecture. For a datafile to be consistent, every block in the datafile must have been checkpointed and closed. In normal running, the datafiles are inconsistent: a number of blocks will have been copied into the database buffer cache, updated, and not yet written back to disk. The datafile itself, on disk, is therefore not consistent with the real-time state of the database; some parts of it will be out of date. To make a datafile consistent, all changed blocks must be flushed to disk, and the datafile closed. As a general rule, this happens only when the database is shut down cleanly, with the IMMEDIATE, TRANSACTIONAL, or NORMAL shutdown options.

An *online* backup is a backup taken while the database is in use. Other terms for online backups are "open," "hot," or "inconsistent" backups. A datafile that is backed up online will not be synchronized with any particular SCN, nor is it synchronized with the other datafiles or the controlfile. It is backed up while it is in use: being read from by server processes, and written to by DBWn.

Online backups can be whole or partial, be full or incremental, and be carried out with RMAN or with operating system commands. But they can only be done if the database is in archivelog mode. There is absolutely no reason to take the database down for backups. Provided you are running in archivelog mode, online backups are all you will ever need. Online backups are the key to Oracle's capability to run nonstop for months or even years and vital to meeting MTBF targets. There may be a performance drop during an online backup because of the additional disk activity, but apart from that there is no reason for your user community to know anything about it.

Online backups can be done with operating system commands, but this is another case where RMAN is a superior tool. Consider what actually happens if you copy a file with an operating system utility while the file is in use. Take an example where the operating system block size is 512 bytes (the default on many Unix and Windows systems) but the Oracle block size, as determined by the DB_BLOCK_SIZE parameter, is 8KB. Each Oracle block will comprise sixteen operating system blocks.

In this scenario, you initiate an operating system copy, perhaps using the Windows copy command. If the file is many megabytes big, this copy will take several seconds or minutes to complete, and during that time it is more than likely that DBWn will flush some changed blocks from the database buffer cache to the datafile; the file is being changed while it is being copied. The granularity of the operating system copy is the operating system block, but the granularity of the DBWn write is the Oracle block. It is thus possible that the copy command will take the first part of an Oracle block, then DBWn will overwrite the whole Oracle block, and finally the copy command will take the remaining part of the Oracle block. Thus the output file produced by the copy will include what is called a "fractured" block: parts of it will represent different versions. Such a block is completely useless: you have a data corruption.

If you are using operating system utilities to perform online backups, you avoid this problem by putting the tablespace containing the datafile into backup mode, with an ALTER TABLESPACE...BEGIN BACKUP command, for the duration of the copy, as shown in Figure 19-1. From that point on, whenever a server process updates a block in the database buffer cache, rather than writing out the minimal change to the log buffer, it will write out the complete block image to the log buffer. This block image will be read-consistent. Then if it is ever necessary to restore the datafile, any fractured blocks can be replaced with a read-consistent image of the block extracted from the redo logs. Thus you accept that an online backup will have fractured blocks, but Oracle can repair them if necessary. The downside of this is that the rate of redo generation may accelerate astronomically while the tablespace is in backup mode: one whole block, perhaps 16KB, for each change, instead of just a few bytes. You may find that you are log-switching thirty times an hour rather than thirty times a day when you put tablespaces into backup mode, with a consequent drop in performance.

By contrast, online backups with RMAN do not have this problem. RMAN is an Oracle tool and can therefore be aware of what is happening. If RMAN detects that DBWn has updated a block while it was being copied—which is obvious, because the block header SCN will have changed—RMAN will try again, until it gets a read-consistent image of the block.

 EXAM TIP Online backups can only be done if your database is running in archivelog mode.

Online backups can be full or incremental, and they can be done with operating system utilities or RMAN—but there is no doubt that RMAN is superior. Furthermore, online backups can only be done if the database is in archivelog mode. Whichever tool you choose, an online backup will not be synchronized with any particular SCN, nor with the other datafiles and the controlfiles. Online and archived redo log files will always be needed to bring a restored online backup into synchronization with the rest of the database.

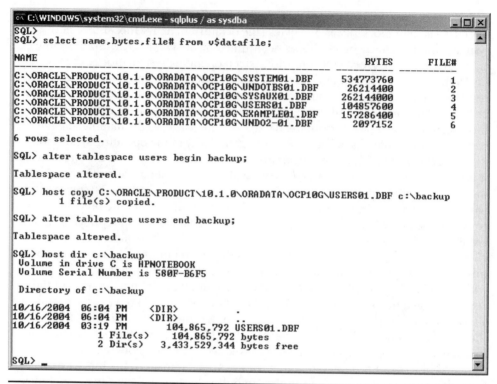

Figure 19-1 Online backup with operating system utilities

Image Copies or Backup Sets

The final terms to become familiar with before looking at the mechanics of backing up are image copies and backup sets. An *image copy* is a backup of a file that is byte for byte the same as the source file. Clearly, an image copy cannot be an incremental backup, nor can it be made to a tape device; in either of these cases, the output file would not be the same as the input file. When taking backups with operating system utilities, unless you use utilities that compress the data or stream it directly to tape, the output files will be image copies. Image copies can be made of datafiles, the controlfile, and the archived logs while the database is open or closed, but as ever, you do not back up the online logs.

A *backup set* is a proprietary structure generated by RMAN. It is a logical structure consisting of one or more physical files, known as *pieces*, which contains one or more database files, which may be datafiles, controlfiles, or archive log files. These three different file types can be combined in one backup set if you wish. The backup set format can be decoded only by RMAN. Thus, once you commit to using RMAN to produce backup sets, you can only ever restore by using RMAN to extract files from your backup sets. However, RMAN can also make image copies. RMAN-generated

PART I

image copies of datafiles, controlfiles, or archive logs will be indistinguishable from image copies made with an operating system command, and if for some reason you want to restore them using operating system commands rather than RMAN, you can do so. Figure 19-2 shows an example of creating a backup set with RMAN.

RMAN backup sets have a number of advantages over image copies, whether you generate the image copies with RMAN or not. Unlike image copies, backup sets can hold incremental backups. But even for a full backup, the pieces that make up the backup set will usually be significantly smaller than image copies. This is because a backup set never contains empty blocks. As RMAN passes through the datafiles, it simply skips blocks that have never been used. A related advantage is that if you wish, you can enable data compression within a backup set. This compression will normally be more efficient than using whatever compression is provided by your operating system or your tape library, because the compression algorithms are optimized for Oracle data formats. Also, RMAN can stream backup sets directly to tape, if you have installed the RMAN drivers for your tape library. This avoids the need to stage the data on disk. While it may be nice to have a disk-based backup because of speed of restore, for large systems it is usually impractical.

 EXAM TIP Image copies can go only to disk. Backup sets can go to disk or tape.

```
C:\WINDOWS\system32\cmd.exe - rman target /                        _ □ ×

RMAN>

RMAN> backup as backupset datafile
2> 'C:\ORACLE\PRODUCT\10.1.0\ORADATA\OCP10G\USERS01.DBF'
3> format 'c:\backup\rman_backup_users01.dbf';

Starting backup at 16-OCT-04
using channel ORA_DISK_1
channel ORA_DISK_1: starting full datafile backupset
channel ORA_DISK_1: specifying datafile(s) in backupset
input datafile fno=00004 name=C:\ORACLE\PRODUCT\10.1.0\ORADATA\OCP10G\USERS01.DB
F
channel ORA_DISK_1: starting piece 1 at 16-OCT-04
channel ORA_DISK_1: finished piece 1 at 16-OCT-04
piece handle=C:\BACKUP\RMAN_BACKUP_USERS01.DBF comment=NONE
channel ORA_DISK_1: backup set complete, elapsed time: 00:00:16
Finished backup at 16-OCT-04

RMAN> host "dir c:\backup";

 Volume in drive C is HPNOTEBOOK
 Volume Serial Number is 580F-B6F5

 Directory of c:\backup

10/16/2004  06:12 PM    <DIR>          .
10/16/2004  06:12 PM    <DIR>          ..
10/16/2004  06:12 PM         4,022,272 RMAN_BACKUP_USERS01.DBF
10/16/2004  03:19 PM       104,865,792 USERS01.DBF
               2 File(s)    108,888,064 bytes
               2 Dir(s)   3,421,454,336 bytes free
host command complete

RMAN> _
```

Figure 19-2 Online backup to a backup set; note the output file size

Both image copies and backup sets of datafiles, controlfile, and archive logs can be online or offline; whole or partial; full or incremental; and made in both archivelog and noarchivelog modes—but backup sets can be generated or restored from only by RMAN.

RMAN Settings

Database Control includes a graphical interface for RMAN that takes you through the process of configuring general settings that will apply to every backup taken, and then settings specific to each backup. There is also an interface to Oracle's scheduling mechanism, which can be used to establish a regular series of backups, such as a whole backup once a week and incremental backups with archive log files once a day. RMAN will run out of the box with no configuration whatsoever, but generally you will adjust a number of settings to your own requirements. For example, the default backup destination is to a disk directory, which may not be suitable. To reach the RMAN interface, from the Database Control database home page take the Maintenance tab and then the Configure Backup Settings link in the Backup/Recovery section to reach the Configure Backup Settings window, which has three tabs: Device, Backup Set, and Policy.

Device Settings

The options for disk backups are the degree of parallelism, the target directory, and whether to generate backup sets or image copies. Parallelism defaults to 1; this means that the RMAN process (which in many ways is a user process like any other) will spawn just one server process, known as a *channel*, to actually create the backup. When selecting a degree of parallelism, points to consider are the number of CPUs and the nature of the disk subsystem. There would be little point in launching numerous channels on a single CPU system with one disk. Even on multiple-CPU computers with striped file systems, you should still be wary of the impact on other users: for an offline backup, you will want the backup to proceed as fast as possible, but for online backups it may be better to slow down the backup in order to limit the amount of resources it will consume. The disk backup location can be any directory; if left blank, it will default to whatever is set by the DB_RECOVERY_FILE_DEST parameter, which will itself have defaulted to the flash_recovery_area directory in your ORACLE_HOME. The next option is whether to generate image copies or backup sets, and if backup sets, then whether to compress the data.

The options for tape backups specify the number of tape drives, any options specific to a tape library, and whether to compress the backup sets. Remember that it is impossible to generate image copies to tape; a tape file is simply not the same as a disk file, so image copies are not an option. Specifying the number of tape drives is equivalent to specifying the degree of parallelism for a disk backup. Your tape library may have a number of drives, and you can choose whether to use some or all of them. This is a matter for negotiation with the system administrators. A tape library is a very expensive piece of equipment, and it may well not be used exclusively for Oracle backups. The system administrators may not be pleased with you if take control of the whole thing, leaving no drives available for other operations that are not related to Oracle.

 TIP There can be political problems with using RMAN. Traditionally, it has been the system administrators who do backups, but with RMAN much of that responsibility transfers to the DBA. Be careful of appearing to take over the system administrators' job.

Then whether you are doing tape or disk backups, in the Host Credentials section you must specify an operating system logon to the machine hosting the database. This is because the RMAN channel(s) will have to assume an operating system identity in order to read and write to the backup destination, be it a directory or a tape library. The operating system identity you give will have to be configured by your system administrators with appropriate permissions on the devices.

Having set up the host credentials, you can test the configuration by clicking the Test Disk Backup and Test Tape Backup buttons. These will check that the devices actually exist, and that using the provided host logon, RMAN can read and write to them.

Backup Set Settings

The first option on the Backup Set Settings tab is the Maximum Backup Piece Size. By default, this is unlimited: the whole backup set will be stored physically in one piece, or file. The size of a backup set cannot be known until the backup is actually known, because RMAN does not back up unused blocks. Use of compression and incrementals makes the size even less predictable. A single file might well be inconveniently large if you are backing up many datafiles and archive logs. For disk backups, your operating system may have limits on the maximum file size, and for tape backups there will certainly be limits on the size of the tape cartridges. In discussion with your system administrators, the maximum piece size needs to be set to something that can be managed sensibly.

You can also specify multiplexing of backup sets, by specifying multiple copies. RMAN will then create multiple copies of each backup set. If your backup destinations are not protected by RAID (in the case of disk backups) or tape mirroring (in the case of tape backups), this gives you an extra level of security.

Policy Settings

The first option on the Policy Settings tab is whether to back up the controlfile and the server parameter (spfile) file whenever a backup of anything else is taken. This is generally considered to be good policy. These are small files, and you can never have too many copies of them. By enabling this auto-backup capability, you can be certain that you will always have an up-to-date copy of these two critical files. The default destination is the DB_RECOVERY_FILE_DEST parameter.

The next option is whether to optimize backups by excluding files that have not changed since the last backup. In practice, this means that any datafiles that are offline or flagged as read-only will be backed up only once and should therefore reduce the time and volume of subsequent backup operations.

Then there is an option "Enable block change tracking for faster incremental backups." This is a new feature of release 10g that can have a huge impact on the time an incremental backup will take. In earlier releases, incremental backups would be much smaller than full backups, but they were not necessarily any faster. This was because RMAN would still have to read the whole datafile in order to determine which blocks had been changed. By checking this option, you start the Change Tracking Writer (or CTWR) background process. This process will write out to a block change tracking file the address of every block that is updated. Then when doing an incremental backup, RMAN can read this file to determine which blocks actually need to be backed up. These blocks can be read with direct access rather than full file scans, thus dramatically reducing the disk I/O workload. This capability can also be initiated from the SQL*Plus command line with an ALTER DATABASE command as shown in Figure 19-3.

The Tablespaces Excluded From Whole Database Backup section lets you nominate one or more tablespaces that should not be backed up during a whole backup operation. Suitable candidates for this would be read-only tablespaces, or perhaps tablespaces whose contents can be easily re-created by means other than a restore. These might be tablespaces containing tables of temporary data, or data that is regularly reloaded through batch operations, or even tablespaces dedicated to indexes that can be regenerated quickly.

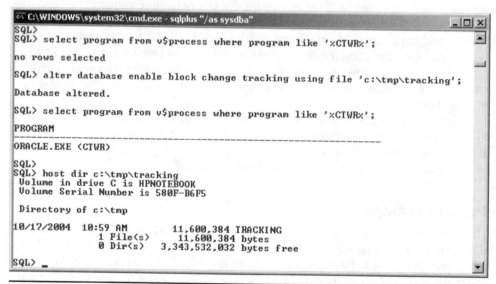

Figure 19-3 Enabling block change tracking for fast incremental backups

Finally, there is the Retention Policy section. RMAN can automatically remove backups that it considers no longer necessary, according to a backup retention policy. The default retention policy is that RMAN will make sure that it has one copy of everything: all the datafiles and each archive log. Using various RMAN commands that are dealt with in detail later, you can list the objects that RMAN thinks need to be backed up (by default, those that have never been backed up, not even once) or instruct RMAN to delete all backups that it considers redundant (by default, all those where there is at least one more recent backup). A more sophisticated retention policy option is the recovery window policy, where RMAN will make sure that it has sufficient whole backups, incremental backups, and archivelog backups to restore the database and recover it to any point in time in the past, by default, thirty-one days.

Scheduling Automatic Backups

From the Database Control database home page, take the Maintenance tab and then the Schedule Backup link in the Backup/Recovery section to reach the Schedule Backup: Strategy window shown in Figure 19-4. Database Control can establish a backup schedule using exclusively default settings; this is known as the Oracle Suggested backup strategy. It will consist of a whole online backup (assuming that your database is in archivelog mode; otherwise, the database will have to be shut down) to the default disk destination, and then incremental backups, also to disk, from then on. These backups will be scheduled to occur overnight. Alternatively, you can choose to create a customized backup strategy, specifying what to back up, where the backups should go, and when and how frequently to make them.

Exercise 19-1: Running a Whole Database Backup

Using Database Control, perform a full, whole, online backup of your database:

1. Connect using Database Control as user SYSTEM. From the database home page, take the Schedule Backup link in the Maintenance section to reach the Schedule Backup: Strategy window.

2. In the Backup Strategy drop-down box, select Customized and click the Whole Database radio button. In the Host Credentials section, enter an operating system username and password. Click Next to reach the Schedule Backup: Options window.

3. Leave everything on defaults: a full, online backup with all archive logs. Click Next to reach the Schedule Backup: Settings window.

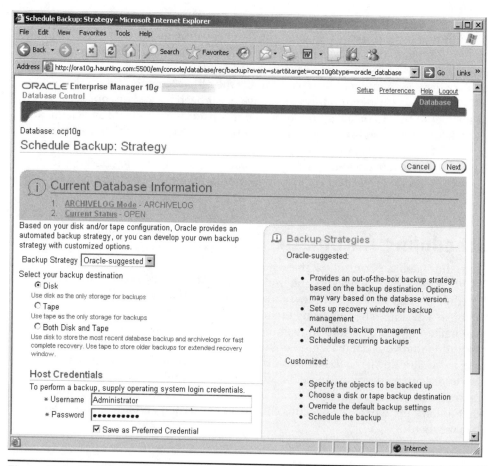

Figure 19-4 The Schedule Backup: Strategy window of Database Control

4. Leave everything on default to schedule a disk backup to your flash recovery area directory. Click Next to reach the Schedule Backup: Schedule window.

5. Leave everything on default to run the backup immediately as a one-off job. Click Next to reach the Schedule Backup: Review window.

6. Click the Submit Job button to launch the backup.

7. Click the View Job button to check how the job is running (see Figure 19-5), and then refresh the browser window to monitor progress.

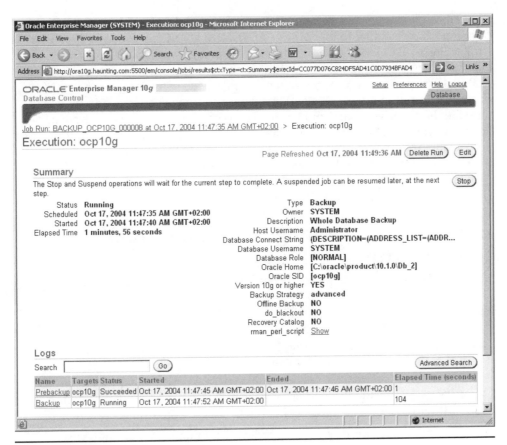

Figure 19-5 Backup job in progress

Controlfile Backup

You have already seen that the controlfile can be backed up as part of a whole database backup and can also be included in any datafile partial backup or archivelog backup. But the controlfile is sufficiently important that another backup option should also be taken regularly. This is the backup to trace. If all copies of the controlfile are destroyed (which, of course, should never happen if your multiplexing strategy is adequate), then rather than restoring a backup of the controlfile, it will sometimes be easier to re-create the controlfile. Furthermore, if any of the settings within the controlfile need to be changed, you may want to re-create it anyway. Such settings include the limits defined at database creation time, such as the maximum number of datafiles that the database can ever have. The backup to trace will generate a controlfile creation script with the CREATE CONTROLFILE command, which can either be run as written or edited if any settings need adjusting. The syntax of the CREATE CONTROLFILE command is very similar to that of the CREATE DATABASE command.

The BACKUP CONTROLFILE TO TRACE command from SQL*Plus, or the Database Control option, will create a file in the directory specified by the USER_DUMP_DEST parameter. You should rename this file to something meaningful (such as create_controlfile_17-10-2004.sql) and copy it to somewhere safe. Ideally, a new trace file should be generated and saved after every structural change to the database. So whenever you add or rename any datafiles or online redo log files, or you create or drop a tablespace, you should back up the controlfile to trace again.

To back up the controlfile through Database Control, from the database home page take the Administration tab. In the Storage section, take the Controlfiles link, and then click the Backup To Trace button.

Exercise 19-2: Backing Up the Controlfile to Trace with SQL*Plus

Using SQL*Plus, perform a controlfile backup-to-trace, and inspect the generated file.

1. Connect with SQL*Plus as user SYSTEM.

2. Issue this command:

   ```
   SQL> alter database backup controlfile to trace;
   ```

3. Locate your user dump destination.

   ```
   SQL> show parameters user_dump_dest;
   ```

4. From an operating system prompt, change to the user dump destination directory.

5. Identify the newest file in the directory. For example, on Windows use

   ```
   dir /od
   ```

   or on Unix,

   ```
   ls -ltr
   ```

   The newly generated trace file will be the last file listed.

6. Open the trace file with any editor you please and study the contents. The critical section is the CREATE CONTROLFILE command, which will resemble this:

   ```
   CREATE CONTROLFILE REUSE DATABASE "OCP10G" NORESETLOGS  ARCHIVELOG
       MAXLOGFILES 16
       MAXLOGMEMBERS 3
       MAXDATAFILES 100
       MAXINSTANCES 8
       MAXLOGHISTORY 454
   LOGFILE
    GROUP 1 (
      'C:\ORACLE\PRODUCT\10.1.0\ORADATA\OCP10G\REDO01.LOG',
      'C:\ORACLE\PRODUCT\10.1.0\ORADATA\OCP10G\REDO01B.LOG'
    ) SIZE 10M,
    GROUP 2 (
      'C:\ORACLE\PRODUCT\10.1.0\ORADATA\OCP10G\REDO02.LOG',
      'C:\ORACLE\PRODUCT\10.1.0\ORADATA\OCP10G\REDO02B.LOG'
    ) SIZE 10M,
    GROUP 3 (
   ```

```
      'C:\ORACLE\PRODUCT\10.1.0\ORADATA\OCP10G\REDO03.LOG',
      'C:\ORACLE\PRODUCT\10.1.0\ORADATA\OCP10G\REDO03B.LOG'
  ) SIZE 10M
-- STANDBY LOGFILE
DATAFILE
  'C:\ORACLE\PRODUCT\10.1.0\ORADATA\OCP10G\SYSTEM01.DBF',
  'C:\ORACLE\PRODUCT\10.1.0\ORADATA\OCP10G\UNDOTBS01.DBF',
  'C:\ORACLE\PRODUCT\10.1.0\ORADATA\OCP10G\SYSAUX01.DBF',
  'C:\ORACLE\PRODUCT\10.1.0\ORADATA\OCP10G\USERS01.DBF',
  'C:\ORACLE\PRODUCT\10.1.0\ORADATA\OCP10G\EXAMPLE01.DBF',
  'C:\ORACLE\PRODUCT\10.1.0\ORADATA\OCP10G\UNDO2-01.DBF'
CHARACTER SET WE8MSWIN1252
;
```

Managing RMAN Backups

RMAN knows what backups it has made and where it has put them. You can find out too. From the Maintenance tab on the database home page, take the Manage Current Backups link in the Backup/Recovery section to bring up the page shown in Figure 19-6.

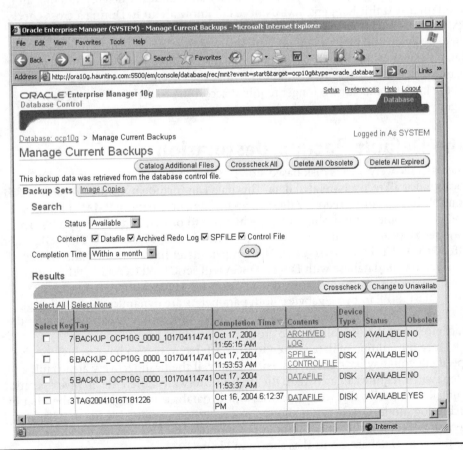

Figure 19-6 Manage Current Backups with Database Control

The figure shows summary information of four backup sets, identified by keys 3, 5, 6, and 7. Backup sets 5 and 6 together make a whole backup: datafiles, controlfile, and spfile. This is an example of how the Database Control interface gives different results from using RMAN from the command line: Database Control will not mix file types in one backup set, but from the command line this is possible. Backup set 3, which was made earlier, contains one or more datafiles. Note that the column "Obsolete" marks backup set 3 as being obsolete; this is because the default retention policy requires only one copy of each object, so the whole backup rendered the earlier partial backup redundant. The column "Pieces" (not shown on the figure because of scrolling; it is off to the right) gives details of the physical files that make up each backup set.

The buttons across the top of the window give access to RMAN's maintenance commands. Catalog Additional Files lets you tell RMAN about backups made with operating system utilities. It is thus possible to have a backup strategy that mixes operating system backups with RMAN backups. Crosscheck All instructs RMAN to check that the backup sets and image copies it has created are in fact still available. It might be, for example, that your tape library automatically deletes files that are a certain age. If this happens, RMAN needs to know about it. During a cross-check, RMAN will read all the tape and disk directories to confirm that the pieces it put there really do still exist; it will not actually read the files and check that they are valid. Related to this is Delete All Expired, which will remove all references to any backups that the cross-check found to be missing. Delete All Obsolete will delete all the backups that are no longer required according to the retention policy. In Figure 19-6, this would mean the backup with key 3.

The Default Backup Destination

The flash recovery area is disk-based storage that Oracle 10g can use as a default location for all recovery-related data. This data can include multiplexed copies of the controlfile and online redo log files; an archive log destination; RMAN backup sets and image copies; and flashback logs, which are to be detailed in Chapter 28. The flash recovery area is controlled by two parameters: DB_RECOVERY_FILE_DEST and DB_RECOVERY_FILE_DEST_SIZE. Neither parameter has a default value, though if you create your database with DBCA, DBCA will set DB_RECOVERY_FILE_DEST to the flash_recovery_area directory in your ORACLE_HOME, and DB_RECOVERY_FILE_DEST_SIZE to two gigabytes. Both parameters are dynamic: you can change the flash recovery areas to another directory at any time, and you can also change the maximum size that it is allowed to grow to.

Once the volume of data written to the flash recovery area has reached the size specified, you may have problems. For example, if the flash recovery area is full and a log switch requires an archive to the flash recovery area, then the archive operation will fail. Eventually, this will cause your whole database to hang. Remember that in archivelog mode, Oracle is not allowed to overwrite an online log file that has not been archived. It is therefore important to monitor the flash recovery area; you can do this with Database Control as shown in Figure 19-7.

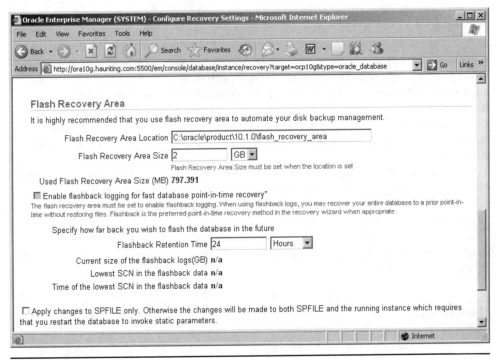

Figure 19-7   Monitoring the flash recovery area with Database Control

The same information can be obtained by querying the view V$RECOVERY_FILE_ DEST, as follows:

```
SQL> select * from v$recovery_file_dest;
NAME                                          SPACE_LIMIT SPACE_USED
--------------------------------------------- ----------- ----------
SPACE_RECLAIMABLE NUMBER_OF_FILES
----------------- ---------------
C:\oracle\product\10.1.0\flash_recovery_area   2147483648  836124672
         4268032               5
```

This query shows the location of the flash recovery area, and that its maximum size is two gigabytes, of which about eight hundred megabytes are being used. There are just five files in the recovery area, but some of them are redundant. These redundant files are taking up about four megabytes of space, which can be overwritten if necessary. As files in the flash recovery area become redundant, they will be replaced by newer files as the space is needed. Both RMAN and the archiver process are intelligent enough to realize when a file in the flash recovery area is no longer needed and can be overwritten.

Chapter Review

This chapter is a basic introduction to the use of RMAN for backup. There is much more to come. RMAN is Oracle's recommended tool for backup and restore. If you wish, you can use operating system utilities as well or instead; however, RMAN is superior in many respects, particularly if it is integrated with an automated tape library. Backups can be online or offline, whole or partial, and (provided they are done with RMAN) full or incremental. All these options are available if the database is in archivelog mode, but in noarchivelog mode you are restricted to offline whole backups.

RMAN can back up datafiles, the controlfile, archivelogs, and the spfile. You never back up online log files. The controlfile requires special consideration for backup and restore, and there is a separate command to back it up: the ALTER DATABASE BACKUP CONTROLFILE command.

RMAN's default destination is the flash recovery area. If you decide to use this default, you must monitor the usage to ensure that there is adequate space, particularly if you are also archiving to it.

Questions

1. What file types can be backed up by RMAN? (Choose four answers.)

   A. Archive log files

   B. Controlfile

   C. Dynamic parameter file

   D. Online log files

   E. Password file

   F. Permanent tablespace datafiles

   G. Static parameter file

   H. Temporary tablespace tempfiles

2. If your database is in noarchivelog mode, which of the following is possible? (Choose the best answer.)

   A. Online backups

   B. Partial backups

   C. Incremental backups

   D. All of the above, but only if you use RMAN

3. Why are RMAN backup sets smaller than image copies? (Choose the best answer.)

   A. They always use compression.

   B. They never include empty blocks.

C. They do not include tempfiles.

D. They can be written directly to tape.

4. Which of the following statements is true about putting multiple files in one backup set? (Choose three answers.)

   A. Each file will be stored in its own piece.

   B. The files in one set must be of the same type.

   C. You can place a limit on the size of the pieces.

   D. You can place a limit on the size of the backup set.

   E. It is impossible to predict the size of the backup set.

   F. You cannot store full and incremental backups in one set.

5. You are configuring RMAN backup settings in Database Control. Which of the following is true? (Choose the best answer.)

   A. The degree of parallelism cannot be greater than the number of CPUs.

   B. The host credentials must be the login for the Oracle owner.

   C. You must enable block change tracking if you want to do incremental backups.

   D. You can specify that backup sets should be compressed.

6. You need to back up the controlfile. What will work? (Choose the best answer.)

   A. Unless you are in archivelog mode, RMAN cannot include it in a backup set.

   B. The ALTER DATABASE BACKUP CONTROLFILE TO TRACE command will make an image copy of the controlfile.

   C. You cannot back up the controlfile; it is protected by multiplexing.

   D. None of the above.

7. What is the "Oracle Suggested" backup strategy? (Choose the best answer.)

   A. Full backup once a week, partial backup once a day

   B. Image copies once a week, incrementals every day

   C. Whole backup once a week, incrementals and archive logs every day

   D. One whole backup, incrementals thereafter

8. Which tablespaces can safely be excluded from RMAN backups? (Choose the best answer.)

   A. Temporary tablespaces

   B. Undo tablespaces

   C. Read-only tablespaces

   D. Index tablespaces

9. What is true about the cross-check command? (Choose the best answer.)

   A. A cross-check will check the validity of the backup pieces.

   B. A cross-check will delete references to files that no longer exist.

   C. A cross-check will verify the existence of backup set pieces.

   D. Cross-checking works only with backup sets, not image copies.

10. If you instruct RMAN to optimize backups, what is the result? (Choose the best answer.)

   A. Datafiles will be backed up only if the retention policy requires it.

   B. Datafiles will be backed up only if they have been changed since the last backup.

   C. Optimization cannot be used with incrementals.

   D. Optimization will have no effect on archivelog backups.

11. Your flash recovery area is full, and you are using it both for backups and as your archive log destination. What will happen? (Choose the best answer.)

   A. The database will hang when the flash recovery area is full.

   B. If you have set it to auto-extend, you will not have a problem.

   C. You cannot resize the flash recovery area online.

   D. The effect will depend on your RMAN retention policy.

12. You want to make a consistent backup. How can you do this? (Choose the best answer.)

   A. You can do this online, if the database is in archivelog mode.

   B. You must close the database first.

   C. You can do this with operating system commands, if you put the tablespaces into backup mode first.

   D. Perform a full, whole, backup and then apply incrementals to synchronize it.

13. What must you do before you can use RMAN with a tape library? (Choose the best answer.)

   A. Install the tape library driver supplied by Oracle.

   B. Migrate all your disk backups to tape.

   C. Obtain the appropriate driver from your hardware vendor.

   D. Transition the database to archivelog mode.

14. Which of the following types of backup can only be done with RMAN, not with operating system commands? (Choose the best answer.)

   A. Cold

   B. Full

C. Hot

D. Incremental

E. Partial

F. Whole

15. Which is the best description of a backup that RMAN would consider to be expired? (Choose the best answer.)

A. A backup that is no longer needed according to the retention policy

B. A backup in the flash recovery area that can be overwritten

C. A backup that has failed on cross-check

D. A backup that has become invalid

Answers

1. **A, B, C, and F.** Of the file types listed, these are the only files RMAN can back up. Note that it can also back up the spfile, and its own backup sets.

2. **C.** Incremental backups are possible in noarchivelog mode, but of course only with RMAN. Partial or online backups cannot be done, no matter what tool you use.

3. **B.** RMAN skips empty blocks as it backs up datafiles.

4. **C, E, and F.** You can decide the size through a setting in the Database Control Configure Backup Settings window. You can't predict the size of the backup set because the skipping of unused blocks makes the output set size undeterminable. And the syntax does not permit storing full and incremental backups in one set.

5. **D.** Compression is available as a Device Setting option in the Configure Backup Settings window, which will be applied as a default to all backup operations; it can be overridden for any particular backup.

6. **D.** None of the preceding choices are correct. A is wrong, because you can always make offline backups. B is wrong because the ALTER DATABASE BACKUP CONTROLFILE TO TRACE command will make a trace file, not an image copy. C is wrong because you can and should back up the controlfile; it is online logs that cannot be backed up.

7. **D.** The Oracle Suggested strategy follows default settings, which call for a whole backup every weekend followed by incremental backups every weekday night.

8. **C.** Tablespaces, such as read-only tablespaces that have not changed since the last backup, can safely be excluded from regular backups, though they must be backed up once.

9. **C.** During a cross-check, RMAN will read all the tape directories to confirm that the pieces exist, and for disk backups, it will read the file headers. In neither case will it scan the files themselves to confirm that they are actually valid.

10. **B.** Optimization consists in backing up only files that have changed. This works independently of the retention policy and the full/incremental distinction.

11. **D.** It may well be that there are files that RMAN considers to be obsolete, in which case they will be overwritten as required.

12. **B.** A consistent backup is one made with the datafiles closed.

13. **C.** It is the tape library vendor who supplies the driver, not Oracle.

14. **D.** Incrementals are an RMAN-only capability; all the others can be done with operating system utilities.

15. **C.** If a cross-check finds that a backup is missing, it will be marked as expired.

CHAPTER 20

Recovering Oracle Databases

In this chapter you will learn how to

- Recover from loss of a controlfile
- Recover from loss of a redo log file
- Recover from loss of a system-critical datafile
- Recover from loss of a nonsystem-critical datafile

It is impossible to corrupt an Oracle database. The mechanism of instance recovery, where redo and undo are used to return the database to a consistent state after an instance failure, guarantees that. It is, however, possible to lose data following media failure—if the DBA has not taken appropriate precautions. The precautions are simple: to run the database in archivelog mode; to multiplex the controlfile, the online logfiles, and the archive log files; and to back up datafiles and archive log files. Following media failure, the backups and the archive logs can be used to recover the database up to the point of the failure, without loss of even one committed row of data. But whereas instance recovery is automatic—indeed, unavoidable—media recovery is a manual process. This chapter will go through elementary recovery techniques. More advanced techniques, applicable to more complex problems, will be covered in later chapters.

Recovery Structures and Processes

Following media failure, there are different techniques for recovery, depending on which files were damaged. The database consists of three file types: the controlfile, the online redo log files, and the datafiles. Recovery from damage to the controlfile or the online redo log files is a trivial exercise, provided that they were multiplexed. Recovery from damage to one or more datafiles is more complex, but still straightforward.

A damaged controlfile can be replaced with a multiplexed copy or re-created with a CREATE CONTROLFILE command. In extreme circumstances, it can be restored from a backup, but this should never be necessary following media failure, if you have followed a suitable multiplexing strategy.

A damaged online redo log file can be regenerated. Oracle provides an ALTER DATABASE CLEAR LOGFILE GROUP # command (where # is the number of the group with a damaged member), which will delete and re-create the members of a logfile group. If the database is running in archivelog mode (and it should be), the logfile group must have been archived before Oracle will permit execution of the clear logfile command. This is because clearing an unarchived log file group would mean that the archive log stream would be missing one logfile, and therefore that recovery would not be possible. There is a variation on the command, ALTER DATABASE CLEAR UNARCHIVED LOGFILE GROUP #, which will delete and re-create a logfile even if it has not been successfully archived, but after executing this command it is absolutely vital to perform a whole database backup.

A damaged datafile requires use of backups and archive logs. Following media failure resulting in damage to a datafile, there are two options for recovery: complete recovery, meaning no loss of data, and incomplete recovery, where you deliberately lose work by stopping the recovery process before it has completed. Incomplete recovery is an advanced procedure dealt with in Chapter 27. Complete recovery is a two-stage process. First, the damaged file must be restored from a backup. Second, the restored file must be recovered, by using redo information in the archive logs to bring it forward in time until it is synchronized with the rest of the database.

EXAM TIP In the Oracle environment, "restore" means to replace a damaged or missing file with a backup; "recover" means to synchronize the file with the rest of the database by use of archive logs.

Since online redo logs are never backed up by RMAN, RMAN cannot be used to recover from damage to them; repairing online logfiles damaged by media failure can by done only with SQL*Plus, or through Database Control. The controlfile and datafiles can be restored and recovered by RMAN; indeed, if you backed them up into backup sets, RMAN is your only option.

To open a database, all the controlfile copies, at least one member of each online logfile group, and all the online datafiles must be present and synchronized. If, during a startup, SMON finds that this is not the case, the startup will not complete. If a controlfile copy is damaged or missing, the startup will stop in NOMOUNT mode. A message is written out to the alert log detailing which copy (or copies) of the controlfile is damaged. Assuming that the controlfiles are fine, SMON proceeds to open the database. During this phase, it checks the headers of all the online datafiles. If any are missing or damaged, appropriate error messages are written out to the alert log, and the database remains in mount mode. If all the online files are present and not damaged, but one or more of them are not synchronized, SMON will attempt to synchronize them by using the online redo logs. This is the process of instance recovery, detailed in Chapter 18, and will happen automatically. If the online logs required are not available, then the database cannot be opened. If one or more datafiles have been restored from a backup, they will almost certainly be so far out-of-date that the online redo logs will not go far enough back in time to recover them: this is when you must use archive log files for the recovery, which is a procedure that must be initiated manually—from SQL*Plus if you are backing up with operating system commands, or with RMAN if (as Oracle strongly advises) you have committed to using RMAN for your backups.

If the media damage occurs while the database is open, the effect will depend on which files were affected. Damage to any controlfile copy will result in the instance terminating immediately. Damage to a datafile that is part of the SYSTEM tablespace or the active undo tablespace will have the same effect. But damage to an online log will not terminate the instance, as long as there is a surviving member of the logfile group. In fact, the instance will continue to function, and your end users will not even notice. But error messages will be written out to the alert log, and the situation should be corrected without delay; such corrections can and should be done online, while people continue to work. Damage to a datafile that is part of a tablespace other than SYSTEM or the active undo tablespace will also not result in an instance failure, but clearly the end users may have problems, because a part of the database will be missing. How your application will react to this is unpredictable—it will depend completely on how the application is structured. The restore and recovery of damaged datafiles can be done online, provided that they are not datafiles belonging to SYSTEM or the undo tablespace. Finally, damage to the tempfiles that make up your temporary tablespaces may not be noticed by the end users at all. Oracle does not validate the existence of tempfiles until they are needed, and a well-tuned database may never need them. This means that tempfiles can be missing for some time before there is any noticeable effect. It also means that a damaged tempfile can be dropped and re-created at any time, unless it happens to be in use at that moment.

As with backups, a restore can be done with RMAN or with operating system utilities. But if your RMAN backups were to backup sets, rather than as image copies, the restore can be done only with RMAN: there is no other way to extract datafiles from a backup set. Recovery after a restore can be carried out with SQL*Plus commands or with RMAN, but the same restriction applies: only RMAN can extract archive logs from a backup set.

Recovery from Media Failure

Restore and recovery following media failure is covered in much greater detail in later chapters and the second OCP examination, but it is necessary to know the rudiments of recovery from simple problems for the first examination too. These simple problems are loss of one copy of a multiplexed controlfile and an online redo log file, and complete recovery following loss of critical and noncritical datafiles.

Recovery from Loss of a Multiplexed Controlfile

As long as a surviving multiplexed copy of the controlfile exists, recovery from loss of a controlfile is simple. Just replace it with a surviving copy of the controlfile. To restore the damaged or missing controlfile copy from a backup would be useless in these circumstances, because all copies of the controlfile must be identical; clearly, a restored copy would not be synchronized with the surviving copies, nor with the rest of the database.

Virtually the moment the damage occurs, the instance will terminate. As ever, the DBA's first reaction to a crashed instance should be to attempt a startup. This will fail, in NOMOUNT mode, with an appropriate error message. The alert log will state which controlfile copy is missing, and also—in the section listing the nondefault initialization parameters—how many controlfiles there actually are, and where they are. At this point, you have three options. First, you could edit the parameter file to remove the reference to the missing or damaged controlfile, as shown in Figure 20-1.

This is fine, but your database will now be running on one fewer multiplexed copies, which will presumably be in breach of your security guidelines. A better option is therefore to replace the damaged file with a copy made from a surviving copy or indeed to change the CONTROL_FILES initialization parameter to replace the reference to the damaged file with a reference to a brand new file, and copy the surviving controlfile to that.

 EXAM TIP Recovering from loss of a controlfile will entail downtime. It cannot be done online.

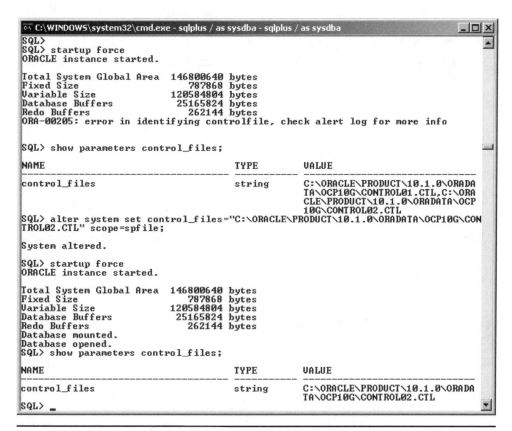

Figure 20-1   Removing the reference to a damaged controlfile

Exercise 20-1: Recovering from Loss of a Controlfile

In this exercise, you will simulate the loss of a multiplexed controlfile and replace it with a copy.

1. Connect to your database with SQL*Plus, and ensure that your controlfile is multiplexed with this query:

   ```
   SQL> select * from v$controlfile;
   ```

   This query must return at least two rows. If it does not, multiplex your controlfile by following the instructions given in Chapter 18, illustrated in Figure 18-5.

2. Simulate damage to a controlfile by crashing the database and renaming one of your controlfiles. Note that on Windows you may have to stop the

Windows service before Windows will let you rename the file, and start it again afterward.

3. Issue a startup command. The startup will stop in nomount mode, with an "ORA-00205: error in identifying controlfile, check alert log for more info" error message.

4. Copy your surviving controlfile to the name and location of the file you renamed.

5. Issue another startup command, which will be successful.

TIP Many DBAs do not like to copy a surviving controlfile over a damaged one, because it is all too easy to copy accidentally the damaged controlfile over the surviving one. It is safer to copy the surviving controlfile to a new file, and edit the control_files parameter to change the reference to the damaged file to the new file.

Recovery from Loss of a Multiplexed Online Redo Log File

Provided that the online redo log files are multiplexed, loss of one member will not cause any downtime, but there will be messages in the alert log telling you that there is a problem. If you can stand the downtime, you can shut down the database and copy a surviving member of the group over the damaged or missing member, but clearly this is not an option if the database is to remain open.

For open recovery, use the ALTER DATABASE CLEAR LOGFILE command to delete the existing files (or at least, those that still exist) and create new ones as shown in Figure 20-2. This can be done only if the logfile is inactive. If you attempt to clear the current logfile group, or the previous one that is still active, you will receive an error. Furthermore, if the database is in archivelog mode, the logfile group must have been archived.

EXAM TIP Recovery from loss of a multiplexed online redo log file can be done while the database is open, and therefore does not entail any downtime.

Exercise 20-2: Recovering a Lost Multiplexed Online Log File

This exercise will simulate loss of a logfile member and then, while the database is open, diagnose the problem and clear it.

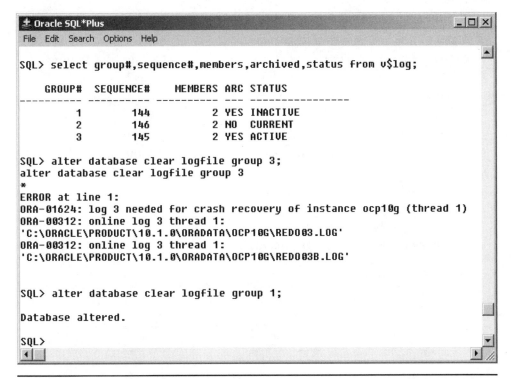

Figure 20-2 Clearing a logfile group with SQL*Plus

1. Using SQL*Plus, connect to your database as user SYS with SYSDBA privilege.

   ```
   SQL> connect / as sysdba;
   ```

2. Observe the state of your online logs with the following query:

   ```
   SQL> select group#,status,member from v$logfile order by group#;
      GROUP# STATUS  MEMBER
   -----------------------------------------------------------------------
           1           C:\ORACLE\PRODUCT\10.1.0\ORADATA\OCP10G\REDO01.LOG
           1           C:\ORACLE\PRODUCT\10.1.0\ORADATA\OCP10G\REDO01B.LOG
           2           C:\ORACLE\PRODUCT\10.1.0\ORADATA\OCP10G\REDO02.LOG
           2           C:\ORACLE\PRODUCT\10.1.0\ORADATA\OCP10G\REDO02B.LOG
           3           C:\ORACLE\PRODUCT\10.1.0\ORADATA\OCP10G\REDO03.LOG
           3           C:\ORACLE\PRODUCT\10.1.0\ORADATA\OCP10G\REDO03B.LOG
   ```

   Confirm that you do have at least two members of each group and that all the
   members have the STATUS column on NULL, as in the example here. If any
   groups do not have two members, multiplex them immediately by following
   the instructions given in Chapter 18, Exercise 18-2. If any members do not
   have a STATUS of NULL, execute the command

   ```
   SQL> alter system switch logfile;
   ```

   a few times to cycle through the groups, and then re-run the query.

3. Shut down the database:

```
SQL> shutdown immediate;
```

4. Using an operating system command, simulate media failure by deleting one of the members. For example, on Windows,

```
SQL> host del C:\ORACLE\PRODUCT\10.1.0\ORADATA\OCP10G\REDO01.LOG
```

or on Unix,

```
SQL> host rm /oracle/product/10.1.0/oradata/ocp10g/redo01.log
```

5. Start up the database and simulate user activity by performing a few log switches.

```
SQL> startup;
SQL> alter system switch logfile;
SQL> alter system switch logfile;
SQL> alter system switch logfile;
```

6. Check the state of your logfile members.

```
SQL> select group#,status,member from v$logfile order by group#;
   GROUP# STATUS  MEMBER
-----------------------------------------------------------------------
        1 INVALID C:\ORACLE\PRODUCT\10.1.0\ORADATA\OCP10G\REDO01.LOG
        1         C:\ORACLE\PRODUCT\10.1.0\ORADATA\OCP10G\REDO01B.LOG
        2         C:\ORACLE\PRODUCT\10.1.0\ORADATA\OCP10G\REDO02.LOG
        2         C:\ORACLE\PRODUCT\10.1.0\ORADATA\OCP10G\REDO02B.LOG
        3         C:\ORACLE\PRODUCT\10.1.0\ORADATA\OCP10G\REDO03.LOG
        3         C:\ORACLE\PRODUCT\10.1.0\ORADATA\OCP10G\REDO03B.LOG
```

Note that the missing file is now marked as being INVALID.

7. Connect to your database as user SYSTEM, using Database Control.

8. From the database home page, take the Administration tab, and then the Redo Logs link in the Storage section to bring up the window shown in Figure 20-3.

9. If the group with the problem (group number 1 in the example shown) is not INACTIVE, use the Switch Logfile choice in the Actions drop-down list and click Go to force log switches until it is inactive.

10. Clear the logfile group by selecting its radio button using the Clear Logfile choice in the Actions drop-down list, and clicking Go.

11. In your SQL*Plus session, confirm that the problem has been fixed.

```
SQL> select group#,status,member from v$logfile order by group#;
   GROUP# STATUS  MEMBER
---------- ------- --------------------------------------------------
        1         C:\ORACLE\PRODUCT\10.1.0\ORADATA\OCP10G\REDO01.LOG
        1         C:\ORACLE\PRODUCT\10.1.0\ORADATA\OCP10G\REDO01B.LOG
        2         C:\ORACLE\PRODUCT\10.1.0\ORADATA\OCP10G\REDO02.LOG
        2         C:\ORACLE\PRODUCT\10.1.0\ORADATA\OCP10G\REDO02B.LOG
        3         C:\ORACLE\PRODUCT\10.1.0\ORADATA\OCP10G\REDO03.LOG
        3         C:\ORACLE\PRODUCT\10.1.0\ORADATA\OCP10G\REDO03B.LOG
```

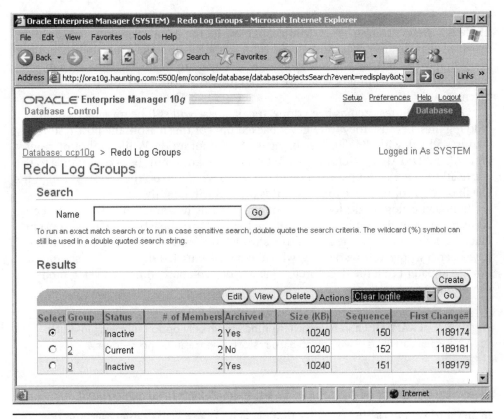

Figure 20-3 Redo logs, as shown in Database Control

Recovery from Loss of Datafiles

Media failure resulting in damage to one or more datafiles requires use of restore and recover routines: a backup of the datafile must be restored, and then archive redo logs applied to it to synchronize it with the rest of the database. There are various options available, depending on whether the database is in archivelog mode or not, and whether the file damaged is one that is critical to Oracle's running or a noncritical file containing "only" user data.

Recovery of Datafiles in Noarchivelog Mode

There is no concept of recovery when in noarchivelog mode, because the archive log files needed for recovery do not exist. Therefore, only a restore can be done. But if a restored datafile is not synchronized with the rest of the database by application of archive redo log files, it cannot be opened. The only option when in noarchivelog mode is therefore to restore the whole database: all the datafiles, and the controlfile. Provided that all these files are restored from a whole offline backup, after the restore you will have a database where all these files are synchronized, and thus a database that can be opened. But you will have lost all the work done since the backup was taken.

Once the full restore has been done, the database will still be missing its online redo log files, because they were never backed up. For this reason, the post-restore startup will fail, with the database being left in mount mode. While in mount mode, issue ALTER DATABASE CLEAR LOGFILE GROUP <group number> commands to re-create all the logfile groups. Then open the database. If you do the restore through the Database Control interface to RMAN, this process will be fully automatic.

In noarchivelog mode, loss of any one of possibly hundreds of datafiles can be corrected only by a complete restore of the last backup. The whole database must be taken back in time, with the loss of user's work. Furthermore, that last backup must have been a whole, offline backup, which will have entailed downtime. It should by now be apparent that the decision to operate your database in noarchivelog mode should not be taken lightly.

EXAM TIP If in noarchivelog mode, your only option following loss of a datafile is a whole database restore. There can be no recovery.

Recovery of a Noncritical File in Archivelog Mode

In an Oracle database, the datafiles that make up the SYSTEM tablespace and the currently active undo tablespace (as specified by the UNDO_TABLESPACE parameter) are considered to be "critical." Damage to any of these will result in the instance terminating immediately. Furthermore, the database cannot be opened again until the damage has been repaired by a restore and recover exercise. Damage to the other datafiles, which make up tablespaces for user data, will not as a rule result in the instance crashing. Oracle will take the damaged files offline, making their contents inaccessible, but the rest of the database should remain open. How your application software will react to this will depend on how it is structured and written.

TIP Is it safe to run your application with part of the database unavailable? This is a matter for discussion with your developers and business analysts, and an important point to consider when deciding on how to spread your segments across tablespaces.

If your backups were done with RMAN, the restore and recovery operation of a damaged datafile will be completely automatic. RMAN will carry out the restore in the most efficient manner possible, making intelligent use of full and incremental backups and then applying the necessary archivelogs. If RMAN is linked to a tape library, it will load the tapes automatically to extract the files it needs.

The restore and complete recovery of a datafile can succeed only if all the archive log files generated since the last backup of the datafile are available. Either they must still be on disk in the archive log destination directories, or if they have been migrated to tape, they will be restored during the recovery operation. RMAN will do the extract from a backup set and restore to disk automatically. If for some reason an archive logfile is missing or corrupted, the recovery will fail, but since archive log destinations and RMAN backup sets can and should be multiplexed, you should never find yourself in this situation. If you do, the only option is a complete restore, and an incomplete recovery up to the missing archive, as described in Chapter 27, which will mean loss of all work done subsequently.

Exercise 20-3: Recovering from Loss of a Noncritical Datafile

First, create a tablespace and a segment within it, and back it up. Then simulate damage to the datafile. Diagnose the problem, and resolve it. The database will stay open for use throughout the whole exercise. At various points you will be asked to supply host operating system credentials, if you have not saved them in previous exercises: give a suitable Windows or Unix login, such as the Oracle owner.

1. Connect to your database as user SYSTEM using SQL*Plus, and create a tablespace. For example, on Windows,

```
SQL> create tablespace noncrit
  2  datafile 'C:\ORACLE\PRODUCT\10.1.0\ORADATA\OCP10G\noncrit.dbf' size 2m;
```

or on Unix,

```
SQL> create tablespace noncrit
  2  datafile '/oracle/product/10.1.0/oradata/ocp10g/noncrit.dbf' size 2m;
```

2. Create a table within the new tablespace and insert a row into it.

```
SQL> create table ex203 (c1 date) tablespace noncrit;
SQL> insert into ex203 values(sysdate);
SQL> commit;
```

3. Using Database Control, connect to your database as user SYSTEM.

4. From the database home page, take the Maintenance tab, then the Schedule Backup link in the Backup/Recovery section.

5. In the Schedule Backup: Strategy window, select Customized in the Backup Strategy drop-down box.

6. Select the Tablespaces radio button, and click Next.

7. In the Schedule Backup: Tablespaces window, click Add.

8. In the Tablespaces: Available Tablespaces window, select the radio button for your new NONCRIT tablespace, and click Select.

9. In the Schedule Backup: Tablespaces window, click Next.

10. In the Schedule Backup: Options window, leave everything on defaults and click Next.

11. In the Schedule Backup: Settings window, leave everything on defaults and click Next.

12. In the Schedule Backup: Schedule window, leave everything on defaults and click Next to schedule an immediate backup.

13. In the Schedule Backup: Review click Submit to run the backup.

14. Simulate a disk failure by corrupting the new datafile. On Windows, open the file with Windows Notepad, delete a few lines from the beginning of the file, and save it; it is important to use Notepad because it is one of the few Windows utilities that will ignore the file lock that Oracle places on datafiles. On Unix you can use any editor you please, such as vi. Make sure that the characters deleted are at the start of the file, to ensure that the file header is damaged.

15. Confirm that the file is damaged by attempting to query the table:

```
SQL> select * from ex203;
select * from ex203
              *
ERROR at line 1:
ORA-01578: ORACLE data block corrupted (file # 7, block # 9)
ORA-01110: data file 7:
'C:\ORACLE\PRODUCT\10.1.0\ORADATA\OCP10G\NONCRIT.DBF'
```

   If the damage is not yet apparent, repeat Step 14 until it is.

16. In your Database Control session, take the Maintenance tab from the database home page, and then the Perform Recovery link in the Backup/Recovery section.

17. In the Perform Recovery: Type window, select Datafiles in the Object Type drop-down box, and click Next.

18. In the Perform Recovery: Datafiles window, the new datafile will be listed. Select it, and click Next.

19. In the Perform Recovery: Review window shown in Figure 20-4, leave everything on defaults and click Submit.

20. When the operation has completed, return to your SQL*Plus prompt and bring the file online, specifying it by name or by number.

```
SQL> alter database datafile 7 online;
```

21. Confirm that the tablespace and the tables within it are now usable, with no loss of data.

```
SQL> select * from ex203;
C1
---------
21-OCT-04
```

22. Tidy up the database.

```
SQL> drop tablespace noncrit including contents and datafiles;
```

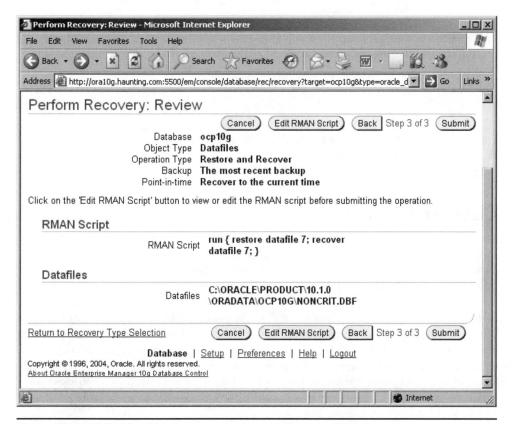

Figure 20-4   RMAN datafile restore and recover, with Database Control

Recovering from Loss of a Critical Datafile

The datafiles that make up the SYSTEM and currently active undo tablespace are
considered critical by Oracle, meaning that it is not possible to keep the database
open if they are damaged. If any portion of the SYSTEM tablespace were not available,
parts of the data dictionary would be missing. Oracle cannot function without a
complete data dictionary. If parts of the undo tablespace were not available, it would
be possible that undo data required for maintaining transactional integrity and
isolation would not be available, and Oracle can't take that chance either. Therefore,
damage to these datafiles will cause the instance to terminate immediately.

 TIP The critical datafiles should be on disk systems with hardware redundancy,
such as RAID level 1 disk mirroring, so that in the case of media failure the
files will survive and the database will remain open.

If the database does crash because of damage to critical datafiles, as ever, the first action is to attempt a startup. This will stop in mount mode, with error messages written to the alert log showing the extent of the damage. To recover, follow the same routine as that for a noncritical file, and then open the database. The restore and recover process is identical to that for a noncritical file, but it must be carried out in mount mode.

 EXAM TIP Loss of a critical datafile will not mean loss of data, but it will mean loss of time.

Chapter Review

This chapter is a basic introduction to recovery techniques. First you saw how to recover from loss of a multiplexed controlfile; this is a simple exercise, but it does involve downtime. Second, you saw how to recover from the loss of a multiplexed online redo log file. This is also simple; and furthermore, it does not involve any downtime at all. Third, you saw the use of RMAN through Database Control to restore and recover datafiles. This is a more complex exercise, but the GUI tool makes it straightforward. If the files are noncritical, the database can remain open and available for use, though segments with extents in the affected files will not be available until the restore and recover is complete and the files are brought back online.

And as a final word, always remember that loss or damage to files resulting from media failure is never a reason to lose data—if the database has been suitably protected by file multiplexing, archiving, and backups.

Questions

1. Loss of which of these files will cause an open database to crash? (Choose three answers.)

   A. A multiplexed controlfile

   B. A multiplexed online logfile

   C. A multiplexed archive log file

   D. An active undo tablespace datafile

   E. An active temporary tablespace tempfile

   F. A datafile from the SYSAUX tablespace

   G. A datafile from the SYSTEM tablespace

   H. A datafile containing critical user data

2. Loss of which of these files will prevent the database from opening? (Choose five answers.)

    A. A multiplexed controlfile

    B. A multiplexed online logfile

    C. A multiplexed archive log file

    D. An active undo tablespace datafile

    E. An active temporary tablespace tempfile

    F. A datafile from the SYSAUX tablespace

    G. A datafile from the SYSTEM tablespace

    H. A datafile containing user data

3. A copy of a multiplexed controlfile is damaged. What should you do? (Choose the best answer.)

    A. Replace it with a surviving copy.

    B. Restore it with RMAN.

    C. Restore it with operating system commands.

    D. Re-create it with the CREATE CONTROLFILE command.

4. How could you diagnose problems with a multiplexed online logfile group member? (Choose the best answer.)

    A. Query the V$LOG view.

    B. Query the V$LOGFILE view.

    C. Query the V$LOGFILE_MEMBER view.

    D. You do not need to diagnose it; the instance will crash when the problem occurs.

5. You issue the command ALTER DATABASE CLEAR LOGFILE GROUP 2 and it fails with the message "ORA-01624: log 2 needed for crash recovery of instance ocp10g (thread 1)." What could be an explanation for this? (Choose the best answer.)

    A. Logfile group 2 has not been archived.

    B. Logfile group 2 is being used for recovery.

    C. Logfile group 2 is active.

    D. The group is not multiplexed.

6. Your database is in noarchivelog mode, and you lose a noncritical datafile. What can you do to minimize loss of data?

    A. Restore the one damaged file, and leave the rest of the database up-to-date.

    B. Restore all the datafiles, but leave the controlfile up-to-date.

    C. Restore the whole database, and clear the online redo logs.

    D. Restore the one damaged file, and apply the online redo logs.

7. In noarchivelog mode, what restore and recover options are available to you? (Choose two answers.)

   A. Whole database restore

   B. Partial restore

   C. Online restore of noncritical datafiles

   D. Offline restore of critical datafiles

   E. Automatic recovery after an instance crash

8. In archivelog mode, which of the following could result in loss of data?

   A. Loss of a nonmirrored datafile that is part of the SYSTEM tablespace

   B. Loss of a nonmirrored datafile that is part of the active undo tablespace

   C. Loss of a nonmultiplexed archive log and a noncritical datafile

   D. Loss of a member from two or more multiplexed online logfile groups

9. Which of the following operations require a database shutdown?

   A. Recovering from loss of a multiplexed controlfile in archivelog mode

   B. Recovering from loss of a multiplexed online redo log file in noarchivelog mode

   C. Restore and recovery of the SYSAUX tablespace

   D. None of the above

10. You have backed up your datafiles and controlfile into a backup set, but your archive logs have not been backed up. If you need to restore and recover a datafile, which of the following routines would work? (Choose two answers.)

    A. Restore with RMAN, recover with SQL*Plus.

    B. Restore and recover with RMAN.

    C. Restore with operating system utilities, recover with SQL*Plus.

    D. Restore with operating system utilities, recover with RMAN.

    E. Restore and recover with SQL*Plus.

11. If media damage destroys a datafile, what will the effect be at the next startup?

    A. The startup will stop in nomount mode.

    B. The startup will stop in mount mode.

    C. It depends on whether the file is part of critical tablespace or a user tablespace.

    D. It depends on whether the database is in archivelog mode.

12. After a whole restore of a database in noarchivelog mode, what must be done before the database can be opened?

    A. The database must be recovered.

    B. The instance must be recovered.

C. The online logs must be cleared.

D. The database can be opened now, but work will have been lost.

13. You issue an ALTER DATABASE CLEAR LOGFILE GROUP 3 command and receive the message "ORA-00350: log 3 of instance ocp10g (thread 1) needs to be archived." What could be a cause of this? (Choose two answers.)

A. The database is not in archivelog mode.

B. The first multiplexed copy of group 3 needs to be archived.

C. If the instance crashed, this group would be needed for instance recovery.

D. An archive log destination is full.

E. The archiver process has failed.

14. During a recovery, it becomes apparent that an archive log is missing. What will be the result?

A. The recovery will succeed, but some data will be missing.

B. The recovery will fail.

C. The recovery will continue, if the damaged file was not from the SYSTEM tablespace or the active undo tablespace.

D. You must issue an ALTER DATABASE CLEAR ARCHIVE LOG FILE command to regenerate the missing archive.

15. Which of the following is correct about using image copies for restore? (Choose the best answer.)

A. You can restore them only with operating system utilities.

B. You can restore them only with RMAN.

C. If they were directed to tape, you can restore them only with RMAN.

D. You can restore them with either RMAN or operating system utilities.

E. Image copies can be used only for whole database restore.

Answers

1. **A, D,** and **G.** Loss of these types of files will typically cause the instance to terminate. The instance will survive the loss of the other file types.

2. **A, D, F, G,** and **H.** For an instance to open, all controlfile copies and online datafiles (no matter what tablespace they are a part of) must be available and synchronized.

3. **A.** It is fine to replace the damaged copy with a surviving copy, because all copies are bound to be identical. Note that B and C cannot be applied to one copy: they would replace all the copies, and then recovery would be necessary to synchronize them with the rest of the database. D is possible, but again it would apply to all copies and is not necessary. So all techniques could work, but A is the best in these circumstances.

4. **B.** This is the view that will point out an invalid logfile.

5. **C.** This is the error generated if you attempt to clear a logfile group before it has become inactive.

6. **C.** This is your only option for a database running in noarchivelog mode. There is no possibility of recovery, because the redo logs needed are not being archived before they are overwritten by log switches.

7. **A and E.** In noarchivelog mode, restoring the whole database is the only option. B, C, and D require the database to be in archivelog mode. Instance recovery is always enabled, no matter what mode the database is running in.

8. **C.** Given the loss of these files, the restore would work, but the recovery would fail.

9. **A.** Any controlfile operation needs downtime.

10. **A and B.** These options are both possible. You must use RMAN to extract files from a backup set, but if the archive logs are still on disk they can be applied with either RMAN or SQL*Plus.

11. **B.** This will be the case with any missing or damaged datafiles, whether critical or not.

12. **C.** This will re-create the online logs; only then can D be done. Neither A nor B is necessary after a whole offline backup, which is the only option for noarchivelog mode.

13. **D and E.** Either one of these conditions could cause this error, because they will cause the archiving to fail.

14. **B.** This should never happen, though, if you have multiplexed archive log destinations as you should.

15. **D.** Image copies don't require the special capabilities of RMAN because they are identical to a copy made with an operating system command.

CHAPTER 21

Managing Globalization in Oracle Databases

In this chapter you will learn how to

- Customize language-dependent behavior for the database and individual sessions
- Specify different linguistic sorts for queries
- Use datetime datatypes
- Query data using case-insensitive and accent-insensitive searches
- Obtain Globalization support configuration information

The Oracle database has many capabilities grouped under the term "Globalization" that will assist a DBA who must consider users of different nationalities. Globalization was known as National Language Support, or NLS, in earlier releases (you will still see the NLS acronym in several views and parameters), but Globalization is more than linguistics: it is a comprehensive set of facilities for managing databases that must cover a wide range of languages, time zones, and cultural variations.

The Need for Globalization

Large database systems, and many small ones too, will usually have a user community that is distributed geographically, temporally, and linguistically. Consider a database hosted in Johannesburg, South Africa, with end users scattered throughout sub-Saharan Africa. Different users will be expecting data to be presented to them in Portuguese, French, and English, at least. They will be in three different time zones. They will have different standards for the formats of dates and numbers. The situation becomes even more complex when the application is running in a three-tier environment: you may have a database in one location, several geographically distributed application servers, and users further distributed from the application servers.

It is possible for a lazy DBA to ignore Globalization completely. Typically, such a DBA will take United States defaults for everything—and then let the programmers sort it out. But this is putting an enormous amount of work onto the programmers, and they may not wish to do it either. The result is an application that works but is detested by a proportion of its users. But there is more to this than keeping people happy: there may well be financial implications too. Consider two competing e-commerce sites, both trying to sell goods all over the world. One has taken the trouble to translate everything into languages applicable to each customer; the other insists that all customers use American English. Which one is going to receive the most orders? Furthermore, dates and monetary formats can cause dreadful confusion when different countries have different standards. Such problems can be ignored or resolved programmatically, but a good DBA will attempt to resolve them through the facilities provided as standard within the database.

Globalization Capabilities

Globalization is a lot more than language support, though languages are certainly a major part of it. Globalization also covers aspects of data presentation, calendars, dates, and much more. Perhaps the most important aspect is how data is actually stored in the database: the character set used.

Character Sets

The data stored in a database must be coded into a character set. A *character set* is a defined encoding scheme for representing characters as a sequence of bits. Some products use the character sets provided by the host operating system. For example,

Microsoft Word does not have its own character sets; it uses those provided by the Windows operating system. Other products provide their own character sets and are thus independent of whatever is provided by the host operating system. Oracle products fall into the latter group: they ship with their own character sets, which is one reason why Oracle applications are the same on all platforms, and why clients and servers can be on different platforms.

A character set consists of a defined number of distinct characters. The number of characters that a character set can represent is limited by the number of bits the character set uses for each character. A single-byte character set will use only one byte per character: eight bits, though some single-byte character sets restrict this even further by using only seven of the eight bits. A multibyte character set uses one, two, or even three bytes for each character. The variations here are whether the character set is fixed-width (for example, always using two bytes per character) or variable width (where some characters will be represented in one byte, other characters in two or more).

How many characters are actually needed? Well, as a bare minimum, you need upper- and lowercase letters, the digits 0 through 9, a few punctuation marks, and some special characters to mark the end of a line, or a page break, for instance. A seven-bit character set can represent a total of 128 (2^7) characters. It is simply not possible to get more than that number of different bit patterns if you have only seven bits to play with. Seven-bit character sets are just barely functional for modern computer systems, but they are usually inadequate. They provide the characters just named, but very little else. If you need to do simple things like using box drawing characters, or printing a name that includes a letter with an accent, you may find that you can't do it with a seven-bit character set. Anything more advanced, such as storing and displaying data in Arabic or Chinese script, will be totally out of the question. Unfortunately, Oracle's default character sets are seven-bit ASCII or seven-bit EBCDIC, depending on the platform: even such widely used languages as French and Spanish cannot be written correctly in these character sets. This is a historical anomaly, dating back to the days when these character sets were pretty much the only ones in use. Eight-bit character sets can represent 256 (2^8) different characters. These will typically be adequate for any Western European language–based system, though perhaps not for some Eastern European languages, and definitely not for many Asian languages. For these more complex linguistic environments, it is necessary to use a multibyte character set.

Unicode character sets deserve a special mention. The Unicode standards are an international standard for character encoding, which is intended to include every character that will ever be required by any computer system. Currently, Unicode has defined more than thirty-two thousand characters. And for completeness, the acronym ASCII is for American Standard Code for Information Interchange, and EBCDIC is Extended Binary Coded Decimal Interchange Code. EBCDIC was developed by IBM (International Business Machines) and is not usually used outside the IBM environment. More acronyms to note are ISO, for the International Standards Organization, and ANSI, for the American National Standards Institute.

Encoding Scheme	Example Character Sets
Single-byte seven-bit	US7ASCII. This is the default for Oracle on non-IBM systems.
	YUG7ASCII. Seven-bit Yugoslavian, a character set suitable for the languages used in much of the Balkans.
Single-byte eight-bit	WE8ISO8859P15. A Western European eight-bit ISO standard character set, which includes the Euro symbol (unlike WE8ISO8859P1).
	WE8DEC. Developed by Digital Equipment Corporation, widely used in the DEC (or Compaq) environment in Europe.
	I8EBCDIC1144. An EBCDIC character set specifically developed for Italian.
Fixed-width multibyte	AL16UTF16. This is a Unicode two-byte character set, and the only fixed-width Unicode character set supported by 10g.
Varying-width single-byte	UTF8. A Unicode character set, where characters may be from one to four bytes. UTF8 is a standard on Unix systems.
Varying-width multibyte	JA16SJIS. Shift-JIS, a Japanese character set, where a shift-out control code is used to indicate that the following bytes are double-byte characters. A shift-in code switches back to single-byte characters.
	ZHT16CCDC. A traditional Chinese character set, where the most significant bit of the byte is used to indicate whether the byte is a single character or part of a multibyte character.
	AL32UTF8. A Unicode varying-width character set.

Table 21-1   Some of the Oracle 10g Character Sets

Oracle 10g ships with more than 250 character sets. Table 21-1 includes just a few examples.

Language Support

The number of languages supported by Oracle depends on the platform, release, and patch level of the product. To determine the range available on any one installation, query the view V$NLS_VALID_VALUES, as follows:

```
SQL> select * from v$nls_valid_values where parameter='LANGUAGE';
PARAMETER                          VALUE
-----------------------------      -----------------------------
LANGUAGE                           AMERICAN
LANGUAGE                           GERMAN
LANGUAGE                           FRENCH
LANGUAGE                           CANADIAN FRENCH
<output abbreviated...>
LANGUAGE                           LATIN SERBIAN
LANGUAGE                           CYRILLIC UZBEK
LANGUAGE                           LATIN UZBEK
LANGUAGE                           CYRILLIC KAZAKH
65 rows selected.
```

The language used will determine the language for error messages and also set defaults for date language and sort orders. The defaults are shown here:

Variable	Default	Purpose
NLS_LANGUAGE	AMERICAN	Language for messages
NLS_DATE_LANGUAGE	AMERICAN	Used for day and month names
NLS_SORT	BINARY	Linguistic sort sequence

The default sort order—binary—is poor. Binary sorting may be acceptable for a seven-bit character set, but for character sets of eight bits or more the results are often inappropriate. For example, the ASCII value of a lowercase letter *a* is 97, and a lowercase letter *z* is 122. So a binary sort will place *a* before *z*, which is fine. But consider diacritic variations: a lowercase letter *a* with an umlaut, *ä,* is 132, which is way beyond *z*; so the binary sort order will produce "a,z,ä"—which is wrong in any language. The German sort order would give "a,ä,z"—which is correct. (Figure 21-1 illustrates how a sort order is affected by the language setting.) Oracle provides many possible sort orders; there should always be one that will fit your requirements. Again, query V$NLS_VALID_VALUES to see what is available:

```
SQL> select * from v$nls_valid_values where parameter='SORT';
PARAMETER                          VALUE
-----------------------------      -----------------------------
SORT                               BINARY
SORT                               WEST_EUROPEAN
SORT                               XWEST_EUROPEAN
SORT                               GERMAN
       <output abbreviated...>
SORT                               SCHINESE_RADICAL_M
SORT                               JAPANESE_M
SORT                               KOREAN_M
87 rows selected.
```

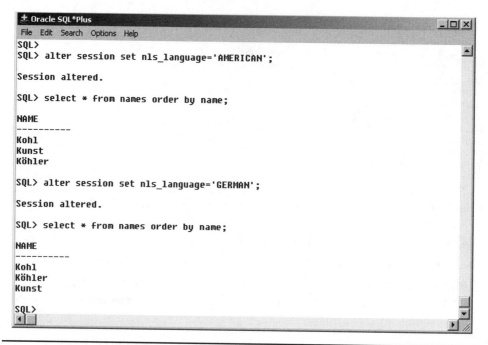

Figure 21-1 Linguistic sorting

Territory Support

The territory selected sets a number of Globalization defaults. To determine the territories your database supports, again query V$NLS_VALID_VALUES:

```
SQL> select * from v$nls_valid_values where parameter='TERRITORY';
PARAMETER                          VALUE
------------------------------     ------------------------------
TERRITORY                          AMERICA
TERRITORY                          UNITED KINGDOM
TERRITORY                          GERMANY
<output abbreviated...>
TERRITORY                          SERBIA AND MONTENEGRO
TERRITORY                          ARGENTINA
TERRITORY                          ECUADOR
TERRITORY                          PHILIPPINES
96 rows selected.
```

The territory selection sets defaults for day and week numbering, credit and debit symbols, date formats, decimal and group numeric separators, and currency symbols. Some of these can have profound effects on the way your application software will behave.

For example, in the U.S. the decimal separator is a point (.), but in Germany and many other countries it is a comma (,). Consider a number such as "10,001". Is this ten thousand and one, or ten and one thousandth? You certainly need to know. Of equal importance is day of the week numbering. In the U.S., Sunday is day 1 and

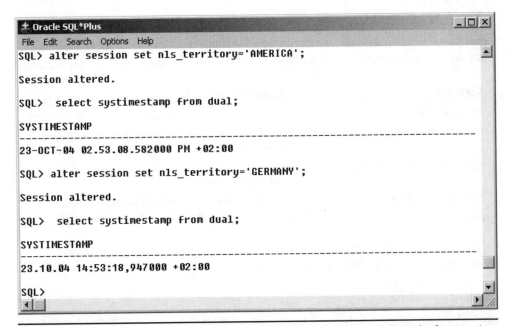

Figure 21-2 Date and time formats, on the twenty-third day of October in the early afternoon in a time zone two hours ahead of Greenwich

Saturday is day 7, but in Germany (and indeed in most of Europe) Monday (or Montag, to take the example further) is day 1 and Sunday (Sonnabend) is day 7. If your software includes procedures that will run according to the day number, the results may be disastrous if you do not consider this. Figure 21-2 illustrates some other territory-related differences in time settings.

These are the defaults for territory-related settings:

Variable	Default / Purpose
NLS_TERRITORY	AMERICA / Geographical location
NLS_CURRENCY	$ / Local currency symbol
NLS_DUAL_CURRENCY	$ / A secondary currency symbol for the territory
NLS_ISO_CURRENCY	AMERICA / Indicates the ISO territory currency symbol
NLS_DATE_FORMAT	DD-MM-RR / Format used for columns of datatype DATE
NLS_NUMERIC_CHARACTERS	.,/ Decimal and group delimiters
NLS_TIMESTAMP_FORMAT	DD-MM-RRHH.MI.SSXFF AM / Format used for columns of datatype TIMESTAMP
NLS_TIMESTAMP_TZ_FORMAT	DD-MM-RRHH.MI.SSXFF AM TZR / Format used for columns of datatype TIMESTAMP WITH LOCAL TIMEZONE

Other NLS Settings

Apart from the language and territory-related settings just described, there are a few more advanced settings that are less likely to cause problems:

Variable	Default / Purpose
NLS_CALENDAR	Gregorian / Allows use of alternative calendar systems
NLS_COMP	BINARY / The alternative of ANSI compares letters using their NLS value, not the numeric equivalent
NLS_LENGTH_SEMANTICS	BYTE / Allows one to manipulate multibyte characters as complete characters rather than bytes
NLS_NCHAR_CONV_EXCP	FALSE / Limits error messages generated when converting between VARCHAR2 and NVARCHAR

Figure 21-3 illustrates switching to the Japanese imperial calendar, with an associated effect on the date display.

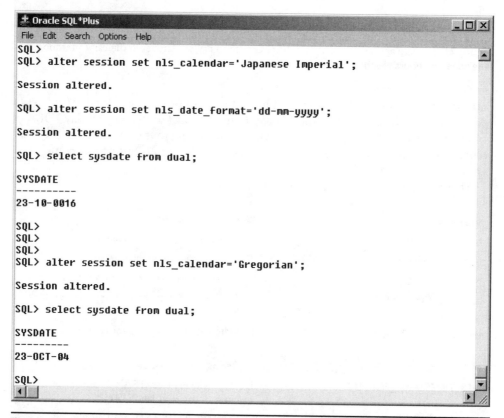

Figure 21-3 Use of the Japanese Imperial calendar, counting years from the ascension of Emperor Akihito to the throne

Using Globalization Support Features

Globalization can be specified at any and all of five levels:

- The database
- The instance
- The client environment
- The session
- The statement

The levels are listed in ascending order of priority. Thus, instance settings take precedence over database settings, and so on. An individual statement can control its own Globalization characteristics, thus overriding everything else.

 EXAM TIP Remember the precedence of the various points where Globalization settings can be specified. On the server side, instance settings take precedence over database settings, but all the server settings can be overridden on the client side: first by the environment, then at the session and statement levels.

Choosing a Character Set

At database creation time, choice of character set is one of the two most important decisions you make. In Chapter 3, as you learned how to create a database, you were told that two points are vital to get right at creation time; everything else can be changed later. Those two were the DB_BLOCK_SIZE parameter, which can never be changed, and the database character set, which it may be possible but not necessarily practicable to change. The difficulty with the DB_BLOCK_SIZE is that this parameter is used as the block size for the SYSTEM tablespace. You can't change that without re-creating the data dictionary: in other words, creating a new database. The database character set is used to store all the data in columns of type VARCHAR2, CLOB, CHAR, and LONG. If you change it, you may well destroy all the data in your existing columns of these types.

It is therefore vital to select, at creation time, a character set that will fulfill all your needs, present and future. For example, if you are going to have data in French or Spanish, a Western European character set is needed. If you are going to have data in Russian or Czech, you should choose an Eastern European character set. But what if you may have both Eastern and Western European languages? Furthermore, what if you anticipate a need for Korean or Thai as well? Oracle provides two solutions to the problem: the National Character Set, and the use of Unicode.

The National Character Set was introduced with release 8.0 of the database. This is a second character set, specified at database creation time, which is used for columns of datatype NVARCHAR2, NCLOB, and NCHAR. So if the DBA anticipated that most of his information would be in English but that some would be Japanese, he could select a Western European character set for the database character set, and a Kanji character set as the National Character Set. With release 9i, the rules changed: from then on, the National Character Set can only be Unicode. This should not lead to any drop in functionality, because the promise of Unicode is that it can encode any character. Two Unicodes are supported as the National Character Set: AL16UTF16 and UTF8. AL16UTF16 is a fixed-width, two-byte character set, and UTF8 is a variable-width character set. The choice between the two is a matter of space efficiency and performance, related to the type of data you anticipate storing in the NVARCHAR2 and NCLOB columns.

It may well be that the majority of the data could in fact be represented in one byte, and only a few characters would need multiple bytes. In that case, AL16UTF16 will nearly double the storage requirements—quite unnecessarily, because one of the two bytes per character will be packed with zeros. This not only wastes space but also impacts on disk I/O. UTF8 will give a huge space saving. But if the majority of the data cannot be coded in one byte, then UTF8 becomes much less efficient because the multibyte characters must be assembled, at run time, from a number of single bytes, with a consequent performance hit. Also, UTF8 will often need three or even four bytes to store a character that AL16UTF16 can encode in two.

The second possibility for a fully multilingual database is to use Unicode as the actual database character set. The supported options are UTF8 and AL32UTF8, which are both variable-width multibyte character sets.

 TIP A Unicode database may make life simpler for developers, because they do not have to worry about which columns to read and write, but there can be performance implications.

The only limitation on the database character set is that it must have either US7ASCII or EBCDIC as a subset. This is because the database character set is used to store SQL and PL/SQL source code, which is written in these characters.

Both the database character set and the National Character Set are specified in the CREATE DATABASE command, as shown in the example script shown in the section "The Database Creation Scripts" in Chapter 3. The defaults are US7ASCII and AL16UTF16. If you create a database using DBCA, DBCA will provide a default for the database character set, which it will pick up from the character set of the host operating system where you are running DBCA. This may be more appropriate than the seven-bit Oracle default, but remember that your clients may be using terminals with a different operating system from the database server. In the Chapter 3 example this is WE8MSWIN1252, a Microsoft Windows eight-bit Western European character set. This was selected by DBCA because it was running on a PC with the Windows "Regional and Language Options" set to "English (US)."

Changing Character Sets

There are many occasions when DBAs have wished that they could change the database character set. Typically, this is because the database was created using the default of US7ASCII, and later on a need arises for storing information using characters not included in that character set, such as a French name. Prior to release 9i there was no supported technique for changing the character set. From 9i onward, there is a supported technique, but there is no guarantee that it will work. It is your responsibility as DBA to carry out thorough checks that the change will not damage the data. The problem is simply that a change of character set does not reformat the data currently in the datafiles, but it will change the way the data is presented. For example, if you were to convert from a Western European character set to an Eastern European character set, many of the letters with the accents common in Western languages would then be interpreted as Cyrillic characters, with disastrous results.

There are two tools provided to assist with deciding on character set change: the Database Character Set Scanner and the Language and Character Set File Scanner. These are independently executable utilities, csscan and lcsscan on Unix, csscan.exe and lcsscan.exe on Windows.

The Database Character Set Scanner will log on to the database and make a pass through the datafiles, generating a report of possible problems. For example,

```
csscan system/manager full=y tochar=utf8
```

This command will connect to the database as user SYSTEM and scan through all the datafiles to check if conversion to UTF8 would cause any problems. A typical problem when going to UTF8 is that a character that was encoded in one byte in the original character set will require two bytes in UTF8, so the data might not fit in the column after the change. The scanner will produce a comprehensive report listing every row that will have problems with the new character set. You must then take appropriate action to fix the problems before the conversion, if possible.

 TIP You must run the csminst.sql script to prepare the database for running the character set scanner.

The Language and Character Set File Scanner is a utility that will attempt to identify the language and character set used for a text file. It will function on plain text only; if you want to use it on, for example, a word processing document, you will have to remove all the control codes first. This scanner may be useful if you have to upload data into your database and do not know what the data is. The tool scans the file and applies a set of heuristics to make an intelligent guess about the language and character set of the data.

Having determined whether it is possible to change the character set without damage, execute the command ALTER DATABASE CHARACTER SET... to make the change. The equivalent command to change the National Character Set is ALTER DATABASE NATIONAL CHARACTER SET.... The only limitation with this command is that the target character set must be a superset of the original character set, but that does not guarantee that there will be no corruptions. That is the DBA's responsibility.

Globalization Within the Database

The database's Globalization settings are fixed at creation time, according to the instance parameter settings in effect when the CREATE DATABASE command was issued and the character set was specified. They are visible in the view NLS_DATABASE_PARAMETERS as shown in Figure 21-4.

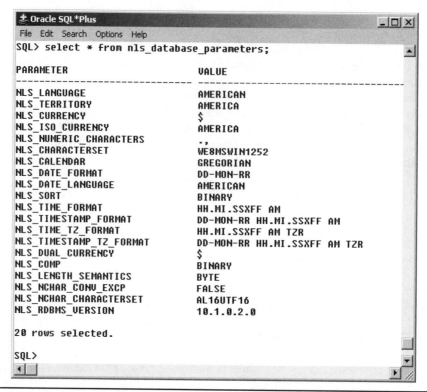

Figure 21-4   Database Globalization settings

Globalization at the Instance Level

Instance parameter settings will override the database settings. In a RAC environment, it is possible for different instances to have different settings, so that, for example, European and U.S. users could each log on to the database through an instance configured appropriately to their different needs. The settings currently in effect are exposed in the view NLS_INSTANCE_PARAMETERS, which has the same rows as NLS_DATABASE_PARAMETERS except for three rows to do with character sets and RDBMS version that do not apply to an instance.

The Globalization instance parameters can be changed like any others, but as they are all static, it is necessary to restart the instance before any changes come into effect.

Client-Side Environment Settings

When an Oracle user process starts, it inspects the environment within which it is running to pick up Globalization defaults. This mechanism means that it is possible for users who desire different Globalization settings to configure their terminals appropriately to their needs, and then Oracle will pick up and apply the settings automatically, without the programmers or the DBA having to take any action. This feature should be used with care, as it can cause confusion because it means that the application software may be running in an environment that the programmers had not anticipated. The internal implementation of this is that the user process reads the environment variables and then generates a series of ALTER SESSION commands to implement them.

The key environment variable is NLS_LANG. The full specification for this is a language, a territory, and a character set. To use French as spoken in Canada with a Western European character set, an end user could set it to

```
NLS_LANG=FRENCH_CANADA.WEISO8859P1
```

and then, no matter what the database and instance Globalization is set to, his user process will then display messages and format data according to Canadian French standards. When the user sends data to the server, he will enter it using Canadian French conventions, but the server will then store it in the database according to the database Globalization settings. The three elements (language, territory, and character set) of NLS_LANG are all optional.

 TIP The DBA has absolutely no control over what end users do with the NLS_LANG environment variable. If the application is Globalization sensitive, the programmers should take this into account and control Globalization within the session instead.

The conversion between server-side and client-side Globalization settings is done by Oracle Net. In terms of the OSI seven-layer model, briefly described in Chapter 12, any required conversion is a layer 6 (presentation layer) function that is accomplished by Oracle Net's Two-Task Common layer. Some conversion is perfectly straightforward and should always succeed. This is the case with formatting numbers, for instance. Other conversions are problematic. If the client and the server are using different character sets, it may not be possible for data to be converted. An extreme case would be a client process using a multibyte character set intended for an Oriental language, and a database created with US7ASCII. There is no way that the data entered on the client can be stored correctly in the much more limited character set available within the database, and data loss and corruption are inevitable.

Exercise 21-1: Making Globalization and Client Environment Settings

This exercise will demonstrate how you, acting as an end user, can customize your environment, in order to affect your Oracle sessions.

1. From an operating system prompt, set the NLS_LANG variable to Hungarian, and also adjust the date display from the default. Using Windows,

```
C:\>set NLS_LANG=Hungarian
C:\>set NLS_DATE_FORMAT=Day dd Month yyyy
```

or on Unix,

```
$ export NLS_LANG=Hungarian
$ export  NLS_DATE_FORMAT=Day dd Month yyyy
```

2. From the same operating system session, launch SQL*Plus and connect as user SYSTEM.

3. Display the current date with

```
SQL> select sysdate from dual;
```

Figure 21-5 shows the complete sequence of steps. Note that in the figure there is a problem with the display of one character in the month name. This is an example of a character used in Eastern European languages that cannot be displayed correctly by a Western European character set.

Session-Level Globalization Settings

Once connected, users can issue ALTER SESSION commands to set up their Globalization preferences. Normally this would be done programmatically, perhaps by use of a logon trigger. The application will determine who the user is and configure the environment accordingly. An alternative to ALTER SESSION is the supplied package DBMS_SESSION. The following examples will each have the same effect:

```
SQL> alter session set nls_date_format='dd.mm.yyyy';
Session altered.
SQL> execute dbms_session.set_nls('nls_date_format','''dd.mm.yyyy''');
PL/SQL procedure successfully completed.
```

Specifications at the session level take precedence over the server-side database and instance settings and will also override any attempt made by the user to configure his session with environment variables. The Globalization settings currently in effect for your session are shown in the V$NLS_PARAMETERS view. The same information, with the exception of the character sets, is shown in the NLS_SESSION_PARAMETERS view.

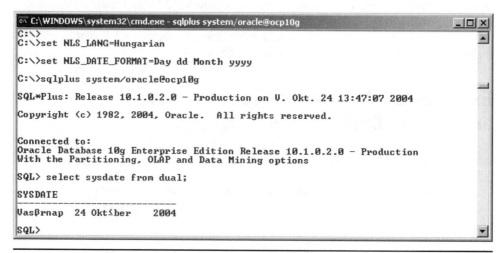

Figure 21-5 Controlling Globalization with client environment settings

Exercise 21-2: Controlling Globalization Within the Session

For this exercise, it is assumed that you have completed Exercise 21-1 and that you are working in the same SQL*Plus session. You will demonstrate how European and U.S. standards can cause confusion.

1. Confirm that your NLS_LANG environment variable is set to a European language. On Windows,

   ```
   SQL> host echo %NLS_LANG%
   ```

   or on Unix,

   ```
   SQL> host echo $NLS_LANG
   ```

2. Set your date display to show the day number:

   ```
   SQL> alter session set nls_date_format='D';
   ```

3. Display the number of today's day:

   ```
   SQL> select sysdate from dual;
   ```

4. Change your territory to the U.S., and again set the date display format:

   ```
   SQL> alter session set nls_territory=AMERICA;
   SQL> alter session set nls_date_format='D';
   ```

5. Issue the query from Step 3 again, and note that the day number has changed with the shift of environment from Europe to America.

Figure 21-6 shows the complete sequence.

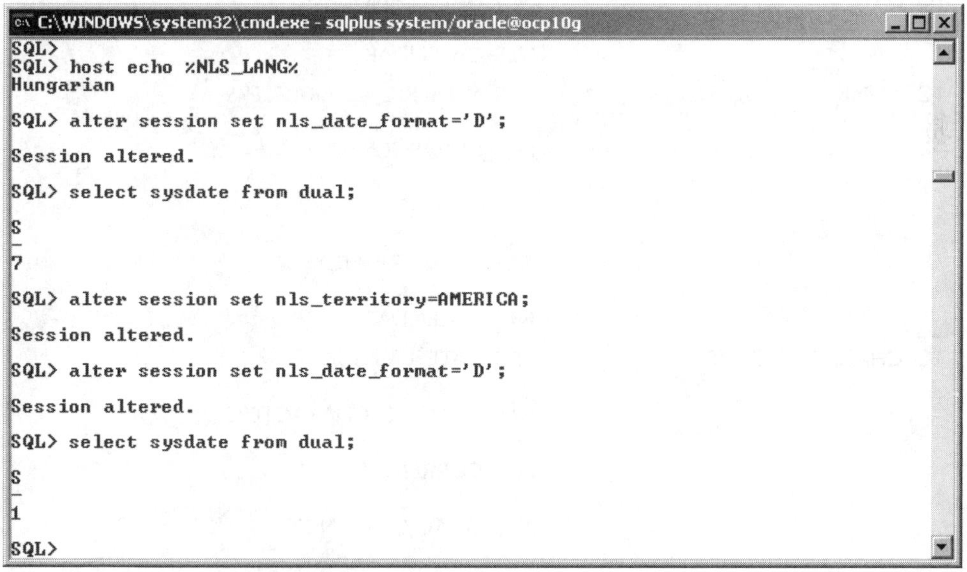

Figure 21-6 Controlling Globalization within a session

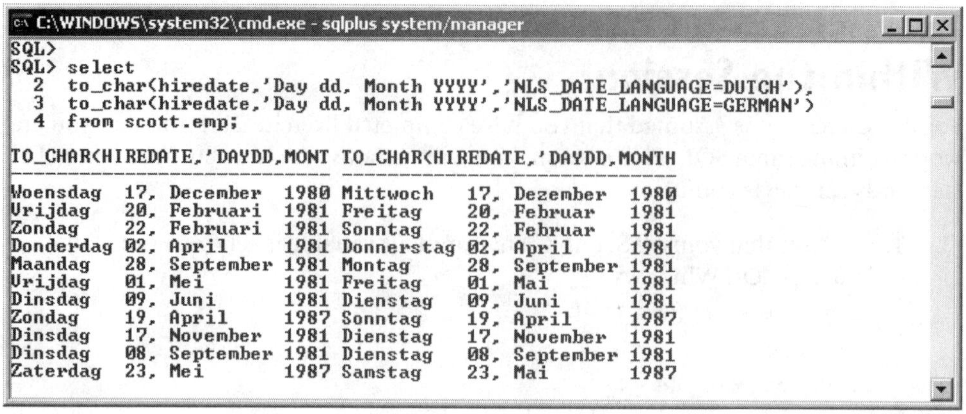

```
C:\WINDOWS\system32\cmd.exe - sqlplus system/manager
SQL>
SQL> select
  2  to_char(hiredate,'Day dd, Month YYYY','NLS_DATE_LANGUAGE=DUTCH'),
  3  to_char(hiredate,'Day dd, Month YYYY','NLS_DATE_LANGUAGE=GERMAN')
  4  from scott.emp;

TO_CHAR(HIREDATE,'DAYDD,MONT TO_CHAR(HIREDATE,'DAYDD,MONTH
---------------------------- -----------------------------
Woensdag  17, December  1980 Mittwoch    17, Dezember  1980
Vrijdag   20, Februari  1981 Freitag     20, Februar   1981
Zondag    22, Februari  1981 Sonntag     22, Februar   1981
Donderdag 02, April     1981 Donnerstag 02, April     1981
Maandag   28, September 1981 Montag      28, September 1981
Vrijdag   01, Mei       1981 Freitag     01, Mai       1981
Dinsdag   09, Juni      1981 Dienstag    09, Juni      1981
Zondag    19, April     1987 Sonntag     19, April     1987
Dinsdag   17, November  1981 Dienstag    17, November  1981
Dinsdag   08, September 1981 Dienstag    08, September 1981
Zaterdag  23, Mei       1987 Samstag     23, Mai       1987
```

Figure 21-7 Using NLS parameters in SQL functions

Statement Globalization Settings

The tightest level of control over Globalization is to manage it programmatically, within each statement. This entails using NLS parameters in SQL functions. Figure 21-7 shows an example.

The SQL functions to consider are the typecasting functions that convert between datatypes. Depending on the function, various parameters may be used.

Function	Globalization Parameters
TO_DATE	NLS_DATE_LANGUAGE
	NLS_CALENDAR
TO_NUMBER	NLS_NUMERIC_CHARACTERS
	NLS_CURRENCY
	NLS_DUAL_CURRENCY
	NLS_ISO_CURRENCY
	NLS_CALENDAR
TO_CHAR, TO_NCHAR	NLS_DATE_LANGUAGE
	NLS_NUMERIC_CHARACTERS
	NLS_CURRENCY
	NLS_DUAL_CURRENCY
	NLS_ISO_CURRENCY
	NLS_CALENDAR

Numbers, dates, and times can have a wide range of format masks applied for display. Within numbers, these masks allow embedding group and decimal separators, and the various currency symbols; dates can be formatted as virtually any combination of text and numbers; times can be shown with or without time zone indicators and as AM/PM or twenty-four hours.

Linguistic Sorting and Selection

Oracle's default sort order is binary. The strings to be sorted are read from left to right, and each character is reduced to its numeric ASCII (or EBCDIC) value. The sort is done in one pass. This may be suitable for American English, but it will give incorrect results for other languages. Obvious problems are diacritics such as *ä* or *à* and diphthongs like *æ*, but there are also more subtle matters. For example, in traditional Spanish, *ch* is a character in its own right that comes after *c*; thus the correct order is "Cerveze, Cordoba, Chavez." To sort this correctly, the database must inspect the following character as well as the current character, if the current character is a *c*.

TIP As a general rule, it is safe to assume that Oracle can handle just about any linguistic problem, but that you as DBA may not be competent to understand it. You will need an expert in whatever languages you are working in to advise.

Linguistic sorting means that rather than replacing each character with its numeric equivalent, Oracle will replace each character with a numeric value that reflects its correct position in the sequence appropriate to the language in use. There are some variations here, depending on the complexity of the environment.

A monolingual sort makes two passes through the strings being compared. The first pass is based on the "major" value of each character. The major value is derived by removing diacritic and case differences. In effect, each letter is considered as uppercase with no accents. Then a second comparison is made, using the "minor" values, which are case and diacritic sensitive. Monolingual sorts are much better than binary but are still not always adequate. For French, for example, Oracle provides the monolingual FRENCH sort order, and the multilingual FRENCH_M, which may be better if the data is not exclusively French.

A technique that may remove confusion is to use Oracle's case and diacritic-insensitive sort options. For example, you may wish to consider these variations on a Scottish name as equivalent:

MacKay
Mackay
MACKAY

To retrieve all three with one query, first set the NLS_SORT parameter to GENERIC_BASELETTER as shown in Figure 21-8. This will ignore case and diacritic variations. Then set the NLS_COMP parameter away from the default of BINARY to ANSI. This instructs Oracle to compare values using the NLS_SORT rules, not the numeric value of the character. The GENERIC_BASELETTER sort order will also

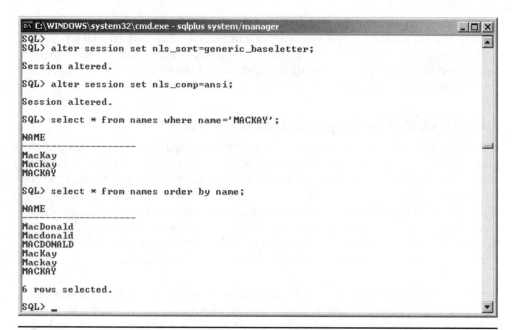

Figure 21-8 Case and accent insensitivity

"correct" what may appear to some as incorrect ordering. A more complex example would require equating "McKay" with "MacKay"; that would require the Locale Builder.

Similarly, all the sort orders can be suffixed with _AI or _CI for accent-insensitive and case-insensitive sorting. For example,

```
SQL> alter session set nls_sort=FRENCH_CI;
```

will ignore upper- and lowercase variations but will still handle accented characters according to French standards.

The Locale Builder

The Globalization support provided as standard by Oracle 10g is phenomenal, but there may be circumstances that it cannot handle. The Locale Builder is a graphical tool that can create a customized Globalization environment, by generating definitions for languages, territories, character sets, and linguistic sorting.

As an example, Oracle does not provide out-of-the-box support for Afrikaans; you could create a customized Globalization to fill this gap, which might combine elements of Dutch and English standards with customizations common in Southern Africa such as ignoring the punctuation marks or spaces in names like O'Hara or Du Toit. To launch the Locale Builder, run

```
$ORACLE_HOME/nls/lbuilder/lbuilder
```

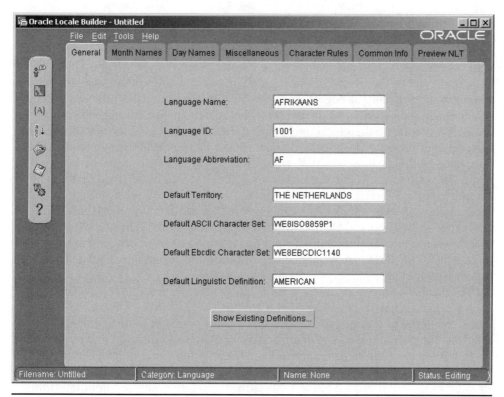

Figure 21-9   Creating a locale with the Locale Builder

on Unix, or

```
%ORACLE_HOME%\nls\lbuilder\lbuilder.bat
```

on Windows to view the dialog box shown in Figure 21-9.

Using Time Zones

Businesses, and therefore databases, must work across time zones. From release 9*i* onward, the Oracle environment can be made time zone aware. This is done by specifying a time zone in which the database operates, and then using the TIMESTAMP WITH TIME ZONE and TIMESTAMP WITH LOCAL TIME ZONE datatypes. The former will be not be normalized to the database time zone when it is stored, but it will have a time zone indicator to show the zone to which it refers. The latter is normalized to the database time zone on storage but is subsequently converted to the client time zone on retrieval. The usual DATE and TIMESTAMP datatypes are always normalized 33to the database time zone on storage and displayed unchanged when selected.

As an example of when time zone processing is important, consider an e-mail database hosted in London, set to Greenwich Mean Time, GMT. A user in Harare (which is two hours ahead of GMT) sends an e-mail at his local time of 15:00; the mail is addressed to two recipients, one in Paris (Central European Time, CET: one hour ahead of GMT with daylight saving time in effect in the Northern hemisphere summer) and the other in Bogotá (which is five hours behind GMT). How do you ensure that the recipients and the sender will all see the mail as having been sent correctly according to their local time zone? If the column denoting when the mail was sent is of datatype TIMESTAMP WITH LOCAL TIME ZONE, then when the mail is received by the database, the time will be normalized to GMT: it will be saved as 13:00. Then when the Bogotá user retrieves it, the time will be adjusted to 08:00 by his user process. When the Paris user retrieves the mail, he will see it as having been sent at either 14:00 or 15:00, depending on whether the date it was sent was in the period between March and October when daylight saving time is in effect. It is possible to do this type of work programmatically, but it requires a great deal of work as well as knowledge of all time zones and any local quirks for daylight saving. The database can do it all for you.

The database time zone can be set at creation time in the CREATE DATABASE command and adjusted later with ALTER DATABASE SET TIME_ZONE=.... If not set, it defaults to the time zone picked up from the host operating system at the time of creation. The client time zone defaults to that of the client operating system, or it can be set with the environment variable ORA_STDZ. Within a session, the time zone can be set with ALTER SESSION SET TIME_ZONE=.... Time zones can always be specified by full name, by abbreviated name, or as a fixed offset, in hours and minutes, from GMT. The last option cannot take account of daylight saving time adjustments. The list of supported time zones is displayed in V$TIMEZONE_NAMES.

Exercise 21-3: Making Time Zone Adjustments

Confirm and adjust your current time zone, using appropriate datatypes. Test the results using appropriate formatting masks.

1. Using SQL*Plus, connect to your instance as user SYSTEM.

2. Identify the database time zone with this query:

   ```
   SQL> select value from v$database_properties where property='DBTIMEZONE';
   ```
   and note the result.

3. Create a table as follows:

   ```
   SQL> create table times (date_std date, date_tz timestamp with time zone,
   date_ltz timestamp with local time zone);
   ```

4. View the list of supported time zones with this query:

   ```
   SQL> select * from $timezone_names;
   ```

5. Adjust your session time zone to something other than the database time zone, for example,

```
SQL> alter session set time_zone='Pacific/Tahiti';
```

6. Set your timestamp with time zone format to twenty-four-hour clock, with abbreviated time zone names with daylight saving variations.

```
SQL> alter session set nls_timestamp_tz_format='YYYY-MM-DD HH24:MI:SS TZD';
```

7. Set your timestamp format to twenty-four-hour clock.

```
SQL> alter session set nls_timestamp_format='YYYY-MM-DD HH24:MI:SS';
```

8. Set your date format to twenty-four-hour clock.

```
SQL> alter session set nls_date_format='YYYY-MM-DD HH24:MI:SS';
```

9. Insert a row into the table created in Step 3.

```
SQL> insert into times values('2004-10-26 15:00:00',
  '2004-10-26 15:00:00 PDT','2004-10-26 15:00:00');
```

10. Display the times.

```
SQL> select * from times;
```

Note that all times read 15:00.

11. Switch your session to the database time zone.

```
SQL> alter session set time_zone=DBTIMEZONE;
```

12. Repeat the query from Step 9, and note that the TIMESTAMP WITH LOCAL TIMEZONE has been adjusted to reflect that your session is now in a different zone.

13. Tidy up.

```
SQL> drop table times;
```

Chapter Review

Globalization capabilities allow you as DBA to customize the Oracle environment to take account of national language and culture variations. This is virtually essential in the modern world, where a database must present data in a variety of formats to suit a range of end users. Globalization parameters can be set at any of five levels: the database, the instance, the client environment, the session, and the statement.

The Globalization settings will influence, among other things, the languages for messages, sort orders, date formats, calendars, names of days and months, and numeric formats. Of vital importance is the choice of character sets, of which there are two. The database character set is used for VARCHAR2, CLOB, CHAR, and LONG columns; the National Character Set is used for NVARCHAR2, NCLOB, and NCHAR columns.

A related topic is time zones. These can now be specified for the database and per session, without ambiguity, if appropriate datatypes are used.

Questions

1. Your database was created with US7ASCII as the database character set, and you later find that this is inadequate. What can you do? (Choose the best answer.)

   A. Re-create the database.

   B. Issue an `alter database character set...` command.

   C. Issue an `alter system character set...` command.

   D. Generate a `create controlfile...` command, edit it to specify a different character set, and re-create the controlfile.

2. What are the options for the National Character Set?

   A. None. It must be AL16UTF16.

   B. It can be any Unicode character set.

   C. It can be either AL16UTF16 or UTF8.

   D. It can be any character set you require.

3. Match each character set with a type:

Character Set	Type
A. AL16UTF16	a. Seven-bit single-byte
B. US7ASCII	b. Eight-bit single-byte
C. UTF8	c. Fixed-width multibyte
D. WE8ISO8859P15	d. Variable-width multibyte

4. Which statements are correct about the TIMESTAMP WITH LOCAL TIME ZONE datatype? (Choose two answers.)

   A. Data is saved with a local time zone indicator.

   B. Data is normalized to the database time zone when it is saved.

   C. On retrieval, data is normalized to the retrieving client's time zone.

   D. On retrieval, data is normalized to the time zone of the client that entered it.

5. Globalization can be set at various levels. Put these in order of precedence, lowest first:

   A. Client environment

   B. Database settings

   C. Instance parameters

   D. Session parameters

   E. Statements

6. The NLS_LANGUAGE and NLS_TERRITORY parameters set defaults for a number of other Globalization parameters. Which of the following is controlled by NLS_LANGUAGE, and which by NLS_TERRITORY? (Two each.)

   A. NLS_DATE_LANGUAGE

   B. NLS_DATE_FORMAT

   C. NLS_NUMERIC_CHARACTERS

   D. NLS_SORT

7. Choose the best description of the Character Set Scanner tool:

   A. It scans character sets to assess their suitability for a particular language.

   B. It scans files to determine the language and character set of the data in them.

   C. It scans datafiles to determine whether the character set can be changed.

   D. It reports on problems a character set change would cause.

8. If the database and the user process are using different character sets, how does data get converted?

   A. Data is not converted, which is why there may be corruptions if the character sets are incompatible.

   B. On data entry, the instance converts data to the database character set. On retrieval, the user process converts to the client character set.

   C. Oracle Net will convert, in both directions.

   D. It depends on various NLS parameters.

9. The database is set to GMT. A client in Buenos Aires (three hours behind GMT) executes these statements at 10:00:00 local time:

```
create table times(c1 timestamp,
c2 timestamp with local time zone);
insert into times values(to_timestamp('10:00:00'),
  to_timestamp('10:00:00'));
commit;
```

   A client in Nairobi (three hours ahead of GMT) executes these statements at 18:00:00 local time:

```
alter session set nls_timestamp_format='hh24:mi:ss';
select * from times;
```

   What will the Nairobi user see for the columns c1 and c2?

   A. 10:00:00 and 16:00:00

   B. 13:00:00 and 16:00:00

   C. 13:00:00 and 10:00:00

   D. 10:00:00 and 13:00:00

10. Study the result of this query:

```
SQL> select * from dates;
C1
--------
03-04-05
```

C1 is a date-type column. How could you determine what the date returned actually means? (Choose two answers.)

A. Query NLS_DATABASE_PARAMETERS.

B. Query NLS_INSTANCE_PARAMETERS.

C. Query NLS_SESSION_PARAMETERS.

D. Set your NLS_DATE_FORMAT to a known value, and re-run the query.

E. Change the query to use TO_CHAR with an NLS parameter.

11. How can you prevent users from causing confusion with, for instance, date and time formats by setting local Globalization environment variables?

A. You can't; the users have control over this.

B. Write logon triggers to set the session environment.

C. Set instance Globalization parameters to override client-side settings.

D. Configure Oracle Net to convert all data sent to and from the database appropriately.

12. Which view will tell you what languages can be supported by your installation? (Choose the best answer.)

A. NLS_DATABASE_PARAMETERS

B. NLS_INSTANCE_PARAMETERS

C. V$NLS_VALID_VALUES

D. V$NLS_LANGUAGES

13. You want to make the order in which sorted names are returned independent of whether the names include accented characters, upper- and lowercase characters, punctuation marks, or spaces. How can you do this? (Choose the best answer.)

A. Set the sort order to GENERIC_BASELETTER, which will ignore such variations.

B. Use the _AI and _CI versions of any of the supported sort orders.

C. Use the Locale Builder to design a custom sort order.

D. This cannot be done.

Answers

1. **B.** Use this command, but test with the character set scanner first.

2. **C.** Either of these Unicode sets is currently allowed.

3. **A-c; B-a; C-d; D-b**

4. **B and C.** This is the datatype that fully normalizes times to and from the database.

5. The correct order is **B, C, A, D, E.** Instance parameters override the database parameters, and then on the client-side environment variables can be overridden by ALTER SESSION commands, and then by individual statements.

6. **A and D.** NLS_DATE_LANGUAGE and NLS_SORT are the two parameters controlled by the NLS_LANGUAGE. The others are two of several controlled by NLS_TERRITORY.

7. **D.** It will, for instance, report if a changed encoding would prevent data from fitting into a column.

8. **C.** Oracle Net will do the conversion to the best of its ability.

9. **B.** The database will normalize the time 10:00:00 from the local time zone at the point of entry, GMT+3, to the database time zone, GMT. Thus both times are saved as 13:00:00 GMT. For retrieval, the timestamp column will be displayed as saved, 13:00:00, but the timestamp with local time zone column will adjust the time to that of the time zone of the client retrieving the data, which is GMT+3.

10. **C and D.** NLS_SESSION_PARAMETERS will show the format used so that you can interpret the output of the query correctly, or you could set the format to a sensible value and re-run the query.

11. **B.** The best option is to write logon triggers, which will prevent any possible confusion caused by the client configuration.

12. **C.** This view will show you the full range of supported languages, as well as all other globalization options.

13. **C.** To remove punctuation marks and spaces as well, you will need to create your own variation with the Locale Builder.

PART II

Oracle Database 10*g*
Administrative II Exam

CHAPTER 22

Configuring Security
for the Listener

In this chapter you will learn how to
- Secure the listener
- Remove the default EXTPROC entry
- Add a separate listener to handle external procedure calls

Chapter 12 covers basic listener configuration: how to create a listener process that will monitor one or more ports on one or more network addresses for incoming connection requests and spawn server processes against one or more instances. This chapter covers three advanced features of the listener: First, how to control administrative access. Second, how to configure the listener to reject connection requests from unauthorized sources. And third, how to set up a listener to run external procedures. These are programs written in C and invoked from a normal database session. In order to understand this capability, you will also read a brief discussion of how to create an external procedure, though this would normally be the responsibility of programmers, not the DBA.

Securing the Listener

Some of the listener control administration commands are protected against execution by unauthorized users. Others are not; any user with execute permissions on the lsnrctl executable can run them. To display the common administration commands, run `lsnrctl help` from an operating system prompt. The commands are shown in the following table:

Command	Protected?
Change_Password	Yes
Exit	No
Quit	No
Reload	Yes
Save_Config	Yes
Services	Yes
Set	Varies according to the parameter being set
Show	Yes
Start	No
Status	Yes
Stop	Yes
Trace	Yes
Version	No

Listener Operating System Authentication

The default security for listener administrative commands is based on operating system user ID. Anyone logged on to the server machine as the user who started the listener has full access to it, including the ability to stop it. By default, no one else can do so. This form of security is always enabled and will take precedence over password security. Thus, even if you do not know the listener password, you can still administer the listener if you know the operating system password of the user who started it. This is exactly analogous to operating system authentication for a SYSDBA connection to a database, which will bypass password file authentication.

Listener Password Authentication

Setting a listener password provides an additional authentication method for giving permission to execute the protected commands, such as STOP. It may well be that the listener is started by scripts running under the operating system ID of the Oracle owner, and that you do not wish to give this login username/password to the junior DBAs. In order to allow them to administer the listener, set a password for it.

Listener passwords can be enabled and set through the Net Manager GUI, through Database Control, with the lsnrctl utility, or by editing the listener.ora file by hand. The last option will not encrypt the password, so it should be used only if the purpose of the password is to prevent mistakes rather than to prevent malicious interference.

To set a password with Database Control, take the Listener link from the database home page, and navigate to the Authentication page as shown in Figure 22-1. Figure 22-2 illustrates how to make the same setting using the Net Manager.

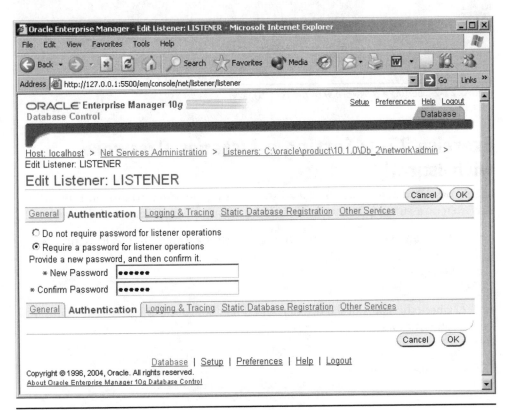

Figure 22-1   Setting a listener password with Database Control

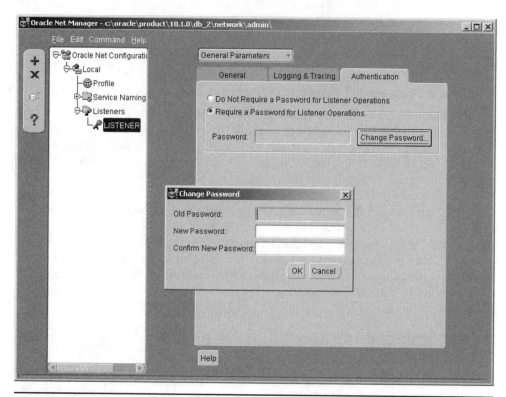

Figure 22-2   Setting a password with the Net Manager

Exercise 22-1: Setting a Listener Password with lsnrctl

Enable password authentication for a listener, using the lsnrctl command-line utility. This exercise assumes that your listener is the default listener, named LISTENER.

1. From an operating system prompt, launch the lsnrctl utility. On Windows,

   ```
   C:\> lsnrctl
   ```

   or Unix,

   ```
   $ lsnrctl
   ```

2. Check the status of the listener, and if it is not running, start it. For example, on Windows,

   ```
   C:\>lsnrctl
   LSNRCTL for 32-bit Windows: Version 10.1.0.2.0 - Production on
   24-JAN-2005 13:06:55
   Copyright (c) 1991, 2004, Oracle.  All rights reserved.
   ```

```
Welcome to LSNRCTL, type "help" for information.
LSNRCTL> status
Connecting to (DESCRIPTION=(ADDRESS=(PROTOCOL=TCP)(HOST=ora10g)(PORT=1521)))
TNS-12541: TNS:no listener
 TNS-12560: TNS:protocol adapter error
  TNS-00511: No listener
   32-bit Windows Error: 61: Unknown error
LSNRCTL> start
Starting tnslsnr: please wait...
```

3. Choose a password (in the example that follows, it is "pass," but this is not displayed) and apply it as shown here. As there is no password currently, press ENTER when prompted for the old password.

```
LSNRCTL>
LSNRCTL> change_password
Old password:
New password:
Reenter new password:
Connecting to (DESCRIPTION=(ADDRESS=(PROTOCOL=TCP)(HOST=ora10g)(PORT=1521)))
Password changed for LISTENER
The command completed successfully
LSNRCTL>
```

4. Save the password to the listener.ora file.

```
LSNRCTL>
LSNRCTL> save_config
Connecting to (DESCRIPTION=(ADDRESS=(PROTOCOL=TCP)(HOST=ora10g)(PORT=1521)))
Saved LISTENER configuration parameters.
Listener Parameter File   c:\oracle\product\10.1.0\db_2\network\
admin\listener.ora
Old Parameter File   c:\oracle\product\10.1.0\db_2\network\admin\
listener.bak
The command completed successfully
LSNRCTL>
```

5. Set your lsnrctl session to use the password, and confirm that you can stop the listener.

```
LSNRCTL>
LSNRCTL> set password pass
The command completed successfully
LSNRCTL> stop
Connecting to (DESCRIPTION=(ADDRESS=(PROTOCOL=TCP)(HOST=ora10g)(PORT=1521)))
The command completed successfully
LSNRCTL>
```

6. Exit from lsnrctl, use an editor to open the listener.ora file, and observe the encrypted password.

```
LISTENER =
  (DESCRIPTION =
    (ADDRESS = (PROTOCOL = TCP)(HOST = ora10g)(PORT = 1521))
  )
#----ADDED BY TNSLSNR 06-NOV-2004 18:31:37---
PASSWORDS_LISTENER = 1AB3AFF023F1126C
#----------------------------------------------
```

PART II

Controlling Database Access

The default listener configuration places no limits at all on who can connect to the database server: all security must be managed within the database or the application. There will be many cases where it is desirable to limit access to users connecting from certain machines or subnets. This can of course be done by a well-configured firewall, but such restrictions can also be enforced by the listener itself.

TIP If your firewall is not capable of proxying Oracle Net traffic securely, then the Oracle Net Connection Manager can be used as a proxy server instead. The Connection Manager is not installed by default; you have to select it in a "custom" installation.

Controlling access to a listener is done through configuring Oracle Net profiles, which are in fact a set of directives in the sqlnet.ora file on the server machine. Remember from Chapter 12 that the sqlnet.ora file is optional on both the client side and the server side; listener security is a case where it becomes necessary. The directives are as follows:

- TCP.VALIDNODE_CHECKING
- TCP.EXCLUDED_NODES
- TCP.INVITED_NODES

Once TCP.VALIDNODE_CHECKING is changed to YES from its default of NO, the other directives are enabled. In practice, it is necessary to set only one of them. If any node is listed in TCP.INVITED_NODES, then all other nodes are implicitly excluded; if any node is listed in TCP.EXCLUDED_NODES, then all other nodes are implicitly invited. If both directives are set and there is a conflict, then the TCP.INVITED_NODES list takes precedence.

The invited and excluded nodes can be listed by name or by IP address, but the syntax does not permit wildcards; each node must be listed individually. For this reason, access control by the listener is most useful in a three-tier environment, where all the sessions are spawned from a small number of application servers with fixed IP addresses. Listing these in the TCP.INVITED_NODES list will ensure that no users can bypass the application servers and make client/server connections to the database. A large client base of PC terminals using dynamically acquired IP addresses cannot easily be controlled in this manner. Note that this mechanism applies only to TCP. Connections from user processes running on the server machine using IPC will always be accepted. The profile can be created either with the Net Manager GUI as shown in Figure 22-3 or by editing the sqlnet.ora file directly.

The directives in sqlnet.ora will be

```
TCP.VALIDNODE_CHECKING = YES
TCP.INVITED_NODES = (as1.haunting.com, as2.haunting.com)
```

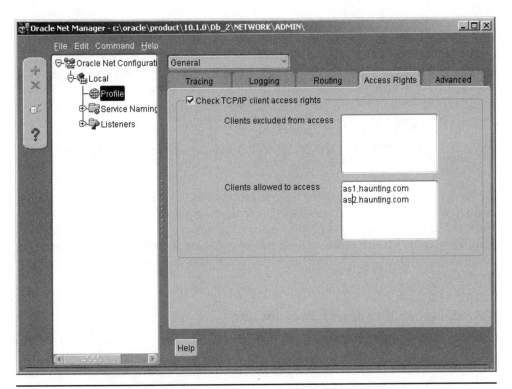

Figure 22-3 Using Net Manager to limit access to the database

 TIP The Connection Manager gives greater control over access, including use of wildcards in both hostnames and IP addresses.

External Procedures

Oracle stored procedures can be written in either PL/SQL or Java. Usually, one or the other of these languages is adequate for any processing that may be required, but there are occasions when developers will wish to use another language. Oracle supports the use of C as a development tool for procedures to be run on the database server and invoked by sessions using the same syntax as that used for invoking a normal PL/SQL procedure.

 EXAM TIP External procedures must be written in C. User process software, linked with the OCI libraries, can be written in C or in C++.

A typical reason for using C would be performance. Neither PL/SQL nor Java stored procedures are directly executable by the operating system; a large element of interpretation is required when stored procedures are invoked. Functions written in C can be compiled down to object code and linked, cutting out the interpretation phase and also making many operations, such as jumps, much quicker.

 TIP It is possible to convert your PL/SQL code to C and then compile and link it, which may give great performance gains. This is the "native compilation" technique, enabled through the PLSQL_CODE_TYPE initialization parameter.

Dynamic link libraries must be dynamically linked to something before the code in them can execute. This is where the listener takes on a special role. Usually, a listener launches server processes. Through the external procedure mechanism, it can also launch a process known as the external procedure agent. This agent has only one function: to dynamically link and run external procedures, in response to invocations by database users.

Creating an External Procedure

There are three steps in creating an external procedure:

- Write, compile, and link the C function.
- Create an Oracle library.
- Create a PL/SQL procedure to call the C function.

The C function itself must be created by the programmers like any other C function. Then it needs to be compiled and linked to the operating system as a shared object library. The result will be a file suffixed according to the conventions of the operating system: .DLL for Windows, or .so for Solaris, or .sl for HP-UX. Take this file and save it to a suitable directory on the database server.

To inform Oracle of the shared object library's existence, issue a CREATE LIBRARY command, such as

```
SQL> create library util_lib as '/OR/newlib/c_utils.so';
```

on Unix or

```
SQL> create library util_lib as 'd:\or\newlib\c_utils.dll';
```

on Windows, which will create a logical pointer, UTIL_LIB, to the physical file delivered by the programmers. In this example, the library resides on the same machine as the database.

TIP It is possible to create a library that points to a file on a remote machine by specifying an AGENT after the filename, where the AGENT is a database link. This would allow you to offload some of the processing from the database server machine to another machine, which might be better optimized for running the external procedures.

Finally, the PL/SQL procedure that will invoke the C function is needed:

```
SQL> create or replace procedure util1 (p1 in out number)
as
language C
name c_util1
library util_lib
parameters (p1 by reference);
```

This PL/SQL procedure can be invoked like any other procedure. It will accept the in/out numeric argument P1 and pass this through by reference to the C function c_util1 in the shared object library referred to by UTIL_LIB. The C function will receive the argument as a pointer, do whatever it has to do, and then return control to PL/SQL. The PL/SQL session will then have access to the changed value of the parameter.

The External Procedure Agent

The *external procedure agent* is an executable file in the ORACLE_HOME/bin directory, called extproc on Unix and extproc.exe on Windows. It is launched on demand by the listener. When an external procedure is invoked by a PL/SQL procedure, the agent will convert the PL/SQL calls into C calls, load the shared library, and execute the function requested. It will raise any exceptions that might occur and return exceptions or arguments back to the PL/SQL environment.

The agent offers some built-in security. By default, the agent can load shared libraries only from the ORACLE_HOME/lib directory, which should be tightly controlled. Otherwise, it would be possible for a malicious user to write a PL/SQL procedure that would invoke C procedures from any of the standard shared libraries available on the server's operating system. It is good practice to restrict the shared libraries that the agent can load by nominating them in the listener.ora file, as shown next.

Configuring the Listener to Launch the Agent

The listener needs to be configured to accept calls to launch the external procedure agent. The mechanism is similar to launching a server process: the agent is launched on demand, one agent per session, and will remain active for the lifetime of the session. Thus, no matter how many external procedure calls are made, the agent has to be launched only once per session. The operating system will use shared memory for the agent, so there will be no memory overhead to launching one agent for each session that requires one, but there will be an impact on the number of processes that the operating system has to manage.

PART II

Just as a database instance must be registered with a listener if a listener is to launch sessions against it, the external procedure agent must also be registered with a listener. Unfortunately this can't be done automatically, as with dynamic instance registration; you will have to configure the listener.ora file, either through the Net Manager GUI as shown in Figure 22-4, through Database Control, or by editing it by hand.

The listener configured in the figure would appear in the listener.ora file as follows:

```
EXT_PROC_LISTENER =
  (DESCRIPTION =
    (ADDRESS = (PROTOCOL = IPC)(KEY = ext_proc1))
  )
SID_LIST_EXT_PROC_LISTENER =
  (SID_LIST =
    (SID_DESC =
      (PROGRAM = extproc.exe)
      (SID_NAME = ext_proc)
      (ORACLE_HOME = c:\oracle\product\10.1.9\db_2)
    )
  )
```

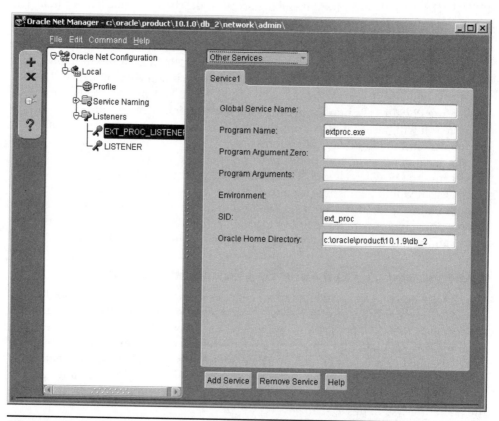

Figure 22-4 Configuring an external procedure agent through the Net Manager

The listener has a name, EXT_PROC_LISTENER in the example. It is perfectly possible to add an external procedure service to the SID list of an existing listener, but it is generally considered good security policy to create a separate listener, with its own listening address(es), specifically for launching external procedures. This listener is only listening on the IPC protocol, so there is no way it can be contacted by any process not running on the database server machine. It is not possible to invoke an external procedure by any other protocol. The IPC "key," which by analogy with TCP is the "port," is called ext_proc1. This must be unique for all IPC services on the server. A hard-coded SID list for the listener is also essential, because external procedure agents cannot register themselves in the manner that database instances can.

The SID list specifies that requests for the ext_proc service will be routed through to the program extproc.exe. The listener then needs to be started in the normal manner, but you may want to start it using an operating system ID other than that of the Oracle owner. The external procedure agents launched by the listener will run with the operating system ID and permissions of the user who started the listener. Security will be considerably improved if you create an operating system user for this purpose with the bare minimum of permissions needed: execute on lsnrctl, the extproc program, and the dynamic link libraries to be loaded, and read (but not write) on listener.ora.

Once a listener has been configured, the client side of Oracle Net needs to be set up so that the server processes can find it when they want to run an external procedure. This will typically be done by inserting an entry in the tnsnames.ora file on the database server. Again, this can be done through the Net Manager or by hand:

```
EXTPROC_CONNECTION_DATA =
  (DESCRIPTION =
    (ADDRESS_LIST =
      (ADDRESS = (PROTOCOL = IPC)(Key = EXTPROC1))
    )
    (CONNECT_DATA =
      (SID = ext_proc)
    )
  )
```

The connection string alias is EXTPROC_CONNECTION_DATA. There is no choice about this: this is the alias that Oracle will always look for to find the address of the external procedure listener. The address is the IPC key EXTPROC1, which must match the listening address specified on the listener configuration file. Then the SID is ext_proc, which the listener will map on to the executable extproc.exe.

EXAM TIP When configuring external procedure services, you can choose the key and the SID name, and you can even nominate your own process to launch, but you must use the IPC protocol and the TNS alias must be EXTPROC_CONNECTION_DATA.

For security, it is advisable to limit the dynamic link libraries that can be run as external procedures. The default security is that the libraries must reside in the ORACLE_HOME/lib directory on Unix or the ORACLE_HOME\bin directory on

Windows. This is better than having no security at all, but it is still somewhat dangerous. It is good practice to nominate the libraries with an additional directive in the SID_DESC section of the listener.ora file; for example,

```
(SID_DESC =
(PROGRAM = extproc)
(SID_NAME = ext_proc)
(ENVS="EXTPROC_DLLS=ONLY:/or/newlib/c_utils.so:/or/newlib/more_utils.so")
)
```

will restrict external procedures to referencing functions in the two named files.

Summary of Responsibilities and Flow Control

These are the essential components for running external procedures:

- **The database**   Responsible for storing information required to locate and execute an external procedure. Both the library alias and the call specification are stored as database objects.

- **The session**   The users' database sessions are responsible for initiating the calls to the external procedures.

- **The listener**   Listens for external procedure requests from database sessions and launches the external procedure agent processes, one per session.

- **The external procedure agent**   Accepts information (arguments, name and location of the library) from the session; loads the shared libraries as required; executes the C functions.

- **The user-provided compiled and linked shared library**   Contains the functions that implement the desired functionality.

- **The library alias**   Records the physical name and location of the shared library, storing it within the database as a library object.

- **The external procedure call specification**   Provides a description of the procedure, including its PL/SQL name and arguments; the library alias; and the C function that implements the procedure. This is stored within the database as a PL/SQL stored procedure.

This is the sequence of events:

- The user invokes the PL/SQL call specification via the EXECUTE command, or any other means.

- The session examines the call specification and finds the name of the shared library and the function within it that implement the procedure, and the number and type of the arguments.

- The session uses the service name EXTPROC_CONNECTION_DATA to look up the Oracle Net connection details to contact the external procedure listener.

- The listener spawns an external procedure agent process to service the request, and returns the address of the new agent to the session.

- The session sends the agent the name of the shared library, the name of the C function within it to run, and the arguments (converted from PL/SQL datatypes to C datatypes).

- The external procedure agent loads the shared library, invokes the C function, converts any returned data to the corresponding PL/SQL datatypes, and returns the data to the session.

Exercise 22-2: Creating a Listener for External Procedure Calls

Create a dedicated listener for servicing external procedure calls, using Database Control.

1. Connect to your database as user SYSTEM using Database Control.

2. Click the Listener link in the General section of the database home page, and then the Net Services Administration link under Related Links to reach the Net Services Administration window.

3. Select Listeners in the Administer drop-down box, and click Go to reach the Host Login window.

4. Enter a suitable operating system username and password, and click Login to reach the Listeners window.

5. Click Create to reach the Create Listener window.

6. Enter a sensibly descriptive listener name, such as **CALLOUT_LISTENER**, and click Add in the Addresses section to reach the Add Address window.

7. Select IPC in the Protocol drop-down box, and then provide a key, such as **EXTPROC1** (this key must be unique on the machine) and click OK to return to the Create Listener window.

8. Click the Other Services link in the General section and then Add to reach the Create Other Service window.

9. Enter **extproc** as the program name and **PLSextproc** as the Oracle System Identifier (SID), and enter your Oracle home directory. Then click OK to return to the Create Listener window.

10. Click OK to create the listener.

11. Select the radio button for your new listener and Start/Stop in the Actions drop-down box. Click Go and then OK to confirm.

12. When the listener has started, take the View Details link to see the output of the startup command as shown in Figure 22-5.

PART II

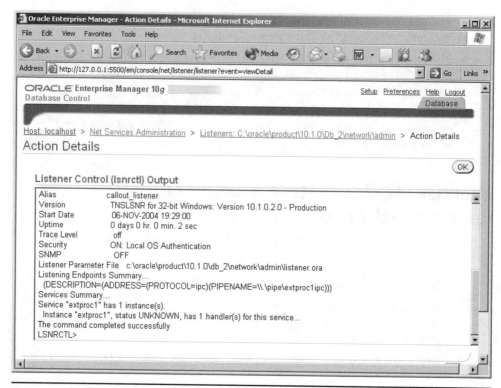

Figure 22-5   Successful start of an external procedure listener

Chapter Review

This chapter covered some advanced features of Oracle Net. First, in order to prevent unauthorized listener administration—which can be either accidental (if there are multiple DBAs working on one machine) or malicious—some listener control commands can be protected by a password. Enabled by default is operating system authentication, meaning that only the operating system user who started a listener can stop it. Setting a password means that anyone can control the listener, provided s/he knows the password.

Second, by default, a listener will connect a user from any node to the database; all security must be handled by the database server itself. You can set up access control within the listener, by coding a list of nodes from which sessions are permitted or rejected. This mechanism is very simple—it cannot use wildcards, for example—but very effective if all the connections should come from a few addresses, as would be the case in an application server environment.

Third, you saw how it is possible for a user to run code written in C as though it were a normal PL/SQL procedure. This is done through Oracle Net, by configuring a listener to launch an agent that can load and run external dynamic link libraries.

Questions

1. Of these four lsnrctl commands, which can be executed by anyone, regardless of whether any security can be configured? (Choose two answers.)

    A. Start

    B. Status

    C. Stop

    D. Version

2. Any of several tools can be used to set a listener password, but it might not be encrypted. Which of the following will encrypt the password? (Choose the best answer.)

    A. Enterprise Manager Database Control

    B. The lsnrctl utility

    C. The Net Manager

    D. All of the above

For the next two questions, examine these entries in the server-side sqlnet.ora file:

```
tcp.validnode_checking=yes
tcp.invited_nodes=pc1.haunting.com,pc2.haunting.com
tcp.excluded_nodes=pc2.haunting.com,pc3.haunting.com
```

3. A user working on pc2.haunting.com attempts to connect. What will happen? (Choose the best answer.)

    A. The session will be established by the listener.

    B. The session will be rejected by the listener.

    C. It will depend on whether the tcp.invited_nodes directive is before or after the tcp.excluded_nodes directive.

    D. The listener would not have started up because of the conflicting entries.

4. A user working on pc5.haunting.com attempts to connect. What will happen? (Choose the best answer.)

    A. The session will be established by the listener.

    B. The session will be rejected by the listener.

    C. The listener would not have started up because of the conflicting entries.

5. If your user community is connecting from PCs using dynamically acquired IP addresses on the class C subnet 10.10.10.*, how can you best limit access to those PCs only? (Choose the best answer.)

    A. Set the tcp.invited_nodes directive to 10.10.10.*

    B. Use a Connection Manager to filter requests.

    C. List all 256 addresses on the subnet as tcp.invited_nodes.

    D. You can't; access control can only work with static addresses.

6. What language(s) can be used to write external procedures? (Choose the best answer.)

   A. C

   B. C++

   C. Java

   D. PL/SQL

   E. Any of the above

7. When will an external procedure agent be launched? (Choose the best answer.)

   A. The first time any user invokes an external procedure, the listener will launch an agent to use for all subsequent calls by all sessions.

   B. The first time a user invokes an external procedure, the listener will launch an agent to use for all subsequent calls by that session.

   C. An agent will be launched for each call made, by any session.

   D. The agent will be launched when the external procedure listener is first started.

8. Information needed to run external procedures is stored on different places. Match the following items to storage places.

Item	Storage Place
A. The C function	a. The database
B. The datatypes of the arguments	b. The dynamic link library
C. The dynamic link library	c. The library object
D. The library object	d. The listener.ora file
E. The location of the dynamic link library	e. The PL/SQL call specification
F. The name of the agent	f. The server's file system
G. The PL/SQL call specification	

9. Which protocol(s) can be used to contact a listener for launching an external procedure agent? (Choose the best answer.)

   A. IPC

   B. TCP

   C. TCP with secure sockets

   D. Named Pipes

   E. All of the above

10. When running an external procedure, place these steps in the correct sequence:

    A. The agent executes the external procedure.

    B. The agent loads the library.

    C. The listener launches an agent.

    D. The request is passed to the listener.

    E. The server process executes a PL/SQL procedure, and looks up a library alias.

    F. The user process invokes a PL/SQL procedure.

Answers

1. **A and D.** Neither Version nor (perhaps surprisingly) Start are protected.

2. **D.** The one technique that will not encrypt the password is editing the listener.ora file by hand.

3. **A.** If both the tcp.invited_nodes and tcp.excluded_nodes directives are present, then tcp.excluded_nodes is ignored by the listener.

4. **B.** If the tcp.invited_nodes directive is present, than all nodes not specifically listed are blocked.

5. **B.** In an environment like this, the Connection Manager is the best option. Choice C would work but would be impossibly clumsy.

6. **A.** C, and not C++, is the only supported language.

7. **B.** Each session will get its own agent, launched when the session first invokes an external procedure.

8. **A-b.** The programmers produce a library file containing the executable code.

    B-e. The PL/SQL call specification details both the PL/SQL datatypes and the C datatypes.

    C-f. The library is just a file, stored in the file system on the server machine.

    D-a. An Oracle library is a database object, stored in the data dictionary.

    E-c. The physical location of the library file is stored as a library object.

    F-d. The agent is the PROGRAM specified in the SID_DESC in listener.ora.

    G-a. Like any other stored procedure, the PL/SQL specification is a procedural object stored in the data dictionary.

9. **A.** IPC is currently the only supported protocol.

10. The sequence is **F, E, D, C, B, A.**

CHAPTER 23

Getting Started with Oracle Recovery Manager (RMAN)

In this chapter you will learn how to

- Configure database parameters that affect RMAN operations
- Change RMAN default settings with CONFIGURE
- Manage RMAN's persistent settings
- Start RMAN utility and allocate channels

Elementary use of the Recovery Manager, RMAN, is described in Chapters 19 and 20. For the second of the two OCP examinations you must demonstrate much greater knowledge of RMAN than that. This is the first of several chapters that go into RMAN to the necessary depth. It details the architecture of the RMAN environment, including its relationship with third-party backup solutions and automated tape robots and with the flash recovery area, and how to configure various options. But first, a summary of RMAN's capabilities.

Recovery Manager Features

It is possible to recover from any disaster without any loss of data if you have a backup of your datafiles and copies of all the archive logs made since the backup was taken. The one exception to this rule is if you lose all copies of the current online redo log file. This should never happen if it is adequately multiplexed—and by configuring Data Guard for zero data loss, even this eventuality can be survived. However, if done manually through operating system and SQL*Plus commands, restore and recovery can be an extremely awkward process. RMAN automates the whole cycle of backup, restore, and recovery through its scripting language and its integration with Database Control. There is no question that RMAN is a better tool for backup and recovery than the alternative user-managed backup techniques. Oracle Corporation strongly advises all users to make use of RMAN.

The objects that RMAN can back up are whole databases, or individual tablespaces and datafiles. The controlfile and the spfile can also be included, as can the archive logs. The only part of the database that is not backed up is the online redo log files: these are protected by multiplexing. These backups can be image copies (where the output file is byte for byte the same as the input file) or backup sets. The backup set is a proprietary format that can be streamed directly to tape and optionally compressed. By combining the use of image copies and backup sets, RMAN can give you an extraordinarily fast recovery. For instance, the first level of backup can be to a disk copy, which is then updated with incremental backup sets and migrated to tape-based backup sets as a second level of backup. RMAN will then select the fastest possible means of restore and recovery from all the available backups.

RMAN can also do things that cannot be done with operating system and SQL*Plus commands. It can do incremental backups, which reduce the volume of backup data dramatically. It can even apply incrementals to whole backups, in effect bringing them forward in time to reduce the recovery time if it is ever needed. The time for an incremental backup may also be much reduced when compared to a full backup. The granularity of a restore and recover operation is the datafile when using traditional methods; the granularity of an RMAN restore and recover can be just one corrupted datafile block. This can reduce the MTTR significantly. Indeed, by using block-level media recovery, it may be possible to detect and repair damage without any downtime at all. Associated with this is corrupt block detection: RMAN will validate the contents of blocks as it scans them, meaning that you may become aware of problems before your end users notice.

Most IT sites will have an automated tape library: a robot system with one or more tape drives capable of storing many tape cartridges. Some are of very limited capacity, with one drive and storage for a dozen cartridges, but others are much more powerful: perhaps a dozen drives and storage for hundreds or thousands of cartridges. Such devices are not cheap—they may have a six-figure price tag—but they are extremely capable. To exploit the full power of RMAN, it needs to be integrated with a tape library. Then the whole backup and recovery cycle can be wholly delegated to RMAN. It will take control of the library and load, read, write, and clear tapes as necessary. The combination of RMAN and a tape library means that the backup routines can run unattended indefinitely, while you can have absolute confidence in the ability to recover from any disaster.

 TIP There are, not infrequently, political problems with the use of RMAN. In many IT installations, it is the system administrators who are responsible for backups. But RMAN transfers that responsibility to the DBAs. You will have to work closely with your system administrators and be aware that they may consider you to be encroaching on their domain.

Recovery Manager Components

The Recovery Manager tool consists of a number of components, some required and some optional. Following an absolutely standard installation of the Oracle software and the creation of a database, it is possible to run the RMAN executable and perform a backup with just two words: BACKUP DATABASE. This will perform a full backup, hot or cold, relying completely on defaults. But to exploit the full power of RMAN, you will certainly need to configure it, and to consider using some of the optional components.

The RMAN Executable

The interactive tool used to manage RMAN is rman.exe on Windows or rman on Unix, in the ORACLE_HOME/bin directory. This provides a command-line interface to RMAN. In some ways it is a user process like any other. It connects to a database via a listener and a server process, prompts for commands from the user, and sends them to the instance for execution. The executable can be run from the same ORACLE_HOME as the database that is being backed up, or it can be run from another computer anywhere on the network, provided that the versions of the RMAN executable and the target database match.

An alternative user interface tool is to use Database Control, which gives a graphical interface. Whichever interface you use, you are in fact invoking PL/SQL procedures. RMAN is implemented with the package DBMS_BACKUP_RESTORE. This package is kernelized, meaning that it is part of the instance itself. This is a very significant feature: you do not need to have an open database in order to use RMAN. Normal PL/SQL stored procedures are stored within the data dictionary, so if the database isn't open, you can't get to them. Because the RMAN procedures are part of the kernel, they are always available so long as the instance exists in memory. This means that even if the database is so severely damaged that you cannot even mount it—because you have lost all your controlfiles—the RMAN executable will still have access to the procedures it needs to carry out a restore operation.

 TIP Ensure that the RMAN executable version matches the version of the target database that is being backed up, but the RMAN executable doesn't have to be the same release as the catalog database.

The Target Databases

The "target" is the database that you intend to back up, or to restore and recover. The RMAN executable can connect to only one target at a time; if you are running multiple databases, you connect to each in turn. The controlfile of the target stores information that RMAN needs. RMAN reads the controlfile to determine the physical structure of the database: the location of the datafiles to be backed up. Also stored in the controlfile are details of archived logs, which RMAN must also back up. RMAN itself writes to the target database controlfile details of the backups that it has performed, so that in the event a restore and recovery are necessary, the information on the location of the backups will be available. If the target database is completely destroyed, including all copies of the controlfile, it will still be possible for RMAN to restore it, provided that RMAN has been configured appropriately.

Server Processes and Channels

RMAN connects to an instance through a normal server session and process, which invokes the PL/SQL procedures. But there are more server processes than that.

Whenever a backup or restore operation is initiated, at least one "channel" will be launched. A *channel* is a server process that does the work of copying files. By launching multiple channels, backup and restore operations can be parallelized. Note that the RMAN executable and its session does not itself perform the backup: it is a control process that invokes PL/SQL procedures in the target database that will launch additional server processes, the channels, on the target server to do the work. These channel processes are of two types: *disk channels* that are capable of backing up to (or restoring from) disk destinations, and *System Backup to Tape* (known as *SBT*) channels that are capable of working with tape devices, such as an automated tape library. Channels can be launched manually using the ALLOCATE CHANNEL command, or RMAN can launch channels automatically according to preconfigured defaults.

A third type of server process is the *polling process*. This is launched automatically whenever a backup or restore operation is running. The polling process monitors and reports on the progress of the operation.

The RMAN Repository

The *repository* is a store of metadata about the target database and its backups. It contains details of the physical structure of the database: the locations of the datafiles; details of all the backups that have been made; and RMAN's persistent configuration settings. The repository is always stored in the controlfile of the target database, and optionally in a Recovery Catalog as well.

If the repository is lost, then RMAN is crippled. Your backups will be fine, but RMAN won't know where they are. However, it should still be possible to rebuild the repository and continue to work, provided appropriate precautions have been taken.

The Recovery Catalog

RMAN's repository is always written to the target database's controlfile, but it can also be written out to a separate Oracle database. This database is known as the Recovery Catalog. Using RMAN with a Recovery Catalog enhances its capabilities substantially.

First, and perhaps most important, with a Recovery Catalog you are no longer dependent upon the target database controlfile. What if all copies of the controlfile are destroyed? Your backups are perfect, but without a repository, RMAN will never be able to find them. In fact, it may be possible to survive this situation: you can instruct RMAN to scan your backup devices and locate and identify any backups, but a far preferable situation is to have the repository always available in a Recovery Catalog database, on a separate machine from the target.

Second, the Recovery Catalog can store RMAN scripts. Without a Recovery Catalog, you can still use scripts but they have to be stored as operating system files on the machine where you are running the RMAN executable.

Third, if you are supporting many databases, one Recovery Catalog can be used to store metadata about all of them. It becomes a centralized repository of all your backup and restore information. Note that one Catalog can be used with databases on any platform. You could, for example, run the RMAN executable on a Windows PC and connect to a Recovery Catalog in a database on a Unix host, and then connect to a series of target databases on Windows, Unix, VMS, and any other platform.

And last, there is no limit to the length of time for which a Recovery Catalog can retain this metadata. The controlfile-based repository will retain data for only the time specified by the instance parameter CONTROL_FILE_RECORD_KEEP_TIME. This defaults to just seven days. You can certainly increase the value of this parameter, but to increase it to, for example, several months would be to use the controlfile for a purpose for which it was never intended: it is meant to be a store of currently relevant information, not a long-term storage place.

The Recovery Catalog database will usually not be a particularly large or busy database, and it will not have very demanding resource requirements, but it will improve RMAN functionality significantly.

Media Management Library

The full power of RMAN can be exploited only if you associate it with an automated tape robot, which can manage your library of tape cartridges. Given such a library, RMAN can automate completely the backup and restore cycle. To use a tape library, the Oracle instance must be linked to a device driver supplied by the vendor of the library. With earlier releases this required relinking the Oracle executables, but from release 9i onward the tape library driver is dynamically linked. The driver will come with instructions on how to link it. Once a Media Management Library driver has been linked to Oracle, you can launch channels of type SBT_TAPE, which will be able to use the tape library and indeed control it completely.

RMAN can work with all the mainstream tape library devices and software, such as those supplied by IBM, Veritas, or Hewlett Packard. The Oracle Backup Solutions Program (or BSP) certifies third-party products as being compatible with RMAN; any vendor who is a member of the Oracle BSP can supply a fully supported backup solution.

When using a tape library, you will encounter some product-specific variations in the way that channels must be configured. For example, if using an Omniback library, you must supply certain parameters, as in this example of an RMAN command to back up the whole database:

```
run {
allocate channel 'omni_0' type 'sbt_tape'
parms 'ENV=(OB2BARTYPE=Oracle8,OB2APPNAME=ocp10g,OB2BARLIST=test1)';
allocate channel 'omni_1' type 'sbt_tape'
parms 'ENV=(OB2BARTYPE=Oracle8,OB2APPNAME=ocp10g,OB2BARLIST=test1)';
backup incremental level 0 filesperset 1
format 'test1<ocp10g_%s:%t:%p>.dbf'
database;
}
```

This RMAN command allocates two channels, named omni_0 and omni_1, of type sbt_tape and uses them to back up the database. The incremental level is zero, meaning back up everything. The number of files per set is one, which instructs RMAN to place each input file in its own backup set; this is a requirement for Omniback. The format string generates unique names for each output file. The product-specific items are the parameters set for each channel, on the lines beginning "parms." These set the environment that is required by the Omniback library. These are the OB2BARTYPE parameters, which must be set to "Oracle8". This sounds wrong, but the Omniback Oracle driver was written for release 8 and has not been updated since. The OB2APPNAME must be set to the name of the database, and OB2BARLIST must be set to the name of the script itself. But as this example shows, for the most part RMAN is platform independent and you need not concern yourself with the details of the tape library.

The Auxiliary Database

In normal usage, RMAN will work with a target database, and (if you have created it) a Recovery Catalog database. In some circumstances, you may wish to use an auxiliary database as well. An *auxiliary database* is a new database created by RMAN, from a backup of the target database.

An auxiliary database could be created in order to copy the target, for example, to create a test or development database identical to the production system. Such a database would be a complete restore.

It is also possible to create an auxiliary that is a subset of the target. This is necessary if you want to carry out what is called a tablespace point-in-time recovery, or TSPITR. This is a technique whereby just one tablespace can be taken back in time, without affecting the rest of the database. The auxiliary database is created and used as a temporary storage area while the operation is in progress.

Finally, an auxiliary database can be created to be used as a standby database. A standby database is a copy of the production database on a remote machine that is continuously updated with the redo generated by the production database. Then, in the event of a disaster, you can switch over to the standby database without any loss of data and minimal downtime.

The Flash Recovery Area

The *flash recovery area* is a disk destination that is used by Oracle as a storage location for all recovery- and fault tolerance–related files. RMAN will use it as a default location for backups. Remember that the flash recovery area is not intended for RMAN's exclusive use; it is also, typically, used for multiplexed online logfiles, for a controlfile copy, and as an archive log destination.

The advantage of directing RMAN backups to the flash recovery area is that Oracle can manage space in the recovery area very effectively: when it fills up, Oracle will automatically delete any files within it that are obsolete, according to whatever rules for obsolescence you establish.

Configuring RMAN

Using RMAN can be trivially simple. The out-of-the-box configuration will carry out a perfect hot backup with just six words, as in this Unix example:

```
$ rman
Recovery Manager: Release 10.1.0.2.0 - Production
Copyright (c) 1995, 2004, Oracle.  All rights reserved.
RMAN> connect target
connected to target database: OCP10G (DBID=3385973595)
RMAN> backup database;
Starting backup at 11-NOV-04
using target database controlfile instead of Recovery Catalog
allocated channel: ORA_DISK_1
channel ORA_DISK_1: sid=146 devtype=DISK
channel ORA_DISK_1: starting full datafile backupset
channel ORA_DISK_1: specifying datafile(s) in backupset
input datafile fno=00001 name=/oracle/product/10.1.0/oradata/opc10g/system01.dbf (xxx)
<output abbreviated...> (xxx)
channel ORA_DISK_1: starting piece 1 at 11-NOV-04
channel ORA_DISK_1: finished piece 1 at 11-NOV-04
```

```
piece handle=/oracle/product/10.1.0/flash_recovery_area/ocp10g/backupset/2004_
11_11/O1_MF_NNNDF_TAG20041111T183217_0S750KOL_.BKP comment=NONE
channel ORA_DISK_1: backup set complete, elapsed time: 00:10:15
Finished backup at 11-NOV-04
RMAN> exit
Recovery Manager complete.
$
```

To try this example, from an operating system prompt run the RMAN executable by entering **rman**. Then from the RMAN prompt, enter **connect target**. This will use operating system authentication to connect you to the local database as user SYS. Then the **backup database;** command instructs RMAN to carry out a complete backup of the database. When the backup is complete, **exit** returns you to the operating system prompt. This six-word backup runs entirely on defaults. Two defaults to note are the channel allocation and the use of the flash recovery area. One channel is launched, of type disk, and the output file is one piece, in a directory within the flash recovery area. This backup is absolutely reliable, but in practice you will always configure RMAN to your own requirements.

Environment Variables and Instance Parameters

The RMAN executable will pick up some settings from the operating system environment in which you launch it. In the preceding example, the date is displayed as "11-NOV-04". If there were an environment variable set as follows,

```
nls_date_format=dd-mm-yy hh24:mi:ss
```

then the date would be displayed as, for instance, "11-11-04 18:26:59". This use of date/time formats is not merely of significance for the display of RMAN's output; it will also be used as the format mask for date/time parameters for operations such as restore and recover.

Another environment variable of significance is NLS_LANG. This can be used to inform RMAN of the database character set. If the database is mounted or open, this doesn't matter; RMAN will read the controlfile to find out what the character set is. But if the database is only in nomount mode, then RMAN will assume the default of US7ASCII, which may not be correct. To avoid possible problems, set the variable before launching RMAN. For example,

```
$ export NLS_LANG=american_america.we8iso8859p15
```

on Unix, or

```
C:> set NLS_LANG=american_america.we8iso8859p15
```

on Windows.

Within the instance, three parameters may be of significance.

CONTROL_FILE_RECORD_KEEP_TIME will limit the number of days that the target database's controlfile will "remember" information about archive logs generated and RMAN backups made. If you are using a Recovery Catalog, this is not so important. As long as information is transferred from the controlfile into the Catalog before it gets overwritten in the controlfile, everything will be fine. The default of seven days will usually be adequate in these circumstances: the information will be transferred (using the RESYNC CATALOG command) whenever RMAN connects to the target, which will generally be much more frequently than seven days. But if you are not using a Recovery Catalog, then this parameter must be changed to a greater value.

DB_RECOVERY_FILE_DEST and DB_RECOVERY_FILE_DEST_SIZE control the location and maximum size of the flash recovery area. If these parameters are defined, they set the default location for RMAN backups and for archive logs. The flash recovery area must be monitored to make sure that it does not fill up. RMAN can apply retention policies to files in the recovery area, and it can overwrite files it considers to be obsolete if it needs to, but if the flash recovery area does fill up, then archiving will fail and this will eventually cause the database to hang.

Connecting to Databases

The RMAN executable can connect to local databases (either targets or the Recovery Catalog) or to remote databases using an Oracle Net connect string. Consider some examples of syntax:

```
C:\> rman target sys/oracle@ocp10g catalog rman/rman@catdb
```

This example runs the executable on a Windows machine and connects to a target identified by the alias "ocp10g" as user SYS (password ORACLE), while connecting concurrently to a Recovery Catalog identified by the alias "catdb" as user rman (password RMAN). The connection to a target will generally need to be as a user with the SYSDBA, or at least the SYSOPER, privilege. This is because it may well be necessary to issue STARTUP or SHUTDOWN commands. The connection to the Recovery Catalog must be as the user who owns the Recovery Catalog schema. The same result could be achieved as follows:

```
C:\>rman
Recovery Manager: Release 10.1.0.2.0 - Production
Copyright (c) 1995, 2004, Oracle.  All rights reserved.
RMAN> connect target sys/oracle@ocp10g
connected to target database: OCP10G (DBID=3385973595)
RMAN> connect catalog rman/rman@catdb
connected to Recovery Catalog database
RMAN>
```

It is also possible to invoke RMAN from the operating system command line with a script of RMAN commands. When the script completes, RMAN will terminate and return control to the operating system shell. This is a technique you can use to schedule a backup with the Unix cron command, or the Windows AT command. On Unix,

```
$ rman target / log /logs/rman.log append cmdfile=/scripts/rman_script.rcv
```

will launch the RMAN executable and connect to a local database as a target, whichever is specified by the ORACLE_SID environment variable: the first forward slash is the instruction to do this. The output of the RMAN session will be written to the file

/logs/rman.log, appending to it if the file already exists; if the log were not specified, the output would go to the standard output device. Then the script /scripts/rman_script.rcv will run. This will be a series of RMAN commands. This example does not use a Recovery Catalog. The default mode of operation for RMAN is not to use a Recovery Catalog, but it is possible to specify this explicitly:

```
$ rman target / nocatalog
```

will connect without a Recovery Catalog to a local database target as user SYS with operating system authentication, and

```
c:\> rman
RMAN> connect target sys/oracle@ocp10g nocatalog
```

will do the same but over a network connection, using password file authentication. The "nocatalog" keyword gives compatibility with earlier releases, when it was not enabled by default, and also makes your scripts self-documenting.

TIP In RMAN, you cannot abbreviate the "connect" command to "conn," as you can in SQL*Plus. Try it—you will get an error.

Configuring Persistent Settings

RMAN comes preconfigured with default settings that will work, but probably not in exactly the way you want. It is possible to control everything in your RMAN sessions with scripts or with sequences of interactive commands that will override these default settings, but usually you will want to reconfigure the defaults so that they are, in general, applicable to most of your work. This will make the scripts and sequences much simpler from then on. You do this by configuring persistent settings for your target databases. Each target has its own set of persistent settings: they are stored in the target database repository: in the target's controlfile and (optionally) in the Recovery Catalog.

To see the current default settings for a target, use the SHOW command. In Figure 23-1, the RMAN executable is launched on a Windows machine, and then a connection is made to the local database. The SHOW ALL command displays the current settings, all of which are on the installation defaults, as is indicated by the "# default" suffix on every line.

Some out-of-the-box defaults are particularly important. First, the RETENTION POLICY is set to REDUNDANCY 1. This means that RMAN will always attempt to have one copy of every datafile and archive log. Second, DEFAULT DEVICE TYPE is DISK. Unless specified otherwise, all backups will go to a disk directory, not to any tape device. Third, DEVICE TYPE DISK PARALLELISM 1 BACKUP TYPE TO BACKUPSET says that when backing up to disk, only one channel will be used, and that the backup will be to the proprietary backup set format, not to an image copy.

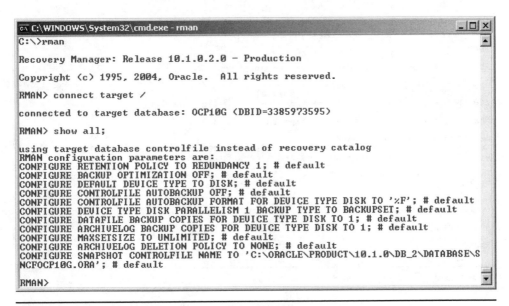

```
C:\WINDOWS\System32\cmd.exe - rman                                    _ □ X

C:\>rman

Recovery Manager: Release 10.1.0.2.0 - Production

Copyright (c) 1995, 2004, Oracle.  All rights reserved.

RMAN> connect target /

connected to target database: OCP10G (DBID=3385973595)

RMAN> show all;

using target database controlfile instead of recovery catalog
RMAN configuration parameters are:
CONFIGURE RETENTION POLICY TO REDUNDANCY 1; # default
CONFIGURE BACKUP OPTIMIZATION OFF; # default
CONFIGURE DEFAULT DEVICE TYPE TO DISK; # default
CONFIGURE CONTROLFILE AUTOBACKUP OFF; # default
CONFIGURE CONTROLFILE AUTOBACKUP FORMAT FOR DEVICE TYPE DISK TO '%F'; # default
CONFIGURE DEVICE TYPE DISK PARALLELISM 1 BACKUP TYPE TO BACKUPSET; # default
CONFIGURE DATAFILE BACKUP COPIES FOR DEVICE TYPE DISK TO 1; # default
CONFIGURE ARCHIVELOG BACKUP COPIES FOR DEVICE TYPE DISK TO 1; # default
CONFIGURE MAXSETSIZE TO UNLIMITED; # default
CONFIGURE ARCHIVELOG DELETION POLICY TO NONE; # default
CONFIGURE SNAPSHOT CONTROLFILE NAME TO 'C:\ORACLE\PRODUCT\10.1.0\DB_2\DATABASE\S
NCFOCP10G.ORA'; # default

RMAN>
```

Figure 23-1 The preconfigured RMAN default persistent settings

To change a default, use the CONFIGURE command:

```
RMAN> CONFIGURE DEFAULT DEVICE TYPE TO sbt_tape;
new RMAN configuration parameters:
CONFIGURE DEFAULT DEVICE TYPE TO 'SBT_TAPE';
new RMAN configuration parameters are successfully stored
RMAN>
```

From now on, all backups will be directed to the tape library, unless specified otherwise in the individual backup command.

TIP The output of SHOW is formatted as a script. You can copy/paste the lines, edit them, and then execute them.

Channel Allocation

A *channel* is a process launched on the target by RMAN for the purpose of transferring data to and from a backup device. At least one channel must be allocated before a backup or restore command can be executed. Channels are of two types: disk channels that can work with disk directories and SBT channels that can work with tape devices. The SBT interface provides a layer of abstraction between RMAN and the tape device itself; if the device driver has been correctly installed, then RMAN can use the tape device without needing to know anything about its characteristics.

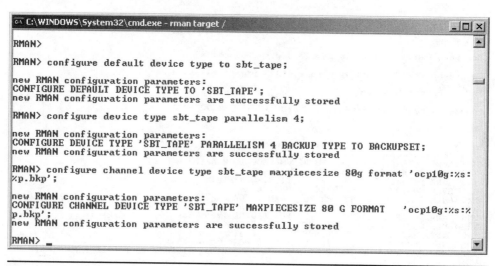

Figure 23-2 Configuring channel defaults

Channels can be allocated for each backup and recovery operation, or they can be configured with default settings to be applied to all operations, unless specifically overridden.

In Figure 23-2, first the default device is changed from disk to tape. From this point on, all backups will go to the tape library. Note that RMAN automatically sets the backup type to BACKUPSET, as it is impossible to write image copies to tape. Then the degree of parallelism for tape backup is set to 4. This means that four tape channels will be allocated automatically. The optimum degree of parallelism can be set only after discussion with the system administrators, but clearly it will be related to the number of tape drives available. The maximum size of a backup piece is then restricted to 80GB. This might be related to the capacity of the tape cartridges. The names of the pieces—the actual physical files produced—are defined by the FORMAT specification, which includes the variables %s and %p that will generate unique names based on the backup set number and the piece number within the set.

 TIP Set numbers continually increment for each target. Piece numbers start at 1 for each set and increment from there.

All the configured defaults can be overridden for any RMAN operation, but configuring sensible defaults means that the scripts you write later can be much more brief and simple than they would be otherwise.

The channel control options are as follows:

- **CONNECT** is an Oracle Net connect string. Unlikely to be of relevance in a single-instance environment, this option is useful for clustered databases. The instance to which the RMAN executable connects need not be the instance against which the channel is launched. Thus, for a RAC database, you can spread the load of backups across all your instances.

- **DURATION** controls the amount of time for the job, specified in hours and minutes. It can also influence the speed with which it will run, by using one of the following additional keywords: MINIMIZE TIME specifies that the backup will run at full speed, perhaps finishing before the duration is over. This would normally be used for tape backups, because it is generally advisable to stream to tapes as fast as possible. MINIMIZE LOAD will monitor the backup speed and reduce it if it seems likely that it will finish before the duration is over. This would be used for disk backups, to reduce the impact on users caused by very high rates of disk I/O. PARTIAL allows RMAN to terminate a backup that has not completed within the DURATION without signaling an error; normal behavior would be to terminate the backup with an error report.

- **FORMAT** fixes the path and filename for the backup pieces or image copies created by the channel. A number of variables can be used to generate unique filenames.

- **MAXOPENFILES** limits the number of input files that RMAN can open at once. The default is 8.

- **MAXPIECESIZE**, specified in bytes (default), kilobytes (K), megabytes (M), or gigabytes (G), restricts the size of the pieces into which a backup set is divided. The size of a backup set is hard to predict with any certainty because of compression, incrementals, and the fact that empty blocks are never included. Clearly, this is meaningless for an image copy backup. Related to this is CONFIGURE MAXSETSIZE, which will apply to all channels.

- **PARMS** can be used to set whatever variables are needed for an SBT_TAPE channel.

The DEVICE TYPE configuration can set, for your tape and disk channels, the default degree of parallelism—or how many channels to launch—and the type of backup to generate. This may be the standard BACKUPSET, as in Figure 23-2, COMPRESSED BACKUPSET, or (for disk channels) COPY, which will generate image copies.

What RMAN Will Back Up

Each backup operation will specify the objects to be backed up. If the objects are one or more datafiles, tablespaces, or archive logs, then RMAN will do exactly what it is told to do. But if the object is the whole database, then you can configure certain exclusions and optimization, to reduce the volume and time of the backups. There is also a very special feature you can enable: the controlfile auto-backup.

Some tablespaces do not need backing up regularly. These may be tablespaces with noncritical data (training systems, perhaps) or data that it is simpler to re-create than to restore and recover (such as tablespaces devoted solely to indexes, if they are not too large). There may also be read-only and offline tablespaces; these are static and need be backed up only once. RMAN can handle these exceptions to the full backup with the EXCLUDE directive, which takes a list of objects to ignore, and backup optimization, which will ignore objects that are still identical to the state they were in at the last backup.

In Figure 23-3, first the tablespace EXAMPLE is nominated as a tablespace to be omitted during a whole database backup. Then backup optimization is enabled, which lets RMAN decide to omit any objects that have not changed since the last backup. This will usually mean that read-only and offline tablespaces as well as archive logs are not backed up repeatedly. Finally, controlfile auto-backup is enabled. The SHOW ALL command confirms the changes. Note that the #default comment has been removed from the relevant settings.

The controlfile auto-backup is vital if you are not using a Recovery Catalog. The RMAN repository is stored in the target database controlfile, so what will happen if all copies of the controlfile are destroyed? This is not a problem with a Recovery Catalog, but without one RMAN is now crippled. The backups needed for a complete restore and recovery may all exist, but RMAN will not be able to find them. By default RMAN will always back up the controlfile whenever you back up the system tablespace, and by adding the keywords INCLUDE CURRENT CONTROLFILE, it can be included in every other backup as well. However, to restore it you will still need a current controlfile and therefore a mountable database, in order for RMAN to read its repository and locate the backup.

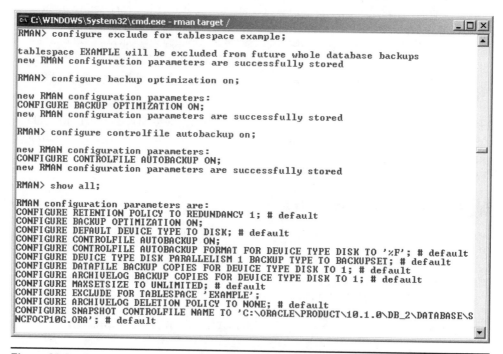

Figure 23-3   Configuring exclusions, optimization, and controlfile auto-backup

Enabling the auto-backup avoids this problem. It instructs RMAN always to back up the controlfile as part of any backup operation; RMAN will generate in image form a file with a well-known name and place it in a well-known directory.

It will then be possible to restore it with the command RESTORE CONTROLFILE FROM AUTOBACKUP, which can be executed in NOMOUNT mode. Remember that RMAN is implemented with kernelized PL/SQL procedures and so is available in NOMOUNT mode. If the controlfile is gone, NOMOUNT is as far as Oracle can get. This command will search for the well-known filename without the need for any repository, and restore it. The well-known filename is based on the DBID and by default is stored in the flash recovery area.

TIP It is possible to change the well-known filename to something not so well known with CONFIGURE CONTROLFILE AUTOBACKUP FORMAT, but if that is done, you will have to record the change and direct RMAN toward it if a restore is ever needed.

Once an autobackup of the controlfile has been located and restored, it will be possible to mount the database and RMAN can then bootstrap itself up and do a normal full restore and recover. Thus it is possible to restore the whole database, even if the RMAN repository has been lost.

Configuring Retention of Backups

The default configuration is REDUNDANCY 1. This means that RMAN will always attempt to have one backup (image copy or in a backup set) of every datafile, every archive log, and the controlfile. It does not ever attempt to back up temporary files or online redo logs. The DELETE OBSOLETE command will delete any backups that are considered to be no longer necessary according to the retention policy.

There are two options for retention policy. Configuring a redundancy level instructs RMAN to keep multiple backups of each object, but it does not take account of when the backup was made. For example, if redundancy is set to 4, and if one tablespace is backed up every 6 hours (not unreasonable, if MTTR is considered vital) and another is backed up once a week (perhaps because the data is largely static, and MTTR is not so significant), then the oldest backup of the first tablespace will be only one day old, but that of the other tablespace will be nearly a month old. The implication for an incomplete point-in-time recovery is that it will not in fact be possible to do an incomplete recovery further back than one day, because there will be no backup of the second tablespace, which is older than that. An extra, unscheduled, backup will distort the situation further. Another problem with a redundancy-based retention policy is that it does not permit RMAN ever to delete an archive log backup. The alternative is to configure the retention policy to a recovery window, with, for example,

```
RMAN> configure retention policy to recovery window of 30 days;
```

From this point on, RMAN will attempt to ensure that it always has sufficient datafile and archive log backups to do an incomplete recovery to any point in the last month, and that it is permitted to delete any backups that become obsolete as time passes. There will always be at least one backup of every datafile that is at least thirty days old, plus the archive logs needed to recover it.

It is possible to configure the retention policy to NONE, which disables the automatic deletion of backups because none are ever considered obsolete. To set the policy back to the default of REDUNDANCY 1, use the CLEAR command:

```
RMAN> configure retention policy clear;
```

Overriding Configured Defaults

Using the CONFIGURE command to set up RMAN to work the way you will usually want it to work is very useful. It is the out-of-the-box default configuration that makes it possible to back up the whole database with two words: BACKUP DATABASE. But there will be times when you want to set your own rules for an individual backup operation. Consider this command:

```
RMAN> run{
allocate channel d1 type disk format '/u06/backups/example1.bkp';
allocate channel d2 type disk format '/u06/backups/example2.bkp';
backup as compressed backupset
tablespace example include current controlfile;}
```

This command launches two disk channels, even though RMAN might be configured to launch four tape channels. The names of the pieces are hard-coded, overriding whatever default has been configured for disk channels. Then the backup type is a compressed backup set, though image copies might well have been configured as the norm for disk backups. The content of the backup is all the datafiles making up the EXAMPLE tablespace, whether or not this is normally excluded. Finally, the backup set will include the controlfile, irrespective of the auto-backup setting.

To override the retention policy, specify this when making the backup. For example,

```
RMAN > backup datafile 7 keep until time "sysdate+90" nologs;
```

This will instruct RMAN not to consider the backup eligible for deletion for at least ninety days, irrespective of the retention policy. The NOLOGS keyword does, however, permit RMAN to remove the archive logs that would be needed to recover the backup.

Exercise 23-1: Configuring RMAN

Use the Database Control interface to RMAN to configure settings and then clear them from the command-line interface.

1. Connect to your database as user SYSTEM with Database Control.
2. Take the Maintenance tab from the database home page, and then the Configure Backup Settings link in the Backup/Recovery section.

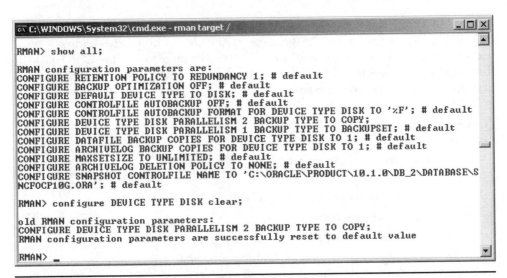

Figure 23-4 Showing and clearing configured defaults

3. In the Disk Settings section, enter **2** in the Parallelism box, and then select the Image Copy radio button to change from the disk defaults of one channel and backup sets.

4. In the Host Credentials section, enter an operating system username and password, if one is not already saved as preferred credentials.

5. Click the OK button to save the changes.

6. From an operating system prompt, launch the RMAN executable and connect in the default NOCATALOG mode, using operating system authentication.

```
rman target /
```

7. Use the SHOW ALL command to display the currently configured settings, and return the disk channel settings to default with the CLEAR command, as in Figure 23-4.

8. Use SHOW ALL again to confirm that the DEVICE TYPE DISK channel settings are back on default.

Chapter Review

This chapter began by summarizing RMAN's capabilities. It should be clear that RMAN is a better tool for backup and recovery than user-managed backups, but to exploit RMAN's capabilities to the full, it is necessary to use it with a Recovery Catalog database and an automated tape library. RMAN consists of a number of components, some of which are optional, but the principles are simple: the RMAN executable connects to a target database and launches channel processes to back it up to tape or disk. The backup files can be image copies of the files, or proprietary format backup sets, optionally, compressed. To make RMAN simple to use, the CONFIGURE command sets defaults for all backup and recovery operations, but these defaults can of course be overridden whenever desired.

Questions

1. After you issue the command
   ```
   CONFIGURE RETENTION POLICY CLEAR;
   ```
   what will the retention policy be set to? (Choose the best answer.)

   A. There will be no retention policy.

   B. Retention policy will be REDUNDANCY 1.

   C. Retention policy will be RECOVERY WINDOW OF 7 DAYS.

   D. Retention policy will depend on the CONTROL_FILE_RECORD_KEEP_TIME.

2. If a connection is made with the RMAN executable with
   ```
   rman target /
   ```
   where will it look for its repository? (Choose the best answer.)

   A. The target database's parameter file only

   B. The target database's controlfile only

   C. The Recovery Catalog only

   D. The Recovery Catalog and the target database's parameter file

   E. The Recovery Catalog and the target database's controlfile only

3. Which is an optional location for the RMAN repository? (Choose the best answer.)

   A. The target database controlfile

   B. The Recovery Catalog controlfile

   C. The Recovery Catalog database

   D. The target database parameter file

4. Match the component (A to I) to the description (a to i).

   A. Auxiliary database

   B. Disk channel

   C. Flash recovery area

   D. Recovery Catalog

   E. RMAN repository

   F. RMAN executable

   G. SBT channel

   H. Tape library driver

   I. Target database

   a. Database to be backed up by RMAN

   b. Database to be created by RMAN

   c. Default location for backups

   d. Optional store of RMAN metadata

   e. Process that can control tape devices

   f. Process that writes to disks

   g. Process that writes to tapes

   h. Required store of RMAN metadata

   i. RMAN controlling process

5. The parameter CONTROL_FILE_RECORD_KEEP_TIME determines how frequently information in the controlfile is overwritten. What is the default value? (Choose the best answer.)

   A. 1 day

   B. 5 days

   C. 7 days

   D. 30 days

6. Which of the following tablespaces could sensibly be excluded from whole online database backups with the CONFIGURE EXCLUDE FOR TABLESPACE... command? (Choose the best answer.)

   A. A user data tablespace, which must be kept online for 24 × 7 availability

   B. Temporary tablespaces

   C. A permanent tablespace used for read-only data

   D. A tablespace used for undo segments

7. Which of the following processes carries out the backup operations? (Choose the best answer.)

   A. The RMAN executable

   B. A channel launched against the Recovery Catalog, if RMAN is using a Recovery Catalog; otherwise, a channel launched against the target database

   C. Always a channel launched against the target database

   D. A tape channel launched by the tape library, if one is being used, or a disk channel launched by RMAN if a tape library is not being used

8. Which of the following objects can be backed up by RMAN? (Select all that apply.)

   A. Archive logs

   B. Controlfile

   C. Datafiles

   D. Dynamic parameter file

   E. Online logs

   F. Password file

   G. Static parameter file

   H. Tables

   I. Tablespaces

   J. Tempfiles

9. How can you control the size of the files RMAN generates for backup sets? (Choose the best answer.)

   A. You can't; backup set size is unpredictable

   B. CONFIGURE MAXSETSIZE;

   C. CONFIGURE CHANNEL...MAXSETSIZE;

   D. CONFIGURE MAXPIECESIZE;

   E. CONFIGURE CHANNEL...MAXPIECESIZE;

10. If you configure the controlfile auto-backup feature, to where will the backup be made?

    A. It will be included in all backup sets

    B. To the Recovery Catalog, if it exists

    C. To the flash recovery area

    D. To the BACKGROUND_DUMP_DEST directory

Answers

1. **B.** CLEARing the retention policy returns it to the default of REDUNDANCY 1.

2. **B.** The repository is always in the target's controlfile, and by default the connection will be in NOCATALOG mode.

3. **C.** The repository is always written to the target's controlfile, and optionally stored in a Recovery Catalog database as well. D, the target database parameter file, is irrelevant to the RMAN repository.

4. The answers are as follows:

A-b. An auxiliary database is one created by RMAN.

B-f. Disk type channel processes are launched by RMAN to write to disk.

C-c. The flash recovery area is a default location for RMAN backups.

D-d. The RMAN metadata is (optionally) stored in the Recovery Catalog.

E-h. RMAN metadata is stored in the RMAN repository.

F-i. The RMAN executable controls all other RMAN processes.

G-g. SBT type channels are launched by RMAN to write to tape devices.

H-e. Tape devices are controlled by a tape library driver.

I-a. Targets are databases backed up by RMAN.

5. **C.** CONTROL_FILE_RECORD_KEEP_TIME defaults to seven days.

6. **C.** Read-only tablespaces need only be backed up once. A tablespace that needs to be available 24 × 7 should certainly not be excluded, and neither should an UNDO tablespace. Temporary tablespaces cannot be backed up by RMAN.

7. **C.** It is the channel that actually does the backup, and channels are launched against the target.

8. **A, B, C, D,** and **I.** The correct objects are archive logs; the controlfile; the datafiles; the dynamic parameter file, or spfile; and tablespaces.

9. **E.** MAXPIECESIZE is the option to restrict the size of the pieces into which a backup set is divided.

10. **C.** Controlfile auto-backups go by default to the flash recovery area. This is the well-known location that RMAN will use, unless you have specifically redirected it elsewhere.

CHAPTER 24

Using RMAN to Back Up Databases

In this chapter you will learn how to

- Use the RMAN BACKUP command to create backup sets and image copies
- Enable block change tracking
- Manage the backups and image copies taken with RMAN with the LIST and REPORT commands

There are four interfaces for using the Recovery Manager (RMAN). First, and the most accessible, is the graphical interface provided by Database Control. Using Database Control for backup and recovery is covered in Chapters 19 and 20. Second, there is a batch mode: using a command file when invoking RMAN from the operating system prompt, or from an operating system scheduler such as cron on Unix or AT on Windows. This will be covered briefly in this chapter. Third, the pipe interface launches an RMAN session and allows another session to control it by issuing appropriate PL/SQL calls. There is a brief description of this technique, but the detail is beyond the scope of the OCP examination. Last, there is the RMAN executable. This is the tool that most DBAs will use. Once the backup routines are well established, they may be formalized as scripts, either command file scripts to be launched from an operating system prompt and run in batch mode or RMAN scripts stored within a Recovery Catalog database. This chapter concentrates on using the RMAN executable to create both full and incremental backup sets and image copies, and to produce various reports of what needs to be backed up, what backups have been taken, and what backups can be safely deleted.

RMAN in Batch Mode

Consider a hypothetical backup regime. It has been agreed with the users that every evening a full online backup should be taken of the database and that this backup should be stored on disk as an image copy, so that it can be restored with minimal delay if necessary. Before this daily backup is taken, the previous day's backup should be moved from disk to tape. The archive logs generated during the day should be migrated to tape at the same time. All the commands necessary to implement this regime can be stored within a text file and invoked by the operating system's scheduler. The file of RMAN commands could be

```
run {
allocate channel t1 type sbt_tape;
allocate channel t2 type sbt_tape;
backup copy of database delete input;
backup archivelog all delete all input;
release channel t1;
release channel t2;
allocate channel d1 type disk;
allocate channel d2 type disk;
backup as copy database;
release channel d1;
release channel d2;}
```

This block of commands first launches two tape channels. The choice of two will be the result of discussions with the system administrators about how the tape library can be used most efficiently. Then these channels are used to back up any existing copies of the database (remember that image copies can be made only to disk destinations) and delete them. This has the effect of transferring the disk backup to tape, where it will be stored as a backup set. Following that, all archive logs are backed up to tape. The DELETE ALL INPUT command instructs RMAN to delete the logs from all the archive log destinations when they have been backed up. Then the tape channels are released, and two disk channels launched. These then take an image copy of the database.

TIP When launching tape channels, both SBT and SBT_TAPE are acceptable syntax.

The script does not include any specification for the name and location of the files generated, nor are there any limits on the size of the backup pieces. These settings will be read from the repository, as configured defaults for the disk and tape type channels.

If the script is saved as daily.rcv, it can be invoked from an operating system prompt thus:

```
rman target / @'daily.rcv'
```

or the command can be registered as a cron job on Unix, or an AT job on Windows.

The RMAN Pipe Interface

One of the many PL/SQL packages supplied with the database is DBMS_PIPE. This is a set of procedures that allow one database session to communicate with another, by creating a data structure in the SGA—the pipe—that one session can put messages on for another session to remove. By using DBMS_PIPE, you can launch an RMAN session and then control it programmatically from another session. All the input of commands that RMAN needs will be written to a pipe by the controlling session; RMAN will read the commands from this pipe, execute them, and write all its output messages to a second pipe that the controlling session will read from.

To use the pipe interface, launch RMAN from the operating system prompt, specifying the PIPE keyword, a name for the pipe, and a target database connect string. For example,

```
rman PIPE rmpipe target sys/oracle@ocp10
```

This will cause RMAN to connect to the target and create two pipes in the instance: the pipe ORA$RMAN_RMPIPE_IN will be monitored by RMAN for user commands, and ORA$RMAN_RMPIPE_OUT will be used by RMAN to write its output. No data will be read from or written to the shell that launched the RMAN executable. The controlling process must use the DBMS_PIPE.PACK and DBMS_PIPE.SEND_MESSAGE procedures to send commands to the ORA$RMAN_RMPIPE_IN pipe, which the RMAN session will read and act upon. The controlling session uses the DBMS_PIPE.RECEIVE_MESSAGE and DBMS_PIPE.UNPACK procedures to read RMAN's output from the ORA$RMAN_RMPIPE_OUT pipe.

This technique, which is fully described in the *Oracle Database Backup and Recovery Advanced User's Guide,* lets you develop a programmatic interface to RMAN.

Backing Up with the RMAN Executable

RMAN can be controlled by the methods just described or by scripts stored within a Recovery Catalog, but whatever method you use, the commands are the same. Before any command can be issued, it is necessary to connect to the target. Throughout this section it is assumed that a connection has been made.

Many commands must be qualified with keywords that will control what the command does. In some cases, these qualifiers can be specified in advance as configured defaults and therefore need not be specified for any one operation. In all the examples that follow, it is assumed that no modifications have been made to the out-of-the-box configuration; the output of the SHOW ALL command would be

```
RMAN> show all;
using target database controlfile instead of recovery catalog
RMAN configuration parameters are:
CONFIGURE RETENTION POLICY TO REDUNDANCY 1; # default
CONFIGURE BACKUP OPTIMIZATION OFF; # default
CONFIGURE DEFAULT DEVICE TYPE TO DISK; # default
CONFIGURE CONTROLFILE AUTOBACKUP OFF; # default
CONFIGURE CONTROLFILE AUTOBACKUP FORMAT FOR DEVICE TYPE DISK TO '%F'; # default
CONFIGURE DEVICE TYPE DISK PARALLELISM 1 BACKUP TYPE TO BACKUPSET; # default
CONFIGURE DATAFILE BACKUP COPIES FOR DEVICE TYPE DISK TO 1; # default
CONFIGURE ARCHIVELOG BACKUP COPIES FOR DEVICE TYPE DISK TO 1; # default
CONFIGURE MAXSETSIZE TO UNLIMITED; # default
CONFIGURE ARCHIVELOG DELETION POLICY TO NONE; # default
CONFIGURE SNAPSHOT CONTROLFILE NAME TO
'/oracle/product/10.1.0/dbs/sncfocp10g.ora'; # default
RMAN>
```

Stand-Alone and Job/Command Block Commands

A minor point that can cause confusion is the use of the command block with RMAN commands. Some commands must be executed directly from the RMAN prompt, but others do not make sense unless they are part of a block of two or more commands, known as a *command block* or a *job*. A command block is started with RUN and delimited with brackets, "{...}". A simple block of two commands is

```
run {
allocate channel d1 type disk;
backup database;}
```

An example of a stand-alone command is CONNECT. It is completely self-contained and can even be specified on the operating system command line when you invoke the RMAN executable. Other stand-alone commands are the commands that manipulate the Recovery Catalog, if you have one. Commands that can be specified only as part of a job include ALLOCATE CHANNEL. There is no sense in allocating a channel unless you intend to use it, so ALLOCATE CHANNEL must be used in a job, where it will be followed by a command that will read or write tapes or disks, such as BACKUP or RESTORE.

Some commands can, however, be issued either stand-alone or within a command block. The BACKUP command is an example. It is impossible to run a backup unless a channel has been allocated, but if automatic channel allocation has been configured as a default, then a BACKUP command can be issued from the RMAN prompt. But if the configured default is not what you want for a particular operation, then you can create a job that includes an ALLOCATE CHANNEL command and then a BACKUP command. The BACKUP command will use the channel allocated within the job rather than those configured as defaults, as in the preceding example of a job.

Creating Backup Sets

Objects can be backed up by RMAN in two ways: as image copies or as backup sets. An image copy backup (detailed in the next section) is identical to the original file. A backup set is a proprietary format that can be manipulated only by RMAN and can be written to disk or (unlike image copies) to tape. The objects that can be backed up as backup sets are the controlfile, the spfile, datafiles, archive logs, image copies, and other backup sets. The syntax for creating backup sets also permits backing up a tablespace, which is implemented as a backup of the datafiles making up the tablespace, or the complete database, which becomes a backup of all the datafiles and the controlfile and spfile.

The choice between backup sets and image copies is generally constrained by available disk resources, and by the requirement for fast restore and recovery. These two constraints will often be in conflict. As a rule, it will be quicker to restore and recover if the backups are image copies. But image copies can be made only to disk, and keeping the necessary disk resources available will not always be possible. By contrast, tape storage capacity is effectively unlimited—but it isn't as fast. However, backup sets have features that make them more attractive: in particular, the ability to make incremental backups. Furthermore, a backup set is always smaller than an image copy. Backup sets of datafiles never include blocks that have not been used, whereas an image copy of necessity includes the complete file. It is possible to reduce the space needed even further by using RMAN's compression capability.

An example of a job to create backup sets would be

```
run {
allocate channel d1 type disk;
backup as compressed backupset
format '/u06/ocp10g/backup/%d_%u.dbf'
duration 8:00 minimize load
filesperset 1
database;
sql 'alter system archive log current';
backup as compressed backupset
format '/u06/ocp10g/backup/%d_%u.arc'
duration 8:00 minimize time
archivelog all delete all input;}
```

This job first launches a single disk channel. The channel will back up the whole database over an eight-hour period. The files produced will be backup sets, compressed with RMAN's binary compression algorithm. The backup sets will be written to a disk directory and uniquely named according to variables that will generate the database name (%d) and an eight-character string that will guarantee uniqueness (%u). The MINIMIZE LOAD keywords instruct RMAN to control the speed of the backup such that it will not finish in less than eight hours; this is to reduce the impact of excessive disk I/O on users. For the same reason, only one channel was launched; parallelizing the backup might make it run more quickly, which would increase the load on the database server. Each database file will be written to its own backup set, which will consist of one piece. Then the job continues by issuing a command to the target that will force a log switch and an archive. A second backup command backs up all existing archive log files into one backup set, removing them from the archive destinations as it does so. This will be done as fast as possible; it is assumed that I/O on archive log destinations will have no impact on users. Both the backup commands will throw an error if the backup does not complete within eight hours; this could be avoided by including the keyword PARTIAL.

Backup sets can also be written directly to tape, as in this example:

```
run (
allocate channel t1 type sbt;
allocate channel t2 type sbt;
allocate channel t3 type sbt;
allocate channel t4 type sbt;
backup format '%d_%u.dbf.arc'
database plus archivelog;}
```

The job launches four channels, capable of writing to the tape library. The number of channels should be related to the number of tape drives in the library. As a rule, it is good practice to write to tape devices as fast as possible, hence the use of multiple channels to parallelize the backup, and no speed restrictions. It is not necessary to specify that the backup should be AS BACKUP SET, because this is the only option when using SBT channels. Image copies cannot be made to tape, though image copies can be backed up as backup sets to tape.

Each channel will generate its own backup set, and they will be generated in parallel. RMAN will apportion the files making up the database and the archive logs across the four channels, and there will be multiple files in each backup set. The job does not specify compression because it is generally more efficient to enable compression within the tape library. The DATABASE PLUS ARCHIVELOG specification instructs RMAN to do the following:

1. Issue an ALTER SYSTEM ARCHIVELOG CURRENT command.

2. Run BACKUP ARCHIVELOG ALL.

3. Back up the whole database.

4. Issue ALTER SYSTEM ARCHIVELOG CURRENT again.

5. Back up the archive logs generated during Step 3 and Step 4.

Archive logs can also be backed up individually, or according to the date they were made. The following command will back up all archive logs that are more than a week old to tape:

```
run {
allocate channel t1 type sbt;
backup as backupset archivelog
until time 'sysdate - 7';}
```

The preceding examples are of online backups, but RMAN can also do offline backups, which are essential if the target is in noarchivelog mode. An RMAN offline backup is done in mount mode. A user-managed offline backup done with operating system utilities is always done when the instance is shut down, because otherwise you cannot guarantee that the datafile and controlfile copies will be read-consistent, but RMAN needs the target database controlfile to be mounted in order to get to its repository. For this reason, RMAN offline backups are done in mount mode. The controlfile backup is taken by making a snapshot read-consistent copy of the controlfile, which is then backed up. This snapshot copy can be controlled by using CONFIGURE SNAPSHOT CONTROLFILE NAME TO.... An example of an offline backup is

```
run {
shutdown immediate;
startup mount;
backup as backupset database;
alter database open;}
```

This job does a clean shutdown (necessary for an offline RMAN backup), mounts the database, and then backs it up as a backup set. (Remember that in NOARCHIVELOG mode only whole backups are possible.) Finally, the job reopens the database.

 EXAM TIP Offline backups are done in mount mode, but the database must have been cleanly shut down first. The backup will fail if the shutdown were a crash or a SHUTDOWN ABORT.

Exercise 24-1: Creating Backup Sets

Use RMAN to create backup sets of various database objects.

1. Connect to your database using RMAN with operating system authentication, in the default NOCATALOG mode. From an operating system prompt, enter

   `rman target / nocatalog`

2. Display the physical structure of the database with the REPORT SCHEMA command. The output will resemble Figure 24-1.

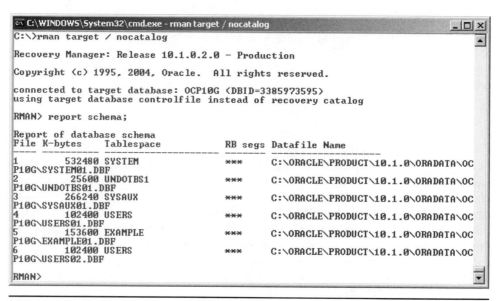

Figure 24-1 The Recovery Manager REPORT SCHEMA command

3. Select a datafile by number (in the examples that follow it is file 6, part of the USERS tablespace) and back it up to a compressed disk backup set in an appropriate directory using one channel. Use a hard-coded name for the backup piece. For example,

```
RMAN> run {
allocate channel d1 type disk;
backup as compressed backupset
format 'C:\ORACLE\PRODUCT\10.1.0\BACKUPS\OCP10G\file6.bus'
datafile 6;}
```

4. Perform a tablespace-level backup of the tablespace that the file is a member of. Use system-generated names for the backup pieces, and limit their size to 50MB each. For example,

```
RMAN> run {
allocate channel d1 type disk
maxpiecesize 50m;
backup as compressed backupset
format 'C:\ORACLE\PRODUCT\10.1.0\BACKUPS\OCP10G\%U.dbf'
tablespace users;}
```

5. Confirm that the file has been backed up twice with the LIST command (as in Figure 24-2) and study the output.

6. Back up the current controlfile into a backup set.

```
RMAN> run {allocate channel d1 type disk;
backup as backupset format 'C:\ORACLE\PRODUCT\10.1.0\BACKUPS\OCP10G\%U.ctl'
current controlfile;}
```

7. Confirm that the backup was created with the LIST command.

```
RMAN> list backup of controlfile;
```

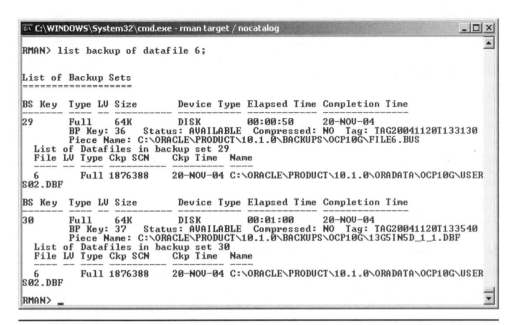

Figure 24-2   Listing the backups of a datafile

Making Image Copies

An image copy of a file is a byte-for-byte identical copy of an individual datafile, controlfile, or archive log file. The result is exactly as though the file had been copied with an operating system utility, though the mechanism is different: RMAN reads and writes in Oracle blocks, not operating system blocks. This means that many of the great features of backup sets (such as incremental backup, compression, writing directly to tape, or controlling the size of the output pieces) cannot be used. But it does mean that a restore can be very fast, because there is no need to extract the file from a backup set. The target database controlfile can be updated to address the image copy instead of the damaged file; in effect, no restore is actually needed if a recent image copy is available. Oracle Corporation's advice is to keep a whole image copy of the database, plus archive logs made since the backup was taken, available in the flash recovery area; this will mean that a full restore is virtually instantaneous, and recovery will be fast as well. However, the economics of disk storage may not make this possible.

Tape channels cannot be used for image copies, but if multiple files are to be copied, then parallelism can be considered. However, thought needs to be put into the degree of parallelism to be used. If all the copies are going to a single nonstriped disk, then there is little point in launching more than one disk channel. Also, the speed of backup to disk can have a negative impact on your users. A full-speed image copy will take up a significant amount of CPU and I/O capacity; this can be avoided by deliberately slowing down the backup process.

Image copies can be made of datafiles, the controlfile, and archive logs. Image copies cannot be made of the spfile.

Although image copies are made on a file-for-file basis, RMAN does let you copy many files with one command. To back up the entire database,

```
RMAN> backup as copy database;
```

If the configured defaults are on default, this command will launch one disk channel and copy all the datafiles and the controlfile to the flash recovery area. The follow-up command would be

```
RMAN> backup as copy archivelog all delete all input;
```

which will move all the archive log files to the flash recovery area.

Using Tags for Backup Sets and Image Copies

A *tag* is a logical name used to reference a backup set or a set of image copies. Whenever a backup set or image copy is made, it is assigned a tag. In earlier Figure 24-2 the first backup set listed, backup set number 29, has been given the tag TAG20041120T133130. The system-generated tags are of little value, but you can override these and specify your own tags. In this example,

```
run {
allocate channel d1 type disk;
backup as compressed backupset
tablespace system,sysaux tag=dd_backup; }
```

the two tablespaces that make up the data dictionary, SYSTEM and SYSAUX, are backed up into one compressed backup set, which is tagged DD_BACKUP. When this backup is no longer required, it can be deleted by tag:

```
RMAN> delete backupset tag=dd_backup;
```

Since tags can be reused, it becomes possible to write generic scripts. For example, if the requirement is to take a whole backup once a month to be kept until the next is taken, then this job can be run at every month end:

```
run {
allocate channel t1 type sbt;
delete backupset tag monthly;
backup as backupset
database tag=monthly; }
```

Incremental Backups

Incremental backups are an example of why RMAN is superior to user-managed backups. When backing up with operating system utilities, the granularity of the backup is the datafile. Datafiles may be many gigabytes in size, and if even one block has been changed, the whole file must be backed up. To make full backups, which include all datafile blocks that have been used, is the default behavior with RMAN, but because RMAN is an Oracle-aware product, it can also make incremental backups.

Many system administrators (irrespective of whether the system is Oracle) dislike the idea of incremental backups, because of the bookkeeping that is necessary. When restoring, you have to know which whole backup to restore, then which cumulative and incremental backups to apply. This can make a restore operation quite complicated, and one thing you want to avoid when doing this type of work is complexity. But RMAN solves the bookkeeping problem by use of its repository. When you issue the command RESTORE DATABASE, RMAN will search the repository and determine which whole backup to use, and then which incrementals to apply. If RMAN is linked to a tape library, this process will be completely automatic: RMAN will load the appropriate tapes and extract whatever files it needs without any human intervention.

 TIP Do not confuse "whole" and "partial," meaning all of the database or a part of it, with "full" and "incremental," meaning every block of the object or only changed blocks. Either a whole or a partial backup can be full or incremental.

The mechanism for incremental backups is based on the system change number, or SCN. Whenever a data block is updated, the block header is updated with the current SCN. Whenever a backup is taken, the backup is marked in the repository as having been taken at a particular SCN. Thus when making an incremental backup, all RMAN has to do is compare the SCNs in the blocks of the datafile with the SCN of the last backup of the datafile to determine if the block has been changed and should therefore be included in an incremental backup. Clearly, incremental backups apply only to datafile backups, not controlfile or archive log backups. Image copies are always full backups; an incremental image copy could not be an image copy of the original.

Why should you consider incremental backups? There are three major reasons: time, space, and the impact on end users. The time for a backup to complete may not be important to the users, but it can be very important to the system administrators. Automated tape libraries are very expensive pieces of equipment and may well be used for backing up systems other than the Oracle databases. If the time required for an RMAN backup can be reduced, there will be savings in the tape library resources needed. Even though the default operation of RMAN is to scan the whole datafile when backing it up incrementally in order to identify which blocks have changed, there will still be time savings because in virtually all cases it is the writing to tape that is the bottleneck, not the reading of the files. By enabling block change tracking (detailed later in the next section), which obviates the need to scan the whole file, the time for the backup can be reduced dramatically. The volume of an incremental backup will usually be substantially less than the volume of a full backup. As discussed previously, backup sets are always smaller than the source files, or image copies, because they never include empty blocks that have never been written to and can, optionally, be compressed. But incremental backups may well be just a small fraction of the size of a full backup set. This will reduce the impact on the tape library or the disk resources needed. The impact on users is largely dependent on the excessive disk I/O needed for a full backup. When block change tracking is enabled, an incremental backup can use direct access to changed blocks, which will reduce the strain on disk I/O resources substantially.

Incremental backups come in three forms. An incremental level 0 backup isn't incremental at all. Level 0 means a full backup, which will contain every used datafile block. The difference comes with subsequent incrementals: a full backup can't be used as the base for a level 1 backup. A differential level 1 backup, which is the default type of incremental, contains only data blocks modified since the last incremental level 1 backup (cumulative or differential), or blocks modified since the last level 0 backup if there has not been an intervening level 1 backup. A cumulative level 1 incremental backup will contain only the blocks modified since the last level 0 backup.

TIP Previous releases of RMAN used incremental levels 0–4 to give similar functionality to the DIFFERENTIAL and CUMULATIVE options. These still work but are provided only for backward compatibility.

As an example of an incremental backup strategy, consider this diagram:

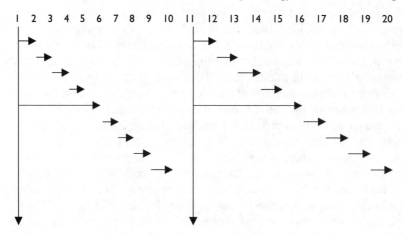

A ten-day incremental backup strategy:

Day 1:	Level 0 incremental
Days 2, 3, 4, 5:	Differential level 1
Day 6:	Cumulative level 1
Days 7, 8, 9, 10:	Differential level 1
Day 11:	Start a new cycle with a level 0 incremental

The cycle starts on day 1 with a level 0 incremental backup. This will be used as a base for subsequent level 1 backups and could be made as follows:

```
RMAN> backup incremental level 0 database;
```

On days 2, 3, 4, and 5 a differential backup will capture just the blocks changed in one day:

```
RMAN> backup incremental level 1 differential database;
```

On day 6 a cumulative backup will capture all changes since the level 0 backup:

```
RMAN> backup incremental level 1 cumulative database;
```

On days 7, 8, 9, and 10 repeat the differential backup before starting another ten-day cycle on day 11 with a new level 0 backup.

Should a restore be necessary, RMAN will extract files from the level 0 backup and apply incrementals in whatever is the most efficient way to re-create the damaged datafiles. This strategy ensures that there will never be more than one day of archive logs to be applied following a restore operation, even though the time and volume of the daily backups is substantially reduced from what it would be if full backups were taken each day. This example does not include backup of the archive logs; they will also have to be protected, but the assumption is that the last day's logs are still on disk in the archive log destinations.

Combining Incremental Backups and Image Copies

It is possible to apply incremental backups to image copies. This is an extremely powerful technique for minimizing restore and recovery time, while still getting the benefits of incremental backups.

The fastest way to restore is to take image copies, because you don't actually have to restore at all. If a datafile is damaged, you simply tell Oracle to use the copy instead. But image copies can only be full backups, not incremental, and you may not wish to inflict the workload of a full whole database copy on your users very frequently. But with infrequent image copies, a large amount of redo may have to be applied from archive logs if the backup is ever needed. The answer is to take just one database copy—this is the only copy you will ever need to make—and then update it from incremental backup sets. The result is an image copy that is regularly updated, meaning that you will be able to restore and recover without having to extract files from backup sets, and having to apply only a minimum of archive logs.

The original copy is taken as usual, with the exception that a tag is required:

```
RMAN> backup as copy incremental level 0
database tag db_whole_copy;
```

Then on a regular basis (typically, daily) perform an incremental backup and apply it to the copy. An example of the syntax is

```
run{
allocate channel d1 type disk;
backup incremental level 1
for recover of copy with tag db_whole_copy
database tag db_copy_upd;
recover copy of database with tag db_whole_copy;
delete backupset tag db_copy_upd;}
```

This job first launches a disk channel. (It does not make sense to work with tape channels for this type of operation.) Then it takes an incremental backup of the database, applies it to the copy, and deletes the incremental backup set. The use of tags to identify the backups relevant to the image copy means that this process will not interfere with a normal backup schedule of datafiles and archive logs.

Block Change Tracking

Incremental backups will always be smaller than full backups, but the time saving may not be as great as you might expect. This is because the default behavior of an incremental backup is to scan the entire datafile being backed up in order to determine which blocks need to be extracted. There is an advantage to this: it allows RMAN to check for block corruption, as discussed in Chapter 30, but there are many occasions when you would prefer that the incremental backup proceed much faster. This can be done by enabling block change tracking.

Block change tracking relies on starting an additional background process: the Change Tracking Writer, or CTWR. This process records the address of each block that has been changed in a file called the *change tracking file.* If block change tracking has been enabled, then RMAN will read the change tracking file when doing an incremental backup to determine which blocks need to be backed up. This is far faster than scanning the whole file.

The change tracking file will be created in a location specified by the DBA, or by default it will go to the DB_CREATE_FILE_DEST directory. It is initially sized at 10MB and will grow in 10MB increments, but unless the database is over one terabyte or is a clustered database, 10MB will be adequate. The file size is not proportional to the amount of update activity. Changed block addresses are stored long enough to allow fast incremental backup of up to eight level 0 backups. There may be a minimal performance overhead to enabling block change tracking, but if incremental backups are being used, Oracle Corporation advises enabling it.

To enable and monitor block change tracking, use the ALTER DATABASE command and the V$BLOCK_CHANGE_TRACKING view, as in Figure 24-3.

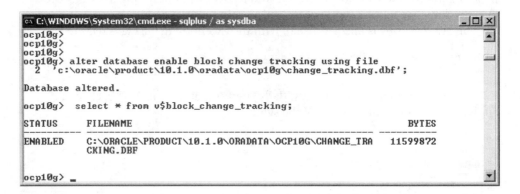

Figure 24-3 Block change tracking

Managing and Monitoring RMAN Backups

The RMAN executable provides facilities for reporting on what backups have been made and what backups are required. The same information can also be obtained through the Database Control interface, or it is possible to query the RMAN repository directly by querying various views that are populated from it. If you are using a Recovery Catalog, this is another source of information. RMAN can also physically remove backups from tape and disk.

The LIST, REPORT, and DELETE Commands

As a general rule, LIST tells you about backups that have been made, whereas REPORT tells you what needs to be backed up. The following table shows some examples of LIST:

Command	Function
RMAN> list backup;	List all your backup sets.
RMAN> list copy;	List all your image copies.
RMAN> list backup of database;	List all your whole database backup sets, whether full or incremental.
RMAN> list backup of datafile 1; RMAN> list backup of tablespace users;	List the backup sets that include datafile I and the backups that include the USERS tablespace.
RMAN> list backup of archivelog all;	List all archive log backup set backups. Use this command or the next to investigate backups of archive logs.
RMAN> list copy of archivelog from time='sysdate - 7';	List all image copies of archive logs generated in the last 7 days.
RMAN> list backup of archivelog from sequence 1000 until sequence 1050;	List all backup sets containing archive logs of log switch sequence numbers 1000–1050.

As you can see, there is a wide range of keywords and syntax available. At any stage, BACKUP and COPY are interchangeable, depending on whether you want to list backup set backups or image copy backups. Note that LIST makes no distinction between whether the backups are on disk or tape. Any of the preceding examples can be suffixed with VERBOSE, which is applied by default, or SUMMARY, as shown in Figure 24-4.

To change the format of the dates and times in the output of LIST, set the environment variable NLS_DATE_FORMAT before launching the RMAN executable. For example, on Unix,

```
$ export NLS_DATE_FORMAT=dd-mm-yy hh24:mi:ss
```

or on Windows,

```
C:\> set NLS_DATE_FORMAT=dd-mm-yy hh24:mi:ss
```

will change the date/time display to the European standard.

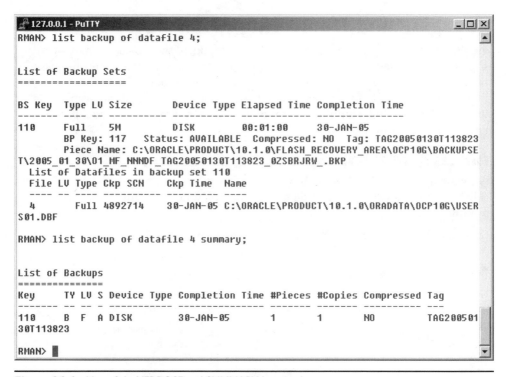

Figure 24-4 Use of the VERBOSE and SUMMARY keywords

The REPORT command interrogates the target database to determine what needs to be backed up. This requires contrasting the physical structure of the database and the archived logs that have been generated with the backup sets and copies as recorded in the repository, and applying a retention policy. The retention policy can be that configured as a default, or it can be specified as part of the REPORT command. This table shows some examples:

Command	Function
RMAN> report schema;	List the datafiles (but not the controlfile or archived logs) that make up the database.
RMAN> report need backup;	Apply the configured retention policy and list all the datafiles and archive log files that need at least one backup to conform to the policy.
RMAN> report need backup days 3;	List all objects that haven't been backed up for three days. Use this command or the next to ignore the configured retention policy.
RMAN> report need backup redundancy 3;	List all files of which there are not at least three backups.

The REPORT OBSOLETE command takes things a step further: it contrasts the RMAN backups that have been taken with the retention policy and lists all those that can be deleted because they are no longer required. This command works in conjunction with DELETE OBSOLETE, which will remove the records of any such backups from the repository and physically remove the backup files from disk or tape. For example,

```
RMAN> report obsolete;
```

will apply the configured retention policy and list all copies and backup sets that are no longer required. Then,

```
RMAN> delete obsolete;
```

will remove the backups deemed surplus to requirements.

```
RMAN> report obsolete redundancy 2;
```

lists all backups that take the number of backups of an object to three or more. Then to remove the superfluous backups,

```
RMAN> delete obsolete redundancy 2;
```

The DELETE command can also be used to remove individual backups, by number or by tag:

```
RMAN> delete backupset 4;
RMAN> delete copy of datafile 6 tag file6_extra;
```

The Dynamic Views

A number of views populated from the target database controlfile can be used to report on RMAN's backups. By querying these, you can develop your own reports, rather than relying on RMAN's LIST command.

View	Displays
v$backup_files	One row for each file that has been backed up, which may be a datafile, the spfile, the controlfile, or an archive log. Also, one row for each piece that RMAN has created. The column FILE_TYPE distinguishes which type of file the row refers to.
v$backup_set	One row per backup set
v$backup_piece	One row per backup piece
v$backup_redolog	One row for each archived log that has been backed up
v$backup_spfile	One row for each backup that has been made of the spfile
v$backup_device	Names of SBT devices that have been linked to RMAN
v$rman_configuration	One row for every configuration setting, excluding all those on default

Join columns in the various views will let you construct comprehensive reports on what has been backed up, where the backups are located, and the volume and type of each backup.

Exercise 24-2: Managing Backups

After setting RMAN qualifiers back to defaults, use the BACKUP, LIST, REPORT, and DELETE commands to create and remove backups.

1. Connect to your database with RMAN, in the default NOCATALOG mode. From an RMAN prompt,

   ```
   RMAN> connect target /
   ```

2. Ensure that your retention policy is set to the default, REDUNDANCY 1.

   ```
   RMAN> configure retention policy clear;
   ```

3. Delete all your backup sets and image copies.

   ```
   RMAN> delete backupset all;
   RMAN> delete copy all;
   ```

   If any backups are listed, enter YES to confirm deletion.

4. List the items that need backing up, according to the configured retention policy.

   ```
   RMAN> report need backup;
   ```

   will list all your datafiles.

5. Choose a datafile, and back it up. In the example that follows, file 6 has been chosen:

   ```
   RMAN> backup datafile 6;
   ```

   Repeat the command to take a second backup of the same file.

6. Repeat the command from Step 4. The file that has been backed up will not be listed.

7. List your backups with

   ```
   RMAN> list backup;
   ```

8. Report and delete the backup that is unnecessary according to the configured retention policy.

   ```
   RMAN> report obsolete;
   RMAN> delete obsolete;
   ```

Chapter Review

Concentrating on the use of the RMAN executable, this chapter detailed how to make backups with Recovery Manager. Backups can be online or offline, whole or partial, full or incremental, and taken as backup sets or image copies. Incremental backups can be greatly accelerated by enabling block change tracking. A particularly useful feature is the ability to apply an incremental backup set to an image copy of the database, enabling you to keep an up-to-date image copy of the database to satisfy subsequent recovery requirements.

The LIST command queries the repository to give details of what backups have been taken. The REPORT command details what backups need to be taken, and what backups are considered obsolete. The DELETE command can remove backups, either individually on demand, or intelligently by applying the retention policy.

Finally, if the RMAN LIST command is not good enough, various views based on the target database controlfile let you query the repository directly.

Questions

1. Which tool or tools can be used as interfaces to the Recovery Manager? (Choose all that apply.)

   A. Database Control

   B. The DBMS_PIPE package

   C. *i*SQL*Plus

   D. The RMAN executable

   E. SQL*Plus

2. Why will this command block fail? (Choose the best answer.)

   ```
   run {
   connect target sys/oracle@ocp10g;
   backup database including current controlfile;}
   ```

   A. A connection as SYS must be as SYSDBA.

   B. Specifying INCLUDE CURRENT CONTROLFILE cannot be done when the whole database has already been specified.

   C. CONNECT cannot appear in a command block.

   D. There is no ALLOCATE CHANNEL command.

3. Some attributes of a backup apply only to backup sets, only to image copies, or to both. Mark the following attributes as being applicable to backup sets only; image copies only; or both.

   A. Can be updated from incremental backups.

   B. Can be incremental backups.

   C. Can be written to tape.

   D. Can be made without requiring tablespace hot backup mode.

   E. Can include all blocks of a datafile.

   F. Can be of the controlfile.

4. You issue the RMAN command,

   ```
   BACKUP AS BACKUPSET DATAFILE 1 PLUS ARCHIVELOG;
   ```

What will happen if there is a log switch during the backup? (Choose the best answer.)

A. The filled logfile group will not be archived until the backup has completed.

B. The filled logfile group will be archived but not included in the backup.

C. The filled logfile group will be archived and included in the backup.

D. The syntax is wrong: archive logs must be backed up into their own backup set.

5. Which of the following statements, if any, are correct about RMAN offline backups? (Choose all correct answers.)

A. The database must be in NOMOUNT mode.

B. The database must be in MOUNT mode.

C. The backup will fail if the shutdown mode was SHUTDOWN IMMEDIATE.

D. NOARCHIVELOG databases can only be backed up offline.

E. ARCHIVELOG databases cannot be backed up offline.

F. Offline backups can be incremental.

6. You are running this command block daily:

```
run {
allocate channel t1 type sbt;
backup as backupset archivelog all delete input;}
```

and you notice that some archive logs remain on disk. What could be the cause of this? (Choose the best answer.)

A. Tape channels cannot write to disks, and they therefore cannot delete from them.

B. You need two channels, one to copy and one to delete.

C. There are multiple archive log destinations.

D. The retention policy does not permit immediate deletion.

7. You perform a full backup on Sunday, an incremental level 0 backup on Monday, an incremental level 1 differential backup on Tuesday, an incremental level 1 cumulative backup on Wednesday, and an incremental level 1 cumulative backup on Thursday. Which blocks will be included in the Thursday backup? (Choose the best answer.)

A. All blocks changed since Sunday

B. All blocks changed since Monday

C. All blocks changed since Tuesday

D. All blocks changed since Wednesday

8. When you enable block change tracking, which process is responsible for recording blocks that have been changed? (Choose the best answer.)

   A. Database writer

   B. Log writer

   C. The server process making the change

   D. A new background process

9. Which of the following commands will tell you about backup sets that are no longer needed according to your retention policy? (Choose the best answer.)

   A. LIST EXPIRED BACKUPSET;

   B. LIST OBSOLETE BACKUPSET;

   C. REPORT EXPIRED BACKUPSET;

   D. REPORT OBSOLETE;

   E. None of the above

10. Which of the following is correct about the REPORT SCHEMA command? (Choose the best answer).

    A. It will list the schema objects in the database.

    B. It will list the datafiles of the database.

    C. It will list the datafiles and controlfile of the database.

    D. It will list the schema objects and the datafiles.

11. You issue this command:

    ```
    BACKUP AS COPY DATABASE PLUS ARCHIVELOG DELETE INPUT;
    ```

    What will happen? (Choose the best answer.)

    A. There will be an error, because DELETE INPUT is not valid for a backup of anything other than archive logs.

    B. The backup will succeed, and the database and archive logs will be deleted.

    C. The backup will succeed, and all the archive logs will be deleted.

    D. The backup will succeed, and only the archive logs in the primary destination will be deleted.

12. You have issued the command

    ```
    configure device type disk parallelism 3;
    ```

    and then execute this job:

    ```
    run {
    allocate channel t1 type disk;
    allocate channel t2 type disk;
    backup format '/backup/%U'
    datafile 1,2,3,4,5;}
    ```

What degree of parallelism will you get? (Choose the best answer.)

A. Three parallel streams, because the configured default is greater than the number of channels requested

B. Two parallel streams, because only two channels will be launched

C. One stream only, because there is only one format specifier for the output file

D. Five parallel streams, because there are five files nominated and a total of five channels: three configured default channels, and two manually allocated

13. A number of V$ views can be queried to report on RMAN backups. Where is the information for these views stored?

A. In the target database controlfile only

B. In the target database controlfile only, unless there is a Recovery Catalog

C. In the Recovery Catalog controlfile only, if you are using a Recovery Catalog

D. In the Recovery Catalog controlfile and the target database controlfile, if you are using a Recovery Catalog

Answers

1. **A, B,** and **D.** The Database Control, the DBMS_PIPE package, and the RMAN executable are all possible interfaces to the Recovery Manager.

2. **C.** CONNECT is a stand-alone command and cannot appear in a command block.

3. Only image copies can be updated from incremental backups (A) or will contain all blocks of a datafile (E). Only backup sets can be incremental (B) or written to tape (C). Either type can be made without requiring hot backup mode (D) and can be made of the controlfile (F).

4. **C.** Archiving will continue as normal and the archive will be included in the backup.

5. **B, D,** and **F.** RMAN offline backups are done in MOUNT mode. NOARCHIVELOG databases can only be backed up offline, but for ARCHIVELOG databases it is always a possibility. Finally, the incremental mechanism can work whether the database is open or mounted.

6. **C.** To remove logs from all destinations, you must specify ...DELETE ALL INPUT;.

7. **B.** All blocks changed since Monday will be included. The catch is that a full backup cannot be used as a base for an incremental backup: only a level 0 incremental backup (which will be the same as a full backup) can be used.

8. **D.** The new background process is the Change Tracking Writer, or CTWR, which is responsible for recording blocks that have been changed.

9. **D.** REPORT OBSOLETE does this by contrasting the RMAN backups that have been taken with the retention policy.

10. **B.** "Schema" is an ambiguous term in the Oracle environment. In the RMAN context, it refers to the datafiles, not the objects owned by a user.

11. **D.** Unless you specify DELETE ALL INPUT, only the archive logs in the primary destination will be deleted. The DELETE command can be specified for, but is never applied to, datafile backups.

12. **B.** The configured default is ignored if there is an ALLOCATE CHANNEL command.

13. **A.** The V$ views associated with the RMAN repository are populated from the target database controlfile, and nowhere else.

CHAPTER 25

Diagnosing Oracle Database Issues

In this chapter you will learn how to

- Use the alert log and database trace files for diagnostic purposes
- View alerts using Enterprise Manager
- Adjust thresholds for tracked metrics
- Control the size and location of trace files

There are two distinct sources of alert information in the Oracle database. First, the various background processes will generate trace files when they encounter certain error conditions. Associated with these trace files is the alert log, which contains messages regarding certain significant events that do not warrant generating an actual error report. You as DBA have minimal control over these trace and alert files: the background processes write to them when necessary. Second, there is the alert system running within the database. This is completely configurable, though in many cases the out-of-the-box configuration will be adequate. It is also possible to generate trace files of an individual session. These can be used to analyze user activity, in particular to diagnose the efficiency of the code that is being run.

The Alert Log

From the moment an instance is started, a stream of critical messages, as well as certain informational ones, is written out to the alert log. The location is determined by the BACKGOUND_DUMP_DEST parameter, but the name cannot be changed. It is

```
alert_<SID>.log
```

where <SID> is the name of the instance.

The parameter is dynamic, meaning it can be changed without shutting down the instance. The directory must exist, and the operating system Oracle owner must have write permission to it: Oracle will verify this by creating a new alert logfile immediately in the nominated directory. Also, the directory may not be the root directory.

 EXAM TIP The alert log, along with any background trace files, is written to the destination specified by the BACKGROUND_DUMP_DEST parameter.

The informational messages in the alert log will include these items:

- All startup and shutdown commands, with the time and mode of the operation. The startup times will include the timings of the transitions from NOMOUNT to MOUNT to OPEN, which are of vital importance for assessing whether the mean-time-to-recover figure matches standards agreed with the users.

- All operations involving physical structures: ALTER DATABASE commands such as creating, dropping, and renaming datafiles and redo logs. Resize operations on datafiles and taking datafiles on and offline are also recorded.

- Tablespace operations, such as DROP and CREATE. Also putting tablespaces into and out of hot backup mode for user-managed backups.

- All log switches and archives, including the names of the affected files.

- The nondefault initialization parameters used to start the instance. Also any subsequent ALTER SYSTEM commands that change parameters.

Thus the alert log contains a continuous history of operations affecting the structure of the database and the instance. It does not include any standard SQL statements, such as DML or DDL commands. It will, however, include some warnings and errors. The more common of these follow:

- **Checkpoint incomplete** Make no mistake—checkpoints always complete. But if your database is performing log switches so frequently that Oracle wants to start a checkpoint before the previous checkpoint has completed, then this error will be signaled. It is indicative of logfiles being far too small and will result in the database hanging until the checkpoint does finish.

- **Unable to open file** This will occur at the transition from NOMOUNT to MOUNT if there is a problem with any copy of the controlfile, or while transitioning from MOUNT to OPEN if there is a problem with an online logfile member or a datafile.

- **Corrupt block** Not a nice message! If a block of a datafile is found to be damaged, its address (file number and the block number within the file) is written out.

- **Problems with archiving** These include an archive log destination being full or unavailable.

- **Deadlocks** Such events occur when badly written software sets up a logically impossible situation, causing two sessions to block each other.

The alert log can be viewed from an operating system prompt, by navigating to the directory specified as the BACKGROUND_DUMP_DEST and opening it with any editor you wish. Consider this extract from an alert log:

```
Wed Oct 20 14:48:16 2004
ORA-00202: controlfile:
'C:\ORACLE\PRODUCT\10.1.0\ORADATA\OCP10G\CONTROL01.CTL'
ORA-27041: unable to open file
O/S-Error: (OS 2) The system cannot find the file specified.
Wed Oct 20 14:48:16 2004
Controlfile identified with block size 0
Wed Oct 20 14:48:19 2004
ORA-205 signalled during: alter database mount exclusive...
Wed Oct 20 14:48:37 2004
Shutting down instance (abort)
```

This depicts something you hope you will never see: an instance terminating because a controlfile copy has been destroyed. The error stack begins with ORA-00202, which says that there is a problem with a controlfile. Then ORA-27041 expands on this by saying that the problem is with opening the file. The error descends to the operating system error, which is Windows error 2: the file cannot be found. As any problem with a controlfile results in the instance being terminated immediately, the message stream concludes with an "abort."

Many of the messages in the alert log will include references to a trace file that will give more detailed information. For example, this extract from an alert log depicts a problem with a corrupted block:

```
Thu Oct 21 14:45:36 2004
Hex dump of (file 7, block 93) in trace file
c:\oracle\product\10.1.0\admin\ocp10g\udump\ocp10g_ora_3688.trc
Corrupt block relative dba: 0x01c00009 (file 7, block 93)
Bad header found during buffer read
Data in bad block:
 type: 32 format: 0 rdba: 0x20202020
```

```
last change scn: 0x2020.20012020 seq: 0x7 flg: 0x20
spare1: 0x20 spare2: 0x20 spare3: 0x1020
consistency value in tail: 0x20202020
check value in block header: 0x2020
block checksum disabled
Reread of rdba: 0x01c00009 (file 7, block 93) found same corrupted data
```

The block with the problem is the ninety-third block of datafile 7. By querying the DBA_EXTENTS view, you can work out which segment this block is a part of; this may be significant when planning how to recover from this situation. A full block dump, which may have some information that can be used to reconstruct the damaged data, is written to a trace file in the USER_DUMP_DEST directory.

An alternative method of viewing the alert log is to use Database Control. From the database home page, the Alert Log link in the Diagnostic Summary section shows a parsed form of the alert, with all errors displayed and formatted in a helpful manner (see Figure 25-1).

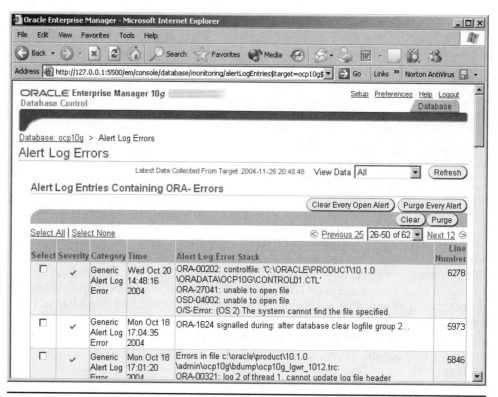

Figure 25-1   Database Control view of alert log error messages

Background Trace Files

The background processes that make up an Oracle instance will write out trace files to the BACKGROUND_DUMP_DEST directory whenever they encounter problems. Here is an example of such a file:

```
Dump file c:\oracle\product\10.1.0\admin\ocp10g\bdump\ocp10g_dbw0_3100.trc
Thu Oct 21 14:40:56 2004
ORACLE V10.1.0.2.0 - Production vsnsta=0
vsnsql=13 vsnxtr=3
Oracle Database 10g Enterprise Edition Release 10.1.0.2.0 - Production
With the Partitioning, OLAP and Data Mining options
Windows XP Version V5.1 Service Pack 2
CPU             : 1 - type 586
Process Affinity: 0x00000000
Memory (A/P)    : PH:253M/510M, PG:1588M/2019M, VA:1803M/2047M
Instance name: ocp10g
Redo thread mounted by this instance: 1
Oracle process number: 4
Windows thread id: 3100, image: ORACLE.EXE (DBW0)
*** SERVICE NAME:() 2004-10-21 14:40:56.738
*** SESSION ID:(168.1) 2004-10-21 14:40:56.738
ORA-01157: cannot identify/lock data file 7 - see DBWR trace file
ORA-01110: data file 7:
'C:\ORACLE\PRODUCT\10.1.0\ORADATA\OCP10G\NONCRIT.DBF'
ORA-27041: unable to open file
OSD-04002: unable to open file
O/S-Error: (OS 2) The system cannot find the file specified.
```

All trace files have a header giving the name of the file and information about the release of Oracle that generated it and the operating system. Following that is the actual error; in this case, DBWn is reporting that a file is missing. The naming convention for trace files is the name of the instance ("ocp10g" in the example), the name of the process that generated it ("dbw0," the first database writer), the operating system process number on Unix or thread number on Windows of the generating process (3100 in the preceding example), and a suffix of ".trc".

Unlike the alert log, trace files always mean an error—often a critical one. For instance, if a controlfile copy is damaged, the process detecting the problem will write out a trace file and then the instance will terminate.

The only control the DBA has over trace files is where to put them, and a limit on their maximum size. They will be written to the directory specified by the BACKGROUND_DUMP_DEST parameter, and another parameter, MAX_DUMP_FILE_SIZE, sets an upper limit to their size. The MAX_DUMP_FILE_SIZE parameter defaults to UNLIMITED, or it can be set to an integer or a string value. If it is just an integer, Oracle will use the operating system block size as the units. Alternatively, the string can be an integer suffixed with K or M, in which case the integer will be interpreted as kilobytes or megabytes. Thus, if your operating system block size is 512 bytes and you want to limit trace files to 5MB, these are equivalent:

```
SQL> alter system set max_dump_file_size=10000;
SQL> alter system set max_dump_file_size='5m';
```

Note that this maximum file size does not apply to the alert log; that will continue to grow until you trim or delete it.

Server-Generated Alerts

The server-generated alert system is a completely configurable mechanism that monitors the database, the instance, and user's sessions and issues warnings when certain limits are reached and when certain events occur. The monitoring is internal to the instance and based on a large number of metrics that are calculated and observed continuously. The background process that does this is the manageability monitor (or MMON) process, assisted by the manageability monitor light (or MMNL) process.

A "metric" is a statistic converted into a meaningful figure. Most statistics are useless on their own. For example, the number of disk reads is a statistic; what you need to know is the number of disk reads per second, which is a metric. Similarly, knowing that segments in a tablespace occupy so many gigabytes may be interesting, but what you really need to know is when the space used reaches a certain proportion of the space available, which requires comparing the space used with the total available space. In earlier releases of the database the conversion of statistics to useful metrics usually had to be done by the DBA; now Oracle does it for you, storing the results in the Automatic Workload Repository, or AWR, in the SYSAUX tablespace.

Different metrics are calculated with different frequencies. The tablespace space usage metric is one of the less frequently calculated figures: only every ten minutes, because space problems do not usually emerge suddenly. By contrast, CPU usage per second is indeed computed every second. Metrics data is generally written to the AWR every hour, but if the memory structures in the SGA used for staging the metrics information fill up within the hour, then the write to the AWR will be more frequent. This is a case where the MMNL process would take action.

Alert Types

Alerts are classed as threshold and nonthreshold. A *threshold* alert refers to a situation that builds up over time. Tablespace usage is a threshold alert: you could configure the alert system to send you a warning alert when a tablespace becomes 95 percent full, and a critical alert when it reaches 99 percent full. These alerts are also referred to as "stateful" alerts because they persist for some time until cleared, either because the problem resolves itself or because you take appropriate action, such as adding more space to the tablespace. *Nonthreshold* alerts inform you of events that occurred unpredictably. Such an alert is the "ORA-1555: snapshot too old" error that is signaled when a query fails because the undo data it needs has been overwritten. When this type of error occurs, it is resolved immediately—in the case of ORA-1555, by canceling the query—and the alert becomes a historical record. Nonthreshold alerts are also referred to as "stateless" alerts, because they do not persist: they occur, and are gone.

The metrics for which alerts can be configured are listed in the view V$ALERT_ TYPES; there are more than a hundred of them. Many of the more useful metrics are "x per second"–type metrics; these all have names suffixed "_ps". To list them,

```
SQL> select internal_metric_name from v$alert_types where
internal_metric_name like '%_ps';
INTERNAL_METRIC_NAME
-----------------------------
transactions_ps
physreads_ps
physwrites_ps
physreadsdir_ps
physwritesdir_ps
physreadslob_ps
physwriteslob_ps
redosize_ps
logons_ps
<output truncated....>
```

Warning and critical alerts can be configured for all of these, and for many more.

The Alert System Architecture

The instance itself accumulates the statistics used by the alert system. There is no overhead to collecting these statistics, and they will be collected automatically if the initialization parameter STATISTICS_LEVEL is set to TYPICAL, which it should always be. Setting STATISTICS_LEVEL to BASIC will disable collection of these statistics, and much more, with no performance benefit. The only possible performance hit involved in collecting this information is when it is written to the AWR on disk, but as that will happen only once an hour, it is not an issue. Setting STATISTICS_LEVEL to ALL will enable the collection of fantastically detailed information about SQL executions; it is possible that this may impact on performance, and therefore it would not normally be done at the instance level but rather at the session level when carrying out advanced SQL statement tuning exercises.

Retrieving the statistics for calculating metrics is done by the background process MMON. As this process is part of the instance, it has direct access to the data structures storing the information. This bypasses the overhead of having, for instance, to populate views in response to a query.

While monitoring the statistics and calculating the metrics, MMON will compare the metrics to the configured alert thresholds. If a metric breaks a threshold, MMON will write an appropriate message to a queue. If a stateless alert event occurs, MMON will also write a message to a queue. Queues are a feature of the database that allows sessions to communicate with each other. A queue is implemented as a table with an object column: the definition of the object defines the structure of the message. Any session (with appropriate permissions) can subscribe to a queue, meaning that it can de-queue (or read) the messages and take action based upon them. The queue used for alerts is a predefined queue called ALERT_QUE. This is a multiconsumer queue, meaning that many sessions can subscribe to the queue and de-queue messages from it. The message will be purged from the queue only after all subscribers have received it. The principle consumer of the ALERT_QUE is the Database Control Enterprise Manager Daemon, and the action it will take (apart from displaying the alerts it has de-queued on the database home page) could be to send an e-mail message or an SMS to the DBA. In an advanced environment, you could write your own alert handler by creating another subscriber to ALERT_QUE.

It should now be clear why the server alert system is so efficient. It uses in-memory statistics that are accessed directly; there is no need to transfer the information to a session via a V$ view, as is the case when you query views yourself. The alerts are written out to a queue that any subscribing client can read and take action upon. So the server is monitoring itself—internally, and automatically.

One final point to note is that if there is a problem with a queue, the alert system can still function: the message will be written to the alert log instead. This is the only point of contact between the alert log and the server alert system.

 EXAM TIP The alert log is completely separate from the server alert system.

Viewing Alert Information

Alert information can be viewed by querying two data dictionary views. DBA_OUTSTANDING_ALERTS will list all stateful alerts that have been raised and not yet dealt with. Once cleared, the alerts are removed from this view and entered into DBA_ALERT_HISTORY. Stateless alerts go directly to DBA_ALERT_HISTORY. This query,

```
SQL> select reason,object_type type,object_name name from
dba_outstanding_alerts;
REASON                                                TYPE        NAME
--------------------------------------------------    ----------  -----
Metrics "Current Open Cursors Count" is at 1266       SYSTEM      SYSTEM
Tablespace [USERS] is [99 percent] full               TABLESPACE  USERS
```

shows two outstanding alerts. The first refers to the number of open cursors, which is an alert relating to the system, or instance, and the second states that the USERS tablespace is 99 percent full. These alerts will remain in this view until cleared by the number of open cursors reducing (perhaps as sessions disconnect) or by space becoming available in the tablespace, either by adding space to it or by dropping or shrinking some of the objects within it.

An alternative view of the alerts is given by Database Control. Figure 25-2 shows how alert information is displayed by the Database Control on the database home page. The system alerts are shown in the alerts section, and space management alerts are indicated in the space usage section. To drill down to the detail of a system alert, double-click on the message for the alert to see the detail, as shown in Figure 25-3.

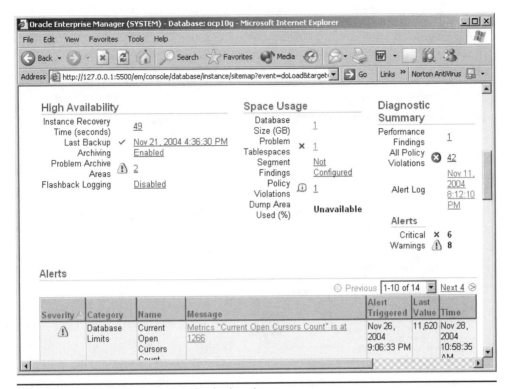

Figure 25-2 Alert information on the database home page

To drill down to the space problems, take the Numeric link (value 1 in the example shown in Figure 25-2) next to the text "Problem Tablespaces" to see the detail of the problems (see Figure 25-4).

Setting Up Notification Rules

It is all very well to be able to view alerts by querying views or using Database Control, but a better technique is to enable the alert notification mechanism, which will typically send e-mails to the DBA when certain alerts are raised. This is configured within Database Control. From the database home page, take the Preferences link at the top right. In the Preferences window, shown in Figure 25-5, enter all the e-mail addresses that might need to receive notifications.

Then take the Rules link. A wizard (Figure 25-6) will walk you through the process of creating or editing rules that will be used to determine the action Database Control will take when an alert is raised: selecting the metrics (and their severities) for which you would like to be e-mailed notifications.

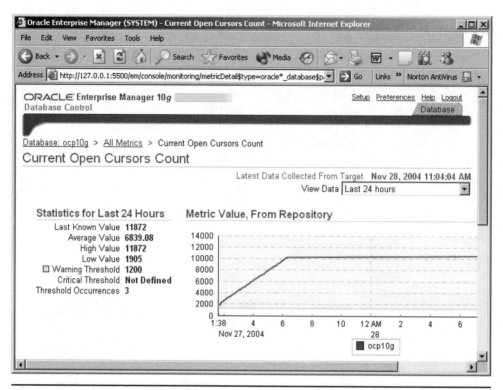

Figure 25-3 Detail of the open cursors alert

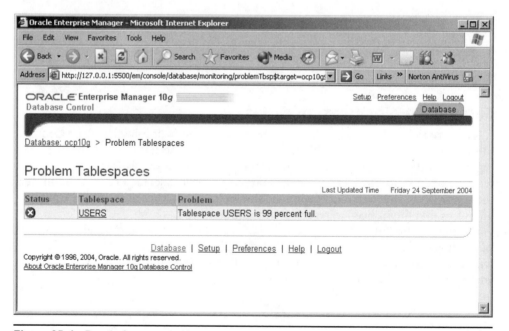

Figure 25-4 Detail of a space problem

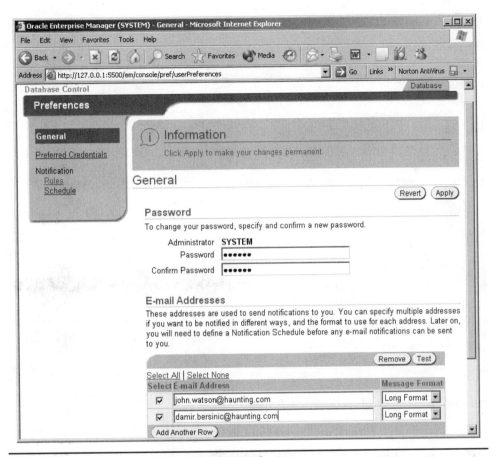

Figure 25-5   Setting e-mail addresses for alert notifications

Editing Thresholds

The standard alerts come with preconfigured thresholds. For tablespace usage, a warning alert will be issued when a tablespace is 85 percent full, and a critical alert will be issued when it is 97 percent full. To view all the alerts and any thresholds that have been set, from the Database Control home page, take the Manage Metrics link in the Related Links section. An alternative interface is provided by the DBMS_SERVER_ ALERT package, which includes a procedure SET_THRESHOLD that can be used to set the criteria for issuing warning and critical alerts. Using the procedure requires extensive use of constants to define the metric to be evaluated, the operators (such as "greater than...") and the values; these are detailed in the *PL/SQL Packages and Types Reference* manual. In the following exercise, you will work with three constants:

- **dbms_server_alert.tablespace_pct_full**   Nominates which metric to monitor
- **dbms_server_alert.operator_ge**   A comparison operator, "greater than or equal to"
- **dbms_server_alert.object_type_tablespace**   The type of object being monitored

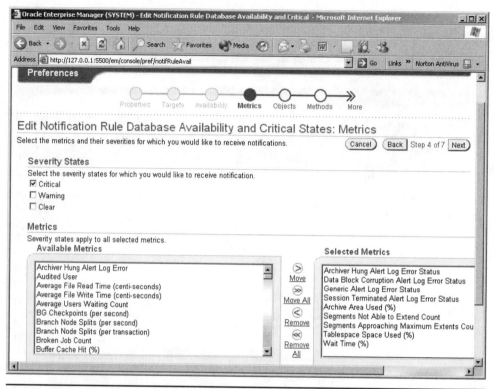

Figure 25-6 Selection of metrics for notification

Exercise 25-1: Setting, Viewing, and Clearing Alerts

Use both the DBMS_SERVER_ALERT API and Database Control to manage the alert system.

1. Connect to your database with SQL*Plus as user SYSTEM, and create a tablespace that is 1MB big.

```
SQL> create tablespace small datafile 'small.dbf' size 1m;
```

2. Set the warning and critical alerts for this tablespace to 50 percent and 75 percent respectively.

```
SQL> execute dbms_server_alert.set_threshold(-
metrics_id=>dbms_server_alert.tablespace_pct_full,-
warning_operator=>dbms_server_alert.operator_ge,-
warning_value=>'50',-
critical_operator=>dbms_server_alert.operator_ge,-
critical_value=>'75',-
observation_period=>1,consecutive_occurrences=>2,-
instance_name=>null,-
object_type=>dbms_server_alert.object_type_tablespace,-
object_name=>'SMALL');
```

This will signal an alert when the SMALL tablespace usage is greater than or equal to 50 percent and 75 percent, if the situation persists for more than one minute and occurs in two consecutive observation periods.

3. Create a table and insert sufficient rows to cause space usage to exceed the warning threshold.

```
SQL> create table toobig (c1 char(1000)) tablespace small;
SQL> begin
for n in 1..500 loop
insert into toobig values('a row');
end loop;
commit;
end;
/
```

4. Connect to your database as user SYSTEM with Database Control. From the database home page, take the Administration tab and then the Tablespaces link in the Storage section to reach the Tablespaces page.

5. Click the SMALL link and then the Thresholds tab to display the current settings, as in Figure 25-7.

6. Return to the database home page, and in the Alerts section look for a warning about space usage for the SMALL tablespace. It may be necessary to wait a few minutes and refresh the screen, as tablespace usage is checked only every ten minutes.

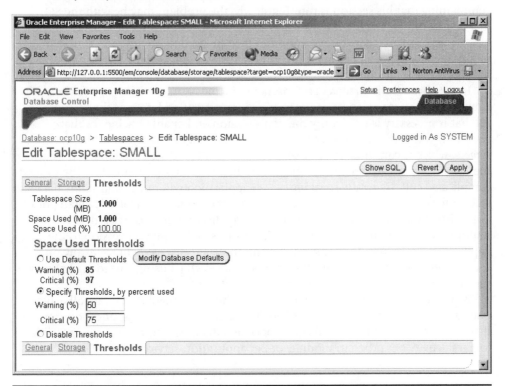

Figure 25-7   Tablespace usage thresholds

7. From your SQL*Plus session, run this query:

```
SQL> select object_name,reason from dba_outstanding_alerts;
```

and note that the SMALL tablespace is listed as being over-full.

8. Fix the problem by adding a datafile to the tablespace.

```
SQL> alter tablespace small add datafile 'small2.dbf' size 2m;
```

9. Refresh the Database Control screen, and note that the alert has disappeared. Again, it may be necessary to wait a few minutes.

10. Confirm that the row has also been removed from the DBA_OUTSTANDING_ALERTS view by repeating the query from Step 7.

11. Confirm that the alert has been transferred to the alert history view.

```
SQL> select object_name, reason,suggested_action,resolution from
dba_alert_history where object_name='SMALL';
```

12. Tidy up by dropping the tablespace.

```
SQL> drop tablespace small including contents and datafiles;
```

User Trace Files

Background trace files are generated automatically when a problem occurs. User trace files are only generated on demand, when you want to track exactly what a session is doing. Usually trace files are used to help with application tuning. If a user is complaining that his session is running slowly, the problem may be with the SQL that he is running. Tracing the session will allow you to see what he was doing and how he was doing it. This information can then be used to identify the SQL that might be causing problems, and these problem statements can be referred back to the programmers for tuning.

In a dedicated client/server environment, tracing is simple. The connection between a user process and a server process is persistent and defines the session. All that is necessary is to identify the user's session and enable tracing for that session. If you are using shared server, each session will be cut across all the shared servers, which means that any one session's trace will be distributed in the trace files generated by each shared server process. In a web environment, it can be more complicated still. Generally speaking, a web application will not establish one database session for each user; rather, the application itself will create a relatively small pool of persistent database sessions, which may be dedicated server or shared server, and multiplex a large number of user sessions over this pool. The user session to the application server may be persistent, but the application server will route any one user request over any available database session, which (if using shared server) may then be serviced by any shared server process.

By using the more advanced tracing capabilities, it is possible to trace all activity, one database session's activity, or one logical session through an application server that may have been multiplexed over a pool of database sessions. It is also possible to trace activity per program module, or per application service.

Instance-Level SQL Tracing

There are two instance parameters that control tracing. SQL_TRACE, which defaults to FALSE, can be set to enable tracing of every SQL statement executed against the instance. USER_DUMP_DEST specifies the directory to which the trace files will be written. Each server process will generate its own stream of trace information, corresponding to a session in a dedicated server environment. In a shared server environment there will be one trace file per shared server, which will contain tracing information for all the statements executed by that shared server for all the sessions it has been servicing. To enable instance-wide tracing,

```
SQL> alter system set sql_trace=true;
```

The trace files generated will be named <SID>_ora_<SPID>.trc, where <SID> is the name of the instance and <SPID> is the Unix process number, or Windows thread number, of the server process that is generating the trace. To identify the session responsible for generating any particular trace file, join the views V$SESSION to V$PROCESS as follows:

```
SQL> select s.username,s.sid,p.spid from v$session s, v$process p
where s.paddr=p.addr;
```

Then use the spid value to find the trace file relevant to each session.

TIP Think long and hard before enabling tracing for the whole instance. The volume of trace generated will be immense.

Session-Level SQL Tracing

Tracing for one session can be enabled interactively by the session itself, or for any session programmatically. Whatever method is used, the trace file will be generated in the USER_DUMP_DEST directory and named with the process ID number of the server process, as just described. To enable tracing for your session, give the command

```
SQL> alter session set sql_trace=true;
```

run whatever SQL statements you are interested in, and then switch off tracing with

```
SQL> alter session set sql_trace=false;
```

But this is no use when a user reports a problem. S/he will not be working with SQL*Plus, but with package software that will not permit issuing commands such as this. To enable tracing for any one user's session, find the session's identifier and serial number and then use the DBMS_MONITOR package. For example, if user JOHN complains that his session is running slowly, run this query to identify his session:

```
SQL> select sid,serial# from v$session where username='JOHN';
       SID    SERIAL#
---------- ----------
       162         14
```

Of course, if JOHN is logged on several times, you may need to select additional columns, such as PROGRAM and TERMINAL, from V$SESSION to make sure you get the right session. Then use the SID and SERIAL# as follows:

```
SQL> execute dbms_monitor.session_trace_enable( -
session_id=>162,serial_num=>14);
```

This will cause the session to start writing out trace information until you issue

```
SQL> execute dbms_monitor.session_trace_disable( -
session_id=>162,serial_num=>14);
```

 TIP Analyzing the content of a trace file is a complex task, but essential to working out exactly what a user was doing, and how he was doing it.

Tracing with Database Control

The DBMS_MONITOR package has procedures that will let you enable tracing at these levels:

- **Session level**   As just described, any one database session can be traced. But if in a web environment many application server sessions are being serviced by a small number of database sessions, this may not be precise enough to identify which users are actually impacting on system performance.

- **Module level**   Different program modules will be generating different levels of activity.

- **Client ID level**   In a web environment, the database may not know who the user that executes any particular statement is, because many end-user application server sessions are being multiplexed through a pool of database sessions. But the application server does know, by assigning an application client ID to each client session. It is possible to trace activity per client ID, even though one client ID's statements will be serviced by any and all of the pool of database sessions.

- **Service level**   Users may be connecting to the database through different service names registered with the Database Listener. Service tracing will identify which service name is being most heavily used, and therefore which groups of users are taking the most resources.

- **Action** The work done by a particular PL/SQL procedure can be tracked, no matter who is executing it.

While it is possible to trace at these levels using DBMS_MONITOR, it is much easier to enable tracing through Database Control. From the database home page, take the Performance tab and then the Top Consumers link in the Additional Monitoring Links section. From there, you can view activity by session, module, service name, web client ID, or PL/SQL procedure. To gain the full benefit if this, your programmers will have to use the DBMS_APPLICATION_INFO package to name their modules and actions, but once this is done each can be traced.

In Figure 25-8, it can be seen that two sessions (both using database username JOHN) are responsible for most of the physical and logical I/O. Not visible in the figure because they are scrolled off to the right are buttons for enabling and disabling tracing. The other tabs will show activity per service, per module, per action, or per web client.

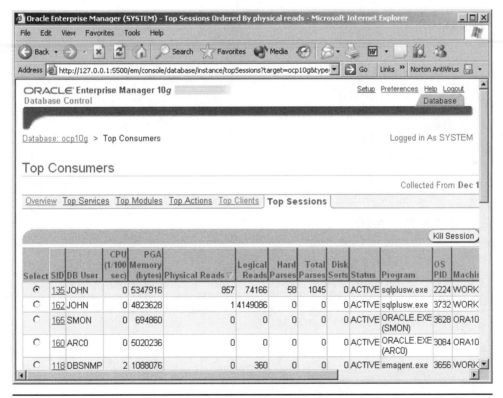

Figure 25-8 Session monitoring with Database Control

Chapter Review

The Oracle database will generate a great deal of diagnostic information by default. This includes the alert log: a chronological list of certain critical events, such as startup and shutdown, and any physical changes to the database or changes to instance parameters. Then there are the background trace files, generated by the background processes when they detect errors. You as DBA have no control over what is written to the alert log or to background trace files: Oracle writes out whatever it needs to write out.

For proactive monitoring, you can use the server alert system. This is preconfigured with alerts for a number of metrics, such as tablespace usage, but can be configured to monitor and report on many more metrics. The alerts raised can be viewed through data dictionary views on the Automatic Workload Repository or through Database Control, or they can be e-mailed to a list of nominated e-mail addresses.

Finally, if necessary you can enable tracing of database activity by each database user, or by individual program modules no matter which users are using them. There is an API, DBMS_MONITOR, and a graphical user interface available to support this tracing functionality.

Questions

1. The location of the alert log is controlled by a parameter. Which one? (Choose the best answer.)

   A. AUDIT_FILE_DEST

   B. BACKGROUND_DUMP_DEST

   C. CORE_DUMP_DEST

   D. DB_CREATE_FILE_DEST

   E. USER_DUMP_DEST

2. What will be written to a background trace file? (Choose the best answer.)

   A. Critical errors

   B. Informational messages about background process activity

   C. User activity information

   D. It will depend on whether the SQL_TRACE parameter has been set

3. If a "stateless," or "nonthreshold," alert condition is raised, where will it be displayed? (Choose the best answer.)

   A. In the alert log

   B. In a background trace file, generated by the process that detected it

   C. In a user trace file, generated by the session that detected it

   D. In the DBA_OUTSTANDING_ALERTS view

   E. In the DBA_ALERT_HISTORY view

4. To enable collection of metrics for all the server alerts, what should the STATISTICS_LEVEL parameter be set to? (Choose the best answer.)

   A. BASIC

   B. TYPICAL

   C. ALL

   D. Either TYPICAL or ALL

   E. Any of BASIC, TYPICAL, or ALL

5. When the server alert system raises an alert, what will it do? (Choose all that apply.)

   A. Write it out to the alert log.

   B. E-mail the alert to registered alert recipients.

   C. Record the alert in the Automatic Workload Repository.

   D. Invoke the appropriate procedure in DBMS_SERVER_ALERT.

6. Which of the following commands will be written to the alert log? (Choose four answers.)

   A. ALTER SESSION SET SQL_TRACE=TRUE;

   B. ALTER SYSTEM SET SHARED_POOL_SIZE=400M;

   C. ALTER TABLESPACE USERS BEGIN BACKUP;

   D. ALTER DATABASE DATAFILE 10 RESIZE 1000M;

   E. DROP TABLESPACE EXAMPLE CASCADE;

   F. DROP USER SCOTT CASCADE;

   G. DROP TABLE HR.EMPLOYEES;

   H. SET AUTOTRACE ON;

7. Your users are connecting to the database through the shared server mechanism, and you want to trace one user's session. How can this be done? (Choose the best answer.)

   A. Enable tracing for his user process.

   B. Trace the dispatcher servicing his session.

   C. You can trace his session if you can identify the session's SID and SERIAL#.

   D. You cannot trace individual sessions through shared server.

8. Which process is responsible for updating metrics? (Choose the best answer.)

   A. MMON, the manageability monitor

   B. SMON, the system monitor

   C. PMON, the process monitor

   D. The server processes

9. Under which of the following circumstances must you subscribe to the ALERT_QUE queue? (Choose the best answer.)

   A. To receive e-mail notifications of alerts

   B. To view alerts in Database Control

   C. To write your own alert handler

   D. To clear alerts from the ALERT_QUE queue manually

10. A SHUTDOWN ABORT is issued. By default, where will this be recorded? (Choose the best answer.)

   A. As an alert in the ALERT_QUE queue

   B. In the alert log

   C. As a user trace file

   D. As background trace file

Answers

1. **B.** The alert log is written to the BACKGROUND_DUMP_DEST.

2. **A.** Background trace files are generated when a background process encounters a severe problem, critical to the running of the instance.

3. **E.** Stateless alerts are displayed in the DBA_ALERT_HISTORY view. They are never in the DBA_OUTSTANDING_ALERTS view, because they are solved as soon as they occur.

4. **D.** Either TYPICAL or ALL will enable collection of the metrics used by the server alert system. BASIC will disable the server alert system.

5. **B and C.** Server alerts are recorded in the AWR and mailed to anyone registered to receive them.

6. **B, C, D, and E.** All ALTER SYSTEM and ALTER DATABASE commands are written out to the alert log, so B and D are correct. Tablespace operations are also written out, so C and E are correct too.

7. **C.** A shared server session is still a session, so you enable tracing for the SID and SERIAL# that uniquely identify the session.

8. **A.** It is the manageability monitor that updates the AWR with metrics.

9. **C.** Subscribing to the queue is only needed if you want to write your own routines to capture alert.

10. **B.** All SHUTDOWN commands are recorded in the alert log, and nowhere else.

CHAPTER 26

Recovering from Noncritical Losses

In this chapter you will learn how to
- Recover temporary tablespaces
- Recover a redo log group member
- Recover index tablespaces
- Recover read-only tablespaces
- Re-create the password file

This is the first of several chapters that go into detail on the various techniques for recovering from disasters, either man-made or out of your control. Never forget that the mechanism of redo and rollback used for instance recovery, as detailed in Chapter 18, makes it absolutely impossible to corrupt an Oracle database. This is not just something said by salesmen—it is a fact. This reliability is why people use the Oracle database (and why it isn't cheap). But if there is media damage—damage to the disks storing the database files—it is possible to lose data. You can protect against this by running your database in archivelog mode; by multiplexing your controlfile, online redo log files, and archive log files; and by backing up your datafiles and archive log files.

Loss of any number of any database files is no excuse for losing data. An adequate backup regime will always let you restore and recover without loss of a single row of committed data, but the restore and recovery cycle may be time consuming and may involve downtime. There are some files whose loss can be tolerated without going through the restore and recover process: known as "noncritical" losses, such losses are covered in this chapter.

 EXAM TIP Loss of undo data is definitely critical. Just because undo data is transient, that doesn't mean that it doesn't matter.

Recovering from Loss of a Temporary Tablespace

A temporary tablespace is one used for storing "temporary" data. It is not necessary to back up temporary tablespaces, and indeed RMAN will never back them up. If you try to put a temporary tablespace into hot backup mode with ALTER TABLESPACE... BEGIN BACKUP; you will get an error. Since temporary tablespaces cannot be backed up, if damaged they cannot be restored—they must be replaced, instead.

Temporary Data

What is temporary data? It is data that exists only for the duration of one database session, possibly for less than that. It is private to the session and totally inaccessible to any other users. Temporary data usually comes in two forms: sort data and global temporary tables.

Sort data is generated when an operation requiring rows to be sorted, such as the use of the ORDER BY clause in a select statement or when creating indices, cannot proceed completely in memory. In an ideal world all sorts will occur in memory, but if memory is limited and the volume of data to be sorted is large, then the sort operation must process rows in batches and write out each sort run to disk before sorting the next batch. Then the multiple sort runs on disk are merged to produce a final listing of all the data, in the correct order. The sort runs are private to the session doing the sort—there is no possible reason for any other session to access them, and indeed this is impossible.

Global temporary tables are a powerful feature of Oracle that your programmers can use. A global temporary table's definition is visible to all sessions (hence "global") and can be populated with rows by any and all sessions, but the rows are visible only to the session that inserted them. Many sessions can make use of the temporary table's definition at once, but each session will see only its own rows. Global temporary tables are cleared when the session terminates. If only a few rows are inserted into a global temporary table, it will be stored in the session's memory, but if a large amount of data is being manipulated in global temporary tables, then—just as with sort data—it will be written out to a temporary tablespace.

Since temporary data persists only for the duration of the session that created it, there is no requirement to save the data permanently, or to recover it in the event of a disaster. For this reason, temporary data is not written to the regular tablespaces that store permanent objects. It is stored, for the duration of the session that created it only, in temporary segments in temporary tablespaces.

 EXAM TIP Working with temporary data does not generate undo or redo.

Temporary Space Configuration

To list your temporary tablespaces and their tempfiles and sizes, run this query:

```
SQL> select t.name,d.name,d.bytes from v$tablespace t, v$tempfile d
where t.ts#=d.ts#;
```

An alternative query against a data dictionary view would be

```
SQL> select tablespace_name,file_name,bytes from dba_temp_files;
```

Every database will have one temporary tablespace nominated as the default temporary tablespace. This is the one used by all users who have not been specifically assigned a temporary tablespace. To identify it,

```
SQL> select property_value from database_properties where
property_name='DEFAULT_TEMP_TABLESPACE';
```

Each user will have a designated temporary tablespace, possibly the database default temporary tablespace. To list them,

```
SQL> select username,temporary_tablespace from dba_users;
```

The dynamic performance view V$TABLESPACE and the data dictionary view DBA_TABLESPACES list all tablespaces, whether temporary or permanent. DBA_TABLESPACES does, however, have a column CONTENTS that distinguishes between them.

EXAM TIP The files that make up temporary tablespaces are listed in the dynamic performance view V$TEMPFILE and the data dictionary view DBA_TEMP_FILES. The files of permanent tablespaces are listed in V$DATAFILE and DBA_DATA_FILES. Both types of tablespace are included in V$TABLESPACE and DBA_TABLESPACES.

Damage to a Tempfile

The tempfiles that make up temporary tablespaces are used very differently from the datafiles that make up permanent tablespaces. All writing to datafiles is done by the DBWn process, and if a datafile is damaged or not available when the database is opened, the database will not open—it will remain in mount mode. Tempfiles are not written to by the DBWn, or indeed by any background process—they are written to by the server processes servicing the sessions that need some temporary space. For this reason, even if a tempfile is not available at startup time, the database will still open. DBWn will, however, write a message such as this to the alert log:

```
Fri Dec 03 20:27:23 2004
Errors in file /oracle/admin/ocp10g/bdump/ocp10g_dbw0_2228.trc:
ORA-01186: file 202 failed verification tests
ORA-01157: cannot identify/lock data file 202 - see DBWR trace file
ORA-01110: data file 202: '/oracle/oradata/tempfiles/ts1.dbf'
```

This message indicates that the tempfile is damaged; the trace file will give more detailed information. As far as users are concerned, the database will appear to be functioning normally. The problem will only become apparent when a session requires some temporary space:

```
ocp10g> create global temporary table gt1 as select * from sh.sales;
            *
create global temporary table gt1 as select * from sh.sales
ERROR at line 1:
ORA-01157: cannot identify/lock data file 202 - see DBWR trace file
ORA-01110: data file 202: '/oracle/oradata/tempfiles/ts1.dbf'
```

In this example, a session tries to create and populate a global temporary table, but the attempt fails because the table is too large to be accommodated in the session's private memory and must be written to the user's temporary tablespace. The session detects that the tempfile making up the temporary tablespace is not available, and returns an error.

TIP It is possible for an application to run for some time without users' becoming aware that there is a problem with a temporary file. However, you as DBA should pick up the problem immediately from monitoring the alert log.

Restoring a Temporary Tablespace

Temporary tablespaces, and the tempfiles that make them up, cannot be backed up. The Recovery Manager, RMAN, ignores them completely; if you run the REPORT SCHEMA command to show the files that make up the database, the tempfiles will not be listed. For user-managed backups, if you attempt to put a temporary tablespace into hot backup mode, you will get an error:

```
ocp10g> alter tablespace temp_ts1 begin backup;
alter tablespace temp_ts1 begin backup
                 *
ERROR at line 1:
ORA-03217: invalid option for alter of TEMPORARY TABLESPACE
```

So if you can't back up a tempfile, how can you restore it? The answer is that you can't—but you can re-create it as shown in Figure 26-1:

1. Add another tempfile to the damaged temporary tablespace.
2. Take the damaged tempfile offline.
3. Drop the damaged file.

An alternative approach would work at the tablespace level, rather than the datafile level, as shown in Figure 26-2:

1. Create a new temporary tablespace.
2. Switch your users over to the new temporary tablespace via the ALTER DATABASE command.
3. Drop the damaged tablespace.

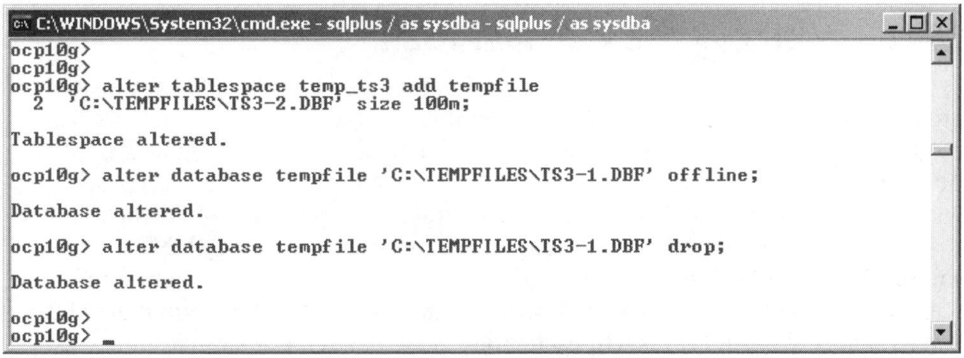

```
C:\WINDOWS\System32\cmd.exe - sqlplus / as sysdba - sqlplus / as sysdba
ocp10g>
ocp10g>
ocp10g> alter tablespace temp_ts3 add tempfile
  2  'C:\TEMPFILES\TS3-2.DBF' size 100m;

Tablespace altered.

ocp10g> alter database tempfile 'C:\TEMPFILES\TS3-1.DBF' offline;

Database altered.

ocp10g> alter database tempfile 'C:\TEMPFILES\TS3-1.DBF' drop;

Database altered.

ocp10g>
ocp10g>
```

Figure 26-1   Replacing a damaged tempfile

```
C:\WINDOWS\System32\cmd.exe - sqlplus / as sysdba - sqlplus / as sysdba    _ □ X
ocp10g>
ocp10g>
ocp10g>
ocp10g> create temporary tablespace temp_ts4
  2  tempfile 'C:\TEMPFILES\TS4-1.DBF' size 100m;

Tablespace created.

ocp10g> alter database default temporary tablespace temp_ts4;

Database altered.

ocp10g> drop tablespace temp_ts3 including contents and datafiles;

Tablespace dropped.

ocp10g> _
```

Figure 26-2 Replacing a damaged temporary tablespace

TIP Creating temporary tablespaces and tempfiles is very fast, because the files are not formatted. A multigigabyte tempfile will be created in seconds.

Recovering from Loss of an Online Redo Log File

An Oracle database requires at least two online log file groups, each with at least one valid member, to function. You may need more than two groups for performance reasons, and you should certainly have more than one member per group for security. Not just data security—your job security, as well. Provided that the groups do have multiple members, the database will survive the loss of any member. Since online log files cannot be backed up, if a member gets damaged it cannot be restored—but it can be replaced.

Online Redo Log File Configuration

Two views describe the configuration of your online redo log. V$LOG has one row per group, and V$LOGFILE has one row per member.

The first query in Figure 26-3 shows that the database has three logfile groups, numbered 1, 2, and 3. There is no technical reason for the numbers being consecutive, and they will not necessarily be used in numerical order: these are merely the numbers that happened to be chosen when the groups were created. The SEQUENCE# column shows which log switch number each group is at; the group with the highest number will be the current group, while the lowest number belongs to the group that will be overwritten at the next log switch. Each group is 10MB—remember that the size is specified at the group level, not at the member level. Each group is multiplexed: two members. Then you can see that the database is configured for archivelog mode, and that only the current group is not archived. The status column informs you that right now the LGWR is streaming out redo to group 2. Group 3, however, is still ACTIVE.

```
ocp10g>
ocp10g>
ocp10g>
ocp10g> select group#,sequence#,bytes,members,archived,status from v$log;

    GROUP#  SEQUENCE#        BYTES    MEMBERS ARC STATUS
---------- ---------- ---------- ---------- --- ----------------
         1        278   10485760          2 YES INACTIVE
         2        280   10485760          2 NO  CURRENT
         3        279   10485760          2 YES ACTIVE

ocp10g> select group#,status,member from v$logfile order by group#;

    GROUP# STATUS  MEMBER
---------- ------- --------------------------------------------
         1         C:\ORACLE\ORADATA\REDOA\REDO1A.LOG
         1         C:\ORACLE\ORADATA\REDOB\REDO1B.LOG
         2         C:\ORACLE\ORADATA\REDOA\REDO2A.LOG
         2         C:\ORACLE\ORADATA\REDOB\REDO2B.LOG
         3         C:\ORACLE\ORADATA\REDOA\REDO3A.LOG
         3         C:\ORACLE\ORADATA\REDOB\REDO3B.LOG

6 rows selected.

ocp10g>
ocp10g>
```

Figure 26-3   Logfile configuration

This means that changes exist in group 3 referring to blocks in the database buffer
cache that have not yet been written to disk by the DBWR: they are still "dirty," and
so in the event of an instance failure, these changes in group 3 would be needed for
instance recovery. In due course, those blocks will be written to disk, and then group
3 will become INACTIVE.

The second query in Figure 26-3 shows the individual logfile group members. You
already know from V$LOG that each group has two members, but now you can see
their names and that they are in different directories. Ideally, they would be on
different devices. The STATUS column for each member is NULL, meaning that the
member is fine. The STATUS column in V$LOG tells you what is happening to the
members of a group, but it is the STATUS column in V$LOGFILE that tells you
whether any one member is actually usable.

Damage to an Online Redo Log File Member

Your online redo log is the guarantee that the database will never be corrupted.
Provided that there is at least one valid member of the current group (and of any
previous group that is still ACTIVE), you will never have a corrupted database. If the
redo log file groups are multiplexed, then damage to an individual member is not
critical—the database will even remain open. But this is a risky position to be in.
Presumably, you have company standards that state, for example, "all production
databases must have an online redo log multiplexed to three destinations on different
devices." If a member gets damaged, you need to diagnose the problem and take
appropriate action immediately in order to re-comply with the standard.

If all copies of the current logfile group are damaged, the instance will terminate immediately. It will also terminate if at a log switch all copies of the group being made current are damaged. If there is still a valid member of the group, the instance will remain open, and your users will not be aware of any problem—but there will be indications that something is wrong. First, the view V$LOGFILE will show the damaged or missing member as being INVALID. Second, the background processes will report the problem. Consider this extract from an alert log:

```
Sat Dec 04 11:01:09 2004
Errors in file c:\oracle\admin\ocp10g\bdump\ocp10g_lgwr_3216.trc:
ORA-00316: log 1 of thread 1, type 0 in header is not log file
ORA-00312: online log 1 thread 1: 'C:\ORACLE\ORADATA\REDOA\REDO1A.LOG'
Sat Dec 04 11:08:20 2004
Private_strands 7 at log switch
Thread 1 advanced to log sequence 282
  Current log# 3 seq# 282 mem# 0: C:\ORACLE\ORADATA\REDOA\REDO3A.LOG
  Current log# 3 seq# 282 mem# 1: C:\ORACLE\ORADATA\REDOB\REDO3B.LOG
Sat Dec 04 11:08:21 2004
ARC1: Evaluating archive   log 1 thread 1 sequence 281
Sat Dec 04 11:08:21 2004
Errors in file c:\oracle\admin\ocp10g\bdump\ocp10g_arc1_1080.trc:
ORA-00313: open failed for members of log group 1 of thread 1
Sat Dec 04 11:08:21 2004
Errors in file c:\oracle\admin\ocp10g\bdump\ocp10g_arc1_1080.trc:
ORA-00313: open failed for members of log group 1 of thread 1
Committing creation of archivelog
'C:\ORACLE\ARCHIVE2\ARCH_C9D1DB5B_1_537705766_281.LOG'
Committing creation of archivelog
'C:\ORACLE\ARCHIVE1\ARCH_C9D1DB5B_1_537705766_281.LOG'
```

At 11:01:09, the LGWR detected a problem with the header of a log file member: this is the ORA-00316 message. The file exists but is damaged; the ORA-00312 message tells you that the damaged file is C:\ORACLE\ORADATA\REDOA\REDO1A.LOG, which is part of group 1. LGWR also produced a trace file, which may have more detailed information. But the instance remains open. Then at 11:08:20 there was a log switch, to group 3 at sequence number 282. Both members of this group open successfully. If the database were not in archivelog mode, the errors would stop here (at least, until group 1 were needed again—at which point they would be repeated), but in this database, once the log switch completes the archive process ARC1 attempts to archive group 1, at 11:08:21. It too detects the problem, and it writes out a trace file. Note that the archive does succeed. The archiver process generates the archive log file (two copies, to two different directories) from the surviving member of group 1.

Re-creating a Damaged Online Log File Member

You have two options: either drop the damaged member and add a replacement member, or clear the group. Figure 26-4 demonstrates both techniques, continuing the preceding example. First the damaged member is dropped, and then the physical file is deleted from disk. Then a new member is added. This will have fixed the problem. The alternative approach is to use the CLEAR LOGFILE command, which

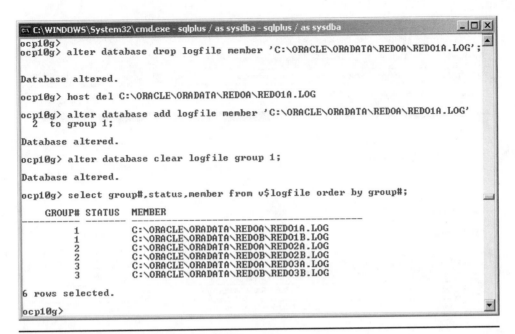

```
C:\WINDOWS\System32\cmd.exe - sqlplus / as sysdba - sqlplus / as sysdba        _ □ X
ocp10g>
ocp10g> alter database drop logfile member 'C:\ORACLE\ORADATA\REDOA\REDO1A.LOG';

Database altered.

ocp10g> host del C:\ORACLE\ORADATA\REDOA\REDO1A.LOG

ocp10g> alter database add logfile member 'C:\ORACLE\ORADATA\REDOA\REDO1A.LOG'
  2  to group 1;

Database altered.

ocp10g> alter database clear logfile group 1;

Database altered.

ocp10g> select group#,status,member from v$logfile order by group#;

   GROUP# STATUS    MEMBER
   ------ ------    ------------------------------------------
        1           C:\ORACLE\ORADATA\REDOA\REDO1A.LOG
        1           C:\ORACLE\ORADATA\REDOB\REDO1B.LOG
        2           C:\ORACLE\ORADATA\REDOA\REDO2A.LOG
        2           C:\ORACLE\ORADATA\REDOB\REDO2B.LOG
        3           C:\ORACLE\ORADATA\REDOA\REDO3A.LOG
        3           C:\ORACLE\ORADATA\REDOB\REDO3B.LOG

6 rows selected.

ocp10g>
```

Figure 26-4   Replacing damaged online logfile members

will create a new group by replacing all the members and reusing the old members'
filenames. Either way, the end result is a fully functional group.

The choice between DROP/ADD and CLEAR will usually be dictated by
circumstances. If there is no damage at all to the disks, only to the file, then CLEAR
is simpler and devoid of any chance of error. Oracle will not let you clear a logfile
group that needs to be archived, or one that is still current or active. But if there is
damage to the disk, then the CLEAR will fail because Oracle will not be able to re-
create the file in its original location. This is when you will DROP the original member,
physically delete it if it still exists, and then ADD a replacement member in a different
disk location. The danger comes with the manual deletion of the damaged file—it is
frighteningly easy to make a mistake and delete the wrong file.

It is also possible to DROP and ADD log file members through database control.
From the database home page, take the Administration tab, and the Redo Log Groups
link in the Storage section. Select the radio button for the group with the problem,
and click Edit. This will take you to the Edit Redo Log Group window shown in
Figure 26-5, where the damaged member can be removed and a replacement added.

TIP Database Control will not physically delete old files from disk. You must
still do that by hand.

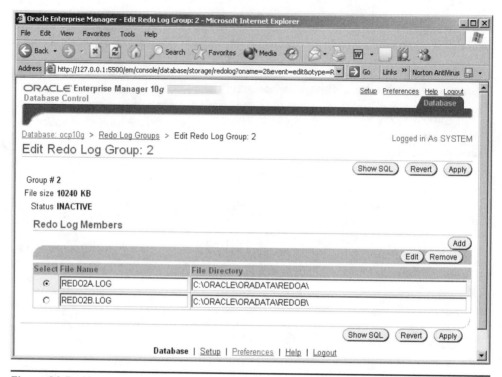

Figure 26-5   Managing online redo log file members with Database Control

Recovering from Loss of an Index Tablespace

Index data is real data that must be protected. Any transaction affecting a table will also affect the indexes on the table; all actions on indexes generate undo and redo, in exactly the same manner that actions on tables generate undo and redo. The only exception is index creation and rebuild, where you can switch off redo generation by using the NOLOGGING option.

Where index data may be different from table data is that it can be regenerated from the base tables. This does not mean that index data is not important. Indexes are as important a part of your database as any other, and vital for maintaining data integrity and database performance. Furthermore, if an index is not available, the table will be locked for nearly all DML operations: you will not be able to do any inserts or deletes, and updates will fail if they affect the indexed column(s). Sure, you can still query the table—but performance may be appalling, because without an index all access will be through full table scans. Nonetheless, there may be circumstances when you decide that it would be quicker and easier to re-create indexes than to restore and recover the tablespace containing them. In this sense, indexes can be considered "noncritical" data and need not be included in your backup and recovery routines.

The Index Tablespace(s)

For indexes to be considered noncritical, it is vital to create one or more tablespaces specifically for your index segments. This is generally considered to be good practice, anyway. Under normal working conditions, your user sessions will be accessing tables and indexes concurrently. If the tables and indexes are in the same tablespace, they will share the same datafiles, and this will limit the degree of concurrency that the operating system and hardware can provide. If they are in separate tablespaces with separate datafiles (ideally, on separate physical devices), performance will improve. Most applications will already be structured in this manner. For example, the Oracle E-Business Suite of applications (up to release 11.5.9) is, by default, structured with two tablespaces per module: one for the tables, the other for the associated indexes. Enforcing the rule that only indexes go into the index tablespaces will be a matter of discipline, and you must check regularly that the rule is being adhered to by running queries such as the following:

```
SQL> select owner,segment_name,segment_type from dba_segments where
tablespace_name='INDX' and segment_type <> 'INDEX';
```

(This example, like all following examples, assumes that the index tablespace is called INDX.)

If you are confident that index data is the only data in a particular tablespace, then you can exclude it from your backup routines. This decision is not to be embarked upon lightly, and you must compare the time it would take to rebuild all the indexes with the time it would take to restore and recover any damaged datafiles.

TIP Index-organized tables are indexes! But do not put them in the index tablespace: they must be backed up, restored, and recovered along with regular heap tables.

If the database is running in noarchivelog mode, then index tablespaces are the only case where, in the event of damage to a datafile, you do not need to do a full restore and lose all the work done since the backup. Remember that in noarchivelog mode, there is no such concept as recovery: all you can do is whole backups, and whole restores. This is the exception: if the damage is restricted to index tablespaces, then you can drop and re-create them and keep the database current.

Damage to an Index Tablespace

If an index is not available because of media damage, your end users will receive messages along these lines:

```
ocp10g> insert into hr.regions values (99,'United Kingdom');
insert into hr.regions values(99,'United Kingdom')
            *
ERROR at line 1:
ORA-00376: file 7 cannot be read at this time
ORA-01110: data file 7: '/oracle/oradata/indexdata/indx_01.dbf'
```

This message will be generated whenever any insert or delete operation is attempted against a table with an index in the damaged tablespace, and updates will succeed only if they do not affect the indexed columns. In effect, you can consider the tables locked. Queries will generate errors if they attempt to use the missing indexes. The problems will also extend to constraints. DML against a child table in a foreign key relationship requires that the primary key index of the parent table be available. If it is not, then the child table will be locked for DML as well, even if its indexes are still available. The only exception is updates that do not affect the constrained columns.

Apart from errors being reported to user sessions, damage to an index tablespace datafile will also show up through the usual messages in the alert log and background trace files, and entries in the dynamic performance views. To investigate the preceding error further, query the dynamic performance views V$DATAFILE and V$RECOVER_FILE as follows:

```
SQL> select name,status from v$datafile where file#=7;
NAME                                            STATUS
----------------------------------------------- -------
/oracle/oradata/indexdata/indx_01.dbf           RECOVER
SQL> select online_status,error from v$recover_file where file#=7;
ONLINE_STATUS ERROR
------------- -----------------------------------
OFFLINE       FILE NOT FOUND
```

The first query tells you that the file is in trouble; the second tells you what is wrong. Note that the file has been taken offline automatically. With previous versions of the database, it was necessary to do this manually.

It may be that the index tablespace consists of several datafiles, only one of which is damaged. In these circumstances, the effects on your application will depend very precisely on where any particular index happens to have extents. Generally, to have predictable results, it is advisable to take the whole tablespace offline if any one file is damaged:

```
SQL> alter tablespace INDX offline immediate;
```

The IMMEDIATE keyword instructs Oracle to take the tablespace offline without attempting to flush any dirty buffers from the tablespace to disk. This is usually a requirement; otherwise, the OFFLINE command will fail when Oracle finds that it cannot write to the datafile. Taking the tablespace offline is in any case a precursor to the rebuilding operation.

 EXAM TIP OFFLINE IMMEDIATE is allowed only when ARCHIVELOGMODE is enabled.

Recovering an Index Tablespace

An index tablespace can be restored and recovered like any other tablespace, provided that you are running the database in archivelog mode. This section describes an alternative approach: rather than repairing the damage through restore and recover, simply drop the tablespace, re-create it, and regenerate the indexes. Bear in mind that this may be a very time-consuming operation. Indexing tables of many millions or billions of rows can take hours, even days. The routine is as follows:

1. Take the damaged tablespace offline.
2. Determine which indexes were in the damaged tablespace.
3. Drop the tablespace and delete its datafiles.
4. Create a new tablespace.
5. Generate all the indexes in it.

To determine which indexes were in the tablespace, query the data dictionary view DBA_SEGMENTS:

```
SQL> select owner,segment_name from dba_segments where
tablespace_name='INDX' and segment_type='INDEX';
```

To drop the tablespace, use

```
SQL> drop tablespace indx including contents and datafiles;
```

which will drop all references to the tablespace and its datafiles from the data dictionary and the controlfile, drop all the objects in the tablespace, and remove the physical files from disk.

Create a new tablespace with whatever characteristics are appropriate. For example,

```
SQL> create tablespace indx datafile
'/oracle/oradata/indexdata/indx_01.dbf' size 100m
extent management local uniform size 128k
segment space management auto
nologging;
```

The generation of the indexes is the hardest part. Just how good is your application documentation? Do you have scripts ready-written for exactly this circumstance? Many applications will have some kind of "system maintenance" menu, which will include an option to rebuild indexes. If so, you do not have a problem. Just run it. If your documentation includes all the index creation scripts, again you do not have a problem.

But if there is no documentation or you suspect that it may not be accurate, you can still construct scripts to rebuild the indexes. This is because the DDL describing indexes is stored in the data dictionary, not in the index, and is therefore still available even though the indexes and their tablespace have been destroyed. As a last resort, you can run queries joining the views DBA_INDEXES to DBA_IND_COLUMNS to work out what columns of what table each index was built on, and also retrieve what type (B*Tree or bitmap) of index it was, and any other characteristics, such as UNIQUE or COMPRESSED. But if this is necessary, it must have been done before the drop of the tablespace: the INCLUDING CONTENTS clause will drop the index definitions from the data dictionary.

A technique that may be better is to use Data Pump to extract the index creation statements, again before the drop of the tablespace. This command will use Data Pump export to extract all the index definitions in the HR schema to a Data Pump dump file to be located in whatever directory DP_DIR maps onto:

```
$ expdp hr/hr directory=dp_dir dumpfile=ind.dmp include=index
```

Then this Data Pump import will extract the DDL for creating the indexes from the dump file and write it out to a file IND.SQL, again in the DP_DIR directory:

```
$ impdp hr/hr directory=dp_dir dumpfile=ind.dmp sqlfile=ind.sql
```

Having acquired the necessary index creation statements by one means or another, run them—but don't forget to check that they all nominate the correct, newly created, tablespace. To speed up the creation, consider the use of PARALLEL and NOLOGGING.

To enable parallelism, specify PARALLEL and optionally a degree in the index creation statement:

```
SQL> create index hr.rname_idx on hr.regions(region_name)
tablespace indx parallel 8;
```

Enabling parallelism in index creation allows the server session that is building the index to take a number of parallel execution servers (eight in the example) and divide the work among them. A "producer" group of parallel servers will read the table, each scanning a range of rows, and pass them to a "consumer" set of parallel servers that will sort the rows, each producing their own index. Then the resulting index pieces are merged to produce the final complete index. The number of parallel servers to be used can be hard-coded (as in the example) or not specified, in which case the database optimizer will make an intelligent guess as to how many parallel servers to use in order to generate the index in the shortest possible time. Demanding too many parallel servers is not good; it will impact adversely on other users and may indeed slow down the index creation. Unless you are confident in your ability to tune parallelism (bearing in mind such matters as the disk configuration, the number of CPUs, the structure of the table, and the workload on the system), it is generally better to trust the optimizer.

The NOLOGGING attribute can be specified in addition to or instead of the PARALLEL keyword:

```
SQL> create index hr.rname_idx on hr.regions(region_name)
tablespace indx nologging;
```

This instructs Oracle not to generate redo during the index creation. Of course, all subsequent DML against the index will generate redo—you can never switch off redo generation for normal work—but disabling redo generation during the index creation will make the creation run much faster.

As soon as an index is created, Oracle will start using it. In earlier releases of the database, it was necessary to analyze the newly created indexes to gather optimizer statistics on them, but release 10g will gather these statistics automatically during the index creation.

Exercise 26-1: Using Index Tablespaces

Create an index tablespace, simulate its loss, and recover without using a backup.

1. Connect to your database with SQL*Plus as user SYSTEM.

2. Create a tablespace for indexes. Specify any convenient directory for the datafile. For example,

   ```
   SQL> create tablespace indx datafile 'c:\oracle\oradata\indx01.dbf'
   size 10m;
   ```

3. Create a table in the default tablespace, and an index in the new tablespace.

   ```
   SQL> create table indtest (c1 number);
   SQL> create index ind1 on indtest(c1) tablespace indx;
   ```

4. Simulate the loss of the datafile.

   ```
   SQL> alter database datafile 'c:\oracle\oradata\indx01.dbf' offline drop;
   ```

5. Demonstrate that the index is not available, and that DML can no longer proceed against the table.

   ```
   SQL> insert into indtest values(1);
   ERROR at line 1:
   ORA-00376: file 7 cannot be read at this time
   ORA-01110: data file 7: 'C:\ORACLE\ORADATA\INDX01.DBF'
   ```

6. Drop the index tablespace.

   ```
   SQL> drop tablespace indx including contents and datafiles;
   ```

7. Show that the table is usable, now that the index has been dropped.

   ```
   SQL> insert into indtest values(1);
   ```

8. Re-create the index tablespace and the index.

   ```
   SQL> create tablespace indx datafile 'c:\oracle\oradata\indx01.dbf'
   size 10m;
   SQL> create index ind1 on indtest(c1) tablespace indx;
   ```

9. Tidy up.

   ```
   SQL> drop tablespace indx including contents and datafiles;
   SQL> drop table indtest;
   ```

Recovering from Loss of a Read-Only Tablespace

Making a tablespace read-only prevents any DML operations against the objects in that tablespace. You can't create objects in it either, but you can drop them. From the DBA's point of view, the purpose of making a tablespace read-only is to eliminate the need for regular backup of a large volume of static information thereafter. From the applications view, it is to ensure that historical data cannot be modified. Whatever the reason, the effect within the controlfile is to freeze the file headers of the datafiles making up the tablespace. When the command ALTER TABLESPACE...READ ONLY; is issued, the datafiles are checkpointed (all dirty buffers written to disk), the current system change number or SCN is noted, and the file headers (which store that SCN) are frozen.

A requirement for a file to be usable is that it should be synchronized with the rest of the database: the SCN in its header must be up-to-date. Read-only tablespace datafiles are the exception to this rule. Oracle will open a read-only tablespace datafile, even though the SCN is out-of-date. But it won't let you write to it. Remember that absolutely nothing happens to the files at the operating system level. The read-only attribute is set purely within the Oracle environment and has nothing to do with operating system access modes.

 EXAM TIP You can drop objects from read-only tablespaces. Why? Because a DROP updates the data dictionary, not the object itself. And the data dictionary certainly isn't in a read-only tablespace.

Backing Up a Read-Only Tablespace

Read-only tablespaces need to be backed up only once, and this should be done immediately after changing the tablespace status. It is still perfectly possible to back up the datafiles on a regular schedule, but there is no point. If you are using user-managed backups, you can't put the tablespace into hot backup mode. Issuing ALTER TABLESPACE...BEGIN BACKUP; will generate the error

```
ORA-01642: begin backup not needed for read only tablespace....
```

The RMAN Recovery Manager can also back up read-only tablespaces, but if you enable backup optimization with

```
RMAN> CONFIGURE BACKUP OPTIMIZATION ON;
```

then RMAN will back up the files only to whatever is required by the RETENTION POLICY setting. For example, if your retention policy is "redundancy 3," RMAN will back it up three times, and never again. If your retention policy is a recovery window, RMAN will back it up only once.

Recovering a Read-Only Tablespace

The problem with restoring and recovering a read-only tablespace is how the controlfile handles it. If the tablespace is read-only at the time the damage to its datafile occurs, and if the backup of the datafile was made while the tablespace was read-only, then there is no problem: just restore the backup over the damaged file. There is no possible loss of data, and nothing else needs to be done apart from bringing the file online, if indeed it ever went offline. This is why loss of a read-only tablespace is considered noncritical.

Where you will run into trouble is if the status of the tablespace was changed from read-only to read/write, or the other way round, between the backup being made and the damage occurring that requires a restore.

Imagine a situation where a tablespace is made read-only on 1 January and later backed up. Then on 1 July it is made read/write, perhaps to move another table into it. Then something goes wrong, and a file gets damaged. You know very well that the only redo that needs to be applied to the file to make it current is the few hours of redo generated since the tablespace was made read-write. But when you restore the backup, Oracle will demand every archive log generated from 1 January. This is because the file header was frozen back then, and as far as Oracle is concerned, the backup you have restored is six months old and must be made current. Do you have those six months of archive logs? You had better hope so, because otherwise the datafiles can never be brought online. Even if the tablespace has been backed up during the six months, that will not help you, because every backup will have the same 1 January SCN in its file header.

The solution is that you must always take a fresh backup of a tablespace the moment you change its status from read-only to read/write.

Recovering from Loss of the Password File

The password file is one of the files that cannot be backed up by RMAN. This is not a limitation of RMAN—it is a logical impossibility. When RMAN connects you to a database, you will usually be connecting with the SYSDBA privilege, which requires either operating system authentication or a password file. For RMAN to restore the file it uses to establish a database connection would not make any sense.

The password file on Unix is

```
$ORACLE_HOME/dbs/orapw<SID>
```

and on Windows it is

```
%ORACLE_HOME%\database\PWD<SID>.ora
```

where <SID> is the name of the instance. On Windows, it is possible to control the location and name of the password file with the ORA_<SID>_PWFILE Registry variable.

Damage to the Password File

Loss of the password file is not critical. It is always possible to connect to a database with the SYSDBA privilege with operating authentication; a password file provides a secondary means of authentication, if operating system authentication is not possible. Operating system authentication takes precedence: as Figure 26-6 illustrates, if you are

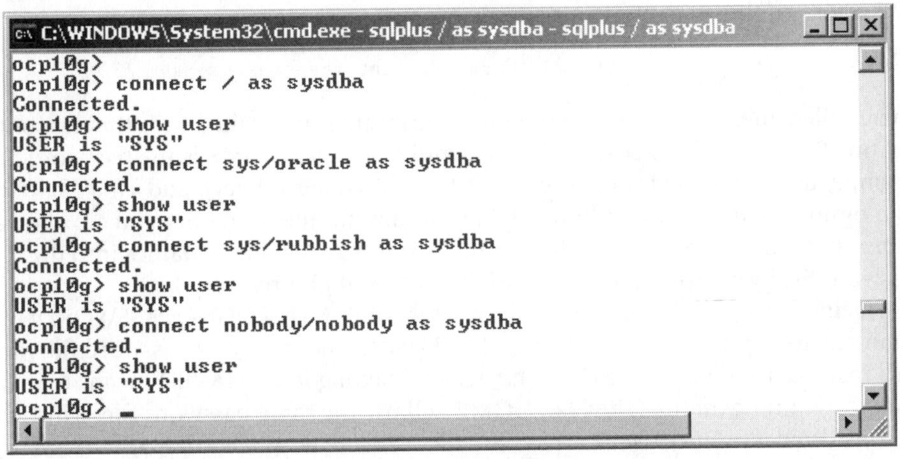

Figure 26-6 Operating system authentication overrides password file authentication.

logged onto the server machine as a member of the operating system group that owns the Oracle software, you can always connect with SYSDBA privileges no matter what username and password you supply.

Nonetheless, a password file is generally considered necessary for most databases. To gain a SYSDBA connection across a network, it is essential. If you are running SQL*Plus on your PC and administering a database on the other side of the planet, you will never actually log on to the operating system of the machine hosting the database, so operating system authentication is not an option. Database Control itself—even though the daemon runs on the same machine as the database—connects over Oracle Net, so it too needs a password file.

If the password file is damaged, the database will continue to function as normal, except that remote SYSDBA connections will not be possible. But if the database is shut down, then startup will fail when the instance tries to read the password file. To get around the problem in the short term, set the REMOTE_LOGIN_PASSWORDFILE instance parameter to NONE. This will prevent Oracle from looking for a password file, and the instance will open normally. This is a static parameter, so to change it, while in nomount mode you must use

```
SQL> alter system set remote_login_passwordfile=none scope=spfile;
```

and then restart.

Replacing the Password File

It is possible to back up the password file with normal operating system backup procedures. Your system administrators' regular backups of the ORACLE_HOME directory will have copies of it, and so you can restore it with no problems. An alternative is to re-create it, by re-running the command used to create it in the first place. If you cast your mind back to the scripts generated by the Database Configuration Assistant when you created the database, you will remember that the database creation scripts include a call to the utility that creates the password file, but if you no longer have a copy of those scripts, it is a simple matter to run it again:

```
orapwd file=<filename> password=<password> entries=<max_users>
```

where <filename> is the name of the file to be created, as detailed near the start of the section "Recovering from Loss of the Password File," <password> is the password to be embedded in the file for the user SYS (it can be changed later), and <max_users> is an optional parameter that limits the maximum number of names you are allowed to insert into the password file: the default is four. You will insert names into the password file by granting users the SYSDBA or SYSOPER privilege.

Having re-created the password file, reset the REMOTE_LOGIN_PASSWORDFILE parameter to use it. The usual setting is EXCLUSIVE, meaning one password file for each instance running off the ORACLE_HOME. Setting it to SHARED means that all instances running off the ORACLE_HOME will use the same password file, which can be considered a security risk.

EXAM TIP Unless REMOTE_LOGIN_PASSWORDFILE is set to SHARED or EXCLUSIVE, the password file is ignored.

Chapter Review

Media failure is damage to the files that make up the database. Some files can be damaged without necessitating the use of restore and recovery routines, and without causing the instance to terminate. Such losses are known as "noncritical." Noncritical files can be replaced, rather than being restored. The noncritical files are temporary tablespace tempfiles, multiplexed online redo log files, and perhaps files from tablespaces dedicated to index data. Read-only tablespaces can also be considered noncritical, in the sense that they do not need to be backed up according to the same schedules as the rest of the database. Finally, the password file is noncritical, because it can always be re-created when necessary.

Questions

1. Some files can be damaged without causing the instance to crash. Which? (Select all that apply.)

    A. A multiplexed controlfile copy

    B. A multiplexed online log file

    C. A multiplexed archive log file

    D. A nonmultiplexed archive log file

    E. A nonmultiplexed online log file, if there are at least two other logfile groups

2. If a tempfile is missing, what will happen at instance startup? (Choose the best answer.)

    A. The file will be re-created automatically.

    B. The database will not open.

    C. The database will open, but an error will be signaled when the tempfile is needed.

    D. The database will open, but all sorts will proceed in memory.

3. Which types of file can be considered noncritical? (Choose the best answer.)

    A. Temporary datafiles

    B. Undo datafiles

    C. Multiplexed controlfiles

    D. All of the above

4. If a log file member is damaged, how will you know? (Choose two answers.)

   A. The STATUS column of V$LOG

   B. The STATUS column of V$LOGFILE

   C. The STATUS column of V$LOGFILE_MEMBER

   D. The alert log will have a message to this effect

   E. The Database Control Redo Log Groups window will show the error

5. If an index tablespace is unavailable, what will be the effect on the associated tables? (Choose the best answer.)

   A. All DML will fail, but you will be able to SELECT from them.

   B. Some DML will succeed, and some index searches will fail.

   C. UNIQUE and PRIMARY KEY constraints will not be enforced.

   D. Both SELECT and DML can continue, but with reduced performance.

6. You make a tablespace read-only. Which of the following commands will succeed against objects in the tablespace? (Choose the best answer.)

   A. INSERT

   B. UPDATE

   C. DELETE

   D. DROP

   E. None of the above

7. Which of these statements is correct? (Choose all the correct answers.)

   A. Writing to a temporary tablespace does not generate REDO.

   B. Generating UNDO data does not generate REDO.

   C. Specifying NOLOGGING for an index disables REDO for DML against the index.

   D. Specifying NOLOGGING for a tablespace disables REDO for all objects in the tablespace.

8. The password file is damaged. Which of the following statements is correct? (Choose the best answer.)

   A. You can still connect as SYSDBA using data dictionary authentication.

   B. You cannot connect as SYSDBA unless you set the REMOTE_LOGIN_PASSWORDFILE parameter to NONE.

   C. You must re-create the password file before you can connect as SYSDBA.

   D. You can always use operating system authentication instead of password file authentication.

9. If a read-only tablespace is damaged, how should it be recovered? (Choose the best answer.)

   A. Read-only tablespaces can be re-created if necessary.

    B. Restore the datafiles, and apply archive redo logs.

    C. Restore the datafiles, and bring them online.

    D. Making a tablespace read-only means that the datafile cannot be damaged.

10. An index tablespace is damaged and you choose to use the DROP/RECREATE approach. Which of the following steps are *not* necessary to recover it? (Choose two answers.)

    A. Drop the indexes.

    B. Take the tablespace offline.

    C. Drop the tablespace.

    D. Create the tablespace.

    E. Recover the tablespace.

    F. Create the indexes.

Answers

1. **B, C, and D.** The instance will survive the loss of a multiplexed logfile or any archive log file. Damage to any controlfile will cause the instance to crash, as will loss of a nonmultiplexed online redo log file.

2. **C.** The database will open, but an error will be written to the alert log. The first time the tempfile is needed for a disk sort, an error will be generated: sorts that can proceed in memory will be fine.

3. **A.** Of the file types listed, only temporary files are noncritical. The files making up the undo tablespace are definitely critical: undo data is as important as any other data. Any controlfile damage will immediately cause the instance to terminate.

4. **B and D.** It is the V$LOGFILE view that tells you whether a log file member is invalid, and a message also goes to the alert log.

5. **A.** Some queries will continue, if they do not attempt to use the indexes. Any DML involving the indexed columns will fail, because Oracle will not be able to maintain the indexes. Therefore the tables will be locked.

6. **D.** You can't change objects in read-only tablespaces, but you can drop them because a DROP affects only the data dictionary, not the tablespace containing the object.

7. **A.** All DML against any permanent objects generates REDO and UNDO, but you can disable these for index creation. Undo and redo are not generated for temporary objects. Changes to undo segments generate REDO, as for any other permanent object. Setting NOLOGGING at the tablespace level sets a default that redo should not be generated for the creation of tables, partitions, and indexes in the tablespace.

8. **D.** Operating system authentication is always available.

9. **C.** All that is needed is to restore the files; no application of redo is necessary.

10. **B** and **E.** You do not have to take the tablespace offline, nor do you have to recover it. You must drop the indexes and the tablespace, though this can in fact be done with one command: DROP TABLESPACE...INCLUDING CONTENTS. Creating the tablespace and the indexes are the other required steps.

CHAPTER 27

Incomplete Database Recovery

In this chapter you will learn how to

- Recover the controlfile
- Explain reasons for incomplete recovery
- Perform incomplete recovery using Enterprise Manager
- Perform incomplete recovery using RMAN
- Perform incomplete recovery using SQL
- Perform database recovery following a RESETLOGS operation

Whenever the database is damaged, you have a choice to make: are you going to try for a complete recovery, meaning no loss of data, or an incomplete recovery, meaning that you will lose data? In most circumstances, you will do a complete recovery. To commit to an incomplete recovery is a very serious decision.

This chapter begins with a review of the procedure for a complete recovery, followed by a discussion of when an incomplete recovery may be necessary. Then all the options for incomplete recovery are detailed and the various tools and techniques examined. The controlfile is a special case for recovery. Depending on circumstances, sometimes it can be recovered with no effect on the rest of the database, but sometimes it requires the technique used for incomplete recovery. Either way, no data will actually be lost.

Complete Recovery

If a backup of the datafiles and copies of all necessary archive logs, the online redo logs, and the controlfile are available, then the database can survive damage to any number of any datafiles without losing any data. The logs—both online and archived—and the controlfile should always be available because they should be multiplexed to different devices. Backups can also be multiplexed automatically if made with RMAN, but if your backups are user-managed, then they must be protected by your system administrators.

There are four steps to complete recovery:

1. Take the damaged datafile(s) offline.
2. Restore the damaged datafile(s).
3. Recover the damaged datafile(s).
4. Bring the recovered datafile(s) online.

This routine assumes that the datafiles damaged do not include files that are part of either the SYSTEM tablespace or the currently active UNDO tablespace. Damage to either of these will result in the instance terminating. In that case, the first and fourth steps—taking the files offline and bringing them back online—are not necessary, because the restore and recovery must be done with the database in mount mode. Another variation is if the datafiles must be restored to a different location—in that case, the files will need to be renamed within the controlfile before the recovery. Restore and recover can also be done at the tablespace level, rather than at the datafile level.

For complete recovery, the controlfile should be the current controlfile. This is because the current controlfile will have all the details needed for the complete recovery: the location of the archive log files and the current system change number. All the archive log files generated since the backup was taken will be needed to apply changes to the restored files, and the online log files will be needed to apply the remaining changes not yet archived. If any logfiles are missing, the complete recovery will fail. If the current controlfile is missing, the situation is not irretrievable—but the recovery will be more awkward, because the information describing the current state of the database will not be available.

The restore of the damaged files results in files that are out-of-date, unsynchronized with the rest of the database. The recovery applies all the redo since the backup was made: both committed and uncommitted changes are applied to the restored files. The final stage of recovery is rolling back the uncommitted changes. This occurs automatically and makes the restored files fully consistent with the rest of the database.

This is an RMAN command block that will do a complete recovery of one tablespace, called EXAMPLE:

```
RMAN> run {
sql "alter tablespace example offline immediate";
restore tablespace example;
recover tablespace example delete archivelog;
sql "alter tablespace example online";}
```

The first command takes the whole tablespace offline. This is not essential but is generally good policy. It might be that only one of several files that make up the EXAMPLE tablespace is damaged, and strictly speaking it is only that one file that needs to be offlined; but to leave the other datafiles and the tablespace online can give unpredictable results, as some of the objects in the tablespace may then be available while others are not. Taking a tablespace offline will cause Oracle to checkpoint the tablespace. This means that DBWn will write all dirty blocks for that tablespace to the datafiles. This will fail if a datafile is damaged—hence the use of the keyword IMMEDIATE, which instructs Oracle not to checkpoint the tablespace. The second command instructs RMAN to restore the most recent backup of the EXAMPLE tablespace: all the datafiles for the tablespace will be restored. The third command will restore any archive logs needed that are no longer on disk, apply them, and delete them. It will also apply redo from the online log files as necessary and then roll back any changes that were uncommitted at the time the file was damaged. The fourth command makes the completely recovered tablespace available for use. This whole restore and recover can be done while the database is open and in use.

 TIP If you take a tablespace offline while the database is open, how will your application react? Is it possible to run the application in these circumstances? Your system documentation should cover this eventuality. If it doesn't, the documentation needs to be improved by someone—probably you.

When Is Incomplete Recovery Necessary?

An incomplete recovery means losing data. The whole database is taken back in time by a restore of all the datafiles, and then it is not completely recovered. Rather than applying all the redo generated since the backup was taken, you deliberately stop the application of redo at some point, to produce a version of the database that is not up-to-date. All work done from that point is lost. There are only two reasons for performing an incomplete recovery: either complete recovery is impossible or you deliberately decide to lose data.

Complete recovery will not be possible unless all archive logs generated from the time of the backup are available, as well as the online redo logs. If an archive log is missing or corrupted, then recovery will stop at that point.

 TIP It may in fact be possible to continue recovery after a corruption is encountered in an archive log, but some data blocks will be marked corrupted. This is an advanced procedure that is not covered in the OCP exam.

Complete recovery should never fail because of missing archive or online log files. Both file types can and should be multiplexed to different devices, making their total loss impossible, but it can happen. If so, incomplete recovery up to the point at which the missing or damaged redo data is needed is your only option.

 EXAM TIP Incomplete recovery is necessary if there is a missing archive log, or if all copies of the current online redo log are missing.

To decide to lose data deliberately is a course of action taken after user error. It may be that a user has committed a transaction that is inappropriate to the business requirements. Such errors could include perfectly normal mistakes—we all make mistakes—while using package software, but more commonly they are errors when using tools such as SQL*Plus. Omitting a WHERE clause when issuing an UPDATE or DELETE statement will result in the whole table being affected, not just one row; if this change is committed, perhaps by exiting from the tool, then the changes are irreversible. As far as Oracle is concerned, it is a committed transaction and can never be rolled back. Worse still is issuing DDL commands. These include an implicit COMMIT statement. It is frighteningly easy to, for example, drop a table in one schema when you think you are connected to another.

Following a user error, you can restore the whole database and recover it up to the point just before the error, thus producing a version of the database without the mistake, but also, without all the correct work done since.

 EXAM TIP It is not possible to skip the recovery of a bad transaction and recover all other work.

A special case of incomplete recovery is recovery of the controlfile. Ideally, all recovery operations will be conducted using the current controlfile, but there are circumstances when this isn't possible and a backup of the controlfile must be restored. There are two possible reasons for this: either all copies of the current controlfile have been lost and it is not possible to run a CREATE CONTROLFILE command to re-create it, or the current controlfile does not accurately describe the version of the database you want to restore, typically, because changes such as dropping tablespaces have occurred since taking the backup. The syntax for recovery using a backup controlfile does include the UNTIL keyword, which would usually indicate an incomplete recovery—even though the recovery may in fact be complete.

The Method for Incomplete Recovery

Whether you are using user-managed backup and recovery procedures or RMAN, there are four steps to incomplete recovery:

1. Mount the database.
2. Restore all the datafiles, and optionally the controlfile.
3. Recover the database UNTIL a time, sequence, or change number.
4. Open with RESETLOGS.

The first contrast with complete recovery is that complete recovery can be done with the database open, unless the damaged files are critical. The critical files are those making up the SYSTEM tablespace and the active UNDO tablespace. Incomplete recovery can be done only in mount mode.

All incomplete recovery operations begin with a restore of all datafiles. This is the second contrast with complete recovery: for complete recovery, you restore only the damaged datafiles; for incomplete recovery you must restore them all. The datafiles do not have to be restored from the same backup, but they must all be older than the point to which you wish to recover. Do not, under any circumstances, restore the online redo logs. If you followed the advice given in earlier chapters, you will not have backed up the online redo logs, so it is impossible to restore them even by accident, but if you have backed up the online logs, restoring them may be disastrous.

The controlfile will have to be restored as well if the physical structure of the current database is different from the structure of the version being restored. For example, if a tablespace has been accidentally dropped, the current controlfile will know nothing about it. Restoring the datafiles that make up the tablespace won't help: the current controlfile will ignore them, and not include them in the recovery. Do not restore the controlfile unless you have to; it may complicate matters if you do.

Apply redo from archive and (if necessary) online logs to the desired point. This is the third contrast with complete recovery. For complete recovery, you apply all the redo to bring the restore right up-to-date; for incomplete recovery, you stop the recovery at whatever point you want. There are options for specifying the point to which you want to recover.

Finally, open the database with RESETLOGS. This will reinitialize the online redo log files, creating a new incarnation of the database. An incarnation of a database is a version of the database with a new thread of redo, beginning at log switch sequence number 1. This is the final contrast with complete recovery. After a complete recovery, the database is exactly as it was before the problem occurred, but after an incomplete recovery it is a different incarnation. Backups and archive logs are specific to an incarnation and those generated by one incarnation must be kept separate from those generated by a previous incarnation.

 EXAM TIP You must be connected AS SYSDBA to do an incomplete recovery. No normal user, and not even a SYSOPER user, can do this.

Incomplete Recovery Options

Having mounted the database and restored all the datafiles and (if necessary) the controlfile, you have three options for incomplete recovery:

- Until time
- Until system change number
- Until log sequence number

The UNTIL TIME option will apply redo to roll the datafiles forward until a particular time. The precision is to the second. This option would usually be used to correct user error. If a user made an irreversible mistake and the time the mistake was made is known, then a time-based recovery to just before the mistake may be the best option.

The UNTIL SCN option (it is UNTIL CHANGE for user-managed backups, UNTIL SCN when using RMAN—but the results are the same) can be used if the exact system change number when the error was made is known. By using advanced tools such as the Log Miner utility or by using the Flashback capability to be detailed in Chapter 29, it is possible to identify exactly the SCN at which a transaction was committed. The recovery can be stopped precisely before the problem, thus losing the minimum possible amount of data.

The UNTIL SEQUENCE option (it is UNTIL CANCEL when using user-managed backups, UNTIL SEQUENCE when using RMAN) is used if an archive log file or an online log file group is missing; it will recover all work up to the log switch into the missing file or group.

 EXAM TIP The syntax for incomplete recovery differs between SQL*Plus and RMAN. SQL*Plus uses UNTIL CANCEL and UNTIL CHANGE, where RMAN would use UNTIL SEQUENCE and UNTIL SCN. They both use UNTIL TIME.

Incomplete Recovery Best Practices

As with complete recovery, the best practice is indeed to practice. The procedure is completely reliable, but the slightest mistake may be disastrous. It is vital to follow all the steps with great care. When doing an incomplete recovery, you do not want to have any doubts about the procedure to be followed; it is frequently said that most problems with incomplete recovery are caused by the DBA making a mistake.

Before starting an incomplete recovery, if at all possible perform a whole closed backup of the database. This means that whatever happens during the restore and recover operation, you will be no worse off than before and can try again. At the very least, back up all the archive logs. The backup should be closed in order to prevent any users doing any work, because such work will be lost after the incomplete recovery. For this reason, it is vital to close the database as soon as you decide that an incomplete recovery is needed.

After a successful incomplete recovery, carry out another whole backup. With release 10*g* of the database, this is not strictly speaking necessary (it was essential with earlier releases) but is still good policy.

Check that the incomplete recovery really was successful. For example, it may be that the user says the error occurred at 10:00, and so you recover until 09:59. But then you find that the user's watch is not synchronized with the server's clock, and that in fact as far as the database is concerned the error occurred at 09:58, and your recovery has repeated it. Check that the operation was successful before allowing users to connect, perhaps by opening the database with STARTUP RESTRICT. You do not want them to lose more work, if you have to repeat the exercise.

Remove any archive logs from the previous incarnation of the database (you should have backed them up already) to prevent any possibility of mixing up logs from before and after the recovery.

Incomplete Recovery with User-Managed Backups

If you are making user-managed backups, then you must restore with operating system commands and recover with SQL*Plus. Whenever an incomplete recovery is necessary, shut down the database straight away, and if possible back it up. Then follow the four steps described at the beginning of the preceding section, "The Method for Incomplete Recovery," using whatever recovery option is appropriate. The examples that follow assume that the controlfile does not need to be restored: that the current controlfile does correctly describe both the current database and the version of the database that is to be restored. This will be the case unless datafiles have been created, renamed, or dropped between the time of the backup and the time of the problem being detected. If the controlfile must be restored, then alternative syntax is needed.

UNTIL TIME Recovery

A time-based incomplete recovery is typically needed after user error, such as committing a bad transaction or dropping a database object. In order to minimize the loss of data, close the database immediately after the problem is reported. There is no point in even letting users finish their transactions, because they will be lost anyway.

Assume that investigation shows that the problem occurred at thirty-five minutes past six in the afternoon, on the tenth of December 2004. First shut down and mount the database:

```
SQL> shutdown immediate;
SQL> startup mount;
```

Then use whatever operating system utility is appropriate to restore all the datafiles. You must also restore any archive log files that will be needed and are no longer available on disk. Then,

```
SQL> recover database until time '2004-12-10:18:34:00';
```

This command will cause Oracle to inspect the restored datafiles and request all the archive logs generated from the time of the oldest restored file up to the time specified. If the archive logs are still available in the location(s) that the ARCn process put them, or if you have restored them to those same location(s), you can accept the default filenames that Oracle presents you with. You can even use "RECOVER AUTOMATIC DATABASE UNTIL...," which will automatically look for the archive log files in the default location and not prompt you for anything. Otherwise, you will have to specify the files by name. If the recovery is up to a very recent time (which one hopes it is) the recovery will also need to extract redo from the current online log file group as well; Oracle will locate and apply that last bit of redo automatically.

Note that there are no options for the format of the UNTIL TIME. It must be CCYY-MM-DD:HH24:MI:SS, irrespective of your session's NLS_DATE_FORMAT setting. Finally,

```
SQL> alter database open resetlogs;
```

and now users can connect.

UNTIL CANCEL Recovery

A cancel-based recovery is typically needed after a complete recovery has failed: the complete recovery required an archive or online log that was missing. In that case, your only option is incomplete recovery, up to (but not including) the log switch sequence number of the missing log. This number will have been reported when you attempted the complete recovery.

Assume that a datafile was damaged, and during complete recovery you were asked for an archive log of sequence number 10305. You attempted to restore it from tape, but it was corrupted. Perform the first two steps of incomplete recovery as already described, but then the RECOVER command will be

```
SQL> recover database until cancel;
```

As you are prompted for the archive logs, apply them until you are prompted for sequence number 10305. At that point, instead of entering the name of the file or accepting the name suggested, enter the word **CANCEL**. Recovery will stop, following which you can open the database with RESETLOGS.

This procedure is also used if all copies of the current redo log file group are lost. After a disaster such as that, the database will crash immediately. On restarting, it will stop in mount mode. Query the view V$LOG to ascertain the sequence number of the current, missing, logfile group and perform an UNTIL CANCEL recovery up to that number.

UNTIL CHANGE Recovery

Recovery until an exact system change number is required for some advanced Oracle options unrelated to loss of data, such as instantiating a replicated database or a standby database. It is rarely used as part of normal system maintenance, because you do not usually know the exact SCN when a problem occurred. The syntax to recover up to (but not including) a system change number is, for example,

```
SQL> recover database until change 309121;
```

 EXAM TIP Recovery stops at the SCN before the one specified. The SCN given is not applied.

Incomplete Recovery Using RMAN

Conceptually, incomplete recovery with RMAN is the same as with user-managed backups: it is the same four steps. But it is much easier. If RMAN is integrated with a Recovery Catalog database and an automated tape library, you do not have to worry at all about the names and locations of the backups of the datafiles or of the archive logs, and it is impossible to make mistakes. Even without these features, RMAN is still simple and totally reliable. The following examples assume that you are not using a Recovery Catalog and that the backups are still available where RMAN put them.

Use of a Recovery Catalog would mean that RMAN could go further back in time than if you are relying on the controlfile-based repository, which is limited to the number of days specified by the CONTROLFILE_RECORD_KEEP_TIME instance parameter. If there is no tape library, then you will have to load the appropriate tapes manually.

RMAN will automatically apply restore optimization. This means that if an appropriate version of the file is already available, then RMAN will not restore it. Thus you will generally find that read-only tablespaces and archive logs that are still on disk where the ARCn process put them don't get restored.

UNTIL TIME Recovery

This RMAN command block will perform the full incomplete recovery cycle up to a specified time:

```
RMAN> run{
allocate channel d1 type disk;
allocate channel t1 type sbt_tape;
shutdown immediate;
startup mount;
sql "alter session set nls_date_format=''dd-mon-yyyy hh24:mi:ss''";
set until time '10-dec-2004 18:34:00';
restore database;
recover database;
alter database open resetlogs;}
```

Note that unlike SQL*Plus when used for incomplete recovery, RMAN is aware of your session setting for the NLS_DATE_FORMAT parameter, which will be picked up from environment variables or, to prevent any possibility of confusion, can be specified in the run block. In the example there are two channels allocated, one for disk and one for tape, so that RMAN can access backups on both media types.

PART II

As with any RMAN restore and recover operation, RMAN will automatically select the most efficient method. This will mean restoring the full backup of each datafile that is closest to (but not after) the recovery time specified. Then RMAN will apply any incremental backups that will bring the files closer to the time, and finally it will apply any archive and online redo logs needed to reach the time exactly. As a rule, it is quicker to apply incrementals than to apply archive logs. RMAN will consider both image copies and backup sets when planning the recovery strategy. Any backup sets of archive logs on tape are first extracted from tape and the archive logs restored to disk, and then the logs are applied to the database.

UNTIL SEQUENCE Recovery

This example assumes that a logfile of sequence number 10305 is missing. This could be because the sole archive log destination disk was damaged before the archive log was migrated to tape, or it could be that a disaster destroyed all copies of the current logfile group. In the former case, the problem would become apparent during an attempted complete recovery; in the latter case, the database instance would crash immediately and the problem would be seen at the next attempted startup. Either way, this run block will do the incomplete recovery:

```
RMAN> run {
shutdown immediate;
startup mount;
set until sequence 10305 thread 1;
restore database;
recover database;
alter database open resetlogs; }
```

In this example, there are no allocate channel commands: you are using the configured default channels. RMAN will consult its repository to identify backups of all the datafiles that predate log switch sequence number 10305, and restore them. Then it will restore and apply all the archive log files up to (but not including) 10305 and open the database with RESETLOGS.

The specification of UNTIL SEQUENCE must include both the log switch sequence number and the thread number. For a single instance environment, the thread number is always 1, but in a clustered environment each instance will generate its own thread of redo, which will have its own series of log switch sequence numbers, so the thread must be specified as well to identify which sequence you are referring to.

 EXAM TIP The log sequence number specified is *not* applied; recovery stops at the end of the previous log.

UNTIL SCN Recovery

The recovery until an exact system change number (SCN) is rarely used as part of normal restore and recover procedures, simply because it is unusual to know the SCN when a problem occurred. The technique is, however, required when creating copies of databases to be used in a Replication, Data Guard, or Streams environment.

These advanced capabilities (which are beyond the scope of the Oracle Certified Professional examination, but are included in the more advanced Oracle Certified Master practicum) require a copy of the primary database that is synchronized to an exact, known SCN, so the propagation of transactions from the primary database can be started from that same point.

For completeness, if recovery to an exact system change number is needed, the syntax is the same as for time- or cancel-based recovery, with the exception of the UNTIL clause:

```
RMAN> run{
...
set until scn 309121;
...
}
```

Exercise 27-1: Performing an Incomplete Recovery with RMAN

Perform a full backup, simulate a user error, and then perform an incomplete recovery to a time just before the error. Test that the recovery was successful after opening the database.

1. Connect to your database as user SYSTEM with SQL*Plus.

2. Ensure that your database is in archivelog mode with archiving enabled.

   ```
   SQL> select log_mode from v$database;
   SQL> select archiver from V$INSTANCE;
   ```

   If these queries do not return ARCHIVELOG and STARTED, follow the steps in Exercise 18-3 in Chapter 18 to correct the situation.

3. Enable the display of the time in the SQL*Plus prompt.

   ```
   SQL> set time on;
   10:23:15 SQL>
   ```

4. Create a table.

   ```
   10:24:01 SQL> create table test_rec as select * from all_users;
   ```

5. Connect to your database with RMAN as user SYS using operating system authentication.

   ```
   rman target /
   ```

6. Carry out a full backup, using your configured defaults.

   ```
   RMAN> backup database;
   ```

7. In your SQL*Plus session, note the time, and then drop the table and confirm its absence.

   ```
   10:35:30 SQL>
   10:35:30 SQL> drop table test_rec;
   Table dropped.
   10:35:44 SQL> select count(*) from test_rec;
   select count(*) from test_rec
                        *
   ERROR at line 1:
   ORA-00942: table or view does not exist
   ```

8. In your RMAN session, run this command block, recovering to just before the drop of the table:

```
RMAN> run {
2> shutdown immediate;
3> startup mount;
4> sql "alter session set nls_date_format=''yy-mm-dd hh24:mi:ss''";
5> set until time '04-12-11 10:35:30';
6> restore database;
7> recover database;
8> alter database open resetlogs;}
```

9. In your SQL*Plus session, reconnect as user SYSTEM (your session will have been terminated by the SHUTDOWN) and confirm that the table has been recovered, and that the log switch sequence number has been reset.

```
10:49:25 SQL> select count(*) from test_rec;
  COUNT(*)
----------
        33
10:49:56 SQL> select group#,sequence#,status from v$log;
    GROUP#  SEQUENCE# STATUS
---------- ---------- ----------------
         1          0 UNUSED
         2          1 CURRENT
         3          0 UNUSED
```

10. In your RMAN session, carry out a fresh backup by repeating Step 8.

11. Tidy up by dropping the table.

```
10:50:05 SQL> drop table test_rec;
```

Incomplete Recovery Using Enterprise Manager

The Recovery Wizard in Enterprise Manager Database Control can also do an incomplete recovery. First, it is necessary to connect to Database Control as a user with the SYSDBA privilege, as in Figure 27-1. No normal user can perform an incomplete recovery. Not even a user with the SYSOPER privilege can do this (although a SYSOPER user can do a complete recovery).

From the database home page, select the Maintenance tab and then the Perform Recovery link in the Backup/Recovery section to reach the Perform Recovery: Type window, as in Figure 27-2. Here you must select Whole Database in the Object Type drop-down box, and the radio button for "Recover to the current time or a previous point-in-time." You must also supply an operating system logon with appropriate permissions on any hardware device that will be used, if you have not already saved your preferred credentials.

On the Perform Recovery: Point-in-time window, shown in Figure 27-3, you can choose the time, system change number, or log switch sequence number up to which to recover. Then the Review window (Figure 27-4) shows the RMAN script that will be executed.

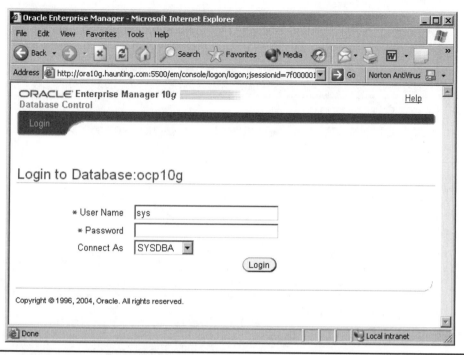

Figure 27-1 Connect to Database Control with the SYSDBA privilege.

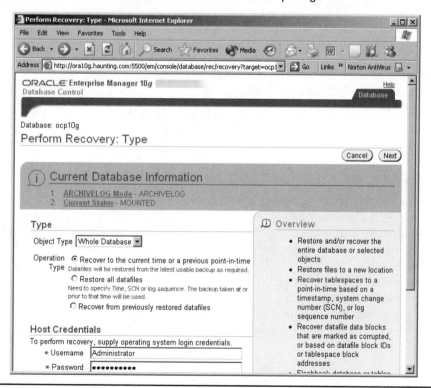

Figure 27-2 Initiate the incomplete recovery procedure.

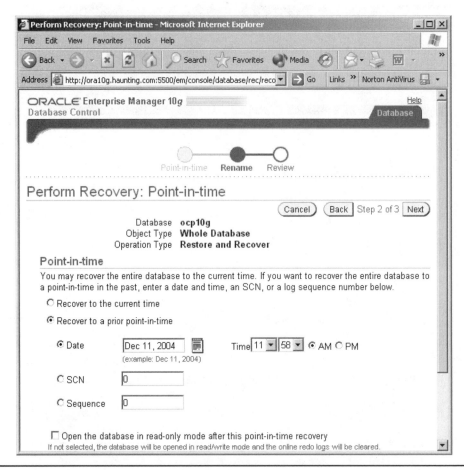

Figure 27-3   Select the incomplete recovery time, sequence, or SCN.

Recovery of the Controlfile

One point to emphasize right away is that recovery of the controlfile should be a very rare occurrence. The controlfile is (or should be) protected by multiplexed copies on different devices. It should be impossible to lose all copies of the controlfile. But if all copies of the current controlfile are lost, it can either be restored from a backup or be re-created.

If you are using user-managed backups and have the appropriate script available, re-creation is the simplest option: just issue a CREATE CONTROLFILE command. Restoring a backup of the controlfile requires applying redo to synchronize the restored controlfile with the rest of the database. Following a datafile restore, this is simple—

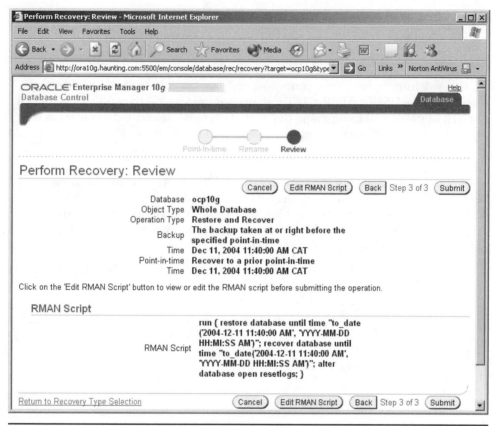

Figure 27-4 Submit the restore and recovery job.

because the current controlfile knows what archive logs are needed and where they are. But if you have restored the controlfile, it won't know anything about changes since it was backed up. Oracle will do its best and make intelligent guesses about archive logs, but it can get confused. In particular, if the final stage of the restore requires the online redo logs, you will have to tell the recovery process which ones to apply.

If you are using RMAN backups, restore and recovery of the database using a backup controlfile is simple. RMAN can work out what to do—probably better than you can.

A special case when it is necessary to restore the controlfile even if it has not been damaged is when doing an incomplete recovery to a point in time when the physical structure of the database was different from the current structure. This would be the case if a tablespace has been dropped.

Creating a New Controlfile

Issuing this command should be part of your regular maintenance routine:

```
SQL> alter database backup controlfile to trace;
```

This will inspect the current controlfile and generate a trace file in the directory specified by the USER_DUMP_DEST instance parameter. This trace file will contain a CREATE CONTROLFILE command that will, if executed, re-create the control as it is right now. As with all user trace files, the name will be of the form

```
<SID>_ora_<SPID>.trc
```

where <SID> is the name of the instance, and <SPID> is the Unix process number, or Windows thread number, of the server process for your session. The trace file is well documented, with comments describing its purpose and how and when to use the CREATE CONTROLFILE command within it. Here is an example of the CREATE CONTROLFILE command:

```
CREATE CONTROLFILE REUSE DATABASE "OCP10G" NORESETLOGS ARCHIVELOG
    MAXLOGFILES 16
    MAXLOGMEMBERS 3
    MAXDATAFILES 100
    MAXINSTANCES 8
    MAXLOGHISTORY 454
LOGFILE
  GROUP 1 (
    '/u01/oradata/ocp10g/redo1b.log',
    '/u01/oradata/ocp10g/redo1a.log'
  ) SIZE 10M,
  GROUP 2 (
    '/u01/oradata/ocp10g/redo2b.log',
    '/u01/oradata/ocp10g/redo2a.log'
  ) SIZE 10M
-- STANDBY LOGFILE
DATAFILE
  '/u01/oradata/ocp10g/system01.dbf',
  '/u01/oradata/ocp10g/undotbs01.dbf',
  '/u01/oradata/ocp10g/sysaux01.dbf',
  '/u01/oradata/ocp10g/users01.dbf',
  '/u01/oradata/ocp10g/example01.dbf',
  '/u01/oradata/ocp10g/users02.dbf'
CHARACTER SET US7ASCII
;
```

This command will create new controlfiles in the locations specified by the CONTROL_FILES instance parameter. Note that the command does not include any mention of read-only tablespaces or of temporary tablespaces. There are additional commands in the trace file to generate these.

TIP Always generate a CREATE CONTROLFILE trace whenever you make any changes to the physical structure of the database, and keep the files somewhere safe. Then you will always be able to create a controlfile that can be used with any restored version of the database.

Re-creating the controlfile may be necessary for reasons other than recovery. In the preceding example, the MAXDATAFILES setting is 100. It may be that the database is expanding, and the number of datafiles is already into the nineties. In that case, at your next maintenance window, you should generate the script, edit it to increase the MAXDATAFILES setting, and re-create the controlfile. This can be done only during a maintenance slot, because the command can only be run with the instance in NOMOUNT mode. Another reason would be to change the database name, which can be done by inserting the SET keyword before DATABASE in the CREATE CONTROLFILE command and specifying a new name.

Restoring a Controlfile with User-Managed Backups

To back up the controlfile with user-managed backups, either the database must be closed, or you must use this command:

```
SQL> alter database backup controlfile to '<FILENAME>';
```

where <FILENAME> is the name of the backup to be created. This will create a binary copy of the controlfile, identical to the controlfile at the time you ran the command. You cannot back up the controlfile of an open database in any other way. This is because, unlike datafiles, the controlfile is not protected by redo; it is therefore necessary to get a read-consistent version of the file, which cannot be guaranteed if you copy it with operating system utilities.

To restore a backup of the controlfile, copy it to the locations specified by the CONTROL_FILES instance parameter and start the database in mount mode with STARTUP MOUNT. Then issue this command:

```
SQL> recover database until cancel using backup controlfile;
```

You will be prompted for archive logs: apply them until recovery fails. It will fail because you will be prompted for an archive log that does not exist: this is the sequence number of the current online log, which has not yet been archived. At that point you must enter the name of one of the members of the current online log group. If you do not know which group was current, try a member of each group in turn; eventually, you will name the correct one and the recovery will complete. Then you can open the database with RESETLOGS, without losing any data. Loss of the controlfile is where the incomplete recovery syntax does in fact result in a complete recovery, though you do still have to create a new incarnation of the database.

The RECOVER DATABASE UNTIL...USING BACKUP CONTROLFILE syntax is also used when doing an incomplete recovery if the structure of the database being restored is different from current. If that is the case, you must restore the controlfile as well as all the datafiles. The application of redo until the point desired will then proceed as normal.

Restoring the Controlfile with RMAN

RMAN can back up the controlfile in several ways:

```
RMAN> backup as copy current controlfile;
RMAN> backup as backupset current controlfile;
RMAN> backup tablespace system include current controlfile;
RMAN> configure controlfile autobackup on;
```

The first two commands will back up the controlfile as an image copy or in a backup set. The controlfile can also be included in a backup set by appending INCLUDE CURRENT CONTROLFILE to the specification of a datafile or a tablespace backup, as in the third example. The controlfile cannot be included in a backup of archive logs. The fourth command will configure RMAN to make an automatic backup of the controlfile and the spfile to a well-known filename and location whenever any other backup operation is run.

RMAN stores its repository in the target database's controlfile. So if the controlfile cannot be mounted, RMAN can't read its repository—and therefore, it is completely crippled. It is a recursive problem: you need the repository to perform a restore, but you need to perform the restore to get to the repository. There are two ways around this. First, if you have a separate Recovery Catalog database, that will have a copy of the repository. It is then trivial for RMAN to locate the controlfile backups and to restore and recover them. If you do not have a Recovery Catalog database, then it is vital that you configure the controlfile auto-backup facility. By default, the auto-backup will go to the flash recovery area, if it is configured. Failing that, it will use a platform-specific location (for instance, it is the $ORACLE_HOME/dbs directory on Unix). If you wish, you can use CONFIGURE CONTROLFILE AUTOBACKUP FORMAT... to nominate a directory and filename for the auto-backups, but if you do this, you must record it, as RMAN will not be able to locate it automatically when you need to restore.

The RMAN code is kernelized: you can run RMAN even with the database in nomount mode, which is as far as you can get without a controlfile. This means that you always have access to the command

```
RMAN> restore controlfile from autobackup;
```

RMAN will go to the default location and attempt to locate the most recent auto-backup. The system-generated name of the auto-backup backup set has embedded within it the timestamp of the backup and the database identifier number, or DBID. If only one database makes auto-backups to the destination, RMAN will automatically retrieve the most recent and restore it. If multiple databases share the same auto-backup destination (as would be the case if several databases have a common flash recovery area), then you must provide the DBID so that RMAN can restore the correct controlfile.

To find your DBID,

```
SQL> select dbid from v$database;
      DBID
----------
3385973595
```

This should be part of your most basic documentation. Then to restore and recover the controlfile,

```
RMAN> run {
startup nomount;
set dbid 3385973595;
restore controlfile from autobackup;
alter database mount;
recover database;
alter database open resetlogs;}
```

As when restoring from a user-managed backup, you have to finish the operation with a resetlogs, creating a new incarnation of the database—but in fact the recovery is complete, in the sense that no data will have been lost.

Exercise 27-2: Carrying Out Controlfile Auto-Backup and Restore

Use RMAN to configure controlfile auto-backup, simulate loss of the controlfile, and restore it.

1. Connect to your database with RMAN, using operating system authentication.

   ```
   RMAN> connect target /
   ```

2. Configure the auto-backup facility.

   ```
   RMAN> configure controlfile autobackup on;
   ```

3. Perform a full backup and exit from RMAN.

   ```
   RMAN> backup database;
   RMAN> exit;
   ```

   Note that at the end of the database backup, the controlfile and spfile are backed up into a separate backup set.

4. Connect to your database as SYSDBA with SQL*Plus.

   ```
   SQL> connect / as sysdba;
   ```

5. Locate your controlfiles and note your database identifier.

   ```
   SQL> select name from v$controlfile;
   SQL> select dbid from v$database;
   ```

6. Abort the instance.

   ```
   SQL> shutdown abort;
   ```

7. Using an operating system command, delete the controlfile(s) listed in Step 5. If you are working on Windows, you may have to stop the Windows service to do this, and then start it again.

8. Attempt to open the database. It will stop in nomount mode.

   ```
   SQL> startup;
   ```

9. Connect with RMAN, as in Step 1.

10. Issue this command block,

```
RMAN> run {
shutdown abort;
startup nomount;
set dbid 3385973595;
restore controlfile from autobackup;
alter database mount;
recover database;
alter database open resetlogs;}
```

substituting your DBID, listed in Step 5, for the example DBID of 3385973595.

11. From an operating system prompt, confirm that the controlfiles you deleted in Step 7 have been restored.

Recovery Through RESETLOGS

With all versions of the Oracle database prior to release 10g, incomplete recovery required a fifth step: a full backup. This was because all backups and archive logs were specific to a database incarnation, and it was not possible to use a backup made before a resetlogs operation after the resetlogs. Make no mistake about this: before 10g, this backup was absolutely essential and was part of the incomplete recovery procedure. Until the backup was made, you were at risk of losing more data.

With release 10g, you can use backups taken before an incomplete recovery; backups and redo from a previous incarnation are valid for the current incarnation. This means that if a datafile is damaged shortly after an incomplete recovery and before the next backup, you can restore the datafile again from the backup used for the incomplete recovery, apply redo from the archive logs of the previous incarnation up to the point of the incomplete recovery, and then apply redo from the current incarnation to do a complete recovery.

For recovery through a resetlogs to work, it is vital that the names generated for the archive log files let Oracle distinguish between logs produced by the different incarnations. These names are controlled by the instance parameter LOG_ARCHIVE_FORMAT. A reasonable setting would be

```
SQL> alter system set log_archive_format='arch_%d_%t_%r_%s.log';
```

These are the variables:

- **%d**   The DBID, in hexadecimal
- **%t**   The thread number (always 1, unless it is a clustered database)
- **%r**   The incarnation number
- **%s**   The log switch sequence number

To assist you in tracking what has been happening with resetlogs operations, various views now include a column, RESETLOGS_ID, to identify which incarnation the row refers to. Of particular importance, this is present in V$DATABASE, where it will show you the current incarnation number, and V$ARCHIVED_LOG, where each archive is flagged as belonging to a particular incarnation.

Chapter Review

Incomplete recovery is a serious, irreversible, procedure. There are usually only two reasons for doing this: either you deliberately want to lose data, or you tried a complete recovery and it failed. You will want to lose data if the data is erroneous: a user made a mistake. Remember that "mistakes" can include DBA-type errors, such as accidentally dropping tables or even tablespaces. A complete recovery will fail if an archive log file is missing, or if all copies of the current online log file are missing.

Incomplete recovery consists of four steps:

1. Mount the database.
2. Restore all the datafiles.
3. Recover the database until the desired point.
4. Open the database with a resetlogs.

Depending on circumstances, you may need to restore the controlfile as well as the datafiles. Never restore the online logs. The three options for the recovery step are until a time, until a log switch sequence number, or until a system change number. The resetlogs command option creates a new database incarnation: a new stream of redo.

You can do an incomplete recovery whether you are using user-managed backups or RMAN, but RMAN is undoubtedly easier and less error prone. The graphical interface provided for RMAN by Database Control may make it even simpler.

Restoring and recovering the controlfile is a special topic. It is often easier to re-create than to restore, because the restore requires the syntax for incomplete recovery and the use of archive and online redo logs. No data should be lost, though.

Finally, an important new feature of release 10*g* of the database is that you can now do a subsequent complete recovery using backups and redo from a previous incarnation, if you are unfortunate enough to have to do this. But it is still considered good policy to make a full backup as soon as possible after an incomplete recovery.

Questions

1. Which of the following file types are not restored when doing an incomplete recovery? (Choose all that apply.)

   A. Controlfile

   B. Datafiles for permanent tablespaces

   C. Datafiles for undo tablespaces

   D. Online redo log files

   E. Server parameter file

   F. Tempfiles for temporary tablespaces

2. It is now 15:00, on Tuesday. A bad transaction was committed in your database at about 14:30. Investigation shows that the tables and indexes affected were on just two tablespaces: the rest of the database is fine. The two tablespaces and several others were backed up last night, but some tablespaces are backed up only on the weekend. Your database is in archivelog mode, with log switches about every ten minutes. Which of the following statements is correct? (Choose the best answer.)

A. You can do an incomplete restore and recovery to 14:29, of just the two tablespaces. The loss of data will be about 30 minutes of work in those tablespaces.

B. You must restore the whole database from the weekend backup and recover to 14:29. You will lose about 30 minutes of work.

C. You must restore the whole database and do an incomplete recovery canceling the application of the archive log that was active at 14:30. You will lose about ten minutes of work.

D. You can restore some tablespaces from last night, the others from the weekend, and recover to 14:29. You will lose about 30 minutes of work.

3. You are doing a point-in-time recovery with SQL*Plus. What format should you use for the date/time in your RECOVER DATABASE UNTIL... statement? (Choose the best answer.)

A. yyyy-mm-dd:hh24:mi:ss

B. mm-dd-yyyy:hh24:mi:ss

C. It will depend on your NLS_DATE_FORMAT setting

D. It will depend on your NLS_TERRITORY setting

4. Under which of the following circumstances is an incomplete recovery necessary? (Choose two answers.)

A. You lose all copies of your current online log file group.

B. You lose a critical tablespace: SYSTEM, and/or the currently active UNDO tablespace.

C. A user makes a bad transaction, and the instance crashes before he can issue the ROLLBACK statement.

D. A datafile is created, used, and destroyed before it gets backed up.

E. You back up a tablespace, drop it, and then want to get to the objects that were in it.

5. Which of the following are valid syntax for the UNTIL clause of the RECOVER DATABASE command when it is issued from SQL*Plus? (Choose three answers.)

A. ...UNTIL CANCEL;

B. ...UNTIL CHANGE <system change number>;

C. ...UNTIL SCN <system change number>;

D. ...UNTIL SEQUENCE <sequence number>;

E. ...UNTIL TIME <time>;

F. ...UNTIL XID <transaction number>;

6. To do an incomplete recovery, what open mode must the database be in? (Choose the best answer.)

   A. Incomplete recovery can be done only with the database CLOSED.

   B. Incomplete recovery can be done only in NOMOUNT mode.

   C. Incomplete recovery can be done only in MOUNT mode.

   D. Incomplete recovery can be in OPEN mode, if the database is in archivelog mode.

   E. SQL*Plus can do incomplete recovery only in CLOSED mode; RMAN can do it in any mode.

7. Which of these RMAN RECOVER commands will apply all redo for a nonclustered database up to and including that in log switch number 90? (Choose the best answer.)

   A. RECOVER DATABASE UNTIL SEQUENCE 90;

   B. RECOVER DATABASE UNTIL SEQUENCE 91;

   C. RECOVER DATABASE UNTIL SEQUENCE 90 THREAD 1;

   D. RECOVER DATABASE UNTIL SEQUENCE 91 THREAD 1;

8. You lose your controlfile while the database is open, and it is not multiplexed. What should you do? (Choose the best answer.)

   A. Restore the datafiles and controlfile, and perform an incomplete recovery. You will not lose any data.

   B. Restore the datafiles and controlfile, and perform a complete recovery. You will not lose any data.

   C. Re-create the controlfile. You will not lose any data.

   D. You can restore the controlfile or re-create it, but you must do an incomplete recovery because losing all copies of the controlfile will mean losing data.

9. Examine the following RMAN script carefully. Which line will result in an error? (Choose the best answer.)

   A. `run {`

   B. `sql "alter session set nls_date_format=''dd-mm-yyyy hh24:mi:ss''";`

   C. `restore database;`

   D. `recover database until time '10-12-2004 15:30:00';`

   E. `alter database open resetlogs;}`

10. Which users can perform an incomplete recovery? (Choose the best answer.)

    A. Only SYS

    B. Only SYS or SYSTEM

    C. Any user connected with operating system authentication

    D. Any user who has the SYSDBA privilege

    E. Any user with either the SYSDBA or the SYSOPER privilege

11. When using RMAN to restore a controlfile auto-backup, you may need to supply a piece of information. What? (Choose the best answer.)

    A. The database name

    B. The approximate time of the latest backup

    C. The database ID

    D. The instance name

    E. The instance number

12. You are using RMAN to perform incomplete recovery. Which of the following is the best sequence to follow? (Choose the best answer.)

    A. shutdown abort / backup / startup mount / restore / recover / open resetlogs

    B. shutdown abort / startup mount / restore / recover / open resetlogs / backup

    C. shutdown immediate / backup / startup mount / restore / open resetlogs / recover

    D. shutdown immediate / backup / restore / recover / open resetlogs / backup

    E. shutdown immediate / backup / startup nomount / restore / recover / open resetlogs / backup

13. You issue the command ALTER DATABASE BACKUP CONTROLFILE TO TRACE;. Where will the trace file be generated? (Choose the best answer.)

    A. In the flash recovery area, if it has been configured

    B. In the BACKGROUND_DUMP_DEST directory

    C. In the USER_DUMP_DEST directory

    D. In a platform-specific location, such as $ORACLE_HOME/dbs on Unix

14. After a RESETLOGS, what will have changed? (Choose all that apply.)

    A. There will be a new database incarnation number.

    B. The system change number will be reset.

    C. The log switch sequence number will be reset.

    D. The database ID will be changed.

    E. The instance number will be changed.

    F. All previous backups and archive logs will be invalid.

15. You issue the command

```
alter system set log_archive_format='arch_%d_%t_%r_%s.log';
```

For each of the variables that will be used in the archive log file names, choose one of the descriptions.

Variable	Description
a. %d	A. The database name
b. %t	B. The redo log file group number
c. %r	C. The SCN where the archive log starts
d. %s	D. The database ID
	E. The checkpoint number where the archive log starts
	F. The thread number of the instance
	G. The incarnation of the database
	H. The log switch sequence number

Answers

1. **A, B,** and **C.** You must restore all the datafiles and, depending on circumstances, the controlfile.

2. **D.** The files do not have to come from the same backup, and recovery will be faster if you restore your most recent backups of each datafile. Incomplete recovery means restoring the whole database and then applying redo to bring all the files forward to the same point.

3. **A.** When doing incomplete recovery with SQL*Plus, you have no options with the date format.

4. **A** and **E.** If you lose all copies of the current logfile group, you will have to do an incomplete recovery up to the last log switch, so A is correct. E is the other correct answer, because you cannot completely recover some tablespaces while leaving others as of a previous time.

5. **A, B,** and **E.** When using SQL*Plus, you can RECOVER UNTIL CANCEL or CHANGE or TIME. SCN and SEQUENCE are used in RMAN, and it is not possible to recover until a particular transaction number.

6. **C.** It doesn't matter what tool you use; incomplete recovery is done in MOUNT mode.

7. **D.** The sequence number specified is not applied, so the SEQUENCE must be 91. Even if the database is single-instance, not RAC, you must still specify the thread number.

8. **C.** The best option is to re-create the controlfile. A would also work but is not the best answer because of the difficulty and downtime.

9. **D.** The error is in the RECOVER DATABASE command. In RMAN, you must first use SET UNTIL... and then simply RECOVER DATABASE;.

10. **D.** The SYSDBA privilege is required, granted either with operating system authentication or password file authentication. The user is immaterial. SYSOPER can do complete recovery, but not incomplete recovery.

11. **C.** If multiple databases are making controlfile auto-backups to the same destination (typically, a shared flash recovery area), then you have to supply the database ID.

12. **B.** The only sequence that will work is B. Remember that the database must be in mount mode for any RMAN operation. The backup at the end is optional, but good practice.

13. **C.** The trace file is generated in response to a command issued by your user process; therefore, it goes to the USER_DUMP_DEST.

14. **A and C.** RESETLOGS resets the log switch sequence number and changes the database incarnation number. In previous versions, all previous backups and archive logs were rendered useless, but this is no longer the case. The SCN continues unchanged, and the database ID and the instance number are not affected.

15. **a-D.** The variable %d is the database ID, in hexadecimal.
    b-F. The variable %t is the instance thread number.
    c-G. The variable %r is the database incarnation number.
    d-H. The variable %s is the log switch sequence number.

CHAPTER 28

Using Oracle Flashback Database

In this chapter you will learn how to

- Determine which flashback technology to use for each recovery situation
- Configure and use Flashback Database
- Monitor the Flashback Database
- Use the Enterprise Manager Recovery Wizard to flash back a database
- Manage (or maintain) the llash recovery area

A long time ago (in a galaxy far away...also known as Oracle 5) every version of every data block could be logged to a Before Image file. This provided the rollback function, which was handled at the block level rather than the transaction level. It did give the capability to "roll back" the entire database, but the performance overhead was generally unacceptable. In Oracle 6 the mechanism was replaced with the transaction level before image logging in rollback (nowadays, "undo") segments. This method writes out pre-update versions of data in a row-oriented rather than blocked-based fashion; the undo segments contain the bare minimum of information needed to construct SQL statements that will reverse the effect of the original SQL statements. Block-level logging is now provided again in release 10g as Flashback Database, but in a fashion that has minimal performance overhead. The Flashback Database capability lets you "rewind" the database to some point in the past, by backing out (in reverse chronological order, at the block level) all the changes made to the datafiles.

This chapter deals with Flashback Database, but there are also other Flashback technologies available. These are summarized here in order to position Flashback Database correctly; they are dealt with in detail in Chapter 29.

The Different Flashback Technologies

There are three distinct Flashback technologies available, each implemented with a different underlying architecture. Each technology has different capabilities and limitations, but there is overlapping functionality between them. The typical reason for using any type of flashback technology is to correct mistakes; it is vital to understand what type of flashback technology is appropriate for correcting different types of errors.

Flashback Database

Flashback Database is, by analogy, like pressing a rewind button on the database. The current database is taken as the starting point, and it is taken back in time, change by change, reversing all work done sequentially. The end result is as if you had done an incomplete recovery: all work subsequent to the flashback point is lost, and indeed the database must be opened with RESETLOGS. Clearly, this is a very drastic thing to do. It allows you to back out changes that resulted in corruptions in a business sense: inappropriate transactions, such as running your year-end archive-and-purge routines before running your end-of-year reports.

If you have experienced physical corruption within the database or loss of media, Flashback Database will not help; for that, you must use traditional, complete, recovery methods. Flashback Database is an alternative to incomplete recovery following user error—perhaps a more flexible and much faster alternative.

 EXAM TIP Flashback Database will not back out physical corruption, only logical corruption caused by user error.

Flashback Query: Versions, Transaction, and Table

There are three flashback techniques based on the use of undo segments. The first flashback capability was initially introduced with release 9*i* of the database and is substantially enhanced in release 10*g*. Flashback Query (the release 9*i* feature) lets you query the database as it was at some time in the past, either for one select statement or by taking your session temporarily back in time so that all its queries will be against a previous version of the database. This can be used to see the state of the data before a set of transactions was committed. What did the tables look like half an hour ago? This can be invaluable in tracking down the cause of business data corruptions, and it can also be used to correct some mistakes: by comparing the current and previous versions of a table, you can see what was done incorrectly. Flashback Versions makes it possible to select all versions of a row over a period of time, to show a history of what has happened to the row, when it happened, who did it, and the transaction identifiers of the transactions that made each change.

The second technique, Flashback Transaction, automates the repair process. Once you have used Flashback Versions Query to identify which transaction caused the problem, Oracle can construct SQL statements that will reverse the changes. This is not the same as rolling back a committed transaction! It is impossible to roll back a committed change, because the rules of a relational database do not permit this. But it is possible to construct another transaction that will reverse the effect of the first, erroneous, transaction. Unlike Flashback Database, Flashback Transaction does not mean data loss: all other work done remains in effect, and the database stays current.

The third flashback technique based on undo data is Flashback Table. Having determined that inappropriate work has been committed against one table, you can instruct Oracle to reverse all changes made to that table since a particular point in time, while leaving all other tables current.

Throughout any Flashback Query operation, the database remains open and all objects (including those involved in the flashback) are available for use. Transactional integrity and constraints are always enforced, which means that the flashback operation might fail. For example, if a flashback of a transaction requires doing an insert, then the primary key must not be in use. Flashing back one table may not be possible if it has foreign key constraints; you will have to flash back all the related tables in one operation.

 EXAM TIP Flashback Query, in all its variations, relies on the use of UNDO segments.

Flashback Drop

It is now possible to "un-drop" a table. This is implemented by mapping the DROP command onto a RENAME command. Rather than actually being dropped, the table is renamed to a system-generated name; it is only actually dropped later, when its storage space is needed for a live object. If necessary, and if its storage space has not been reused, the object can be renamed back to its original name and thus restored. Without this capability, the only way to get a table back after a drop was to do an incomplete recovery to the point in time just before the table was dropped. This was usually time consuming and meant the loss of all work done subsequently. The new Flashback Database capability achieves the same result as incomplete recovery and should be much faster, but work done on other tables following the drop is lost and the database will be unavailable until the operation is completed.

Flashback Drop lets you reinstate the table as it was at the time that it was dropped, with no loss of data whatsoever; the database remains current. This does not require any use of backups, and neither is there any downtime for users. Note that Flashback Drop is specifically for the DROP command; you cannot flash back a TRUNCATE command. Along with the table itself, any associated indexes and permissions will also be restored.

 EXAM TIP You cannot flash back a table truncation, only a table drop.

When to Use Flashback Technology

Human error has always been the most difficult type of error from which to recover. This is because as far as the database is concerned, human error is not an error at all. The "error" is just another committed transaction, and the rules of a relational database (the *D* for "Durable" of the ACID test) do not allow Oracle to back out committed transactions. Depending on the nature of the error, the different Flashback technologies may help you to recover, while minimizing downtime and loss of data.

The most drastic flashback technique is Flashback Database. Consider using this only when you would also consider using incomplete recovery; the effect is the same, though the downtime will typically be much less. Examples would include dropping a user or a tablespace on the production system when you thought you were connected to the test system. A table truncation (though not a table drop) would also be a time to use Flashback Database.

Flashback Drop will restore a table (together with its indexes and grants) to the state it was in at the time of the drop. Note that this will not restore a truncated table, only one that has been completely dropped. There is no downtime involved, other than the obvious fact that until the table is un-dropped, no one can get to it, and no work will be lost. Unlike Flashback Database, Flashback Drop does not require any configuration; it is always available, unless you specifically disable it.

For finer granularity of recovery, consider Flashback Table and Flashback Transaction. These should not affect the users at all, other than that the work reversed is gone—which is presumably the desired outcome. Like Flashback Drop, the Flashback Query, Transaction, and Table facilities are always available without any configuration other than granting appropriate privileges. They may, however, require some tuning of undo management.

In some cases, you will have a choice of Flashback technologies. Consider an example where a batch job is run twice. Perhaps you import a few hundred thousand

invoices into your accounting system from your billing system every day, and through some mistake and lack of validation the same billing run is imported twice. If the import is done as one huge transaction, then Flashback Transaction will reverse it. But if it is done as many small transactions, rather than reversing them all it may be easier to do a table-level flashback of all the tables affected. It may be that some of the billing system interface tables are dropped after the run, but Flashback Drop will recover them. But if the run involves a truncation, the only option is Flashback Database. Also, it may be that the error was not discovered for some time and a significant amount of work has been done on the basis of the erroneously imported data; then Flashback Database may be the only way to ensure that you end up with
a database that is consistent in business terms.

When choosing a Flashback technique, always remember that Oracle will guarantee transactional integrity, but that the results in business terms may not be what you want. Flashback Database, or indeed incomplete recovery, is the only way to guarantee absolutely the integrity of the database and conformity with your business rules, but the price in lost time and data may be very high.

EXAM TIP In the case of media damage, such as losing a datafile, no flashback technology can help. That is what the standard backup, restore, and recovery procedures are for.

Flashback Database Architecture

Once Flashback Database is enabled, images of altered blocks are copied from time to time from the database buffer cache to a new memory area within the SGA, the *flashback buffer*. This flashback buffer is flushed to disk, to the flashback logs, by a new background process: the Recovery Writer, or RVWR. There is no change to the usual routine of writing changes to the log buffer, which the LGWR then flushes to disk; flashback logging is additional to this. Unlike the redo log, flashback logging is not a log of changes; it is a log of complete block images.

EXAM TIP Unlike redo logs, the flashback logs cannot be multiplexed and are not archived. They are created and managed automatically.

Critical to performance is that not every change is copied to the flashback buffer, only a subset of changes. If all changes to all blocks were copied to the buffer, then the overhead in terms of memory usage and the amount of extra disk I/O required to flush the buffer to disk would be crippling for performance. Internal algorithms limit which versions of which blocks are placed in the flashback buffer, in order to restrict its size and the frequency with which it will fill and be written to disk. These algorithms are intended to ensure that there will be no performance hit to enabling Flashback Database: they guarantee that even very busy blocks are logged only infrequently.

When conducting a database flashback, Oracle will read the flashback logs to extract the versions of each changed database block, and copy these versions back into the datafiles. As these changes are applied to the current database in reverse chronological order, this has the effect of taking the database back in time, by reversing the writes that the DBWn process has done.

Since not every version of every changed block is copied into the flashback buffer and hence to the flashback logs, it is not possible to flash back to an exact point in time. It may be that a block was changed many times, but that the flashback log has only a subset of these changes. Consider the case where block A was changed at 10:00 and again at 10:05, but that only the 10:00 version is in the flashback log. Block B was changed at 10:05 and at 10:20, and both versions are in the flashback log. All the changes have been committed. It is now 11:00, and you want to flash back to 10:15. The flashback operation will restore the 10:00 version of block A and the 10:05 version of block B: it will take each changed block back as close as it can to, but no later than, the desired time. Thus Flashback Database constructs a version of the datafiles that is just before the time you want. This version of the datafiles may well be totally inconsistent: as in this example, different blocks will be at different system change numbers, depending on what happened to be available in the flashback log. To complete the flashback process, Oracle then uses the redo log. It will recover all the blocks to the exact time requested (in the example, only block A needs recovery), thus synchronizing all the datafiles to the same SCN. The final stage is to roll back any transactions that were uncommitted at the point, exactly as occurs at the last stage of an incomplete recovery.

So database flashback is in fact a combination of several processes and data structures. First, you must allocate some memory in the SGA (which will be automatic—you cannot control how large the buffer is) and some space on disk to store the flashback data, and start the RVWR process to enable flashback logging. Then when doing a flashback, Oracle will use the flashback logs to take the database back in time to before the time you want, and then apply redo logs (using whatever archive redo log files and online redo log files are necessary) in the usual fashion for incomplete recovery to bring the datafiles forward to the exact time you want. Then the database can be opened with a new incarnation, in the same manner as following a normal incomplete recovery.

 EXAM TIP Flashback Database requires archivelog mode and the use of ALTER DATABASE OPEN RESETLOGS to create a new incarnation of the database.

Flashback Database requires archivelog mode, because without the availability of the archive log stream it would not be possible to convert the inconsistent version of the database produced by application of flashback logs to a consistent version that can be opened. So what is the benefit of Flashback Database over incomplete recovery, which also requires archivelog mode? It is in the speed and convenience with which you can take the database back in time.

An incomplete recovery is always time consuming, because part of the process is a full restore. The time for an incomplete recovery is to a large extent proportional to the size of the database. By contrast, the time needed for a database flashback is largely proportional to the number of changes that need to be backed out. In any normal environment, the volume of changed data will be tiny when compared to the total volume of data, so a flashback should be many times faster. Furthermore, Flashback Database is very easy to use. Once configured, flashback logging will proceed completely unattended, and a database can be flashed back very easily with one command. There are none of the possibilities for error inherent in a traditional restore and recover operation.

Configuring Flashback Database

Configuring a database to enable Flashback Database does require downtime: there is a command that can be issued only while the database is in mount mode. To configure Flashback Database, follow these steps:

1. Ensure that the database is in archivelog mode.

   Archivelog mode is a prerequisite for enabling Flashback Database. Confirm this by querying the V$DATABASE view:

   ```
   SQL> select log_mode from v$database;
   ```

2. Set up a flash recovery area.

   The flash recovery area is the location for the flashback logs. You have no control over them other than setting the flash recovery area directory and limiting its size. It is controlled with two instance parameters: DB_RECOVERY_FILE_DEST specifies the destination directory; DB_RECOVERY_FILE_DEST_SIZE restricts the maximum amount of space in bytes that it can take up. Remember that the flash recovery area is used for purposes other than flashback logs, and it will need to be sized appropriately. For example,

   ```
   SQL> alter system set db_recovery_file_dest='/flash_recovery_area';
   SQL> alter system set db_recovery_file_dest_size=8G;
   ```

3. Set the lifespan for the flashback retention target.

   This setting is controlled by the DB_FLASHBACK_RETENTION_TARGET instance parameter, which specifies a time in minutes (the default is one day). The flashback log space is reused in a circular fashion, older data being overwritten by newer data. This parameter instructs Oracle to keep flashback data for a certain number of minutes before overwriting it:

   ```
   SQL> alter system set db_flashback_retention_target=240;
   ```

   It is only a target (four hours in this example), and if the flash recovery area is undersized, Oracle may not be able to keep to it. But in principle, you should be able to flash back to any time within this target.

4. Cleanly shut down and mount the database.

   ```
   SQL> shutdown immediate;
   SQL> startup mount;
   ```

5. Enable flashback logging.

   While in mount mode,

   ```
   SQL> alter database flashback on;
   ```

   This will start the RVWR process and allocate a flashback buffer in the SGA. The process startup will be automatic from now on.

6. Open the database.

```
SQL> alter database open;
```

Logging of data block images from the database buffer cache to the flashback buffer will be enabled from now on.

The preceding steps configure Flashback Database using SQL*Plus. It can also be done through Database Control.

Exercise 28-1: Configuring Flashback Database with Database Control

Use Database Control to enable Flashback Database.

1. Connect to your database with Database Control as user SYS.

2. From the database home page, take the Maintenance tab, then the Configure Recovery Settings link in the Backup/Recovery section.

3. In the Flash Recovery Area section shown in Figure 28-1, nominate a directory for the flash recovery area and a maximum size. Check the Enable Flashback Logging check box, and specify a flashback retention time.

4. Click Apply. This will lead to a prompt to restart the database, which you must accept to complete the configuration.

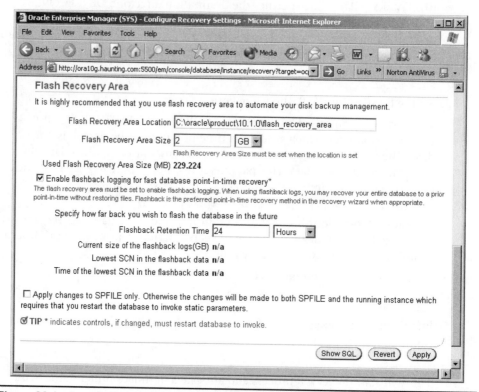

Figure 28-1   Enabling Flashback Database with Database Control

Monitoring Flashback Database

The flashback retention target is only a target; there is no guarantee that you could actually flash back to a time within it. Conversely, you might be able to flash back to beyond the target. The possible flashback period is a function of how much flashback logging information is being generated per second, and how much space is available to store this information before overwriting it with more recent data.

The most basic level of flashback monitoring is to confirm that it is actually enabled:

```
SQL> select flashback_on from v$database;
```

On Unix you can see the RVWR process as an operating system process; on Windows it will be another thread within the ORACLE.EXE process.

To monitor the current flashback capability and estimate the space needed for flashback logs to meet your target, query the V$FLASHBACK_DATABASE_LOG view. V$FLASHBACK_DATABASE_STAT gives a historical view of the rate of disk I/O for the datafiles, the online redo log files, and the flashback log files.

In Figure 28-2, the first query shows the setting for the retention target in minutes, as specified by the DB_FLASHBACK_RETENTION_TARGET instance parameter. Then there is the actual space being taken up by flashback log data, and an estimate (based on recent patterns of activity) of the space needed to meet the target. In order to keep to the target of one day (1440 minutes), 425MB of flashback log would be needed, but currently there is only 60MB of data.

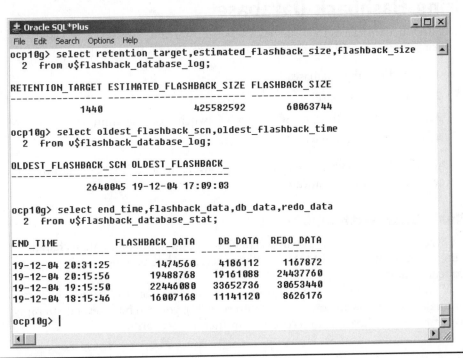

Figure 28-2   Monitoring Flashback Database

The second query shows exactly which SCN and time the flashback logs could take the database back to. If the flash recovery area is sized appropriately and the retention target is realistic, then there will be a sensible relationship between the time shown in this query and the current time less the retention target.

The third query shows the price you are paying for enabling Flashback Database, in terms of the bytes of I/O that it necessitates per hour. The top row will always be an incomplete hour, up to the current time. In the example, the database is generating about 20MB of flashback data per hour, which is consistent with the estimate of the first query. The impact of this on performance will need to be discussed with your system administrators, bearing in mind whether the system is I/O bound or not. For comparison, the view also shows the I/O related to normal database activity. The view will have one row per hour since the instance was started.

The size of the flashback buffer is outside the DBA's control, but to see the current size, query the V$SGASTAT view:

```
SQL> select * from v$sgastat where name like 'flashback%';
POOL            NAME                             BYTES
-----------     ------------------------------   ----------
shared pool     flashback generation buff        1493012
```

Flashback Database can also be monitored through Database Control. Navigate to the Configure Recovery Settings window as in Exercise 28-1, and you will see the equivalent information, with the exception of the flashback buffer size.

Using Flashback Database

There are three interfaces to Flashback Database: SQL*Plus, RMAN, and Database Control. Whichever tool you choose to use, the method is the same:

1. Shut down the database.
2. Mount the database.
3. Flash back to a time, an SCN, or a log switch sequence number.
4. Open the database with RESETLOGS.

Provided that all archive logs required are available, a flashback operation will proceed completely automatically.

Flash Back with SQL*Plus

The SQL*Plus flashback syntax will accept either a timestamp or a system change number argument; unlike RMAN, it will not accept a date or a log switch sequence number.

If you are not sure exactly what time you need to go back to (you will be very fortunate if you know the exact timestamp or SCN), you can have several attempts, by combining flashback with recovery. Consider this scenario:

It is 20 December 2004. At about 10:00 a junior DBA dropped an important schema on the production database, when s/he thought s/he was logged on to the test database. The error is noticed within ten minutes, but it is a big, busy database in a call center, used for taking orders, and every second of processing counts. The first step is to shut down the database:

```
SQL> shutdown abort;
```

There is no point in using any other type of shutdown; all work in progress is going to be lost anyway, and you need to minimize the downtime. Then take the database back to 10:00 as follows:

```
SQL> startup mount;
SQL> flashback database to timestamp
to_timestamp('20-12-04 10:00:00','dd-mm-yy hh24:mi:ss');
SQL> alter database open read only;
```

Note that unlike RECOVER DATABASE UNTIL TIME, this command is sensitive to NLS settings for the timestamp format. While the database is in READ ONLY mode, you can run a query against the dropped schema. If you discover that the schema is still there, perhaps you can recover a bit more user data:

```
SQL> shutdown abort;
SQL> startup mount;
SQL> recover database until time '2004-12-20:10:02:00';
SQL> alter database open read only;
```

You run your test query again, and you discover that after recovering two more minutes of data the schema is gone: it must have been dropped between 10:00 and 10:02. So you split the difference:

```
SQL> shutdown abort;
SQL> startup mount;
SQL> flashback database to timestamp
to_timestamp('20-12-04 10:01:00','dd-mm-yy hh24:mi:ss');
SQL> alter database open read only;
```

If the schema is not there now, flash back a few seconds further. If it is there, do a few seconds of recovery. You can repeatedly issue flashback and recover commands until you find the time that you want, testing by running queries while in read-only mode. When you get to a point you are satisfied with, do one final shutdown and open with RESETLOGS to create a new incarnation of the database that can be opened for normal use:

```
SQL> shutdown abort;
SQL> alter database open resetlogs;
```

This method will minimize the loss of data and may take only a few minutes. An incomplete recovery might take hours, particularly if you need to have several tries before you get to the right time.

Flash Back with RMAN

Within the Recovery Manager environment you have three options: you can flash back to a time, to an SCN, or to a log switch sequence number, as in these examples:

```
RMAN> flashback database to time =
to_date('20-12-04 10:00:00','yy-mm-dd hh24:mi:ss');
RMAN> flashback database to scn=2728665;
RMAN> flashback database to sequence=2123 thread=1;
```

Apart from the minor changes in syntax, RMAN flashback is the same as SQL*Plus flashback. In particular, you can use the same technique of repeatedly applying flashback and recovery until you find the optimal point to open the database.

Flash Back with Database Control

If Flashback Database has been enabled, then Database Control will be aware of this. If you request a point-in-time recovery, Database Control will suggest flashback by default if there is sufficient information in the flashback logs, but you can elect to do an incomplete recovery instead if you wish. The assumption is that flashback is generally much faster than incomplete recovery.

The options for database flashback are to a time, to an SCN, or to a log switch sequence number. The only limitation to be aware of is that the granularity of the time-based flashback with Database Control is only to the minute, whereas RMAN can flash back to a second and SQL*Plus can flash back to a timestamp, which can be to a millionth of a second.

Exercise 28-2: Using Flashback Database with Database Control

Simulate a bad transaction against a table, and flash back the database to before the transaction. This exercise assumes that Exercise 28-1 has been completed, so that flashback logging is running.

1. Connect to your database with SQL*Plus as user SYSTEM.

2. Create a table, and count the rows within it.

   ```
   SQL> create table test as select * from from dba_users;
   SQL> select count(*) from test;
   ```

3. Note the current system time, and delete all rows from the table, as in Figure 28-3.

4. Connect to your database with Database Control as user SYS.

5. From the database home page take the Maintenance tab, and the Perform Recovery link in the Backup/Recovery section.

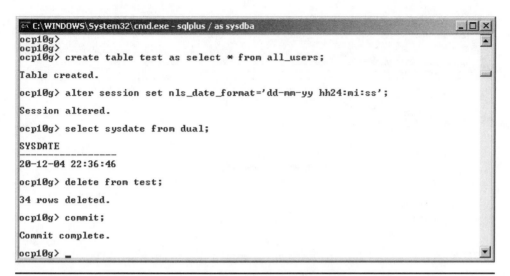

Figure 28-3 Simulate a bad transaction.

6. In the Perform Recovery: Type window, select Whole Database in the Object Type drop-down box, and the "Recover to the current time or a previous point-in-time" radio button. Click Next to continue.

7. Accept the request to restart the database, and when prompted click Perform Recovery to reach the Perform Recovery: Type window. Click Next to continue.

8. In the Perform Recovery: Point-in-Time window shown in Figure 28-4, review the details regarding flashback. Select the "Recover to a prior point-in-time" radio button, and enter the time noted in Step 3. Click Next to continue.

9. In the Perform Recovery: Flashback window shown in Figure 28-5, accept the default to use flashback rather than incomplete recovery. Click Next to continue.

10. In the Perform Recovery: Review window, study the RMAN script that will be executed and click Submit.

11. When the flashback operation is compete, return to your SQL*Plus session and re-run the query in Step 2 to confirm that the table is as it was before the bad transaction.

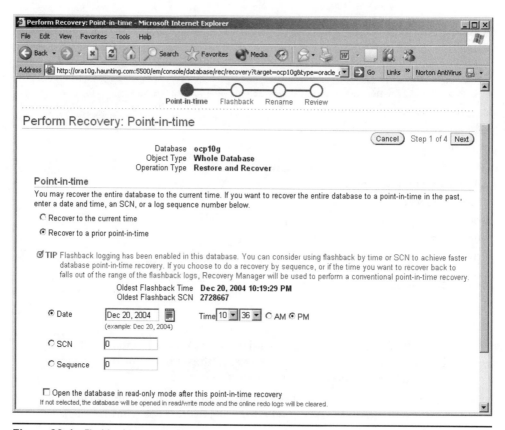

Figure 28-4 Flashback recovery

Managing the Flash Recovery Area

The flash recovery area is a default location for all recovery-related files. These can include archive logs, RMAN backups, controlfile auto-backups, multiplexed controlfile and redo log copies, and the flashback log files. All these files can be redirected elsewhere if you wish, except for the flashback logs; the DBA has no control over these, and a flash recovery area must be defined if Flashback Database is enabled. The flash recovery area can be located in either a file system directory (Oracle will create its own subdirectories within this) or an ASM disk. The flash recovery area can only be a disk destination; therefore, you must monitor its usage and back it up to tape.

Space Usage Within the Flash Recovery Area

The maximum size that the flash recovery area can grow to is limited by the parameter DB_RECOVERY_FILE_DEST_SIZE. If the flash recovery area fills, the effect on the database will depend on how it is being used. If archive logs are being written to the

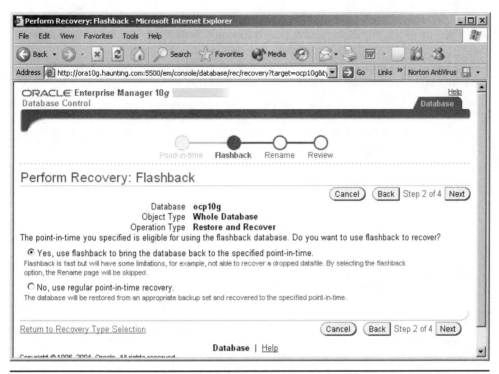

Figure 28-5 Choice of flashback as against incomplete recovery

flash recovery area, then all DML will cease because archiving will become impossible. If only RMAN backups are going to the flash recovery area, then the database will not be affected at all, though the backups will fail. If Flashback Database has been enabled, when the flash recovery area fills then DML will not be affected, but the flashback capability will be reduced because Oracle will not be able to retain enough flash data to meet the defined DB_FLASHBACK_RETENTION_TARGET.

The view V$RECOVERY_FILE_DEST gives an overall picture of space usage:

```
NAME                                                SPACE_LIMIT
--------------------------------------------------- -----------
SPACE_USED SPACE_RECLAIMABLE NUMBER_OF_FILES
---------- ----------------- ---------------
C:\oracle\product\10.1.0\flash_recovery_area          2147483648
1278850560        300611072              73
```

In this example, the size of the flash recovery area has been limited to 2GB. The files in the area, 73 of them, take up 1279MB, of which 301MB is "reclaimable," meaning that the space is occupied by backup files considered to be obsolete, according to the RMAN retention policy.

Database Control also shows flash recovery area information, as a metric. This shows the proportion of space used over the last twenty-four hours (or since instance startup). From the database home page, take the Maintenance tab, then the All Metrics link in the Related Links section. This can display a graph of the percentage of space used, as in Figure 28-6.

 TIP The "space used" figure is space used by your database. If you have put non-database files in the flash recovery directory, Oracle will know nothing about them.

To make the space considered "reclaimable" available for use, from an RMAN prompt execute

```
RMAN> delete obsolete;
```

This will physically delete all backups that RMAN no longer deems necessary according to its retention policy.

Certain backup commands can also clear files off disk as they execute:

```
RMAN> backup ... delete input;
```

Here, the DELETE INPUT keywords instruct RMAN to remove files as they are backed up. This would normally be used when backing up archive log files to tape, or when migrating disk backup sets to tape.

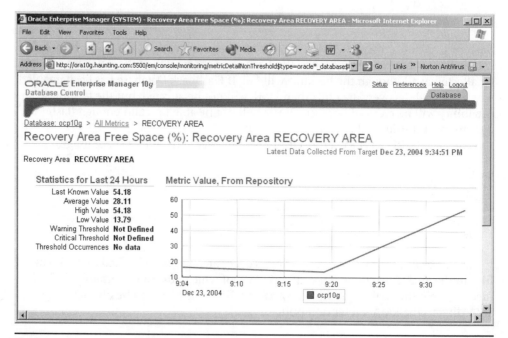

Figure 28-6 Space used in the flash recovery area

It is possible (and sometimes convenient) to use the same physical directory as the flash recovery area for several databases. In that case, you will have to monitor the overall disk usage with operating system utilities. Each database will know about its own allowance of space, as set by the DB_RECOVER_FILE_DEST_SIZE parameter, and its current space usage, but there is no way for the databases to be aware of each others' activity.

Oracle Corporation advises that the flash recovery area should be large enough for your most recent full whole backup, plus any incremental backups and archive logs needed to recover the backup. In other words, you should be able to store enough information in the recovery area to perform a restore and recover without needing to use tapes. In addition, there will need to be space for flashback logs, multiplexed controlfile and online redo log files, and a controlfile auto-backup.

Backing Up the Flash Recovery Area

The flash recovery area is not intended for long-term storage, only a short-term store of data needed for immediate, very fast, recovery, either complete or incomplete, or for use by Flashback Database. For long-term backups, the contents of the flash recovery area should be migrated to tape.

It is possible to back up some files in the flash recovery area using operating system utilities, so long as you take care that the files are not actually in use while you do it. For the flashback logs, this is impossible unless you actually shut down the database. For the other file types, it is a matter of coordinating the backup with other work. But it will always be easier to back up the flash recovery area with RMAN.

There are two RMAN commands relevant to the flash recovery area. The first,

```
RMAN> backup recovery area:
```

backs up all recovery files created in the flash recovery area that can be backed up:

- Full and incremental backup sets
- Datafile and archive log file image copies
- Controlfile auto backups
- Archive logs

It will not back up the following file types:

- Flashback logs
- Current controlfile
- Online redo log files

Flashback logs cannot be backed up, other than by using operating system utilities with the database closed. The current controlfile must be backed up using the appropriate RMAN or SQL*Plus commands. Online redo log files are never backed up.

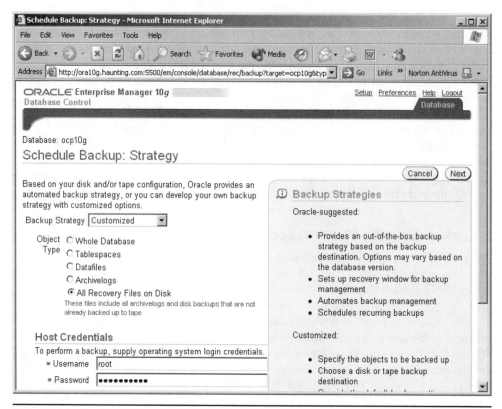

Figure 28-7   Backing up recovery files with Database Control

The second RMAN command related to the flash recovery area,

```
RMAN> backup recovery files;
```

extends the first command to include all recovery files, whether or not they are in the flash recovery area. Both commands in the examples assume that there are configured defaults for the channels. The commands can be suffixed with DELETE ALL INPUT to free up the disk space.

Database Control also has an interface to recovery file backup. From the database home page, take the Maintenance tab, and then the Schedule Backup link in the Backup/Recovery section. From the Schedule Backup: Strategy page shown in Figure 28-7, select a Customized backup strategy and the All Recovery Files On Disk radio button.

Limiting the Amount of Flashback Data Generated

Enabling Flashback Database may have an effect on online performance. The algorithm Oracle uses to restrict the amount of data written out to the flashback logs is designed to minimize the impact on performance, but (particularly on a system that is I/O bound) you may want to restrict it further. In some circumstances, you could also find that the volume of flashback data generated to meet the target is excessive. It is possible to exclude tablespaces from flashback logging, but the recovery process is then a little more complex.

Excluding Tablespaces from Flashback

By default, if Flashback Database is enabled then flashback data is recorded for all tablespaces, but you can set the attribute with

```
SQL> alter tablespace <tablespace_name> flashback off;
```

which can be executed at any time, or

```
SQL> alter tablespace <tablespace_name> flashback on;
```

which can be executed only when the database is in mount mode. To view the status of flashback, there is a column in the V$TABLESPACE view:

```
SQL> select tablespace_name,flashback_on from v$tablespace;
```

Note that the information is displayed in a dynamic performance view, not the data dictionary view DBA_TABLESPACES, because flashback is enabled through the controlfile, not the data dictionary.

Candidate tablespaces for excluding from flashback are tablespaces where you can tolerate a long period of downtime in comparison to the rest of the database; tablespaces you can drop whenever you please; or tablespaces that can be restored and recovered very quickly.

Flash Back When Tablespaces Are Not Logging Flashback Data

If one or more tablespaces are not generating flashback data, then before carrying out a flashback operation the files making up the tablespaces must be taken offline. Then the flashback, including the implicit recovery, can proceed as normal. Remember that offline datafiles are ignored by RECOVER; it is the same with FLASHBACK.

You will not be able to open the database (with or without RESETLOGS) until you have either dropped the datafiles making up the offlined tablespaces or restored and recovered them to the same point as the flashback. To drop them is a drastic action, but if it is a tablespace that you can just drop and re-create, and reinstantiate the objects within it, then this will minimize the downtime. Otherwise, after the flashback bring the datafiles making up the tablespace online. Then restore them, and do an incomplete recovery up to the time to which you flashed back. This will synchronize all the datafiles, and you can then open with RESETLOGS.

Excluding some tablespaces from flashback logging will help with online performance, but the price you pay is that you will have to do a partial restore as part of the recovery process. This will generally still be quicker than the full restore needed for an incomplete recovery.

Chapter Review

This chapter covered Flashback Database. It is a powerful capability, allowing you to "rewind" the database: to back out all work done, in reverse order, and take the database back in time. The end result is as though you had done an incomplete recovery, but whereas incomplete recovery is a process that may take hours, a flashback might take only a few minutes.

Enabling Flashback Database will start a new background process: the Recovery Writer, or RVWR. There will also be a flashback buffer allocated in the SGA, and from then on block images will be written out to a new disk-based data structure, the flashback logs. You have no control over any of these components beyond setting the location of the flash recovery area, which will be used (among other things) for the flashback logs. You can instruct Oracle to retain enough flashback data to flash back for a certain period, but whether Oracle can actually do that will be dependent on the space available in the flash recovery area.

You must monitor the flash recovery area to see how full it is getting, and reclaim space regularly by deleting no longer needed backups and archive logs. It must also be backed up regularly to stable storage.

Questions

1. Under which of these circumstances might Flashback Database be of use? (Choose the best answer.)

   A. To recover a dropped table

   B. To recover a dropped schema

   C. To recover a damaged datafile

   D. To reverse a bad transaction

   E. All of the above

2. Which of the following is correct about Flashback Database? (Choose two correct answers.)

   A. You should set the FLASHBACK_BUFFER_SIZE parameter.

   B. You must create the flashback log files.

   C. You must set the DB_RECOVERY_FILE_DEST parameter.

   D. You must issue ALTER SYSTEM FLASHBACK ON.

   E. You must issue ALTER DATABASE FLASHBACK ON.

3. Why is archivelog mode required to enable Flashback Database? (Choose the best answer.)

   A. Because the redo log data is needed to reverse changes

   B. To recover to an exact time after flashback

   C. Because ARCn processes are needed to write flashback data

   D. Archivelog mode is optional, it is not required

4. What state must the database be in to turn on the Flashback Database feature? (Choose the best answer.)

   A. Shutdown

   B. Nomount

   C. Mount

   D. Open

5. Which of the following commands is not necessary for a Flashback Database operation? (Choose all that apply.)

   A. Alter database open readonly

   B. Alter database open resetlogs

   C. Flashback database to...

   D. Recover database until...

   E. Shutdown

   F. Startup mount

6. What tool(s) can be used to perform a database flashback? (Choose the best answer.)

   A. Database Control and RMAN

   B. Database Control and SQL*Plus

   C. RMAN and SQL*Plus

   D. Database Control, RMAN, and SQL*Plus

7. You have set the DB_FLASHBACK_RETENTION_TARGET to one day, but the flash recovery area does not have room for this much flashback data. What will happen? (Choose the best answer.)

   A. The database will hang until space is freed up.

   B. It will depend on whether AUTOEXTEND has been enabled for the flash recovery area.

   C. The database will continue to function, but flashback operations may fail.

   D. If any backups in the flash recovery area are not needed according to the retention policy, they will be automatically removed.

8. A user error has occurred, but the effects are limited to one tablespace. You want to flash back this one tablespace, but not the others. What must you do? (Choose the best answer.)

   A. Execute ALTER TABLESPACE...FLASHBACK OFF for all the other tablespaces, and then flash back the database.

   B. Take the other datafiles offline, flash back the database, and bring the other datafiles online.

    C. Flash back the whole database, and then do complete recovery of the other tablespaces.

    D. It is not possible to flash back one tablespace and leave the rest of the database current.

9. Within RMAN, you issue the command BACKUP RECOVERY AREA. What files in the recovery area will be backed up? (Choose all that apply.)

    A. RMAN backup sets

    B. RMAN image copies

    C. Archive redo logs

    D. Multiplexed online redo logs

    E. Multiplexed controlfile copies

    F. Controlfile auto-backups

    G. Flashback logs

10. You have enabled Flashback Database, but you suspect that flashback logging is impacting adversely on performance. What could you do? (Choose the best answer.)

    A. Reduce the DB_FLASHBACK_RETENTION_TARGET parameter.

    B. Tune the frequency of RVWR writes.

    C. Stop flashback logging for some tablespaces.

    D. Investigate the flashback log multiplexing and archiving strategy.

    E. Tune the flashback buffer.

Answers

1. **B.** The only way to recover a dropped schema (other than incomplete recovery) is Flashback Database. No flashback technology will help with physical corruption. A dropped table would be better fixed with Flashback Table, and a bad transaction, with Flashback Transaction.

2. **C and E.** The DB_RECOVERY_FILE_DEST instance parameter permits the instance to use a recovery area, and ALTER DATABASE FLASHBACK ON starts the Recovery Writer. There is no such parameter as FLASHBACK_BUFFER_SIZE, and the flashback logs are created automatically. Remember too that flashback is an attribute of the database, not the instance.

3. **B.** Flashback is only approximate; redo is needed to reach the precise point required. Note that redo can never be used to reverse changes, only to redo them, and that the flashback data is written by the RVWR process, not by the archiver processes.

4. **C.** No options here, the database must be in mount mode to issue ALTER DATABASE FLASHBACK ON.

5. **A and D.** The optional steps are to OPEN READONLY and to RECOVER DATABASE UNTIL.

6. **D.** Any of the three tools listed can be used: Database Control, RMAN, and SQL*Plus.

7. **C.** The retention target is only a target, and Oracle will continue to function even if it cannot be met—but your flashbacks may fail. The database will hang, though, if it is not possible to archive logs. AUTOEXTEND is an attribute that can be applied to datafiles, not the flash recovery area. Backups will be automatically removed only if you instruct RMAN to do it.

8. **D.** The whole database must be synchronized before it can be opened. Executing ALTER TABLESPACE...FLASHBACK OFF restricts tablespaces from generating flashback data. The other alternatives won't work because the other datafiles will not be synchronized.

9. **A, B, C, and F.** The file types that cannot be backed up with this command are online logs and the flashback logs (which are never backed up), and the current controlfile (for which you must use the BACKUP CURRENT CONTROLFILE command).

10. **C.** This will reduce the volume of flashback data written to disk, but will also mean that flashback operations may take a little longer and be a little more complicated. Reducing the DB_FLASHBACK_RETENTION_TARGET parameter will not have an effect on performance, only on how far you can flash back. The tuning options are impossible; Oracle controls these. And investigating the strategy is useless because flashback logs cannot be multiplexed or archived.

CHAPTER 29

Recovering from User Errors

In this chapter you will learn how to

- Recover a dropped table using Flashback technology
- Manage the recycle bin
- Perform a Flashback Table operation
- Recover from user errors using Flashback Versions Query
- Perform transaction-level recovery using Flashback Transaction Query

The previous chapter introduced Flashback Database, a powerful but drastic feature that is functionally equivalent to an incomplete recovery. This chapter covers the other flashback technologies available in an Oracle 10*g* database. These are not as extreme as Flashback Database in that they do not entail either downtime or loss of data. They are still, however, very powerful techniques for recovering from errors by backing out changes that you would prefer not to have been committed.

The flashback technologies discussed here are, first, Flashback Drop, enabled by the way the DROP TABLE command is used and implemented, and second, various ways of exploiting the UNDO capability: Flashback Versions Query, Flashback Table Query, and Flashback Transaction Query.

Flashback and the ACID Test

Remember the ACID test, described in Chapter 9. This is part of the rules to which a relational database must conform, and is critical to an understanding of the flashback technologies: both their capabilities and their limitations.

All DML transactions are terminated with either a COMMIT or a ROLLBACK statement. Until then, while the transaction is in progress, the principle of transaction isolation (the *I* of the ACID test) as implemented by Oracle guarantees that no one, other than the session carrying out the transaction, can see the changes it has made.

Furthermore, the principle of atomicity (the *A* of the ACID test) guarantees that the session can terminate the transaction with a ROLLBACK, which will reverse the changes completely; no other session will have any knowledge that the changes were ever made. If the transaction is terminated with a COMMIT, then the changes will be immediately visible to all other sessions. The only exception to this is any sessions that for reasons of read consistency (the *C* of the ACID test) need to be protected from the changes. Furthermore, once a transaction is committed, it must be absolutely impossible for the database to lose the changes; this is the *D*, for durable, of the ACID test.

In many ways, DDL commands are transactions like any other. The rules of a relational database require that the effect of committed DDL can never be reversed, and all DDL is committed, automatically. You have no control over this; the COMMIT is an integral part of all DDL commands.

Flashback Drop provides a means whereby you can reverse the effect of a DROP TABLE command, but there is no guarantee that it will succeed. This will depend on other activity in the database since the DROP was executed. You can use the various Flashback Query commands to reverse DML commands, but again, whether this will succeed will depend on what other activity has occurred in the intervening time. It is impossible to roll back a committed transaction, whether DML or DDL. The ACID test does not permit this. The flashback technologies rely on constructing another transaction that will reverse the impact of the original transaction, but it may be that this new transaction will fail, because of other, incompatible committed changes.

Flashback Drop

Accidentally dropping a table is terrifyingly easy to do. It is not just that you can drop the wrong table because of a typing error; it could be the right table, but you are connected to the wrong schema, or logged onto the wrong instance. You can reduce the likelihood of this by setting your SQL*Plus prompt, for example,

```
SQL> set sqlprompt "_user'@'_connect_identifier> "
SYSTEM@ocp10g>
```

TIP To set your sqlprompt automatically for all SQL*Plus sessions, put the preceding command into the glogin.sql file, in the ORACLE_HOME/sqlplus /admin directory.

Flashback Drop lets you reinstate a previously dropped table (but not a truncated table!) exactly as it was before the drop. All the indexes will also be recovered, and also any triggers and grants. Unique, primary key, and not-null constraints will also be recovered, but not foreign key constraints.

EXAM TIP The Flashback Drop command applies only to tables, but all associated objects will also be recovered, except for foreign key constraints.

The Implementation of Flashback Drop

In earlier releases of the Oracle Database, when a table was dropped all references to it were removed from the data dictionary. If it were possible to see the source code for the old DROP TABLE command, you would see that it was actually a series of DELETE commands against the various tables in the SYS schema that define a table and its space usage, followed by a COMMIT. There was no actual clearing of data from disk, but the space used by a dropped table was flagged as being unused and thus available for reuse. Even though the blocks of the table were still there, there was no possible way of getting to them because the data dictionary would have no record of which blocks were part of the dropped table. The only way to recover a dropped table was to do a point-in-time recovery, restoring a version of the database from before the drop when the data dictionary still knew about the table.

In release 10g of the Oracle database, the implementation of the DROP TABLE command has been completely changed. Tables are no longer dropped at all; they are renamed.

In Figure 29-1, you can see that a table, OLD_NAME, occupies one extent of 64KB, which starts in the seventeenth block of file six. After the rename to NEW_NAME, the storage is exactly the same; therefore, the table is the same. Querying the view DBA_OBJECTS would show that the table's object number had not changed either.

The release 10g implementation of the DROP TABLE command has been mapped internally onto a RENAME command, which affects the table and all its associated indexes, triggers, and constraints, with the exception of foreign key constraints, which are dropped. Foreign key constraints have to be dropped for real. If they were maintained, even with a different name, then DML on the non-dropped parent table would be constrained by the contents of a dropped table, which would be absurd.

Grants on tables do not have names, so they can't be renamed. But even though when you grant a privilege you specify the object by name, the underlying storage of the grant references the object by number. As the object numbers don't get changed by a RENAME operation, the grants are still valid.

As far as normal SELECT and DML statements are concerned, a dropped table is definitely dropped. There is no change to any other commands, and all your software will assume that a dropped table really is gone. But now that DROP is in fact a RENAME, it becomes possible to un-drop, by renaming the table back to its original name. However, this is not guaranteed to succeed. It may be that the space occupied by the dropped table has been reused. There are also complications if in the interim period another table has been created, reusing the same name as the dropped table.

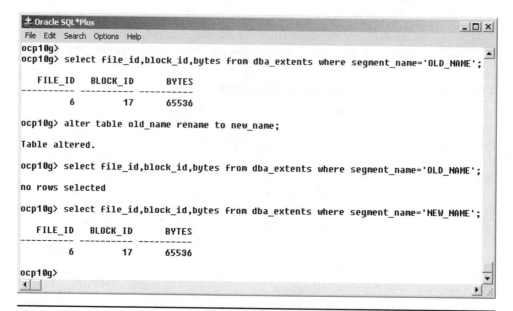

Figure 29-1 Renaming tables with SQL*Plus

The dropped objects can be queried, by looking at the "recycle bin" to obtain their new names. This is a listing of all objects that have been dropped, mapping the original table and index names onto the system-generated names of the dropped objects. There is a recycle bin for each user, visible in the USER_RECYCLEBIN data dictionary view, or for a global picture, you can query DBA_RECYCLEBIN. The space occupied by the recycle bin objects will be reused automatically when a tablespace comes under space pressure (after which time the objects cannot be recovered), or you can manually force Oracle to really drop the objects with the PURGE command.

 TIP There are no guarantees of success with Flashback Drop, but it may well work. The sooner you execute it, the greater the likelihood of success.

Using Flashback Drop

Consider the example in Figure 29-2. This is the most basic use of Flashback Drop. The DROP command renames the table to a system-generated name, and Flashback Drop brings it back. Variations in syntax are

```
SQL> drop table <table_name> purge;
SQL> flashback table <table_name> to before drop rename to <new_name>;
```

The first command really will drop the table. The PURGE keyword instructs Oracle to revert to the true meaning of DROP: all references to the table are deleted, and it can never be brought back. The second command will flash back the table but give it a new name. This would be essential if, between the drop and the flashback, another table had been created with the same name as the dropped table. Note that although a table can be renamed during a flashback, it cannot change the schema: all flashback operations occur within the schema to which the object belongs. The indexes, triggers, and constraints that are flashed back along with the table keep their recycle bin names. If you want to return them to their original names, you must rename them manually after the flashback.

There are two points to emphasize here. First, Flashback Drop can only recover from a DROP. It cannot recover from a TRUNCATE. Second, if you drop a user with, for example,

```
SQL> drop user scott cascade;
```

you will not be able to recover any of SCOTT's tables with flashback. The drop of the schema means that Oracle cannot maintain the objects at all, even in the recycle bin, because there is no user to connect them to.

Database Control also has an interface to Flashback Drop. From the database home page, take the Maintenance tab and then Perform Recovery in the Backup/ Recovery section. In the drop-down box for Object Type, select Tables, and then the

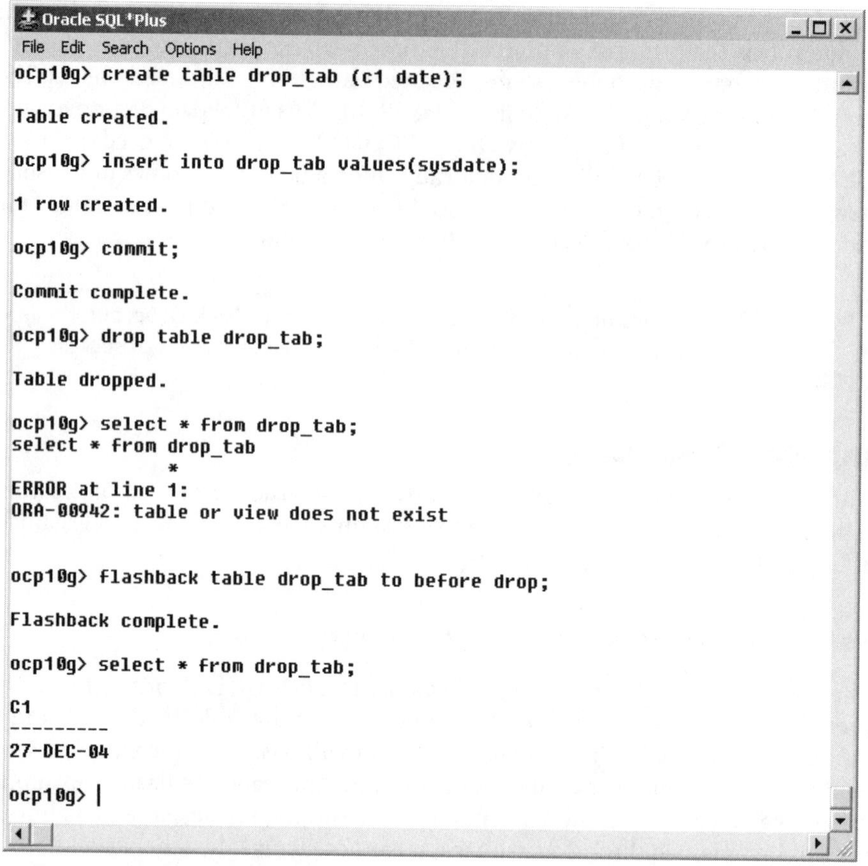

Figure 29-2 Using Flashback Drop

radio button for Flashback Dropped Tables. This will take you to the Perform Recovery: Dropped Objects Selection window, where you can view all the dropped tables in your database. From here you can select from the dropped tables or go on to recover them, as shown in Figure 29-3.

If a table is dropped and then another table is created with the same name and then also dropped, there will be two tables in the recycle bin. They will have different recycle bin names, but the same original name. By default, a Flashback Drop command will always recover the most recent version of the table, but if this is not the version you want, you can specify the recycle bin name of the version you want recovered, rather than the original name. For example,

```
SQL> flashback table "BIN$sn0WEwXuTum7c1Vx4dOcaA==$0" to before drop;
```

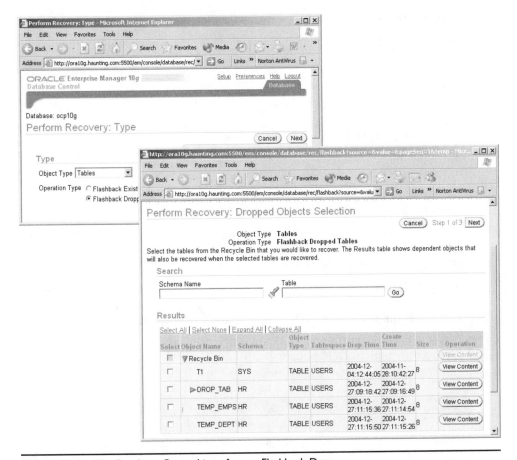

Figure 29-3 The Database Control interface to Flashback Drop

Exercise 29-1: Using Flashback Drop with SQL*Plus

Create a new schema, and a table within it. Drop the table, and then recover it with Flashback Drop.

1. Connect to your database as user SYSTEM with SQL*Plus.

2. Create a user for this exercise.

```
SQL> create user dropper identified by dropper;
SQL> grant connect,resource to dropper;
SQL> connect dropper/dropper;
```

3. Create a table, with an index and a constraint, and insert a row.

```
SQL> create table names (name varchar2(10));
SQL> create index name_idx on names(name);
SQL> alter table names add (constraint name_u unique(name));
SQL> insert into names values ('John');
SQL> commit;
```

4. Confirm the contents of your schema.

```
SQL> select object_name,object_type from user_objects;
SQL> select constraint_name,constraint_type,table_name from user_constraints;
```

5. Drop the table.

```
SQL> drop table names;
```

6. Re-run the queries from Step 4. Note that the objects and the constraints do still exist but that they now have system-generated names, all prefixed with BIN$.

7. Query your recycle bin to see the mapping of the original name to the recycle bin names.

```
SQL> select object_name,original_name,type from user_recyclebin;
```

8. Demonstrate that it is possible to query the recycle bin but that you cannot do DML against it, as in Figure 29-4. Note that the table name must be enclosed in double quotes to allow SQL*Plus to parse the nonstandard characters correctly.

9. Recover the table with Flashback Drop.

```
SQL> flashback table names to before drop;
```

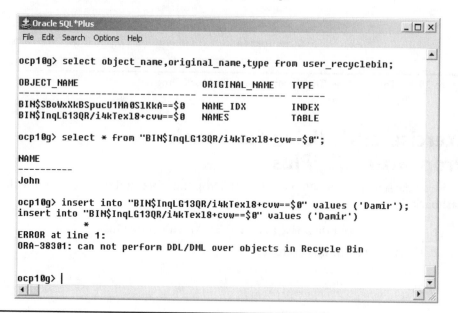

Figure 29-4 Querying the recycle bin

10. Re-run the queries from Step 4. Note that the index and the constraint have retained their recycle bin names.

11. Rename the index and constraint to the original names. In these examples, substitute your own recycle bin names:

```
SQL> alter index "BIN$SBoWxXkBSpucU1MA0SlKkA==$0" rename to name_idx;
SQL> alter table names rename constraint "BIN$PfhO1XqPTrewRb5+ToED1Q==$0"
to name_u;
```

12. Confirm the success of the operation by re-running the queries from Step 4.

13. Connect as user SYSTEM, and drop the DROPPER schema.

```
SQL> connect system/oracle;
SQL> drop user dropper cascade;
```

14. Query the DBA_RECYCLEBIN view to demonstrate that all the objects owned by user DROPPER really are gone.

```
SQL> select count(*) from dba_recyclebin where owner='DROPPER';
```

Managing the Recycle Bin

The recycle bin is a term given to the storage space used by dropped objects. You can ignore the recycle bin completely—its management is automatic, both in terms of transferring objects into it when they are dropped, and removing them permanently when the space is needed in the tablespace for live objects. But there may be circumstances when you will need to be aware of the contents of the recycle bin and how much space they are taking up.

 TIP The recycle bin can be disabled with a hidden parameter.

Querying the Recycle Bin

Each user has his own recycle bin: s/he can always view dropped tables in his or her own schema. The simplest way is the SHOW RECYCLEBIN command:

```
SQL> show recyclebin;
ORIGINAL NAME RECYCLEBIN NAME                        OBJECT TYPE  DROP TIME
------------- ------------------------------         ------------ -----------
DROP_TAB      BIN$vWMhmt3sTcqJ9WhSREM29g==$0 TABLE   2004-12-27:09:18:42
TEMP_DEPT     BIN$OLp3r9zPRRe6KSjs7Ee3gQ==$0 TABLE   2004-12-27:11:15:50
TEMP_EMPS     BIN$DKaQ10DDSty8hXQH2Xniwg==$0 TABLE   2004-12-27:11:15:36
```

This shows that the current user has three dropped tables: their original names, their recycle bin names, and the time they were dropped. For more detailed information, query the data dictionary view USER_RECYCLEBIN, or DBA_RECYCLEBIN for a global view:

```
SQL> select owner,original_name,type,droptime,can_undrop, space from
dba_recyclebin;
```

OWNER	ORIGINAL_NAME	TYPE	DROPTIME	CAN	SPACE
SYS	T1	TABLE	2004-12-04:12:44:05	YES	8
DROPPER	T1	TABLE	2004-12-27:11:23:21	YES	8
HR	DROP_TAB	TABLE	2004-12-27:09:18:42	YES	8
HR	TEMP_EMPS	TABLE	2004-12-27:11:15:36	YES	8
HR	TEMP_DEPT	TABLE	2004-12-27:11:15:50	YES	8

The critical column is CAN_UNDROP. Oracle is under no obligation to keep dropped tables or indexes: the Flashback Drop facility is purely a convenience that Oracle provides; it is not part of the relational database standard. If Oracle needs the space being occupied by a dropped object to allocate more space to a live object, it will take it; from that point, the dropped object can no longer be recovered with Flashback Drop, and it will be removed from the view. The SPACE column (in units of datafile blocks) shows how much space is taken up by the dropped object.

Having identified the dropped table's name in the recycle bin, it can be queried like any other table, though you will have to enclose its name in double quotes because of the nonstandard characters used in recycle bin names. But always remember that you have a limited (and unpredictable) time during which you can do this. If you think it is likely that a dropped table will be needed, you should recover it immediately.

 EXAM TIP Flashback Drop is not enabled for tables stored in the SYSTEM tablespace: such tables will not be reported by the queries described in the preceding text, because they are dropped and purged immediately.

Reclaiming Space from the Recycle Bin

Space taken up by dropped objects is in an ambiguous state: it is assigned to the object, but Oracle can overwrite it at will. The normal diagnostics regarding space usage will ignore space occupied by the recycle bin. This means that your "tablespace percent full" alerts will not fire until the warning and critical space usage levels are reached by live objects. Furthermore, if your datafiles have the AUTOEXTEND attribute enabled, Oracle will not in fact autoextend the datafiles until all space occupied by dropped objects has been reassigned: it will overwrite the recycle bin in preference to increasing the datafile size.

Consider this example: a 1MB tablespace, called SMALL, has been completely filled by one table, called LARGE. The space usage alerts will have fired, and querying DBA_FREE_SPACE reports no space available. Then the table is dropped. The alert will clear itself and DBA_FREE_SPACE will report that the whole tablespace is empty, but querying the recycle bin, or indeed DBA_SEGMENTS, will tell the truth, as in Figure 29-5.

This apparently contradictory state is resolved by Oracle reusing space as it needs it. If space is required in the tablespace for a new segment, then it will be taken, and it will no longer be possible to retain the dropped table. If there are many deleted objects in the recycle bin, Oracle will overwrite the object that had been in there for

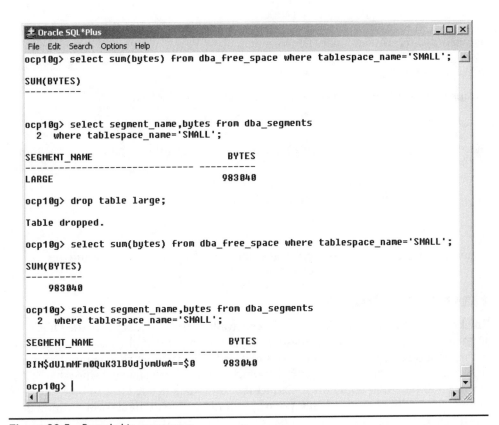

Figure 29-5   Recycle bin space usage

the longest time. This FIFO, or first in, first out, algorithm assumes that objects dropped recently are most likely candidates for a flashback.

It is also possible to remove deleted objects permanently using the PURGE command in its various forms:

```
drop table <table_name> purge
```

means drop the table and do not move it to the recycle bin, and

```
purge table <table_name>
```

means remove the table from the recycle bin. If there are several objects with the same original name, the oldest is removed. Avoid this confusion by specifying the recycle bin name instead. Use

```
purge index <index_name>
```

to remove an index from the recycle bin; again, you can specify either the original name, or the recycle bin name. The form

```
purge tablespace <tablespace_name>
```

means remove all dropped objects from the tablespace; the form

```
purge tablespace <tablespace_name> user <user_name>
```

means remove all dropped objects belonging to one user from the tablespace; the form

```
purge user_recyclebin
```

means remove all your dropped objects; and the form

```
purge dba_recyclebin
```

means remove all dropped objects. You will need DBA privileges to execute this.

Flashback Query

The basic form of Flashback Query has been available since release 9i of the Oracle Database: you can query the database as it was at some time in the past. The principle is that your query specifies a time that is mapped onto a system change number, an SCN, and that whenever the query hits a block that has been changed since that SCN, it will go to the undo segments to extract the undo data needed to roll back the change. This rollback is strictly temporary and only visible to the session running the Flashback Query. Clearly, for a Flashback Query to succeed, the undo data must be available.

In release 10g of the database, Flashback Query has been enhanced substantially, and it can now be used to retrieve all versions of a row, to reverse individual transactions, or to reverse all the changes made to a table since a certain time. It is also possible to guarantee that a flashback will succeed, but there is a price to be paid for enabling this: it may cause transactions to fail.

 EXAM TIP All forms of Flashback Query rely on undo data to reconstruct data as it was at an earlier point in time.

Basic Flashback Query

Any one select statement can be directed against a previous version of a table. Consider this example:

```
ocp10g> select sysdate from dual;
SYSDATE
-----------------
27-12-04 16:54:06
ocp10g> delete from regions where region_name like 'A%';
```

```
2 rows deleted.
ocp10g> commit;
Commit complete.
ocp10g> select * from regions;
REGION_ID REGION_NAME
--------- ------------------------
        1 Europe
        4 Middle East and Africa
ocp10g> select * from regions as of timestamp to_timestamp('27-12-04
16:54:06','dd-mm-yy hh24:mi:ss');
REGION_ID REGION_NAME
--------- ------------------------
        1 Europe
        2 Americas
        3 Asia
        4 Middle East and Africa
ocp10g> select * from regions as of timestamp to_timestamp('27-12-04
16:54:06','dd-mm-yy hh24:mi:ss') minus select * from regions;
REGION_ID REGION_NAME
--------- ------------------------
        2 Americas
        3 Asia
```

First, note the time. Then delete some rows from a table and commit the change. A query confirms that there are only two rows in the table, and no rows where the REGION_NAME begins with A. The next query is directed against the table as it was at the earlier time: back then there were four rows, including those for "Asia" and "Americas." Make no mistake about this: the two rows beginning with A are gone; they were deleted, and the delete was committed. It cannot be rolled back. The deleted rows you are seeing have been constructed from undo data. The final query combines real-time data with historical data, to see what rows have been removed. The output of this query could be used for repair purposes, to insert the rows back into the table.

While being able to direct one query against data as of an earlier point in time may be useful, there will be times when you want to make a series of selects. It is possible to take your whole session back in time by using the DBMS_FLASHBACK package:

```
ocp10g> execute dbms_flashback.enable_at_time(-
> to_timestamp('27-12-04 16:54:06','dd-mm-yy hh24:mi:ss'));
PL/SQL procedure successfully completed.
ocp10g>
```

From this point on, all queries will see the database as it was at the time specified. All other sessions will see real-time data, but this one session will see a frozen version of the database, until the flashback is cancelled:

```
ocp10g> execute dbms_flashback.disable;
PL/SQL procedure successfully completed.
ocp10g>
```

While in flashback mode, it is impossible to execute DML commands. They will throw an error. Only SELECT is possible.

How far back you can take a Flashback Query (either one query, or by using DBMS_FLASHBACK) is dependent on the contents of the undo segments. If the undo data needed to construct the out-of-date result set is not available, then the query will fail with an "ORA-08180: no snapshot found based on specified time" error.

The syntax for enabling Flashback Query will accept either a timestamp or an SCN. If you use an SCN, then the point to which the flashback goes is precise. If you specify a time, it will be mapped onto an SCN with a precision of three seconds.

 EXAM TIP You can query the database as of an earlier point-in-time, but you can never execute DML against the older versions of the data.

Flashback Table Query

Conceptually, a table flashback is simple. Oracle will query the undo segments to extract details of all rows that have been changed, and then it will construct and execute statements that will reverse the changes. The flashback operation is a separate transaction that will counteract the effect of all the previous transactions, if possible. The database remains online and normal work is not affected, unless row locking is an issue. This is not a rollback of committed work; it is a new transaction designed to reverse the effects of committed work. All indexes are maintained, and constraints enforced: a table flashback is just another transaction, and the usual rules apply. The only exception to normal processing is that by default triggers on the table are disabled for the flashback operation.

A table flashback will often involve a table that is in a foreign key relationship. In that case, it is almost inevitable that the flashback operation will fail with a constraint violation. To avoid this problem, the syntax permits flashback of multiple tables with one command, which will be executed as a single transaction with the constraint checked at the end.

The first step to enabling table flashback is to enable row movement on the tables. This is a flag set in the data dictionary that informs Oracle that rowids may change. A rowid can never actually change, but a flashback operation may make it appear as though it has. For instance, in the case of a row that is deleted, the flashback operation will insert it back into the table: it will have the same primary key value, but a different rowid.

In the example that follows, there are two tables: EMP and DEPT. There is a foreign key relationship between them, stating that every employee in EMP must be a member of a department in DEPT.

First, insert a new department and an employee in that department, and note the time:

```
ocp10g> insert into dept values(50,'SUPPORT','LONDON');
1 row created.
ocp10g> insert into emp values(8000,'WATSON','ANALYST',7566,'27-DEC-
04',3000,null,50);
1 row created.
```

```
ocp10g> commit;
Commit complete.
ocp10g> select sysdate from dual;
SYSDATE
-----------------
27-12-04 18:30:11
```

Next delete the department and the employee, taking care to delete the employee first to avoid a constraint violation:

```
ocp10g> delete from emp where empno=8000;
1 row deleted.
ocp10g> delete from dept where deptno=50;
1 row deleted.
ocp10g> commit;
Commit complete.
```

Now attempt to flash back the tables to the time when the department and employee existed:

```
ocp10g> flashback table emp to timestamp to_timestamp('27-12-04
18:30:11','dd-mm-yy hh24:mi:ss');
flashback table emp to timestamp to_timestamp('27-12-04 18:30:11','dd-mm-yy
hh24:mi:ss')
                  *
ERROR at line 1:
ORA-08189: cannot flashback the table because row movement is not enabled
```

This fails because by default row movement, which is a prerequisite for table flashback, is not enabled for any table, so enable it, for both tables:

```
ocp10g> alter table dept enable row movement;
Table altered.
ocp10g> alter table emp enable row movement;
Table altered.
```

and now try the flashback again:

```
ocp10g> flashback table emp to timestamp to_timestamp('27-12-04
18:30:11','dd-mm-yy hh24:mi:ss');
flashback table emp to timestamp to_timestamp('27-12-04 18:30:11','dd-mm-yy
hh24:mi:ss')
*
ERROR at line 1:
ORA-02091: transaction rolled back
ORA-02291: integrity constraint (SCOTT.FK_DEPTNO) violated - parent key not
found
```

This time the flashback fails for a more subtle reason. The flashback is attempting to reverse the deletion of employee 8000 by inserting him, but employee 8000 was in department 50, which has been deleted and so does not exist. Hence the foreign key violation. You could avoid this problem by flashing back the DEPT table first, which would insert department 50. But if your flashback involves many tables and many

DML statements, it may be logically impossible to find a sequence that will work. The answer is to flash back both tables together:

```
ocp10g> flashback table emp,dept to timestamp to_timestamp('27-12-04
18:30:11','dd-mm-yy hh24:mi:ss');
Flashback complete.
```

This succeeds because both the tables are flashed back in one transaction, and the constraints are only checked at the end of that transaction, by which time, the data is logically consistent.

The flashback could still fail for other reasons:

- Primary key violations will occur if a key value has been reused between a delete and the flashback.

- An "ORA-08180: no snapshot found based on specified time" will be raised if there is not enough undo information to go back to the time requested.

- If any rows affected by the flashback are locked by other users, the flashback will fail with "ORA-00054: resource busy and acquire with NOWAIT specified."

- The table definitions must not change during the period concerned; flashback cannot go across DDLs. Attempting to do this will generate "ORA-01466: Unable to read data – table definition has changed."

- Flashback does not work for tables in the SYS schema. Try to imagine the effect of flashing back part of the data dictionary....

If a table flashback fails for any reason, the flashback operation will be cancelled: any parts of it that did succeed will be rolled back, and the tables will be as they were before the flashback command was issued.

Variations in the syntax allow flashback to a system change number, and firing of DML triggers during the operation:

```
SQL> flashback table emp,dept to scn 6539425 enable triggers;
```

Table flashback can also be initiated by Database Control. From the database home page, take the Maintenance tab and then the Perform Recovery link in the Backup/Recovery section. Select Tables in the Object Type drop-down box, and then the Flashback Existing Tables radio button to invoke the Flashback Table Wizard. However table flashback is initiated, it is always recorded in the alert log.

Flashback Versions Query

A row may have changed several times during its life. Flashback Versions Query lets you see all the committed versions of a row (but not any uncommitted versions), including the timestamps for when each version was created and when it ended. You can also see the transaction identifier of the transaction that created any given version of a row, which can then be used with Flashback Transaction Query. This information is exposed by a number of pseudo-columns that are available with every table.

Pseudo-columns are columns appended to the row by Oracle internally; they are not part of the ISO standards for a relational database, but they can be very useful. One pseudo-column is the row ID: the unique identifier for every row in the database, that is used in indexes as the pointer back to the table. These pseudo-columns are relevant to flashback:

- **VERSIONS_STARTSCN**   The SCN at which this version of the row was created, either by INSERT or by UPDATE

- **VERSIONS_STARTTIME**   The timestamp at which this version of the row was created

- **VERSIONS_ENDSCN**   The SCN at which this version of the row expired, either because of DELETE or UPDATE

- **VERSIONS_ENDTIME**   The timestamp at which this version of the row expired

- **VERSIONS_XID**   The unique identifier for the transaction that created this version of the row

- **VERSIONS_OPERATIONS**   The operation done by the transaction to create this version of the row, either INSERT or UPDATE or DELETE

To see these pseudo-columns, you must include the VERSIONS BETWEEN keywords in your query. For example, Figure 29-6 shows all versions of the row for employee 8000.

The versions are sorted in descending order of existence: they must be read from the bottom up. The bottom row shows that employee 8000 was inserted (the *I* in the last column) at SCN 2902882 by transaction number 05002D00AD020000. The employee was given an ENAME of WATSON and a SAL of 3000. This version of the row existed until SCN 2902915, which takes us to the third row. At this SCN, the row

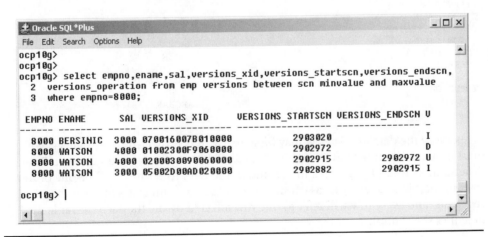

Figure 29-6   Flashback Versions Query

was updated (the *U* in the last column) with a new salary. This version of row persisted until SCN 2902972, when it was deleted, as shown in the second row. The VERSIONS_ENDSCN column is always null for a deletion. The top row of the result set shows a new insertion, which reuses the employee number. For this row, the VERSIONS_ENDSCN is also null, because the row still exists, in that version, as at the end of the time range specified in the query.

In the example in Figure 29-6, the VERSIONS BETWEEN uses two constants for the SCN. MINVALUE instructs Oracle to retrieve the earliest information in the undo segments; MAXVALUE will be the current SCN. In other words, the query as written will show all versions that can possibly be retrieved, given the information available. The syntax will also accept a range specified with two timestamps:

```
SQL> select empno,ename,sal,versions_xid,versions_starttime,
versions_endtime,versions_operation from emp versions between
timestamp to_timestamp(systimestamp - 1/24) and systimestamp
where empno=8000;
```

This example will select all versions of employee number 8000 that existed during the last hour.

Flashback Transaction Query

Flashback Table Query and Flashback Versions Query use undo data for an object. Flashback Transaction Query analyzes the undo by a different dimension: it will retrieve all the undo data for a transaction, no matter how many objects it affects. The critical view is FLASHBACK_TRANSACATION_QUERY, described here:

```
ocp10g> describe flashback_transaction_query
 Name                                      Null?     Type
 ----------------------------------------- --------  ---------------------
 XID                                                 RAW(8)
 START_SCN                                           NUMBER
 START_TIMESTAMP                                     DATE
 COMMIT_SCN                                          NUMBER
 COMMIT_TIMESTAMP                                    DATE
 LOGON_USER                                          VARCHAR2(30)
 UNDO_CHANGE#                                        NUMBER
 OPERATION                                           VARCHAR2(32)
 TABLE_NAME                                          VARCHAR2(256)
 TABLE_OWNER                                         VARCHAR2(32)
 ROW_ID                                              VARCHAR2(19)
 UNDO_SQL                                            VARCHAR2(4000)
```

Because the data in this view may be sensitive, it is protected by a privilege: you must have been granted SELECT ANY TRANSACTION before you can query it. By default, this privilege is granted to SYS and to the DBA role. There will be one or more rows in this view for every transaction whose undo data still exists in the undo segments, and every row will refer to one row affected by the transaction. Table 29-1 describes the columns.

Column Name	Description
XID	The transaction identifier. This is the join column to the pseudo-column VERSIONS_XID displayed in a Flashback Versions Query
START_SCN	The system change number at the time the transaction started
START_TIMESTAMP	The timestamp at the time the transaction started
COMMIT_SCN	The system change number at the time the transaction was committed
COMMIT_TIMESTAMP	The timestamp at the time the transaction was committed
LOGON_USER	The Oracle username of the session that performed the transaction
UNDO_CHANGE#	The undo system change number. This is not likely to be relevant to most work
OPERATION	The DML operation applied to the row: INSERT, UPDATE, or DELETE
TABLE_NAME	The table to which the row belongs
TABLE_OWNER	The schema to which the table belongs
ROW_ID	The unique identifier of the row affected
UNDO_SQL	A constructed statement that will reverse the operation. For example, if the OPERATION were a DELETE, then this will be an INSERT

Table 29-1   Flashback Transaction Query Columns

A one-line SQL statement might generate many rows in FLASHBACK_TRANSACTION_ QUERY. This is because SQL is a set-oriented language: one statement can affect many rows. But each row affected will have its own row in the view. The view will show committed transactions and also transactions in progress. For an active transaction, the COMMIT_SCN and COMMIT_TIMESTAMP columns are NULL. Rolled-back transactions are not displayed.

Take an example where a salary was multiplied by eleven, rather than being incremented by ten percent:

```
SQL> update emp set sal =sal*11 where empno=7902;
1 row updated.
SQL> commit;
Commit complete.
```

Later, it is suspected that there was a mistake made. So query the versions of the row:

```
SQL> select ename,sal,versions_xid from emp versions between scn
  2  minvalue and maxvalue where empno=7902;
ENAME            SAL VERSIONS_XID
---------- ---------- ----------------
FORD           33000 06002600B0010000
FORD            3000
```

This does indicate what happened, and it gives enough information to reverse the change. But what if the transaction affected other rows in other tables? To be certain, query FLASHBACK_TRANSACTION_QUERY, which will have one row for every row affected by the transaction. A minor complication is that the XID column is type RAW, whereas the VERSIONS_XID pseudo-column is hexadecimal, so you must use a type-casting function to make the join:

```
SQL> select operation,undo_sql from flashback_transaction_query
where xid=hextoraw('06002600B0010000');
OPERATION   UNDO_SQL
----------  ---------------------------------------------------------
UPDATE      update "SCOTT"."EMP" set "SAL" = '3000' where ROWID =
            'AAAM+yAAEAAAAAeAAM';
```

This query returns only one row, which confirms that there was indeed only one row affected by the transaction, and provides a statement that will reverse the impact of the change. Note the use of a ROWID in the UNDO_SQL statement. Provided that there has been no reorganization of the table, this will guarantee that the correct row is changed.

Exercise 29-2: Using Flashback Query with Database Control

Create a table, execute some DML, and then investigate and reverse the changes.

1. Connect to your database as user SYSTEM using SQL*Plus.

2. Create a table and enable row movement for it.
   ```
   SQL> create table countries (name varchar2(10));
   SQL> alter table countries enable row movement;
   ```

3. Insert some rows as follows.
   ```
   SQL> insert into countries values('Zambia');
   SQL> insert into countries values('Zimbabwe');
   SQL> insert into countries values ('Zamibia');
   SQL> commit;
   ```

   Correct the spelling mistake, but omit the WHERE clause.
   ```
   SQL> update countries set name= 'Namibia';
   SQL> commit;
   ```

4. Connect to your database as user SYSTEM with Database Control.

5. From the database home page, take the Maintenance tab and then the Perform Recovery link in the Backup/Recovery section to reach the Perform Recovery: Type window.

6. In the Object Type drop-down box, choose Tables, and select the Flashback Existing Tables radio button. Click Next to reach the Perform Recovery: Point-in-time window.

7. Select the "Evaluate row changes and transactions to decide on point in time" radio button, and enter **SYSTEM.COUNTRIES** as the table, as in Figure 29-7. Click Next to reach the Perform Recovery: Flashback Versions Query Filter window.

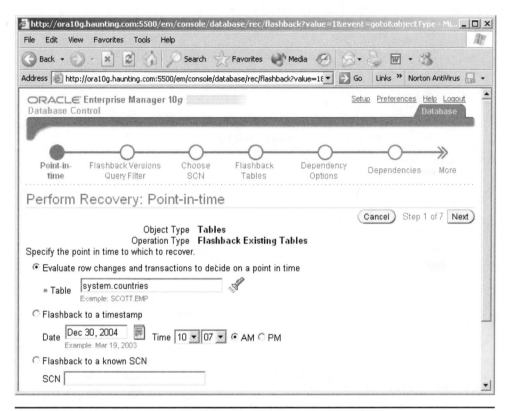

Figure 29-7 Select a table for Flashback Query.

8. In the "Step 1" section, highlight the column NAME and click the Move link to select it for the query. In the "Step 2" section, enter **WHERE NAME LIKE '%'** in order to see all rows. In the "Step 3" section, select the Show All Row History radio button.

   Click Next to reach the Perform Recovery: Choose SCN window shown in Figure 29-8.

9. Note that there are two transactions: the first did the three inserts; the second updated the rows. Select the radio button for one of the "Namibia" rows, and click Next to reach the Perform Recovery: Flashback Tables window.

10. Click Next to reach the Perform Recovery: Review window. Click Show Row Changes to see what will be done by this operation, and Show SQL to see the actual FLASHBACK TABLE statement. Click Submit to execute it.

11. In your SQL*Plus session, confirm that the rows are now back as when first inserted, complete with the spelling mistake.

    ```
    SQL:> select * from countries;
    ```

12. Tidy up.

    ```
    SQL> drop table countries;
    ```

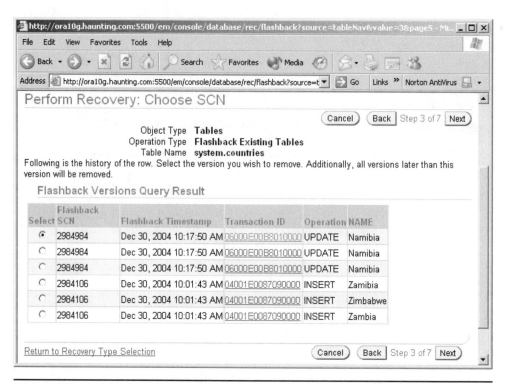

Figure 29-8 Flashback Versions Query

Flashback and Undo Data

Flashback query in its various forms relies entirely on undo data. You are asking Oracle to present you a version of the data as it was some time ago; if the data has been changed since that time, Oracle must roll back the changes. To do this, Oracle needs the undo data that protected the change. Whether the query will succeed will depend on whether that undo data is still available. Consider Figure 29-9. The first query asks for a view of the table as it was forty minutes ago, and it succeeds. This is because there is at least forty minutes of undo data available in the undo segments. The second query attempts to go back forty days, and it fails. In virtually all databases, it would be completely unrealistic to expect Flashback Query to work over such a long period. You would need an undo tablespace the size of Jupiter to store that much undo data.

Undo data is generated as necessary according to the transaction workload: at busy times of day you may be generating many megabytes of undo per second; at other times you may be generating virtually no undo at all. As undo data can be overwritten once the transaction is completed, the age of the oldest undo data available in the undo tablespace will vary depending on workload. A comprehensive discussion

```
Oracle SQL*Plus
File Edit Search Options Help
ocp10g>
ocp10g>
ocp10g> select count(*) from hr.regions as of timestamp (systimestamp - 40/1440);

  COUNT(*)
----------
         4

ocp10g> select count(*) from hr.regions as of timestamp (systimestamp - 40);
select count(*) from hr.regions as of timestamp (systimestamp - 40)
                                *
ERROR at line 1:
ORA-08180: no snapshot found based on specified time


ocp10g> |
```

Figure 29-9 Flashback Query and undo data

of this was included in Chapter 16 with reference to the "ORA-1555: snapshot too old" error, and this is equally relevant to Flashback Query.

To guarantee that a Flashback Query will always succeed for a given period, set the RETENTION GUARANTEE attribute for the undo tablespace, in conjunction with the UNDO_RETENTION instance parameter. This will ensure that you can always flash back the number of seconds specified, but the price you will pay is that if your undo tablespace is not sized adequately for the transaction workload, then the database may hang for DML. As discussed in Chapter 16, you must monitor the V$UNDOSTAT view to calculate the necessary size.

Chapter Review

The Flashback technologies detailed in this chapter have been Flashback Drop and the various options for Flashback Query. These are completely different from the Flashback Database described in Chapter 28.

Flashback Drop lets you "undrop" a table, together with any associated objects. It is actually implemented by renaming dropped objects rather than physically dropping them, which puts them in the recycle bin. They are only actually dropped when the space they occupy is needed for live objects, or by the use of the PURGE command. There is no guarantee that a Flashback Drop will succeed; this will depend on whether the space used by the dropped object has been reused.

Flashback Query allows you to query the database as it was at some time in the past; it is implemented by the use of undo data. The simplest version of Flashback Query is to use the AS OF keyword in a SELECT statement. Flashback Versions Query displays all versions of a row between two times, with various pseudo-columns to identify what happened. Flashback Table Query uses the Flashback Versions Query data to reverse changes made to a table; Flashback Transaction Query uses it to reverse changes made by a transaction. By default there is no guarantee that a Flashback Query will succeed, but by setting the RETENTION GUARANTEE attribute for your undo tablespace, you can change this.

These Flashback technologies are online operations; your end users will not notice that they are in progress. They are enabled automatically and are always available when the applicable privileges have been granted.

Questions

1. Different Flashback technologies use different data structures. For each technology, A to G, choose the data structure, a to e, upon which it relies.

A. Use of DBMS_FLASHBACK	a. The redo log (online and/or archive)
B. Flashback Database	b. Undo segments
C. Flashback Drop	c. The recycle bin
D. Flashback Table Query	d. The flashback log
E. Flashback Transaction Query	e. RMAN backups, in the flash recovery area
F. Flashback Version Query	
G. SELECT ... AS OF	

2. When you drop a table, what objects will go into the recycle bin? (Select all that apply.)

   A. The table

   B. Grants on the table

   C. Indexes on the table

   D. All constraints on the table

   E. All constraints on the table except foreign key constraints

3. After dropping a table, how can you access the rows within it? (Choose the best answer.)

   A. Query the table using the AS OF syntax.

   B. Query the table using the BEFORE DROP syntax.

   C. Query the table using its recycle bin name.

   D. You can't query it until it has been recovered.

4. If a table has been dropped and then another table created with the same name, which of the following statements is correct? (Choose the best answer.)

   A. You must rename the new table before you can flash back the dropped one.

   B. You can flash back the dropped table if you specify a new name for it.

C. You can flash back the dropped table into a different schema.

D. You must drop the new table before flashing back the old one.

5. Under which of the following circumstances will Flashback Drop work? (Choose the best answer.)

A. When a table has been truncated

B. When a table has been purged

C. When a user has been dropped

D. When an index has been dropped

E. None of the above

6. There are two tables in the recycle bin with the same original name. What will happen if you issue a FLASHBACK TABLE <original_name> TO BEFORE DROP command? (Choose the best answer.)

A. The command will return an error.

B. The oldest recycle bin table will be recovered.

C. The newest recycle bin table will be recovered.

D. You can't have two tables in the recycle bin with the same original name.

7. If a Flashback Table operation violates a constraint, what will happen? (Choose the best answer.)

A. The row concerned will not be flashed back, but the rest of the operation will succeed.

B. The flashback operation will hang until the problem is fixed.

C. The flashback operation will be rolled back.

D. You must disable constraints before a table flashback.

8. What is the best technique to flash back two tables in a foreign key relationship? (Choose the best answer.)

A. Flash back the child table, and then the parent table.

B. Flash back the parent table, and then the child table.

C. Flash back both tables in one operation.

D. This is not an issue; foreign key constraints are not protected by flashback.

9. Why and when must you enable row movement on a table before a flashback operation? (Choose the best answer.)

A. Flashback Drop requires row movement, because all the rows in the table will have a different object number.

B. Flashback Query requires row movement, because the rows will have new ROWIDs picked up from the undo segment.

   C. Flashback Transaction requires row movement, because any affected rows
      may be moved as the transaction is reversed.

   D. Flashback Table requires row movement, because any affected rows may be
      moved as the changes are reversed.

10. Study the following screen. Which statements are correct? (Choose two answers.)

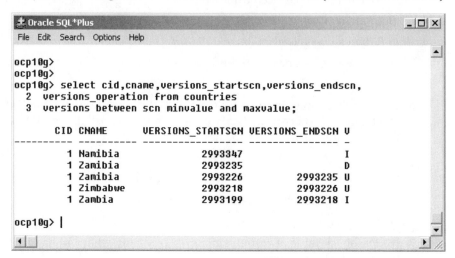

   A. The delete of Zamibia and the insert of Namibia are uncommitted
      changes.

   B. There cannot be a unique constraint on CID for this sequence to be
      possible.

   C. There is currently only one row in the table.

   D. If another session queried the table, it would see Zambia.

   E. If another session queried the table, it would see Namibia.

11. What information can you extract from the pseudo-columns displayed by a
    Flashback Versions Query? (Choose all that apply.)

   A. The timestamps marking the beginning and end of a version's existence

   B. The SCNs marking the beginning and end of a version's existence

   C. The DML operation that created the version

   D. The Oracle user that executed the DML

   E. The transaction that the DML was part of

   F. The statement necessary to reverse the DML

   G. The statement necessary to repeat the DML

12. Which of the following statements are correct about flashback, undo, and retention? (Choose two answers.)

    A. Setting RETENTION GUARANTEE on a user data tablespace will ensure that a Flashback Drop will succeed, if carried out within the UNDO_RETENTION period.

    B. Setting RETENTION GUARANTEE on an undo tablespace will ensure that a Flashback Query will succeed, if carried out within the UNDO_RETENTION period.

    C. RETENTION GUARANTEE defaults to true for undo tablespaces, and false for user data tablespaces.

    D. Flashback Database will always succeed, if the DB_FLASHBACK_RETENTION_TARGET instance parameter is less than the RETENTION_GUARANTEE period.

    E. Setting the RETENTION_GUARANTEE attribute can cause DML to fail.

13. Which view will display details of all transactions, as extracted from the undo segments? (Choose the best answer.)

    A. ALL_TRANSACTIONS

    B. DBA_TRANSACTIONS

    C. FLASHBACK_TRANSACTION_QUERY

    D. UNDO_TRANSACTION_QUERY

14. Which tools can be used to flash back the drop of a table? (Choose all that apply.)

    A. SQL*Plus

    B. Database Control

    C. RMAN

    D. All of the above

15. A Flashback Table operation needs to update a row that another user is already updating. What will happen?

    A. The session doing the flashback will hang until the other session commits or rolls back his change.

    B. The flashback operation will not start unless it can get exclusive access to the table.

    C. The flashback operation will complete, but with an error message stating that the row could not be flashed back.

    D. The flashback operation will fail, with error message stating that a row or table was locked.

16. When querying DBA_OBJECTS, you see that a user owns an object whose name is BIN$Af3JifupQXuKWSpmW0gaGA==$0. What is true about this object? (Choose the best answer.)

    A. It is the user's recycle bin and contains his dropped tables.

    B. It is the user's recycle bin and contains his deleted rows.

    C. It is a dropped table or index and will be purged automatically when its space is needed.

    D. It is a dropped table or index and should be purged manually, because it is taking up space that may be needed for other objects.

Answers

1. **A, D, E, F, and G-b.** Of the seven technologies, five rely on undo segments and are all variations of Flashback Query.
   B-d. Flashback Database uses the flashback logs.
   C-c. Flashback Drop uses the recycle bin.
   Neither the redo log (a) nor your backups (e) have anything to do with flashback.

2. **A and C.** The only items that go into the recycle bin are the table and its indexes. Grants are preserved, but they remain in the data dictionary. The same is true of constraints, except for foreign key constraints, which are dropped.

3. **C.** You can query the table using its system-generated name.

4. **B.** The table must be renamed as part of the flashback to avoid a conflict.

5. **E.** The FLASHBACK DROP command can be applied only to tables, not indexes. Furthermore, the table must not have been purged. Note that you cannot flash back a TRUNCATE, because a truncation does not put anything in the recycle bin.

6. **C.** Oracle will recover the most recent table.

7. **C.** Table flashbacks are implemented as one transaction, which (like any other transaction) will be rolled back if it hits a problem. To disable constraints would be a way around the difficulty but is certainly not a requirement for flashback, and probably not a good idea.

8. **C.** The only way to guarantee success is to flash back both tables together.

9. **D.** Only Flashback Table requires row movement.

10. **C and E.** There is no WHERE clause in the query, so you are seeing the whole table. Versions of rows are always sorted with the newest (or current) version first, so starting from the bottom you can see that a row was inserted; updated twice; deleted; and then another inserted.

11. **A, B, C,** and **E.** The information is in the columns VERSIONS_STARTTIME, VERSIONS_ENDTIME, VERSIONS_STARTSCN, VERSIONS_ENDSCN, VERSIONS_OPERATIONS, and VERSIONS_XID. D and F can be extracted with a Flashback Transaction Query, but G cannot be done with any flashback technology.

12. **B** and **E.** Enabling the retention guarantee ensures that flashback queries will succeed, even if that means blocking DML.

13. **C.** The other views do not exist.

14. **A** and **B.** Flashback Drop can be accessed through SQL*Plus or Database Control only. RMAN can do Flashback Database, but no other flashback operations.

15. **D.** Table flashback requires row locks on every affected row, but unlike with normal DML, if the lock cannot be obtained, rather than waiting it will cancel the whole operation and roll back what work it did manage to do.

16. **C.** This is the naming convention for dropped tables and indexes, which are overwritten when the tablespace comes under space pressure.

CHAPTER 30

Detecting and Recovering from Database Corruption

In this chapter you will learn how to
- Define block corruption and list its causes and symptoms
- Detect database corruptions using the utilities ANALYZE and DBVERIFY
- Detect database corruptions using the DBMS_REPAIR package
- Implement the DB_BLOCK_CHECKING parameter to detect corruptions
- Repair corruptions using RMAN

Sometimes the Oracle blocks that make up a datafile get corrupted. You may be fortunate enough to go though your whole career and never see a corrupted block—or you may be hit by any number of them tomorrow. It is impossible for the DBA to prevent corruptions from occurring, but he can detect them and perhaps mitigate the impact of them on end users. And provided that an adequate backup strategy is in place, he can repair the damage.

It is also possible for a block of an online redo log file, an archive redo log file, or even the controlfile to be corrupted, but managing this is totally beyond the control of the DBA. These files are protected by multiplexing, which should be sufficient. The level of redundancy is specified by your organization's standards, and any further fault tolerance, such as RAID mirroring, is a matter for your system administrators.

This chapter deals with datafile corruption. Although the cause of datafile corruption may be beyond your control, surviving it with no loss of data (and possibly with no downtime either) is certainly within the DBA domain.

Block Corruption and Its Causes

Blocks may be corrupted in two ways: either media corruption or logical (also known as "software") corruption.

A media-corrupt block is a block where the contents of the block make no sense whatsoever: its contents do not match the format expected by Oracle, according to the formatting rules for the tablespace and the objects within it. When a datafile is created, it is formatted into Oracle blocks, of whatever block size was chosen for the tablespace. This is the first level of formatting. A second level occurs when the block is actually used. When an object is allocated an extent, the blocks in the extent are not further formatted, but as the high-water mark of the object is advanced into the new extent, then the blocks receive a second level of formatting, as they take on the characteristics required for that particular segment. If, because of damage to the disks, this formatting is lost, then the block will be "media corrupt."

A logically corrupt block is a block where the Oracle formatting is correct—the block does have the correct header area and a data area—but the contents of the block are internally inconsistent. For example, the block header of a table block includes a row directory, stating where each row begins. If when attempting to find a row, there isn't one, this will be a logical corruption—an Oracle internal error, rather than a media problem.

If the causes of block corruption were fully known, the problem would never occur. As a general rule, block corruption is a hardware or operating system problem. A problem in the I/O system can mean that somewhere in the chain of cause and effect between the DBWn process instructing the operating system to write a block to disk and a server process receiving the block from the operating system in response to a read request, the block has been damaged. It is also possible for a fault in memory to be flushed, accurately, to disk. If block corruptions are reported consistently, then the problem is almost certainly hardware or operating system related.

Logical corruption is also usually hardware related, but it is possible—though extremely rare—for a bug within Oracle itself to cause Oracle to create an inconsistent block. If the hardware and operating system diagnostics do not show any problems, then check the Metalink web site for any known problems with your release of the server software. Any bugs relating to block corruption will have been widely reported, and a patch will be available.

Parameters Relating to Block Corruption

There are two instance parameters that will assist in detecting corrupted blocks: DB_BLOCK_CHECKSUM, which defaults to TRUE, will help detect damage introduced by the disk or I/O systems. DB_BLOCK_CHECKING, which defaults to FALSE, will help detect damage introduced by faulty memory.

With DB_BLOCK_CHECKSUM on TRUE, whenever the DBWn process writes a block to disk it will compute a checksum for the block and include it in the block header. When a server process reads a block, if the checksum is present it will recalculate it and compare. This will mean that any damage occurring in the time between the DBWn writing the block and its being read back will be detected. For normal running on reliable hardware, this should be adequate and will have only a minimal impact on performance. Oracle Corporation advises leaving this parameter on default, so that any damage caused while the block is on disk, or corruptions introduced during the write and read process, will be detected. Even when this parameter is on false, checksumming is still enabled for the SYSTEM tablespace.

EXAM TIP Checksumming and block checking are always enabled for the SYSTEM tablespace, no matter to what these parameters are set.

Setting DB_BLOCK_CHECKING to TRUE will have an impact on performance, and Oracle Corporation advises leaving it on default unless there are specific problems related to corruptions occurring in memory. When set to TRUE, the Oracle processes will check the block for consistency every time the buffer containing the block is accessed. This will mean that if corruptions are occurring in memory, they will be detected immediately, but the price is high—perhaps as much as 10 percent of processing capacity. As with checksumming, block checking is always enabled for the SYSTEM tablespace irrespective of the setting of this parameter.

TIP Oracle Corporation advises leaving both these parameters on default, unless instructed otherwise by Oracle Support.

Detecting Block Corruptions

A corrupted block may be detected by your users when they try to read it, but ideally you will have detected it before any user notices the problem. There are utilities that will help with this.

The examples that follow are from a Windows system, based on a tablespace called DAMAGED with a datafile DAM.DBF. The tablespace was created and a table, CORRUPT_TAB, created within it, and a primary key constraint added. This caused the creation of an index, called CORR_PK, on the constrained column. Then the file was deliberately damaged by using an editor to change a few bytes of some blocks of the CORRUPT_TAB table. This is a reasonable simulation of either media or logical corruption: the file still exists and is of the correct size, but the contents have been damaged externally to Oracle. The index, however, is not directly affected.

The Corrupted Block Error Message

Figure 30-1 shows the message you hope you will never see, an ORA-01578 telling you that there is a corrupted block.

The first query succeeds. This is because although the query appears to request a full table scan, in fact Oracle can execute the query without reading the table at all. There is a primary key constraint on the table, which means that Oracle can count the number of rows by scanning the index, not the table. It will usually be quicker to do this. The second query, which requires reading the table itself, fails with an ORA-01578 error message that lists the address of the corrupted block. The message is

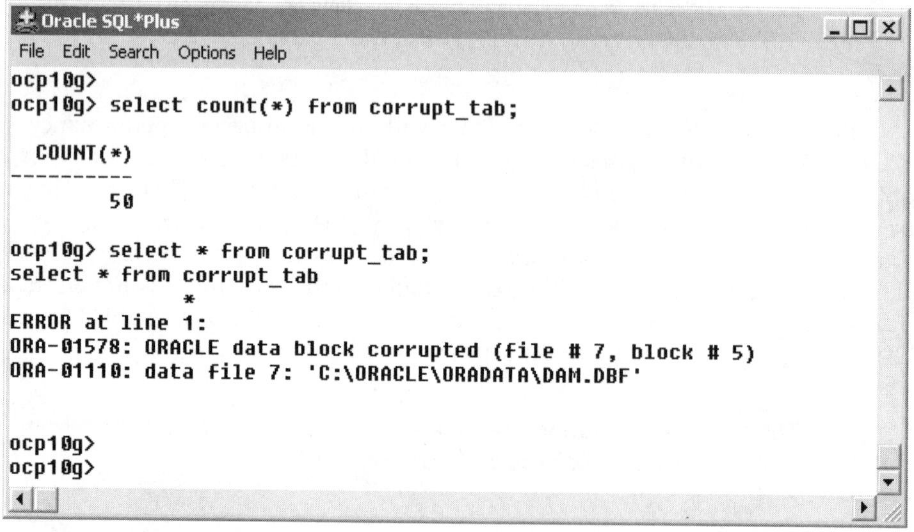

Figure 30-1   A corrupt block encountered during a full table scan

returned to the session that detected the problem, but there is also this message in the alert log:

```
Hex dump of (file 7, block 5) in trace file
c:\oracle\product\10.1.0\admin\ocp10g\udump\ocp10g_ora_3508.trc
Corrupt block relative dba: 0x01c00004 (file 7, block 5)
Bad header found during buffer read
Data in bad block:
 type: 16 format: 2 rdba: 0x01c02004
 last change scn: 0x2020.20267bf9 seq: 0x2 flg: 0x04
 spare1: 0x20 spare2: 0x20 spare3: 0x2020
 consistency value in tail: 0x7bf91002
 check value in block header: 0x2cbf
computed block checksum: 0x0
Reread of rdba: 0x01c00004 (file 7, block 5) found same corrupted data
Thu Dec 16 14:25:40 2004
Corrupt Block Found
        TSN = 21, TSNAME = DAMAGED
        RFN  7, BLK = 5, rdba = 29360132
        OBJN = 52077, OBJD = 52077, OBJECT= , SUBOBJECT =
        Segment Owner= , Segment Type =
```

This tells you again the file and block number, and at the end another vital piece of information: the number of the object that the block is part of, in this case object number 52077. To identify the object, run

```
SQL> select owner,object_name,object_type from dba_objects where object_id=52077;
```

An alternative query to identify the object would be to match the data block address against the DBA_EXTENTS view. To identify which segment includes an extent that covers the fifth block of the seventh datafile,

```
ocp10g> select owner,segment_name,segment_type from dba_extents where
  2  file_id=7 and 5 between block_id and block_id + blocks;
OWNER                SEGMENT_NAME     SEGMENT_TYPE
-------------------- ---------------- ------------------
HR                   CORRUPT_TAB      TABLE
```

This is an example of a problem that could have existed for some considerable time. Unless the corruption is in the header blocks of the datafile, it will only be detected when the block is read by a server process. Generally, you should aim to detect such problems before a user hits them.

The DBVERIFY Utility

DBVERIFY is an external utility run from an operating system prompt to verify datafiles (see Figure 30-2). It can be run against files while they are in use, or against image copies made with user-managed backups or by RMAN. It cannot verify online or archive redo logs, nor the controlfile, nor RMAN backup sets. The files to be verified can exist on a conventional file system, or on Automatic Storage Management disks, or on raw devices; the syntax is identical except that for a raw device you must tell DBVERIFY a range of blocks to look at, because it will have no other way of knowing where the file ends. The only required argument is the name of the file to verify—the optional arguments START and END let you specify a range of blocks to be verified.

The executable for DBVERIFY is $ORACLE_HOME/bin/dbv on Unix, %ORACLE_HOME%\bin\dbv.exe on Windows. In the output, a block is referred to as a page. The output (with the possible exception of "Total Pages Influx") is self-explanatory: details of every block found to be corrupt, followed by a summary of the state of all blocks. If "Total Pages Influx" is greater than zero, it is not an indication of any problem; it merely shows that while DBVERIFY was running against an open file, it encountered a block that was currently being written to by the DBWn process. When that happens, it will re-read the block until it gets a consistent image. "Total Pages Influx" is the number of times it had to do this.

If you are using RMAN to back up your datafiles, DBVERIFY is not needed, because RMAN will perform its own verification. DBVERIFY is essential if you are using user-managed backups, in order to determine that the backups are actually usable.

 EXAM TIP DBVERIFY works against datafiles, live or backup, but nothing else.

```
C:\WINDOWS\System32\cmd.exe                                          _ □ ×

C:\oracle\product\101~1.0\oradata\ocp10g>dbv file=dam1.dbf

DBVERIFY: Release 10.1.0.2.0 - Production on Sat Jun 4 15:34:34 2005

Copyright (c) 1982, 2004, Oracle.  All rights reserved.

DBVERIFY - Verification starting : FILE = dam1.dbf

Page 5 is marked corrupt
Corrupt block relative dba: 0x01c00004 (file 7, block 5)
Bad header found during dbv:
Data in bad block:
 type: 16 format: 2 rdba: 0x01c02004
 last change scn: 0x2020.20267bf9 seq: 0x2 flg: 0x04
 spare1: 0x20 spare2: 0x20 spare3: 0x2020
 consistency value in tail: 0x7bf91002
 check value in block header: 0x2cbf
 block checksum disabled


DBVERIFY - Verification complete

Total Pages Examined       : 130
Total Pages Processed (Data) : 20
Total Pages Failing   (Data) : 1
Total Pages Processed (Index): 0
Total Pages Failing   (Index): 0
Total Pages Processed (Other): 4
Total Pages Processed (Seg)  : 0
Total Pages Failing   (Seg)  : 0
Total Pages Empty           : 106
Total Pages Marked Corrupt  : 1
Total Pages Influx          : 0

C:\oracle\product\101~1.0\oradata\ocp10g>
```

Figure 30-2   Running DBVERIFY

The ANALYZE Command

The primary purpose of ANALYZE is to gather statistics that will be used by the optimizer to work out the most efficient way of executing a SQL statement. But it does have another use: checking whether a table or an index is corrupted. There are three forms of the command:

```
SQL> analyze table <tablename> validate structure;
SQL> analyze index <indexname> validate structure;
SQL> analyze table <tablename> validate structure cascade;
```

When validating the structure of a table, ANALYZE verifies the integrity of each of the data blocks and rows; when validating the structure of an index, it verifies the integrity of the data blocks and the index keys. The CASCADE option will verify both the table and any associated indexes. The check will be of all blocks below the high-water mark of the segments, so unlike DBVERIFY it will not warn you of problems in space not yet used.

 TIP CASCADE can be a very time-consuming process for large objects because it checks to ensure each index entry points to a valid table row.

Two side effects of ANALYZE...VALIDATE STRUCTURE are that for partitioned tables it will check that rows are in the correct partition, and for indexes it will compute the ratio of space devoted to active index entries and space wasted because the index entries refer to deleted rows. To see the latter information, query the view INDEX_STATS.

The DBMS_REPAIR Package

DBMS_REPAIR is a set of procedures that will check objects for problems and make the objects usable again.

Before you can do anything with it, you must create a table that DBMS_REPAIR uses to store its output:

```
SQL> exec dbms_repair.admin_tables(-
table_name=>'REPAIR_CORRUPT_TAB',-
table_type=>dbms_repair.repair_table,-
action=>dbms_repair.create_action);
```

This procedure call creates a table REPAIR_CORRUPT_TAB, which will store details of any problems encountered when checking a table. The table's name must be prefixed with REPAIR_ and will be created in the SYS schema. Then invoke the CHECK_OBJECT procedure as in Figure 30-3.

If any blocks in a table are found to be corrupted, the details of which block and the object affected will be written out to the repair table. There will also be a suggestion as to how to repair the damage: in the example, by marking the block as "software corrupt." This would not repair the damage in the sense of correcting the damage, but

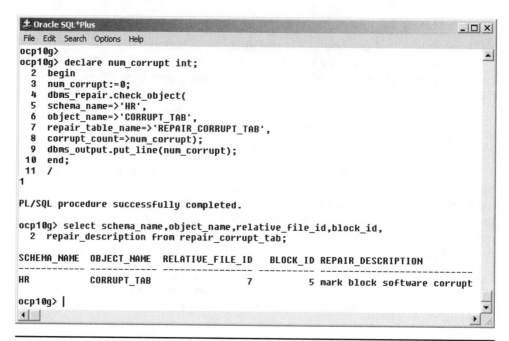

Figure 30-3 Using DBMS_REPAIR to verify a table

it would make the object usable again, which may be better than having statements fail repeatedly with ORA-01578.

To follow the advice, use DBMS_REPAIR.FIX_CORRUPT_BLOCKS to mark the damaged blocks as corrupted, then DBMS_REPAIR.SKIP_CORRUPT_BLOCKS to instruct Oracle to ignore any blocks so marked. This will allow sessions to access the object without any errors, though the data in the damaged blocks will be missing. This can result in unexpected effects, as in Figure 30-4.

The routine in the figure has made the table usable, in the sense that it can now be scanned without errors—but some data is missing. In the example, every row is gone. But as far as the index is concerned, the rows still exist. This imbalance should be corrected by rebuilding all the table's indexes with ALTER INDEX...REBUILD ONLINE. Before you do this, consider the possibilities of interrogating the indexes by running queries that only select the indexed columns, to retrieve as much information as possible regarding the missing rows. Depending on the degree of redundancy between indexes and table (how many columns are actually included in one index or another?), you may be able to reconstruct a significant amount of each missing row.

TIP DBMS_REPAIR provides a way of making damaged tables usable without any downtime, but the price you pay is losing the data. Before deciding to do this, consider the extent of the damage, the effect on the business, and whether a restore and recover operation would be more appropriate.

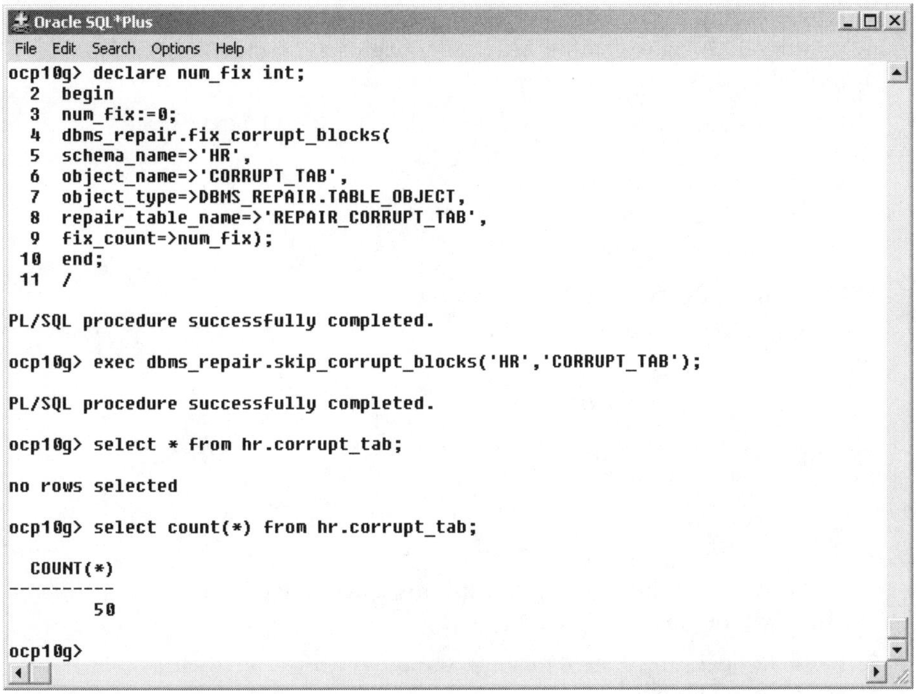

```
± Oracle SQL*Plus                                                    _ □ x
File  Edit  Search  Options  Help
ocp10g> declare num_fix int;
  2  begin
  3  num_fix:=0;
  4  dbms_repair.fix_corrupt_blocks(
  5  schema_name=>'HR',
  6  object_name=>'CORRUPT_TAB',
  7  object_type=>DBMS_REPAIR.TABLE_OBJECT,
  8  repair_table_name=>'REPAIR_CORRUPT_TAB',
  9  fix_count=>num_fix);
 10  end;
 11  /

PL/SQL procedure successfully completed.

ocp10g> exec dbms_repair.skip_corrupt_blocks('HR','CORRUPT_TAB');

PL/SQL procedure successfully completed.

ocp10g> select * from hr.corrupt_tab;

no rows selected

ocp10g> select count(*) from hr.corrupt_tab;

  COUNT(*)
----------
        50

ocp10g>
```

Figure 30-4 Repairing a table with corrupted blocks

Exercise 30-1: Checking for Block Corruptions

Create a tablespace and a table, and confirm that there are no corrupt blocks.

1. Connect to your database with SQL*Plus as user SYSTEM.

2. Create a tablespace called NEW_TBS. For example, on Unix,

   ```
   SQL> create tablespace new_tbs datafile
   '/oracle/oradata/new_tbs.dbf' size 2m;
   ```

   or on Windows,

   ```
   SQL> create tablespace new_tbs datafile
   '\oracle\oradata\new_tbs.dbf' size 2m;
   ```

3. Create a table within the new tablespace, and identify which blocks in which files the table is occupying.

   ```
   SQL>  create table new_tab tablespace new_tbs as
   select * from all_users;
   Table created.
   SQL> select extent_id,file_id,block_id,blocks from dba_extents
     2  where owner='SYSTEM' and segment_name='NEW_TAB';
    EXTENT_ID    FILE_ID   BLOCK_ID      BLOCKS
   ---------- ---------- ---------- ----------
            0          9          9          8
   SQL>
   ```

In this example, the table has just one extent, extent_id 0, which is in file number 9, the new datafile. The extent begins at block number 9 and is 8 blocks big. Your results may differ from this.

4. Connect as SYS, and use DBMS_REPAIR to create the repair table.

```
SQL> exec dbms_repair.admin_tables(-
table_name=>'REPAIR_TABLE',-
table_type=>dbms_repair.repair_table,-
action=>dbms_repair.create_action,-
tablespace=>'NEW_TBS');
```

5. Check the NEW_TAB table for corruptions.

```
SQL> declare num_corrupt int;
  2  begin
  3  dbms_repair.check_object(
  4  schema_name=>'SYSTEM',
  5  object_name=>'NEW_TAB',
  6  repair_table_name=>'REPAIR_TABLE',
  7  corrupt_count=>num_corrupt);
  8  end;
  9  /
PL/SQL procedure successfully completed.
```

6. To confirm that there are no corruptions, query the table REPAIR_TABLE. There will be no rows.

7. From an operating system prompt, use DBVERIFY to verify the table. For example, on Unix,

```
$ dbv file=/oracle/oradata/new_tbs.dbf blocksize=8192
```

or on Windows,

```
C:\> dbv file=\oracle\oradata\new_tbs.dbf blocksize=8192
```

The output will resemble this:

```
DBVERIFY - Verification complete
Total Pages Examined          : 256
Total Pages Processed (Data) : 1
Total Pages Failing   (Data) : 0
Total Pages Processed (Index): 0
Total Pages Failing   (Index): 0
Total Pages Processed (Other): 10
Total Pages Processed (Seg)  : 0
Total Pages Failing   (Seg)  : 0
Total Pages Empty            : 245
Total Pages Marked Corrupt   : 0
Total Pages Influx           : 0
```

Recovering Corrupt Blocks with RMAN

If you are making user-managed backups, you cannot perform a block recovery, because the granularity of a user-managed restore is the datafile. If one block of a file many gigabytes big is corrupted, you must restore and recover the entire datafile through the usual routine:

- Take the damaged file offline.

- Restore the file from a backup made before the corruption occurred.

- Recover the file completely.

- Bring the recovered file online.

This can be done with zero data loss, but the impact on your users, in terms of downtime, may be enormous. RMAN backups open the possibility of block-level restore and recovery, perhaps with no downtime at all.

 EXAM TIP Block media recovery is applicable only to datafile blocks. If a block of an online log file, an archive log file, or a controlfile is corrupted, you must have a multiplexed copy available if you ever need to recover.

Detection of Corrupt Blocks

RMAN will detect corrupt blocks as it performs backup operations. A user-managed backup routine will generally detect a hardware corruption, because the operating system utility you are using will have a problem reading the file, but it cannot detect software corruption: damage where the file is still readable by the operating system but the contents would not make sense to Oracle. RMAN, being an Oracle-aware tool, will verify the contents of data blocks as it reads them; unless instructed otherwise, it will terminate the backup as soon as it hits a corrupt block. If you wish, you can run RMAN backups that specify a tolerance for corrupted blocks. If this is done, then rather than throwing an error and terminating the backup immediately when a corruption is detected, RMAN will continue to back up the datafile but will record the addresses of any corruptions it encounters in its repository. This example instructs RMAN to continue a backup as long as no more than one hundred corrupt blocks are encountered:

```
RMAN> run {
set maxcorrupt for datafile 7 to 100;
backup datafile 7;}
```

The details of corrupt blocks are visible in two places. The view V$DATABASE_BLOCK_CORRUPTION shows the address of the cause of the problem: the datafile file number and block number. The address of the block in the backup is recorded in V$BACKUP_CORRUPTION for backup set backups, or in V$COPY_CORRUPTION if the backup were to an image copy. In normal running, you would not use the SET MAXCORRUPT keywords. Without them, the backup will fail and you will thus be made aware of the problem immediately. Then re-run the backup with SET MAXCORRUPT and after completion query the views to determine the extent of the damage.

By default, RMAN will always check for physical corruption, known as "media corruption" in the non-RMAN world. An example of this would be a block that Oracle cannot process at all: an invalid checksum, or a block full of zeros. RMAN can also be instructed to check for logical corruption, also known as "software corruption,"

PART II

as well. These checks will occur whenever a file is backed up, whether as an image copy or into a backup set. To override the defaults,

```
RMAN> backup nochecksum datafile 7;
```

will not check for physical corruption, and

```
RMAN> backup check logical datafile 6;
```

will check for logical as well as physical corruption.

Block Media Recovery

If RMAN has detected a block corruption, it can do Block Media Recovery, or BMR. BMR changes the granularity of a restore and recovery operation from the datafile to just the damaged blocks. This has two huge advantages over file restore and recover: first, the file does not have to be taken offline; normal DML can continue. Second, the mean time to recover is much reduced, since only the damaged blocks are involved in the operation, not the whole file. The only downtime that will occur is if a session happens to hit a block that is actually damaged and has not yet been recovered.

The BMR mechanism provides RMAN with a list of one of more blocks that need recovery. RMAN will extract backups of these blocks from a backup set or an image copy and write them to the datafile. Then RMAN will pass through the archive logs generated since the backup and extract redo records relevant to the restored blocks and apply them. The recovery will always be complete—it would be logically impossible to do an incomplete recovery; incomplete recovery of just one block would leave the database in an inconsistent state. If a session hits a corrupted block before the BMR process has completed, then it will still receive an ORA-01578 error, but it is quite possible that the BMR operation will be complete before any users are aware of the problem.

 EXAM TIP BMR can be applied to any data block whatsoever. Unlike DBMS_REPAIR, it is not restricted to tables and indexes; LOB and UNDO segments can also be block-recovered.

The BLOCKRECOVER Command

The BLOCKRECOVER command always specifies a list of one or more blocks to be restored and recovered, and it optionally specifies the backup from which the restore should be made. For example, this command,

```
RMAN> blockrecover datafile 7 block 5;
```

Instructs RMAN to restore and recover the one specified block from the most recent backup set or image copy of the file (see Figure 30-5). The syntax would also accept a list of blocks in several files:

```
RMAN> blockrecover datafile 7 block 5,6,7 datafile 9 block 21,25;
```

```
C:\WINDOWS\System32\cmd.exe - rman target /                          _ □ ×

RMAN> blockrecover datafile 7 block 5;

Starting blockrecover at 18-DEC-04
using channel ORA_DISK_1

channel ORA_DISK_1: restoring block(s)
channel ORA_DISK_1: specifying block(s) to restore from backup set
restoring blocks of datafile 00007
channel ORA_DISK_1: restored block(s) from backup piece 1
piece handle=C:\ORACLE\PRODUCT\10.1.0\FLASH_RECOVERY_AREA\OCP10G\BACKUPSET\2004_
12_17\O1_MF_NNNDF_TAG20041217T215642_0W6GHUL6_.BKP tag=TAG20041217T215642
channel ORA_DISK_1: block restore complete
failover to previous backup

channel ORA_DISK_1: restoring block(s)
channel ORA_DISK_1: specifying block(s) to restore from backup set
restoring blocks of datafile 00007
channel ORA_DISK_1: restored block(s) from backup piece 1
piece handle=C:\ORACLE\PRODUCT\10.1.0\FLASH_RECOVERY_AREA\OCP10G\BACKUPSET\2004_
12_16\O1_MF_NNNDF_TAG20041216T164507_0W37UNXY_.BKP tag=TAG20041216T164507
channel ORA_DISK_1: block restore complete

starting media recovery
media recovery complete

Finished blockrecover at 18-DEC-04

RMAN>
```

Figure 30-5   Block media recovery with RMAN

There may be doubt regarding the integrity of the backups. In that case, you can instruct RMAN to restore the block(s) from a backup that is known to be good:

```
RMAN> blockrecover datafile 7 block 5 from backupset 1093;
```

will restore from the nominated backup set, which could also be specified by a tag:

```
RMAN> blockrecover datafile 7 block 5 from tag monthly_whole;
```

If the damage is more extensive, then two other options for BMR will simplify the process. First, provided that RMAN has populated the view V$DATABASE_BLOCK_CORRUPTION by running a backup with MAXCORRUPT set to greater than zero, then the CORRUPTION LIST option will instruct RMAN to restore and recover every block listed in the view. Second, to ensure that the backup(s) used for the restore are from a time before the corruption occurred, there is the UNTIL option. For example,

```
RMAN> blockrecover corruption list until time sysdate - 7;
```

instructs RMAN to restore and recover every block that has been discovered to be damaged by a previous backup operation, using only backups made at least one week ago.

EXAM TIP In the BMR context, the keyword UNTIL does not denote an incomplete recovery! It means that the restore must be from a backup made before a particular date (or sequence number or SCN).

Exercise 30-2: Carrying Out a Block Media Recovery

1. Connect to your database with RMAN, using operating system authentication.

   ```
   rman target /
   ```

2. Back up the datafile created in Exercise 30-1, Step 2, either by name or by specifying the file number listed by the query in Exercise 30-1, Step 3, and tag the backup. For example,

   ```
   RMAN> backup datafile 9 tag file9;
   ```

3. From your SQL*Plus session, force a log switch and archive.

   ```
   SQL> alter system archive log current;
   ```

4. Perform a block recovery of some of the blocks assigned to the NEW_TAB table. Choose any blocks covered by the extent listed by the query in Exercise 30-1, Step 3. For example,

   ```
   RMAN> blockrecover file 9 block 10,11,12 from tag 'file9';
   ```

5. Tidy up by dropping the tablespace.

   ```
   SQL> drop tablespace new_tbs including contents and datafiles;
   ```

Dealing with Corruptions

The first step is to identify that a corruption has in fact occurred. You could wait for users to report ORA-01578 errors, or you can detect corruptions in advance by running DBVERIFY against your live datafiles and your user-managed backups. RMAN will also detect corruptions: by default, the RMAN backup will fail when it hits a corrupted block.

Having located one or more corrupt blocks, you must identify the object to which they belong. Or if you know the object that is damaged, then the DBMS_REPAIR .CHECK_OBJECT procedure can scan the object to identify the corrupted blocks.

Once the extent of the damage is known, you can decide what action to take. Provided that you have an adequate backup strategy in place, either user-managed or with RMAN, you will always be able to carry out a complete recovery. The only exception would be if the corruption occurred so long ago that it is included in all your backups. By default this is not possible with RMAN, but it could occur with user-managed backups if you don't ever verify them with DBVERIFY. A normal complete recovery involves downtime: any objects with extents in the datafile being restored and recovered will not be available for use until the recovery is finished. There are other techniques that will avoid this.

If the damage is limited to an index, you can drop the index and re-create it. This may be transparent to your end users, though if the index is used for enforcing a unique or primary key constraint, the constraint will have to be disabled and the table locked for DML until the index is rebuilt by re-enabling the constraint:

```
ocp10g> alter table corrupt_tab disable validate constraint corr_pk;
Table altered.
ocp10g> delete from corrupt_tab;
delete from corrupt_tab
       *
ERROR at line 1:
ORA-25128: No insert/update/delete on table with constraint
(HR.CORR_PK) disabled and validated
ocp10g> alter table corrupt_tab enable validate constraint corr_pk;
Table altered.
ocp10g>
```

If the damage is to a table, you can consider using the DBMS_REPAIR package to fix the table. This will make the table usable, but the rows in the damaged blocks will be gone. Also you must rebuild all associated indexes, but this can be done online. This decision to lose data is a grave one, but the zero downtime may sometimes make it the best option.

Finally, if you are using RMAN for your backups, you have the possibility of a complete block recovery, with no downtime. This is often the best answer.

While fixing the data damage caused by a corruption, you must also identify and fix the cause of the problem. This problem is likely to be due to faults occurring in the server machine's I/O systems, on its disks, or in its memory: this type of error is outside the database administration domain. Your system administrators will have appropriate diagnostic tools to check all of these. There is also a remote possibility that some releases of the Oracle database software on some platforms may have bugs that can cause software corruptions; these will be documented on Metalink, and there will be patches available to correct the problem.

Chapter Review

Database block corruption should never occur. But it does happen. Oracle will, by default, detect media corruptions that occurred during a block's sojourn on disk; by setting the DB_BLOCK_CHECKING parameter, you can extend its checking to include software corruptions, or with DB_BLOCK_CHECKSUM you can disable the physical check. If a server process detects an error, it will return an ORA-01578 message to the session, and a message goes to the alert log.

A good DBA will proactively detect corruptions before the users hit them, by using DBVERIFY to scan datafiles, or by monitoring the success of his RMAN backups. Then, depending on the extent of the damage and the objects damaged, he has the choice between a restore and complete recovery of the datafiles affected; or simply marking the damaged blocks as corrupted with DBMS_REPAIR; or dropping and re-creating the object. A better solution, if using RMAN for backups, may be block media recovery.

Questions

1. You have these parameter settings:

   DB_BLOCK_CHECKSUM=true
   DB_BLOCK_CHECKING=false

   Which of these statements are correct? (Choose all the correct answers.)

   A. Checksums will be calculated and checked whenever a block is accessed in the database buffer cache.

   B. Checksums will be calculated and checked whenever a block is accessed on disk.

   C. Blocks of the SYSTEM tablespace will always be checked for internal consistency.

   D. Blocks of the SYSTEM, SYSAUX, and active UNDO tablespaces will always be checked for internal consistency.

   E. No blocks will be checked for internal consistency.

2. If a table has corrupted blocks but the primary key index does not, what will be the effect on SELECT statements? (Choose two correct answers.)

   A. Index searches may succeed, depending on what columns are selected.

   B. Index searches may succeed, depending on what rows are selected.

   C. Full table scans may succeed, depending on what columns are selected.

   D. Full table scans may succeed, depending on what rows are selected.

3. Which of the following file types can DBVERIFY verify? (Choose three answers.)

   A. Offline datafiles

   B. Online datafiles

   C. Datafile image copies

   D. RMAN backup sets

   E. Online redo log files

   F. Archive redo log files

4. DBVERIFY reports that a block is INFLUX. What does this mean? (Choose the best answer.)

   A. It is an error denoting a type of corruption.

   B. DBVERIFY could not check the block because it was in use.

   C. DBVERIFY did check the block after a retry.

   D. It indicates that the image of the block on disk is not the same as the image in memory.

5. You issue the command

   ```
   analyze table tab1 cascade;
   ```

   What will be analyzed? (Choose the best answer.)

A. The table TAB1 and any child tables related to it by a foreign key constraint

B. The table TAB1 and any parent tables related to it by a foreign key constraint

C. The table TAB1 and all tables, parent or child, to which it is related

D. The table TAB1 and its indexes

E. The table TAB1 and all its partitions

F. All of the above

6. Which of the following is true about the DBMS_REPAIR package? (Choose the best answer.)

A. You can use it to reconstruct the data contained within a corrupted block by block media recovery.

B. You can use it to reconstruct the data contained within a corrupted block by extracting data from relevant index blocks.

C. You can use it to scan datafiles, but not individual objects.

D. It can make objects usable, but it cannot retrieve lost data.

7. You want to repair a table with corrupted blocks using DBMS_REPAIR. This requires four procedure calls. Put them in the correct order:

A. DBMS_REPAIR.ADMIN_TABLES

B. DBMS_REPAIR.CHECK_OBJECT

C. DBMS_REPAIR.FIX_CORRUPT_OBJECT

D. DBMS_REPAIR.SKIP_CORRUPT_BLOCKS

8. Which of the following statements are correct about Block Media Recovery (BMR)? (Choose two answers.)

A. BMR can be performed only with RMAN.

B. BMR can be performed only with SQL*Plus.

C. Both RMAN and SQL*Plus can be used for BMR.

D. BMR is always a complete recovery.

E. BMR is always an incomplete recovery.

F. BMR can be either complete or incomplete; the DBA decides.

9. If, during an RMAN backup, a corrupt block is encountered, what will happen? (Choose the best answer.)

A. The backup will fail.

B. The backup will succeed.

C. It depends on the MAXCORRUPT setting.

    D. If the corruption is in the SYSTEM tablespace, the backup will fail; otherwise, it will continue, but the address of the corrupt block will be written to the RMAN repository.

10. To what file types is BMR applicable? (Choose the best answer.)

    A. Archive log files

    B. Controlfiles

    C. Datafiles

    D. Online logfiles

    E. Tempfiles

    F. All of the above

11. What will be the effect of issuing this command:

```
blockrecover corruption list until time sysdate - 7;
```

    (Choose the best answer.)

    A. The recovery will be up to but not including the system change number of the time specified.

    B. The recovery will be up to and including the system change number of the time specified.

    C. The recovery will be complete, but the restore will be from before the time specified.

    D. The recovery will be of all blocks entered onto the corruption list before the time specified.

    E. The recovery will be of all blocks entered onto the corruption list after the time specified.

12. You are running BMR against some corrupted blocks of a table, while the database is open. What will be the effect on users' work? (Choose three correct answers.)

    A. Index searches may succeed, depending on what columns are selected.

    B. Index searches may succeed, depending on what rows are selected.

    C. Full table scans may succeed, depending on what columns are selected.

    D. Full table scans may succeed, depending on what rows are selected.

    E. If a session hits a block being recovered, it will hang until the recovery completes.

    F. If a session hits a block being recovered, it will report an ORA-01578 error.

Answers

1. **B and C.** DB_BLOCK_CHECKSUM enables calculation and checking of checksums as they are read from and written to disk, not memory. Irrespective of the DB_BLOCK_CHECKING setting, internal consistency checking is always enabled for the SYSTEM tablespace, but for others only when the parameter is on TRUE.

2. **A and B.** Index searches will succeed if they only need rows from valid blocks or if the query can be satisfied solely from the columns on the index.

3. **A, B, and C.** DBVERIFY can verify any datafile: online, offline, or a backup copy, but nothing else.

4. **C.** An INFLUX block is one that DBWn was writing while DBVERIFY was trying to verify it. This is not an error, and DBVERIFY will try again until it gets a consistent read.

5. **D.** In the ANALYZE context, CASCADE means the table plus its indexes. If the table happens to be partitioned, all partitions are always checked.

6. **D.** Perhaps unfortunately, DBMS_REPAIR can only make objects usable—it cannot actually repair damaged data.

7. **A, B, C, and D.** The order is alphabetical: A creates the table used to store block addresses. B checks all the blocks. C marks corrupted blocks. D instructs Oracle to ignore blocks so marked.

8. **A and D.** The BLOCKRECOVER command is only available through RMAN, and either recovery is complete or it fails.

9. **C.** By default, RMAN will fail when it hits a corrupt block, but you can override this by setting MAXCORRUPT to a number greater than zero.

10. **C.** BMR is solely applicable to datafiles; they are the only file type to which redo can be applied.

11. **C.** BMR is always complete, and UNTIL specifies the age of the backups to be restored.

12. **A, B, and F.** The index searches will succeed if they can be satisfied purely with the indexed columns, or if they do not include rows in the corrupted blocks. If a session hits a block that is being recovered, it will throw an error.

CHAPTER 31

Tools for Oracle Database 10*g* Tuning

In this chapter you will learn how to

- Use the database advisors to gather information about your database
- Use the SQL Tuning Advisor to improve database performance
- Use automatic undo retention tuning

Database tuning is an extremely skillful task requiring many years of experience. Apart from an understanding of the Oracle instance and database architecture, it also requires intimate knowledge of the hardware, the operating system, and the application. Tuning is a holistic exercise: you cannot tune one aspect of the environment without considering all other aspects.

To assist the DBA with tuning, Oracle collects a vast amount of statistical information about database activity and performance. Interpreting this information correctly is the heart of the tuning process. Oracle database release 10g includes several "advisors" that will assist the novice DBA in this interpretation and also save experienced DBAs from the necessity of checking for certain common, and basic, performance problems.

The Advisor Methodology

The advisors will help to identify the causes of performance problems, and suggest solutions. It is vital to distinguish between causes and symptoms: much effort can be wasted on treating symptoms rather than causes. For example, a simple statistical analysis of activity on the database might show that disk I/O is the bottleneck—the one part of the environment that is slowing down everything else. At first sight, it would seem reasonable to attempt to optimize the disk I/O; one could restructure the physical storage to change the RAID striping strategy, or even install faster disks. But this is tuning the symptom, not the cause. The cause of the problem is not the disks; the cause is the need for disk I/O. It could be that the database is running queries that are doing full table scans, rather than indexes: adding an index might eliminate the need for the disk I/O, which is a far better solution than merely making excessive disk I/O happen a bit faster.

The advisors attempt to perform a root cause analysis. They identify a problem and suggest a solution by following an expert system perfected over many years by enumerable DBAs. At the heart of the tuning methodology is the use of wait events. A wait event is something that causes either one session or the whole instance to hang. There are more than eight hundred different wait events in a 10g database, but for convenience they are grouped into classes.

To see which event class has caused the bulk of the problems, query the V$SYSTEM_WAIT_CLASS view:

```
ocp10g> select wait_class,total_waits,time_waited
  2  from v$system_wait_class order by time_waited;
WAIT_CLASS                      TOTAL_WAITS TIME_WAITED
------------------------------- ----------- -----------
Network                                  33           0
Commit                                   31          84
Configuration                          8185         116
Concurrency                              19         307
Other                                   271        3822
System I/O                             2319        4860
User I/O                               5425       29780
Idle                                   8612     3185078
8 rows selected.
```

This query shows that the worst problem by far is "Idle" events. However, idle events are not a problem; they represent processes hanging because they don't have anything to do. For example, a server process will be idle if it is waiting to receive an instruction from a user process. So of the real problems, disk I/O, both for user sessions and for background processes, is the worst.

The advisors attempt to go beyond simple statements of symptoms, as in the preceding query, by identifying possible causes of the problems: in the case just described, they might suggest restructuring the SGA to allow more memory for the database buffer cache, or creating additional indexes; either of these could reduce the need for disk I/O, which might be a better solution than just speeding up the disk subsystem. The advisors take this broader view of the situation by considering the whole instance and the activity within it.

All performance tuning is based on statistics. The level of detail of statistics gathered is controlled by the instance parameter STATISTICS_LEVEL. This has three possible settings: BASIC, TYPICAL, and ALL. TYPICAL is the default. The TYPICAL level of statistics will gather all statistics that can be collected without an impact on performance; this is usually the level that is sufficient for tuning. Setting the parameter to ALL will force collection of additional statistics that may be of value for advanced SQL statement tuning, but the collection of which may also slow down statement execution. The BASIC setting prevents most statistics collection but will not significantly improve performance.

 TIP Leave the STATISTICS_LEVEL instance parameter on default. This will collect all the statistics usually required, without any performance impact. Set it to ALL only for short periods when you are doing particularly detailed analysis.

The Automatic Database Diagnostic Monitor (ADDM)

A background process called the manageability monitor, or MMON, flushes statistics from memory to disk on a regular schedule, by default, every sixty minutes. MMON writes statistics to the tables in the SYSAUX tablespace that make up the Automatic Workload Repository, the AWR. This is known as a statistics "snapshot." Whenever a snapshot is taken, the MMON also runs the ADDM. This will generate a report on activity and possible problems between this snapshot and the time of the last snapshot, so by default, you have access to tuning reports covering every hour.

The default frequency of snapshots is hourly, with a retention period of seven days. These defaults can be changed through database control, or through the DBMS_WORKLOAD_REPOSITORY API. To change the retention to two weeks and the frequency to every twenty minutes, from a SQL*Plus prompt run this command (note that the units are minutes):

```
ocp10g> execute dbms_workload_repository.modify_snapshot_settings(-
> retention=>20160,interval=>20);
```

To return to the default values, execute the procedure with NULLs for the two arguments. To view or change these settings through Database Control, from the Administration page take the Automatic Workload Repository link in the Workload section, and click Edit.

 EXAM TIP Snapshots are by default gathered by MMON and saved to the AWR every hour; therefore the ADDM runs, by default, every hour.

To view the ADDM reports, from any Database Control screen take the Advisor Central link in the Related Links section at the bottom of the page. The Advisor Central window gives access to all the advisors and recent reports, as in Figure 31-1.

Select a report to see the results. Figure 31-2 shows the summary for an ADDM report. This shows that the most serious problem detected, responsible for nearly 90 percent of waits, has to do with writing to the online redo log files. The next most serious problem is excessive disk I/O on datafiles, caused by the database buffer cache being undersized. For each problem, clicking the description will lead to a window giving more detail on the problem and suggestions of what to do about it.

You can also generate an ADDM report covering the time between any two snapshots, either through Database Control or by using the DBMS_ADVISOR API.

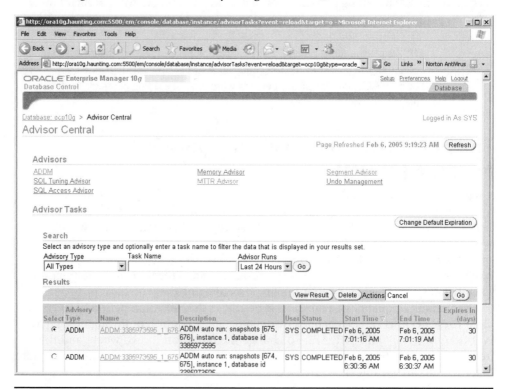

Figure 31-1 Advisor Central

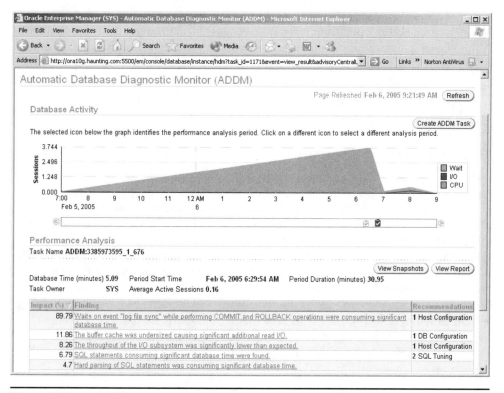

Figure 31-2 An ADDM report

The Advisors

The ADDM is one of several tools to be used for tuning a database, but it will usually be the first. Frequently, its recommendations will include a suggestion that you run one or more other advisors. There are six advisors:

- **SQL Tuning Advisor** Inspects SQL statements and the objects they address, and makes recommendations regarding possibly inefficient coding methods and missing or incorrect object statistics.

- **SQL Access Advisor** Generates suggestions for changing the indexing and materialized view strategy, in an attempt to reduce the number of block visits that will be necessary to run certain statements.

- **Memory Advisor** Predicts the effect on disk I/O of resizing the database buffer cache and the PGA aggregate target, and can also compute the optimal size for the shared pool.

- **MTTR (Mean Time to Recover) Advisor** Estimates the effect on disk I/O of demanding various minimum startup times after an instance crash.

- **Segment Advisor**   Inspects segments and recommends which could benefit from a shrink operation. It can also be used for estimating the space that will be required for tables and indexes at segment creation time, depending on the anticipated number of rows.

- **Undo Advisor**   Determines how large the undo tablespace needs to be in order to guarantee that transactions will not run out of undo space, and that queries will not fail with read consistency errors.

The SQL Tuning Advisor

It is often said that SQL statement tuning is the most important part of database tuning. There is little point in optimizing disk and memory usage to make a query that addresses several million blocks run more quickly, if the query could be rewritten to address just a few dozen blocks. With regard to SQL tuning, Oracle Corporation makes a clean break between the DBA's domain and the developers' domain: the DBA is responsible for identifying the SQL statements that are causing problems. These are the statements that are being executed many times (perhaps millions of times an hour), the statements that are consuming a substantial amount of CPU time, and the statements that are responsible for the bulk of the memory I/O and the disk I/O. Then it is the developers' responsibility to tune them. In practice, these two roles often overlap: your developers will need assistance in writing efficient SQL.

The SQL Tuning Advisor takes as its input one or more SQL statements. These can come from four sources:

- **Top SQL**   This is the SQL cached in the SGA right now.
- **SQL tuning sets**   This is a set of statements that can be built up from a number of sources, such as the current SGA; a snapshot in the AWR; or a group of statements entered by hand.
- **Snapshots**   Included in the information written to the AWR by the MMON are the high-load SQL statements running during the period.
- **Preserved snapshots**   Regular AWR snapshots are only stored for a period, but preserved snapshots, also known as "baselines," are stored in the AWR indefinitely and can also be used as input to the SQL Tuning Advisor.

The Advisor can make recommendations in four areas:

- **Optimizer statistics**   The Advisor will inspect the statistics on the objects being used by the statements, and if any have missing or out-of-date statistics, it will recommend an analysis.
- **SQL profiling**   This is a highly advanced capability of the advisor: it will partially run the statements to test various execution plans, and gather execution statistics to be used in conjunction with the object statistics.

- **Access path analysis**   The Advisor will investigate the possibilities of using extra indexes. The recommendations may include running the SQL Access Advisor, which can do a more comprehensive analysis.

- **SQL structure analysis**   There are certain constructs that are known to be inefficient compared to others that will deliver the same result. The advisor will identify such constructs and suggest alternative ways of structuring the statement.

To run the SQL Tuning Advisor, take its link from the Advisor Central window, and select a source (in the example following, the source is "Top SQL," the SQL currently in the SGA) and a time period, as in Figure 31-3.

In Figure 31-3, one SELECT statement consumed 64 percent of resources in a five-minute period. This statement needs to be tuned. Click it to run the Advisor against it. An example of typical recommendations is given in Figure 31-4, which suggest that a table should be analyzed and an index created. Note that the second recommendation is an instruction to run the Access Advisor.

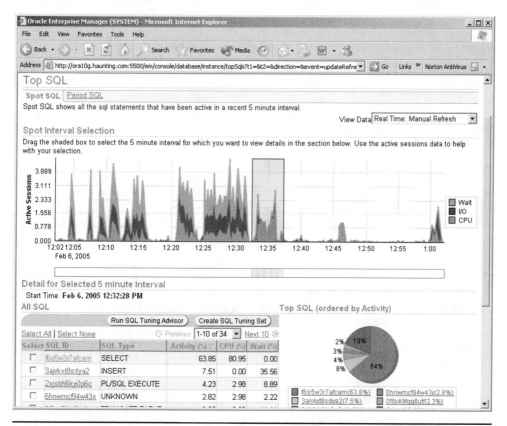

Figure 31-3   The Top SQL window of the SQL Tuning Advisor

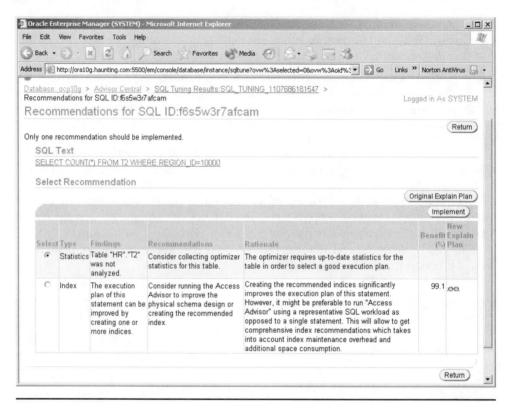

Figure 31-4 SQL Tuning Advisor recommendations

The SQL Access Advisor

As does the SQL Tuning Advisor, the Access Advisor takes a workload from the current SGA, a snapshot, or a SQL tuning set. The analysis will test the effect of using additional indexes and (if requested) materialized views. It also considers storage characteristics, and dropping unused indexes and materialized views.

TIP Materialized views are an advanced capability of the database, which in effect pre-run all or part of a query and save the results so that they can be used subsequently for all queries that address the same data.

The recommendations include scripts that can be used to generate any suggested indexes and materialized views.

The Memory Advisor

More detail on sizing memory structures for optimal performance will be given in Chapter 34; for now, concentrate on the graphical tools provided by Database Control.

There are three memory advisors: the Shared Pool Advisor, the Database Buffer Cache Advisor, and the Program Global Area Advisor. To reach these advisors, first take the Memory Advisor link from the Advisor Central window, as in Figure 31-5.

This shows the current settings for the most important system global area components. Note that Automatic Shared Memory Management is "Disabled." Only as long as it is disabled do you have access to the SGA memory advisors. Once you enable it (as you will in Chapter 34), the Advice buttons will disappear. After that, you can still get to the advisors—but only through views and an API, not through Database Control.

Taking the Advice button for the shared pool will generate a graph, as shown in Figure 31-6.

The Shared Pool Advisor plots estimates of parse time saved against various sizes of the shared pool. A significant amount of time is taken up in an instance by parsing SQL statements, and if the shared pool is large enough to cache already parsed code, then the code can be reused, thus saving time that would be required to parse it again. In the preceding example, it can be seen that increasing the shared pool to 90MB would help, but at that point the benefits level off. It can also be seen from the shape of the curve that reducing the size of the shared pool would be bad; if it is necessary to reduce the size of the SGA (perhaps because the system is swapping), it might be preferable to look for savings elsewhere.

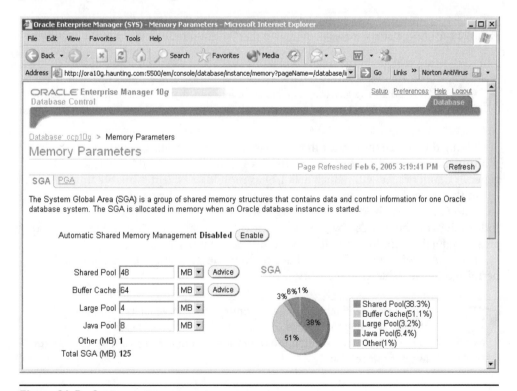

Figure 31-5   Setting memory parameters

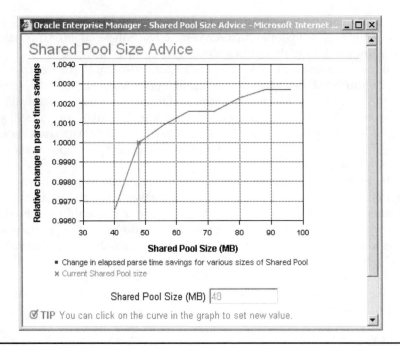

Figure 31-6 Advice on the shared pool

 TIP An oversized shared pool is bad for performance, so do not make it larger than the advisor suggests. An oversized shared pool requires excessive resources for management and can impact on search times to retrieve objects.

Taking the Advice button for the database buffer cache will generate a graph plotting the estimated relative change in disk I/O for various buffer cache sizes. In general, a larger cache will reduce disk I/O as more data is kept available in memory.

In the example shown in Figure 31-7, you can see that the database buffer cache is already optimally sized: making it larger would not have an impact on disk I/O. Indeed, it could be reduced by several megabytes without causing problems, but too great a reduction would cause disk I/O to increase exponentially.

The PGA Advisor gives similar advice on how much memory Oracle should be permitted to use for session memory.

 TIP Always remember that your computer will have limits on the amount of RAM available for Oracle to use. There is little point in assigning memory to the Oracle structures, if the operating system is going to have to page (or swap) it out to disk.

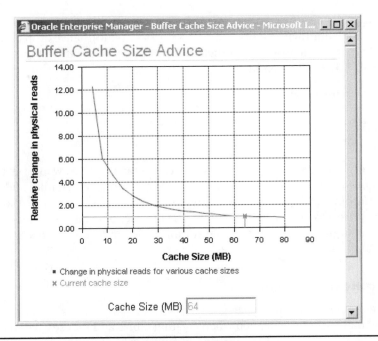

Figure 31-7   The Database Buffer Cache Advisor

The Mean Time to Recover Advisor

As you know from earlier chapters, it is impossible to corrupt an Oracle database
through any sort of instance failure. Any damage that occurs because of a crash is
always repaired on the next startup by the SMON, through the mechanism of using
the online logfiles to reinstantiate all work in progress at the time of the crash that
had not yet been written to disk. This recovery occurs during the transition of the
database from MOUNT to OPEN, and until it has been completed, users cannot
connect. But even though the instance recovery is automatic and guarantees no
corruptions, it can be a slow process requiring a considerable amount of downtime.

If a database is being run to a service level agreement with a clause such as "in the
event of a power failure, the database must be available for logon within X minutes of
power being restored," then it is vital to limit the downtime needed for instance
recovery. This time is dependent on two factors: how much redo will have to be read,
and how many I/O operations will be necessary on datafiles. To reduce these factors,
Oracle must write out dirty buffers from the database buffer cache to disk: only those
buffers that were dirty at the time of the crash need to be reconstructed by reading them
off disk, applying the redo changes, and finally cleaned by writing them back to disk.

In normal running, the DBWn will write out dirty buffers according to algorithms
designed to maximize performance (these are detailed in Chapter 34), but if this
would result in a too-long recovery time, you can set the instance parameter FAST_
START_MTTR_TARGET. This is set in seconds and instructs the DBWn to write out

dirty blocks at a rate sufficient to ensure that recovery would take no longer than the time nominated. But there is a price to pay: a possible performance drop caused by the disk I/O that Oracle would not otherwise have done. To see the estimates, query the V$INSTANCE_RECOVERY view:

```
ocp10g> select recovery_estimated_ios ios, actual_redo_blks redo,
target_mttr, estimated_mttr, writes_mttr from  v$instance_recovery;
       IOS       REDO TARGET_MTTR ESTIMATED_MTTR WRITES_MTTR
---------- ---------- ----------- -------------- -----------
       642      18081         180            172         900
```

This query shows that if the instance were to crash right now, on startup the recovery process would have to perform 642 I/O operations on datafiles and apply 18081 blocks of redo. The target mean time to recover has been set to 180 seconds, but in fact Oracle would need 172 seconds. The number of database writes that DBWn has done (in addition to those it would normally do) in its efforts to keep to the target is 900.

The Segment Advisor

The Segment Advisor is in three parts.

Size estimates can be generated when creating tables and indexes, based on the DDL defining the objects and the anticipated number of rows. This is an option when you create a table through Database Control.

After creation, growth trend estimates can be generated subsequently by Database Control, using information stored in the AWR.

Recommendations on whether a segment should be shrunk can be generated based on the statistics on the object, which include the amount of free space in the blocks allocated to it. By making use of historical information stored in the AWR, the Advisor can make an intelligent decision about whether free space within the segment should be kept (rather than being returned to the tablespace through a shrink) because it is likely to be needed again.

The Undo Advisor

Your undo tablespace should always be large enough to guarantee that transactions have enough space for their undo data, and enough additional space that long-running queries can always retrieve the data they need for read consistency. The Undo Advisor tells you exactly how large it should be.

The advisor can be viewed through Database Control by taking the appropriate link from the Advisor Central window, but it is also very easy to see from the SQL prompt. The V$UNDOSTAT view tells you all you need to know:

```
ocp10g> select begin_time,end_time, undoblks, maxquerylen,
ssolderrcnt,nospaceerrcnt from v$undostat;
BEGIN_TI END_TIME   UNDOBLKS MAXQUERYLEN SSOLDERRCNT NOSPACEERRCNT
-------- --------   -------- ----------- ----------- -------------
20:51:31 20:58:06       2221          12           0             0
20:41:31 20:51:31     107347         177           0             0
```

```
20:31:31 20:41:31      48349        678           0              0
20:21:31 20:31:31       3716         23           0              0
20:11:31 20:21:31       6020          4           0              0
20:01:31 20:11:31      88123       1223           0              0
19:51:31 20:01:31      94407         65           0              0
19:41:31 19:51:31       5312          5           0              0
19:31:31 19:41:31       4401          0           0              0
19:21:31 19:31:31       5184         67           0              0
19:11:31 19:21:31      21793        187           0              0
```

The V$UNDOSTAT view displays statistics for ten-minute intervals, from instance startup time. The preceding query selects the number of blocks of undo generated per ten minutes, and also the longest query that completed in the ten minutes. Also selected are the number of snapshot-too-old errors that will have caused queries to fail and no-space errors that will have caused transactions to fail—zero in both cases.

The Undo Advisor graphs the space required to support queries of varying length according to the highest rate of undo generation, using the algorithm detailed in Chapter 16 on managing undo.

Exercise 31-1: Using the SQL Tuning Advisor

Simulate identifying an extremely inefficient statement, and observe the advisor's recommendations.

1. Connect to your database using SQL*Plus as user system.

2. Create a table, and then insert some rows into it.

   ```
   ocp10g> create table t1 (c1 number, c2 char(1000));
   Table created.
   ocp10g> begin
     2   for i in 1..5000 loop
     3   insert into t1 values (i,'a');
     4   end loop;
     5   commit;
     6   end;
     7   /
   PL/SQL procedure successfully completed.
   ```

3. Flush all buffers from the database buffer cache, and run a query against the table.

   ```
   ocp10g> alter system flush buffer_cache;
   System altered.
    ocp10g> select max(c1) from t1;
      MAX(C1)
   ----------
         5000
   ```

4. Determine the SQL_ID of the statement. The SQL_ID is the unique identifier for any SQL statement in the library cache of the SGA.

   ```
   ocp10g> select sql_id from v$sql where sql_text='select max(c1) from t1';
   SQL_ID
   -------------
   62hp8nsjwjgvm
   ```

5. Connect to your database with Database Control as user SYSTEM.

6. Take the Advisor Central link in the Related Links section, and then the link SQL Tuning Advisor. Take the SQL Tuning Sets link.

7. In the SQL Tuning Sets window, select Spot SQL in the Create SQL Tuning Set From drop-down box, and click Go. You will see your statement's SQL_ID, though not necessarily in the first statements shown. In the example shown in Figure 31-8, it is in the second page of statements. Select its check box, and click the Run SQL Tuning Advisor button.

8. In the Schedule Advisor window, leave everything on default and click OK.

9. When the advisor has completed, click View Recommendations. The recommendations will vary depending on how your database is configured; typically, they will include analyzing the table or building an index (see Figure 31-9).

10. Follow the advice, and repeat Steps 3–8. Note that the recommendations should change, or that the advisor will report that no further recommendations can be made.

11. Tidy up by dropping the table.

```
ocp10g> drop table t1;
Table dropped.
```

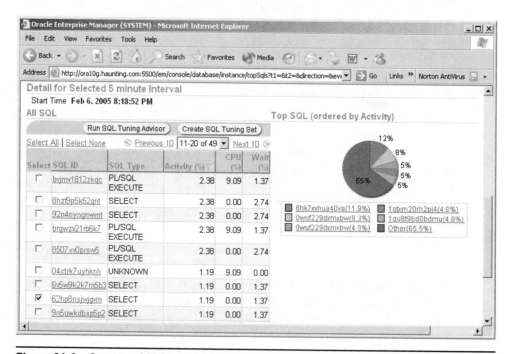

Figure 31-8   Creating a SQL Tuning Advisor job

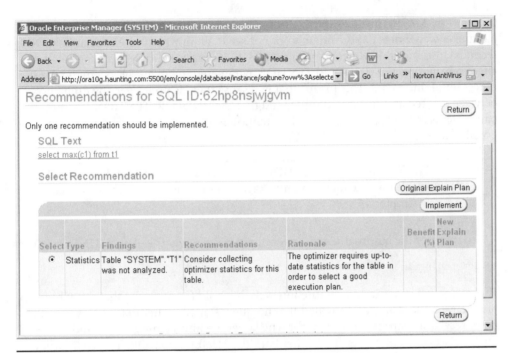

Figure 31-9 SQL Tuning Advisor recommendations

Automatic Undo Retention Tuning

Undo data is stored in the undo tablespace, the tablespace nominated by the UNDO_ TABLESPACE instance parameter. This tablespace should be sized according to the rate at which undo data is being generated and the length of the queries running in the database, as detailed in Chapter 16. But even if the undo tablespace is inadequately sized and therefore comes under space pressure, automatic undo retention tuning will tend to minimize problems.

Undo data generated by a transaction must always be kept until the transaction commits. This is an absolute; under no circumstances will Oracle ever overwrite undo data that might be needed to roll back a transaction. This data is known as "active" undo data. Once a transaction has committed, its undo data is no longer active, but it could still be needed to support long-running queries that began before the transaction. Data that may be needed for this purpose is known as "unexpired" undo data. "Expired" undo is data that is no longer needed either to roll back a transaction or to be read by queries.

Active undo will never be overwritten, and ideally expired undo can be safely overwritten at any time. Unexpired undo can be overwritten, but at the risk (not the certainty) of causing queries to fail with the "ORA-1555: snapshot too old" error. The point at which data transitions from "unexpired" to "expired" is controlled by the instance parameter UNDO_RETENTION. With release 9i of the Oracle database,

Oracle would overwrite any expired undo. This meant that if the UNDO_RETENTION parameter were not set appropriately (or not set at all, in which case it defaults to 900 seconds), there would be great danger of ORA-1555 errors. Release 10g of the database effectively ignores the UNDO_RETENTION parameter; it will always overwrite the oldest bit of undo data. This means that in a sense there is no longer any difference between expired and unexpired undo, and that the UNDO_RETENTION instance parameter is redundant, because undo retention is automatically tuned for the longest possible query.

 TIP The UNDO_RETENTION parameter is still important if you intend to enable the retention guarantee capability of an undo tablespace, as discussed in Chapter 16.

To monitor the automatic undo retention tuning, query the view V$UNDOSTAT:

```
select begin_time,end_time,tuned_undoretention from v$undostat;
```

This query will show, in ten-minute intervals, how old (in seconds) the oldest block of inactive undo data was. Provided that no query started earlier than that, you will never receive a snapshot-too-old error. The larger the undo tablespace is, and the less the transaction workload is, the further back the TUNED_UNDORETENTION will be.

Chapter Review

Database tuning is a skilled and time-intensive process, but the advisors provided with release 10g of the Oracle database can assist. The starting point should be the ADDM. This runs every time a snapshot of statistics is collected, by default, every hour. The ADDM will highlight any performance problems, either giving specific advice or suggesting that you run one of the other advisors to drill down further to the root cause of the problem.

The provided advisors are as follows:

- The SQL Tuning Advisor
- The SQL Access Advisor
- The Segment Advisor
- The Mean Time to Recover Advisor
- The Undo Advisor
- The Memory Advisor

All the advisors, and the ADDM, rely on information stored in the Automatic Workload Repository, the AWR. This is updated with snapshots of statistical information at regular intervals by the manageability monitor (the MMON) background process, which also runs the ADDM automatically every time a snapshot is created.

Questions

1. When are ADDM reports generated? (Choose the best answer.)

   A. On demand, through Database Control or the Advisor API

   B. Automatically, whenever a snapshot is collected

   C. Both on demand and automatically when a snapshot is collected

   D. ADDM does not generate reports; it recommends running other advisors

2. To enable the use of the Automatic Database Diagnostic Monitor and all the tuning advisors, to what must the STATISTICS_LEVEL instance parameter be set? (Choose the best answer.)

   A. NONE

   B. BASIC

   C. TYPICAL

   D. ALL

   E. BASIC, TYPICAL, or ALL

   F. TYPICAL or ALL

3. Which advisors can recommend index segment creation? (Choose two correct answers.)

   A. The SQL Tuning Advisor

   B. The SQL Access Advisor

   C. The Segment Advisor

   D. The Automatic Database Diagnostic Monitor

4. For which memory structures are there advisors? (Choose all that apply.)

   A. Database buffer cache

   B. Large pool

   C. Log buffer

   D. Program global areas

   E. Shared pool

5. The ADDM and the advisors use snapshot statistics. Where are these stored? (Choose the best answer.)

   A. In the SYSTEM tablespace

   B. In the SYSAUX tablespace

   C. They are stored by Database Control

   D. They are accumulated in memory and cleared on shutdown

Answers

1. **C.** ADDM generates reports automatically whenever an AWR snapshot is collected, and you can also generate reports covering other periods on demand.

2. **F.** To enable the advisors, the STATISTICS_LEVEL must be either TYPICAL or ALL.

3. **A** and **B.** Both the SQL Tuning Advisor and the SQL Access Advisor can recommend index creation. The Segment Advisor advises on existing segments, not new ones, and the ADDM does not itself recommend index creation, though it may advise using another advisor that will.

4. **A, B, D,** and **E.** There is no log buffer advisor.

5. **B.** Snapshots are stored in the Automatic Workload Repository, in the SYSAUX tablespace.

CHAPTER 32

Monitoring and Managing Storage

In this chapter you will learn how to

- Tune redo writing and archiving operations
- Issue statements that can be suspended upon encountering space condition errors
- Reduce space-related error conditions by proactively managing tablespace usage
- Reclaim wasted space from tables and indexes using the segment shrink functionality
- Estimate the size of new tables and indexes
- Use different storage options to improve the performance of queries
- Rebuild indexes online

Space management is a major part of a DBA's day-to-day work. You must ensure that there is enough storage space available for all the Oracle segments. If a segment fills and cannot expand, users will receive errors; also, poor space management can also have performance implications.

In previous releases of the Oracle database, space management was to a large extent a manual process that required constant monitoring. A good DBA would automate this process as far as possible by writing a suite of scripts to generate regular reports on space usage, picking up potential problems before they occurred. Release 10g of the database includes many tools for automating this monitoring, and for generating advice on how performance can be improved.

Chapter 3 summarizes Oracle's storage architecture: how tablespaces abstract the physical data storage in datafiles from the logical data storage in segments, and more detail is provided in Chapters 6 and 8. This chapter shows how to monitor and optimize storage, in order to prevent errors and improve performance.

Online and Archive Redo Log File Storage

The redo log has a dual purpose: the online log files are essential to prevent database corruptions in the event of an instance failure, and the archive log files are required for recovery in the event of media failure. You cannot run a database safely without multiplexed copies of your redo log. But a poorly configured redo log can also cause performance degradation and can even cause the whole instance to hang. Throughout this section, it is assumed that your database is running in archivelog mode, with two logfile groups of two members each, and archiving to two destinations.

Disk I/O and the Online Redo Log Files

The discussion of commit processing in Chapter 9 details when the LGWR process will write redo data in memory to the online redo log files on disk. The performance-critical aspect of the LGWR process is that when a user issues a commit statement, the session will hang until the LGWR has flushed the log buffer to disk. This is one of the ultimate bottlenecks in the Oracle environment: you cannot do DML faster than the log writer can flush the log buffer to disk.

Whenever the LGWR process flushes the log buffer to disk, it issues a parallel write request to the operating system. If the multiplexed copies of the online log file group are on separate physical disk devices, then the operating system can in fact do a parallel write—but if both members are on the same device, then the write will have to be sequential: first one member, then the other. This contention for disk I/O will double the time required before the operating system can return "write complete." It will also reduce the fault tolerance of the system; if you lose one disk, you will lose both members of the group.

On a high-throughput system, your system administrators should optimize the performance of the devices used for online redo log file members. Because they are (or should be) protected by multiplexing, they are perfectly suited to RAID 0 striping, but the ideal is RAID 0+1, as discussed in Chapter 33.

TIP Store your online log file members on separate devices, and use operating system striping to optimize performance.

If possible, do not locate online log files on the same devices as datafiles, because that too will cause contention. You do not want the situation where the one LGWR process is contending for access to its logfiles with hundreds of server processes and the DBWn that are accessing the datafiles.

Log Switches and Performance

Another problem that can occur with the online log is not directly related to file I/O. This is the effect of a log switch. The LGWR writes out redo data in very nearly real time, and when you say COMMIT, it is real time. The DBWn, however, writes on a very lazy algorithm: as little as possible, as rarely as possible. This gap between LGWR and DBWn is the amount of redo data that will have to be processed to back out corruptions in the event of an instance crash. To control the length of the gap, use the FAST_START_MTTR_TARGET instance parameter. The smaller the figure you set this to, the faster your recovery time will be—but the more performance will deteriorate, because DBWn is forced to write out blocks faster.

One guarantee that Oracle provides is that if the instance crashes, there will always be enough redo data available in the online log files to bring the database forward in time to the point of the crash. To ensure this, the LGWR is not allowed to overwrite a logfile group before the DBWn has written all the data blocks that were affected by changes in the logfile to disk. DBWn must therefore write out dirty buffers from the database buffer cache with each log switch, to advance the checkpoint position through the time that the log switch occurred. A side effect of this is that frequent log switches force DBWn to do a lot more disk I//O than it would do otherwise.

If the logfiles are small, then there will be frequent log switches: this forces DBWn to write out dirty buffers to the datafiles, with a resultant deterioration in performance. The ideal situation is that DBWn writes should be driven by your requirements for recovery time, not by log switching. Database Control includes an advisor that will check whether the frequency of log switching is forcing DBWn to write out data blocks faster than it would do otherwise.

To reach this advisor, take the Administration tab on the database home page, then the Redo Logs link in the Storage section. Select Sizing Advice in the Actions drop-down box, and the advisor will present a recommended size for the groups, based on recent activity, that will ensure that log switches will not be any more frequent than the need to meet the FAST_START_MTTR_TARGET setting (see Figure 32-1). Your logfile groups should be at least this size; making them larger will not degrade performance, but making them smaller definitely will.

Archive Log Files and Performance

Online redo log files must be copied to archive redo log files when they fill. It is not possible to overwrite an online log until it has been archived. In a high-throughput system, you will locate your online redo log files on your fastest devices; therefore, your archive redo log files will be on slower devices. This situation is unavoidable,

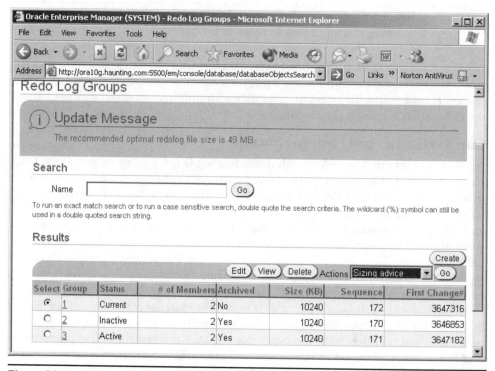

Figure 32-1 The redo log file sizing advisor

and it may well be that at times of peak activity you are generating online redo faster than it can be copied to archive redo. If the archiver processes cannot keep up with the log writer process, the instance will hang until the archiver catches up.

To minimize the effects of this, first, never locate archive log files on the same devices as online log files. To do so would be a guarantee of contention: the LGWR process would be trying to write to the same disk that the ARCn process was writing to.

Second, always launch at least as many archiver processes as you have archive destinations. The number of ARCn processes is controlled by the instance parameter LOG_ARCHIVE_MAX_PROCESSES, which defaults to 2.

Third, if there are still problems, add more online log file groups. This will give you more time before any one group must be overwritten, and it will help the database over a sudden burst of high activity.

Space Errors and Resumable Statements

Users should never experience errors to do with space: proactive monitoring of space usage should avoid the problem. But it does happen. The default behavior in the event of a statement hitting a space problem is that the statement is rolled back and an error is returned to the session. This behavior can be modified such that the statement will suspend, giving the DBA an opportunity to fix the problem. The statement will then resume and (one hopes) run to completion.

Common Space-Related Errors

When a segment fills up, Oracle will automatically allocate another extent to it in one of the datafiles that make up the tablespace the segment resides within. If all the datafiles are full, the extent allocation will fail and an error will be returned to the user. If a datafile has the AUTOEXTEND attribute set, rather than generating an error, Oracle will go to the operating system and increase the size of the datafile, allocating the new extent in the newly acquired space. This will continue until the file reaches its maximum size or the disk fills up. Then the user will receive an error.

Segments in dictionary-managed tablespaces may have a MAXIMUM EXTENTS setting; if a segment fills and it has reached this limit, an error will be generated. This does not occur for segments in locally managed tablespaces, because in a locally managed tablespace this setting is always on UNLIMITED.

Undo space can also be a problem. Even if the segments a user is working on have plenty of space, if the undo tablespace has no more free space (i.e., space that is not required for protecting active transactions), there will be an error. This should not occur if you are using automatic undo management and the undo tablespace is sized correctly, as described in Chapter 16.

Even SELECT statements can generate space errors. This happens if the statement requires a sort that spills to disk, and the user's temporary tablespace fills up. This should be avoided by using automatic PGA memory management (as described in Chapter 34) and sizing the temporary tablespaces appropriately.

Whenever a space-related error occurs, the statement that caused it will be rolled back. If the statement is part of a multistatement transaction, the rest of the transaction will remain intact. Well-written code will have exception clauses that catch space errors and handle them in an elegant manner, but no exceptions clause can prevent the rollback.

Some of the most costly space errors occur during database administration work. Consider the case where you have to create an index on a large table. This might take hours and then fail before completion because the tablespace fills up. So you extend the tablespace and try again. After a few more hours, it fails because the undo tablespace fills up. So you extend that and try a third time. This time it fails because of temporary space. Repeated space errors can waste a phenomenal amount of time.

Autoextension of Datafiles

Either at datafile creation time or subsequently with the ALTER DATABASE DATAFILE <file_name> AUTOEXTEND ON command you can specify that a file will automatically extend when full. To see whether and how AUTOEXTEND is enabled for a file, query the DBA_DATA_FILES view:

```
SQL> select file_name,bytes,autoextensible,increment_by,maxbytes
from dba_data_files;
FILE_NAME                   BYTES AUT INCREMENT_BY         MAXBYTES
-------------------- ---------- --- ------------ ----------------
/oradata/users01.dbf  102629376  NO            0                0
/oradata/undo01.dbf   524288000 YES            1      34359721984
/oradata/users02.dbf    1048576 YES          128         10485760
/oradata/bigfile1.dbf   1048576 YES            1   35184372064256
<output truncated...>
```

This query shows that the file /oradata/users01.dbf is currently 100MB. It will not automatically extend.

The file /oradata/undo01.dbf is currently 500MB and will autoextend in increments of one block up to a maximum size of 32GB. If autoextension is enabled with no controls, a datafile in a small file tablespace will extend in units of one block up to a maximum of the block size (in this case, 8KB) multiplied by 4194304.

The datafile /oradata/users02.dbf is also autoextensible, but in a controlled fashion. It is currently 1MB big, and when full, it will extend in units of 128 blocks (or 1MB) up to a maximum size of 10MB.

The final example is of a datafile that makes up a bigfile tablespace, created as autoextensible with no controls. The default upper limit is again dependent on the block size; for 8KB blocks, it is 32TB.

 TIP Enabling autoextension may avoid errors, but should not be necessary in a well-managed database. If you must do it, always specify sensible values for the increment size and the maximum size.

To modify a datafile to enable autoextension, use an ALTER DATABASE command such as

```
SQL> alter database datafile '/oradata/users01.dbf' autoextend on
next 10m maxsize 200m;
```

This command instructs Oracle to increase the file size in units of 10MB, up to a maximum size of 200MB.

Enabling autoextension of datafiles will avoid a large number of space errors, but a far better option is to prevent them occurring at all by proactive management.

Resumable Statements

A session, or indeed the whole instance, can be configured to suspend statements that hit space problems, rather than reversing them and generating an error. To the user, it will appear as though the statement is hanging in the middle of execution. The DBA can then fix the problem (for example, by adding more space to a datafile), and the statement will then start running again. It will carry on from where it had left off, with no loss of processing time other than the time for which it was suspended. By default, statements will be suspended for two hours. If the problem has not been fixed in that time, the error will be generated and the statement rolled back.

 TIP While a statement is suspended, any row locks it may be holding will be maintained. It will also hold any undo or temporary space it has already acquired. Remember this when setting the resumable timeout.

To enable resumable statements, use an ALTER SESSION command, such as

```
SQL> alter session enable resumable timeout 60 name 'AR archive';
```

The optional keywords TIMEOUT and NAME let you specify how long, in seconds, to suspend operations before generating an error and a name for the suspended session. The example here will suspend any statements that hit space problems for up to one minute. If the problem is resolved in that time, the statement will resume. If not, the error will be generated. The name "AR archive" will be used as a label in the view describing the suspended session. Reissuing the ENABLE RESUMABLE command at various points in a process with different names will help identify the point in the code at which the problem occurred. Because a suspended session may be tying up resources and could therefore impact on other users, a user must be granted the RESUMABLE privilege before he can enable resumable statements.

To enable resumable statements at the instance level, set the instance parameter RESUMABLE_TIMEOUT. This will cause all sessions that hit space problems to hang for the duration of the timeout given, unless the problem is fixed first. This is the only way to enable resumable statements other than interactively: there is no API that lets you enable resumable statements programmatically, for your own session or for anyone else.

To track statement suspension, you can either query views or make use of a trigger. Whenever a statement is suspended, a row is entered into the DBA_RESUMABLE view. This view will give details of the statement, the problem, and the timings:

```
ocp10g> desc dba_resumable;
 Name                                     Null?    Type
 ---------------------------------------- -------- -----------------
 USER_ID                                           NUMBER
 SESSION_ID                                        NUMBER
 INSTANCE_ID                                       NUMBER
 COORD_INSTANCE_ID                                 NUMBER
 COORD_SESSION_ID                                  NUMBER
 STATUS                                            VARCHAR2(9)
 TIMEOUT                                           NUMBER
 START_TIME                                        VARCHAR2(20)
 SUSPEND_TIME                                      VARCHAR2(20)
 RESUME_TIME                                       VARCHAR2(20)
 NAME                                              VARCHAR2(4000)
 SQL_TEXT                                          VARCHAR2(1000)
 ERROR_NUMBER                                      NUMBER
 ERROR_PARAMETER1                                  VARCHAR2(80)
 ERROR_PARAMETER2                                  VARCHAR2(80)
 ERROR_PARAMETER3                                  VARCHAR2(80)
 ERROR_PARAMETER4                                  VARCHAR2(80)
 ERROR_PARAMETER5                                  VARCHAR2(80)
 ERROR_MSG                                         VARCHAR2(4000)
```

There will be one row in this view for every statement that has been, or is currently, suspended. The first two columns identify the username and session; the next three, the instances involved (only relevant in a RAC database, where several instances may be running different parts of a parallel operation). The STATUS of the statement tells you whether it is currently suspended, or it is running again after a problem occurred and was fixed, or the statement did in fact terminate because the problem wasn't fixed within the timeout. The START/SUSPEND/RESUME_TIME columns show when the statement started to run and the most recent suspension and resumption times.

A statement might be suspended and resumed many times, but you can see only the current or last suspension. The NAME column is the name given in the ENABLE RESUMABLE statement. The SQL_TEXT is the statement itself. Finally, there are the details of the error condition that was raised. This is the error that would have been returned to the session, and that will be returned if the problem is not fixed within the TIMEOUT. If you do not wish to fix the problem, use the DBMS_RESUMABLE .ABORT procedure to terminate the statement and return the error message to the session immediately.

Information is also visible in the V$SESSION view. The EVENT column of a suspended session will be populated with "statement suspended, wait error to be cleared" while a suspension is in progress.

When a session is suspended, a system event is raised: the AFTER SUSPEND event. This can be used to fire a database trigger. The action the trigger takes can be merely informative, such as sending an alert message to the DBA, or it can investigate the cause of the problem and attempt to fix it. For example,

```
SQL> create trigger suspend_message
  2  after suspend on database
  3  begin
  4  utl_mail.send(
  5  sender=>'suspend alert',
  6  recipients=>'dba@haunting.com',
  7  message=>'session suspended!');
  8  end;
  9  /
```

This trigger uses the UTL_MAIL package to send a simple e-mail whenever a session is suspended. The trigger must be created in the SYS schema.

TIP Before using UTL_MAIL, you must set the SMTP_OUT_SERVER instance parameter to nominate the address of your e-mail server.

To investigate the cause of the error, the trigger must use the DBMS_RESUMABLE .SPACE_ERROR_INFO function, which will return details of the problem:

```
FUNCTION SPACE_ERROR_INFO RETURNS BOOLEAN
 Argument Name                  Type                    In/Out
 ---------------------------    ---------------------   ------
 ERROR_TYPE                     VARCHAR2                OUT
 OBJECT_TYPE                    VARCHAR2                OUT
 OBJECT_OWNER                   VARCHAR2                OUT
 TABLE_SPACE_NAME               VARCHAR2                OUT
 OBJECT_NAME                    VARCHAR2                OUT
 SUB_OBJECT_NAME                VARCHAR2                OUT
```

Depending on the ERROR_TYPE and the OBJECT_TYPE, the trigger could take action appropriate to the object, such as resizing a datafile.

TIP Test an AFTER SUSPEND trigger thoroughly, not forgetting that the trigger itself could run into a space management problem. For example, if the disk is full, the trigger will not be able to extend a datafile.

Exercise 32-1: Using Resumable Statements

Simulate a space error, and demonstrate how enabling resumable statements avoids it.

1. Connect to your database as user SYSTEM with SQL*Plus.

2. Create a small tablespace.

```
SQL> create tablespace small datafile 'small1.dbf' size 1m;
```

3. Create a table in the tablespace.

```
SQL> create table toobig (c1 char(1000)) tablespace small;
```

4. Force an error by filling the tablespace.

```
ocp10g> begin
  2  for i in 1..1000 loop
  3  insert into toobig values('a');
  4  end loop;
  5  end;
  6  /
begin
*
ERROR at line 1:
ORA-01653: unable to extend table SYSTEM.TOOBIG by 8 in tablespace SMALL
ORA-06512: at line 3
```

5. Enable resumable statements for your session.

```
SQL> alter season enable resumable;
```

6. Reissue the anonymous PL/SQL block of Step 4. The session will hang.

7. In another window, connect as user SYSTEM and query the DBA_RESUMABLE view.

```
SQL> select error_msg,status,sql_text from  dba_resumable;
ERROR_MSG
-----------------------------------------------------------------------

STATUS    SQL_TEXT
--------- -----------------------------
ORA-01653: unable to extend table SYSTEM.TOOBIG by 8 in tablespace SMALL
SUSPENDED INSERT INTO TOOBIG VALUES('a')
```

8. Fix the problem by adding a datafile to the SMALL tablespace.

```
SQL> alter tablespace small add datafile 'small2.dbf'  size 10m;
```

9. In your first session, note that the insert has now completed successfully.

10. Tidy up.

```
SQL> drop tablespace small including contents and datafiles;
```

Use of Alerts to Monitor Tablespace Usage

Far better than either enabling autoextension of datafiles or relying on resumable statements is ensuring that tablespaces never fill up in the first place. To do this, you must monitor tablespace usage. To see the amount of free space in your tablespaces, query the DBA_FREE_SPACE view:

```
SQL> select tablespace_name, sum(bytes) from dba_free_space
group by tablespace_name;
```

EXAM TIP Space occupied by recycle bin objects is reported as "free" in the DBA_FREE_SPACE view.

Monitoring free space used to be a regular part of a DBA's job, but with release 10g of the database it can be automated by the alert system. The alert system is enabled by the manageability monitor, or MMON, background process. Management information is accumulated in memory during normal running and periodically flushed to disk by the MMON process. The data is stored on disk in the Automatic Workload Repository, a set of tables in the SYSAUX tablespace.

The alert system comes preconfigured with thresholds on tablespace usage that will trigger a warning alert when a tablespace reaches 85 percent full and a critical alert when it becomes 97 percent full. The mechanism is intelligent enough to consider space currently in use for temporary tablespaces and undo tablespaces, rather than the actual space occupied by temporary or undo segments. For regular tablespaces, it will ignore space occupied by recycle bin objects. The tablespace usage alert is checked every ten minutes. If the datafiles of a tablespace are autoextensible, then the alert is based on a comparison of the used space with the maximum size of the files, not the current size.

The thresholds of 85 percent and 97 percent are a database-wide default, which can be changed either globally or for individual tablespaces. There is no way to adjust the ten-minute frequency of monitoring. To set thresholds for a tablespace with Database Control, from the database home page take the Administration tab, and then the Tablespaces link in the Storage section. Selecting the Tablespace radio button and clicking Edit will take you to the Edit Tablespace window shown in Figure 32-2, where you can set the thresholds for the one tablespace or adjust the database-wide defaults.

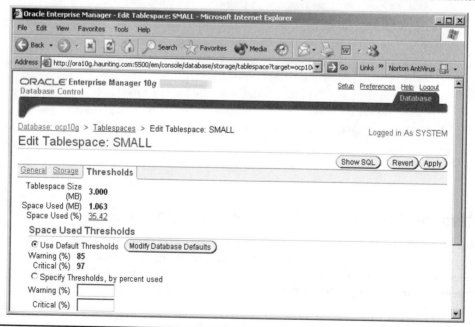

Figure 32-2 Setting tablespace usage thresholds

EXAM TIP The 85 percent and 97 percent values are default alert thresholds for all tablespaces. You can change this database default or override it for individual tablespaces.

Alerts may be seen in various ways. It is, for example, possible to configure the database to send e-mails or pages when an alert is raised. The default behavior is merely to report the alert through Database Control. All recent alerts are displayed on the database home page. Alerts can also be viewed in the DBA_OUTSTANDING_ALERTS view. When an alert is cleared—for example, by adding another file to a full tablespace—the alert is removed from the DBA_OUTSTANDING_ALERTS view and transferred to the DBA_ALERT_HISTORY view.

Exercise 32-2: Using Tablespace Usage Alerts

Create a tablespace, and make use of the alert system to monitor its usage.

1. Connect to your database as user SYSTEM with SQL*Plus.

2. Create a tablespace with one small datafile.
   ```
   SQL> create tablespace small datafile 'small.dbf' size 1m;
   ```

3. Create a table in the tablespace.
   ```
   SQL> create table toobig (c1 char(1000)) tablespace small;
   ```

4. Fill the tablespace by inserting some rows into the table.
   ```
   SQL> begin
     2  for i in 1..1000 loop
     3  insert into toobig values('a');
     4  end loop;
     5  end;
     6  /
   ```
   This will cause an ORA-01653 error, because the table will have filled the tablespace.

5. Connect to your database as user SYSTEM with Database Control.

6. On the database home page, note the "Problem Tablespaces" in the Space Usage section. This will say that there is (at least) one problem tablespace, shown as a link. You may have to wait a few minutes and refresh the screen before this is updated, due to the ten-minute gap between space usage checks. Then take the link to see the problem tablespace, as in Figure 32-3.

7. In your SQL*Plus session, query the outstanding alerts view.
   ```
   SQL> select object_name,reason from dba_outstanding_alerts;
   OBJECT_NAME    REASON
   -------------- ----------------------------------------
   SMALL          Tablespace [SMALL] is [93 percent] full
   ```

8. Fix the problem by adding a second datafile to the tablespace.
   ```
   SQL> alter tablespace small add datafile 'small2.dbf' size 2m;
   ```

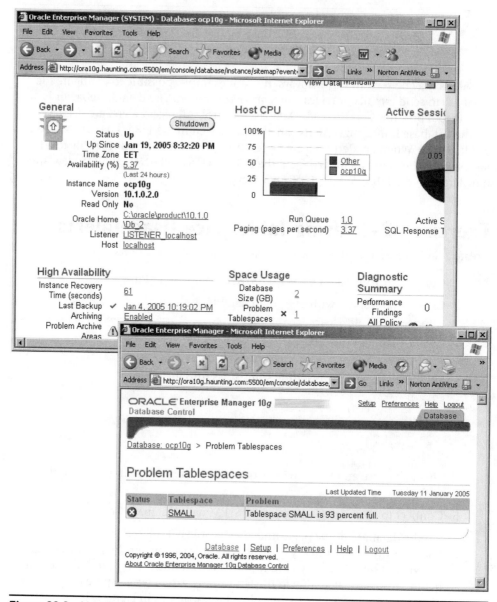

Figure 32-3 Identifying tablespaces under space pressure

9. Refresh the Database Control window and re-run the query of Step 7, and you will see that the alert has been cleared. Again, there may be a delay of up to ten minutes.

10. Tidy up.

```
SQL> drop tablespace space small including contents and datafiles;
```

Monitoring and Managing Segment Sizes

As rows are inserted into a table, Oracle will allocate more extents to the table as necessary. When rows are deleted, these extents are not deallocated. They remain part of the table. This mechanism gives rise to two possible problems.

First, while extents can be allocated dynamically, it will generally be more efficient to allocate enough space to the table in the first place. If you know that a table will grow to 100GB, it will be better to allocate 100GB of space initially than to rely on Oracle to add many extents as the segment grows. But it is difficult to estimate the physical size that a table will grow to, even if you do have an estimate for the number of rows. The Database Control Segment Advisor can do this for you.

Second, because deletions do not deallocate space, it is possible for a table to occupy far more space than the actual number of rows currently in it requires. This is not only a waste of storage, it can also impact badly on performance. A full table scan must scan the whole table, whether or not the rows have been deleted.

Indexes face similar problems. It is extremely difficult to estimate in advance the size of an index, and large amounts of DML will result in an index whose efficiency has deteriorated.

Database control includes advisors that can scan objects and recommend whether they are occupying far more space than necessary; at segment creation time the advisors can estimate the amount of space that a segment will require, given its structure and the number of rows expected.

Estimating Segment Sizes

When you create a table or an index with Database Control, an advisor can estimate the space that will be needed. When creating a table, after defining the columns take the Estimate Table Size button and enter the number of rows expected in the page shown in Figure 32-4. A similar option is available in the wizard for creating indexes.

Shrinking Table Segments

As rows are inserted into a table, the extents that make up the table will fill. When all the extents are full, Oracle will allocate another extent, and so on. The high water mark, or HWM, is a marker in a segment for the last block that has ever been used. When a table is created, the HWM is set to the beginning of the segment. As rows are inserted, the HWM is pushed up. When the HWM reaches the end of the initial extent, a new extent is added to the table. More inserts will push the HWM up through the new extent. This is normal table growth.

As rows are deleted, space is freed up within the segment, but the segment itself retains the space it has been allocated, and the HWM does not move. Extents are not returned to the tablespace and made available for other segments. New insertions can reuse the space below the HWM that has been freed up by deletions, but in many cases segments will end up occupying far more space than is needed for their current contents because the blocks below the HWM are very sparsely populated. This results in a waste of storage capacity and also causes performance problems. Full table scans always scan up to the HWM.

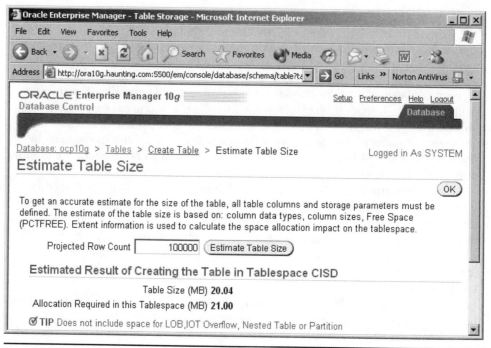

Figure 32-4 Table size estimate

EXAM TIP A full table scan takes several hours to complete. You delete all the rows, and scan again. How long will the second scan take? Exactly as long as the first.

The ALTER TABLE SHRINK SPACE command will reorganize a table in order to compact rows into as few blocks as possible. Rows in blocks toward the end of the table are moved to free space in blocks toward the beginning of the table. Once all possible movements have been done, the HWM is moved down as far as it can go and all extents above the newly positioned HWM are returned to the tablespace. The result is a table that has a much smaller number of blocks than before, all of which are packed with rows as tightly as possible. This minimizes the space required and optimizes the performance of full table scans.

A segment shrink operation is implemented internally as a series of insert and delete DML operations. To move a row, a copy of the row is inserted into a new location and deleted from its original location. It follows from this that indexes will be maintained, and that row locks will be required while the move is in progress—but these locks are only transitory, and the segment remains available for use by other users. Unless another session happens to require access to a row while it is being moved, no one will notice that a shrink is in progress. If another session does hit a row that is being moved, there will be a momentary delay until the move is completed and the lock is released.

The final stage of a shrink operation is a DDL operation. Once all rows possible have been moved from the end of the segment toward the beginning, there will be a large number of blocks (one hopes, many extents) toward the end of the segment that are completely empty. The shrink ends by moving the HWM from its current position to the last block that is now in use, and deallocating all extents above the new HWM position. This will minimize the space usage of the segment and optimize full table scans.

Insert and delete triggers do not fire as a result of segment shrink operations, because the data itself does not change. Before a shrink can be done, row movement must be enabled for the table, as it must be for enabling table flashback. A segment shrink can only be applied to heap structured tables, which must be in tablespaces that use automatic segment space management (ASSM). These are standard tables, partitioned tables, materialized view container tables, and materialized view log tables. There are also some limitations on the datatypes of the table.

In summary, only tables in ASSM tablespaces can be shrunk, and of those, these cannot be shrunk:

- Clustered tables (described later)
- Tables with columns of type LONG
- LOB segments (though the table itself can be shrunk)
- Tables with on-commit materialized views (because triggers are disabled)
- Tables with ROWID materialized views (because rowids change)
- IOT mapping tables and IOT overflow segments (described later)
- Tables with function-based indexes
- Heap tables for which row movement has not been enabled

A table shrink can be initiated from Database Control or the SQL*Plus command line. There are two options that can be specified on the command line, CASCADE and COMPACT. CASCADE will shrink the table and its indexes. COMPACT stops the shrink after the row compaction phase and before the shift of the HWM. The HWM move may be noticed by your end users, because it does require a (very brief) table lock. To avoid this impact, shrink your tables in normal running time with the COMPACT keyword, and then repeat the shrink without COMPACT at your next maintenance slot. The second shrink will be very fast, because the work of moving the rows has already been done. Figure 32-5 demonstrates shrinking a table in one operation.

Shrinking Index Segments

As DML is applied to indexed columns, the indexes tend to become inefficient due to wasted space. This is because of the manner in which Oracle's B*Tree indexes are maintained: once space is allocated in a block for an index entry, even if the row to which the index entry refers is deleted, the space remains assigned. It may well be that after a protracted period there are many blocks in an index that are only partially full of live entries, the rest of the space being taken up by deleted entries. This means that

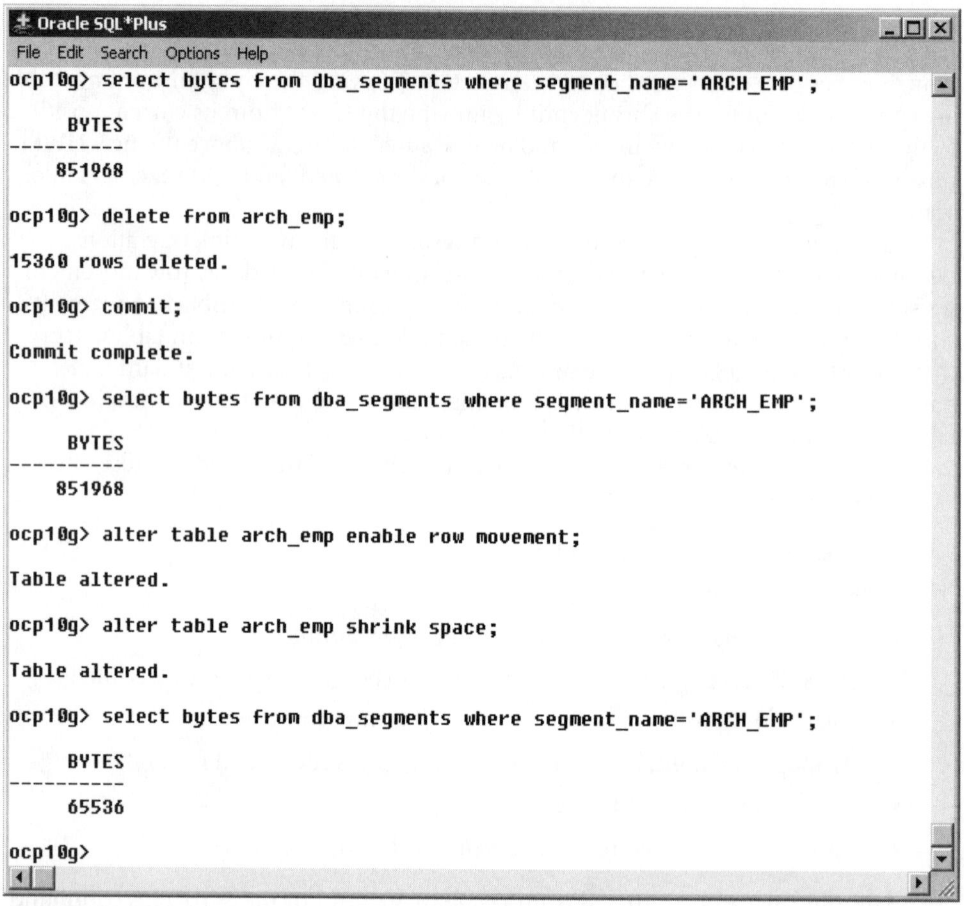

```
 Oracle SQL*Plus                                                      _ □ ×
 File  Edit  Search  Options  Help
ocp10g> select bytes from dba_segments where segment_name='ARCH_EMP';    ▲

     BYTES
----------
    851968

ocp10g> delete from arch_emp;

15360 rows deleted.

ocp10g> commit;

Commit complete.

ocp10g> select bytes from dba_segments where segment_name='ARCH_EMP';

     BYTES
----------
    851968

ocp10g> alter table arch_emp enable row movement;

Table altered.

ocp10g> alter table arch_emp shrink space;

Table altered.

ocp10g> select bytes from dba_segments where segment_name='ARCH_EMP';

     BYTES
----------
     65536

ocp10g>                                                                  ▼
```

Figure 32-5 Using the SHRINK SPACE command

even though there is "unused" space in the blocks that are already part of the index, new insertions will require new blocks to be assigned. To see if this is a problem, analyze the index with the VALIDATE STRUCTURE option and then query the INDEX_STATS view:

```
ocp10g> analyze index i1 validate structure;
Index analyzed.
ocp10g> select lf_rows_len,del_lf_rows_len from index_stats
  2  where name='I1';
LF_ROWS_LEN DEL_LF_ROWS_LEN
----------- ---------------
     283780          144516
```

This shows that about 280KB of space is devoted to index entries, but that about half of it is in fact used by entries that refer to deleted rows. The effect of an index shrink (which in previous releases of the database was known as a "coalesce") is to make the space used by deleted entries available for reuse. The mechanism of moving rows by paired inserts and deletes that shrinks a table cannot be applied to an index, because the index keys must remain in the same place relative to each other: you cannot actually move anything. The shrink, or coalesce, scans the leaf blocks of the index and by compacting the entries for live rows makes the space previously used for deleted rows available for reuse:

```
ocp10g> alter index i1 shrink space;
Index altered.
ocp10g> analyze index i1 validate structure;
Index analyzed.
ocp10g> select lf_rows_len,del_lf_rows_len from index_stats
  2  where name='I1';
LF_ROWS_LEN DEL_LF_ROWS_LEN
----------- ---------------
     139264               0
```

After the shrink, no space is occupied by deleted entries, but if you were to query the DBA_SEGMENTS view, you would find that the size of the segment had not changed. Applying the SHRINK SPACE command to indexes will prevent unnecessary growth of the index but does not actually reduce the size of the index. To do that, you must rebuild it, which is a much more serious operation.

The SHRINK command, when applied to an index, is functionally identical to the older COALESCE command:

```
ocp10g> alter index i1 coalesce;
Index altered.
```

Rebuilding Index Segments

An index shrink, or coalesce, may help with releasing space within an index, but it does not actually return any space to the tablespace. It is, however, a quick and easy operation. An index rebuild creates a completely new index. This will be as efficient as it can be: occupying the minimum amount of space, and having the shallowest possible depth.

To rebuild an index, use the ALTER INDEX...REBUILD ONLINE command:

```
ocp10g> select bytes from dba_segments where segment_name='I1';
    BYTES
----------
   327680
ocp10g> alter index i1 rebuild online;
Index altered.
ocp10g> select bytes from dba_segments where segment_name='I1';
    BYTES
----------
   262144
```

If you do not specify ONLINE, the table will be locked for DML for the duration of the rebuild, which on a large table could mean hours of downtime. During the course of the rebuild you will need up to twice the storage, because both the original and the rebuilt versions of the index coexist while the rebuild is in progress.

 TIP If you have the storage space, always rebuild an index rather than dropping and re-creating it. Index creation requires a sort, but a rebuild can use the keys in the old index, which are already in order.

It is also possible to rebuild an index into a different tablespace. This command,

```
ocp10g> alter index i1 rebuild online tablespace idx_ts;
```

will move the index from its present location into the IDX_TS tablespace.

Monitoring Index Usage

Indexes can improve the performance of queries dramatically, but they can be bad for the performance of DML operations. Whenever the value of an indexed column is changed, not only must the block containing the row be read into memory and changed, but blocks of the index must be manipulated as well. As a general rule, a DBA aims to have only the minimum number of indexes needed to support queries.

Many databases will have indexes that are not being used. For instance, they may have been created for reports that are no longer generated, or perhaps to support certain once-off operations, and have never been dropped. It may also be that the optimizer has realized that for some tables it is actually quicker to use full table scans rather than indexes; this would typically be the case if the tables were small, or if the number of distinct values in the indexed column were low. Every unused index is slowing down the database, for no purpose.

To find out if an index is being used, enable monitoring for the index. Wait for a period, and then check whether it has been used within that period by querying the V$OBJECT_USAGE view. This will have one row for every index in your schema whose usage is being monitored. If the index has not been used, consider dropping it. Take care with the period you choose. It might be that an index is not used during the week but is vital for end-of-week reporting, so leave monitoring running for a full workload cycle before making any decisions. Bear in mind, however, that if an index is used only rarely, it may be worth creating it when needed and dropping it afterward, rather than maintaining it at all times.

 EXAM TIP The index monitoring facility tells you only if an index has been used, not when, or how often, or by which statements.

The example in Figure 32-6 demonstrates enabling monitoring for an index, checks whether the index was used by a query, and then disables monitoring.

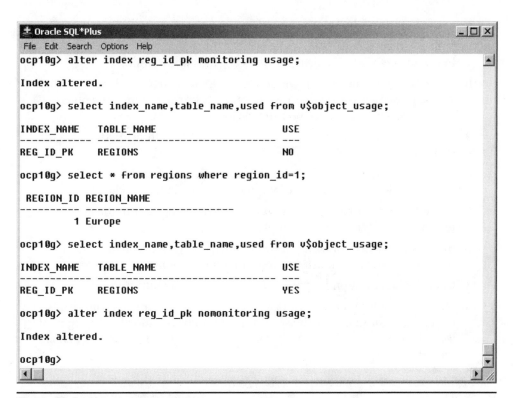

Figure 32-6 Using index monitoring

Exercise 32-3: Using the Database Control Segment Advisor to Shrink a Table

Simulate space wastage within a table, and use Database Control to diagnose and fix the problem.

1. Connect to your database with SQL*Plus as user SYSTEM.

2. Create an ASSM tablespace, a large table within it, and delete all the rows.

   ```
   SQL> create tablespace assm_ts datafile 'assm_ts.dbf'
   size 10m segment space management auto;
   SQL> create table wasted_space tablespace assm_ts as
   select * from dba_objects;
   SQL> delete from wasted_space;
   SQL> commit;
   ```

3. Check the size of the object.

   ```
   SQL> select bytes from user_segments where segment_name = 'WASTED_SPACE';
   ```

4. Connect to your database with Database Control as user SYSTEM.

5. From the database home page, take the Advisor Central link in the Related Links section, and then the link for Segment Advisor.

6. In the Segment Advisor window, select the radio buttons for Schema Objects and Complete Analysis Of All Segments, and click Continue.

7. In the Segment Advisor: Schema Objects window, click Add.

8. In the Schema Objects: Add window, enter SYSTEM as the Schema, and WASTED_SPACE as the Object Name, and click Search. When the object is retrieved, check its check box and click OK and Next.

9. In the Segment Advisor: Options window, leave everything on default and click Next.

10. In the Segment Advisor: Schedule window, select Standard in the Schedule Type drop-down box. Leave everything else on default, and click Next.

11. In the Segment Advisor: Review window, click Submit to run the task, and return to the Advisor Central window.

12. In the Advisor Central window, you will see that your Segment Advisor task has been created. Click Refresh to see that it has completed.

13. Click the radio button for your task, and the View Results button.

14. Study the result of the advisor task, as in Figure 32-7, which recommends that the table be shrunk. Note the space that would be reclaimed if the segment were shrunk. Also, take the Show SQL button to see the statements that are required.

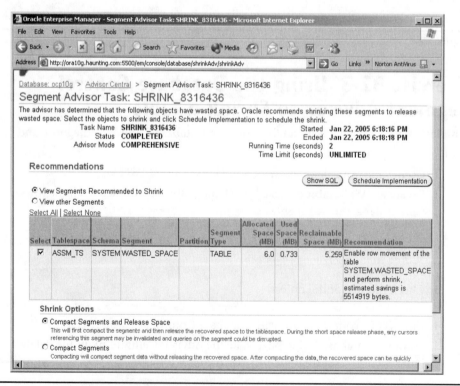

Figure 32-7   Results of a Segment Advisor task

15. Click Schedule Implementation, and submit the job to run immediately.

16. When the job has completed, return to your SQL*Plus session and run the query from Step 3 to confirm that the segment's size has been reduced.

17. Tidy up.

```
SQL> drop tablespace assm_ts including contents and datafiles;
```

Alternative Table Storage Structures

The standard table type in the Oracle database is the heap table. A *heap* consists of variable-length rows in random order; there is no structure to the physical storage. When you create a table, you can demand a heap, but there is little point in doing so because it is what you will get by default anyway. The syntax is

```
SQL> create table heap_tab (c1 date) organization heap;
```

Oracle provides other, more advanced, table structures that can yield significant performance and manageability benefits. These are the index-organized table, or IOT, and three forms of clustered table: index clusters, hash clusters, and sorted hash clusters. Selection of table type is a matter for the DBA and the system designers. Your users, the programmers, have no way of knowing whether a table is a heap or a more sophisticated structure; their code will run unchanged.

 TIP Although the benefits of using these table types can be enormous, it is vital to get it right. Selecting a structure that is inappropriate can be disastrous.

Oracle also supports partitioning of tables. Partitioning divides one logical table into multiple physical segments. There are a number of partitioning options available that can give vast manageability and performance benefits in large databases, but as partitioning is available only as a separately licensed add-on to the Enterprise Edition of the database, it is not covered in the OCP curriculum.

Index-Organized Tables (IOTs)

An *index-organized table (IOT)* looks like a table to the programmers, but the segment structure used to store it is an index. The leaf blocks of a normal B*Tree index segment hold index key values, in order, matched with ROWIDs. These ROWIDs are pointers to the physical addresses of the rows in a heap table segment. An IOT is a B*Tree index, but the leaf blocks contain the key values, followed by the rest of the row; the row itself is stored in the index, and there is no heap table.

Access to rows in an IOT is faster than access to a heap table through an index: rather than searching an index to retrieve a ROWID pointer to a table and then retrieving the row, one operation—the index search—does it all. There are also space savings, in that only one segment is needed, not two.

A more subtle advantage of IOTs over heaps is that the REBUILD ONLINE functionality of an index can be applied to the table. When a heap table is reorganized with the MOVE TABLE command, the table is locked for the duration of the move, and all its indexes must be rebuilt afterward. For an IOT, you can issue MOVE TABLE <table name> ONLINE and there will be no table lock, because the operation is actually implemented as an online index rebuild. Secondary indexes will also survive intact.

There are some limitations on IOTs:

- The table must be created with a primary-key, nondeferrable, constraint. This is used to create the index that holds the table.

- An IOT cannot be a clustered table.

- Composite partitioning cannot be applied to an IOT.

- Columns of type LONG cannot be defined in an IOT.

Access to rows in an IOT by the primary key is extremely fast. Access through secondary keys can be less than optimal, depending on the DML that has been applied to the table. This is because of the way ROWIDs are used. All rows in heap tables are uniquely identified throughout the whole database by a ROWID. This is a pseudo-column that you can select if you wish:

```
ocp10g> select rowid,region_id,region_name from hr.regions;
ROWID               REGION_ID REGION_NAME
------------------- ---------- -----------------------
AAAMAcAAFAAAAANAAA          1 Europe
AAAMAcAAFAAAAANAAB          2 Americas
AAAMAcAAFAAAAANAAC          3 Asia
AAAMAcAAFAAAAANAAD          4 Middle East and Africa
```

Every row has a physical location: it is in a certain block of a certain file. Encrypted within the ROWID is information that can be used to find this. Rows in an IOT do not have a ROWID; they exist only in the index. This means that there is no ROWID for an index entry in a secondary index to point to. Since version 8i of the database, this problem has been solved. You can create secondary indexes on IOTs, but they may not be very efficient. The secondary index structure contains the key value as usual, and then a "guess" as to the physical location of the row. This guess will have been correct when the index was created, but as the IOT undergoes DML, the guess may become wrong, because natural maintenance of the IOT will have caused leaf nodes to split as inserts are done; unlike rows in a heap table, rows in IOTs do not have a fixed location. To cover up for this, a secondary IOT index also stores the primary key value of the row. So when you use an IOT's secondary index, your server process searches the secondary index to retrieve the guess for the physical address of the row, and if the row is still there, you read it immediately. If it is not there, your session reverts to using the primary key to locate the row. So in effect, you may have to search two indexes: first the secondary index, and then the IOT itself.

The primary key–based row identifier is known as the Universal Rowid, the UROWID data type. UROWIDs are also used to store references for rows in remote, non-Oracle, databases. To see them, query the ROWID pseudo-column as in the preceding example. It is not possible for a row to have both a ROWID and a UROWID, so the one pseudo-column is used for both.

When UROWIDs become out-of-date, the performance of the secondary indexes on IOTs will become less efficient. To correct this situation, either rebuild the secondary index with the usual ALTER INDEX...REBUILD ONLINE command or try the less resource-intensive ALTER INDEX...UPDATE BLOCK REFERENCES command.

A normal B*Tree index will usually have many index entries per leaf block of the index. This is because an index entry consists of only the key columns of the table, plus the ROWID pointer. If the key columns are only a few bytes long, Oracle will be able to pack dozens or even hundreds of them into each index block. This changes with an IOT, because the whole row must go into the index blocks. An index with only a few key values per block will be very large, and the searches will not be fast. To avoid this problem, IOTs can be created with an "overflow" segment. The assumption is that in most cases, your programmers will require access to only a few of the table's columns on a regular basis. These columns are stored in the IOT. The remaining, rarely accessed, columns are stored in a separate segment.

Consider an example of a table of employees. The HR application will continuously search this table on employee number for validation that the number exists, and to retrieve the employees' names. It is vital that access to the name by number should be as fast as possible. It is only rarely that the application requires the other columns. The table could be created as follows:

```
ocp10g> create table emp_iot
  2   (emp_no number,
  3    emp_name varchar2(20),
  4    emp_dept number,
  5    emp_address varchar2(500),
  6    emp_hist varchar2(1000),
  7    constraint emp_pk primary key(emp_no))
  8    organization index
  9    including emp_name
 10    tablespace hr_tabs
 11    overflow tablespace hr_over;
```

The first seven lines are a standard table creation, including the definition of a primary key constraint. Line 8 overrides the heap default and is the only requirement for creating an IOT. Line 9 specifies that only the columns up to and including the column EMP_NAME, that is to say just the employees' names and numbers, should actually be stored in the IOT; all remaining columns will be stored in a separate overflow segment. Note that it is possible for the overflow segment to be in a different tablespace.

With this structure, all employee number lookups that retrieve only the employee name can be satisfied from the IOT, and the IOT entries will be small; therefore, there will be many of them per block. Only if a query retrieves additional columns is it necessary to go to the overflow segment.

An alternative syntax is to specify PCTTHRESHOLD rather than INCLUDING. This specifies that no more than a certain percentage of a block should be occupied by any one row; any columns that do not fit in this percentage will go to the overflow segment. Setting PCTTHRESHOLD to 20 will guarantee at least five rows per leaf block of the IOT.

TIP How often do you see "SELECT *" in code? One hopes, never! You should always select columns by name if possible, particularly when using IOTs. "SELECT *" against an IOT means that you will always go to the overflow segment, so you might as well not have bothered to make it an IOT in the first place.

The storage of an overflow segment is actually a heap table. To see the full logical and physical structures involved in IOTs, you must query a number of data dictionary views. Continuing the example of the IOT we just created,

```
ocp10g> select table_name,tablespace_name,iot_name,iot_type
from user_tables;
TABLE_NAME            TABLESPACE_NAME IOT_NAME        IOT_TYPE
-------------------- --------------- --------------- ----------------
EMP_IOT                                               IOT
SYS_IOT_OVER_53978   HR_OVER         EMP_IOT         IOT_OVERFLOW
```

A query against DBA_TABLES shows that the table created, EMP_IOT, does not in fact have any physical existence; it does not exist in a tablespace, only as a logical structure. The table that does exist is the overflow segment, with a system-generated name.

```
ocp10g> select index_name,tablespace_name,index_type,table_name
from user_indexes;
INDEX_NAME       TABLESPACE_NAME INDEX_TYPE      TABLE_NAME
---------------- --------------- --------------- ----------------
EMP_PK           HR_TABS         IOT - TOP       EMP_IOT
```

There is an entry in the DBA_INDEXES view for an index named after the primary key constraint. This is in fact the actual IOT. A query against DBA_SEGMENTS will show what is really going on:

```
ocp10g> select segment_name,tablespace_name,segment_type from
user_segments;
SEGMENT_NAME         TABLESPACE_NAME SEGMENT_TYPE
-------------------- --------------- ----------------
EMP_PK               HR_TABS         INDEX
SYS_IOT_OVER_53978   HR_OVER         TABLE
```

A final topic to cover with IOTs is the use of secondary bitmap indexes. Secondary B*Tree indexes became possible with release 8i, secondary bitmap indexes, with release 9i. But it is necessary to create another segment, the mapping table. The mapping table is a heap-organized table that stores logical rowids of the index-organized table; each mapping table row stores one logical rowid for the corresponding index-organized table row. Then the bitmap indexes are in fact built on this mapping table, not on the underlying IOT. As with B*Tree secondary indexes, if the logical rowids become out-of-date, the efficiency of the index will deteriorate as Oracle has to revert to a primary key index search to retrieve the row. To create a mapping table, either specify MAPPING TABLE when you create the table or add it later with a move command:

```
ocp10g> alter table emp_iot move mapping table;
Table altered.
```

This will reorganize the IOT and generate a mapping table. If the mapping table already exists, it will be rebuilt with updated UROWIDs. To see the physical implementation,

```
ocp10g> select segment_name,tablespace_name,segment_type from
user_segments;
SEGMENT_NAME          TABLESPACE_NAME  SEGMENT_TYPE
--------------------  ---------------  ------------------
SYS_IOT_MAP_53978     HR_TABS          TABLE
EMP_PK                HR_TABS          INDEX
SYS_IOT_OVER_53978    HR_OVER          TABLE
```

It will now be possible to create a secondary bitmap index:

```
ocp10g> create bitmap index emp_dept_idx on emp_iot(emp_dept);
Index created.
```

Creation and management of IOTs, in all their variations, are fully supported by Database Control. Clusters, described next, are not.

Index-Clustered Tables

An *index cluster* is a group of tables stored in one physical segment. All the tables must be linked by a common key; typically, an index cluster will be used to denormalize tables in foreign key relationships. It may well be that rows in a child table are only ever accessed through the foreign key; in that case, storing both the parent and the child table in one cluster will improve performance. A cluster is created with a cluster index, and then the tables created within the cluster must have columns that can be mapped onto the columns of the cluster index.

As with IOTs, the programmers need know nothing about clusters. They will address the tables as usual, including join conditions. But internally, Oracle will store the child rows with the parent rows, and it will therefore not need to perform the join. For example, consider this worked example of a table of staff members and a separate table of address lines:

```
ocp10g> create cluster staff_clust (sno number) index;
Cluster created.
ocp10g> create index staff_idx on cluster staff_clust;
Index created.
ocp10g> create table staff(
  2   sno number,
  3   sname varchar2(20),
  4   constraint staff_pk primary key (sno))
  5*  cluster staff_clust (sno);
Table created.
ocp10g> create table address_lines(
  2   sno number constraint addr_fk references staff,
  3   lno number,
  4   ltext varchar2(100))
  5   cluster staff_clust (sno);
Table created.
```

First, the cluster segment and the index are created. These will be the only segments. Then two tables, parent and child, are created in the cluster. To see the logical storage that the programmers will address,

```
ocp10g> select table_name,tablespace_name,cluster_name from user_tables;
TABLE_NAME           TABLESPACE_NAME CLUSTER_NAME
-------------------- --------------- ---------------
STAFF                USERS           STAFF_CLUST
ADDRESS_LINES        USERS           STAFF_CLUST
```

and to see the physical storage,

```
ocp10g> select segment_name,tablespace_name,segment_type from user_segments;
SEGMENT_NAME         TABLESPACE_NAME SEGMENT_TYPE
-------------------- --------------- ------------------
STAFF_PK             USERS           INDEX
STAFF_CLUST          USERS           CLUSTER
STAFF_IDX            USERS           INDEX
```

Access to the lines of an address will only ever be through the staff number, so clustering the address lines with the staff records makes perfect sense. Note that there is no need for an index on the ADDRESS_LINES table with this structure; the cluster index will be all that is needed.

Hash-Clustered Tables

Like index clusters, *hash clusters* can be used to denormalize tables, but in many cases they will be used for single tables. This is because the hash cluster access method is totally different from normal index access, and it can give huge benefits irrespective of any advantages to be gained from denormalizing data.

A hash cluster is created with a cluster key, as is an index cluster, but rather than creating an index on this key, Oracle will use it to construct a hashing algorithm. Whenever a row is inserted into a table in the hash cluster, Oracle will assign a physical location based on the hash value of the key. This results in the fastest possible method of retrieval: hash key access. When you search for a row on the key column, rather than having to search an index to find the location of the row, Oracle can calculate its location from the hash value. This is CPU intensive rather than I/O intensive and will be far faster.

The drawback with hash clusters is that hash key retrieval is only efficient if you search for rows using the equality predicate on the key. Range searches, or get-next-record type operations, will almost certainly result in a full cluster scan, because the hashing of rows will have spread them randomly throughout the cluster. It is also inadvisable to use hash clusters if you do not have a reasonably accurate idea of the number of rows you expect to insert. The syntax for cluster creation requires an estimate of how many rows, and this is used to construct the hashing algorithm. If you specify a thousand rows and then insert a million rows, the efficiency of the cluster will degrade dramatically, because the hash buckets will be too large. The same problem may arise if the distribution of key values is very uneven.

To work with the same example used previously, consider this command:

```
ocp10g> create cluster staff_clust(sno number)
  2  hashkeys 10000;
Cluster created.
```

This cluster will operate efficiently for up to 10,000 distinct key values. Use the same statements as in the previous example to create the tables.

Sorted Hash-Clustered Tables

The *sorted hash cluster* is conceptually similar to a hash cluster. The cluster segment is created with a hashing algorithm, tables created in the cluster, and the inserted rows randomly distributed according to the value of the column mapped onto the cluster key. The difference is that when creating the cluster, in addition to specifying the columns to be used for the cluster key, you also nominate one or more columns to be used for ordering rows with the same cluster key. This guarantees that the rows will always be returned in the correct order, without the need for any sorting. In the example of the ADDRESS_LINES table, both the index cluster and the hash cluster described in preceding sections will give very efficient retrieval, but the lines will have to be sorted to get them in the correct order. Using a sorted hash cluster, that is no longer necessary:

```
ocp10g> create cluster addr_clust(sno number, lno number sort)
  2  hashkeys 10000 single table;
Cluster created.
ocp10g> create table address_lines(
  2  sno number,
  3  lno number,
  4  ltext varchar2(100))
  5  cluster staff_clust (sno,lno);
Table created.
```

Using these structures, you can select the address lines for a staff member, in the correct order, without the use of any indexes or any sorting. It is undoubtedly the fastest way to retrieve and order data, provided that you access the table using an equality predicate on the cluster key columns. In the example, the cluster is a SINGLE TABLE cluster. Specifying this is optional, but if you do intend to put only one table in the cluster, using this clause will let Oracle construct the cluster more efficiently.

As with the other cluster types, your programmers need know nothing about these structures; they will write normal code with the usual ORDER BY clauses, but no sorting will actually happen.

Chapter Review

This chapter opened with a discussion of the redo log and performance. First, multiplexed online and archive log files should be distributed across devices to avoid contention. Second, online log files should be adequately sized to prevent too-frequent log switches from forcing excessive DBWn activity.

PART II

Moving on to tablespaces and datafiles, these should be adequately sized for the anticipated size of the objects that will be created within them. The default behavior if a session hits a space-related problem is for the statement to be rolled back, and an error returned to the user process. You can change this by enabling the suspension of statements that hit space problems through the ENABLE RESUMABLE command at the session level, or for the whole instance with the RESUMABLE_TIMEOUT instance parameter.

It is, however, better to ensure that space problems never arise in the first place. One approach for this is to enable automatic extension of datafiles, but the best method is to monitor your tablespace usage and take appropriate action before an error occurs. The preconfigured tablespace usage alerts will help with this.

As tables undergo DML, they may acquire more space than they actually need. Indexes also will tend to deteriorate in efficiency with use. Oracle provides the table shrink capability, which will reorganize the space within a table to minimize the wasted space. Indexes too can be reorganized, either by coalescing or by rebuilding. It may indeed be that some indexes serve no purpose and can be dropped; you can identify such indexes by enabling index usage monitoring.

The final section of the chapter is a discussion of various possible table structures. The programmers have no knowledge of these, but they can give huge performance improvements if used appropriately.

IOTs give extremely fast primary key–based access to tables, but there are some restrictions. They can be used with secondary B*Tree indexes, and even bitmapped indexes, but the efficiency of these may deteriorate through their reliance on Universal Rowids.

Index clusters are an excellent structure for storing tables in foreign key relationships, provided you only ever get to the child table through the foreign key. Hash clusters offer the fastest possible data retrieval, if you use the equality predicate on the primary key. Range searches will be bad. Sorted hash clusters are optimal where access is not by primary key and rows should be returned in a particular order.

Questions

1. There is a redo log file advisor. What sort of advice will it give you? (Choose the best answer.)

   A. The maximum advisable size for your online log file members

   B. The minimum advisable size for your online log file members

   C. Recommendations on multiplexing for fault tolerance

   D. Recommendations on the number of logfile groups

   E. All of the above

2. How can you enable the suspension and resumption of statements that hit space errors? (Choose all the correct answers, if any.)

   A. Issue an ALTER SESSION ENABLE RESUMABLE command.

   B. Issue an ALTER SYSTEM ENABLE RESUMABLE command.

C. Set the instance parameter RESUMABLE_STATEMENTS.

D. Set the instance parameter RESUMABLE_TIMEOUT.

E. Use the DBMS_RESUMABLE.ENABLE procedure.

F. None of the above.

3. If a statement is suspended because of a space error, what will happen when the problem is fixed? (Choose the best answer.)

A. After the resumable timeout has expired, the statement will continue executing from the point it had reached.

B. After the resumable timeout has expired, the statement will start executing from the beginning again.

C. The statement will start executing from the beginning immediately after the problem is fixed.

D. The statement will continue executing from the point it had reached immediately after the problem is fixed.

4. You receive an alert warning you that a tablespace is nearly full. What action could you take to prevent this becoming a problem, without any downtime for your users? (Choose two correct answers.)

A. Purge all recycle bin objects in the tablespace.

B. Shrink the tables in the tablespace.

C. Shrink the indexes in the tablespace.

D. Move one or more tables to a different tablespace.

E. Move one or more indexes to a different tablespace.

5. Which process is responsible for sending the alert when a tablespace usage critical threshold is reached? (Choose the best answer.)

A. Database Control

B. The DBMS_SERVER_ALERT package

C. MMON, the manageability monitor process

D. The server process of the session that detected the problem

E. DBWn, the Database Writer, when it detects the problem

6. A tablespace has reached its critical usage threshold. What will happen to the alert message? (Choose the best answer.)

A. The alert will be sent every ten minutes, until it is cleared.

B. The alert will remain in the DBA_OUTSTANDING_ALERTS view for a maximum of twenty-four hours.

C. The alert will be reported every twenty-four hours, if it is not cleared.

D. The alert will be posted to DBA_ALERT_HISTORY after it has been reported.

E. The alert will be posted to DBA_ALERT_HISTORY once it is cleared.

7. What must you do before executing a table shrink operation? (Choose the best answer.)

   A. Compact the table.

   B. Disable triggers on the table.

   C. Disable row movement for the table.

   D. Enable row movement for the table.

   E. Disable the primary key constraint on the table.

8. Which of the following statements describe the effect of the command

   ```
   alter table emp shrink space compact cascade;
   ```

   (Choose the best answer.)

   A. The table EMP will be compacted and reduced in size, as will all associated indexes, materialized views, and materialized view logs.

   B. The table EMP will be compacted only, as will all associated indexes, materialized views, and materialized view logs.

   C. The operation will apply to the EMP table and its indexes only. No space will be returned to the tablespace.

   D. The statement will fail because you cannot specify both COMPACT and CASCADE in one SHRINK command.

9. Which of the following will cause a table shrink to fail? (Choose four answers.)

   A. The tablespace is not ASSM.

   B. The table does not have a primary key.

   C. The table has a column of type LONG.

   D. The table has a column of type BLOB.

   E. Row movement has not been enabled for the table.

   F. The table has indexes, and you do not specify CASCADE.

   G. It is an index-organized table.

   H. It is a clustered table.

10. What tool is provided to tell you how often an index segment is being used? (Choose the best answer.)

    A. The Segment Advisor in Database Control

    B. The ALTER INDEX MONITORING USAGE facility

    C. The INDEX_STATS view

    D. There is no tool for this

11. How can you reduce the amount of space that an index segment is occupying? (Choose the best answer.)

    A. Coalesce the index.

    B. Shrink the index.

C. Rebuild the index.

D. Shrink the index's table, with the CASCADE option.

12. Suppose you create a table with this command:

```
create table emp_iot
(emp_no number,
emp_name varchar2(20),
emp_address varchar2(500),
emp_hist varchar2(1000),
constraint emp_pk primary key(emp_no))
organization index
including emp_name
overflow
mapping table;
```

How many segments will be created? (Choose the best answer.)

A. 1

B. 2

C. 3

D. 4

E. None, the command will fail because no tablespaces are specified

13. What will happen if you query a table in a sorted hash cluster and include an ORDER BY clause to sort the data on the column(s) specified as the cluster sort key? (Choose the best answer.)

A. The statement will fail because you cannot use an ORDER BY clause on the columns used as the cluster sort key.

B. The rows will be sorted.

C. There will be no sort performed, because the cluster index will be used to return the rows in sorted order.

D. The ORDER BY clause will be ignored.

14. If you create an index cluster and a cluster index, and then a table in the cluster and an index on the table, how many segments will you have? (Choose the best answer.)

A. 1

B. 2

C. 3

D. 4

Answers

1. B. The redo log advisor will calculate the minimum size of the online log file groups needed to avoid excessive checkpointing activity.

2. A and D. Resumable statements can be enabled interactively for one session or for all sessions with the RESUMABLE_TIMEOUT instance parameter.

3. **D.** If resumable statements have been enabled, then a statement that hits a problem will hang either until the problem is fixed, in which case it will continue from where it stopped, or until the resumable timeout is reached, in which case it will be aborted.

4. **B and E.** Both shrinking tables and moving indexes (which can be done online) to a different tablespace will solve the problem with no downtime. It won't help to purge recycle bin objects because dropped objects are not counted as used space by the alert system. Shrinking the indexes will not help because an index shrink doesn't return space to the tablespace; only a rebuild will do that. Moving the tables would solve the problem, but with downtime—there would be a table lock, and the indexes would be broken.

5. **C.** Alerts are sent by MMON. Database Control reports alerts; it doesn't generate them. DBMS_SERVER_ALERT is used to configure the alert system. Server processes can detect a problem, but only reports it to the session. And DBWn has no connection to the alert system.

6. **E.** Alert messages are visible in DBA_OUTSTANDING_ALERTS until they are cleared, when they go to DBA_ALERT_HISTORY.

7. **D.** The only requirement is to enable row movement. Compaction is part of the shrink process, and disabling triggers is unnecessary because the shrink itself will take care of not firing triggers. Primary key constraints are not relevant to shrinking.

8. **C.** The COMPACT keyword instructs Oracle not to shift the HWM and free up space, and the CASCADE keyword means shrink the indexes too, but neither of these will return space to the tablespace. The first two choices are both wrong because they assume that CASCADE will affect objects other than indexes.

9. **A, C, E, and H.** ASSM and row movement are requirements for shrinking, but the shrink will still fail if the table contains LONG columns or is clustered.

10. **D.** There is no tool that will tell you how often an index has been used. The closest to a correct answer is B, but index monitoring will tell you only if an index has been used, not how often.

11. **C.** A rebuild is the only way to reclaim space from an index. The other answers are all the same: they will free space within the index, not reduce its size.

12. **C.** There will be three segments: the IOT index segment, the mapping table heap segment, and the overflow heap segment.

13. **D.** The ORDER BY clause will be ignored because the rows will be returned in order anyway. No sort is needed.

14. **C.** There will be three segments: the cluster segment, the cluster index segment, and the index segment.

CHAPTER 33

Managing Storage with Automatic Storage Management

In this chapter you will learn how to

- Set up initialization parameter files for ASM and database instances
- Execute SQL commands with ASM filenames
- Start up and shut down ASM instances
- Administer ASM disk groups
- Use RMAN to migrate your database to ASM

Automatic Storage Management, or ASM, is a facility provided with the Oracle database for managing your disks. It is an Oracle-aware logical volume manager, or LVM, that can stripe and mirror database files and recovery files across a number of physical devices. This is an area where the database administration domain overlaps with the system administration domain.

Many databases will not use ASM: they will store their files on the volumes provided by the operating system, which may well be managed by an LVM. But if you do not have a proper logical LVM, as will probably be the case with low-end systems running on, for example, Linux or Windows, then ASM provides an excellent (and bundled) alternative to purchasing and installing one. On high-end systems, ASM can work with whatever LVM is provided by the operating system.

NOTE Most of the examples in this chapter are for Windows. This is because ASM on Windows functions perfectly with a standard installation of Oracle straight out of the box. On Linux, there may be some additional steps; these are beyond the scope of the OCP examination but are briefly described at the end of the chapter.

Before going into the details of ASM architecture and configuration, following is a brief discussion of logical and physical volume management. This is not intended to be any sort of comprehensive treatment (which is not necessary for the OCP exam) but rather the minimum information needed to appreciate the purpose of ASM.

The Purpose of a Logical Volume Manager

Your database server machine will have one or more disks, either internal to the computer or in external disk arrays. These disks are the physical volumes. In virtually all modern computer installations, there is a layer of abstraction between these physical volumes and the logical volumes. Logical volumes are virtual disks, or file systems, that are visible to application software, such as the Oracle database. Physical volumes are presented to the software as logical volumes by the operating system's *logical volume manager*, or *LVM*.

Even the simplest computer nowadays will probably be using some sort of LVM, though it may be extremely limited in its capabilities. In the case of a Windows PC, you may well have only one disk, partitioned into two logical drives: perhaps a C: drive formatted with the FAT32 file system, and a D: drive formatted with the NTFS file system. Thus one physical volume is presented to you by Windows as two logical volumes. Larger installations may have dozens or hundreds of disks. By using an LVM to put these physical volumes into arrays that can be treated as one huge disk area and then partitioned into as many (or as few) logical volumes as you want, your system administrators can provide logical volumes of whatever size, performance, and fault tolerance is appropriate.

RAID Levels

If the physical volumes are mapped one-to-one onto logical volumes, the performance and fault tolerance of the logical volumes is exactly that of the physical volumes. RAID, in its various levels, is intended to enhance performance and fault tolerance by exploiting the presence of multiple physical volumes. There are four levels to consider in most environments.

RAID level 0 is optimal for performance but suboptimal for fault tolerance. A RAID 0 array consists of one or more logical volumes cut across two or more physical volumes. Theoretically, this will improve logical disk I/O rates and decrease fault tolerance by a proportion equal to the number of physical volumes. For example, if the array consists of four disks, then it will be possible to read and write all them concurrently; a given amount of data can be transferred to the logical volume in a quarter of the time it would take if the logical volume were on only one disk. But if any of the four disks is damaged, the logical volume will be affected, so it is four times more likely to fail than if it were on only one disk.

RAID level 1 is optimal for fault tolerance. There may be performance gains, but that is not why you use it. Where RAID 1 is definitely suboptimal is cost. A RAID 1 array consists of one or more logical volumes mirrored across two or more disks: whenever data is written to the logical volume, copies of it will be written concurrently to two or more physical volumes. If any one physical volume is lost, the logical volume will survive because all data on the lost physical volume is available on another physical volume. There may be a performance improvement for read operations if it is possible to read different data from the mirrors concurrently; this will depend on the capabilities of the LVM. The cost problem is simply that you will require double the disk capacity—more than double, if you want a higher degree of mirroring. In the four-disk example, the logical volume will be equivalent in size to only two of the physical disks, but you can lose any one disk, and possibly two disks, before the logical volume is damaged.

RAID level 5 is a compromise between the performance of RAID 0 and the fault tolerance of RAID 1. The logical volume is cut across multiple physical volumes (so concurrent read and writes are possible), and a checksumming algorithm writes out enough information to allow reconstruction of the data on any one physical volume, if it gets damaged. Thus you do not get all the performance gain of RAID 0, because of the checksumming overhead; in particular, write operations can be slow because each write operation needs to calculate the checksum before the write can take place. You do not get all the fault tolerance of RAID 1, because you can survive the loss of only one disk. In the four-disk example, the logical volume will be equivalent in size to three physical volumes, and if any one of the four is lost, the logical volume will survive.

RAID 0+1 is optimal for both fault tolerance and performance: you mirror your striped disks. In the four-disk example, your system administrators would create one logical volume striped across two of the physical disks and mirror this to the other two disks. This should result in double the performance and double the safety (and double the price) of mapping one logical volume directly onto one physical volume.

Volume Sizes

Physical volumes have size restrictions. A disk is a certain size, and this cannot be changed. Logical volumes may have no size restrictions at all. If your LVM allows you to put a hundred disks of 100GB each into a RAID 0 array, then your logical volume will be 10TB big. (It will also perform superbly, but it will not be very tolerant against disk failure.) Furthermore, logical volumes can usually be resized at will, while the system is running.

Choice of RAID Level

Many system administrators will put all their physical volumes into RAID 5 arrays. This is simple to do and provides a certain amount of fault tolerance and perhaps a small performance improvement, but this may not be the best practice for an Oracle database. As the DBA, you should take control of the RAID strategy and apply different levels to different file types.

Some files are critical to the database remaining open: the files that make up the SYSTEM tablespace, the active UNDO tablespace, and the controlfile copies. Damage to any of these will cause the database to crash. Some files are critical for performance: the online redo log files and the controlfiles. I/O on these can be a serious bottleneck. By considering the characteristics of each file, a RAID strategy should become apparent. For example, the SYSTEM and UNDO tablespaces should be on RAID 1 volumes, so that they will always be available. The online redo logs are protected by multiplexing, so you don't have to worry about hardware fault tolerance, but performance is vital, so put them on RAID 0 volumes. The controlfile copies are critical for performance, but if any copy is damaged, the database will crash; thus, RAID 0+1 could be appropriate. Your other datafiles could perhaps go on RAID 5 volumes, unless they are particularly important or volatile.

ASM Compared with Third-Party LVMs

ASM has a huge advantage over other logical volume managers: it is aware of the nature of Oracle database files. This means it can make more intelligent decisions about how to manage the files than a third-party product.

First, when a logical volume is cut across several physical volumes in what are called "stripes," a decision must be made on the size of the stripe. Different file types will perform better with different stripe sizes: ASM is aware of this and will stripe them appropriately.

Second, ASM can handle files individually, whereas all other LVMs work at the volume level: they are not aware of the files within the volume. So with a third-party LVM, you have to specify RAID attributes per volume. ASM can specify the attributes per file, so you can for instance have three-way mirroring for your SYSTEM tablespace datafiles but no mirroring at all for your temporary tablespaces' tempfiles, all within the same logical volume.

Third, ASM is in principle the same on all platforms, and it is bundled with the database. You do not have to learn (and perhaps purchase) different volume managers for different platforms. Any configuration you do is portable, within the limits of device naming conventions.

Fourth, there is the question of availability. Some operating systems come with an LVM as standard. With AIX on IBM hardware, for example, use of the LVM is not an option—it is compulsory. With other vendor's operating systems, the LVM may be a separately licensed option, or there may not be one at all—you will have to buy a third-party product. ASM is always available and should bring significant performance and manageability benefits to systems that do not have an LVM; on those that do, it will add an extra, Oracle-aware, layer to space management that will further enhance performance while reducing the management workload.

The ASM Architecture

Implementing ASM requires a change in the instance architecture. It even requires another instance. There is an instance parameter INSTANCE_TYPE that defaults to RDBMS. An RDBMS instance is a normal instance, used for opening a database and accepting user sessions. Setting this parameter to ASM will start an Automatic Storage Management instance, which is very different. An ASM instance is not used by end users; it controls access to ASM files stored on ASM disk groups, on behalf of the RDBMS instances. These files are functionally the same as non-ASM database files: they are datafiles, controlfiles, logfiles, and recovery files, but they are stored in the ASM logical volume manager environment, not in the file systems provided by your operating system.

The ASM Disks and Disk Groups

An ASM *disk group* is a pool of ASM disks managed as one logical unit. As with any other LVM, ASM takes a number of physical volumes and presents them to Oracle as one or more logical volumes. The physical volumes can be actual disks, or they can be volumes managed by a volume manager that is part of your operating system. Either way, they will not be formatted with any file system; they must be raw devices. ASM will take the raw devices and put them into a number of ASM disk groups. A disk group is the logical volume.

 EXAM TIP ASM disks must be raw devices, without a file system, but they do not need to be actual disks. They can be disks, partitions of a disk, or logical volumes managed by an LVM.

For example, on a Linux system you might have six SCSI disks, of 36GB each. You could decide to use one of them, /dev/sda, for the root file system and utilities. Then use /dev/sdb for the $ORACLE_HOME directories, and then /dev/sdc, /dev/sdd, /dev/sde, and /dev/sdf for the database files. You would create a file system on each disk and format it—probably as ext3—and then mount the file systems onto directory mount points in the root file system. This is all very well, but you are wasting the performance potential of the machine. It will be extremely difficult to balance the I/O evenly across the four disks used for the database, and you will have to monitor which files have the most activity and try to keep them separate. Also, one disk may fill up while the others have plenty of space.

The equivalent Windows example would be drive C: for Windows itself, and drive D: for the ORACLE_HOME. Then drives E:, F:, G:, and H: would be dedicated to database files. Probably all the disks would be formatted as NTFS.

If you were to put the four disks dedicated to the database into one RAID 0 logical volume, you would get better performance, and a system that requires much less monitoring and management. But it may be that you do not have a logical volume manager. Enter ASM....

To use ASM, you would not format the four disks to be used for database files. The root file system and the ORACLE_HOME file system must be managed as normal; you cannot use ASM volumes for anything other than database files. Then you would launch an ASM instance and set instance parameters such that it will find the four raw volumes and place them into one ASM disk group. This group will contain the database, with whatever RAID characteristics you want.

EXAM TIP You can use ASM only for database files, not for your Oracle home or for anything else.

The size of the ASM disk group is the sum of the size of the ASM disks, but depending on what degree of fault tolerance is specified, the size available for use will be less. The default fault tolerance is single mirror, meaning that, to continue our example, the end result will be 72GB of space available for the database. This degree of mirroring can be changed for the whole group, or for individual files within it.

Disks can be added and removed from a disk group dynamically, within certain limits. In general, if the operating system and hardware can handle adding or removing disks while the computer is running, then ASM can handle this as well.

The ASM Instance

When using non-ASM files, an RDBMS instance will locate and open its files itself. In the ASM environment, these tasks are carried out by an ASM instance on behalf of the RDBMS instance. But even in an ASM environment, the RDBMS instance will always do its own I/O; its server processes will read the datafiles, its DBWn process will write to the datafiles, and the LGWR will write to the online redo log files.

EXAM TIP Normal disk activity does not go through the ASM instance. ASM is a management and control facility that makes the files available; it does not do the actual I/O work.

In some respects, an ASM instance is an instance like any other. It has an SGA and some of the usual background processes. But it cannot mount or open a database; all it can do is locate and manage ASM disks. Many instance parameters are not legal for an ASM instance. Usually, the parameter file (which may be a dynamic spfile or a static pfile) will have only half a dozen parameters. Because it cannot mount or open a database, it will never be able to read a data dictionary; for this reason, you can only connect to it with password file or operating system authentication, as SYSOPER or as SYSDBA.

It is possible to have more than one ASM instance running on one computer, but there is no value in doing this. You should create one ASM instance per computer and use it to manage all the ASM disks available to that computer on behalf of all the RDBMS instances running on the computer.

An ASM instance will have two background processes in addition to the usual processes. These are the RBAL and the ARBn processes, used to handle rebalancing activity—the movement of data between ASM disks in an ASM disk group, in response to adding or removing a disk to or from the group. If a new device is added to a group, ASM will detect this and initiate an operation to bring the disk into use. This will mean moving data onto the disk, to take account of the increased possibilities for striping and to include the new disk in spreading the I/O workload evenly. The RBAL process coordinates this rebalancing, and the ARBn processes (several of these may be launched automatically) do the work. Also, if a disk leaves an ASM disk group, either by design or because of a hardware failure, a rebalancing operation is necessary. In either case, the redistribution of data will occur without users being aware of the problem.

To create and configure disk groups, you must first connect to the ASM instance and start it. Having created the groups, the ASM instance will then wait for requests from RDBMS instances for access to files.

The RDBMS Instance

An RDBMS instance that is using ASM files functions as normal, except that it will have two additional background processes: RBAL and ASMB. The RBAL process opens the ASM disks, which it will locate through the ASM instance. The ASMB process connects to the ASM instance by creating a session against it, via a server process. This session is responsible for the continuing communication between the RDBMS instance and the ASM instance; in effect, the RDBMS instance becomes a client to the ASM server. The information passed over this session will be requests for physical changes, such as file creation, deletion, or resizing, and also various statistics and status messages.

It is not necessary to inform the RDBMS instance of the name of the ASM instance. When an ASM instance starts, it registers its name and the names of the ASM disk groups it is managing with the Cluster Synchronization service. This is why the Oracle cluster services must be running, even if the node and instance are not clustered. The RDBMS instance does know the names of the disk groups that it is using; these names are embedded in the ASM filenames stored (like any other filenames) in the RDBMS instance's controlfile, and this lets the ASMB process instance locate the ASM instance managing those groups by interrogating the Cluster Synchronization service.

Commonly, an RDBMS instance will require access to only two disk groups: one for its live database files, the other for its flash recovery area.

The ASM Files

Files in ASM disk groups are managed by the ASM instance on behalf of the RDBMS instances. They are created, read, and written by the RDBMS instances. The files types that will commonly be stored as ASM files include any or all of these:

- Controlfile
- Initialization parameter file
- Online redo log files
- Archive redo log files
- Datafiles
- Tempfiles
- RMAN backup sets
- RMAN image copies
- Flashback logs
- Controlfile autobackups
- Data Pump dump files

As this list shows, the whole database can be stored on ASM disks, as can all recovery-related files; you can direct the flash recovery area to an ASM disk group.

 EXAM TIP ASM does not manage the Oracle binaries, nor the alert log, trace files, or password file.

All ASM files are striped across all the ASM disks in the group. The allocation of space is by *allocation unit*, or *AU*. The standard AU size is 1MB, and for files where data access tends to take the form of reasonably large disk I/O operations, such as datafiles or archive log files, the striping is also in 1MB units. This is known as "coarse" striping. For files where read and write requests are generally for smaller units of I/O, such as online logs and the controlfile, the AUs themselves are striped across the disks in 128KB stripes, in what is known as "fine" striping. Thus there will be lower latency in satisfying the (typically, small) requests for reads and writes of these file types, because the one small request can be split up into several even smaller requests directed to each disk in parallel.

The syntax for creating and managing ASM files is exactly the same as for file system–based files. All ASM files are created and managed by the RDBMS instance, using the usual commands. The only difference is in the filename: when creating a database file, you specify only the name of the disk group to which the file should be directed, and ASM will generate the actual filename and manage the physical locations.

There is a one-to-one relationship between a database file and an ASM file. If your database has 200 datafiles using conventional file system storage, it will still have 200 datafiles when you convert to ASM. But they will no longer exist as individual files that you can see with operating system utilities. In fact, normal operating system commands will not be able to see anything at all within the ASM disks, because they are not formatted with a file system. This means that the only way to get at ASM files is through Oracle utilities. This is not a problem at all, but it does mean that you must use RMAN to back up your ASM datafiles, archive logs, and controlfiles.

ASM files can coexist with files stored within file systems. There is no reason why a tablespace should not consist of one ASM file and one conventional file, but there would be no purpose in such an arrangement. However, this does mean that it is possible to migrate a database to ASM over time, by moving the various files whenever convenient. Because you cannot write to an ASM disk group with any operating system tools, for datafiles this move must be accomplished with RMAN through a backup and restore operation. To move online logs, create new members in an ASM disk group and drop the old members.

Creating Raw Devices

Your system administrators will be responsible for creating the raw devices to be given to ASM. These may be whole disks, partitions of a disk, or RAID devices provided by a logical volume manager. Whatever they are, there will be an operating system syntax that lets Oracle address them: a Unix raw device will be addressed through a block device driver in the /dev directory; Windows will address it through a \\.\ path name. On a Windows PC, you could use the Microsoft Management Console Disk Management snap-in to create the devices. On a Linux PC, you could use the fdisk utility. Larger systems will have an LVM, either part of the operating system or a third-party product such as Veritas.

Exercise 33-1: Creating Raw Devices (Windows)

On a Windows PC, create two raw partitions. The examples that follow are only suggestions; your Windows administrators will be able to advise on the details for your computer.

1. From the Start button, navigate to Settings | Control Panel | Administrative Tools | Computer Management | Disk Management.

   Figure 33-1 shows a PC with one disk, Disk 0. The disk has three partitions. The first is just 24MB, formatted with the FAT32 file system. The second partition is 24.41GB, formatted with NTFS. The third partition is 3.91GB, and Windows can't understand it (in fact, it is a Linux ext3 partition). And then there is 8.91GB of disk space that is not allocated at all.

   NOTE If your PC does not have any unallocated space, use a partition management tool such as PartitionMagic from Symantec to reduce the size of an existing partition to provide some unallocated space, or install another disk.

2. Right-click the unallocated space, and launch the New Partition Wizard. Click Next to proceed.

3. When prompted to create a partition, choose to create an extended partition, not a primary partition. Click Next to continue.

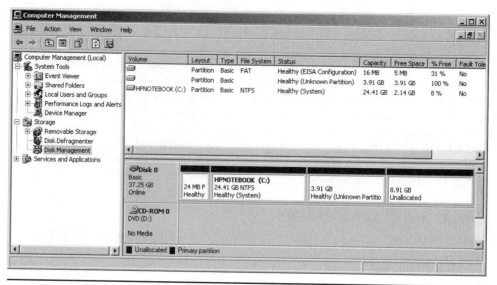

Figure 33-1 Windows disk partitions

4. When prompted for the size of the partition, choose the maximum size available. Click Next to continue, and Finish to see the partition information shown in Figure 33-2.

5. Right-click the free space in the new partition, and select New Logical Drive to launch the New Partition Wizard again, and click Next to continue.

6. Select the radio button for Logical Drive. Click Next to continue.

7. When prompted for a partition size, enter a size that is less than half of the maximum space available; 4000MB in this example. Click Next to continue.

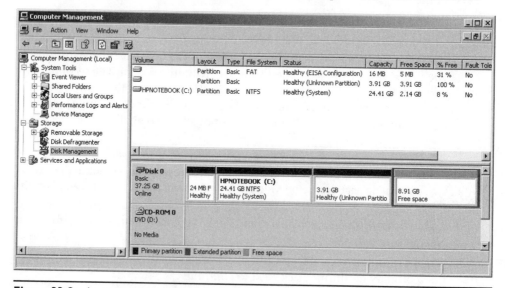

Figure 33-2 An empty extended partition

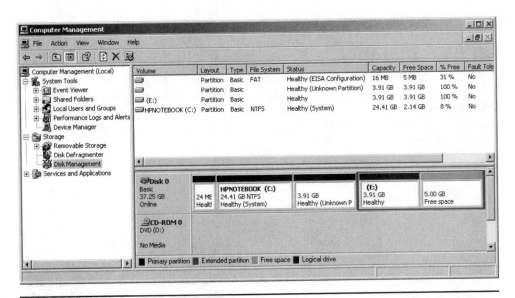

Figure 33-3   A drive E:, with no file system

8. Select the radio button to assign a drive letter, and accept whatever letter is suggested. Click Next to continue.

9. Select the radio button for Do Not Format This Partition, and click Next to continue.

10. Click Finish to confirm. The logical drive, with no file system, will appear as in Figure 33-3.

11. Repeat Steps 5–10 to create a second unformatted logical drive in the extended partition (see Figure 33-4).

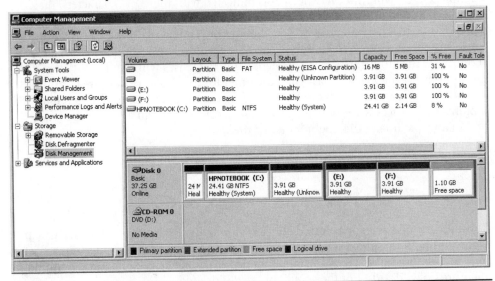

Figure 33-4   Two unformatted logical drives, E: and F:, of 4GB each

Creating, Starting, and Stopping an ASM Instance

An ASM instance is controlled by an instance parameter file, as is an RDBMS instance, but there are strict limits on the parameters that can be included. Many will cause an ASM instance to have errors on startup, so keep the parameter file as small as possible. The parameters most likely to be needed (and often all that are required) are in the table that follows:

Parameter	Required?	Description
instance_type	Yes	Must be ASM for an ASM instance. Default is RDBMS
instance_name	No	Must be prefixed with "+". Defaults to the ORACLE_SID environment variable
asm_power_limit	No	Controls resources to be used for rebalancing operations. Default is 1, the lowest
asm_diskstring	Yes	List of paths identifying the disks to be given to ASM
asm_diskgroups	No	Disk groups to be mounted on startup. Default is NULL

An ASM parameter file for Windows might take this form:

```
instance_name='+asm'
instance_type='asm'
asm_diskstring='\\.\*:'
asm_diskgroups=dgroupA,dgroupB
background_dump_dest='d:\oracle\admin\dump\asm'
```

The instance name must be prefixed with a "+" symbol, on all platforms. On Windows, this must also be specified when creating the Windows service for the instance. The syntax for the ASM_DISKSTRING will be platform specific. In the example, Oracle will find every device, as indicated with the "\\.\" characters, that includes the ":" character in its name. All Windows disk devices that have been assigned a drive letter will have a ":" in their name. The two nominated disk groups must exist; if this is the first startup of the ASM instance, omit this parameter and set it only after the groups have been created. Many databases will require only two disk groups: one for the live database files, the other for the flash recovery area. Wildcard characters (such as the asterisk in the preceding example) can be used to let ASM find a number of devices without having to name them all individually.

A Linux parameter file might look like this:

```
instance_name='+asm'
instance_type='asm'
asm_diskstring='/dev/md2','/dev/md3','/dev/md4','/dev/md5'
asm_diskgroups=dgroupA,dgroupB
remote_login_passwordfile=exclusive
```

This time the disk string has four distinct values, rather than using wildcards, which will let it find four named RAID devices. The two nominated disk groups must exist and be composed of the RAID volumes named in diskstring. In this example, there are no wildcards, but they could be used if desired.

To start the instance, you must connect to it as SYSDBA and issue a STARTUP command. The connection can be made by setting the ORACLE_SID environment variable to the instance name (not forgetting that it must be prefixed with a "+" symbol), or if a password file has been created and enabled as in the preceding example, you can connect with password file authentication. The startup will first go through NOMOUNT, where the instance is built in memory. Then the MOUNT will locate the disks found by the ASM_DISKSTRING and open the disk groups specified by ASM_DISKGROUPS. There is no OPEN for an ASM instance.

 TIP The size of an ASM instance can, as in the preceding examples, be left completely on default. This will result in an instance of about 100MB. In most circumstances this is both sufficient and necessary.

RDBMS instances use files in disk groups managed by the ASM instance. If the ASM instance has not started and mounted the disk groups, then the RDBMS instances cannot open. It is therefore necessary to ensure, through your operating system utilities, that the ASM instance starts before the RDBMS instances that are dependent upon it. Similarly, if the ASM instance shuts down, then the dependent RDBMS instances must shut down also. When a SHUTDOWN command is issued to an ASM instance, before it shuts down the command is propagated to all dependent RDBMS instances. They will then shut down with the same mode, and only then will the ASM instance shut down. The exception to this rule is SHUTDOWN ABORT. Issuing this to an ASM instance will terminate it immediately, and the RDBMS instances will then terminate with ABORT when they detect that the ASM instance is no longer available.

 EXAM TIP If an RDBMS instance fails, the ASM instance will not be affected. If an ASM instance fails, the RDBMS instances will abort.

Exercise 33-2: Creating an ASM Instance (Windows)

Create a parameter file and use it to start an ASM instance. All this exercise should be done from an operating system prompt.

1. From an operating system prompt, run the ORADIM utility to create a Windows service for the ASM instance.

   ```
   C:\> oradim -new -asmsid +ASM -startmode manual
   ```

2. In your ORACLE_HOME\database directory, use Windows Notepad to create a file called INIT+ASM.ORA with just these three lines:

   ```
   instance_name='+asm'
   instance_type='asm'
   asm_diskstring='\\.\*:'
   ```

3. Set your ORACLE_SID environment variable to the ASM instance name.

   ```
   c:\> set ORACLE_SID=+ASM
   ```

4. Connect to the ASM instance with SQL*Plus as SYSDBA, and start the instance.

```
C:\>sqlplus / as sysdba
SQL*Plus: Release 10.1.0.2.0 - Production on Mon Jan 3 22:52:26 2005
Copyright (c) 1982, 2004, Oracle.  All rights reserved.
Connected to an idle instance.
SQL> startup
ASM instance started
Total System Global Area  100663296 bytes
Fixed Size                   787648 bytes
Variable Size              99875648 bytes
Database Buffers                  0 bytes
Redo Buffers                      0 bytes
ORA-15110: no diskgroups mounted
SQL>
```

5. Confirm that ASM has found the disks.

```
SQL> select path,total_mb from v$asm_disk;
PATH            TOTAL_MB
----------    ----------
\\.\E:              4000
\\.\F:              4000
\\.\C:             24999
```

In this example, the ASM_DISKSTRING parameter specified every device with a colon in its name, so the instance has found the three logical drives C:, E:, and F:.

Creating ASM Disk Groups

Disk groups are created by an ASM instance and then used by an RDBMS instance. To create a disk group, as a minimum give the group a name and a list of disks that have been discovered by the ASM disk string and are therefore visible in the V$ASM_DISK view:

```
SQL> create diskgroup dg1 disks '/dev/sdc', '/dev/sdd', '/dev/sde', '/dev/sdf';
```

If you nominate a disk that is already part of a disk group, the command will fail. The default level of redundancy provided by ASM is "normal" redundancy, meaning that each AU is mirrored once. All files will be striped across all the disks for maximum performance. For normal redundancy, the group must have at least two disks, and the effective size of the group will be half the total space allocated.

In the preceding example, which continues the Linux four-SCSI-disk example discussed earlier, the result will be a disk group with an effective size of 72GB. Every file created in the group will (unless specified otherwise) be striped and mirrored with RAID 0+1. The stripe size will be selected by ASM according to the type of file: online redo log files and controlfile copies will be fine striped; datafiles and archive logs will be coarse striped.

To override the default NORMAL redundancy, meaning single mirror, add the keywords HIGH REDUNDANCY or EXTERNAL REDUNDANCY to the CREATE DISKGROUP command. HIGH REDUNDANCY will create three copies of every allocation unit (and therefore requires a minimum of three disks), and EXTERNAL

REDUNDANCY will not mirror at all: the assumption is that there is an underlying LVM that is doing whatever level of RAID is deemed appropriate.

Redundancy can be taken a step further by putting ASM disks within a disk group into failure groups. When ASM mirrors extents, it will never mirror an extent to another disk in the same failure group. This means that you are better protected against the failure of multiple disks. By default, each disk is considered to be its own failure group; this gives ASM complete freedom to mirror that disk's data onto any other disk in the group. However, if some disks are connected at the hardware level, typically by being attached to the same controller, you would not want ASM to mirror between them. Using failure groups forces ASM to create mirrors on a different subset of the disks within the group. An example of this is

```
SQL> create diskgroup dgroupa normal redundancy
failgroup controller2 disk '/dev/rdsk/c2*'
failgroup controller3 disk '/dev/rdsk/c3*';
```

This command creates a disk group consisting of all the disk devices matched by the wildcards given, which is all the disks hanging off the second and third controllers. But the use of failure groups instructs ASM never to mirror data between two disks that are on the same controller.

Exercise 33-3: Creating a Disk Group (Windows)

Use the ASM instance created in Exercise 33-2 to create a disk group with the two raw volumes created in Exercise 33-1.

1. From an operating system prompt, set your ORACLE_SID environment variable to the ASM instance.

   ```
   C:\> set ORACLE_SID=+ASM
   ```

2. Connect to your ASM instance with SQL*Plus with the SYSDBA privilege using operating system authentication.

   ```
   c:\> sqlplus / as sysdba
   ```

3. Create a disk group, nominating the two raw volumes.

   ```
   SQL> create diskgroup dg1 disk '\\.\E:','\\.\F:';
   ```

4. Confirm the creation of the group by querying the relevant views.

   ```
   SQL> select name,group_number,type,state,total_mb from v$asm_diskgroup;
   NAME     GROUP_NUMBER TYPE    STATE         TOTAL_MB
   -------- ------------ ------  -----------   ----------
   DG1                 1 NORMAL MOUNTED            8000
   SQL> select path,group_number,total_mb from v$asm_disk;
   PATH     GROUP_NUMBER   TOTAL_MB
   -------- ------------ ----------
   \\.\C:              0      24999
   \\.\E:              1       4000
   \\.\F:              1       4000
   ```

   In this example, the group has NORMAL redundancy, so the total space available, 8GB, will be effectively halved. The group is MOUNTED, meaning that it is available for use. The second query shows that of the three disk devices discovered, E: and F: have been assigned to a disk group.

5. To ensure that the disk group is mounted automatically when the ASM instance starts, add this line to the ASM instance parameter file created in Exercise 33-2, Step 2:

```
asm_diskgroups=dg1
```

 EXAM TIP The views V$ASM_DISK and V$ASM_DISKGROUP are only populated in an ASM instance. They are always empty in an RDBMS instance.

Creating and Using ASM Files

The ASM disk groups are created in the ASM instance; the ASM files are created in the RDBMS instance. The normal commands for creating datafiles, tempfiles, and logfiles can all take a disk group name in place of a filename. For example,

```
SQL> create tablespace new_tbs datafile '+dg1' size 100m;
SQL> alter tablespace system add datafile '+system_dg' size 1000m;
SQL> alter database add logfile group 4 '+dg_log1','+dg_log2' size 100m;
```

The first of these commands creates a new tablespace with one datafile in the disk group DG1. The second command adds a datafile to the SYSTEM tablespace, in a disk group created specially for the SYSTEM datafiles; this will probably be a disk group created with HIGH redundancy. The third command creates a new online logfile group, with two members in different disk groups; these will be groups with EXTERNAL redundancy, because you can rely on the multiplexing to provide fault tolerance.

To direct archive logs to ASM, set the LOG_ARCHIVE_DEST parameters to point to disk groups:

```
SQL> alter system set log_archive_dest_1='location=+dg_arc1';
SQL> alter system set log_archive_dest_2='location=+dg_arc2';
```

It is also possible to direct the flash recovery area to an ASM disk group:

```
SQL> alter system set db_recovery_file_dest='+dg_flash';
```

In all these examples, you do not specify a filename, only a disk group. ASM will generate the actual filenames according to its own conventions. If you wish, you can see the names by querying views such as V$DATAFILE, V$LOGFILE, or V$ARCHIVED_LOG, but there is little value in this. A feature of ASM is that it gives you complete independence from the physical storage: there is no reason for you to want to know the actual filenames. It is possible to interpret the system-generated names, but they are not any sort of physical path.

Exercise 33-4: Using ASM for Datafiles

Create a tablespace in the disk group created in Exercise 33-3.

1. Connect to your RDBMS instance with SQL*Plus as user SYSTEM. Ensure that your ORACLE_SID environment variable is set to the name of your RDBMS instance first.

2. Create a tablespace with a datafile in your ASM disk group.

```
SQL> create tablespace new_tbs datafile '+dg1' size 100m;
```

3. Find the filename of the new datafile.

```
SQL> select file_name from dba_data_files where tablespace_name='NEW_
TBS';
FILE_NAME
----------------------------------------
+DG1/ocp10g/datafile/new_tbs.257.1
```

Note that the system-generated filename is prefixed with the name of the disk group, followed by the database name, the type of file, the tablespace name, and a unique numeric identifier.

ASM and RMAN

Since ASM files are created on raw devices managed by Oracle, there is no way that you can back up ASM files with operating system utilities: no regular operating system command or utility can see the contents of an ASM disk, because it has no file system installed upon it. You must use RMAN. The RMAN backup and restore and recover commands do not change at all when using ASM; wherever you would use a filename, enter the ASM filename. If your backup scripts specify tablespace names, or the whole database, then they will run unchanged.

Apart from being required for regular backup and recovery procedures, RMAN is also the only tool available for migrating a database from conventional file system storage to ASM storage. The examples that follow assume that you have three disk groups: group dgroup1 is for your datafiles; groups dgroup2 and dgroup3 are for control and online log files.

To migrate the controlfile, change the CONTROLFILES instance parameter to point toward your disk groups and then shut down the database and start it in NOMOUNT mode:

```
SQL> alter system set controlfiles='+dgroup2','+dgroup3' scope=spfile;
SQL> shutdown immediate;
SQL> startup nomount;
```

Then launch RMAN, and restore the controlfile from its original location:

```
RMAN> restore controlfile from '/u1/ocp10g/ctrl1.con';
```

From an RMAN prompt, this script will migrate all your datafiles to an ASM disk group:

```
shutdown immediate;
startup mount;
backup as copy database format '+dgroup1';
switch database to copy;
alter database open;
```

To migrate the redo logs, create new members in your disk groups and drop the old members:

```
SQL> alter database add logfile member '+dgroup2','+dgroup3' to group 1;
SQL> alter database drop logfile member
'/u02/ocp10g/log1a.rdo','/u03/ocp10g/log1b.rdo';
```

Finally, you must move your temporary tablespace tempfiles. Since these cannot be backed up, the technique is to drop them and create new files on a disk group. It may be simpler just to drop the whole temporary tablespace and create a new one.

 EXAM TIP RMAN is the only tool you can use to back up ASM files. User-managed backups are not possible.

ASM and Linux

The code that implements ASM is the ASMLib library. For Linux, this library is implemented as a set of Linux packages, some of which may be specific to different releases of the Linux operating system. Generally, this means that to use ASM on Linux, you must do some research on Metalink to locate the correct version of the ASMLib for your Linux installation. For example, there are different packages for Red Hat AS 3 and SLES 8. Do not worry about reliability—ASM on Linux works as well as on any other platform; the issues are only to do with getting it installed.

The URL to obtain the various versions of the ASM libraries (correct as of the time of writing) is

```
http://www.oracle.com/technology/tech/linux/asmlib/index.html
```

Once the ASMLib is installed, ASM will function exactly as on any other platform. A workaround is to use operating system files that simulate raw disks. This is not a supported routine but is adequate for learning or demonstration purposes:

1. From a Linux prompt, create the files.

   ```
   $ dd if=/dev/zero of=_file_disk1 bs=1k count=1000000
   $ dd if=/dev/zero of=_file_disk2 bs=1k count=1000000
   ```

   These commands will create two virtual disk files of 1GB each.

   ```
   $ ls -l
   total 200208
   -rw-r--r--    1 oracle    dba       1024000000 Mar 19 23:58 _file_disk1
   -rw-r--r--    1 oracle    dba       1024000000 Mar 19 23:58 _file_disk2
   ```

2. As the root user, associate loop devices with the files.

   ```
   # losetup /dev/loop1 _file_disk1
   # losetup /dev/loop2 _file_disk2
   ```

3. Bind raw devices to the loop devices.

   ```
   # raw /dev/raw/raw1 /dev/loop1
   /dev/raw/raw1:  bound to major 7, minor 1
   # raw /dev/raw/raw2 /dev/loop2
   /dev/raw/raw2:  bound to major 7, minor 1
   ```

4. Change the ownership and mode of the raw devices.

   ```
   # chown oracle:dba /dev/raw/raw1
   # chown oracle:dba /dev/raw/raw2
   # chmod 660 /dev/raw/raw1
   # chmod 660 /dev/raw/raw2
   ```

5. Create an ASM instance as normal, setting the ASM_DISKSTRING instance parameter to point to the simulated raw devices.

```
asm_diskstring='/dev/raw/raw1','/dev/raw/raw2'
```

Chapter Review

ASM is an Oracle-aware logical volume manager. It can work with logical volumes created by an operating system–provided LVM, or it can work with raw devices. To use ASM, this is the sequence:

1. Using operating system utilities, create the raw devices.

2. Create and start the ASM instance.

3. In the ASM instance, create the ASM disk groups, using the raw devices.

4. In the RDBMS instance, create datafiles in the ASM disk groups.

The first step is platform specific. Subsequent steps are the same on all platforms.

ASM files are, by default, striped with the equivalent of RAID 0+1; all files are cut across all disks in the group to maximize performance, and every allocation unit is mirrored onto two disks. The stripe size is determined by the type of file: coarse stripes of 1MB for datafiles and archive logs, where I/O operations tend to be large, and fine stripes of 128KB for online redo logs and the controlfile, where I/O operations tend to be smaller.

An ASM instance is a type of instance dedicated to managing ASM disk groups. You can connect to it only as SYSDBA or SYSOPER, because it never mounts and opens a database; it mounts disk groups, which are then available to RDBMS instances. If the ASM instance shuts down, the RDBMS instances that are using it will also shut down.

The only tool for backing up, or indeed for migrating to, ASM files is RMAN.

ASM is available for all platforms, but the details of installation may vary. For example, on Windows ASM works straight out of the box, but on Linux you may have to do some extra configuration.

Questions

1. What mode must an ASM instance be in before an RDBMS instance can access ASM files? (Choose the best answer.)

A. NOMOUNT

B. MOUNT

C. OPEN

D. Either MOUNT or OPEN

2. What file types and directories can be stored with ASM? (Choose all that apply.)

A. Alert log

B. Controlfiles

    C. Datafiles

    D. Online redo log files

    E. Oracle home directory

3. Which of the following recovery files can be stored with ASM? (Choose all that apply.)

    A. Archive redo log files

    B. RMAN backup sets

    C. RMAN image copies

    D. User-managed backups

    E. The flash recovery area

4. Which of the following parameters is required for an ASM instance? (Choose the best answer.)

    A. ASM_DISKGROUPS

    B. ASM_POWER_LIMIT

    C. INSTANCE_NAME

    D. INSTANCE_TYPE

5. How should you migrate your online redo logs to ASM storage? (Choose the best answer.)

    A. Copy the files to an ASM disk group, and use RENAME to update the controlfile.

    B. Use RMAN to transfer them to an ASM disk group, and SWITCH to update the controlfile.

    C. Create new members in an ASM disk group, and drop the old members.

    D. Online logs cannot use ASM storage.

6. If you abort an ASM instance, what will be the effect on RDBMS instances that make use of disk groups managed by the aborted instance? (Choose the best answer.)

    A. ASM is a single point of failure, and therefore the RDBMS instances will also abort.

    B. The RDBMS instances will remain open, but any ASM datafiles will be inaccessible.

    C. RDBMS instances that have already opened ASM files will not be affected, but no new RDBMS instances will be able to open.

    D. The RDBMS instances will hang until the ASM instance is restarted.

7. What are the default characteristics of ASM files? (Choose the best answer.)

    A. The files will be striped for performance but not mirrored for safety.

    B. The files will be mirrored for safety but not striped for performance.

    C. The files will be both striped and mirrored.

    D. The files will be neither striped nor mirrored.

8. What happens when you open an ASM instance? (Choose the best answer.)

    A. The ASM disk groups are made available to RDBMS instances.

    B. The ASM disks are opened.

    C. The ASM files are opened.

    D. You cannot open an ASM instance.

9. What statement is correct about ASM and logical volume managers (LVMs)? (Choose the best answer.)

    A. ASM is itself an LVM and cannot work with a third-party LVM.

    B. ASM can use LVM volumes, if they are formatted with a file system.

    C. You can use ASM for striping, and the LVM for mirroring.

    D. You can use ASM for mirroring, and the LVM for striping.

10. What does the RBAL process do? (Choose the best answer.)

    A. It rebalances data across the disks in an ASM disk group when a disk is added or removed.

    B. It coordinates rebalancing activity.

    C. It opens and closes ASM disks.

    D. It depends on whether it is the RBAL process of an ASM instance or of an RDBMS instance.

11. Which of the following techniques is valid for backing up files on ASM disks? (Choose all that apply.)

    A. If the files are mirrored, split the mirror, back up the split copy, and re-instantiate the mirror.

    B. Put the tablespaces into hot backup mode, and copy the ASM datafiles.

    C. Connect to the ASM instance with RMAN, and back up as normal.

    D. Connect to the RDBMS instance with RMAN, and back up as normal.

12. How can you connect to an ASM instance? (Choose the best answer.)

    A. By using operating system authentication only

    B. By using password file authentication only

    C. By using data dictionary authentication only

    D. None of the above are correct

13. What does ASM stripe? (Choose the best answer.)

    A. Files across all disk groups

    B. Disks across all disk groups

    C. Disk groups across all disks

    D. Files across all disks in a group

    E. Allocation units across all disks in a group

14. Some operations can only be carried out when connected to an ASM instance, while others can only be carried out when connected to an RDBMS instance. Mark each of these operations as being "ASM" or "RDBMS."

    A. Creating ASM datafiles

    B. Creating ASM disk groups

    C. Backing up ASM datafiles

    D. Mounting the ASM instance

15. If an RDBMS instance that is using ASM files crashes, what will the ASM instance do? (Choose the best answer.)

    A. The ASM instance will abort.

    B. The ASM instance will recover the files that the RDBMS instance had open, and remain available for other RDBMS instances.

    C. The ASM instance will recover the files that the RDBMS instance had open, and shut down cleanly.

    D. Nothing.

Answers

1. **B.** An ASM instance must be mounted before an RDBMS instance can use the ASM files. You cannot open an ASM instance.

2. **B, C,** and **D.** You can use ASM for database files, such as the controlfile, datafiles, and online log files. Your Oracle home and the alert and trace files must be on conventional storage.

3. **A, B, C,** and **E.** Archive logs, RMAN backups, and indeed the whole flash recovery area can be on ASM. You cannot direct user-managed backups to ASM, because operating system utilities cannot write to ASM devices.

4. **D.** The only essential parameter is INSTANCE_TYPE.

5. **C.** The only method is to create new files, because you can't copy to an ASM disk group, and RMAN cannot back up online log files.

6. **A.** The ABORT command will be propagated to all the RDBMS instances.

7. **C.** By default, files are both striped and mirrored. You can disable the mirroring, but not the striping, by using the EXTERNAL REDUNDANCY option when you create the disk group.

8. **D.** You cannot open an ASM instance.

9. **C.** This is probably the best way to use ASM: to rely on an LVM to provide fault tolerance and ASM to provide Oracle-aware striping performance.

10. **D.** There is an RBAL process in both an ASM instance and the RDBMS instances that are using it. A describes the ARBn process, B is RBAL in an ASM instance, and C is RBAL in an RDBMS instance.

11. **D.** Absolutely normal RMAN backups, when you are connected to the RDBMS instance as the target, are the only way to back up ASM files.

12. **D.** ASM instances do not open a database, so you cannot use data dictionary authentication, but either password file or operating system authentication will work.

13. **D.** ASM stripes files across all disks in the group.

14. **B** and **D; A** and **C.** The ASM instance operations are B and D; the RDBMS operations are A and C.

15. **D.** An ASM instance operates independently of the RDBMS instances that are using it.

CHAPTER 34

Monitoring and Managing Memory

In this chapter you will learn how to

- Implement Automatic Shared Memory Management
- Manually configure SGA parameters for various memory components in the SGA
- Use Automatic PGA Memory Management

An Oracle instance consists of memory structures and processes. An understanding of the purpose of the various memory structures and how they are used by the processes is a vital part of a database administrator's knowledge. Appropriate configuration of memory usage is vital for performance.

This chapter discusses the memory structures that make up an Oracle instance: the shared memory that is the System Global Area, or SGA, and the Program Global Area, or PGA, that is private to each session. These memory structures can be controlled manually (which was the only option in earlier releases of the Oracle database), or you can enable self-tuning mechanisms. If you enable the automatic management of SGA and PGA, you should be able to ensure that all available memory is used to the best effect, while guaranteeing that the server will never need to swap.

The System Global Area

In operating system terms, the System Global Area (SGA) is shared memory. The implementation of shared memory is platform specific. For example, on Solaris your system administrators must configure shared memory by kernel settings in the /etc/system file and any changes require a reboot to take effect; but on Linux shared memory can be configured dynamically with the sysctl utility. The memory that makes up the SGA is shared by all background and server processes.

The SGA is divided into several memory structures. There are three required components of the SGA:

- The shared pool
- The log buffer
- The database buffer cache default pool

There are also a number of optional SGA components:

- The large pool
- The streams pool
- The Java pool
- The database buffer cache keep pool
- The database buffer cache recycle pool
- The database buffer cache nK block size pools

All of these are detailed in the following sections. As with all components of the instance, the SGA memory structures are controlled by instance parameters. Many of these are dynamic, meaning that to an extent (and within certain limitations) the SGA can be reconfigured without any downtime. Some can even be controlled automatically, by enabling the Automatic Shared Memory Management capability. Others are static and cannot be changed without shutting down the instance. SGA configuration is critical to performance; there are advisors that will assist in determining what sizes are appropriate for some of the SGA memory structures.

The overall size of the SGA can be determined by querying the V$SGASTAT view:

```
SQL> select sum(bytes)/(1024*1024) size_in_mb from v$sgastat;
```

The size of the SGA can vary as components are resized, but it can never exceed the limit set by the instance parameter SGA_MAX_SIZE. The actual size will always be equal to or less than this parameter. If this parameter is not set, then it defaults to the size of the SGA at startup, so by default, the SGA can shrink but not expand. The effect at the operating system level of the SGA_MAX_SIZE parameter is platform specific. For example, on Linux Oracle will take virtual memory up to the SGA_MAX_SIZE setting when the instance starts, and then if the current size of the SGA is less than SGA_MAX_SIZE, Oracle instructs Linux to page out all the difference. So you will find that your system appears to be swapping, but this is not a problem because only memory that is allocated but not needed is swapped out. On Windows, the memory allocated is that actually used, so if SGA_MAX_SIZE is greater than the SGA, this has no significance at all.

TIP Give yourself some room to maneuver by setting the SGA_MAX_SIZE instance parameter to a figure greater than that you think you need, but remember that there may be side effects of which your system administrators need to be aware.

SGA components are, with the exception of the log buffer, sized in granules. A *granule* is an area of contiguous memory. The granule size is platform specific and varies according to the total size of the SGA. Typical granule sizes are 4MB if the total SGA is no bigger than 1000MB or 16MB if it is larger, but there are platform variations. For instance, on Windows, the granule size is 8MB for an SGA greater than 1GB.

TIP You can query the V$SGAINFO view to see the granule size that is being used by an instance.

When setting the instance parameters that control the size of SGA components you can specify any figure you please, but what you get will be a multiple of granules: the figure will be rounded up to the next whole granule. The exception is the log buffer: since this will usually need to be smaller than one granule, for performance reasons, what you ask for is what you get.

The Shared Pool

The *shared pool* is a required element of the SGA. It is sized according to the SHARED_POOL_SIZE instance parameter, rounded up to the next granule boundary. However, there are certain limitations at the lower end of the size range. If you try to set it to an impossibly low value, the instance will not start:

```
ocp10g> alter system set shared_pool_size=2m scope=spfile;
System altered.
ocp10g> startup force
ORA-00371: not enough shared pool memory, should be at least 62198988 bytes
ocp10g>
```

In this example, a shared pool of at least 60MB is necessary before the instance can start.

TIP If you find yourself with an instance that cannot start (as in this example), use the CREATE PFILE FROM SPFILE command to generate a text parameter file, edit it to change the parameter that is preventing the startup, and then use CREATE SPFILE FROM PFILE to generate an spfile that will work.

The shared pool is divided into a number of memory structures. The DBA has no control over the sizing of these; Oracle itself will manage the shared pool structures dynamically within the limit specified by the SHARED_POOL_SIZE instance parameter. To view the current memory allocations, query the V$SGASTAT view as in Figure 34-1.

In Figure 34-1, the shared pool consists of thirty-six components. These are some of the more important ones:

- **The sql area and the library cache**   Together, these make up what will often be the largest part of the shared pool. This is a cache of recently executed SQL statements, both the text of the statements and the parsed forms with an execution plan.

- **The row cache**   This cache, also commonly referred to as the data dictionary cache, is made up of data dictionary information (table structures, users, constraints, grants, and more) that are being used to parse SQL statements.

- **The ASH (Active Session History) buffers**   This is information regarding recent activity by users. Used for performance diagnosis, it is regularly flushed to the Automatic Workload Repository in the SYSAUX tablespace.

- **Various PL/SQL areas**   PL/SQL code, including triggers, is loaded into the shared pool from the data dictionary for execution.

- **The flashback generation buffers**   This is memory used for the flashback database buffers, before they are flushed to the flashback logs.

All the shared pool components are sized automatically by the instance; you have no control over the size of any one component.

A shared pool that is too small is very bad for performance, but do not make it larger than necessary. An oversized shared pool is also bad for performance. To determine how large the shared pool should be, use the Shared Pool Advisor. This concentrates on the library cache. The algorithms Oracle uses to allocate memory in the shared pool favor the library cache the least, so if there is enough memory for an

Figure 34-1   SGA memory allocations

optimally sized library cache, you can assume that there is enough memory for everything
else. To enable the advisor, set the instance parameter STATISTICS_LEVEL to TYPICAL,
which is the default, and query the V$SHARED_POOL_ADVICE view:

```
SQL> select shared_pool_size_for_estimate "size",
  2   shared_pool_size_factor "factor",
  3   estd_lc_time_saved "saving"
  4   from v$shared_pool_advice;
     size     factor     saving
---------- ---------- ----------
      400         .5    788,794
      480         .6    790,444
      560         .7    791,191
      640         .8    791,589
      720         .9    791,793
```

800	1.0	791,917
880	1.1	792,013
960	1.2	792,070
1,040	1.3	792,106
1,120	1.4	792,122
1,200	1.5	792,139
1,280	1.6	792,156
1,360	1.7	792,171
1,440	1.8	792,181
1,520	1.9	792,187
1,600	2.0	792,199

20 rows selected.

This view shows the amount of library cache parsing time that would be saved if the shared pool were a certain size, returning up to twenty rows for estimates from half the current size to double the current size. You should set the SHARED_POOL_SIZE instance parameter to the value where the time saving stabilizes. In the preceding example the shared pool is currently 800MB, which is clearly much bigger than necessary: it can be halved to 400MB without any significant deterioration in the time saved.

This advisor can also be accessed through Database Control, by clicking the Advice button shown in Figure 34-2 in the section "Automatic Shared Memory Management" later in this chapter.

The Database Buffer Cache

Server processes copy datafile blocks into the *database buffer cache*. If blocks in the cache are changed, the DBWn process will write them back to the datafiles. This process was described in Chapter 9, which detailed what happens in memory and on disk when DML commands are executed. The default instance configuration treats the database buffer cache as one area of memory used for caching blocks of all segments, but it is possible to optimize the use of the database buffer cache by dividing it into different areas, known as pools, and caching blocks of different segments in these different pools. But before going into this, you will read more about the algorithms that Oracle uses to determine which buffers to copy blocks into, and which buffers to write back to disk.

 EXAM TIP All the database buffer cache sizing parameters are dynamic, but the SGA_MAX_SIZE parameter limits the amount of space you can allocate to the cache without having to downsize other SGA components or restart the instance.

The LRU List and the Checkpoint Queue

Every buffer in the database buffer cache will be in one of three states: pinned, dirty, or free.

A *pinned* buffer is a buffer that is in use. At this precise moment, a process is working on the block in the buffer, and until it has finished with the block, no other process can get to it.

A *dirty* buffer is a buffer containing a block whose image in the buffer is not the same as the image on disk. The block has been copied into the cache, it has been updated, but it has not yet been written back to disk. It is possible for a server process to gain access to the block (to pin it) and to apply another update, but it is not possible for a server process to copy another block from disk over a dirty buffer. It must first be cleaned, by DBWn writing it back to disk.

A *free* buffer is a negative definition: it is neither dirty, nor pinned. This means that it is either unused or clean. When the instance first starts, all the buffers will be unused, but within minutes every buffer will have something in it. In practice, there are no unused buffers. A clean buffer is one containing a block whose image in the buffer is the same as the image on disk. Either the block has been copied into the cache and not changed, or it has been changed ("dirtied") and subsequently the DBWn process has cleaned it by writing it back to disk.

When a server process needs to read data into memory, it must find the block on disk and then find a free buffer in the database buffer cache into which to copy it. Blocks cannot be copied into pinned buffers, because they are protected by a locking mechanism, and they cannot be copied into dirty buffers, because if they were, the changes made to the dirty buffer would be overwritten. Free buffers can be overwritten, because the data they contain is also available on disk. Once a dirty buffer has been cleaned by DBWn, it becomes free.

There will be many free buffers in the cache at any time. Which one will a server process choose to overwrite when it needs to copy a block into memory? This is critical for performance. The selection is based on the Least Recently Used, or LRU, list. Every buffer has an address, and the LRU list has an entry for every buffer. The LRU list sorts the entries according to when they were last accessed. So a buffer that was accessed just a moment ago will be at the most recently used end of the LRU list, and the buffer that hasn't been touched for the longest time will be at the least recently used end of the LRU list. Some buffers will be very busy, because many server processes are reusing the blocks they contain; these buffers may be pinned, dirty, or free, but they will always be toward the most recently used end of the LRU list. The blocks at the least recently used end of the list are occupying space for no purpose; a session must have needed the blocks once, or they wouldn't be in the cache, but no servers need them now. When a server needs to copy a block into memory, it goes to the least recently used end of the LRU list and takes the first free buffer that it finds. This means that popular data is always in memory; only buffers that hold data that is not in frequent use are overwritten.

A second list of buffers is the checkpoint queue. This is a list of dirty buffers, waiting to be written to disk by the DBWn process. It is populated by server processes searching for free buffers. When a server process looks for a free buffer, starting at the least recently used end of the LRU list, whenever it finds a dirty buffer in the course of its search it will transfer its address to the checkpoint queue. So the checkpoint queue is a list of buffers that are dirty and also not recently used. From time to time, the DBWn will copy all buffers on the checkpoint queue to disk, thus making them clean, or free, and available for reuse. This means that a very busy buffer, one that is being continuously updated, will never be written to disk, because it will always be at the most recently used end of the LRU list and thus never found by a server process searching for a free buffer. This very simple mechanism allows Oracle to keep disk I/O to a minimum: DBWn will write only data that is both static and dirty. Unchanged buffers are never written to disk, and dirty buffers are written only if they haven't been touched for some time.

In normal running, the DBWn will clean the checkpoint queue for one of two reasons. First, a server process may take too long to find a free buffer ("too long" is controlled by internal parameters), in which case it will signal the DBWn to flush the buffers on the checkpoint queue to disk. Second, the checkpoint queue may have become too long: no one server process has had a problem, but overall a large number of dirty buffers have been found by server processes searching for free buffers. Either way, once DBWn has copied the buffers on the checkpoint queue to disk, they become free and the server processes can then use them. If the database is static, with no searches for free buffers occurring, another mechanism comes into play. DBWn has a three-second time-out: every three seconds it will copy some dirty buffers to disk, irrespective of whether they have been encountered by servers looking for free buffers. It will traverse the LRU list, writing first the dirty buffers that have not been recently used. But eventually, the whole cache will be cleaned.

The end result of these algorithms is that DBWn writes as little data as it can get away with—and always writes relatively static data in preference to volatile data.

The only time that all dirty buffers get written to disk in one operation is when a database checkpoint occurs. This is signaled by an orderly shutdown, or when you issue the ALTER SYSTEM CHECKPOINT command. Tablespace checkpoints, where all the dirty buffers for one tablespace get written to disk, occur automatically as a result of certain tablespace operations:

- Dropping the tablespace
- Making the tablespace read-only
- Putting the tablespace into hot backup mode
- Taking the tablespace offline

 EXAM TIP Many people think that a log switch triggers a checkpoint. It doesn't. It used to, but that behavior changed with release 8i, when incremental checkpointing was introduced. Now the checkpoint position continues to advance smoothly according to the algorithms described in the preceding section, with no special activity at log switch time.

The Default, Keep, and Recycle Pools

The database buffer cache can be divided into up to three "pools." A *pool* is a distinct area in the database buffer cache used for caching particular objects: any one segment will be cached in only one pool. Each pool has its own LRU list and checkpoint queue.

All instances must have a database buffer cache default pool. This is the pool sized by the DB_CACHE_SIZE instance parameter. The default pool is the only required pool, and all segments (whether table, index, undo, lob, or any other segment type) are by default cached in the default pool. In some circumstances, having only one pool can be a limitation on performance, because the blocks of all the segments will be cached within it; they will be competing for space in the cache.

In most database systems, there will be some segments where many sessions are accessing the same blocks repeatedly, and other segments where the blocks are accessed only once. For example, it may be that a large fact table is being read by many sessions, but that any one block of the table is being accessed only once. But the small-dimension tables hanging off the fact table will be repeatedly scanned by all the sessions. There is little point in retaining the blocks of the fact table in memory, because they aren't being reaccessed, whereas the dimension tables would ideally be in memory all the time. A similar situation can arise with indexes: all users scan the index, but they each require different blocks of the table. For optimal memory usage, the index blocks would be kept in the cache permanently, but the table blocks would be read into memory, and then the buffer would be either flushed back to disk or overwritten immediately.

With one pool, the default pool, Oracle treats all segments equally: blocks are read into memory, and if they are not accessed repeatedly they will—eventually—drop down the LRU list to the least recently used end of the list, and the buffer will be reused. The ideal situation would be that blocks of segments that are repeatedly accessed are always in memory, and blocks that are unlikely to be reaccessed drop straight down to the bottom of the LRU list and so are reused immediately. This behavior can be forced by creating multiple buffer cache pools.

To ensure that the blocks of some segments are always kept in memory, create a database buffer cache "keep" pool, and instruct Oracle to cache those segments in this keep pool. The keep pool is created by setting the DB_KEEP_CACHE_SIZE instance parameter. The keep pool should be large enough to store all the objects that you intend to cache in it. This means that the stable running state of the instance will have all the blocks of the keep pool segments in memory all the time. Suitable candidate objects for the keep pool might be small-dimension tables or indexes on large fact tables.

To ensure that blocks that are unlikely to be reaccessed are pushed out of memory as quickly as possible, create a database buffer cache "recycle" pool by setting the DB_RECYCLE_CACHE_SIZE instance parameter. This should be relatively small, so that a block that is read into memory will be overwritten very soon.

Having created keep or recycle buffer cache pools by setting the DB_KEEP_CACHE_SIZE and DB_RECYCLE_CACHE_SIZE parameters, you can specify that a particular segment should be cached in them at segment creation time, or for an existing segment with an ALTER command, by using the STORAGE clause:

```
SQL> alter table emp(storage buffer_pool recycle);
SQL> alter index emp_name_idx(storage buffer_pool keep);
SQL> create index emp_mgr_idx on emp(mgr) storage(buffer_pool keep);
```

 TIP Using keep and recycle pools can be very good for performance, but it is important to know how your data is being accessed. To put this into perspective, use of keep and recycle pools is not supported by Oracle Corporation for the Oracle E-Business Suite.

The Nonstandard Block Size Pools

Oracle permits the use of multiple block sizes within a database, but for every block size you use you must create a pool of cache buffers of that size: you cannot cache an 8KB block in a 4KB buffer. The possible block sizes are 2KB, 4KB, 8KB, 16KB, and 32KB. The choice of the standard block size is made at database creation time and can never be changed. If it is unsuitable, you must create a new database with a more appropriate block size. It is set by the DB_BLOCK_SIZE parameter, which defaults to 2KB. The DB_BLOCK_SIZE is used for formatting the SYSTEM and SYSAUX tablespace datafiles. After database creation, tablespaces can be formatted into other block sizes, provided that a database buffer cache pool of buffers of that size has been created.

To create these additional pools, set one or more of these parameters:

- DB_2K_CACHE_SIZE
- DB_4K_CACHE_SIZE
- DB_8K_CACHE_SIZE
- DB_16K_CACHE_SIZE
- DB_32K_CACHE_SIZE

 EXAM TIP You cannot set the DB_nK_CACHE_SIZE parameter, where n is your standard block size. This will throw an error. The standard block size cache is set with DB_CACHE_SIZE, DB_RECYCLE_CACHE_SIZE, and DB_KEEP_CACHE_SIZE.

Support for multiple block sizes means that you can create tablespaces with different block sizes in an attempt to optimize performance. For example, the standard block size might be 8KB, which is often said to be a good choice for most databases. But if you are storing audio CDs in the database as BLOBs, then each access to a CD will be a continuous read/write of up to 700MB. This type of access may be more efficient if the blocks are 32KB, so you could create a tablespace formatted into 32KB blocks and use that to store the LOB segments.

TIP Block size support is platform specific. For instance, the largest block size possible on Windows is 16KB.

Use of multiple block sizes also means that it is possible to transport tablespaces of different block sizes from one database to another. For example, you might have one database using a 4KB standard block size, and another using 8KB standard block size. By creating additional buffer pools formatted in the other block size, you will be able to copy tablespaces between the databases.

TIP Oracle Corporation advises that the primary reason for supporting the use of multiple block sizes is for transportable tablespaces, not for performance tuning.

To create a tablespace of a nonstandard block size, specify the block size in the tablespace creation command:

```
ocp10g> create tablespace ts_16k datafile 'ts_16k.dbf' size 400m
  2  blocksize 16k;
create tablespace ts_16k datafile 'ts_16k.dbf' size 400m
*
ERROR at line 1:
ORA-29339: tablespace block size 16384 does not match configured block sizes
```

This fails because there is no buffer cache pool formatted into 16KB buffers. To create one,

```
ocp10g> alter system set db_16k_cache_size=4m;
System altered.
```

This will succeed provided the increase in size of the SGA (only 4MB in the example) does not take it over the limit set by the SGA_MAX_SIZE parameter. If the SGA is already at that limit, then either another SGA component must be reduced in size, or the change will require a shutdown.

Then create the tablespace by reissuing the preceding command. All objects created in the tablespace will be formatted in 16KB blocks and cached in the 16KB buffer cache pool. You can use nonstandard block sizes for user data tablespaces and undo tablespaces, but not temporary tablespaces.

EXAM TIP Only the standard block size pool can be divided into default, keep, and recycle. The nonstandard block size pools are default only.

Sizing the Database Buffer Cache

As a general rule, the larger the database buffer cache is, the more data blocks can be cached in memory and therefore the less disk I/O will be needed. Disk I/O is the limiting factor in performance of many database systems. But the structure of the application and the nature of the work being done will limit the benefits of a large database buffer cache. If users are not going to reaccess blocks, then there is no point in caching them. The cache should be large enough to cache blocks that are repeatedly accessed, but not so large that it caches blocks that are used only once. To assist in estimating how large the cache should be, you can consult a Database Buffer Cache Advisor.

Provided that the STATISTICS_LEVEL parameter is on TYPICAL or ALL, you have access to the Database Buffer Cache Advisor through the V$DB_CACHE_ADVICE view, which will have twenty rows for each pool you have created. Each row predicts the estimated number of physical reads that would be necessary if the cache were a certain size, ranging from one tenth of the current size to double the current size:

```
SQL> select name,size_for_estimate, size_factor, estd_physical_reads
from  v$db_cache_advice;
NAME        SIZE_FOR_ESTIMATE SIZE_FACTOR ESTD_PHYSICAL_READS
---------- ------------------ ----------- -------------------
DEFAULT                  80          .1    3296,275,577
DEFAULT                 160          .2    1197,244,495
DEFAULT                 240          .3     571,762,504
DEFAULT                 320          .4     258,223,630
DEFAULT                 400          .5     178,347,651
DEFAULT                 480          .6     146,103,881
DEFAULT                 560          .7     131,742,725
DEFAULT                 640          .8     127,894,451
DEFAULT                 720          .9     124,493,254
DEFAULT                 800           1     122,117,170
DEFAULT                 880         1.1     118,988,621
DEFAULT                 960         1.2     116,470,955
DEFAULT                1040         1.3     114,001,803
DEFAULT               1,120         1.4     111,294,674
DEFAULT               1,200         1.5     108,580,193
DEFAULT               1,280         1.6     106,112,377
DEFAULT               1,360         1.7     103,996,510
DEFAULT               1,440         1.8     102,112,565
DEFAULT               1,520         1.9     100,159,402
DEFAULT               1,600           2     100,018,331
20 rows selected.
```

This example shows that there is only one pool configured, the default pool, and that it is currently 800MB. If memory on the server is tight, the pool could be reduced to perhaps 600MB without the disk I/O increasing excessively, but taking it lower than 400MB would be disastrous. If there is spare memory on the server, the default pool could certainly be increased to perhaps 1200MB, but there would be minimal benefit from going much above that.

This advisor can also be accessed through Database Control, by taking the Advice button shown in Figure 34-2 in the section "Automatic Shared Memory Management" later in this chapter.

The Log Buffer

The use of the log buffer was covered in detail in Chapter 9. It is used as a very short term staging area for all changes applied to blocks in the database buffer cache by server processes, before they are streamed to disk by the LGWR process. Remember what will cause LGWR to write:

- When a user commits a transaction. This is the guarantee that data can never be lost; the user's session will hang until the write is complete.
- When the log buffer is one-third full. This is for performance: to force the LGWR to write in near real time, even if transactions are not committing.
- Just before the DBWn writes. This is to prevent corruption: DBWn is not allowed to write anything, unless the changes are already in the redo log on disk.
- Every three seconds. There is a three-second time-out, so that in the highly unlikely event that none of the three preceding triggers has fired, LGWR will still write in close to real time.

The log buffer is sized by the LOG_BUFFER parameter, which is static. The default is platform specific and related to the number of CPUs. On Windows, for example, if CPU_COUNT is set to one, the LOG_BUFFER will default to 256K, but with CPU_COUNT on eight the LOG_BUFFER will default to 2MB.

Other SGA Areas

The shared pool, the database buffer cache default pool, and the log buffer are the three required components of the SGA. The following components are optional.

The Large Pool

The purpose of the *large pool* is to reduce the strain on the shared pool. If you create a large pool, then various processes that would otherwise use shared pool memory will automatically use the large pool instead. Among these are the following processes:

- **Shared server processes** As discussed in Chapter 13, if you configure the shared server, the session UGAs will be stored in the large pool.
- **Parallel execution servers** If you have enabled parallel query and DML, the parallel servers will communicate via the large pool.
- **I/O slave processes** If you have enabled database writer slaves or tape I/O slaves, they will communicate through the large pool.
- **RMAN** The RMAN channel processes use the large pool for caching buffers during backup and restore operations.

If you do not create a large pool, your instance will still function—but perhaps not as efficiently. The large pool is sized by the LARGE_POOL_SIZE parameter, which is dynamic. To monitor large pool usage, query the V$SGASTAT view:

```
ocp10g> select * from v$sgastat where pool='large pool';
POOL          NAME                                BYTES
-----------   -------------------------   ----------
large pool    free memory                      6258688
large pool    CTWR dba buffer                    61440
large pool    krcc extent chunk              2068480
```

If there is consistently a large amount of free memory, you could consider reducing the size of the pool. In this example, note that some space has been allocated to the "CTWR dba buffer." This is memory used by the Change Tracking Writer process, needed to allow RMAN to do fast incremental backups.

If the LARGE_POOL_SIZE instance parameter has not been explicitly set, the default depends on other parameters. For example, if parallelism has been enabled within the database, a large pool will be created.

The Java Pool

The *Java pool* is optional, in that you do not need it if you do not run any stored Java procedures. However, a number of standard Oracle-supplied components are written in Java, so the Java pool is usually considered a necessary part of the instance.

Java stored procedures are loaded from the data dictionary into the shared pool, as are PL/SQL stored procedures. The purpose of the Java pool is to provide room for the run-time memory structures used by a Java application, in particular the heap space needed to instantiate Java objects. The Java pool is controlled by three instance parameters:

- **JAVA_POOL_SIZE**   This parameter creates the Java pool. It is dynamic, within the limits imposed by the SGA_MAX_SIZE. The default is 24MB.

- **JAVA_MAX_SESSIONSPACE_SIZE**   This is a static parameter, restricting the amount of space in the Java pool that any one session is allowed to occupy.

- **JAVA_SOFT_SESSIONSPACE_LIMIT**   This too is static, and it may help with monitoring Java pool usage before imposing a hard limit with JAVA_MAX_SESSIONSPACE_SIZE. If a session's Java pool memory usage goes above the soft limit, a message is written out to a trace file.

To monitor Java pool usage, query the V$SGASTAT view:

```
ocp10g> select * from v$sgastat where pool='java pool';
POOL          NAME                                BYTES
-----------   -------------------------   ----------
java pool     joxs heap                         233856
java pool     free memory                    15266240
java pool     joxlod exec hp                  5471424
```

The Streams Pool

Streams is an advanced capability of the database that is not part of the OCP curriculum. This is a very brief summary, all that is necessary to complete the description of the SGA.

All changes made to the database are captured in the redo log as physical change records: changes to be applied to blocks. Physical change records are not ordered or grouped in any fashion that can be applied to logical structures such as tables; they can be applied only to the physical datafiles. Streams processes the redo log to extract logical change information, such as the changes applied to tables by transactions, from the redo log stream. These changes are stored as logical change records that can be propagated to other databases and so applied to tables at remote sites.

The instance parameter STREAMS_POOL_SIZE creates an area of memory that is used by the Streams processes for both the capture and the application of logical change records.

Automatic Shared Memory Management

Tuning the SGA is one of the most critical aspects of performance tuning. There are advisors available within the database to assist with tuning the SGA (as displayed in the views V$SHARED_POOL_ADVICE and V$DB_CACHE_ADVICE), but tuning the SGA manually is still a time-consuming task. Furthermore, different SGA configurations may be suited to different patterns of work. It may well be that an SGA that is perfectly tuned for a normal daytime workload will not be optimal for nighttime reporting runs or end-of-month batch processing. For the OLTP workload, a large database buffer cache will minimize the disk I/O, but the reporting and batch processing jobs might benefit more from a large pool, needed for parallel processing.

Inappropriate memory allocations can cause more serious problems than performance issues—they can cause processes to fail. If there is not enough space in the shared pool for an operation, it will fail with an "ORA-04031: unable to allocate n bytes of shared memory" error. The same will occur if the large pool runs out of space.

The Automatic Shared Memory Management capability (introduced with release 10g of the database) relieves the DBA of the burden of having to monitor the usage and manage the sizing of the major SGA components. Once an overall target for the size of the SGA has been set, Oracle itself will monitor memory usage and adjust the sizing of various SGA components automatically in response to the workload.

Four memory structures that are often referred to as auto-tune components are managed by Automatic Shared Memory Management:

- Database buffer cache default pool, DB_CACHE_SIZE
- Shared pool, SHARED_POOL_SIZE
- Large pool, LARGE_POOL_SIZE
- Java pool, JAVA_POOL_SIZE

If the parameters controlling these structures are not set or are set to zero, then Oracle has complete freedom to resize them, dynamically, up or down according to demand. If they have been set, the settings given specify a minimum level below which automatic management will not reduce them.

These other structures must always be sized manually:

- Database buffer cache keep pool, DB_KEEP_CACHE_SIZE
- Database buffer cache recycle pool, DB_RECYCLE_POOL_SIZE
- Database buffer cache nonstandard block size pools, DB_nK_CACHE_SIZE
- Streams pool, STREAMS_POOL_SIZE
- Log buffer, LOG_BUFFER

To enable Automatic Shared Memory Management, set the instance parameter SGA_TARGET. This specifies a total size for the SGA. At instance startup time, Oracle will allocate memory for SGA structures according to the parameters given, both for the automatically managed components and the manually managed components; any missing parameters will be set on defaults. If the total size of the SGA thus created exceeds the SGA_TARGET, then automatic memory management is disabled. If the total at startup is less than the target, Oracle will resize the four automatically managed components upward on demand until the target is reached. From then on, Oracle will monitor the usage of the four components and if necessary transfer memory from one to another in order to ensure that the distribution is optimal for performance and to avoid ORA-04031 errors.

The behavior on subsequent startups depends on the initialization parameter file being used. If the instance was started with a dynamic spfile, then Oracle will write to the file the current settings of the parameters for the four automatically managed components. This allows Oracle to "remember" the settings, and at the next startup they will be used. This saves the running time needed for Oracle to determine what the best settings are. If the instance was started with a static pfile, then automatic memory management will still work, but the current settings will be lost at shutdown, and the self-tuning process will have to start from the beginning at the next startup.

Enabling Automatic Shared Memory Management by setting the SGA_TARGET instance parameter starts an additional background process: the Memory Manager, or MMAN. MMAN observes the system and the workload to determine the ideal memory distribution. The checks are made every few minutes.

 EXAM TIP Automatic Shared Memory Management requires that the STATISTICS_LEVEL instance parameter to be on TYPICAL, the default, or ALL. Without this, the information MMAN needs will not be gathered.

To enable Automatic Shared Memory Management through Database Control, from the database home page take the Administration tab, and the Memory Parameters link in the Instance section, as in Figure 34-2.

In this window you can set the parameters for the various memory structures, or view the advisors. Clicking the Enable button will prompt for a value for the SGA_TARGET, and once set, the automatic management will take over.

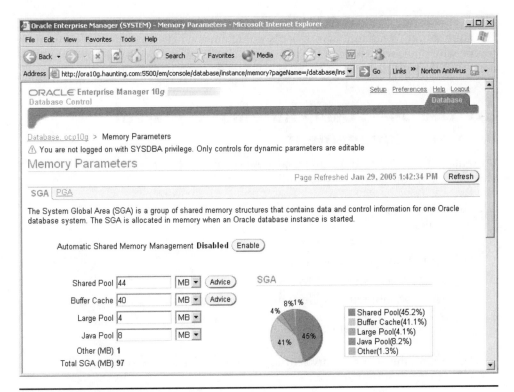

Figure 34-2 SGA sizing with Database Control

 EXAM TIP The SGA_TARGET is the total size of the whole SGA, including any manually managed components—not just the total size of the four automatically managed components.

The SGA_TARGET is the size that the SGA will be—this may well be less than the SGA_MAX_SIZE instance parameter. SGA_TARGET is a dynamic parameter, but you cannot raise it above the SGA_MAX_SIZE setting. If you attempt to set the SGA_TARGET above the SGA_MAX_SIZE for a running instance, the command will fail:

```
ocp10g> alter system set sga_target=200m scope=memory;
alter system set sga_target=200m scope=memory
*
ERROR at line 1:
ORA-02097: parameter cannot be modified because specified value is invalid
ORA-00823: Specified value of sga_target greater than sga_max_size
```

If you set the parameter in the spfile by using the SCOPE=SPFILE clause, the command will succeed, and at the next startup the SGA_MAX_SIZE will be adjusted to the SGA_TARGET.

To disable Automatic Shared Memory Management, set the SGA_TARGET to zero. The automatically managed components will retain their current size until the next restart, when they will revert to the values specified by their parameters, or to their defaults if the parameters have been removed from the initialization file.

Exercise 34-1: Using Automatic Shared Memory Management

Clear all manual SGA settings, and enable Automatic Shared Memory Management. This exercise requires the use of an spfile.

1. Connect to your database with SQL*Plus as user SYS with the SYSDBA privilege.

   ```
   SQL> connect / as sysdba;
   ```

2. Confirm that you are using an spfile.

   ```
   SQL> show parameters spfile;
   ```

   If this does not return a filename, convert your instance to use an spfile.

   ```
   SQL> create spfile from pfile;
   SQL> shutdown abort;
   SQL> startup;
   ```

3. Remove the SGA memory settings from the spfile for the automatically managed components.

   ```
   SQL> alter system reset shared_pool_size scope=spfile sid='*';
   SQL> alter system reset large_pool_size scope=spfile sid='*';
   SQL> alter system reset java_pool_size scope=spfile sid='*';
   SQL> alter system reset db_cache_size scope=spfile sid='*';
   ```

4. Determine the current size of the SGA.

   ```
   SQL> select sum(bytes) from v$sgastat;
   ```

5. Set the SGA_TARGET to a value similar to that returned by the query in Step 4. In this example, 100MB.

   ```
   SQL> alter system set sga_target=100m scope=spfile sid='*';
   ```

6. Restart the instance, and again check the size of the SGA.

   ```
   SQL> startup force;
   ORACLE instance started.
   Total System Global Area   134217728 bytes
   Fixed Size                     787828 bytes
   Variable Size                91224716 bytes
   Database Buffers             41943040 bytes
   Redo Buffers                   262144 bytes
   Database mounted.
   Database opened.
   ocp10g> select sum(bytes) from v$sgastat;
   SUM(BYTES)
   ----------
    101713268
   ```

Note that in this example the SGA size reported by the STARTUP command is 128MB. This is not the current size of the SGA; it is the value of the SGA_MAX_SIZE parameter and is the largest that the SGA can grow to. The actual allocated SGA is 100MB, as specified by the SGA_TARGET.

7. Display the sizes of the various SGA components.

```
SQL> show parameters db_cache_size;
NAME                                 TYPE        VALUE
------------------------------------ ----------- ------
__db_cache_size                      big integer 40M
db_cache_size                        big integer 0
```

Note that the parameter DB_CACHE_SIZE is on zero, as specified in Step 3, but that there is another parameter: the strangely named __DB_CACHE_SIZE. This double-underscore parameter is the internal setting maintained by MMAN: it is the current size of the database buffer cache default pool, and if the instance is shut down, this value (which may be changed by MMAN at any time) will be used as the starting point for self-tuning subsequently.

8. Repeat the SHOW command for the other automatically managed parameters.

```
SQL> show parameters large_pool_size;
NAME                                 TYPE        VALUE
------------------------------------ ----------- ----------
__large_pool_size                    big integer 4M
large_pool_size                      big integer 0
SQL> show parameters shared_pool_size;
NAME                                 TYPE        VALUE
------------------------------------ ----------- ----------
__shared_pool_size                   big integer 44M
shared_pool_size                     big integer 0
SQL> show parameters java_pool_size;
NAME                                 TYPE        VALUE
------------------------------------ ----------- ----------
__java_pool_size                     big integer 8M
java_pool_size                       big integer 0
```

9. Reconcile the actual memory usage to the target by summing up the values for the four double-underscore parameters. In the preceding output, they come to 96MB. This is 4MB, or one granule, less than the SGA target. The "spare" granule will contain the log buffer, along with the structures known as the "fixed size" element of the SGA. If your instance has any of the non-automatically managed SGA components configured, remember to include them in the calculation.

The Program Global Area

Every session has access to the shared SGA, but it will also have access to a block of memory that is private to the session. This is the Program Global Area, or PGA. The PGA stores data and control information for each session and is used only by the server process servicing the session. A PGA is created when a session starts. The information in the PGA includes bind information; session variables; stack space; cursors; and (perhaps most important) the sort space used for sorting, joining, and aggregating rows.

When using shared server, a large part of the PGA (the part known as the UGA) goes into the large pool (or the shared pool, if the large pool has not been configured). This was discussed in Chapter 13. However, the majority of Oracle installations do not need the shared server, so each session has its own PGA, taken from the operating system's free memory pool.

PGAs are of variable size; the amount of PGA space that a session needs at any given moment is dependent on the nature of the work it is doing. With earlier releases of the database, PGA management was very crude and could result in extremely inefficient use of memory, but from release 9*i* onward it can be automated. There are two parameters to set:

- **WORKAREA_SIZE_POLICY** This should be set to AUTO, which is now the default (the default was MANUAL in release 9*i*).

- **PGA_AGGREGATE_TARGET** This is the total amount of memory that Oracle will use for all the sessions' PGAs; it defaults to 20 percent of the SGA size.

In discussion with your system administrators, you will come to a decision about the amount of memory that can be allocated to Oracle before system performance will degrade because of swapping. After subtracting the amount needed for the SGA, you can set the PGA_AGGREGATE_TARGET to the remainder.

As sessions require PGA memory, Oracle will allocate them memory until the total allocated PGA across all sessions is equal to the PGA_AGGREGATE_TARGET. From this point on, if a session requires more PGA, or if a new session connects, Oracle will take memory from another session's PGA that is no longer required by that session. As the need for PGA is usually transient, this mechanism should ensure that every session has access to the memory it needs, when it needs it.

If a session needs more PGA than it currently has, the total allocation is already at the target, and no session has unused PGA that can be reassigned, there are two possibilities. If the memory requirement is invariable, as for example when a session requires stack space, then Oracle will allocate it and break the target. This should be avoided at all costs; it implies that the target is far too low. If the requirement is not absolute, then Oracle will refuse to allocate more memory, and the session will make use of temporary space in the session's temporary tablespace instead. This impacts on performance, through the extra disk I/O, and should be avoided if possible.

To monitor PGA usage, there are two critical views. V$PGASTAT gives an overall picture of PGA usage:

```
ocp10g> select * from v$pgastat;
NAME                                          VALUE UNIT
-------------------------------------- ---------- ------
aggregate PGA target parameter             104857600 bytes
aggregate PGA auto target                   75497472 bytes
global memory bound                           524288 bytes
total PGA in use                            25165824 bytes
total PGA allocated                         53518336 bytes
maximum PGA allocated                       64432128 bytes
```

```
total freeable PGA memory                      524288 bytes
PGA memory freed back to OS                         0 bytes
total PGA used for auto workareas                   0 bytes
maximum PGA used for auto workareas            483328 bytes
total PGA used for manual workareas                 0 bytes
maximum PGA used for manual workareas               0 bytes
over allocation count                            3266
bytes processed                             273463296 bytes
extra bytes read/written                            0 bytes
cache hit percentage                              100 percent
16 rows selected.
```

These are some rows to highlight:

- **Aggregate PGA target parameter**   This is set to 100MB.

- **Aggregate PGA auto target**   Of the 100MB, only 74MB can be automatically managed; the rest is non-negotiable, for example, stack space.

- **Total PGA in use**   At this moment, only about one quarter of the PGA is actually being used.

- **Total PGA allocated**   About half the PGA is allocated—more than the previous figure, implying that some could be reassigned if necessary.

- **Total freeable PGA memory**   If necessary, 0.5MB of allocated PGA could be reassigned, or returned to the operating system.

- **Over allocation count**   This should always be zero: it is the number of times that Oracle had to go over the target. Raise the target if this figure is increasing.

- **Cache hit percentage**   This should be tending toward 100 percent. It reflects the number of times sessions could work purely in PGA, without having to use temporary space on disk. Raise the target if this figure is increasing and the system has spare memory.

V$PGA_TARGET_ADVICE makes predictions regarding the effect of changing the target:

```
ocp10g> select pga_target_for_estimate "size",
  2  pga_target_factor "factor",
  3  estd_extra_bytes_rw/1000000 "extra Mb r/w",
  4  estd_overalloc_count "over alloctions"
  5  from v$pga_target_advice;
       size     factor  extra Mb r/w over allocations
 ---------- ---------- ------------- ----------------
        128        0.1     119.558.2           10,590
        256        0.3     112,984.8            7,657
        512        0.5      96,472.4            5,528
        768        0.8      78,932.9            3,824
      1,024        1.0      13,997.6                0
      1,229        1.2       9,019.4                0
      1,434        1.4       8,281.3                0
      1,638        1.6       7,352.9                0
      1,843        1.8       6,525.9                0
      2,048        2.0       6,048.9                0
      3,072        3.0       6,048.9                0
      4,096        4.0       6,048.9                0
```

| 6,144 | 6.0 | 6,048.9 | 0 |
| 8,192 | 8.0 | 6,048.9 | 0 |

In this example, the PGA aggregate target is currently 1GB. This is the absolute minimum for performance: if it were reduced, Oracle would not be able to stick to it—as shown by the predictions regarding over-allocations. If the target were raised, the amount of disk I/O on temporary tablespaces would reduce by many gigabytes, as more operations could proceed in memory—but there would be no point in raising the target above 2GB, because there is no further improvement from then on.

The PGA Advisor can also be accessed through Database Control, by taking the PGA tab shown in Figure 34-2. This will show a graphical representation of the V$PGA_TARGET_ADVICE view.

It is possible to disable automatic PGA management, by setting the WORKAREA_ SIZE_POLICY instance parameter to MANUAL. You can do this at the session level, as well as for the whole instance. In this case, the size of a PGA is limited by these parameters:

SORT_AREA_SIZE
HASH_AREA_SIZE
BITMAPMERGE_AREA_SIZE
CREATE_BITMAP_AREA_SIZE

These parameters are ignored when using automatic PGA management. Apart from the difficulty of predicting suitable values for these settings, a far worse problem is that PGAs managed in this manner grow but never shrink. Oracle cannot reassign memory from one PGA to another, unless automatic PGA management is enabled. Oracle Corporation strongly advises using automatic PGA management.

Chapter Review

This chapter has covered memory management: the SGA and the PGA.

The SGA is an area of shared memory accessed by all the background and server processes. The required components of the SGA are the shared pool, the log buffer, and the database buffer cache default pool. Optional components are the large pool, the Java pool, the streams pool, and the other pools within the database buffer cache. A PGA is private to a session. It contains the session data: call stack, cursors, session variables, bind information, and SQL work areas such as sort space.

Both the SGA and the PGAs can be manually configured, but a better option is to use automatic management.

Automatic management of the SGA is enabled by setting the SGA_TARGET parameter; the MMAN process will then resize SGA components dynamically to achieve the optimal distribution of memory between components. Only four components can be automatically managed: the shared pool, the large pool, the Java pool, and the database buffer cache default pool.

PGA automatic management is enabled by default. Oracle resizes all the PGAs up (according to demand) and down (as memory is needed elsewhere) in an attempt to ensure that all sessions have as much memory as they need, without taking the total allocation over the limit set by the PGA_AGGREGATE_TARGET.

Questions

1. Some SGA components are required; others are optional. Which of the following are required? (Choose all that apply.)

    A. Database buffer cache default pool

    B. Database buffer cache keep pool

    C. Database buffer cache recycle pool

    D. Java pool

    E. Large pool

    F. Log buffer

    G. Shared pool

    H. Streams pool

2. Some SGA components can be dynamically resized, while others can be changed only by a shutdown/startup of the instance. Which of the following parameters are static? (Choose all that apply.)

    A. DB_CACHE_SIZE

    B. DB_KEEP_CACHE_SIZE

    C. DB_RECYCLE_CACHE_SIZE

    D. JAVA_POOL_SIZE

    E. LARGE_POOL_SIZE

    F. LOG_BUFFER

    G. SGA_MAX_SIZE

    H. SGA_TARGET

    I. SHARED_POOL_SIZE

3. If you enable Automatic Shared Memory Management, which SGA components will be managed automatically? (Choose four correct answers.)

    A. Database buffer cache default pool

    B. Database buffer cache keep pool

    C. Database buffer cache recycle pool

    D. Java pool

    E. Large pool

    F. Log buffer

    G. Shared pool

    H. Streams pool

4. Which of the following commands will force a database checkpoint? (Choose two correct answers.)

   A. ALTER SYSTEM CHECKPOINT

   B. ALTER SYSTEM SWITCH LOGFILE

   C. STARTUP FORCE

   D. SHUTDOWN IMMEDIATE

5. Your database was created with the DB_BLOCK_SIZE parameter on the default of 2048. You have decided that this is too small, and that 8KB would be better. What can you do? (Choose the best answer.)

   A. Set the parameter DB_8K_CACHE_SIZE to create a buffer cache pool of 8KB buffers, and use the DBMS_SPACE_ADMIN package to convert the tablespaces.

   B. Export the whole database, change the DB_BLOCK_SIZE to 8196, restart the instance, and import the database back in.

   C. Export the whole database, create a new database with a DB_BLOCK_SIZE of 8196, and import the database into it.

   D. You can convert all the tablespaces, except for SYSTEM and temporary tablespaces.

6. Space in the SGA is allocated in granules. If the granule size is 4MB and you attempt to start an instance with the parameter setting DB_CACHE_SIZE=5M, how big will your database buffer cache be? (Choose the best answer.)

   A. 4MB

   B. 5MB

   C. 8MB

   D. The instance will not start, because SGA components must be a multiple of the granule size

7. Space in the SGA is allocated in granules. If the granule size is 4MB and you attempt to start an instance with the parameter setting LOG_BUFFER=1048576, how big will your log buffer be? (Choose the best answer.)

   A. 1MB

   B. 4MB

   C. It will revert to the default size for the platform and number of CPUs

   D. The instance will not start

8. The log writer flushes the log buffer to disk. What will cause it to do this? (Choose three correct answers.)

   A. A user committing a transaction

   B. When the buffer is two-thirds full

C. When the buffer is one-third full

D. When there are too many dirty buffers

E. A three-second timeout

F. Issuing an ALTER SYSTEM FLUSH LOG_BUFFER command

9. You set parameters as follows:

```
SGA_MAX_SIZE=256m
SGA_TARGET=128m
SHARED_POOL_SIZE=64m
DB_CACHE_SIZE=64m
KEEP_CACHE_SIZE=32m
LARGE_POOL_SIZE=32m
```

What will happen when you attempt to start the instance? (Choose the best answer.)

A. The instance will not start, because the memory requested for the components is above the SGA_TARGET.

B. The instance will not start, because you cannot specify component sizes if you enable Automatic Shared Memory Management with SGA_TARGET.

C. The instance will start, but the components will be reduced in size by Automatic Shared Memory Management to limit the total size to the SGA_TARGET.

D. The instance will start, with the components sized as requested.

10. You set parameters as follows:

```
SGA_MAX_SIZE=800m
SGA_TARGET=1000m
DB_KEEP_CACHE_SIZE=400m
```

and leave the other SGA sizing parameters on default. How much memory can Oracle assign to the auto-tuned components? (Choose the best answer.)

A. 400MB

B. 600MB

C. 800MB

D. 1000MB

11. If you set the sizes for the four automatically tuned SGA components, which of the following is true? (Choose the best answer.)

A. Automatic Shared Memory Management is disabled.

B. The sizes given will be the minimum size of the components, if you enable Automatic Shared Memory Management.

C. The sizes given will be the maximum size of the components, if you enable Automatic Shared Memory Management.

D. You must set the sizes to zero before enabling Automatic Shared Memory Management.

12. Which process is responsible for Automatic Shared Memory Management? (Choose the best answer.)

   A. MMAN

   B. MMON

   C. MMNL

   D. PMON

   E. SMON

13. To what must the STATISTICS_LEVEL parameter be set if you are to enable Automatic Shared Memory Management? (Choose the best answer.)

   A. BASIC

   B. TYPICAL

   C. ALL

   D. TYPICAL or ALL

   E. BASIC, TYPICAL, or ALL

14. Which of the following statements is correct about Automatic PGA Management? (Choose two correct answers.)

   A. Servers can share access to PGAs.

   B. PGA memory usage will never go above the PGA_AGGREGATE_TARGET setting.

   C. PGAs will grow and shrink according to demand.

   D. You can have some sessions' PGAs automatically managed, and others manually managed.

15. Which of the following is not part of the PGA? (Choose the best answer.)

   A. Bind information

   B. Parsing information

   C. Session variables

   D. Sort space

Answers

1. **A, F, and G.** The required components of the SGA are the database buffer cache default pool, the log buffer, and the shared pool. The others are optional, though by default you will get a Java pool and (depending on other parameters) possibly a large pool.

2. **F and G.** The static parameters are LOG_BUFFER and SGA_MAX_SIZE.

3. **A, D, E, and G.** The four automatically managed components are the database buffer cache default pool, the Java pool, the large pool, and the shared pool.

4. **A and D.** Database checkpoints can be forced with ALTER SYSTEM CHECKPOINT and will occur naturally upon an orderly shutdown, such as SHUTDOWN IMMEDIATE. A log switch will not trigger a checkpoint with the 10g release. STARTUP FORCE includes a SHUTDOWN ABORT, so there is no checkpoint.

5. **C.** You can never change the DB_BLOCK_SIZE after database creation, so the only option is to create a new database. There is no way to convert a tablespace from one block size to another.

6. **C.** The cache will be 8MB because the requested size of 5MB will be rounded up to the next granule boundary.

7. **A.** The log buffer will be 1MB, as requested. It is the one SGA component that is not sized in granules.

8. **A, C, and E.** Log writer will write on COMMIT, when the log buffer is one-third full, and every three seconds. Too many dirty buffers is a trigger for the database writer, not the log writer. There is no such command as ALTER SYSTEM FLUSH LOG_BUFFER, though there are commands ALTER SYSTEM FLUSH SHARED_POOL and ALTER SYSTEM FLUSH BUFFER_CACHE.

9. **D.** The settings for the components take precedence over the setting for the target, which will be ignored.

10. **B.** The SGA_TARGET includes both automatically and manually managed components, so the 400MB assigned to the keep pool must be subtracted from the 1000MB total. So the best answer is 600MB. It is the "best" answer, but possibly not completely accurate—there will be a granule required for, among other things, the log buffer.

11. **B.** Manually setting sizes for automatically tuned components sets a minimum size below which MMAN will not reduce the components.

12. **A.** MMAN, the Memory Manager, is responsible for implementing Automatic Shared Memory Management. MMON, manageability monitor, is responsible for writing statistics to the Automatic Workload Repository and generating ADDM reports. MMNL, Manageability Monitor Light, flushes ASH data to the AWR. PMON monitors sessions, and SMAN monitors the instance.

13. **D.** Automatic Shared Memory Management requires a STATISTICS_LEVEL of TYPICAL or ALL.

14. **C and D.** Automatic PGA management lets PGAs grow and shrink. It can be set for the instance or per session. The other choices are wrong because PGAs are always private to the session and because the target is only a target—there may be times when Oracle cannot keep to it.

15. **B.** Parsing information is stored in the shared pool, where all sessions have access to it.

CHAPTER 35

Managing Oracle Database Resources

In this chapter you will learn how to

- Configure the Resource Manager
- Assign users to Resource Manager groups
- Create resource plans within groups
- Specify directives for allocating resources to consumer groups

Many computer systems will have several groups of users, each with different standards for the level of service they require. If the system as a whole is highly stressed, it may be impossible to deliver the desired level of service to all groups. But if a priority structure can be negotiated, then it should be possible to guarantee a certain level of service to certain groups—perhaps at the expense of other groups.

In a mainframe environment, the operating system itself handles allocating resources to tasks. A *transaction processing (TP)* monitor will ensure that high-priority jobs get the processing power they need. But simpler operating systems such as Unix or Windows may not have proper resource scheduling capabilities. Oracle's Resource Manager brings mainframe-style resource management capabilities to all supported Oracle platforms, meaning that you as DBA can guarantee that certain groups of database users will always receive a certain level of service, no matter what the overall workload on the database may be.

The Need for Resource Management

Operating systems like Unix or Windows use a very simple algorithm to assign resources to different processes: round-robin time slicing. To the operating system, there is really no difference between any of the background processes that make up the Oracle instance and any of the many server processes that support user sessions: as far as the operating system is concerned, a process is a process; it will be brought onto CPU, given a few cycles of CPU time, and then switched off CPU so that the next process can be brought on. The operating system has no way of knowing that one server process is supporting a session doing completely trivial work, while another server process is supporting a session doing work critical to the survival of the organization. A more immediate problem that all DBAs come across is that one bad query can kill the database. The Resource Manager provides a mechanism whereby the operating system's time-slicing algorithm can be adjusted, to ensure that some users receive more processing capacity than others—and to ensure that the one query does not destroy performance for everyone else. The underlying mechanism is to place a cooperative multitasking layer controlled by Oracle on top of the operating system's preemptive multitasking system.

Throughout this chapter, the environment is assumed to be that of a telesales organization. There are several groups of users: of particular interest are the data entry clerks and the management accountants.

There may be two hundred data entry clerks in the call center, taking orders over the telephone. If their database sessions are running slowly, this is disastrous for the company. Customers will dial in only to be told "you are number 964 in the queue, your call is important to us, please do not hang up...." This is happening because the data entry clerks cannot process calls fast enough: they take an order, they click the Submit button, and then they wait...and wait...and wait...for the system to respond. This is costing money.

On the other hand, the management accountants' work is not so urgent. Perhaps an advertisement has been run on one local radio station, and the response in terms of sales inquiries needs to be evaluated before running the advertisement nationwide. This is important work, but it doesn't have to be real time. If the reports take ten minutes to run instead of five, does it really matter?

TIP Do not adjust the priorities of Oracle processes by using the Unix nice command, or the Windows equivalent. Oracle assumes that the operating system is treating all processes equally, and if you interfere with this there may be unexpected (and disastrous) side effects.

What is needed is a technique for ensuring that if the database sessions supporting the data entry clerks need computing resources, they get them—no matter what. This could mean that at certain times of day when the call center is really busy, the clerks need 100 percent of computing resources. The Resource Manager can handle this, and during that time of peak usage the sessions supporting the management accountants may hang completely. But during other times of day, when the call center is not busy, there will be plenty of resources available to be directed to the management accountants' work.

At month end, another task will become top priority: the end-of-month billing runs, and the rollover of the ledgers into the next accounting period. The Resource Manager needs to be versatile enough to manage this, too.

Clearly, the Resource Manager is only necessary in highly stressed systems, but when you need it, there is no alternative.

The Resource Manager Architecture

Users are placed in Resource Manager consumer groups, and Resource Manager plans, consisting of a set of directives, control the allocation of resources across the groups. You are using the Resource Manager whether you know it or not; it is configured by default in all databases from release 8i onward, but the default configuration has no effect on normal work.

Consumer Groups

A Resource Manager consumer group is a set of users with similar resource requirements. One group may contain many users, and one user may be a member of many groups, but at any given moment, each session will have one group as its effective group. When a user first creates a session, his default consumer group membership will be active, but if he is a member of multiple groups, he can switch to another group, activating his membership of that group.

In the telesales example, the two hundred data entry clerks could be in a group called OLTP, and the half-dozen management accountants could be in a group called DSS. Some users could be in both groups; depending on what work they are doing, they will activate the appropriate group membership. Other groups might be BATCH, to be given top priority for month-end processing, and LOW for people who happen to have accounts on the system but are of no great significance.

There are five groups created by default when a database is created:

- **SYS_GROUP** This is a group intended for the database administrators. By default, the SYS and SYSTEM users only are in this group.

- **DEFAULT_CONSUMER_GROUP** This is a group for all users who have not been specifically granted membership of any other group. By default, all users other than SYS and SYSTEM are in this group, and this membership is active when they first create a session.

- **OTHER_GROUPS** This is a group that all users are members of, used as a catch-all for any sessions that are in groups not listed in the active Resource Manager plan.

- **LOW_GROUP** This group is intended for low-priority sessions.

- **AUTO_TASK_CONSUMER_GROUP** This group is intended for running system maintenance jobs.

To view the groups in your database, query the views DBA_RSRC_CONSUMER_GROUPS and DBA_USERS. The latter shows the initial consumer group set for each user at connect time (see Figure 35-1).

Resource Manager Plans

A Resource Manager plan is of a certain type. The most basic (and most common) type of plan is one that allocates CPU resources, but there are other resource allocation methods. Many plans can exist within the database, but only one plan is active at any one time. This plan applies to the whole instance: all sessions are controlled by it.

```
C:\WINDOWS\System32\cmd.exe - sqlplus / as sysdba

ocp10g> select CONSUMER_GROUP,COMMENTS from dba_rsrc_consumer_groups;

CONSUMER_GROUP                  COMMENTS

OTHER_GROUPS                    consumer group for users not included in any group
DEFAULT_CONSUMER_GROUP          consumer group for users not assigned to any group
SYS_GROUP                       Group of system sessions
LOW_GROUP                       Group of low priority sessions
AUTO_TASK_CONSUMER_GROUP        System maintenance task consumer group

ocp10g> select username, initial_rsrc_consumer_group from dba_users;

USERNAME                        INITIAL_RSRC_CONSUMER_GROUP

SYSTEM                          SYS_GROUP
SYS                             SYS_GROUP
OLAPSYS                         DEFAULT_CONSUMER_GROUP
SI_INFORMTN_SCHEMA              DEFAULT_CONSUMER_GROUP
MGMT_VIEW                       DEFAULT_CONSUMER_GROUP
ORDPLUGINS                      DEFAULT_CONSUMER_GROUP
WKPROXY                         DEFAULT_CONSUMER_GROUP
CSMIG                           DEFAULT_CONSUMER_GROUP
```

Figure 35-1 Resource Manager consumer groups

In the telesales example, there could be three plans. A daytime plan would give top priority to the OLTP group. At times of peak activity, with the system working to full capacity, it is possible that the sessions of users in other groups would hang. At night, a different plan would be activated that would guarantee that the DSS jobs would run, though perhaps still not with the priority of the OLTP group. A month-end plan would give 100 percent of resources to the BATCH group.

A plan consists of a number of directives. Each directive assigns resources to a particular group at a particular priority level. Three plans are configured at database creation time:

- The INTERNAL_PLAN has only one directive, which has no practical effect. It states that the group OTHER_GROUPS can have 100 percent of CPU resources at priority level 1. All plans must have a directive for OTHER_GROUPS, which picks up all users in groups not specifically allocated any resources by the plan. So this plan, enabled by default, will result in all users having equal priority.

- The SYSTEM_PLAN has three directives (see Figure 35-2). The first states that at priority level 1, the highest priority, the SYS_GROUP consumer group can take 100 percent of CPU resources. At level 2, OTHER_GROUPS can have 100 percent, and at level 3 the LOW_GROUP can take 100 percent. This plan ensures that if SYS or SYSTEM needs to do something, it will get whatever resources it needs to do it. Any resources it does not need will "trickle down" to the OTHER_GROUPS.

- The INTERNAL_QUIESCE plan has a particular purpose covered at the end of the chapter: it will freeze all sessions except those of the SYS_GROUP members.

To enable a plan, use the RESOURCE_MANAGER_PLAN instance parameter. By default, this parameter is NULL, which means that the INTERNAL_PLAN is the plan in effect. This has no effect on priorities.

 EXAM TIP The instance parameter RESOURCE_LIMITS has nothing to do with the Resource Manager. It pertains to the older method of controlling resources, through database profiles.

Resource Manager Configuration Tools

There is an API that can be used to administer the Resource Manager; it also provides a Database Control interface. The API consists of two packages: DBMS_RESOURCE_MANAGER_PRIVS and DBMS_RESOURCE_MANAGER. DBMS_RESOURCE_MANAGER_PRIVS is used to put users into consumer groups and also to grant the system privilege necessary to administer the Resource Manager (see Figure 35-3).

To give user JOHN the capability of administering the Resource Manager,

```
SQL> execute dbms_resource_manager_privs.grant_system_privilege
('JOHN', 'ADMINISTER_RESOURCE_MANAGER', FALSE);
```

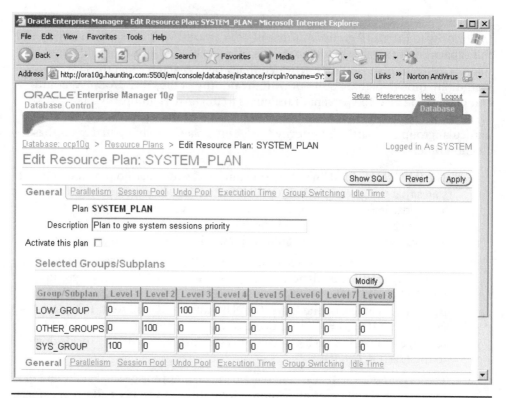

Figure 35-2　The SYSTEM_PLAN, displayed with Database Control

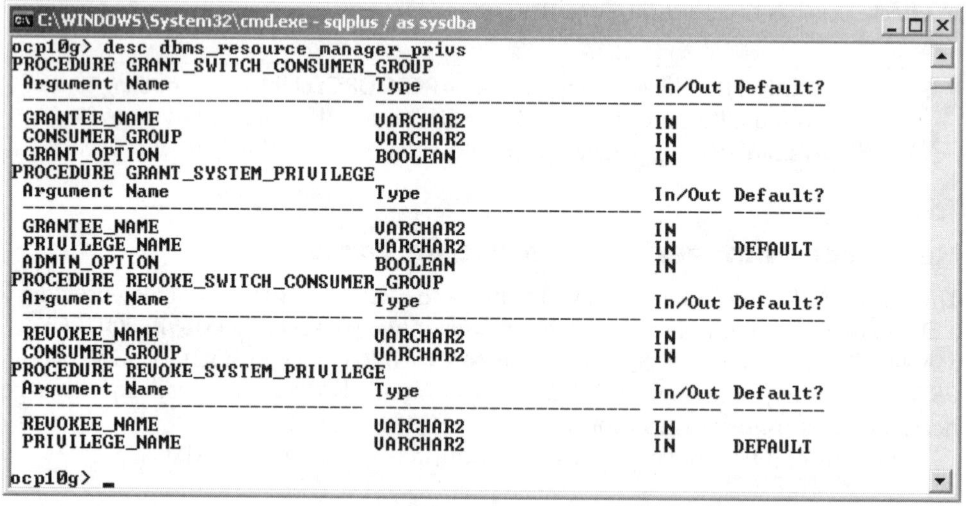

Figure 35-3　The DBMS_RESOURCE_MANAGER_PRIVS package

DBMS_RESOURCE_MANAGER is used to create consumer groups, plans, and directives. It is also used to create the "pending area." Before any work can be done with Resource Manager objects, you must create a pending area. This is an area of memory in the SGA, used for storing the objects while they are being configured. A plan may consist of many directives, and each directive is created independently; it would therefore be possible to create a totally impossible plan, one that might, for example, allocate 500 percent of CPU. The pending area is provided to prevent this possibility: the plan is created in the pending area, and then when complete it is validated to check that it does make sense. Only then does the plan get saved to the data dictionary.

To reach the Database Control interface to the Resource Manager, from the database home page take the Administration tab, and then follow the links in the Resource Manager section.

Managing Users and Consumer Groups

A pending area is needed to create consumer groups, but not to put users into groups. If you use Database Control, the pending area will be managed for you; if you use the API directly, you must explicitly create it. Database Control does itself use the API, but the GUI front end makes it much simpler to use and has validations that should make it impossible to create a logically inconsistent Resource Manager environment.

At connect time, a session will pick up the initial consumer group assigned to that user. If the user is a member of multiple consumer groups, the session can be switched to a different consumer group later on. This can be done either manually or by using more advanced techniques automatically according to the work that the session is doing.

Any user can switch his active consumer group to any of the groups of which he is a member by using the SWITCH_CURRENT_CONSUMER_GROUP procedure in the DBMS_SESSION package. Alternatively, a user with the privilege to administer the Resource Manager can switch another session over, by using one of two procedures in the DBMS_RESOURCE_MANAGER package. The SWITCH_CONSUMER_GROUP_FOR_USER procedure will switch all sessions logged on with a particular username, or SWITCH_CONSUMER_GROUP_FOR_SESS will switch one particular session, identified by SID and SERIAL#:

```
SQL> exec dbms_resource_manager.switch_consumer_group_for_sess(-
session_id=>209,session_serial=>10223,consumer_group=>'OLTP');
```

 EXAM TIP The DBMS_RESOURCE_MANAGER_PRIVS package includes the procedure to put someone in a group, but it is procedures in DBMS_SESSION and DBMS_RESOURCE_MANAGER that can change a user's active consumer group.

Exercise 35-1: Managing Users in Resource Consumer Groups

Create some users and consumer groups, view the configuration, and test the consumer group switching for a user who is a member of multiple groups.

1. Connect to your database as user SYSTEM using SQL*Plus.

2. Create some users and grant them the CONNECT role.

   ```
   SQL> grant connect to clerk identified by clerk;
   SQL> grant connect to acct identified by acct;
   SQL> grant connect to batch identified by batch;
   SQL> grant connect to mgr identified by mgr;
   ```

3. Connect to your database as user SYSTEM using Database Control.

4. From the database home page, take the Administration tab, and then the Resource Consumer Groups link in the Resource Manager section, to see the five default groups.

5. Click Create to reach the Create Resource Consumer Group window.

6. Enter **OLTP** for the consumer group name, and **group for telesales clerks** as the description. Click Add to display a listing of all users in the database.

7. Check the selection boxes for users CLERK and MGR, and click Select to return to the Create Resource Consumer Group window.

8. Check the Initial Group box for the CLERK user, but not for the MGR user.

9. Click Show SQL, and study the output (see Figure 35-4). Note the use of the pending area. Click Return to return to the Create Resource Consumer Group window.

10. Click OK to create the group, and assign the users to it.

11. Create two more groups, with users as follows:

    Group DSS, members ACCT and MGR, initial group for ACCT
    Group BATCH, members BATCH and MGR, initial group for BATCH

12. From your SQL*Plus session, check the groups and the memberships.

    ```
    SQL> select CONSUMER_GROUP,COMMENTS from  dba_rsrc_consumer_groups;
    CONSUMER_GROUP            COMMENTS
    ------------------------  ----------------------------------------
    OTHER_GROUPS              consumer group for users not included in
                             any group in the active top-plan
    DEFAULT_CONSUMER_GROUP    consumer group for users not assigned to
                             any group
    SYS_GROUP                 Group of system sessions
    LOW_GROUP                 Group of low priority sessions
    AUTO_TASK_CONSUMER_GROUP  System maintenance task consumer group
    OLTP                      group for telesales clerks
    DSS                       group for management accountants
    BATCH                     group for batch jobs
    SQL> select * from DBA_RSRC_CONSUMER_GROUP_PRIVS;
    ```

```
GRANTEE     GRANTED_GROUP            GRANT_OPTION INITIAL_GROUP
----------  ------------------------ ------------ -------------
MGR         DSS                      NO           NO
MGR         OLTP                     NO           NO
MGR         BATCH                    NO           NO
ACCT        DSS                      NO           YES
BATCH       BATCH                    NO           YES
CLERK       OLTP                     NO           YES
PUBLIC      LOW_GROUP                NO           NO
PUBLIC      DEFAULT_CONSUMER_GROUP   YES          YES
SYSTEM      SYS_GROUP                NO           YES
```

13. In your SQL*Plus session, start the Resource Manager by enabling the SYSTEM_PLAN.

```
SQL> alter system set resource_manager_plan=system_plan;
```

14. In a second SQL*Plus session, connect as user CLERK.

15. In the first session, confirm that CLERK's consumer group is DSS.

```
SQL> select username,resource_consumer_group from v$session;
```

16. In the second session, connect as user MGR and run this code block to activate your membership of the DSS group:

```
SQL> declare old_grp varchar2(30);
  2  begin
  3  dbms_session.switch_current_consumer_group('DSS',old_grp,TRUE);
  4  end;
  5  /
```

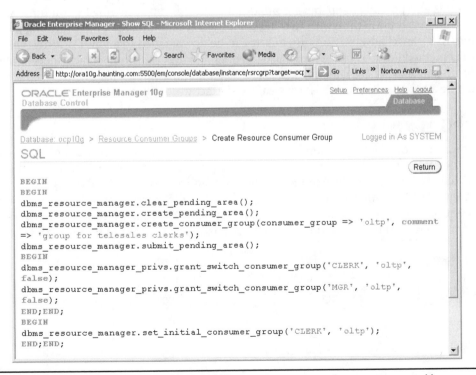

Figure 35-4 Use of the Resource Manager API to manage groups and users, as generated by Database Control

17. In the first session, repeat the query of Step 15 to confirm that MGR is in the DSS group.

18. In the first session, switch the MGR user over to the OLTP group.

```
SQL> execute
dbms_resource_manager.switch_consumer_group_for_user('MGR','OLTP');
```

19. In the first session, repeat the query of Step 15 to confirm that MGR has been switched over to the OLTP group.

Resource Manager Plans

A plan consists of a set of directives that divide resources between consumer groups. There are several principles that can be used to control this:

- CPU method
- Number of active sessions
- Degree of parallelism
- Operation execution time
- Idle time
- Volume of undo data

It is also possible to enable automatic consumer group switching by combining operation execution time with CPU usage: a session that initiates a long-running job that will impact adversely on other users can be downgraded to a lower priority. The CPU method is known as an "emphasis" method, because the effect will vary depending on system activity. The other methods are "absolute" methods, meaning that you define a hard limit, which is always enforced exactly as written.

CPU Method

Continuing the telesales example, the daytime plan would give maximum resources to the OLTP group. All other sessions will hang, if the OLTP users really do need the whole machine. The only exception is the SYS_GROUP. You should always give the SYS_GROUP priority over anything else: if you, the DBA, need to do something on the production system (such as rebuilding a broken index, or doing a restore and recover), then you should be able to do it as fast as possible. The plan could look like this:

Priority Level	Group	CPU %
1	SYS_GROUP	100
2	OLTP	100
3	DSS BATCH	50 50
4	OTHER_GROUPS	100

There are eight possible priority levels; this plan uses four of them. All CPU resources not used at one level trickle down to the next level. When this plan is active, the SYS_GROUP at level 1 can, if necessary, take over the whole machine; all other sessions will hang. But this shouldn't happen; in normal running, no CPU cycles will be taken by the SYS_GROUP, so the whole machine will be available at level 2, where the OLTP users can use it all. Any CPU resources they do not need drop down to level 3, where they are divided 50/50 between the DSS and the BATCH sessions. If, after they have taken what they need, there is still some capacity left, it will be available to members of other groups. It is possible, at times when the OLTP users are working nonstop and CPU usage has hit 100 percent, that the DSS and BATCH sessions will hang.

 EXAM TIP The total CPU allocated at each level cannot exceed 100 percent. If it does, the pending area will fail to validate and the plan will not be saved to the data dictionary. It is possible to have a plan that allocates less than 100 percent at a level, but there is little purpose in doing this.

The nighttime plan will have different settings:

Priority Level	Group	CPU %
1	SYS_GROUP	100
2	OLTP	50
	DSS	25
	BATCH	25
3	OTHER_GROUPS	100

As with the daytime plan, if the SYS_GROUP needs to do something, it will get top priority. But at level 2, the DSS and BATCH users are guaranteed processing time. They still do not have as high a priority as the OLTP group, but their sessions will not hang. The month-end plan might change this further:

Priority Level	Group	CPU %
1	SYS_GROUP	100
2	BATCH	100
3	DSS	50
	OLTP	50
4	OTHER_GROUPS	100

When this plan is active, the BATCH jobs will take priority over everyone else, taking the whole machine if necessary. This would be advisable if the month-end processing actually means that the system is not usable, so it is vital to get it done as fast as possible.

TIP If the CPU is not running at 100 percent usage, then these plans will have no effect. They have an impact only if the CPU capacity cannot satisfy the demands upon it.

A variation on the CPU method is that the "group" can itself be a plan. It is possible by this method to set up a hierarchy, where a top-level plan allocates resources between two or more subplans. These subplans can then allocate resources between consumer groups. A case where this might be applicable would be an application service provider. Perhaps you have installed an application such as an accounting suite, and you lease time on it to several customers. Each customer will have his own groups of users. Your top-level plan will divide resources between subplans for each customer, perhaps according to the amount they are paying for access to the service. Then within that division, the customers can each allocate resources between their consumer groups.

EXAM TIP Every plan must include a directive for the group OTHER_ GROUPS; otherwise, the validation will fail and you cannot save the plan from the pending area to the data dictionary.

To create a plan such as the daytime plan just described requires a series of procedure calls through the API. The first step is to create the pending area:

```
SQL> exec dbms_resource_manager.create_pending_area;
```

You then create the plan:

```
SQL> exec dbms_resource_manager.create_plan(-
plan=>'DAYTIME',comment=>'plan for normal working hours');
```

and the directives within it:

```
SQL> exec dbms_resource_manager.create_plan_directive(-
plan=>'DAYTIME',group_or_subplan=>'SYS_GROUP',cpu_p1=>100,-
comment=>'give sys_group users top priority');
SQL> exec dbms_resource_manager.create_plan_directive(-
plan=>'DAYTIME',group_or_subplan=>'OLTP',cpu_p2=>100,-
comment=>'give oltp users next priority');
SQL> exec dbms_resource_manager.create_plan_directive(-
plan=>'DAYTIME',group_or_subplan=>'DSS',cpu_p3=>50,-
comment=>'dss users have half at level 3');
SQL> exec dbms_resource_manager.create_plan_directive(-
plan=>'DAYTIME',group_or_subplan=>'BATCH',cpu_p3=>50,-
comment=>'batch users have half at level 3');
SQL> exec dbms_resource_manager.create_plan_directive(-
plan=>'DAYTIME',group_or_subplan=>'OTHER_GROUPS',cpu_p4=>100,-
comment=>'if there is anything left, the others can have it');
```

Finally, validate the pending area and (if the validation returns successfully) save the plan to the data dictionary:

```
SQL> exec dbms_resource_manager.validate_pending_area;
SQL> exec dbms_resource_manager.submit_pending_area;
```

To activate the plan,

```
SQL> alter system set resource_manager_plan=daytime;
```

This plan will be displayed in Database Control as in Figure 35-5.

The Active Session Pool Method

It may be that investigation has shown that a certain number of jobs can be run concurrently by one group of users with no problems, but that if this number is exceeded, then other groups will have difficulties. For example, it might be that the telesales company has six management accountants, logging on with Oracle usernames in the DSS group. If one, two, or even three of them generate reports at the same time, everything is fine, but if four or more attempt to run reports concurrently, then the OLTP users begin to suffer.

The active session pool method of the Resource Manager lets the DBA limit the number of statements that will run concurrently for one group, without restricting the actual number of logins. To continue the example, all six accountants can be connected, and if three of them submit reports, they will all run, but if a fourth submits a job, it will be queued until one of the other three finishes. The nighttime plan would remove all restrictions of this nature.

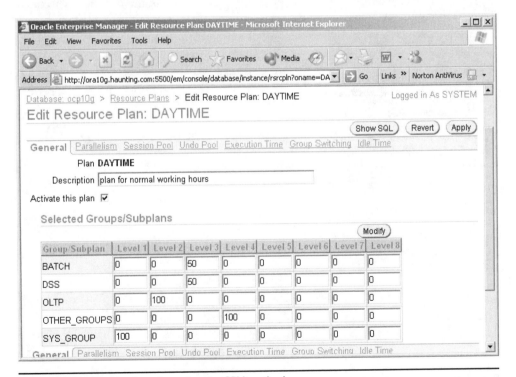

Figure 35-5 The daytime plan, using the CPU method

An *active session* is defined as a session that is running a query, or a session that is in an uncommitted transaction. If parallel processing has been enabled, the individual parallel processors do not count against the session pool; rather, the entire parallel operation counts as one active session. By default, a session will be queued indefinitely, but if you wish, you can set a time limit. If a session from the pool does not become available within this limit, the statement is aborted and an error returned to the session that issued it.

EXAM TIP A session that is not actually doing anything will still count against the active session pool for the group if it has made a change and not committed it.

To enable the active session pool, either use the API directly or go through Database Control, as in Figure 35-6. In this example, when the daytime plan is active, BATCH users are limited to only one active session. If a second BATCH user issues any kind of SQL statement before the first has completed, it will be queued until the first statement has finished. DSS users are limited to three concurrent statements, but they are queued for only five minutes. If a session waits longer than that, an error will be returned.

To monitor the effect of the active session pool, a column CURRENT_QUEUE_ DURATION in V$SESSION will show for every queued session the number of seconds

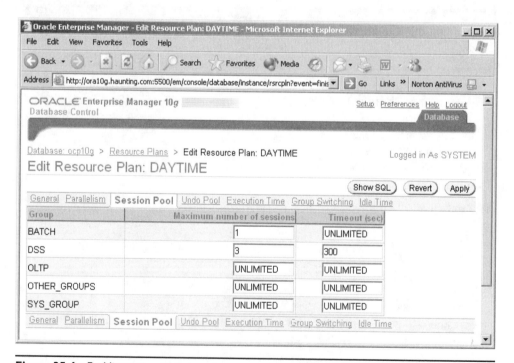

Figure 35-6 Enabling active session pools

it has been waiting. The view V$RSRC_CONSUMER_GROUP gives a global picture, showing how many sessions for each group are queued at any given moment.

Limiting the Degree of Parallelism

Parallel processing, both for SELECT statements and for DML, can greatly enhance the performance of individual statements, but the price you pay may be an impact on other users. To enable parallel processing, you must, as a minimum

- Create a pool of parallel execution servers, with the PARALLEL_MAX_SERVERS instance parameter.

- Enable parallelism for each table, with the ALTER TABLE <table name> PARALLEL command.

- Enable parallel DML for your session with ALTER SESSION ENABLE PARALLEL DML (parallel query will be enabled automatically for the session, if parallelism is set for the table).

- Either set the instance parameter PARALLEL_AUTOMATIC_TUNING=TRUE or specify a degree of parallelism with hints in each statement.

The problem is that once you enable parallel processing, you cannot stop anyone from using it. It may be that your management accountants have discovered that if they run a query with the degree of parallelism set to fifty (and you cannot control this—it is done by hints in the code they write), then the report generates faster. But do you really want one session to take fifty parallel execution servers from the pool? That may not leave enough for other work. Furthermore, the query may now run faster but cripple the performance of the rest of the database. The Resource Manager can control this, by setting a hard limit on the number of parallel processors that each session of any one group is allowed to use. In the daytime plan, for instance, you might limit the DSS and BATCH groups to no more than five per session, even if they ask for fifty. The nighttime plan would remove this restriction.

As with all Resource Manager limits, this can be set through the API or through Database Control, as Figure 35-7 illustrates.

Controlling Jobs by Execution Time

The problem of one large job killing performance for everyone else is well known in the database world. The Resource Manager solves this by providing a mechanism whereby large jobs can be completely eliminated from the system at certain times.

In Figure 35-8, for the daytime plan severe limits have been placed on the maximum execution time of statements submitted by all users except the SYS_GROUP. Any jobs submitted by the DSS or BATCH users will be cancelled if they would not complete in one minute. An even more severe restriction is applied to the OLTP group. Because OLTP has been given a much higher priority at the CPU level, a large job submitted by an OLTP user would be much more serious than one submitted by other users (the

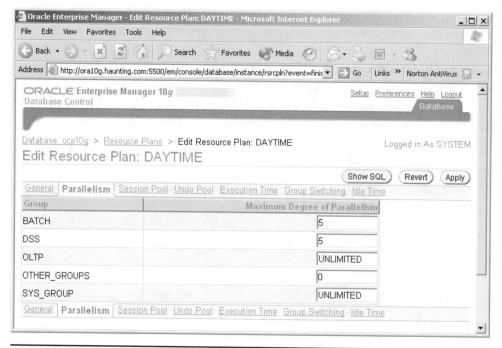

Figure 35-7   Restricting parallelism

OLTP sessions are meant to be used for running small, fast queries and transactions), so this setting will eliminate any job that would take more than ten seconds to complete.

The length of time that a statement will take is estimated by the optimizer. This relies on the statistics on the tables and is another reason for making sure that all your tables do have valid statistics. If the statistics are not accurate, the Resource Manager could make mistakes: it might block jobs that would in fact be quick, and permit jobs that are long-running.

The nighttime plan would remove these restrictions, so that the long-running queries and batch jobs could go through when online performance is less important.

Terminating Sessions by Idle Time

Sessions that are not doing anything waste machine resources. Every session consists, on the server side, of a server process and a PGA. Even if the session is not executing a statement, the operating system must still bring it onto the CPU according to its round-robin time-slicing algorithm. This is known as a *context switch*. Every context switch forces the computer to do a lot of work as registers are loaded from main memory, the state of the session checked, and then the registers cleared again. If the PGA has been paged to disk, that too must be reloaded into main memory. The shared server mechanism, detailed in Chapter 13, will help to reduce idle processes, but it can't do anything about the number of sessions. The UGAs (in the SGA, remember)

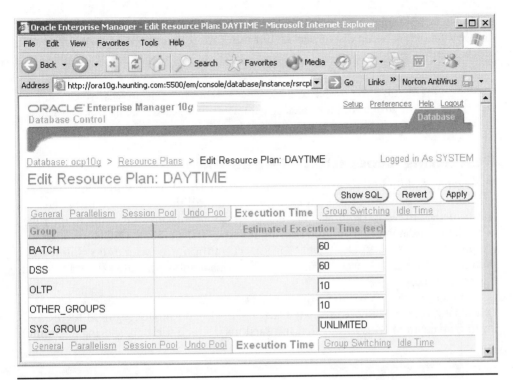

Figure 35-8   Controlling execution times

will still be taking up memory, and Oracle still has to check the state of the session on a regular basis.

The Resource Manager can disconnect sessions that are not working, according to two criteria. The first is simply idle time: how long is it since the session executed a statement? The second is more sophisticated: it not only checks how long since a session executed a statement, but also whether the session is holding any record or table locks that are blocking other sessions, which is a much more serious problem.

Remember from Chapter 17 that a record lock enqueue held by one session will cause another session that needs to lock the same row to hang indefinitely; this can cause the whole database to grind to a halt. It is possible for the DBA to detect this problem, identify the session that is holding the lock, and kill it—but this is a tricky procedure. By using the Resource Manager, you can configure automatic killing of any sessions that block other sessions for more than a certain length of time.

An important point is that "idle time" is time that the server process has been idle, not time that the user process has been idle. For example, your management accountant might be using a spreadsheet as his user process: he will have downloaded some information to it, to work on locally before saving it back to the database. While this is going on, the server process is indeed idle, but the user could be working flat-out in the spreadsheet. He will not be pleased if, when tries to pass the information back, he finds that you have disconnected him and perhaps lost all his work in progress.

In Figure 35-9, all groups except SYS_GROUPS have been given reasonable amounts of idle time before being disconnected, but much more aggressive settings if they are blocking other sessions.

TIP It is also possible to disconnect sessions by using profiles, which you must enable with the instance parameter RESOURCE_LIMITS. However, the Resource Manager is a better tool for this.

Restricting Generation of Undo Data

Management of undo data was covered in Chapter 16. All DML statements must generate undo data, and this data must be stored until the transaction has been committed or rolled back. Oracle has no choice about this; it is according to the rules of a relational database. If you have configured the UNDO_RETENTION instance parameter and set the RETENTION GUARANTEE attribute for your undo tablespace, then the undo data may well be kept for some considerable time after the transaction has committed.

All your undo data will be written to a single undo tablespace, unless (against Oracle Corporation's advice) you are using the outdated rollback segment method of undo management. This means that transactions from all users are sharing a common

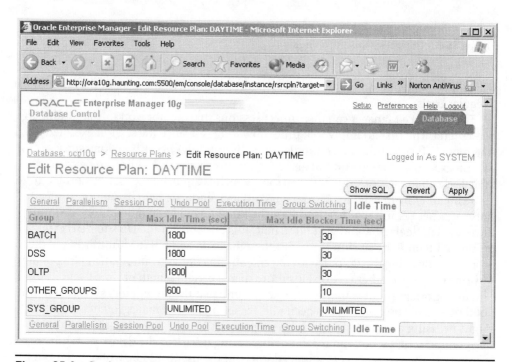

Figure 35-9 Configuring idle time disconnection with Database Control

storage area. A potential problem is that one badly designed transaction could fill this storage area, the undo tablespace.

Programmers should not design large, long-running transactions. In business terms, though, huge transactions may be necessary to preserve the integrity of the system. For example, an accounting suite's nominal ledger cannot be partly in one accounting period, and partly in the next: this is an impossibility in accountancy. So the rollover from one period to the next could mean updating millions of rows in thousands of tables over many hours, and then committing. This will require a huge undo tablespace and will also cause record-locking problems as the big transaction blocks other work. The answer is to break up the one business transaction into many small database transactions programmatically. If this is a problem, go back to the developers; there is nothing you as DBA can do to fix it.

As DBA, however, you can prevent large transactions by one group of users from filling up the undo tablespace. If your batch routines do not commit regularly, they will write a lot of undo data that cannot be overwritten. If too many of these batch jobs are run concurrently, the undo tablespace can fill up with active undo. This will cause all transactions to cease, and no more transactions can start, until one of them commits. The Resource Manager provides a mechanism whereby the undo tablespace can in effect be partitioned into areas reserved for different consumer groups.

Your calculations on undo generated per second and your desired undo retention (as derived from the V$UNDOSTAT view, and your requirements for the flashback query capability) might show that the undo tablespace should be, for example, 8GB. To be safe, you size it at 12GB. But to ensure that the small OLTP transactions will always have room for their undo data, you can limit the space used by the BATCH group to, say, 6GB during normal working hours by assigning an undo pool in a Resource Manager plan. To calculate the undo space necessary for individual transactions, you can query the view V$TRANSACTION while the transaction is in progress. The column USED_UBLK shows how much undo is being used by each active transaction.

EXAM TIP The undo pool per group has nothing to do with tablespace quotas, which are assigned per user. You cannot even grant quotas on undo tablespaces.

When the amount of active undo data generated by all sessions of a certain consumer group hits its pool limit (which you can set through Database Control, as shown in Figure 35-10), it will no longer be possible for members of that group to add more undo to current transactions or to start new transactions: they will hang until one transaction commits, thus freeing up space within the pool. Meanwhile, other groups can continue working in the remainder of the undo tablespace. This restricts the effect of generating too much undo to one group, rather than having it impact on all users.

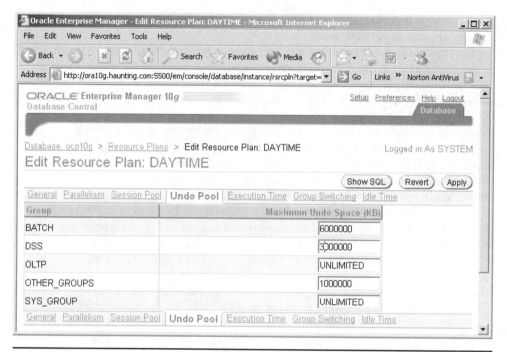

Figure 35-10 Configuring undo pools with Database Control

Automatic Consumer Group Switching

In the discussion of consumer groups, you saw that one user can be a member of multiple groups, and that either the user himself or the system administrator can switch a user's session from one consumer group to another.

Why would one wish to do this? From the user's point of view, he will presumably want to activate his membership in the group that has the highest priority at any given time. So if the daytime plan gives priority to OLTP and the nighttime plan gives priority to DSS, then if you are a member of both groups, you will switch between them as the different plans are activated. So whichever plan is enabled, you will always have the highest priority available to you.

The DBA is going to switch users' sessions for a very different reason: to reduce the impact one session is having on others. This will mean identifying sessions that are causing problems and downgrading them, rather than upgrading them, which is what the user himself would like. It may well be that a job that kills the database if run at normal priority, can run without impacting other sessions if its priority is reduced. Of course, it will take longer to complete, but that may not be a problem (at least, not to everyone else). To do this manually would be extremely difficult, requiring continuous monitoring of sessions and workload. This is exactly what the Resource Manager can do.

Exercise 35-2: Configuring and Testing Automatic Consumer Group Switching

Set up a mechanism that will automatically downgrade all large jobs to a low priority. Do this with Database Control, but whenever possible click the Show SQL button and study the API calls being generated.

1. Connect to your database as user SYSTEM with Database Control.

2. Take the Administration tab on the database home page, and then the Resource Consumer Groups link in the Resource Manager section.

3. Click Create to reach the Create Resource Consumer Group window.

4. Enter **HIGH** as the name of the group, and click Add to display a list of all users.

5. Select the check boxes for the four users you created earlier: ACCT, BATCH, CLERK, and MGR. Click Select.

6. Select the Initial Group check box for all four users, so that when any of them log on they will be in the HIGH group. Click OK to create the group and return to the Resource Consumer Groups window.

7. Click Create to create another group. Name it **MEDIUM**, and again make your four users members of the group. Do not make it the initial group for any of them.

8. Create a third group called **LOW**, and again make your four users members of the group. Do not make it the initial group for any of them.

9. Navigate to the Resource Plans window, and click Create to reach the Create Resource Plan window. Enter **AUTO_SWITCH** as the name of the plan, and click Modify to reach the Select Groups/Subplans window.

10. One by one, select your HIGH, MEDIUM, and LOW groups and move them to the Selected Groups/Subplans section. Click OK to return to the Create Resource Plan window.

11. Enter priorities for the consumer groups at level 1, as shown in Figure 35-11.

12. Take the Group Switching link, and configure switching as in Figure 35-12. This will switch users from their initial group of HIGH down to MEDIUM if a job takes more than ten seconds, and then down to LOW priority if it takes more than a minute at MEDIUM.

13. Click OK to execute the configuration, and return to the Resource Plans window.

14. Select the radio button for the AUTO_SWITCH group, and Activate in the Actions drop-down box. Click Go to activate your new plan. This has the effect of altering the RESOURCE_MANAGER_PLAN instance parameter.

15. In a SQL*Plus session, connect as user CLERK.

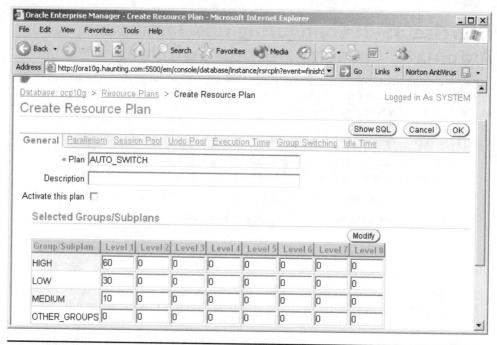

Figure 35-11 Priorities for the AUTO_SWITCH plan

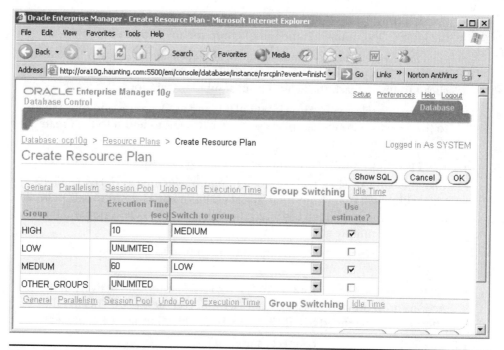

Figure 35-12 Settings for automatic consumer group switching

16. In a second SQL*Plus session, connect as user SYSTEM and confirm that CLERK's active group is HIGH.

```
SQL> select resource_manager_group from v$session where
username='CLERK';
```

17. In the CLERK session, simulate launching a large job by running a query that does a Cartesian join based on a view with many rows.

```
SQL> select count(*) from all_objects,all_objects;
```

18. While the query is running, in your second session reissue the query in Step 16 a few times, and you will see the CLERK session being downgraded from HIGH to MEDIUM, and then to LOW.

19. Tidy up.

```
SQL> alter system set resource_manager_plan='';
```

Additional Features

The Resource Manager is an extremely powerful tool. This final section picks up a few peripheral features, most of which are not available through the Database Control interface.

Quiescing the Database

You have already seen how setting an active session pool can restrict the number of running statements from any consumer group. What if the active session pool were set to zero for all groups? The result would be that all sessions would hang. This is in fact a very useful capability, and it is used by the command ALTER SYSTEM QUIESCE RESTRICTED.

This command activates the Resource Manager plan INTERNAL_QUIESCE, which sets the active session pool for all groups other than the SYS_GROUP to zero. The effect is that statements in progress will continue until they finish, but that no one (other than members of the SYS_GROUP) can issue any more statements. If they do, the session will hang. In effect, the database is frozen for all but the administrators. This can be invaluable to get a stable system for a moment of maintenance work.

To cancel the quiesce, issue ALTER SYSTEM UNQUIESCE.

The quiesce will fail unless one resource plan or another has been active continuously since instance startup. For this reason, you should always set a plan, such as the SYSTEM_PLAN, in your initialization file.

Consumer Group Switching for One Call

Automatic consumer group switching switches a session permanently—unless it is switched back manually. In some cases, this would not be desirable. Consider the case where a large number of users are connected to an application server, which is funneling their application server sessions through a small number of shared database sessions.

In this environment, each user will issue a series of commands through the application server, which may be picked up by any of the database sessions; there is not a persistent link between any one application server session and any one database session. If the Resource Manager is configured as in Exercise 35-2, and if a user issues a long-running job, the database session he happens to be using for that statement will be switched down. This is fine, until the job finally finishes. But having been downgraded, the session will remain downgraded—which will impact on all statements sent through it subsequently, even though they may be short jobs from a different application server user that should be run at high priority.

This problem is unavoidable if you use Database Control to configure the Resource Manager, because of the way Database Control configures the Resource Manager. This is the specification of the DBMS_RESOURCE_MANAGER.CREATE_PLAN_DIRECTIVE procedure:

```
PROCEDURE CREATE_PLAN_DIRECTIVE
Argument Name                   Type            In/Out Default?
------------------------------  --------------  ------ --------
PLAN                            VARCHAR2        IN
GROUP_OR_SUBPLAN                VARCHAR2        IN
COMMENT                         VARCHAR2        IN
CPU_P1                          NUMBER          IN     DEFAULT
CPU_P2                          NUMBER          IN     DEFAULT
CPU_P3                          NUMBER          IN     DEFAULT
CPU_P4                          NUMBER          IN     DEFAULT
CPU_P5                          NUMBER          IN     DEFAULT
CPU_P6                          NUMBER          IN     DEFAULT
CPU_P7                          NUMBER          IN     DEFAULT
CPU_P8                          NUMBER          IN     DEFAULT
ACTIVE_SESS_POOL_P1             NUMBER          IN     DEFAULT
QUEUEING_P1                     NUMBER          IN     DEFAULT
PARALLEL_DEGREE_LIMIT_P1        NUMBER          IN     DEFAULT
SWITCH_GROUP                    VARCHAR2        IN     DEFAULT
SWITCH_TIME                     NUMBER          IN     DEFAULT
SWITCH_ESTIMATE                 BOOLEAN         IN     DEFAULT
MAX_EST_EXEC_TIME               NUMBER          IN     DEFAULT
UNDO_POOL                       NUMBER          IN     DEFAULT
MAX_IDLE_TIME                   NUMBER          IN     DEFAULT
MAX_IDLE_BLOCKER_TIME           NUMBER          IN     DEFAULT
SWITCH_TIME_IN_CALL             NUMBER          IN     DEFAULT
```

When configuring automatic group switching, Database Control uses the SWITCH_TIME argument, which causes the Resource Manager to switch the session permanently. If you configure automatic switching through the API, you can use the SWITCH_TIME_IN_CALL argument instead. This will downgrade the session to the SWTICH_GROUP only for the duration of the statement, returning it to its original group when the slow statement finishes.

Use of the Ratio CPU Method

There is an alternative technique for allocating CPU resources. Rather than coding CPU usage as a percentage, as in the examples earlier in this chapter, you can specify ratios—and let Oracle work out the percentages.

In the telesales example at the start of this chapter, the CPU resources at level 2 for the nighttime plan were

OLTP   50%
DSS   25%
BATCH 25%

If you decide to add a fourth group (call it WEB) and want to make it equal in priority to OLTP, and to double DSS and BATCH, you will have to change all the directives to achieve this:

OLTP   33%
WEB   33%
DSS   17%
BATCH 17%

The ratio method lets you specify proportions. The absolute values have no significance. For example, the original ratios could have been

OLTP   20
DSS   10
BATCH 10

and now, to add the WEB group with a priority equal to OLTP, you only have to add one new directive,

WEB   20

and leave the others unchanged.

Creating a Simple Plan

Historically, the Resource Manager was a mission to set up. It is a very powerful feature of the database, and powerful features are not necessarily easy to use. The Database Control interface provided with release 10g certainly simplifies things in comparison to using the API directly, but there is one procedure call that simplifies it even further. With this one procedure, you can create a plan, the groups, and the directives:

```
SQL> exec dbms_resource_manager.create_simple_plan(-
simple_plan=>'daytime',-
consumer_group1=>'oltp',group1_cpu=>50,-
consumer_group2=>'dss',group2_cpu=>25,-
consumer_group3=>'batch',group3_cpu=>25);
```

This call will create a plan, in this case DAYTIME, which always gives the SYS_GROUP 100 percent of CPU at priority level 1, and the OTHER_GROUPS 100 percent at level 3. Level 2 is divided according to the arguments given. The arguments can create up to eight groups (only three—OLTP, DSS, and BATCH—in the example) and assign them percentages of CPU at level 2.

All other resources, such as parallelism, active sessions, and undo pool, are not configured.

 EXAM TIP The CREATE_SIMPLE_PLAN procedure will do everything. You do not even need to create, validate, and submit a pending area. All you need to do afterward is put users in the groups and activate the plan.

Adaptive Consumer Group Mapping

The default method for assigning sessions to consumer groups is through the Oracle username, as specified by the INITIAL_RSRC_CONSUMER_GROUP displayed in DBA_USERS. The initial group can be changed at any time, either manually or by the automatic consumer group switching capability based on the workload of the statements being executed.

A consumer group can be applied initially according to a number of login attributes and later changed by a number of run-time attributes. By default, only EXPLICIT and ORACLE_USER are available—but there are others. The table that follows lists them all, in order: the first to match is applied. Thus, an explicit setting will always take precedence, but if that has not been done (either manually or automatically), then the Resource Manager will try them in order until it finds one that has been configured.

1	EXPLICIT	Switch to a group either by using the API or by using automatic consumer group switching.
2	SERVICE_MODULE_ACTION	Switch to a group according to the action name being executed, the program module, and the service used to connect.
3	SERVICE_MODULE	Switch to a group according to the service name used to connect and the program module.
4	MODULE_NAME_ACTION	Switch to a group according to the program module and the action within it being executed.
5	MODULE_NAME	Switch to a group according to the program module.
6	SERVICE_NAME	Activate a group at login according to the service name used to connect.
7	ORACLE_USER	Activate a group at login according to Oracle user ID used to connect.
8	CLIENT_PROGRAM	Activate a group at login according to the user process being used to connect.

| 9 | CLIENT_OS_USER | Activate a group at login according to the operating system ID on the client machine. |
| 10 | CLIENT_MACHINE | Activate a group at login according to the name of the client machine. |

To use either MODULE or ACTION as the mapping attribute, your programmers must embed calls in their code to the DBMS_APPLICATION_INFO package to name the modules and the actions within them. This allows the Resource Manager to switch priorities according to what code is being executed. This is invaluable in a Web application, where typically everyone is connecting with the same Oracle username through the same application server.

To use the SERVICE as the mapping attribute, you must ensure that some users connect through one database service, and some through another. This will require setting up multiple service names in the SERVICE_NAMES instance parameter, and configuring the client side of Oracle Net such that different users will request a different service.

The order of the attributes in the preceding table is critical, and it can be changed. Consider a user connected to Oracle from a PC in the management accountants' office (with the machine name DSS_PC1) as Oracle user CLERK. You can use the Resource Manager API to map both the Oracle username and the machine name to a consumer group:

```
SQL> exec dbms_resource_manager.set_consumer_group_mapping(-
(dbms_resource_manager.oracle_user,'CLERK','OLTP');
SQL> exec dbms_resource_manager.set_consumer_group_mapping(-
dbms_resource_manager.client_machine,'DSS_PC1','DSS');
```

By default, according to the preceding table, the user will be assigned to the OLTP group, because his Oracle username takes precedence over the location he has connected from. This could be changed by swapping the order around:

```
SQL> exec dbms_resource_manager.set_consumer_group_mapping_pri(-
EXPLICIT => 1, -
SERVICE_MODULE_ACTION => 2, -
SERVICE_MODULE => 3, -
MODULE_NAME_ACTION => 4, -
MODULE_NAME => 5, -
SERVICE_NAME => 6, -
ORACLE_USER => 10, -
CLIENT_PROGRAM => 8, -
CLIENT_OS_USER => 9, -
CLIENT_MACHINE => 7,);
```

From now on, the machine that the user is working from will determine his active Resource Manager group, no matter what Oracle username he logs in as. The current order of precedence is displayed in the view DBA_RSRC_MAPPING_PRIORITY.

To manage mapping through Database Control, take the Resource Consumer Group Mappings link in the Resource Manager section under the Administration tab.

Chapter Review

This chapter introduced one of the more advanced features of the Oracle database: the ability to control the resources allocated to different database sessions. Oracle does not do preemptive multitasking: it adds a layer on top of the preemptive multitasking provided by the operating system. This layer lets Oracle guarantee a certain level of service to some database users, perhaps at the expense of others. It is not simple to set up, but then it is a very powerful facility.

A Resource Manager plan allocates resources to consumer groups, according to a set of directives. The principle of allocation is, by default, CPU usage, but there are other algorithms that can be used. Users are mapped to groups according, by default, to their username, but again there are other techniques. The active group membership for a session can be changed after login, either manually or automatically. The automatic switch can be based on the length of time a statement will take to execute, or by using a number of other attributes (such as the program module being executed).

Large jobs can be eliminated entirely from the system by a plan, or by using active session pools they can be queued such that no more than a certain number are running at once.

Questions

1. There are several steps involved in setting up the Resource Manager. Put these in the correct order:

   A. Assign users to consumer groups.

   B. Create consumer groups.

   C. Create directives.

   D. Create a pending area.

   E. Create a plan.

   F. Submit the pending area.

   G. Validate the pending area.

2. Which of the following statements, if any, are correct about users and consumer groups? (Choose all that apply.)

   A. One user can only be a member of one consumer group.

   B. One user can be a member of many consumer groups.

   C. The SYS_GROUP is reserved for the user SYS.

   D. By default, the initial group for all users is DEFAULT_CONSUMER_GROUP.

3. Which of the following statements, if any, are correct about Resource Manager plans? (Choose all that apply.)

   A. The default plan is the SYSTEM_PLAN.

   B. The RESOURCE_MANAGER_PLAN instance parameter is static.

C. Different consumer groups can have different active plans.

D. Any one plan can manage up to 16 priority levels.

E. None of the above.

4. Some actions in the Resource Manager API are done with procedures in the package DBMS_RESOURCE_MANAGER_PRIVS, and others, with procedures in the package DBMS_RESOURCE_MANAGER. Mark the following actions accordingly:

A. Granting the privilege to administer the Resource Manager

B. Placing users in groups

C. Removing users from groups

D. Switching your active group

E. Creating consumer groups

F. Configuring how to map sessions to groups

5. Resource Manager plans can use a number of methods to control resources. Which of the following are possible? (Choose three correct answers.)

A. CPU usage

B. Tablespace quota usage

C. Number of active sessions

D. Number of idle sessions

E. Volume of redo data generated

F. Volume of undo data generated

6. A CPU method plan allocates resources at two levels as follows:

> Level 1: SYS_GROUP, 50%   OLTP, 50%
>
> Level 2: DSS, 50%   BATCH, 50%

If the only users logged on are from the BATCH group, what percentage of CPU can they use? (Choose the best answer.)

A. 12.5%

B. 25%

C. 50%

D. 100%

E. The plan will not validate because it attempts to allocate 200% of CPU resources

7. You create a Resource Manager plan limiting the active session pool for the group DSS to 3. What will happen if three members of the group are logged on, and a fourth member attempts to connect? (Choose the best answer.)

A. The new session will not be able to connect until an existing session disconnects.

B. The new session will be able to connect but will hang immediately.

C. The new session will be able to connect but will only be able to run queries, not DML statements.

D. Any statements the new session issues may hang, depending on other activity.

8. If the active Resource Manager plan specifies that sessions belonging to a particular group may only have four parallel execution servers, what will happen if a session in that group issues a statement that requests six parallel execution servers? (Choose the best answer.)

A. The statement will not run.

B. The statement will run with four parallel servers.

C. It will depend on the setting of the PARALLEL_MIN_PERCENT instance parameter.

D. It will depend on the setting of the PARALLEL_AUTOMATIC_TUNING instance parameter.

9. If the active Resource Manager plan limits the time that a statement is allowed to run, what will happen if a statement is allowed to start executing and does not complete within the time? (Choose the best answer.)

A. The statement will be terminated and, if it was a DML statement, rolled back.

B. The statement will be terminated, and if the session is in a transaction, the whole transaction will be rolled back.

C. The statement will continue to run to completion.

D. The statement will stop running, but any work it has done will remain intact.

10. If a session exceeds the idle time permitted by the Resource Manager, what will happen? (Choose the best answer.)

A. The session will issue an auto-commit and terminate.

B. The session will roll back an active transaction and terminate.

C. If the session is not in a transaction, it will terminate immediately; otherwise, it will terminate when the transaction completes.

D. It depends on whether the instance parameter RESOURCE_LIMITS is on TRUE or FALSE.

11. When you use the Resource Manager to define an undo pool, what happens? (Choose the best answer.)

A. If a user exceeds his quota on the undo tablespace, his session will hang.

B. If a user exceeds his quota on the undo tablespace, the statement running will be rolled back but the rest of the statement will remain intact.

C. If a group fills its undo pool, all the group's transactions will hang until one session commits, rolls back, or is terminated.

D. The effect depends on whether RETENTION GUARANTEE is enabled for the undo tablespace.

12. Which of the following statements is correct regarding automatic consumer group switching? (Choose the best answer.)

    A. If a group exceeds its permitted CPU usage, one or more of its sessions will be downgraded.

    B. Switching can be triggered only by SQL statement execution time.

    C. Switching can be triggered by SQL statement execution time, degree of parallelism, or CPU usage.

    D. You can configure whether the switch is permanent, or for one transaction, or for one statement.

13. Your session has been downgraded by the Resource Manager, using automatic consumer group switching. Which of the following statements are correct? (Choose two answers.)

    A. You can only reactivate your original group if you have been granted the appropriate privilege.

    B. If the downgrade was only for one call, you need do nothing.

    C. The system administrator can return your session to your original group using a procedure in DBMS_SESSION.

    D. You can return your session to your original group using a procedure in DBMS_SESSION.

    E. You must disconnect and connect again to reactivate your initial group.

14. The pending area is an area of memory used to configure the Resource Manager before saving the configuration to the data dictionary. For which of these operations must you create, validate, and submit a pending area? (Choose the best answer.)

    A. Adding users to consumer groups

    B. Creating consumer groups

    C. Using the CREATE_SIMPLE_PLAN procedure

    D. None of the above

15. There are a number of session attributes that can be used to map a session to a particular consumer group, other than the Oracle username. Which of the following is not a valid attribute for this purpose? (Choose the best answer.)

    A. The operating system ID on the client machine

    B. The name of the program module being executed

    C. The time of the session logon

    D. The user process

Answers

1. **D, B, E, C, G, F, and A.** The order is D, create a pending area; B, create consumer groups; E, create a plan; C, create directives; G, validate the pending area; F, submit the pending area; A, assign users to groups.

2. **B.** There can be a many-to-many relationship between users and groups.

3. **E.** The default plan is the INTERNAL_PLAN, so A is wrong. B is also wrong, because the parameter is dynamic. C is wrong because the active plan applies to the whole instance. D is wrong too; one plan can have up to eight levels. So none of the answers is correct.

4. **A, B, and C.** DBMS_RESOURCE_MANAGER_PRIVS is used for A, B, and C. D, E, and F. DBMS_RESOURCE_MANAGER handles D, E, and F.

5. **A, C, and F.** Of the methods listed, CPU usage, active sessions, and undo data are possible. You cannot have a plan based on tablespace quotas or redo data. Also, although you can disconnect idle sessions, you cannot have a plan that limits the number of idle sessions.

6. **D.** If no other sessions are connected, then all CPU resources will be available to the connected sessions.

7. **D.** When a session pool is full of active sessions, more sessions can connect—but they will hang immediately until an active session completes its statement.

8. **B.** The statement will run, but with only the number of PX servers permitted by the Resource Manager.

9. **C.** This is an example of the Resource Manager making a mistake, presumably because of poor statistics. The job will continue until completion.

10. **B.** The session will terminate, and any transaction will be rolled back.

11. **C.** Undo pools refer to whole groups, not to individual users or sessions. If a group fills its pool, all sessions that are part of the group will hang until one commits.

12. **B.** Automatic switching is based on a single statement, and you can configure it for that one statement, or for the whole session.

13. **B and D.** B is correct because if the downgrade were for one call, by using the SWITCH_TIME_IN_CALL argument, the session will return to its original group when the statement is complete, and D is correct because the procedure to switch your own session is in DBMS_SESSION.

14. **B.** You need to create, validate, and submit a pending area when creating consumer groups.

15. **C.** There is no way to activate a group membership based on the time the login happened.

CHAPTER 36

Automating Administrative Tasks

In this chapter you will learn how to

- Simplify management tasks by using the Scheduler
- Create a job, program, schedule, and window
- Reuse Scheduler components for similar tasks
- View information about job executions and job instances

There will be many occasions when you as DBA, or your users, need to automate the scheduling and running of jobs. These jobs could be of many kinds—for example, maintenance work, such as database backups; data loading and validation routines; report generation; collecting optimizer statistics; or executing business processes. The Scheduler is a facility that can be used to specify tasks to be run at some point in the future.

The Scheduler can be coupled to the Resource Manager. It can activate Resource Manager plans and run jobs with the priorities assigned to various Resource Manager consumer groups.

In earlier releases of the database, job scheduling capabilities were provided through the DBMS_JOB facility. This is still supported for backward compatibility, but it is not nearly as versatile as the Scheduler.

The Scheduler Architecture

The data dictionary includes a table that is a storage point for all Scheduler jobs. You can query the table through the DBA_SCHEDULER_JOBS view. The job coordinator process, the CJQ0 process, monitors this table and when necessary launches job slaves, the J*nnn* processes, to run the jobs. The CJQ0 process is launched automatically when a job is due; it is deactivated after a sustained period of Scheduler inactivity. The J*nnn* processes are launched on demand, though the maximum number is limited by the JOB_QUEUE_PROCESSES instance parameter; this defaults to 0, but if that value is used, the Scheduler will not function.

The job coordinator picks up jobs from the job queue table and passes them to slaves for execution. It also launches and terminates the slaves according to demand. To see the processes currently running, query the V$PROCESS view. In a Windows instance,

```
ocp10g> select program from v$process where program like '%J%';
PROGRAM
------------------------------------------
ORACLE.EXE (CJQ0)
ORACLE.EXE (J000)
ORACLE.EXE (J001)
```

In a Unix instance, the processes will be separate operating system processes; in a Windows instance, they are threads in the ORACLE.EXE image.

 EXAM TIP The JOB_QUEUE_PROCESSES instance parameter must be greater than zero or the Scheduler cannot run. It is zero by default.

An advanced feature of the Scheduler is to associate it with the Resource Manager. It may be that certain jobs should be run with certain priorities, and this can be achieved by linking a job to a Resource Manager consumer group. It is also possible to use the

Scheduler to activate a Resource Manager plan, rather than having to change the RESOURCE_MANAGER_PLAN instance parameter manually.

The Scheduler can be configured and monitored with an API—the DBMS_SCHEDULER package—or through Database Control.

Scheduler Objects

The most basic object in the Scheduler environment is a *job*. A job can be completely self-contained: it can define the action to be taken, and when to take it. In a more advanced configuration, the job is only a part of the structure consisting of a number of Scheduler objects of various types.

Jobs

A job specifies what to do, and when to do it. The "what" can be a single SQL statement, a PL/SQL block, a PL/SQL stored procedure, a Java stored procedure, an external procedure, or any executable file stored in the server's file system: either a binary executable or a shell script. The "when" specifies the timestamp at which to launch the job, and a repeat interval for future runs.

There are several options when creating a job, as can be seen from looking at the DBMS_SCHEDULE.CREATE_JOB procedure. This procedure is overloaded; it has no less than four forms. Figure 36-1 is a part of the output from a DESCRIBE of the DBMS_SCHEDULER package.

All forms of the CREATE_JOB procedure must specify a JOB_NAME. This must be unique within the schema that the job is created.

Then, taking the first form of the procedure, the JOB_TYPE must be one of PLSQL_BLOCK, STORED_PROCEDURE, or EXECUTABLE. If JOB_TYPE is PLSQL_BLOCK, then JOB_ACTION can be either a single SQL statement or a PL/SQL block. If the JOB_TYPE is STORED_PROCEDURE, then JOB_ACTION must name a stored procedure, which can be PL/SQL, JAVA, or an external procedure written in C, as described in Chapter 22. If the JOB_TYPE is EXECUTABLE, then the JOB_ACTION can be anything that could be run from an operating system command-line prompt: a command, an executable binary file, or a shell script or batch file. The NUMBER_OF_ARGUMENTS parameter states how many arguments the JOB_ACTION should take.

The first form of the procedure continues with details of when and how frequently to run the job. The first execution will be on the START_DATE; the INTERVAL defines a repeat frequency, such as daily, until END_DATE. JOB_CLASS is to do with priorities and integration of the Scheduler with the Resource Manager. The ENABLED argument determines whether the job can actually be run. Perhaps surprisingly, this defaults to FALSE. If a job is not created with this argument on TRUE, it cannot be run (either manually, or through a schedule) without enabling it first. Finally, AUTO_DROP controls whether to drop the job definition after the END_TIME. This defaults to TRUE.

```
Select C:\WINDOWS\System32\cmd.exe - sqlplus system/oracle                    _ □ ×
PROCEDURE CREATE_JOB
 Argument Name                      Type                        In/Out Default?
 ----------------------------       -----------------------     ------ --------
 JOB_NAME                           VARCHAR2                     IN
 JOB_TYPE                           VARCHAR2                     IN
 JOB_ACTION                         VARCHAR2                     IN
 NUMBER_OF_ARGUMENTS                BINARY_INTEGER               IN     DEFAULT
 START_DATE                         TIMESTAMP WITH TIME ZONE IN         DEFAULT
 REPEAT_INTERVAL                    VARCHAR2                     IN     DEFAULT
 END_DATE                           TIMESTAMP WITH TIME ZONE IN         DEFAULT
 JOB_CLASS                          VARCHAR2                     IN     DEFAULT
 ENABLED                            BOOLEAN                      IN     DEFAULT
 AUTO_DROP                          BOOLEAN                      IN     DEFAULT
 COMMENTS                           VARCHAR2                     IN     DEFAULT
PROCEDURE CREATE_JOB
 Argument Name                      Type                        In/Out Default?
 ----------------------------       -----------------------     ------ --------
 JOB_NAME                           VARCHAR2                     IN
 PROGRAM_NAME                       VARCHAR2                     IN
 SCHEDULE_NAME                      VARCHAR2                     IN
 JOB_CLASS                          VARCHAR2                     IN     DEFAULT
 ENABLED                            BOOLEAN                      IN     DEFAULT
 AUTO_DROP                          BOOLEAN                      IN     DEFAULT
 COMMENTS                           VARCHAR2                     IN     DEFAULT
PROCEDURE CREATE_JOB
 Argument Name                      Type                        In/Out Default?
 ----------------------------       -----------------------     ------ --------
 JOB_NAME                           VARCHAR2                     IN
 PROGRAM_NAME                       VARCHAR2                     IN
 START_DATE                         TIMESTAMP WITH TIME ZONE IN         DEFAULT
 REPEAT_INTERVAL                    VARCHAR2                     IN     DEFAULT
 END_DATE                           TIMESTAMP WITH TIME ZONE IN         DEFAULT
 JOB_CLASS                          VARCHAR2                     IN     DEFAULT
 ENABLED                            BOOLEAN                      IN     DEFAULT
 AUTO_DROP                          BOOLEAN                      IN     DEFAULT
 COMMENTS                           VARCHAR2                     IN     DEFAULT
PROCEDURE CREATE_JOB
 Argument Name                      Type                        In/Out Default?
 ----------------------------       -----------------------     ------ --------
 JOB_NAME                           VARCHAR2                     IN
 SCHEDULE_NAME                      VARCHAR2                     IN
 JOB_TYPE                           VARCHAR2                     IN
 JOB_ACTION                         VARCHAR2                     IN
 NUMBER_OF_ARGUMENTS                BINARY_INTEGER               IN     DEFAULT
 JOB_CLASS                          VARCHAR2                     IN     DEFAULT
 ENABLED                            BOOLEAN                      IN     DEFAULT
 AUTO_DROP                          BOOLEAN                      IN     DEFAULT
 COMMENTS                           VARCHAR2                     IN     DEFAULT
```

Figure 36-1 The specification of the CREATE_JOB procedure

If a job is created with no scheduling information, it will be run as soon as it is enabled, and then dropped immediately if AUTO_DROP is on TRUE, which is the default.

The third form of the CREATE_JOB procedure has the job details (the JOB_TYPE, JOB_ACTION, and NUMBER_OF_ARGUMENTS) replaced with a PROGRAM_NAME that points to a program, which will provide these details. The fourth form has the scheduling details (START_DATE, REPEAT_INTERVAL, and END_DATE) replaced with a SCHEDULE_NAME that points to a schedule, which will manage the timing of the runs. The second, and briefest, form of the procedure uses both a program and a schedule.

Programs

Programs provide a layer of abstraction between the job and the action it will perform. They are created with the DBMS_SCHEDULER.CREATE_PROGRAM procedure:

```
PROCEDURE CREATE_PROGRAM
Argument Name            Type                  In/Out Default?
--------------------     -------------------   ------ --------
PROGRAM_NAME             VARCHAR2              IN
PROGRAM_TYPE             VARCHAR2              IN
PROGRAM_ACTION           VARCHAR2              IN
NUMBER_OF_ARGUMENTS      BINARY_INTEGER        IN     DEFAULT
ENABLED                  BOOLEAN               IN     DEFAULT
COMMENTS                 VARCHAR2              IN     DEFAULT
```

By pulling the "what" of a job out of the job definition itself and defining it in a program, it becomes possible to reference the same program in different jobs, and thus to associate it with different schedules and job classes, without having to define it many times. Note that (as for a job) a program must be ENABLED before it can be used.

Schedules

A *schedule* is a specification for when and how frequently a job should run. It is created with DBMS_SCHEDULER.CREATE_SCHEDULE procedure:

```
PROCEDURE CREATE_SCHEDULE
Argument Name       Type                           In/Out Default?
----------------    -------------------------      ------ --------
SCHEDULE_NAME       VARCHAR2                       IN
START_DATE          TIMESTAMP WITH TIME ZONE       IN     DEFAULT
REPEAT_INTERVAL     VARCHAR2                       IN
END_DATE            TIMESTAMP WITH TIME ZONE       IN     DEFAULT
COMMENTS            VARCHAR2                       IN     DEFAUL
```

The START_DATE defaults to the current date and time. This is the time that any jobs associated with this schedule will run. The REPEAT_INTERVAL specifies how frequently the job should run, until the END_DATE. Schedules without an END_DATE will run forever.

The REPEAT_INTERVAL argument can take a wide variety of calendaring expressions. These consist of up to three elements: a frequency, an interval, and possibly several specifiers. The frequency may be one of these values:

YEARLY
MONTHLY
WEEKLY
DAILY
HOURLY
MINUTELY
SECONDLY

PART II

The specifiers can be one of these:

BYMONTH
BYWEEKNO
BYYEARDAY
BYMONTHDAY
BYHOUR
BYMINUTE
BYSECOND

Using these elements of a REPEAT_INTERVAL makes it possible to set up schedules that should satisfy any requirement. For example,

```
repeat_interval=>'freq=hourly; interval=12'
```

will run the job every 12 hours, starting at the START_DATE. The next example,

```
repeat_interval=>'freq=yearly; bymonth=jan,apr,jul,oct; bymonthday=2'
```

will run the job on the second day of each of the named four months, starting as early in the day as resources permit. A final example,

```
repeat_interval=>'freq=weekly; interval=2; byday=mon; byhour=6; byminute=10'
```

will run the job at ten past six on alternate Mondays.

 EXAM TIP One schedule can be applied to many jobs; one program can be invoked by many jobs.

Job Classes

A job class is used to associate one or more jobs with a Resource Manager consumer group, and also to control logging levels. Create a class with the DBMS_SCHEDULER. CREATE_JOB_CLASS procedure:

```
PROCEDURE CREATE_JOB_CLASS
Argument Name                   Type              In/Out  Default?
------------------------------  ----------------  ------  --------
JOB_CLASS_NAME                  VARCHAR2          IN
RESOURCE_CONSUMER_GROUP         VARCHAR2          IN      DEFAULT
SERVICE                         VARCHAR2          IN      DEFAULT
LOGGING_LEVEL                   BINARY_INTEGER    IN      DEFAULT
LOG_HISTORY                     BINARY_INTEGER    IN      DEFAULT
COMMENTS                        VARCHAR2          IN      DEFAULT
```

The JOB_CLASS_NAME is the name to be referenced by the JOB_CLASS argument of the CREATE_JOB procedure. The RESOURCE_CONSUMER_GROUP nominates the group whose resource allocations should be applied to the running job, as determined by the Resource Manager plan in effect whenever the job happens to run. The SERVICE has significance only in a RAC database: you can restrict the job to run only on an instance with a particular service name. The details of logging can also be specified per class.

Windows

A *schedule* specifies exactly when a job should be launched. *Windows* extend the concept of schedules, by giving Oracle more freedom to decide when to run the job. A window opens at a certain time and closes after a certain duration: jobs specified to run in a window may be launched, at Oracle's discretion, at any time during the window. The window itself can open repeatedly according to a schedule. Use of windows is of particular value when combined with classes and the Resource Manager: Oracle can schedule jobs to run within a window according to their relative priorities. Windows also activate Resource Manager plans.

Create windows with the DBMS_SCHEDULER.CREATE_WINDOW procedure:

```
PROCEDURE CREATE_WINDOW
Argument Name           Type                        In/Out  Default?
---------------------- ----------------------- ------ --------
WINDOW_NAME             VARCHAR2                     IN
RESOURCE_PLAN           VARCHAR2                     IN
START_DATE              TIMESTAMP WITH TIME ZONE IN     DEFAULT
REPEAT_INTERVAL         VARCHAR2                     IN
END_DATE                TIMESTAMP WITH TIME ZONE IN     DEFAULT
DURATION                INTERVAL DAY TO SECOND      IN
WINDOW_PRIORITY         VARCHAR2                     IN     DEFAULT
COMMENTS                VARCHAR2                     IN     DEFAULT
```

The RESOURCE_PLAN nominates the Resource Manager plan that will be activated when the window opens. The window will open on the START_DATE and reopen according to the REPEAT_INTERVAL until the END_DATE. The procedure is overloaded; there is a second form that lets you nominate a precreated schedule rather than specifying the schedule here with these three arguments.

The DURATION is an INTERVAL DAY TO SECOND datatype. This will allow a time span to be specified in days, hours, minutes, and seconds. The basic syntax for an INTERVAL DAY TO SECOND column is

```
'<days> <hours>:<minutes>:<seconds>'
```

Note that that there is a space between the days and the hours, and colons between the hours, minutes, and seconds. So this,

```
'1 2:3:4'
```

specifies a time gap of one day, two hours, three minutes, and four seconds.

The PRIORITY argument is intended to manage circumstances where windows overlap, and has two possible values: LOW (the default) or HIGH. Only one window can be in effect at a time, and it will be the window with the higher priority. If two or more overlapping windows have the same priority, the window that opened first will take priority.

Windows share the same namespace as schedules. It is therefore impossible to create a window with the same name as a schedule, but this does mean that wherever you can refer to a schedule, you can also refer to a window. So looking back to the second and fourth forms of the CREATE_JOB procedure in earlier Figure 36-1, it becomes clear that a job can be created to run at any time within a named window, rather than at the precise times specified by a schedule. The window itself will open and close according to a schedule, either a schedule defined within the window or a precreated schedule object.

Privileges

All Scheduler privileges are granted and revoked with the usual GRANT and REVOKE syntax. There are a number of Scheduler-related privileges:

- CREATE JOB
- CREATE ANY JOB
- EXECUTE ANY PROGRAM
- EXECUTE ANY CLASS
- MANAGE SCHEDULER
- EXECUTE ON <job, program, or class>
- ALTER ON <job, program, or schedule>
- ALL ON <job, program, schedule, or class>

Before a user can create any jobs, schedules, or programs, s/he must be granted the CREATE JOB privilege; this includes the ability to create and use his/her own programs and schedules. To create jobs in other schemas, the user will need CREATE ANY JOB. To use Scheduler objects in other schemas, you need the EXECUTE privilege on them. The MANAGE SCHEDULER privilege is needed to create job classes and windows, and to force windows to open or close irrespective of their schedules.

The ready-made role SCHEDULER_ADMIN includes the first five privileges just listed. It is granted to SYSTEM with ADMIN by default.

Creating and Scheduling Jobs

To create and schedule a job with one procedure call, use the CREATE_JOB procedure. For example,

```
begin
dbms_scheduler.create_job(
job_name=>'system.inc_backup',
job_type=>'executable',
job_action=>'/home/usr/dba/rman/whole_inc.sh',
start_date=>trunc(sysdate)+23/24,
repeat_interval=>'freq=weekly;byday=mon,tue,wed,thu,fri;byhour=23',
comments=>'launch weekday incremental backup script');
end;
```

This will create a job that will call a Unix shell script at eleven o'clock every weekday evening, starting today. The job is created in the SYSTEM schema. The operating system permissions on the script will have to be set such that the Oracle owner can run it.

Exercise 36-1: Creating a Job with the Scheduler API

Use the DBMS_SCHEDULER package to create a job, and confirm that it is working.

1. Connect to your database as user SYSTEM using SQL*Plus.

2. Create a table to store times, and set your date format to show the date and time.

```
SQL> create table times (c1 date);
SQL> alter session set nls_date_format='dd-mm-yy hh24:mi:ss';
```

3. Create a job to insert the current time into the table every minute.

```
SQL> begin
  2  dbms_scheduler.create_job(
  3  job_name=>'savedate',
  4  job_type=>'plsql_block',
  5  job_action=>'insert into times values(sysdate);',
  6  start_date=>sysdate,
  7  repeat_interval=>'freq=minutely;interval=1',
  8  enabled=>true,
  9  auto_drop=>false);
 10  end;
 11  /
PL/SQL procedure successfully completed.
```

4. Query the job table to see that the job is scheduled.

```
SQL> select job_name,enabled,to_char(next_run_date,'dd-mm-yy
hh24:mi:ss'),run_count from user_scheduler_jobs;
JOB_NAME                 ENABL TO_CHAR(NEXT_RUN_  RUN_COUNT
------------------------ ----- ----------------- ----------
SAVEDATE                 TRUE  15-01-05 14:58:03          2
```

5. Query the times table to demonstrate that the inserts are occurring.

```
SQL> select * from times;
```

6. Disable the job.

```
SQL> exec dbms_scheduler.disable('savedate');
```

7. Re-run the queries from Steps 4 and 5 to confirm that the job is disabled, and that no more inserts are occurring.

8. Drop the job:

```
SQL> exec dbms_scheduler.drop_job('savedate');
```

Using Programs and Schedules

Programs and schedules let you reuse Scheduler components for similar tasks. Rather than defining each job as a self-contained entity, you create programs and schedules, each of which can be used by many jobs.

The job created in Exercise 36-1 could be split up into a job, a program, and a schedule. To do this through Database Control, from the database home page take the Administration tab. Then in the Scheduler section take the Programs link, click Create, and enter the code you want executed as in Figure 36-2. This can be as long and complicated as you want (bearing in mind that the datatype for PROGRAM_ACTION is VARCHAR2 and so is limited to 4KB).

TIP Keep your JOB_ACTIONs and PROGRAM_ACTIONs as short as possible, preferably just one statement. Do all the work in a procedure invoked by that statement. This will be far easier to maintain than having a large amount of SQL or PL/SQL in your job and program definitions.

If you create a program with the CREATE_PROGRAM procedure, then (just as with jobs) the program will be disabled by default. Change this default either by specifying the ENABLED argument as TRUE when you create the program or by using the ENABLE procedure subsequently:

```
SQL> exec dbms_scheduler.enable('program1');
```

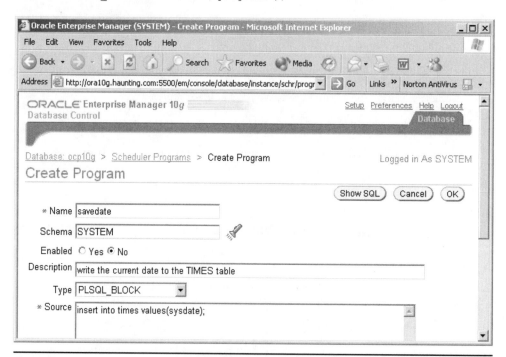

Figure 36-2 Creating a program with Database Control

To create a schedule, take the Schedules link from the Scheduler section, and click Create to view the page shown in Figure 36-3. The GUI interface does not give access to some of the more complicated interval possibilities, such as every third Tuesday, which would be

```
'freq=weekly;interval=3;byday=tue'
```

but it gives access to all that will usually be required.

To create a job, take the Jobs link. The initial window (shown in Figure 36-4) assumes that the job is a PL/SQL block. Taking the Change Command Type button will let you nominate your program. The Schedule link lets you tie the job to a precreated schedule, rather than defining the schedule within the job.

TIP Programs share the same namespace as jobs: you cannot have a program with the same name as a job. The same is true for schedules and windows.

It is also possible to run a job independently of a schedule, by using the RUN_JOB procedure:

```
SQL> exec dbms_scheduler.run_job('savedate');
```

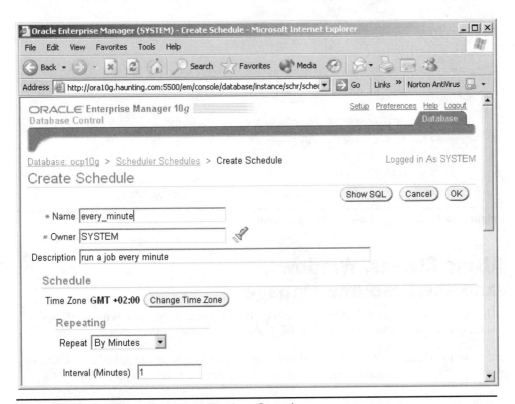

Figure 36-3   Creating a schedule with Database Control

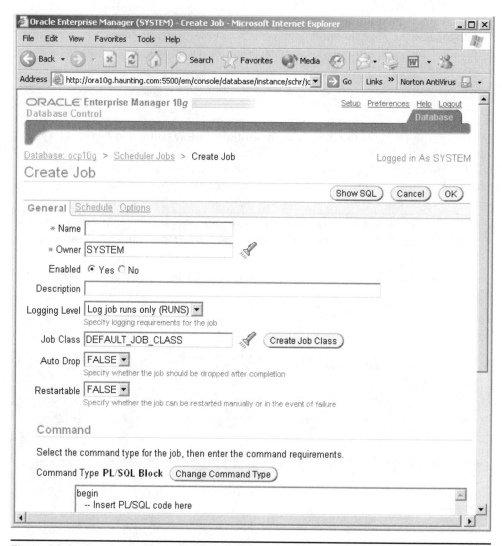

Figure 36-4 Creating a job with Database Control

Using Classes, Windows, and the Resource Manager

The more advanced capabilities of the Scheduler let you integrate it with the Resource Manager, to control and prioritize jobs. These are the relevant components:

- **Job classes** Jobs can be assigned a class, and a class can be linked to a Resource Manager consumer group. Classes also control the logging level for their jobs.

- **Consumer groups** Resource Manager consumer groups are restricted in the resources they can use, being limited in, for instance, CPU usage or the number of active sessions.

- **Resource plans** A Resource Manager plan defines how to apportion resources to groups. Only one plan is active in the instance at any one time.

- **Windows** A window is a defined (probably recurring) period of time, during which certain jobs will run and a certain plan will be active.

- **Window groups** It is possible to combine windows into window groups, for ease of administration.

Prioritizing jobs within a window is done at two levels. Within a class, jobs can be given different priorities by the Scheduler, but because all jobs in a class are in the same consumer group, the Resource Manager will not distinguish between them. But if jobs in different classes are scheduled within the same window, the Resource Manager will assign resources to each class according to the consumer groups for that class.

Using Job Classes

Create a class with Database Control, or through the API. For example,

```
SQL> exec dbms_scheduler.create_job_class(-
job_class_name=>'daily_reports',-
resource_consumer_group=>'dss',-
logging_level=>dbms_scheduler.logging_full);
```

Then assign the jobs to the class, either at job creation time by specifying the JOB_CLASS attribute, or by modifying the job later. To assign a job to a class with the API, you must use the SET_ATTRIBUTE procedure. To put the job REPORTS_JOB into the class just created,

```
SQL> exec dbms_scheduler.set_attribute(-
name=>'reports_job',-
attribute=>'job_class',-
value=>'daily_reports');
```

If there are several jobs in the one class, prioritize them with more SET_ATTRIBUTE calls:

```
SQL> exec dbms_scheduler.set_attribute(-
name=>'reports_job',-
attribute=>'job_priority',-
value=>2);
```

If several jobs in the same class are scheduled to be executed at the same time, the job priority determines the order in which jobs from that class are picked up for execution by the job coordinator process. It can be a value from 1 through 5, with 1 being the first to be picked up for job execution. The default for all jobs is 3. This could be critical if, for example, the class's consumer group has an active session pool that is smaller than the number of jobs: those jobs with the highest priority will run first, while the others are queued.

 EXAM TIP It is not possible to assign priorities by any means other than the SET_ATTRIBUTE procedure of the API.

Logging levels are also controlled by the job's class. There are three options:

- **DBMS_SCHEDULER.LOGGING_OFF**   No logging is done for any jobs in this class.

- **DBMS_SCHEDULER.LOGGING_RUNS**   Information is written to the job log regarding each run of each job in the class, including when the run was started and whether the job ran successfully.

- **DBMS_SCHEDULER.LOGGING_FULL**   In addition to logging information about the job runs, the log will also record management operations on the class, such as creating new jobs.

To view logging information, query the DBA_SCHEDULER_JOB_LOG view:

```
SQL> select job_name,log_date,status from dba_scheduler_job_log;
JOB_NAME      LOG_DATE                            STATUS
------------  ----------------------------------  ------------
PURGE_LOG     16-JAN-05 13-00-03                  SUCCEEDED
TEST_JOB      16-JAN-05 11-00-00                  FAILED
NIGHT_INCR    16-JAN-05 01-00-13                  SUCCEEDED
NIGHT_ARCH    16-JAN-05 01-00-00                  SUCCEEDED
```

More detailed information is written to the DBA_SCHEDULER_JOB_RUN_DETAILS view, including the job's run duration and any error code it returned.

Logging information is cleared by the automatically created PURGE_LOG job. By default, this runs daily and will remove all logging information more than thirty days old.

Using Windows

Create windows either through Database Control or with the CREATE_WINDOW procedure. For example,

```
SQL> exec dbms_scheduler.create_window(-
window_name=>'daily_reporting_window',-
resource_plan=>'night_plan',-
schedule=>'weekday_nights',-
duration=>'0 08:00:00',-
window_priority=>'low',-
comments=>'for running regular reports');
```

This window activates a Resource Manager plan called NIGHT_PLAN. This might be a plan that gives priority to the DSS consumer groups over the OLTP group. It opens according to the schedule WEEKDAY_NIGHTS, which might be Monday through Friday at 20:00. The window will remain open for eight hours; the DURATION argument accepts an INTERVAL DAY TO SECOND value, as does the REPEAT_INTERVAL for a schedule. Setting the priority to LOW means that if this window overlaps with another window, then the other window will be allowed to impose its Resource Manager plan. This would be the case if you created a different window for your end-of-month processing, and the end-of-month happened to be on a weekday. You could give the end-of-month window HIGH priority, to ensure that the end-of-month Resource Manager plan, which could give top priority to the BATCH group, does come into effect.

 EXAM TIP Even if a job has priority 1 within its class, it might still only run after a job with priority 5 in another class—if the second job's class is in a consumer group with a higher Resource Manager priority.

Preconfigured Jobs

There are two jobs configured by default: the PURGE_LOG job that cleans out the Scheduler log, and the GATHER_STATS_JOB that analyzes the database to gather optimizer statistics. To see these jobs, you must connect as user SYS. Using Database Control, take the Administration tab from the database home page, and then the Jobs link in the database section to view the page shown in Figure 36-5.

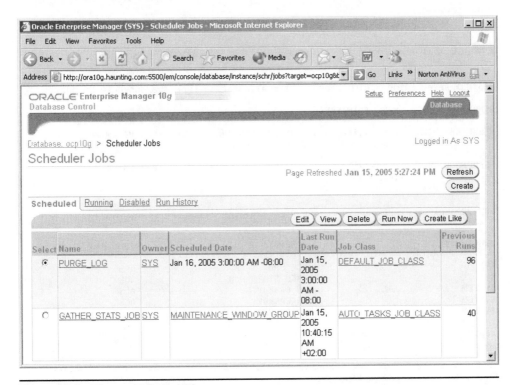

Figure 36-5 The preconfigured jobs

The PURGE_LOG job deletes entries from the Scheduler log, on a daily schedule. The GATHER_STATS_JOB is much more important and is configured in a more sophisticated manner. It is set up to use the preconfigured MAINTENANCE_WINDOW_GROUP, which consists of two windows: the WEEKEND_WINDOW and the WEEKNIGHT_WINDOW. To see the details of these windows, take the link in Database Control or query the DBA_SCHEDULER_WINDOWS view as shown in Figure 36-6.

The first query in the figure shows the two windows that are created by default. The WEEKNIGHT_WINDOW opens at ten in the evening on weekdays and stays open for eight hours. The WEEKEND_WINDOW opens on Saturday at midnight (that is, on Friday night) and stays open for two days. The GATHER_STATS_JOB will run in both of these windows.

What happens if a window closes before a job that is run in the window has completed? The default behavior is that the job will continue until it finishes, but this can be overridden by setting an attribute. The second query in Figure 36-6 shows all the Scheduler jobs in the database, including the attribute STOP_ON_WINDOW_CLOSE. To change this attribute, use the SET_ATTRIBUTE procedure:

```
SQL> exec dbms_scheduler.set_attribute(name=>'full_backup',-
attribute=>'stop_on_window_close',-
value=>'true');
```

This will cause the FULL_BACKUP job to abort if it has not finished by the time its window closes.

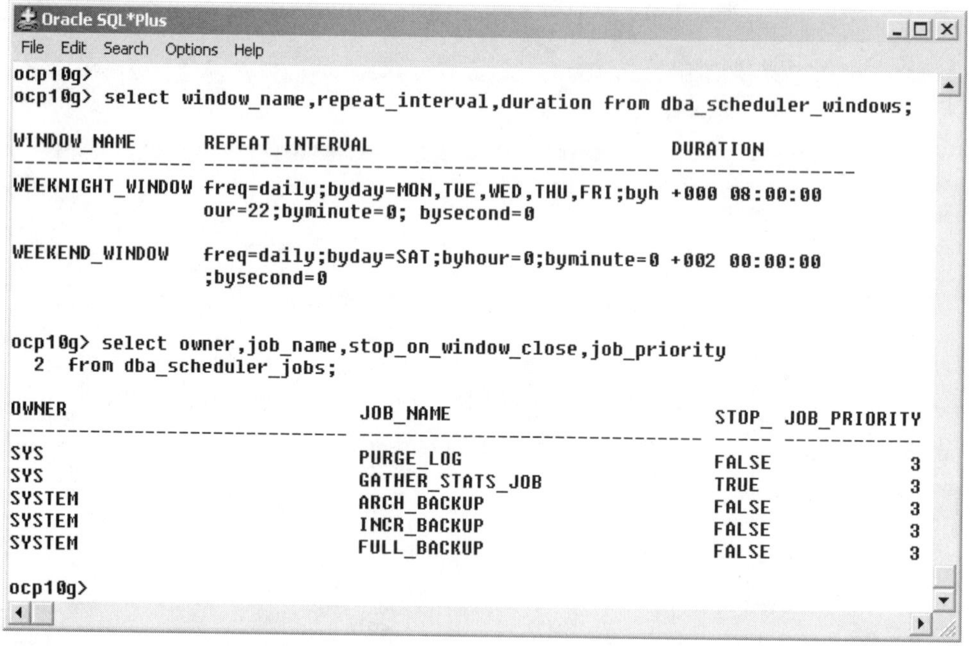

Figure 36-6 Querying the Scheduler views

EXAM TIP The GATHER_STATS_JOB will stop if it has not completed by the time the window it is running in (WEEKNIGHT_WINDOW or WEEKEND_ WINDOW) closes.

Chapter Review

The Scheduler is a tool for running jobs at some point in the future. The jobs can be operating system executable commands or files, or stored PL/SQL or Java procedures, or external procedures. The jobs can be run as a one-off or repeatedly according to a schedule. The basic Scheduler object is the job, though for administrative convenience and to allow reuse of components, the "what" of the job can be pulled out and stored as a program, and the "when" of the job can be stored as a separate schedule.

To integrate the Scheduler with the Resource Manager, assign jobs to classes. These are associated with a Resource Manager group. Then by using windows rather than schedules, you can activate a particular Resource Manager plan for a period of time.

There are two preconfigured jobs. The PURGE_LOG job clears out the Scheduler log; the default level of logging is to log each run of a job. This job runs according to a daily schedule. The GATHER_STATS_JOB is the job that gathers optimizer statistics; this job runs in one of two windows: the WEEKNIGHT_WINDOW or the WEEKEND_ WINDOW. They are part of the preconfigured MAINTENANCE_WINDOW group.

Questions

1. When a job is due to run, what process will run it? (Choose the best answer.)

    A. A CJQ*n* process

    B. A J*nnn* process

    C. A server process

    D. A background process

2. Which of the following is a requirement if the Scheduler is to work? (Choose the best answer.)

    A. The instance parameter JOB_QUEUE_PROCESSES must be set.

    B. A Resource Manager plan must be enabled.

    C. A schedule must have been created.

    D. All of the above.

    E. None of the above.

3. A Scheduler job can be of several types. Choose all that apply:

    A. Anonymous PL/SQL block

    B. Executable operating system file

    C. External C procedure

    D. Java stored procedure

      E. Operating system command

      F. Operating system shell script (Unix) or batch file (Windows)

      G. PL/SQL stored procedure

4. You create a job with this syntax:

```
exec dbms_scheduler.create_job(-
job_name=>'j1',-
program_name=>'p1',-
schedule_name=>'s1',-
job_class=>'c1');
```

  and find that it is not running when expected. What might be a reason for this? (Choose the best answer.)

      A. The schedule is associated with a window, which has not opened.

      B. The job has not been enabled.

      C. The class is part of the Resource Manager consumer group with low priority.

      D. The permissions on the job are not correct.

5. What are the possible priority levels of a job within a class? (Choose the best answer.)

      A. 1 to 5

      B. 1 to 999

      C. HIGH or LOW

      D. It depends on the Resource Manager plan in effect

6. There is a preconfigured job to gather optimizer statistics, the GATHER_STATS_JOB job. This is scheduled to run in both the WEEKNIGHT_WINDOW and the WEEKEND_WINDOW. What will happen if it fails to complete before the window closes? (Choose the best answer.)

      A. It will continue to run to completion.

      B. It will terminate and continue the next time either window opens.

      C. It will terminate and restart the next time either window opens.

      D. The behavior will vary depending on whether it was running in the WEEKNIGHT_WINDOW window or the WEEKEND_WINDOW window.

7. You want a job to run every thirty minutes. Which of the following possibilities for the REPEAT_INTERVAL argument are correct syntactically and will achieve this result? (Choose two answers.)

      A. `'freq=minutely;interval=30'`

      B. `'freq=hourly;interval=1/2'`

      C. `'0 00:30:00'`

      D. `'freq=minutely;byminute=30'`

      E. `'freq=byminute;interval=30'`

8. You create a job class, and you set the LOGGING_LEVEL argument to LOGGING_RUNS. What will be the result? (Choose the best answer.)

   A. There will be a log entry for each run of each job in the class, but no information on whether the job was successful.

   B. There will be a log entry for each run of each job in the class, and information on whether the job was successful.

   C. There will be a single log entry for the class whenever it is run.

   D. You cannot set logging per class, only per job.

9. Which of the following statements (if any) are correct regarding how Scheduler components can be used together? (Choose all that apply.)

   A. A schedule can be used by many jobs.

   B. A job can use many programs.

   C. A class can have many programs.

   D. Job priorities can be set within a class.

   E. Consumer groups control priorities within a class.

   F. A Resource Manager plan can be activated by a schedule.

10. Which view will tell you about jobs configured with the Scheduler? (Choose the best answer.)

    A. DBA_JOBS

    B. DBA_SCHEDULER

    C. DBA_SCHEDULED_JOBS

    D. DBA_SCHEDULER_JOBS

11. If two windows are overlapping and have equal priority, which window(s) will be open? (Choose the best answer.)

    A. Both windows will be open.

    B. Windows cannot overlap.

    C. Whichever window opened first will remain open; the other will remain closed.

    D. Whichever window opened first will be closed, and the other will open.

12. How long will Scheduler logging records be visible in the DBA_SCHEDULER_JOB_LOG view? (Choose the best answer.)

    A. They will remain until the PURGE_LOG job is run.

    B. By default, they will be kept for thirty days.

    C. By default, they will be kept for one day.

    D. By default, the view will be cleared every thirty days.

Answers

1. **B.** Jobs are run by a job slave process. The CJQ0 process is the job queue coordinator, which passes the jobs to the slave for execution.

2. **A.** The only requirement for the Scheduler to function is that there must be at least one job slave process, created with the JOB_QUEUE_PROCESSES parameter. Resource Manager plans and schedules are optional.

3. **A, B, C, D, E, F,** and **G.** All the answers are correct.

4. **B.** As written, the procedure call will not enable the job, so it can't run at all.

5. **A.** Within a class, jobs can have priority 1–5.

6. **C.** The GATHER_STATS_JOB is configured to stop when its window closes. At the next window, it will start again.

7. **A** and **B.** Either will give a half-hour repeat interval.

8. **B.** With logging set to LOGGING_RUNS, you will get records of each run of each job, including the success or failure. The other possible logging levels are NONE, in which case there will be no logging at all, or FULL, which records details for each run and also administrative actions, such as enabling or disabling jobs.

9. **A.** One job can use only one schedule, but one schedule can be used by many jobs

10. **D.** The DBA_SCHEDULER_JOBS view externalizes the data dictionary jobs table, with one row per scheduled job.

11. **C.** If two windows overlap and have equal priority, then the one that opens earlier will be the open window.

12. **B.** The standard configuration for the PURGE_LOG job is to run every day and delete all records more than thirty days old.

APPENDIX

About the CD

The CD-ROM included with this book comes complete with MasterExam and the electronic version of the book. The software is easy to install on any Windows 98/NT/2000/XP computer and must be installed to access the MasterExam feature. You may, however, browse the electronic book directly from the CD without installation. To register for a second bonus MasterExam, simply click the Online Training link on the Main Page and follow the directions to the free online registration.

System Requirements

The software requires Windows 98 or later and Internet Explorer 5.0 or later and 20MB of hard disk space for full installation. The electronic book must be viewed with Adobe Acrobat Reader.

Installing and Running MasterExam

If your computer CD-ROM drive is configured to auto run, the CD-ROM will automatically start up upon inserting the disk. From the opening screen, you may install MasterExam by pressing the MasterExam button. This begins the installation process and creates a program group named LearnKey. To run MasterExam, choose Start | Programs | LearnKey. If the auto run feature does not launch your CD, browse to the CD and click the LaunchTraining.exe icon.

MasterExam

MasterExam provides you with a simulation of the actual exam. The number of questions, the type of questions, and the time allowed are intended to be an accurate representation of the exam environment. You have the option to take an open book exam (including hints, references, and answers), a closed book exam, or the timed MasterExam simulation.

When you launch MasterExam, a digital clock display appears in the upper left-hand corner of your screen. The clock will continue to count down to zero unless you choose to end the exam before the time expires.

The Electronic Book

The entire contents of the Study Guide are provided in a PDF file. Adobe's Acrobat Reader has been included on the CD so you can view it.

Help

A help file can be accessed by clicking the Help button on the main page in the lower left-hand corner. An individual help feature is also available through MasterExam.

Removing Installation(s)

MasterExam is installed to your hard drive. For best results when attempting to remove the program, from the Start menu choose Programs | LearnKey | Uninstall.

Technical Support

For questions regarding the technical content of the electronic book or MasterExam, please visit www.osborne.com or e-mail customer.service@mcgraw-hill.com. For customers outside the United States, e-mail: international_cs@mcgraw-hill.com.

LearnKey Technical Support

For technical problems with the software (installation, operation, removing installations), please visit www.learnkey.com or e-mail techsupport@learnkey.com.

GLOSSARY

Glossary of Acronyms

Full explanations of all the terms used in the Oracle environment can be found in the Oracle Database 10g Documentation. This is available on a CD delivered with your Oracle software, or through the World Wide Web on Oracle Corporation's web site. Issue the URL

```
http://otn.oracle.com
```

and navigate to the database documentation pages; one volume, the *Oracle Database Master Glossary*, summarizes most of the Oracle-specific terms. Many third-party web sites also offer dictionaries of terms used in computing. Of particular interest to Oracle DBAs is the glossary included on the well-known ORAFAQ web site,

```
http://www.orafaq.com
```

This web site is one of the most comprehensive sources of information on the Oracle database in the world.

Following is a list of the acronyms used throughout this book.

ACID   Atomicity, Consistency, Isolation, and Durability. Four characteristics that a relational database must be able to maintain for transactions.

ADDM   Automatic Database Diagnostic Monitor. A tool that generates performance tuning reports based on snapshots in the AWR.

ANSI   American National Standards Institute. A U.S. body that defines a number of standards relevant to computing.

API   Application Programming Interface. A defined method for manipulating data, typically implemented as a set of PL/SQL procedures in a package.

ASCII   American Standard Code for Information Interchange. A standard (with many variations) for coding letters and other characters as bytes.

ASH   Active Session History. A category of information in the AWR, that records details of session activity.

ASM   Automatic Storage Management. An LVM provided with the Oracle database.

ASSM   Automatic Segment Space Management. The method of managing space within segments by use of bitmaps.

AWR   Automatic Workload Repository. A set of tables in the SYSAUX tablespace, populated with tuning data gathered by the MMON process.

BLOB   Binary Large Object. A LOB data type for binary data, such as photographs and video clips.

BMR   Block Media Recovery. An RMAN technique for restoration and recovery of individual data blocks, rather than complete data files.

CET   Central European Time. A time zone used in much of Europe (although not Great Britain) that is one hour ahead of UTC with daylight saving time in effect during the summer months.

CKPT   The Checkpoint Process. The background process responsible for recording the current redo byte address—the point in time up to which the DBWn has written changed data blocks to disk—and for signaling checkpoints, which force DBWn to write all changed blocks to disk immediately.

CLOB   Character Large Object. A LOB data type for character data, such as text documents, stored in the database character set.

CPU   Central Processing Unit. The chip that provides the processing capability of a computer, such as an Intel Pentium or a Sun SPARC.

CTWR   Change Tracking Writer. The optional background process that records the addresses of changed blocks, to enable fast incremental backups.

DBA   Database Administrator. The person responsible for creating and managing Oracle databases—you!

DBCA   The Database Configuration Assistant. A GUI tool for creating, modifying, and dropping instances and databases.

DBID   Database Identifier. A unique number for every database, visible in the DBID column of the V$DATABASE dynamic performance view.

DBMS   Database Management System, often used interchangeably with RDBMS.

DBWn or DBWR   The Database Writer. The background process responsible for writing changed blocks from the database buffer cache to the datafiles. An instance may have up to ten database writer processes, DBW0 through DBW9.

DDL   Data Definition Language. The subset of SQL commands that change object definitions within the data dictionary: CREATE, ALTER, DROP, and TRUNCATE.

DHCP   Dynamic Host Configuration Protocol. The standard for configuring the network characteristics of a computer, such as its IP address, in a changing environment where computers may be moved from one location to another.

DMnn   Data Pump Master process. The process that controls a Data Pump job—one will be launched for each job that is running.

DML   Data Manipulation Language. The subset of SQL commands that change data within the database: INSERT, UPDATE, DELETE, and MERGE.

DNS   Domain Name Service. The TCP mechanism for resolving network names into IP addresses.

DSS   Decision Support System. A database, such as a data warehouse, optimized for running queries, as against a database optimized for OLTP work, which will tend to be more transaction oriented.

DWnn   Data Pump Worker process. One or more of these will be launched for each Data Pump job that is running.

EBCDIC   Extended Binary Coded Decimal Interchange Code. A standard developed by IBM for coding letters and other characters in bytes.

FGA   Fine-Grained Auditing. A facility for tracking user access to data, based on the rows that are seen or manipulated.

GMT   Greenwich Mean Time. Now referred to as UTC, this is the time zone of the meridian through Greenwich Observatory in London.

GUI   Graphical User Interface. A layer of an application that lets users work with the application through a graphical terminal, such as a PC with a mouse.

HTTP   Hypertext Transfer Protocol. The protocol that enables the World Wide Web (both the protocol and the Web were invented at the European Organization for Nuclear Research in 1989), this is a layered protocol that runs over TCP/IP.

HWM   High-Water Mark. This is the last block of a segment that has ever been used; blocks above this are part of the segment but are not yet formatted for use.

IBM   International Business Machines. A well-known computer hardware, software, and services company.

I/O   Input/Output. The activity of reading from or writing to disks—often the slowest point of a data processing operation.

IOT   Index-Organized Table. A table type where the rows are stored in the leaf blocks of an index segment.

IP   Internet Protocol. Together with the Transmission Control Protocol, TCP/IP, the de facto standard communications protocol used for client/server communication over a network.

IPC   Inter-Process Communication Protocol. The platform-specific protocol, provided by your OS vendor, used for processes running on the same machine to communicate with each other.

ISO   The International Organization for Standardization. A group that defines many standards, including SQL.

J2EE   Java 2 Enterprise Edition. The standard for developing Java applications.

JVM Java Virtual Machine. The run-time environment needed for running code written in Java. Oracle provides a JVM within the database, and one will be provided by your operating system.

LDAP Lightweight Directory Access Protocol. The TCP implementation of the X.25 directory standard, used by the Oracle Internet Directory for name resolution, security, and authentication. LDAP is also used by other software vendors, including Microsoft and IBM.

LGWR The Log Writer. The background process responsible for flushing change vectors from the log buffer in memory to the online redo log files on disk.

LOB Large Object. A data structure that is too large to store within a table. LOBs (Oracle supports several types) are defined as columns of a table but physically stored in a separate segment.

LRU Least Recently Used. LRU lists are used to manage access to data structures, using algorithms that ensure that the data that has not been accessed for the longest time is the data that will be overwritten.

LVM Logical Volume Manager. A layer of software that abstracts the physical storage within your computer from the logical storage visible to an application.

MMAN The Memory Manager background process, which monitors and reassigns memory allocations in the SGA for automatically tunable SGA components.

MML Media Management Layer. Software that lets RMAN make use of automated tape libraries and other SBT devices.

MMNL Manageability Monitor Light. The background process responsible for flushing ASH data to the AWR, if MMON is not doing this with the necessary frequency.

MMON The Manageability Monitor background process, responsible for gathering performance-monitoring information and raising alerts.

MTBF Mean Time Between Failure. A measure of the average length of running time for a database between unplanned shutdowns.

MTS Shared Server. Formerly (before release 9i) called Multi-Threaded Server, this is the technique whereby a large number of sessions can share a small pool of server processes, rather than requiring one server each.

MTTR Mean Time to Recover. The average time it takes to make the database available for normal use after a failure.

NCLOB National Character Large Object. A LOB data type for character data, such as text documents, stored in the alternative national database character set.

NetBEUI   NetBIOS Extended User Interface. An enhanced version of NetBIOS.

NetBIOS   Network Basic Input Output System. The network communications protocol that was burnt onto the first network card that IBM ever produced.

NLS   National Language Support. The capability of the Oracle database to support many linguistic, geographical, and cultural environments—now usually referred to as Globalization.

OC4J   Oracle Containers for J2EE. The control structure provided by the Oracle Internet Application Server for running Java programs.

OCA   Oracle Certified Associate. The qualification you will have after passing the first of the two Database 10g examinations, covered in Part I one of this book.

OCI   Oracle Call Interface. An API, published as a set of C libraries, that programmers can use to write user processes that will use an Oracle database.

OCP   Oracle Certified Professional. The qualification you will have after passing the second exam, which is covered in Part II of this book.

ODBC   Open Database Connectivity. A standard developed by Microsoft for communicating with relational databases. Oracle provides an ODBC driver that will allow clients running Microsoft products to connect to an Oracle database.

OLAP   Online Analytical Processing. Work which is select intensive, rather than transactional, involving running queries against a (usually) large database. Oracle provides OLAP capabilities as an option, in addition to the standard query facilities.

OLTP   Online Transaction Processing. A pattern of activity within a database typified by a large number of small, short, transactions.

OS   Operating System. Typically, in the Oracle environment, this will be a version of Unix (perhaps Linux) or Microsoft Windows.

PGA   Program Global Area. The variable-sized block of memory used to maintain the state of a database session. PGAs are private to the session, and controlled by the session's server process.

PL/SQL   Procedural Language / Structured Query Language. Oracle's proprietary programming language, which combines procedural constructs, such as flow control, and user interface capabilities with SQL.

PMON   The Process Monitor. The background process responsible for monitoring the state of users' sessions against an instance.

RAC   Real Application Clusters. Oracle's clustering technology, which allows several instances on different machines to open the same database for scalability, performance, and fault tolerance.

RAID   Redundant Array of Inexpensive Disks. Techniques for enhancing performance and/or fault tolerance by using a volume manager to present a number of physical disks to the operating system as a single logical disk.

RAM   Random Access Memory. The chips that make up the real memory in your computer hardware, as against the virtual memory presented to software by the operating system.

RDBMS   Relational Database Management System, often used interchangeably with DBMS.

RMAN   Recovery Manager. Oracle's backup and recovery tool.

RVWR   The Recovery Writer background process, an optional process responsible for flushing the flashback buffer to the flashback logs.

SBT   System Backup to Tape. An RMAN term for a tape device.

SCN   System Change Number. The continually incrementing number used to track the sequence and exact time of all events within a database.

SGA   System Global Area. The block of shared memory that contains the memory structures that make up an Oracle instance.

SID   (1) System Identifier. The name of an instance, which must be unique on the computer the instance is running on. (2) Session Identifier. The number used to identify uniquely a session logged on to an Oracle instance.

SMON   The System Monitor. The background process responsible for opening a database and monitoring the instance.

SQL   Structured Query Language. An international standard language for extracting data from and manipulating data in relational databases.

SSL   Secure Sockets Layer. A standard for securing data transmission, using encryption, checksumming, and digital certificates.

TCP   Transmission Control Protocol. Together with the Internet Protocol, TCP/IP, the de facto standard communication protocol used for client/server communication over a network.

TCPS   TCP with SSL. The secure sockets version of TCP.

TNS   Transparent Network Substrate. The heart of Oracle Net, a proprietary layered protocol running on top of whatever underlying network transport protocol you choose to use, probably TCP/IP.

UGA   User Global Area. The part of the PGA that is stored in the SGA for sessions running through shared servers.

UI   User Interface. The layer of an application that communicates with end users, nowadays frequently graphical: a GUI.

URL   Uniform Resource Locator. A standard for specifying the location of an object on the Internet, consisting of a protocol; a host name and domain; an IP port number; a path and filename; and a series of parameters.

UTC   Coordinated Universal Time, previously known as Greenwich Mean Time (GMT). UTC is the global standard time zone; all others relate to it as offsets, ahead or behind.

X   As in X Window System, the standard GUI environment used on most computers, except those that run Microsoft Windows.

XML   Extensible Markup Language. A standard for data interchange using documents, where the format of the data is defined by tags within the document.

INDEX

INTERNATIONAL CONTACT INFORMATION

AUSTRALIA
McGraw-Hill Book Company
Australia Pty. Ltd.
TEL +61-2-9900-1800
FAX +61-2-9878-8881
http://www.mcgraw-hill.com.au
books-it_sydney@mcgraw-hill.com

CANADA
McGraw-Hill Ryerson Ltd.
TEL +905-430-5000
FAX +905-430-5020
http://www.mcgraw-hill.ca

GREECE, MIDDLE EAST, & AFRICA
(Excluding South Africa)
McGraw-Hill Hellas
TEL +30-210-6560-990
TEL +30-210-6560-993
TEL +30-210-6560-994
FAX +30-210-6545-525

MEXICO (Also serving Latin America)
McGraw-Hill Interamericana Editores
S.A. de C.V.
TEL +525-1500-5108
FAX +525-117-1589
http://www.mcgraw-hill.com.mx
carlos_ruiz@mcgraw-hill.com

SINGAPORE (Serving Asia)
McGraw-Hill Book Company
TEL +65-6863-1580
FAX +65-6862-3354
http://www.mcgraw-hill.com.sg
mghasia@mcgraw-hill.com

SOUTH AFRICA
McGraw-Hill South Africa
TEL +27-11-622-7512
FAX +27-11-622-9045
robyn_swanepoel@mcgraw-hill.com

SPAIN
McGraw-Hill/
Interamericana de España, S.A.U.
TEL +34-91-180-3000
FAX +34-91-372-8513
http://www.mcgraw-hill.es
professional@mcgraw-hill.es

UNITED KINGDOM, NORTHERN,
EASTERN, & CENTRAL EUROPE
McGraw-Hill Education Europe
TEL +44-1-628-502500
FAX +44-1-628-770224
http://www.mcgraw-hill.co.uk
emea_queries@mcgraw-hill.com

ALL OTHER INQUIRIES Contact:
McGraw-Hill/Osborne
TEL +1-510-420-7700
FAX +1-510-420-7703
http://www.osborne.com
omg_international@mcgraw-hill.com

GET YOUR FREE SUBSCRIPTION
TO ORACLE MAGAZINE

Oracle Magazine is essential gear for today's information technology professionals. Stay informed and increase your productivity with every issue of *Oracle Magazine*. Inside each free bimonthly issue you'll get:

- Up-to-date information on Oracle Database, Oracle Application Server, Web development, enterprise grid computing, database technology, and business trends
- Third-party vendor news and announcements
- Technical articles on Oracle and partner products, technologies, and operating environments
- Development and administration tips
- Real-world customer stories

IF THERE ARE OTHER ORACLE USERS AT YOUR LOCATION WHO WOULD LIKE TO RECEIVE THEIR OWN SUBSCRIPTION TO ORACLE MAGAZINE, PLEASE PHOTOCOPY THIS FORM AND PASS IT ALONG.

Three easy ways to subscribe:

① Web
Visit our Web site at otn.oracle.com/oraclemagazine. You'll find a subscription form there, plus much more!

② Fax
Complete the questionnaire on the back of this card and fax the questionnaire side only to +1.847.763.9638.

③ Mail
Complete the questionnaire on the back of this card and mail it to P.O. Box 1263, Skokie, IL 60076-8263

ORACLE®

FREE SUBSCRIPTION

○ **Yes, please send me a FREE subscription to *Oracle Magazine*.**   ○ **NO**

To receive a free subscription to *Oracle Magazine*, you must fill out the entire card, sign it, and date it (incomplete cards cannot be processed or acknowledged). You can also fax your application to +1.847.763.9638. **Or subscribe at our Web site at otn.oracle.com/oraclemagazine**

○ From time to time, Oracle Publishing allows our partners exclusive access to our e-mail addresses for special promotions and announcements. To be included in this program, please check this circle.

○ Oracle Publishing allows sharing of our mailing list with selected third parties. If you prefer your mailing address not to be included in this program, please check here. If at any time you would like to be removed from this mailing list, please contact Customer Service at +1.847.647.9630 or send an e-mail to oracle@halldata.com.

signature (required)   date

X

name   title

company   e-mail address

street/p.o. box

city/state/zip or postal code   telephone

country   fax

YOU MUST ANSWER ALL TEN QUESTIONS BELOW.

① WHAT IS THE PRIMARY BUSINESS ACTIVITY OF YOUR FIRM AT THIS LOCATION? (check one only)
- ☐ 01 Aerospace and Defense Manufacturing
- ☐ 02 Application Service Provider
- ☐ 03 Automotive Manufacturing
- ☐ 04 Chemicals, Oil and Gas
- ☐ 05 Communications and Media
- ☐ 06 Construction/Engineering
- ☐ 07 Consumer Sector/Consumer Packaged Goods
- ☐ 08 Education
- ☐ 09 Financial Services/Insurance
- ☐ 10 Government (civil)
- ☐ 11 Government (military)
- ☐ 12 Healthcare
- ☐ 13 High Technology Manufacturing, OEM
- ☐ 14 Integrated Software Vendor
- ☐ 15 Life Sciences (Biotech, Pharmaceuticals)
- ☐ 16 Mining
- ☐ 17 Retail/Wholesale/Distribution
- ☐ 18 Systems Integrator, VAR/VAD
- ☐ 19 Telecommunications
- ☐ 20 Travel and Transportation
- ☐ 21 Utilities (electric, gas, sanitation, water)
- ☐ 98 Other Business and Services

② WHICH OF THE FOLLOWING BEST DESCRIBES YOUR PRIMARY JOB FUNCTION? (check one only)
Corporate Management/Staff
- ☐ 01 Executive Management (President, Chair, CEO, CFO, Owner, Partner, Principal)
- ☐ 02 Finance/Administrative Management (VP/Director/ Manager/Controller, Purchasing, Administration)
- ☐ 03 Sales/Marketing Management (VP/Director/Manager)
- ☐ 04 Computer Systems/Operations Management (CIO/VP/Director/ Manager MIS, Operations)
IS/IT Staff
- ☐ 05 Systems Development/ Programming Management
- ☐ 06 Systems Development/ Programming Staff
- ☐ 07 Consulting
- ☐ 08 DBA/Systems Administrator
- ☐ 09 Education/Training
- ☐ 10 Technical Support Director/Manager
- ☐ 11 Other Technical Management/Staff
- ☐ 98 Other

③ WHAT IS YOUR CURRENT PRIMARY OPERATING PLATFORM? (select all that apply)
- ☐ 01 Digital Equipment UNIX
- ☐ 02 Digital Equipment VAX VMS
- ☐ 03 HP UNIX
- ☐ 04 IBM AIX
- ☐ 05 IBM UNIX
- ☐ 06 Java
- ☐ 07 Linux
- ☐ 08 Macintosh
- ☐ 09 MS-DOS
- ☐ 10 MVS
- ☐ 11 NetWare
- ☐ 12 Network Computing
- ☐ 13 OpenVMS
- ☐ 14 SCO UNIX
- ☐ 15 Sequent DYNIX/ptx
- ☐ 16 Sun Solaris/SunOS
- ☐ 17 SVR4
- ☐ 18 UnixWare
- ☐ 19 Windows
- ☐ 20 Windows NT
- ☐ 21 Other UNIX
- ☐ 98 Other
- 99 ☐ None of the above

④ DO YOU EVALUATE, SPECIFY, RECOMMEND, OR AUTHORIZE THE PURCHASE OF ANY OF THE FOLLOWING? (check all that apply)
- ☐ 01 Hardware
- ☐ 02 Software
- ☐ 03 Application Development Tools
- ☐ 04 Database Products
- ☐ 05 Internet or Intranet Products
- 99 ☐ None of the above

⑤ IN YOUR JOB, DO YOU USE OR PLAN TO PURCHASE ANY OF THE FOLLOWING PRODUCTS? (check all that apply)
Software
- ☐ 01 Business Graphics
- ☐ 02 CAD/CAE/CAM
- ☐ 03 CASE
- ☐ 04 Communications
- ☐ 05 Database Management
- ☐ 06 File Management
- ☐ 07 Finance
- ☐ 08 Java
- ☐ 09 Materials Resource Planning
- ☐ 10 Multimedia Authoring
- ☐ 11 Networking
- ☐ 12 Office Automation
- ☐ 13 Order Entry/Inventory Control
- ☐ 14 Programming
- ☐ 15 Project Management
- ☐ 16 Scientific and Engineering
- ☐ 17 Spreadsheets
- ☐ 18 Systems Management
- ☐ 19 Workflow

Hardware
- ☐ 20 Macintosh
- ☐ 21 Mainframe
- ☐ 22 Massively Parallel Processing
- ☐ 23 Minicomputer
- ☐ 24 PC
- ☐ 25 Network Computer
- ☐ 26 Symmetric Multiprocessing
- ☐ 27 Workstation
Peripherals
- ☐ 28 Bridges/Routers/Hubs/Gateways
- ☐ 29 CD-ROM Drives
- ☐ 30 Disk Drives/Subsystems
- ☐ 31 Modems
- ☐ 32 Tape Drives/Subsystems
- ☐ 33 Video Boards/Multimedia
Services
- ☐ 34 Application Service Provider
- ☐ 35 Consulting
- ☐ 36 Education/Training
- ☐ 37 Maintenance
- ☐ 38 Online Database Services
- ☐ 39 Support
- ☐ 40 Technology-Based Training
- ☐ 98 Other
- 99 ☐ None of the above

⑥ WHAT ORACLE PRODUCTS ARE IN USE AT YOUR SITE? (check all that apply)
Oracle E-Business Suite
- ☐ 01 Oracle Marketing
- ☐ 02 Oracle Sales
- ☐ 03 Oracle Order Fulfillment
- ☐ 04 Oracle Supply Chain Management
- ☐ 05 Oracle Procurement
- ☐ 06 Oracle Manufacturing
- ☐ 07 Oracle Maintenance Management
- ☐ 08 Oracle Service
- ☐ 09 Oracle Contracts
- ☐ 10 Oracle Projects
- ☐ 11 Oracle Financials
- ☐ 12 Oracle Human Resources
- ☐ 13 Oracle Interaction Center
- ☐ 14 Oracle Communications/Utilities (modules)
- ☐ 15 Oracle Public Sector/University (modules)
- ☐ 16 Oracle Financial Services (modules)
Server/Software
- ☐ 17 Oracle9i
- ☐ 18 Oracle9i Lite
- ☐ 19 Oracle8i
- ☐ 20 Other Oracle database
- ☐ 21 Oracle9i Application Server
- ☐ 22 Oracle9i Application Server Wireless
- ☐ 23 Oracle Small Business Suite

Tools
- ☐ 24 Oracle Developer Suite
- ☐ 25 Oracle Discoverer
- ☐ 26 Oracle JDeveloper
- ☐ 27 Oracle Migration Workbench
- ☐ 28 Oracle9i AS Portal
- ☐ 29 Oracle Warehouse Builder
Oracle Services
- ☐ 30 Oracle Outsourcing
- ☐ 31 Oracle Consulting
- ☐ 32 Oracle Education
- ☐ 33 Oracle Support
- ☐ 98 Other
- 99 ☐ None of the above

⑦ WHAT OTHER DATABASE PRODUCTS ARE IN USE AT YOUR SITE? (check all that apply)
- ☐ 01 Access
- ☐ 02 Baan
- ☐ 03 dbase
- ☐ 04 Gupta
- ☐ 05 IBM DB2
- ☐ 06 Informix
- ☐ 07 Ingres
- ☐ 08 Microsoft Access
- ☐ 09 Microsoft SQL Server
- ☐ 10 PeopleSoft
- ☐ 11 Progress
- ☐ 12 SAP
- ☐ 13 Sybase
- ☐ 14 VSAM
- ☐ 98 Other
- 99 ☐ None of the above

⑧ WHAT OTHER APPLICATION SERVER PRODUCTS ARE IN USE AT YOUR SITE? (check all that apply)
- ☐ 01 BEA
- ☐ 02 IBM
- ☐ 03 Sybase
- ☐ 04 Sun
- ☐ 05 Other

⑨ DURING THE NEXT 12 MONTHS, HOW MUCH DO YOU ANTICIPATE YOUR ORGANIZATION WILL SPEND ON COMPUTER HARDWARE, SOFTWARE, PERIPHERALS, AND SERVICES FOR YOUR LOCATION? (check only one)
- ☐ 01 Less than $10,000
- ☐ 02 $10,000 to $49,999
- ☐ 03 $50,000 to $99,999
- ☐ 04 $100,000 to $499,999
- ☐ 05 $500,000 to $999,999
- ☐ 06 $1,000,000 and over

⑩ WHAT IS YOUR COMPANY'S YEARLY SALES REVENUE? (please choose one)
- ☐ 01 $500, 000, 000 and above
- ☐ 02 $100, 000, 000 to $500, 000, 000
- ☐ 03 $50, 000, 000 to $100, 000, 000
- ☐ 04 $5, 000, 000 to $50, 000, 000
- ☐ 05 $1, 000, 000 to $5, 000, 000

100103